INTRODUCTION TO ACCOUNTING

INTRODUCTION TO
ACCOUNTING

PETER SCOTT

SECOND EDITION

OXFORD
UNIVERSITY PRESS

OXFORD
UNIVERSITY PRESS

Great Clarendon Street, Oxford, OX2 6DP,
United Kingdom

Oxford University Press is a department of the University of Oxford.
It furthers the University's objective of excellence in research, scholarship,
and education by publishing worldwide. Oxford is a registered trade mark of
Oxford University Press in the UK and in certain other countries

First Edition 2018

Impression: 1

Published in the United States of America by Oxford University Press
198 Madison Avenue, New York, NY 10016, United States of America

British Library Cataloguing in Publication Data
Data available

Library of Congress Control Number: 2020946422

ISBN 978–0–19–884996–4

Printed in Great Britain by
Bell & Bain Ltd., Glasgow

BRIEF TABLE OF CONTENTS

Acknowledgements		xix
Preface		xx
Guided tour of the book		xxii
Guided tour of the online workbook		xxiv
Guide to the lecturer resources		xxvi
Dashboard		xxvii

1	Introduction	1

PART ONE   FINANCIAL ACCOUNTING

2	The statement of financial position	39
3	The statement of profit or loss	76
4	Double-entry bookkeeping 1: debits, credits, T accounts, the trial balance and the financial statements	127
5	Double-entry bookkeeping 2: books of prime entry, accounting systems and other double-entry applications	182
6	The statement of cash flows	253
7	The financing of business	300
8	Ratio analysis 1: profitability, efficiency and performance	320
9	Ratio analysis 2: liquidity, working capital and long-term financial stability	359

PART TWO   COST AND MANAGEMENT ACCOUNTING

10	Cost and management accounting in context	395
11	Product costing: absorption costing	408
12	Relevant costs, marginal costing and short-term decision making	446

13	Standard costing and variance analysis	479
14	Budgeting	508
15	Process costing	549
16	Capital investment appraisal	583
17	Corporate governance and sustainability	616

Appendix	647
Annotated statements	653
Terminology converter	656
Glossary	657
Index	666

FULL TABLE OF CONTENTS

Acknowledgements		xix
Preface		xx
Guided tour of the book		xxii
Guided tour of the online workbook		xxiv
Guide to the lecturer resources		xxvi
Dashboard		xxvii
1	**Introduction**	**1**
	Introduction	2
	What skills do I need?	2
	Types of business organisation	3
	Sole traders	3
	Partnerships	4
	Limited companies	4
	Public limited and private limited companies	9
	What is accounting?	10
	Control, accounting and accountability	12
	The role of accounting information in business decision making	14
	What qualities should accounting information possess?	16
	Materiality	20
	Cost v. benefit	21
	The users of accounting information	22
	Accounting branch 1: financial accounting	22
	Accounting branch 2: cost and management accounting	25
	The structure and regulation of the accounting profession	26
	The International Accounting Standards Board (IASB)	28
	The limitations of accounting information	29
	Appendix: current IFRS and IAS in issue at June 2020	30
	Chapter summary	31
	End-of-chapter questions	32

PART ONE   FINANCIAL ACCOUNTING

2	**The statement of financial position**	**39**
	Introduction	40
	Terminology: statement of financial position/balance sheet	42
	Assets	42
	Assets: faithful representation	43
	Asset recognition: summary of the steps to follow	44
	Assets in the statement of financial position	45
	Non-current assets	46
	Current assets	47
	The distinction between non-current and current assets	49
	Liabilities	50
	Liability recognition: summary of the steps to follow	51
	Liabilities in the statement of financial position	53
	Current liabilities	53
	Non-current liabilities	54
	The accounting equation	56
	Equity	56
	The components of equity	57
	Drawing up the statement of financial position	60
	Guidelines on the approach to adopt in drawing up the statement of financial position	60
	How are assets and liabilities valued?	63
	Historic cost v. fair value	63
	A mixture of original cost and fair value: problems	63
	What does the statement of financial position show?	64
	What the statement of financial position does not show	64
	The dual aspect concept	66
	Chapter summary	69
	End-of-chapter questions	70
3	**The statement of profit or loss**	**76**
	Introduction	77
	Terminology: statement of profit or loss/income statement/statement of financial performance/profit and loss account	78
	Definitions	79
	Income	79
	Expenses	80
	Income in the statement of profit or loss	81
	Expenditure in the statement of profit or loss	83
	Cost of sales	83
	Distribution and selling costs	83

Administration expenses   83

Finance expense   84

Income tax   84

Different categories of profit   85

Statement of profit or loss by nature   87

Notes to the statement of profit or loss in Illustration 3.2   88

Determining the amount of income or expense   89

The accruals basis of accounting   91

Prepayments and accruals: recording transactions in the statement
of profit or loss and statement of financial position   94

Prepayments   94

Accruals   94

Depreciation   96

Residual value and the annual depreciation charge   97

Profits and losses on disposal of non-current assets   98

Methods of depreciation: straight line and reducing balance   99

Which depreciation method is most appropriate in practice?   101

What depreciation is and what depreciation is not   102

Further adjustments to the statement of profit or loss   103

Irrecoverable debts   103

The allowance for receivables   104

Discounts allowed (early settlement discounts)   105

Discounts received (quantity discounts)   105

Sales returns   106

Purchase returns   106

Closing inventory   106

Preparing the statement of profit or loss   107

Drawings and the business entity convention   115

Appendix: methods of calculating the cost of closing inventory   115

First in, first out   116

Last in, first out   116

Weighted average cost   117

Chapter summary   118

End-of-chapter questions   119

**4   Double-entry bookkeeping 1: debits, credits, T accounts,
the trial balance and the financial statements   127**

Introduction   128

The T account   129

Debits   129

Credits   129

Double entry and the accounting equation   130

Posting accounting transactions to T accounts   132

The trial balance   137

Comprehensive example: double entry and the trial balance   139

Julia's trial balance   154

Closing off the T accounts at the end of an accounting period   160

Appendix: separate T accounts for inventory and purchases   171

Chapter summary   173

End-of-chapter questions   174

5   Double-entry bookkeeping 2: books of prime entry, accounting systems and other double-entry applications   182

Introduction   183

Transactions and transaction systems   184

The sales and cash received system   185

    Sales   185

    Credit notes   187

    Cash received   187

    Cash refunds   188

Recording daily sales: the sales day book   188

Value Added Tax (VAT)   190

The double entry to record sales listed in the sales day book   190

Sales returns day book   192

The double entry to record sales returns listed in the sales returns day book   193

The sales ledger   194

Cash received   196

The sales ledger and cash receipts   198

Exercising control: the trade receivables control account   199

The purchases and cash paid system   201

    Purchases   202

    Credit notes   202

    Cash paid   202

    Cash refunds   202

Recording daily purchases: the purchase day book   203

The double entry to record purchases listed in the purchase day book   204

Purchase returns day book   206

The double entry to record purchase returns listed in the purchase returns day book   208

The purchase ledger   208

Cash payments   211

The purchase ledger and cash payments   213

Exercising control: the trade payables control account   214

Exercising control: the bank reconciliation   216

Petty cash   220

The payroll system   222

Gross pay	223
Income tax (PAYE)	223
Employee's national insurance	223
Pension contributions	223
Net pay	224
Employer's national insurance	224
The double entry to record the weekly/monthly payroll	225
The nominal ledger	228
The double entry to record disposals of non-current assets	229
Finding missing figures by using T accounts: incomplete records	232
Potential errors	233
The trial balance does not balance	235
Journals	238
Chapter summary	238
End-of-chapter questions	239
6 The statement of cash flows	**253**
Introduction	254
Statement of cash flows: the IAS 7 presentation format	255
Constructing the statement of cash flows	256
Cash flows from operating activities	257
Cash flows from investing activities	259
Cash flows from financing activities	260
Cash and cash equivalents	262
Profit ≠ cash	263
Start Up's cash flow: scenario 1	263
Start Up's cash flow: scenario 2	264
Cash is cash is cash: the value of statements of cash flows	265
Is the statement of cash flows enough on its own?	266
Preparing the statement of cash flows: the direct method	269
Using T accounts to calculate cash flows	271
Calculating cash received from the trade receivables control account	273
Calculating cash paid to suppliers from the trade payables control account	274
Calculating cash paid for expenses using the expenses T account	276
Preparing the statement of cash flows: the indirect method	278
The indirect method: cash flows from operating activities: inflows or outflows?	280
Inventory	281
Receivables	281
Trade payables	281
Prepayments and accruals	281

Accounting principles and conventions   283

Appendix: further uses for T accounts in the calculation of
figures to include in the statement of cash flows   285

    1 Property, plant and equipment   285

    2 Tax paid during the year   287

    3 Dividends paid   289

    4 Interest received (finance income)   290

    5 Interest paid (finance expense)   291

Chapter summary   292

End-of-chapter questions   292

7 The financing of business   **300**

Introduction   301

Financing business   301

    Capital introduced: sole traders and partnerships   301

    Bank finance: all businesses   302

    Other types of long-term finance: public limited companies   306

Dividends   315

Distributable and non-distributable reserves   315

Chapter summary   316

End-of-chapter questions   316

8 Ratio analysis 1: profitability, efficiency and performance   **320**

Introduction   321

Evaluating financial statements: ratio analysis   322

Why is ratio analysis needed?   323

Ratios, figures or both?   325

The advantages of ratios: summary   326

Profitability ratios   327

    Gross profit percentage   328

    Interpretation of the results   329

    Other profitability ratios   330

Efficiency ratios   332

    Non-current asset turnover   333

    Revenue and profit per employee   334

    Sales and profit per unit of input resource   336

Performance ratios   338

    Earnings per share (EPS)   339

    Price/earnings ratio (the P/E ratio)   340

    Dividend per share (DPS)   342

    Dividend yield   343

    Dividend cover   344

    Will Bunns the Bakers' shareholders be happy with the
company's performance?   345

Return on capital employed   346

The importance of calculating and presenting ratios
consistently   347

How well are we doing? Comparisons with other companies   347

    Undertaking comparisons   349

Appendix: ratios considered in this chapter   349

Chapter summary   352

End-of-chapter questions   353

9 **Ratio analysis 2: liquidity, working capital and long-term
financial stability**   **359**

Introduction   360

Liquidity and the cash flow cycle   361

Liquidity ratios   363

    Current ratio   363

    Quick (acid test) ratio   364

    Current and quick ratios: the traditional view   366

Working capital   367

Working capital ratios   368

    The cash conversion cycle   370

Why is working capital so important?   372

Current liabilities: the timing of payments   373

Capital structure ratios: long-term solvency and financial stability
assessment   375

    Gearing ratio   377

    Debt ratio   377

    Interest cover   378

When are borrowings risky?   378

Appendix: ratios considered in this chapter   381

Chapter summary   383

End-of-chapter questions   383

PART TWO   COST AND MANAGEMENT ACCOUNTING

10 **Cost and management accounting in context**   **395**

Introduction   396

Cost accounting and cost objects: definitions   396

Management accounting: a definition   398

Cost and management accounting v. financial accounting   400

Financial accounting information v. cost and management
accounting information: a comparison   402

Chapter summary   405

End-of-chapter questions   406

11	**Product costing: absorption costing**	**408**
	Introduction	409
	Why is it important to know about costs?	409
	Costs and costing	411
	Setting a selling price	411
	Direct costs, variable costs and marginal costs	412
	Variable cost behaviour: graphical presentation	414
	Fixed costs	414
	Variable costs, fixed costs and total costs	416
	Allocating fixed overhead costs to products: absorption costing	417
	Setting the selling price	420
	Absorption costing and inventory valuation	420
	Absorption costing: overhead allocation	422
	Allocating service department overheads	427
	Method	427
	Administration overheads, marketing overheads and finance overheads: period costs	429
	Problems with absorption costing	429
	Overhead allocation: activity-based costing	430
	How does activity-based costing work?	431
	Absorption costing	432
	Activity-based costing	433
	The limitations and assumptions of costing	435
	Assumption 1: fixed costs are fixed	435
	Assumption 2: variable costs remain the same for all units of production	436
	Assumption 3: costs can be determined with the required precision	437
	Chapter summary	438
	End-of-chapter questions	439
12	**Relevant costs, marginal costing and short-term decision making**	**446**
	Introduction	447
	Decision making: not just selling price	447
	Contribution	448
	Marginal v. absorption costing	449
	Relevant costs and sunk costs	451
	Relevant costs: opportunity cost	452
	Contribution analysis and decision making	453
	Break-even point	453
	Break-even point: graphical illustration	455
	The margin of safety	455
	Sensitivity analysis	456

Target profit   457

Cost-volume-profit analysis   458

High and low fixed costs   459

Contribution analysis, relevant costs and decision making   459

Marketing and selling price   459

Special orders   461

Special orders: additional considerations   463

Outsourcing (make or buy decisions)   464

Outsourcing (make or buy decisions): additional considerations   466

Limiting factor (key factor) analysis   468

Relevant costs, marginal costing and decision making: assumptions   472

Chapter summary   473

End-of-chapter questions   474

13   Standard costing and variance analysis   479

Introduction   480

What is standard costing?   480

Variance analysis   481

Different standards   482

Setting the standard   483

Direct material price and usage variances   487

Direct material total variance   489

Direct material variances: information and control   490

Direct labour rate and efficiency variances   490

Direct labour total variance   492

Direct labour variances: information and control   493

Variable overhead variances   494

Fixed overhead expenditure variance   494

Fixed overhead expenditure variance: information and control   494

Sales variances   495

Sales price variance   495

Sales volume variance   495

Variances: summary   497

Standard costing: limitations   498

Appendix: variable overhead variances   499

Variable overhead total variance   500

Variable overhead expenditure variance   500

Variable overhead efficiency variance   500

Chapter summary   501

End-of-chapter questions   502

14   Budgeting   508

Introduction   509

What is budgeting?   509

Budget objectives and the budgeting process   510

Budgeting: comprehensive example	512
Step 1: setting the strategy and deciding on selling prices	512
Step 2: the sales budget	513
Step 3: calculate the direct costs of budgeted sales	515
Step 4: set the budget for fixed costs	516
Step 5: draw up the budgeted monthly statement of profit or loss	517
Step 6: calculating cash receipts from sales	520
Step 7: calculating cash payments to direct materials suppliers and direct labour	521
Step 8: draw up the monthly cash budget	522
The importance of cash flow forecasts	525
Step 9: draw up the budgeted statement of financial position	526
Conclusions: financing expansion	529
Budgeting flowchart summary	529
Budgetary control: statement of profit or loss	530
Higher sales	532
Direct costs	532
Fixed costs	533
Net profit	533
Budgetary control: cash budget	534
Sensitivity analysis	536
Chapter summary	539
End-of-chapter questions	539
15 Process costing	**549**
Introduction	550
The process account	550
Normal losses in a process	552
Abnormal losses	553
Abnormal gains	554
Disposal costs	556
Normal losses	556
Abnormal losses	557
Selling losses from a process	559
Normal losses	559
Abnormal losses	560
Valuing work in progress at the end of an accounting period	562
Step 1: calculate the equivalent units of production	564
Step 2: calculate the cost per equivalent unit of output and work in progress	564
Step 3: calculate the total cost of output and work in progress	564
Step 4: complete the process account	565
Closing work in progress: varying completion percentages of costs	565

Step 1: calculate the equivalent units of production   565

Step 2: calculate the cost per equivalent unit of output and work
in progress   566

Step 3: calculate the total cost of output and work in progress   567

Step 4: complete the process account   567

Unit costs when there is opening and closing work in progress   568

Valuing finished production and closing work in progress: the first in
first out method   569

Step 1: calculate the equivalent units of production   569

Step 2: calculate the cost per equivalent unit of output and
work in progress   571

Step 3: calculate the total cost of output and closing work
in progress   571

Step 4: complete the process account   572

Valuing finished production and closing work in progress:
the weighted average cost method   573

Step 1: calculate the equivalent units of production   574

Step 2: calculate the cost per equivalent unit of output and
work in progress   574

Step 3: calculate the total cost of output and closing work
in progress   575

Step 4: complete the process account   575

Chapter summary   577

End-of-chapter questions   578

16   Capital investment appraisal   583

Introduction   584

What is capital investment?   584

Why is capital investment appraisal important?   585

What financial information will I need to undertake capital
investment appraisal?   587

Capital investment appraisal techniques: comprehensive example   588

Capital investment appraisal techniques   589

Payback   589

Accounting rate of return (ARR)   592

The time value of money   595

Business investment and the time value of money   597

Net present value   597

Discounted payback   600

Internal rate of return (IRR)   602

Making a final decision   606

Post investment audit   608

Sensitivity analysis   608

Chapter summary   608

End-of-chapter questions   609

17   Corporate governance and sustainability   616

Introduction   617

Corporate governance: a brief history   618

Corporate governance: a definition   619

Corporate governance: the parties involved   619

    The board of directors: executive and non-executive directors   619

    External audit   621

    Internal audit   623

    Stock exchange rules   624

Addressing shareholder concerns   625

    Long-term success v. short-term profits   625

    Company decision making   626

    Board effectiveness   628

    Ensuring the integrity of financial statements   631

    Directors' remuneration   633

    Shareholder communications   634

Corporate social responsibility reporting   635

    Duty to promote the success of the company   637

    The rationale for corporate social responsibility reporting 639

Sustainability and environmental reporting   640

    The rationale for adopting and reporting a sustainability strategy 641

Professional accountants' ethical principles   643

Chapter summary   644

End-of-chapter questions   645

Appendix   647

Annotated statements   653

Terminology converter   656

Glossary   657

Index   666

ACKNOWLEDGEMENTS

Thanks are due to many individuals. Firstly, to all of the staff at Oxford University Press who have been involved with this project. Kehinde Badmus and Felicity Boughton oversaw the day-to-day revisions and updates, but there were many others working tirelessly behind the scenes to bring the book and all its associated resources to its intended audience. Secondly, a big thank you to the reviewers of the first edition who took the time to comment constructively on that first attempt. Their input has informed the development of this second edition and its online workbook. Thirdly, thanks must go to the hundreds if not thousands of students who have, over many years, been the testing ground for the material presented here: their ability to grasp concepts, ideas and techniques served up in various different formats has helped guide me in the formulation of my ideas on the most effective approach to providing the solid foundations upon which later studies in accountancy are built. Fourthly, thanks go to all my former colleagues at De Montfort University for their constant interest, encouragement and enthusiasm for the project. Finally, the deepest debt of gratitude must go to my family, and above all to my wife, Christine, for their forbearance, patience and encouragement during the time it took to develop and write this book.

Peter Scott, October 2020

The author and publisher would like to thank sincerely all those people who gave their time and expertise to review draft chapters throughout the writing process. Your help was invaluable.

Thanks are also extended to those who wished to remain anonymous.

Dr Sandar Win, University of Bedfordshire
Dr Brian Gibbs, University of Bolton
Dr Octavian Ionescu, University of East Anglia
Dr Alaa Alhaj Ismail, Coventry University
David Gilding, University of Leeds
Dr Kelvin Leong, Wrexham Glyndŵr University
Dr Gizella Marton, University of Dundee
Dr Nick Rowbottom, University of Birmingham
Mostafa Abuzeid, University of Sheffield
Barry McCarthy, University College London
Dave Knight, Leeds Beckett University
Nicola Horner, University of the West of England
David Kyle, York St John University
Dr Emer Gallagher, Liverpool John Moores University
Samuel O Idowu, London Metropolitan University
Terry Harris, Durham University
Dr Anwar Halari, The Open University
Gayle Waddell, University of Liverpool
Dr Mariannunziata Liguori, Queen's University Belfast
Dr Pik Kun Liew, University of Essex
Dr Abdelhafid Benamraoui, University of Westminster

Dr Chandana Alawattage, University of Aberdeen
Stephanie Tiller, University of Worcester
Dr Oluseyi O Adesina, Canterbury Christ Church University
Christopher Kelsall, University of Central Lancashire
Ian Andrews, University of Exeter
Wondimu Mekonnen, University of Buckingham
Dr Androniki Triantafylli, Queen Mary University of London
Elizabeth Vokes, University of Northampton
Michael Barker, Coventry University
Chris Soan, Newcastle University
Kevin Burrows, University of Plymouth
Acheampong Charles Afriyie, University of Gloucestershire
Dr Chun Lei Yang, University of Manchester
Dr Naser Makarem, University of Aberdeen
Daniel Johnson, Coventry University
Dr Sayjda Talib, Lancaster University
Susan Lane, University of Bradford
Samuel Hinds, University of Surrey
Dr Akrum Helfaya, Keele University, UK & Damanhour University, Egypt

PREFACE

Accounting: building a solid foundation

Welcome to your study of accounting. This first year of your studies is extremely important as the understanding you develop in the weeks and months ahead and the techniques you learn will provide the foundation upon which both your future studies and your professional career will be built. Everything you study in the next nine months will continue to be relevant in the remainder of your degree studies and throughout your time in the accounting profession and business world. At this initial stage of your studies, the approach to the subject adopted in this package is completely practical: accounting is a 'doing' subject and the best way to learn how it works and what it does is to practise the various techniques and approaches as frequently as possible. You are provided with careful, step-by-step guidance showing you how to construct and evaluate various accounting statements and how to summarise and record accounting information. You are then given numerous further opportunities to apply what you have learnt with a view to enhancing your understanding and ability to produce and interpret accounting information. Only once you have mastered the techniques and practice of accounting can you move forward to look at the more theoretical aspects of the subject and question why things are done as they are. Since many basic accounting tasks are now undertaken by artificial intelligence, it is tempting to ignore these basics and let the machines do the low level work while attention is focused on the higher, more interesting areas of the subject and of accounting and business practice. However, it is always unwise to assume that machines are infallible: the information they produce is only as accurate as the software and the software developers allow. Gaining a full understanding of the foundations of accounting and basic recording practice now will enable you to interrogate all information presented to you much more effectively and to assess its accuracy and completeness before using that information as a basis for decision making and control.

The integrated online workbook: how this package works

This textbook is published with a free online workbook containing a large bank of examples and exercises that relate to, and are thoroughly integrated with, the material in each chapter. (For details on how to access this, please refer to the 'Guided tour of the online workbook'.)

The integration of these online resources with the textbook provides the supportive learning environment necessary to allow you to develop the specialist practical skills required in accounting and business. Clear signposts in the chapters offer you numerous opportunities to reinforce, revisit and revise your understanding of the subject, prompting you to apply your knowledge as you work through each topic. Your understanding of the material will strengthen as approaches and techniques are frequently recapped, including through the use of running examples within both the financial and management accounting parts of the book.

The textbook

The first part of the textbook focuses on financial accounting. You are initially introduced to two of the three key financial accounting statements (the statement of financial position and the statement of profit or loss) and shown how to construct these from first principles. You are then provided with an in-depth and detailed guide to double-entry bookkeeping to show you how the accounting records are built up over the course of the financial year and how these records are then summarised and presented in the statement of profit or loss and the statement of financial position. The third key accounting statement, the statement of cash flows, is then introduced and detailed guidance on how to prepare this statement is offered. Once the financial statements have been put together, accountants must then interpret these statements to determine what information they provide about an entity's profitability and performance and its ability to survive into the future.

The second part of the book deals with cost and management accounting and the ways in which accounting can be used in decision making and in controlling a business's future development through planning and forecasting. The key techniques of costing, budgeting and capital investment appraisal are covered in the requisite depth and detail to provide you with a ready guide to the production and presentation of meaningful information for use both in the running of a business and in the evaluation of its performance. Users of financial statements require reassurance about the accuracy and integrity of the information they are presented with and, in addition, they want to be confident that companies are good corporate citizens who always do the right thing. Therefore, the final chapter provides an introduction to the corporate governance rules, corporate social responsibility reporting and sustainability, topics that you will go on to consider in much greater depth in your degree, your professional studies and throughout your working life.

A note on terminology

Business today is international in its focus. As a result, the accounting terminology adopted throughout this book is that of international accounting standards rather than that of UK standards. Where different terms for the same statements are in common usage, these are noted throughout the book as they arise and summarised in the terminology converter at the back of the book.

GUIDED TOUR OF THE BOOK

Identifying and defining

Learning outcomes

Clear, concise learning outcomes begin each chapter and help to contextualise the chapter's main objectives. This feature can help you plan your revision to ensure you identify and cover all the key concepts.

LEARNING OUTCOMES

Once you have read this chapter and worked through the questions and examples in both this chapter and the online workbook, you should be able to:

- Understand that profit does not equal cash
- Appreciate that without a steady cash inflow from operations an entity will not be able to survive
- Describe the make up of operating, investing and financing cash flows

Key terms and glossary

Key terms are highlighted where they first appear in the chapter and are also collated into a glossary at the end of the book. This provides an easy and practical way for you to revise and check your understanding of definitions.

of accounting to provide you with a very strong foundation on which t e and future professional studies. We shall consider the main financi s, the statement of financial position (balance sheet), the statement of profit or l flows that you will encounter on a daily basis in your professional life. I understanding of accounting and its role in business organisations, we -depth look at how double-entry bookkeeping gathers and analyses

Statement of cash flows A summary of the cash inflows and outflows of an entity for a given period of time.

Statement of financial position A summary of the assets, liabilities and equity of an entity at a particular point in time.

Statement of profit or loss A statement of income and expenditure for a particular period of time. Also referred to

Understanding accounting principles

Illustrations

Illustrations display accounting statements and documents and serve to set out the numbers discussed in the text in an easily readable format. This enables you to follow the explanations closely and to become familiar with the layout of such documents.

Illustration 4.34 (= Illustration 4.10) Julia's bank account

Bank Account

Debit (increases the asset)		£	Credit (decreases the asset)		£
2021			2021		
1 April	Capital account	30,000	1 April	Rent	5,000
30 April	Sales: April	20,000	1 April	Cash register	1,000
31 May	Sales: May	25,000	1 April	Shelving and fittings	12,000
30 June	Sales: June	30,000	5 May	Cost of sales	15,000

In-text examples

Regular practical examples are presented throughout each chapter to illustrate how accounting material is used in a variety of different business contexts. The diversity in cases demonstrates how accounting information can be interpreted in different ways to achieve different ends according to business needs.

EXAMPLE 11.2

Anna is a self-employed carpenter working at home producing handmade wooden dining chairs. Dur the month of June, she produced 30 chairs. What price should she sell her chairs for? She provides you w invoices showing the costs of the materials she used in June:

	£
Wood	540
Glue	18
Screws	30
Sandpaper	12

Totalling up the costs above, Anna has spent £600 on making 30 chairs. Dividing the total costs by the chairs made gives a cost of £20 per chair.

Accounting in practice

'Give me an example' boxes

Topical examples taken from the *Financial Times*, the BBC and other news outlets and numerous references to financial statements from real companies will help your understanding of how the theory being discussed in the chapter plays out in business practice.

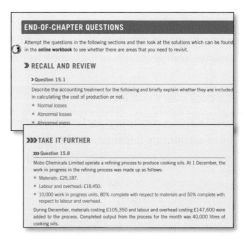

'Why is this relevant to me?' boxes

These short and frequent explanations clarify exactly how the accounting material under discussion will be important and relevant to accounting and business professionals. They are an important reminder of how important even theoretical accounting knowledge will be in enabling you to succeed in your future career, whether it be as an accountant or as a business professional working with accounting information.

Testing and applying understanding

End-of-chapter questions

There is a set of questions at the end of every chapter designed to test your knowledge of the key concepts and practical examples that have been discussed and illustrated. They are divided into three tiers according to difficulty, allowing you to track your progress. Use them during your course to ensure you fully understand the accounting principles and practice before moving on, or when revising to make sure you can confidently tackle the more difficult questions. The solutions are supplied within the **online workbook**, in an easily printable format.

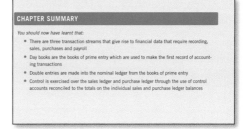

Chapter summary

Each chapter concludes with a bulleted list linking to the learning outcomes, outlining the key points you should take away from the chapter. This provides another useful method of checking that you have covered the key points when you come to revise each topic.

GUIDED TOUR OF THE ONLINE WORKBOOK

Access the interactive online workbook by visiting www.oup.com/uk/scott_financial/.

Resources in the online workbook have been specifically designed to support you throughout your financial accounting studies. References within the textbook indicate the relevant resource accompanying that section or topic, thereby allowing you to reinforce your learning as you progress through the book and ensuring that you take full advantage of this fantastic package.

Summaries of key concepts

Key glossary terms are provided in interactive flashcard format.

Multiple-choice questions

Interactive multiple-choice questions for every chapter give you instant feedback as well as page references to help you focus on the areas that need further study.

Numerical exercises

These exercises, often based in Excel, give you the opportunity to calculate accounting information from given sets of data, thereby practising what is discussed and illustrated in the book.

Go back over this again

Containing a mixture of further examples, written exercises, true or false questions and annotated accounting information, this section provides the perfect opportunity for you to revise and revisit any concepts you might be unsure of.

Show me how to do it

Video presentations, accompanied by a voice-over, allow you to watch practical demonstrations of how more complex accounting tasks are dealt with by the author.

Web links

Arranged by chapter, these web links will take you directly to the websites of the companies and organisations covered in the book, as well as websites of more general accounting interest. Follow the links to learn more about how accounting plays out in the real world of business.

Further reading

Arranged by chapter, this section provides you with a list of additional resources you may wish to consult if you'd like to take your learning further, or simply consider a topic from a different perspective.

GUIDE TO THE LECTURER RESOURCES

Test bank

A wealth of additional multiple-choice questions that can be customised to meet your specific teaching needs.

Lecturer examples and solutions

Additional exercises that can be used alongside the PowerPoint slides in lectures or seminars.

Group tutorial exercises

A range of more detailed, workshop-based activities that students can complete prior to and during tutorials.

Lecturer examination questions and answers

Additional problem solving and suggested essay-based exam questions with accompanying answers.

PowerPoint slides

Illustrated PowerPoint slides for each chapter that can be used in lectures or printed as handouts, and can be easily adapted to suit your teaching style.

DASHBOARD

Dashboard is a cloud-based online assessment and revision tool. It comes pre-loaded with the resources listed in the 'Guide to the lecturer resources', as well as additional questions to use for assessment and functionality to track your students' progress.

Visit www.oxfordtextbooks.co.uk/dashboard/ for more information.

Simple: With a highly intuitive design, it will take you less than 15 minutes to learn and master the system.

Informative: Assignment and assessment results are automatically graded, giving you a clear view of the class's understanding of the course content.

Mobile: You can access Dashboard from every major platform and device connected to the Internet, whether that's a computer, tablet or smartphone.

Gradebook

Dashboard's Gradebook functionality automatically marks the assignments that you set for your students. The Gradebook also provides heat maps that allow you to view your students' progress and quickly identify areas of the course where your students may need more practice or support, as well as the areas in which they are most confident. This feature helps you focus your teaching time on the areas that matter. The Gradebook also allows you to administer grading schemes, manage checklists and administer learning objectives and competencies.

INTRODUCTION

LEARNING OUTCOMES

Once you have read this chapter and worked through the questions and examples in both this chapter and the online workbook, you should be able to:

- Understand the different forms of business organisation and the advantages and disadvantages of each format

- Define accounting and explain what role it plays in business

- Explain the underlying role that accounting plays in informing all business decisions

- Define and discuss the qualities of useful accounting information

- Distinguish between the two branches of accounting, financial accounting and cost and management accounting, and their roles

- State the main users of accounting information and identify what they need from accounting information

- Explain what accounting does not do and the limitations of accounting information

1

INTRODUCTION

Welcome to your study of accounting. You are now taking your first steps on the road to qualifying as a member of the accounting profession with a view to building your career in one or more of the varied roles which accountants fulfil in business and the wider economy. In order to help you fulfil your ambition, this book will introduce you to the key techniques and practical applications of accounting to provide you with a very strong foundation on which to build your further degree and future professional studies. We shall consider the main financial accounting statements, the statement of financial position (balance sheet), the statement of profit or loss and the statement of cash flows that you will encounter on a daily basis in your professional life. In order to underpin your understanding of accounting and its role in business organisations, we shall also be taking an in-depth look at how double-entry bookkeeping gathers and analyses information on the transactions that form the building blocks of these financial accounting statements. However, accounting is not just about the mechanics of putting these accounting statements together: it is also about interpreting those accounting statements to understand what they are telling users about the financial performance and financial position of a business. Likewise, accounting does not just look at the past by presenting historical statements relating to past results and outcomes. Accounting information is also used dynamically to plan for the future and to model possible scenarios and outcomes depending on the courses of action taken.

WHAT SKILLS DO I NEED?

Many students find the thought of accounting worrying as they do not feel they have the necessary mathematical ability to be able to understand or apply the subject in practice. However, do be assured that accounting needs no particular mathematical strengths, just some basic applications of arithmetic and an ability to reason. As long as you can add up, subtract, multiply and divide figures you have all the arithmetical skills you will need to undertake the calculations and apply this subject. The ability to reason is a skill that you will need in every subject of study and it will be fundamental to the success of any career, not just to a career in accounting.

Once you have learnt how to apply the basic techniques, accounting is much more about understanding what the figures are telling you and about interpreting the data in front of you—this requires you to think in a logical fashion and to investigate the meaning beneath the surface. Therefore, it is much more accurate to say that accounting requires the ability to communicate and express your ideas in words rather than being dependent upon mathematical skills.

WHY IS THIS RELEVANT TO ME?   Skills needed to study accounting

- To reassure you that the study of accounting requires no further special skills than those you already possess
- To enable you to appreciate that the study of accounting will further develop the skills you have already acquired in reaching your current level of education

TYPES OF BUSINESS ORGANISATION

Let's start with a review of each of the three main types of business organisation which use ac-counting information. These comprise of sole traders, partnerships and limited companies.

Sole traders

Simple businesses require a simple format. As the name implies, sole traders run their businesses on their own. Sole traders set their businesses up and, while they might employ other people to assist them in the day-to-day running of operations, they take all the business decisions them-selves and assume total responsibility for the success or failure of their businesses. Sole traders have unlimited liability for the debts incurred by their businesses and they could lose everything in a business failure. These losses would extend not only to business assets but also to personal assets such as houses, cars, investments, in fact anything that those sole traders own.

The sole trader format for organising a business is most effective where operations are straightforward and where there are no complexities that could be more efficiently dealt with by adopting a different structure. An example of a sole trader that we will look at will be Julia, a stand-alone retailer, in Chapters 3, 4 and 6. Other examples would be childminders, hair-dressers, market traders, taxi drivers, sports coaches, barristers and accountants working as sole practitioners. All these people operate their businesses on their own and plough a lone furrow as they make their way in the world. There are no special requirements for setting up in business as a sole trader: just start trading. The features of the sole trader business format are summarised in Figure 1.1.

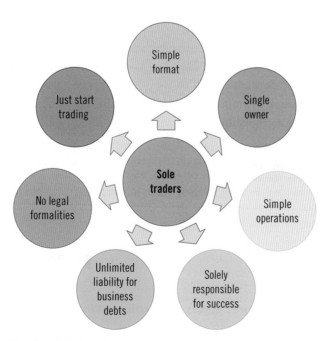

Figure 1.1 The features of the sole trader business format

GO BACK OVER THIS AGAIN!   Are you quite sure that you understand how sole traders operate? Go to the **online workbook** and have a go at Exercises 1.1 to reinforce your understanding of sole traders and how they operate.

Partnerships

Where two or more individuals own and run a business together, then a partnership structure will be adopted for that business. Partnerships are more complex undertakings than sole traders and reflect the fact that one person cannot know everything or be talented in every activity. Thus, in a building firm partnership, one partner might be skilled as a bricklayer and plasterer, one as a plumber and heating engineer, one as an electrician. Similarly, in an accounting partnership, one partner might be knowledgeable in accounts preparation and audit, one in tax and one in insolvency.

The principle in a partnership is that all the partners take part in running the business and enjoy a share of the profits or suffer a share of the losses from that business. You might say that a partnership is two or more sole traders coming together to make a bigger business, with each partner enjoying a share of management and reward from that enlarged business. The problem in a partnership is that the partners have to be certain that they will all be able to work together effectively and that no personality clashes or disputes will cause disruption to the business. Sole traders, of course, do not have this problem. Partnerships, like sole traders, can be set up informally and just start trading. However, given the possibility that there will be disagreements between the partners, it is usual to set out the key terms of the partnership in a written agreement signed by all the partners at the start of the partnership. As was the case with sole traders, partnerships have unlimited liability for the debts incurred by the partnership. This unlimited liability is joint and several which means that each partner is liable collectively for the partnership debts incurred not just by themselves but by their fellow partners as well. Limited liability partnerships (LLPs) can now be set up in the UK as a result of the Limited Liability Partnerships Act 2000. Under this Act, partners in an LLP can place limits on their liability for partnership debts. Further consideration of limited liability partnerships is beyond the scope of the current book. The features of the partnership business format are summarised in Figure 1.2.

GO BACK OVER THIS AGAIN!   Are you confident that you know how partnerships work? Go to the **online workbook** and have a go at Exercises 1.2 to reinforce your understanding of partnerships and how they operate.

Limited companies

Limited companies are much more complex organisations and are subject to much greater regulation and oversight. Given this complexity, let's look at the distinguishing features of limited liability companies (summarised in Figure 1.3) one by one, comparing and contrasting limited companies with sole traders and partnerships.

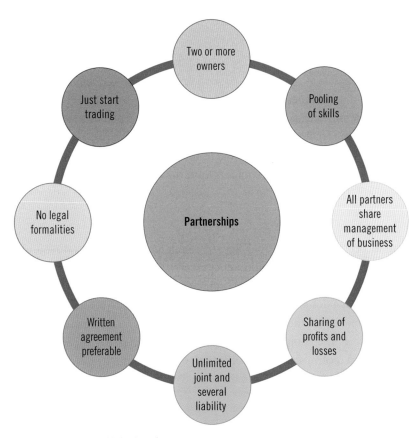

Figure 1.2 The features of the partnership business format

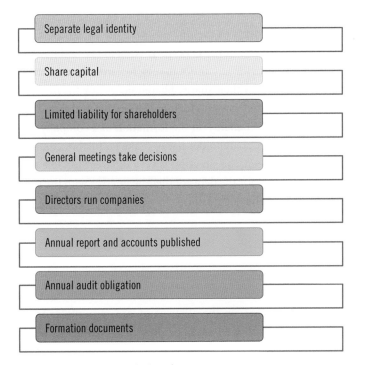

Figure 1.3 The features of the limited liability company business format

Separate legal identity

Limited companies are regarded as separate legal entities with their own name and a perpetual life. Businesses that operate as sole traders or partnerships are considered to be an extension of those individuals and the businesses and their owners are not regarded as distinct legal beings. This separate legal identity means that limited companies can sue and be sued, sign undertakings and enter into contractual obligations in their own name. Sole trader and partnership businesses tend to cease when the owners retire or die, but limited companies carry on indefinitely no matter how many of their directors or shareholders leave the company.

Share capital

Businesses can incorporate themselves as limited companies. Incorporation requires a detailed formal process (see this chapter, Formation documents). On incorporation of a business, shareholders subscribe for shares in the limited company. When individuals subscribe for shares, this gives limited companies a source of finance. While sole traders and partners provide the financing for their businesses and record this in their statements of financial position as capital introduced (Chapter 2, The components of equity), shareholders pay money into the company's bank account and receive shares in proportion to the capital they have invested. This share capital is recorded as issued share capital in the limited company's statement of financial position (Chapter 2, The components of equity).

Limited liability

The great advantage of limited companies over sole traders and partnerships is that the liability of the shareholders to meet the debts of the limited company is restricted to the amount they have subscribed for their shares. If a limited company were to fail and go out of business, then shareholders will not have to provide any more money towards clearing the debts of the company than they have already paid for their shares. Shareholders lose the money they have already paid to acquire their shares, but they have no further liability beyond this. Thus, if a shareholder agreed to purchase one hundred £1 shares on the formation of a company, then, once the £100 has been paid to the company, the shareholder has to make no further contribution to the company should it fail. As we have seen, the situation is very different for sole traders and partnerships who have unlimited liability for the debts of their businesses with the potential to lose both business and personal assets in a business failure.

General meetings

Sole traders and partners own their businesses and answer only to themselves. Sole traders and partners thus make major decisions about their organisations throughout the year as and when the need arises. Limited companies, on the other hand, are accountable to their shareholders. Every year, each and every limited company must hold an annual general meeting (AGM) at which the shareholders come together to consider and vote on various significant resolutions affecting the company. When companies undertake other business transactions which require the agreement of shareholders at other times of the year, the directors will call an extraordinary general meeting (EGM). An EGM is any company meeting other than the annual general meeting. For example, the directors may call an EGM to ask shareholders to approve the takeover of another company. Shareholders have voting rights at the AGM and at EGMs. The size of these voting rights and the power of each shareholder depend upon the number of shares held. For each share held, a shareholder has one vote. The more shares that a shareholder owns, the more power that shareholder can exercise when voting on company resolutions.

Appointment of directors

One of the resolutions voted on at the AGM concerns the appointment of directors of the company. Limited companies, although answerable to their shareholders, are managed and run by directors appointed by the shareholders at the AGM. The directors are elected by the shareholders to run the company on their behalf. If shareholders are not happy with the performance of the current directors, they have the power to vote them out of office at the AGM and appoint different directors in their place. Directors are employees of limited companies placed in a position of trust by the shareholders. Ownership (by shareholders) and management (by directors) are thus separated, a situation that does not apply in the case of sole traders and partnerships. Of course, both directors and other employees can buy shares in their companies and thereby influence the direction and decisions of the companies which employ them. When sole traders and partnerships incorporate their businesses (transfer their business undertakings to limited companies set up for this purpose), the new companies issue shares to these former owners as payment for the assets transferred and to enable the original owners to retain control of their businesses.

Annual accounts

Because of this separation of share ownership and management, the directors of limited companies have a statutory obligation under the Companies Act 2006 to present annual accounts to the shareholders at the AGM. These accounts are a financial record of how the directors have managed the monies and other resources entrusted to them by the shareholders and how they have used those monies and resources to generate profits for shareholders during the past year. As we note later (this chapter, Control, accounting and accountability), the directors present this account of their stewardship of the resources entrusted to them to help shareholders control the directors' actions and prevent them from exceeding their powers. All limited company accounts are filed at Companies House and are available for public consultation.

Auditors and annual accounts

As shareholders do not take part in the day-to-day running of the company, they do not know whether the accounts presented by the directors are a true and fair summary of the financial achievements during the year or not. Therefore, shareholders appoint independent auditors to

1

check the annual report and accounts for inaccuracies, omissions and misrepresentations. These auditors then report to the shareholders on whether the annual report and accounts present a true and fair view of the company's profit or loss for the year and of the state of the company's affairs (the statement of financial position) at the year-end date. The audit report will also state whether the financial statements have been properly prepared in accordance with the relevant financial reporting standards and with the requirements of the Companies Act 2006. Shareholders are empowered by the Companies Act 2006 to choose the auditors they want to conduct the annual audit rather than the auditors that the directors would like to appoint. Auditors of limited companies enjoy various protections against removal by the directors and this enables them to perform their audits efficiently and effectively without fear or favour to the shareholders' benefit. Not every company is required to have an audit. Those companies which must have an audit and those companies for which an audit is optional are specified in the Companies Act 2006. You will learn much more about these audit requirements and about auditing at a later stage in your studies.

Sole traders and partnerships prepare annual accounts, but these are used to determine any tax that is due on profits and to present to banks to support applications for loan and other borrowing facilities. There is no obligation upon sole traders or partnerships to publish their accounts publicly so that the financial affairs of sole traders and partnerships remain private and confidential. The annual accounts for sole traders and partnerships are not audited.

Formation documents

When limited companies are formed, they are registered with the Registrar of Companies. This registration comprises the name of the company and the names of the first directors (the names of the company and the directors can be changed at any time by the submission of the appropriate documentation to Companies House). In addition, two important documents are filed when a company is registered. The first is the Memorandum of Association. This document covers the limited company's objectives and its powers and governs the relationship of the company with the outside world. The second document is the Articles of Association, which covers the internal regulations of the company and governs the shareholders' relationships with each other.

WHY IS THIS RELEVANT TO ME?   Types of business organisation

To enable you as a business professional to:

- Appreciate the different types of business organisation that you will be dealing with during your professional career
- Understand how the different types of business organisation operating in the economy today are set up and run
- Compare and contrast the different types of business organisation you will be dealing with in your professional life

GO BACK OVER THIS AGAIN!   Do you feel confident that you can describe the different features of the various types of business organisations and distinguish between them? Go to the **online workbook** and have a go at Exercises 1.3 to make sure you can describe and distinguish between the different types of business organisation.

SUMMARY OF KEY CONCEPTS   Are you quite happy that you can describe the main features of each of the three different types of business organisations? Go to the **online workbook** to revise these main features with Summary of key concepts 1.1–1.3.

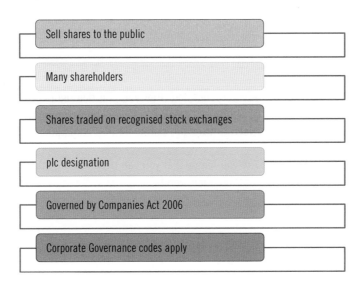

Figure 1.4 The characteristics of public limited companies (plcs)

Public limited and private limited companies

The Companies Act 2006 regulates all limited liability companies. However, there are two types of limited company covered in the Act: private limited companies and public limited companies. The distinctive characteristics of public limited companies are summarised in Figure 1.4. Private limited companies are prohibited from selling their shares to the public and usually have very few shareholders. Public limited companies can issue shares to the public and have many shareholders. The shares of public limited companies (but not those of limited companies which can only be traded privately) are traded on recognised stock exchanges such as those of London, New York, Paris, Hong Kong and Tokyo. Many of the businesses or websites you visit each day are run by public limited companies and these include your bank and the supermarkets in which you buy your food. Private limited companies have the word Limited or Ltd after their names while the names of public limited companies are followed by the letters plc. Look out for these company designations as you browse the web or go out into town.

Public and private limited companies are subject to exactly the same rules in the Companies Act 2006. Both types of limited company produce annual reports and accounts (these are also referred to by the term financial statements). Public limited companies are also subject to stock exchange rules and regulations. A more complex financial reporting regime applies to public limited companies in that they also have to comply with various corporate governance codes, which seek to improve their ethics and accountability. Chapter 17 provides a brief overview of the corporate governance code which currently applies to public limited companies.

WHY IS THIS RELEVANT TO ME?   Public and private limited companies

To enable you as a business professional to:

- Gain an awareness of the distinctive characteristics of the two types of limited company
- Appreciate the differences between public and private limited companies

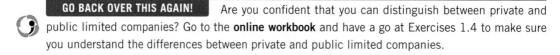

GO BACK OVER THIS AGAIN!   Are you confident that you can distinguish between private and public limited companies? Go to the **online workbook** and have a go at Exercises 1.4 to make sure you understand the differences between private and public limited companies.

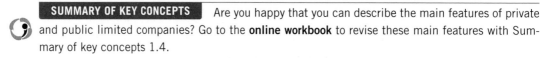

SUMMARY OF KEY CONCEPTS   Are you happy that you can describe the main features of private and public limited companies? Go to the **online workbook** to revise these main features with Summary of key concepts 1.4.

WHAT IS ACCOUNTING?

Let's start with a definition.

Accounting summarises numerical data relating to past events and presents this data as information to managers and other interested parties as a basis for both decision making and control purposes as presented in Figure 1.5.

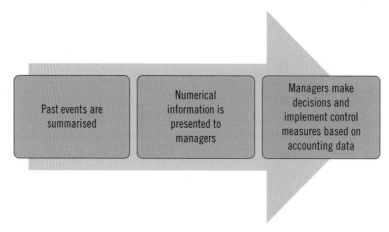

Figure 1.5 What is accounting?

This is quite a lot to take in, so let's unpick the various strands of this definition.

1. Numerical data: accounting information is mostly, but not always, presented in money terms. It could just as easily be a league table of football teams with details of games won, games lost and games drawn, goals for and goals against and points gained, all of which is numerical information. Or it could be a list of schools in a particular area with percentages of pupils gaining five GCSEs grades 1–9 and average A-level points at each school. In a business, it could be the number of units of product produced rather than just their cost, or the number of units sold in a given period of time. The critical point here is that accounting data is presented in the form of numbers.

2. Relating to past events: accounting systems gather data and then summarise these data to present details of what has happened. A league table is a summary of past results. Similarly, a total of sales for the month will be a summary of all the individual sales made on each day of that month and relating to that past period of time.

3. Information presented to managers: managers have the power and authority to use accounting information to take action now to maintain or improve future outcomes. In the same way, if a team is in the middle of the league table but aspires to a higher position, the team manager can take steps to hire better coaches, buy in the contracts of players with higher skill levels and sell the contractual rights of underperforming players. If a school wants to improve their examination results, they will take steps to determine what is preventing better performance and try to correct these deficiencies.

4. As a basis for decision making: accounting information is used to determine what went well and which events did not turn out quite as anticipated. For example, demand for a business's product over the past month might not have reached the levels expected. If this is the case, managers can take steps to determine whether the selling price is too high and should be reduced, whether there are defects in the products that require rectification or whether the product is just out of date and no longer valued by consumers. On the other hand, if demand for a product is outstripping supply, then managers can take the decision to divert business resources to increase production to meet that higher demand.

5. Control purposes: businesses, as we shall see in Chapter 14, prepare budgets prior to the start of an accounting period (usually 12 months) which set out what they aim to achieve in terms of sales, profits and cash flows. A comparison of actual outcomes with the budget will enable managers to decide where the budget was met, where the budget was exceeded and where the budget failed to reach expectations. Then the causes of the last two outcomes can be investigated and action taken to address the reasons behind the underperformance or to take advantage of better than expected results. The future is uncertain, but businesses will still plan by predicting to the best of their ability what they expect to occur in the following months and then compare actual outcomes with what they expected to happen as a means of controlling operations. Published financial statements of companies are used by investors and lenders to determine whether investments should be made in or money lent to those companies.

WHY IS THIS RELEVANT TO ME?   Accounting definition

To enable you as a business professional to:

• Understand what accounting is

• Appreciate that the production of accounting information is not an end in itself but is a tool to enable you to understand, direct and control business, investment, lending or other activities

---

SUMMARY OF KEY CONCEPTS   How clearly have you remembered the definition of accounting given earlier? Go to the **online workbook** to revise this definition with Summary of key concepts 1.5.

GO BACK OVER THIS AGAIN!   If this all still seems very complicated, visit the **online workbook** Exercises 1.5 and 1.6 to enable you to appreciate that you are already working with accounting data on a daily basis.

GO BACK OVER THIS AGAIN!   Are you certain you can define accounting? Go to the **online workbook** Exercises 1.7 to make sure you can say what accounting is and what role it performs in a business context.

CONTROL, ACCOUNTING AND ACCOUNTABILITY

The function of accounting information as a mechanism through which to control outcomes and activities can be illustrated further. Representatives are accountable for their actions to those people who have placed them in positions of power or trust. Accounting information is thus provided so that individuals and organisations can render an account of what they have done with the resources placed in their care. Example 1.1 provides an everyday illustration of these ideas.

EXAMPLE 1.1

Your employer pays your salary into your bank account while various payments are made out of your account to pay your bills and other outgoings. Your bank then provides you with a statement (either online or in paper copy) on a regular basis so that you can check whether they have accounted for your money correctly or not.

In the same way, company directors present financial accounts to shareholders and other interested parties on an annual basis to give an account of how they have looked after the money and other resources entrusted to them and how they have used that money to invest and generate income for shareholders. Local and national governments regularly publish information on the taxes collected and how those taxes have been spent. This information enables politicians to render an account of how taxes collected have been used to provide goods and services to citizens.

Where power and resources are entrusted to others, it is important that they are accountable for what they have done with that power and those resources. If your bank makes mistakes in the management of your account or charges you too much for managing your account, then you can change banks. If shareholders are unhappy with their directors' performance, they will not reappoint them as directors of their company. Instead, they will elect other directors to replace them in the expectation that these new directors will manage their investment much more carefully and profitably. Alternatively, they can sell their shares and invest their money in companies that do provide them with higher profits and higher dividends. If voters are unhappy with how their local and national politicians have taxed them or how they have spent their taxes, they will vote for different representatives with different policies more to their liking.

Persons entrusted by others with resources are in the position of stewards, looking after those resources for the benefit of other parties. Providing an account of their stewardship of those resources helps those other parties control the actions of their stewards. At the same time, accounts enable these other parties to make decisions on whether to continue with their current stewards or to replace them with others who will perform more effectively and provide them with a more efficient and profitable service. These relationships are summarised in Figure 1.6.

WHY IS THIS RELEVANT TO ME?   Control, accounting and accountability

To enable you as a business professional to:

- Appreciate that accounting functions as a control on the actions of others
- Understand how you will be entrusted with a business's resources and that you will be accountable for your stewardship of those resources

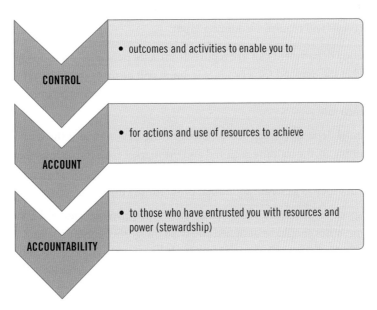

CONTROL
- outcomes and activities to enable you to

ACCOUNT
- for actions and use of resources to achieve

ACCOUNTABILITY
- to those who have entrusted you with resources and power (stewardship)

Figure 1.6 Control, accounting and accountability

1

GO BACK OVER THIS AGAIN!   Are you quite sure you understand how accounting helps with control and accountability? Go to the **online workbook** Exercises 1.8 to make sure you understand the links between accounting, accountability and control.

THE ROLE OF ACCOUNTING INFORMATION IN BUSINESS DECISION MAKING

Businesses are run to make a profit. Businesses that do not make a profit fail and are closed down. In order to achieve this profit aim, businesses need to make and implement decisions on a daily basis. Such decisions might comprise, among others, some or all of the following:

- What products should we produce?
- What services should we provide?
- How much do our products cost to make?
- How much do our services cost to provide?
- What price should we charge for our products or services?
- Should we be taking on more employees?
- How much will the additional employees cost?
- Will the cost of the new employees be lower than the income they will generate?
- Should we be expanding into bigger premises?
- Will the costs of the bigger premises be outweighed by the increase in income?
- How will we finance our expansion?
- Should we take out a bank loan or ask the shareholders to buy more shares?

All of these decisions will require accounting input:

- The marketing department can use reports from sales personnel and consumer evaluations to tell us what the demand for a product is, but it will be up to the accounting staff to tell us what the product costs to make and what the selling price should be in order to generate a profit on each sale.
- The personnel department can tell us about hiring new staff and the legal obligations incurred in doing so, the training required and the market rates for such workers, but it will be the accounting staff who can tell us what level of productivity the new employees will have to achieve in order to generate additional profit for the business.
- The strategy department can tell us what sort of premises we should be looking for, how these new premises should be designed and what image they should present, but it will be the accounting staff who can tell us how many products we will have to make and sell for the new premises to cover their additional costs and the best way in which to finance this expansion.

Accounting is thus at the heart of every decision and every activity that a business undertakes, as shown in Figure 1.7.

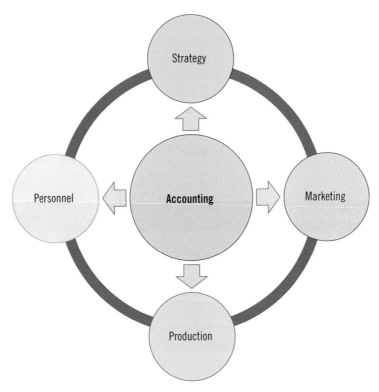

Figure 1.7 Accounting's central role in business activity and business decision making

At this early stage of your studies, it is easy to think of each department in a business just sticking to its own specialist field of expertise, operating in isolation from all the others, concentrating on their own aims and goals. You might reply that you would never think of a business as just a loose grouping of separate departments all doing their own thing with no thought for the bigger picture. But pause for a moment and ask yourself whether you treat all your current year study modules as interlinked or as totally separate subjects? You should see them as interlinked and look to see how all the subjects interact, but it is too easy to adopt a blinkered approach and compartmentalise each different aspect of your studies.

As these decisions and discussion illustrate, all business decisions require input from different departments and information from one department has to be integrated with information from other departments before an overall coordinated plan of action is put into operation. Businesses operate as cohesive entities, with all departments pulling in the same direction rather than each following their own individual pathway. Management make decisions and implement strategies, but underpinning all these decisions and strategies is accounting information.

This central role for accountants and accounting information puts accounting staff under pressure to perform their roles effectively and efficiently. After all, if the information presented by the accounting staff is defective in any way, the wrong decision could be made and losses rather than profits might result. Therefore, accountants have to ensure that the information they provide is as accurate and up to date as possible to enable management to make the most effective decisions.

Ideally, accounting staff will always be striving to improve the information they provide to management as better information will result in more informed and more effective decisions.

To illustrate the importance of the accounting function, take a moment to think what would happen if we did not have accounting information. Businesses would be lost without the vital information provided by accounting. If accounting did not exist, there would be no information relating to costs, no indication of what had been achieved in the past as a point of comparison for what is being achieved now, no figures on which to base taxation assessments, no proof that results are as companies claim they are. In short, if accounting did not exist, someone would have to invent it.

WHY IS THIS RELEVANT TO ME?   The role of accounting information in business decision making

To enable you as a business professional to:

- Appreciate that business decisions depend upon input from different departments and that decisions are not made in isolation by one department acting on its own

- Appreciate the importance of accounting information in business decision making

- Understand that accounting is not a stand-alone department but an integral part of all organisations

---

 MULTIPLE CHOICE QUESTIONS   Are you convinced that you understand what role accounting plays in business decision making? Go to the **online workbook** Multiple choice questions 1.1 to make sure you can suggest how accounting and accounting information would be used in the context of a business decision.

WHAT QUALITIES SHOULD ACCOUNTING INFORMATION POSSESS?

Given the pivotal role of accounting information in business decision making, what sort of qualities should such information possess for it to be useful in making these decisions? Helpfully, the International Accounting Standards Board (IASB) in its *Conceptual Framework for Financial Reporting* provides guidance in this area. The IASB states that financial information should possess the following two fundamental qualitative characteristics:

- Relevance

- Faithful representation

In addition, the IASB's *Conceptual Framework* identifies the following qualitative characteristics that enhance the usefulness of information that is relevant and faithfully represented:

- Comparability

- Verifiability

- Timeliness
- Understandability

This hierarchy of qualitative characteristics is shown in Figure 1.8.

What does each of the above qualitative characteristics represent? Table 1.1 considers the characteristics of each of the two fundamental and four enhancing qualities of financial information. We shall note at relevant points in later chapters the ways in which these *Conceptual Framework* qualitative characteristics apply in practice.

Let's think about how the qualities considered above apply to accounting information. Taking the bank statement (Example 1.1) considered under control, accounting and accountability earlier in this chapter, our thoughts might be as shown in Table 1.2.

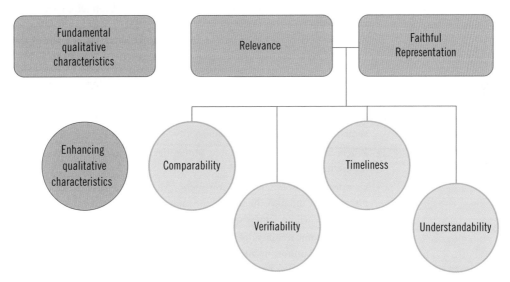

Figure 1.8 The qualitative characteristics of financial information

Table 1.1 The qualities of accounting information

Qualitative characteristic	Considerations
Relevance	• Relevant information is capable of making a difference in the decisions made by users. • Relevant information may be predictive and assist users in making predictions about the future or it may be confirmatory by assisting users to assess the accuracy of past predictions. • Relevant information can be both predictive and confirmatory.

→

1

Qualitative characteristic	Considerations
Faithful representation	• Financial information must not only represent relevant economic phenomena (transactions and events), but it must also faithfully represent the substance of the phenomena that it purports to represent. • Perfectly faithful representation of economic phenomena in words and numbers requires that the information presented must have three characteristics: it must be complete, neutral and free from error. • Do note that free from error does not mean that information must be perfectly accurate. Much accounting information, as you will see throughout your studies, relies on best estimates or the most likely outcomes. The IASB *Conceptual Framework* makes it clear that 'free from error means there are no errors or omissions in the description of the phenomenon, and the process used to produce the reported information has been selected and applied with no errors in the process. In this context, free from error does not mean perfectly accurate in all respects' (IASB *Conceptual Framework for Financial Reporting* paragraph 2.18).
Comparability	• Information should be comparable over time. • The usefulness of information is enhanced if it can be compared with similar information about other entities for the same reporting period and with similar information about the same entity for other reporting periods. • Where information is comparable, similarities and differences are readily apparent. • Comparability does not mean consistency. However, consistency of presentation and measurement of the same items in the same way from year to year will help to achieve comparability. • Similarly, comparability does not mean that economic phenomena must be presented uniformly. Information about the same phenomena will be presented in similar but not in the same ways by different entities. The differences in the presentation of such phenomena will not be so great as to prevent comparability.
Verifiability	• Verifiability provides users with assurance that information is faithfully presented and reports the economic phenomena it purports to represent. • To ensure verifiability, it should be possible to prove the information presented is accurate in all major respects. • The accuracy of information can be verified by observation or recalculation. • Financial information will often be subject to independent audit and the independent auditors will use various techniques and approaches to verify the financial information presented.
Timeliness	• The decision usefulness of information is enhanced if it is available to users in time for it to be capable of influencing their decisions. • The decision usefulness of information generally declines with time although information used in identifying trends continues to be timely in the future.

→

Qualitative characteristic	Considerations
Understandability	• This characteristic should not be confused with simplicity. • As you will see in your future studies, financial accounting can involve very complex calculations, details and disclosures. Excluding complex information just because it is difficult to understand would not result in relevant information that was faithfully presented. Reports that excluded such information would be incomplete and would thus mislead users. • Readers of financial reports are assumed to have a reasonable knowledge of business and economic activities in order to make sense of what they are presented with. If they are unable to understand the information presented, then the IASB recommends using an adviser. • To help users understand information presented, that information should be classified, characterised and presented clearly.

Table 1.2 How your bank statement fulfils the qualities of accounting information

Relevant?	• Your bank statement is capable of making a difference to the decisions you make. Depending on your current level of cash, you are able to decide to spend less, increase the income into your bank account or decide to invest surplus funds in high interest accounts. • Looking at your current income and expenditure, you can predict what is likely to happen in the future in your bank account. Where you have made predictions about what cash you would have left at the end of each month, you can then confirm how accurate or inaccurate those predictions were and make future predictions about how much you will have left at the end of the next month to decide what you should do with these surplus funds. • Accurate predictions in the past will enable you to be confident that your future predictions will be accurate too.
Faithful representation?	• Your bank statement is presented by your bank, so this should be a faithful representation of your income and expenditure (economic phenomena, transactions and events) over a given period of time. • It is in your bank's interest to ensure that the information presented in your bank statement is complete, neutral (the statement just presents the facts of your income and expenditure) and free from error. Any errors you do pick up can be notified to your bank for correction.
Comparable?	• Presentation of your bank statement does not differ over time and is presented in the same format every month so this information is comparable over different periods of time. • This consistency of presentation and measurement of income and expenditure in the same way from month to month and year to year will help to achieve the required comparability.

→

Verifiable?	• The accuracy of your statement can be verified by reference to your list of standing orders, direct debits, debit card transactions, cheques written and income from payslips and other sources. • You can add up your bank statement to make sure the balance at the end of each month is correct (recalculation). • You are thus the auditor of your own bank account, checking and verifying that the information presented is accurate and free from error to ensure that your statement is faithfully presented and reports the substance of the economic phenomena it purports to represent.
Timely?	• Your bank statement is received each month (or you can access it instantly online), so it is presented in time for it to be capable of influencing your decisions. If your bank statement were to be sent annually, this would be much less relevant information as it would be seriously out of date by the time you received it and much less capable of making a difference to the decisions you make. • However, past bank statements are still timely when comparing trends of income and expenditure across different periods of time.
Understandable?	• You can certainly understand your bank statement as it shows you the money going into and out of your account. • You have a reasonable knowledge of your finances so you can make sense of what your bank statement presents you with. If you are unable to understand the information presented, then you can always contact your bank for advice. • To help you understand the information presented, transactions are classified, characterised and presented clearly in your bank statement.

 GO BACK OVER THIS AGAIN!   Are you sure that you can define relevance, faithful representation, comparability, verifiability, timeliness and understandability? Go to the **online workbook**
Exercises 1.9 to make sure you can define these qualities of financial information accurately.

 SUMMARY OF KEY CONCEPTS   Can you state and define the two fundamental and four enhancing qualities of financial information? Go to the **online workbook** to check your grasp of these
qualities with Summary of key concepts 1.6–1.11.

Materiality

A further requirement of financial information for decision-making purposes is that it should
not be overloaded with unnecessary detail. This leads us on to the concept of materiality. The IASB
defines materiality as follows:

> Information is material if omitting it or misstating it could influence decisions that … users … make
> on the basis of … financial information about a specific reporting entity. In other words, materiality
> is an entity-specific aspect of relevance based on the nature or magnitude, or both, of the items to
> which the information relates in the context of an individual entity's financial report.

Source: IASB *Conceptual Framework for Financial Reporting,* paragraph 2.11

How is materiality applied in practice? Example 1.2 provides instances of the circumstances in which an item might be defined as material.

An item could be material by size ('magnitude' in the above definition). If a shop makes £2m of sales a year, then the sale of a 50p carton of milk missed out of those sales will not be material. However, in a steel fabrications business making £2m of sales a year, the omission of a £250,000 sale of a steel frame for a building would be material as it makes up 12.5% of the sales for the year.

As well as size, items can be material by nature. The theft of £5 from the till by a member of staff would be unlikely to be material. However, the theft of £5 from the till by the managing director would be: if you are an investor in the business, this tells you that your investment might not be very safe if the managing director is willing to steal from the business.

MULTIPLE CHOICE QUESTIONS   Are you confident that you can decide whether a piece of information is material or not? Go to the **online workbook** Multiple choice questions 1.2 to make sure you can determine whether information is material or not.

SUMMARY OF KEY CONCEPTS   Can you recall the definition of materiality? Go to the **online workbook** to check your grasp of this definition in Summary of key concepts 1.12.

Cost v. benefit

The IASB recognises that there is a cost in collecting, processing, verifying and disseminating financial information (IASB *Conceptual Framework for Financial Reporting*, paragraphs 2.39–2.43). Therefore, information should only be presented if the benefits of providing that information outweigh the costs of obtaining it. Example 1.3 suggests how you might weigh up the costs and benefits in a practical but non-accounting situation.

You know that there is a wonderful quote in a book that you have read that would really enhance your essay and provide you with a brilliant conclusion. However, you have forgotten where to find this quote and you have not written down the name of the book or the page reference. Your essay must be handed in by 4.00 p.m. today and it is already 3.40 p.m. You still have to print off your essay before handing it in. If your essay is handed in after 4.00 p.m. you will be awarded a mark of 0% and so fail the assignment.

The costs of searching for the quote outweigh the benefits of finding it as you will not receive any marks if your essay is late so you print off your essay and hand it in on time and, when it is returned, you have scored 65% and gained a pass on this piece of coursework.

1

GO BACK OVER THIS AGAIN!   Are you quite certain that you understand how cost v. benefit works? Visit the **online workbook** Exercises 1.10 to reinforce your understanding.

SUMMARY OF KEY CONCEPTS   Do you think you can remember how to define cost v. benefit? Go to the **online workbook** to check your grasp of this definition in Summary of key concepts 1.13.

THE USERS OF ACCOUNTING INFORMATION

As we have seen, accounting is all about providing information to interested parties so that they can make decisions on the basis of that information. But who are the users of this accounting information and what decisions do they make as a result of receiving that information?

Accounting is made up of two branches. The first of these branches provides information to external users and the other provides information to internal users. The information needs of both these user groups differ in important ways as we shall see.

Accounting branch 1: financial accounting

Financial accounting is the reporting of past information to users outside the organisation. This information is presented in the annual report and accounts that all companies are obliged to produce by law, publish on their websites and lodge with the Registrar of Companies at Companies House. Directors of companies produce these annual reports and accounts for issue to shareholders to provide an account of how they have used the resources entrusted to them to generate profits, dividends and value for the shareholders. Even if a business entity is not a company and there is no legal obligation to produce accounts, it will still produce financial statements to provide evidence of what it has achieved over the past year. These accounts will also be used as a basis for enabling the business's managers or owners and its lenders and advisers to make decisions based upon them as well as being used by the taxation authorities to determine the tax due on the profits for the year.

What is the aim of these financial accounts and reports and what do they provide? The International Accounting Standards Board states that the objective of financial reporting (not just financial statements) is as follows.

The objective of general purpose financial reporting is to provide financial information about the reporting entity that is useful to existing and potential investors, lenders and other creditors in making decisions relating to providing resources to the entity. Those decisions involve decisions about:

a) buying, selling or holding equity and debt instruments;

b) providing or settling loans and other forms of credit;

c) or exercising rights to vote on, or otherwise influence, management's actions that affect the use of the entity's economic resources.

Source: IASB *Conceptual Framework for Financial Reporting*, paragraph 1.2

While the IASB focuses on the financial information needs of existing and potential investors, lenders and other creditors, it does envisage that other users might find general purpose financial reports useful:

Other parties, such as regulators and members of the public other than investors, lenders and other creditors, may also find general purpose financial reports useful. However, those reports are not primarily directed to these other groups.

Source: IASB *Conceptual Framework for Financial Reporting*, paragraph 1.10

Financial information is reported to users external to the organisation through three key statements: the statement of financial position, the statement of profit or loss and the statement of cash flows. We shall be studying all three of these financial statements in this book as they will form the bedrock of your professional career in accounting. Chapter 2 will consider the statement of financial position and how this presents the financial position of an entity at a given point in time. Chapter 3 will look at how entities' financial performance is measured and reported in the statement of profit or loss while Chapter 6 will provide a detailed overview of the statement of cash flows. Ways in which users can evaluate these particular financial statements and what they tell them about the performance, the financial stability and the investment potential of entities will be the subject of Chapters 8 and 9. However, our concern at this point is with the users of financial accounts and reports, what those different user groups might use financial reports for and the economic decisions they might base upon them.

As well as the three primary user groups noted by the IASB, other parties who might find general purpose financial statements useful include the following:

• Employees and their representative groups

• Customers

• Governments and their agencies

• The public

What information would each of the identified user groups expect to find in external financial reports that would enable them to make economic decisions? Table 1.3 provides examples of some of the questions that the seven categories of user will ask when looking at financial statements: can you think of additional questions that each user group will ask?

Table 1.3 The external users of financial statements

User group	Examples of questions asked by each user group
Existing and potential investors (this group would include investment advisers)	• What profit has the company made for me in my position as a shareholder/investor? • What financial gains am I making from this company? • Would it be worthwhile for me to invest more money in the shares of this company? • If the company has not done well this year, should I sell my shares or hold onto them? • Does my company comply with all the relevant company and stock market regulations? • Is my company run effectively and efficiently?
Lenders	• Will this company be able to repay what has been lent? • Will this company be able to pay loan instalments and interest as they fall due? • Is this company in danger of insolvency? • What cash resources and cash generating ability does this company have?
Other creditors (this group will include suppliers of goods and services to the entity)	• Will I be paid for goods or services I have supplied? • Will I be paid on time so that I can pay my suppliers? • Will my customer expand so that I can expand, too?
Employees and their representative groups	• How stable is the company I work for? • Is the company I work for making profits? • If the company is making losses, will it survive for the foreseeable future? • What about the continuity of my employment? • Should I be looking for employment elsewhere? • If the company I work for is profitable, will I be awarded a pay rise or a bonus? • What retirement benefit scheme does my company offer to employees? • Is my employer investing in the future prosperity of the business?
Customers	• Will the entity survive in the long term so that it can continue to provide me with goods and services?
Governments and their agencies	• What taxation does this entity pay? • What contribution does this entity make to the economy? • Does this entity export goods to other countries?
The public	• What contribution does this entity make to society? • Does this entity make donations to charity? • If this entity is a major local employer, will they survive into the future to ensure the health of the local economy?

Many questions that users of financial reports ask will be common to all categories of user. For example, investors might ask questions about the ethical and environmental record of the company and whether this is the kind of organisation they would want to be involved with and be seen to be involved with. But ethically and environmentally concerned employees might also ask the same questions and lenders, concerned about their reputation and being seen to do business with unethical organisations, might be looking for the same information. Suppliers and customers will have similar concerns as their image and reputation will be shaped by those they do business with.

Similarly, all user groups will want to know about the availability of cash with which to pay dividends (investors), salaries (employees), loan interest and loan repayments (lenders), goods supplied on credit (suppliers) and taxes due (governments). Even customers and the public will be concerned about the availability of cash, as, without sufficient inflows of cash from trading, companies will collapse.

While users of external financial statements might legitimately ask the questions mentioned, the extent to which such reports provide this information varies. Some financial reports are very detailed in their coverage, others less so. As you gradually become familiar with the content of published financial reports and accounts, your awareness of shortcomings in these documents will increase.

> **WHY IS THIS RELEVANT TO ME?**   The users of accounting information
>
> To enable you as a business professional to understand:
>
> * Who the target audience is for the reports that you will produce
> * Which external parties are interested in the financial information provided by business entities
> * The kinds of answers users of external financial reports expect from the information provided

GO BACK OVER THIS AGAIN!   Are you convinced that you understand what information particular user groups are looking for in published financial reports? Go to the **online workbook** Exercises 1.11 to check your understanding in this area.

SUMMARY OF KEY CONCEPTS   Can you recall the seven user groups of financial accounting information? Go to the **online workbook** to check your knowledge of these user groups with Summary of key concepts 1.14.

SUMMARY OF KEY CONCEPTS   Are you confident that you can state the objective of financial statements? Go to the **online workbook** to check your knowledge of this objective with Summary of key concepts 1.15.

Accounting branch 2: cost and management accounting

Cost and management accounting is concerned with reporting accounting and cost information to users within an organisation. As the name suggests, management accounting information is used to help managers manage the business and its activities. Cost and management accountants are

1

first concerned with the costs that go into producing products and services to determine a selling price for those products and services that will generate a profit for the business. Management accounting information is then used to plan levels of production and activity in the future as well as deciding what products to produce and sell to maximise profits for the business. As well as planning what the business is going to do, management accounting produces reports to evaluate the results of past plans to see whether they achieved their aims and the ways in which improvements could be made.

While financial accounting reports what has happened in the past, management accounting is very much concerned with both the present and the future and how accounting information can be used for short-term decision making and longer-term planning. In this book we will be looking at costs and costing in Chapters 11 and 15, while Chapter 12 will show you how costs and cost behaviour can be used in making short-term decisions. Chapter 13 then considers the technique of standard costing as an aid to quick decision making and performance evaluation. Chapter 14 focuses on the key short-term planning technique of budgeting, while Chapter 16 extends the time horizon to look at the ways in which long-term business planning determines whether a capital project is worth investing in or not.

As we shall see, the format of financial accounting statements is very much prescribed by legislation and the requirements of the International Accounting Standards Board, whereas management accounting statements are presented in the format most appropriate for managers to aid them in their decision making. The distinction between financial and management accounting information will be dealt with in greater detail in Chapter 10.

WHY IS THIS RELEVANT TO ME?   The two branches of accounting

To enable you as a business professional to:

- Appreciate the wide range of internal and external users of accounting information
- Distinguish quickly between financial and management accounting

---

THE STRUCTURE AND REGULATION OF THE ACCOUNTING PROFESSION

Professional accounting bodies have been set up in many countries around the world. These professional accounting bodies are responsible for admitting individuals to membership and for regulation and oversight of their conduct as professional people once they have been accepted as members. Admission to the professional bodies is achieved through a combination of examinations and practical experience. The main professional accounting bodies in the United Kingdom and Ireland are:

- The Association of Chartered Certified Accountants (ACCA)
- The Chartered Institute of Management Accountants (CIMA)

- The Chartered Institute of Public Finance and Accounting (CIPFA)
- The Institute of Chartered Accountants in England and Wales (ICAEW)
- The Institute of Chartered Accountants in Ireland (ICAI)
- The Institute of Chartered Accountants in Scotland (ICAS).

Qualified accountants undertake the preparation of financial statements and reports, the audit of financial statements and the provision of taxation and business advice to individuals and organisations. As professionals, qualified accountants are expected to adhere to high standards of conduct to maintain the standing of the profession and to provide a professional service to their clients, employers and the public. Accountants are expected to behave with integrity, being honest in all their professional and business relationships. They are also expected to be objective, to carry out their duties with due care and competence, to maintain the confidentiality of information acquired in the course of fulfilling their duties and to comply at all times with relevant laws and regulations. Where accountants breach these ethical rules of conduct, their professional bodies will take action to discipline them with warnings, fines and, in the most serious cases, exclusion from membership.

As well as adhering to the professional bodies' expected standards of behaviour and ethical conduct, qualified accountants are expected to ensure that accepted accounting standards have been applied correctly in the presentation of financial information. In the European Union and in the UK accounting standards are set by the International Accounting Standards Board (IASB) for companies listed on a stock exchange and by the UK Financial Reporting Council (FRC) for smaller unlisted and non-public interest companies. Failure to apply these accounting standards correctly will also result in an accountant's professional body taking disciplinary action against a member.

Poor management and dishonest behaviour on the part of directors in the past led to investors losing a lot of money. Governments and stock exchanges around the world responded by setting up various committees to report on the state of corporate governance, the way in which large companies were run and to make recommendations for improvement. As a result of these recommendations, corporate governance codes were formulated to enshrine best practice and to ensure that large companies were run in an open and honest manner to safeguard shareholders' and the general public's interests in those companies. Professional accountants are expected to adhere to and apply these corporate governance codes in businesses in which they work to ensure the transparency of information presented by these companies. Further consideration of corporate governance will be presented in Chapter 17 and this introduction to the topic will form the basis of your future studies in this area.

WHY IS THIS RELEVANT TO ME?   Structure and regulation of the accounting profession

To provide you as a business professional with:

- A quick overview of the accounting profession and the ways in which it is regulated
- An indication of the standards of behaviour to be expected from professional accountants and other persons holding positions of responsibility in companies

1

THE INTERNATIONAL ACCOUNTING STANDARDS BOARD (IASB)

As noted earlier (this chapter, The structure and regulation of the accounting profession), the IASB is responsible for developing and issuing accounting standards. These accounting standards are built upon the principles and definitions set out in the IASB's *Conceptual Framework for Financial Reporting* and must be adhered to by companies when producing and presenting their annual financial statements. We shall see how the definitions in the *Conceptual Framework* inform the content of the three main financial statements in Chapters 2, 3, 4 and 6. The development process for an accounting standard follows the process outlined in Figure 1.9.

The first step in developing a new standard is the identification of a reporting problem. There may be a variety of different approaches to presenting information about a particular item in financial statements. Such variety will lead to a lack of relevant information due to the lack of comparability between the financial statements of different entities. The IASB then develops a draft accounting standard called an Exposure Draft. This Exposure Draft will propose a single approach to the reporting of the particular item in the financial statements to ensure that reporting differences are eliminated. Interested parties then comment on the proposals in the Exposure Draft, supporting or disagreeing with the proposed approach. Once the comment period is complete, the IASB takes all the comments into account when developing the final accounting standard. The standard developed and issued is known as an International Financial Reporting Standard, abbreviated to IFRS. Prior to the establishment of the IASB under its current constitution in 2001, its predecessor body the International Accounting Standards Committee issued statements called International Accounting Standards, abbreviated to IAS. As each IAS is revised in line with current accounting and reporting practice, it is reissued as an IFRS. You will study all the IFRS and IAS in very great detail later on in your degree and professional exams. A complete list of IFRS and IAS in issue at June 2020 is presented in the Appendix to this chapter.

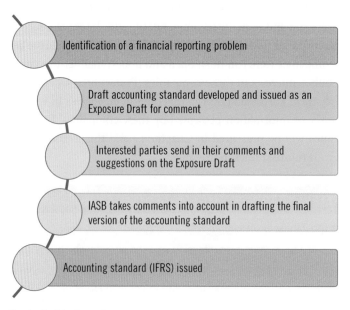

Figure 1.9 The accounting standard development process

WHY IS THIS RELEVANT TO ME?   The international accounting standards board

To enable you as a business professional to:

- Appreciate the process of developing and issuing accounting standards
- Understand the role of the IASB in the accounting standard development process

THE LIMITATIONS OF ACCOUNTING INFORMATION

We have seen that accounting information plays an anchor role in decision making for businesses and other users. However, there are various aspects of business performance that accounting does not cover. While it is important to know what accounting is and what it does, it is just as important to be aware of what accounting does not do.

First, accounting does not provide you with measures of the quality of an organisation's performance. The quality of what an entity produces or provides is measured by its customers and their level of satisfaction with goods and services delivered, their willingness to recommend an organisation's products and the number of times they return to buy more goods or use more services. While measures can be devised to assess recommendations and repeat business, this is not a function that accounting would normally fulfil.

Similarly, a business entity may make a profit, but accounting does not tell us the time, effort and thought that went into delivering the products and services to generate that profit. In the same way, your team may win, draw or lose, but the bare result does not tell you about the quality of entertainment on offer, whether your team played badly but still managed to scrape a vital goal or whether they played brilliantly and were just unlucky.

Second, accounting does not tell you about the pollution and environmental or social damage an entity has caused. Organisations will report redundancies as an internal cost-saving opportunity for the business while ignoring the wider external effects of their actions. Thus, businesses do not report the destruction of communities built around an organisation's operations and all the burdens that this imposes upon families, social services, the National Health Service and the state. Similarly, while companies use air, water and other natural resources in their production processes, there is no formal, legal requirement that they should report on the damage they cause to these resources. Despite the lack of regulation in this last area, we shall look in more detail in Chapter 17 at the current debate surrounding accounting for the environment and sustainability accounting.

Finally, accounting does not provide any valuation or measure of the skills base and knowledge of organisations. Boards of directors will thank their staff for all their hard work and efforts during the previous financial year, but the monetary value of the employees to the business does not feature in financial statements. This is attributable to the fact that valuing staff is exceptionally complex due to the subjective nature of such valuations and the fact that employees do not meet the asset definition and recognition criteria (Chapter 2, Assets). Thus, you might think your financial accounting lecturer is the most organised and most informative tutor you have seen on your course so far, while your friend is grumbling about how uninteresting the lectures

1

and tutorials are and how she cannot follow them. In the same way, while employees, their skills, knowledge and abilities are the most valuable resources in a business, these resources cannot be measured in money or any other numerical terms and so do not appear in the financial statements. As accounting is about measuring items in financial statements, you might find this omission rather odd given the significance of employees to the success or failure of a business. However, it is important to remember that Albert Einstein's famous dictum is just as applicable to accounting as it is to many other disciplines: 'Not everything that can be counted counts. Not everything that counts can be counted.'

WHY IS THIS RELEVANT TO ME?   The limitations of accounting information

To enable you as a business professional to:

- Gain an awareness of the aspects of business performance that accounting does not cover
- Appreciate the limitations of accounting and accounting information
- Understand that accounting and accounting information will not necessarily provide you with all the information you need to make decisions or evaluate an organisation's performance

SUMMARY OF KEY CONCEPTS   Are you confident that you can state the limitations of accounting and accounting information? Go to the **online workbook** to check your knowledge of these limitations with Summary of key concepts 1.16.

APPENDIX: CURRENT IFRS AND IAS IN ISSUE AT JUNE 2020

Listed below are the numbers and titles of all International Financial Reporting Standards and all International Accounting Standards in issue and currently in use at June 2020.

IFRS 1 First-time adoption of International Financial Reporting Standards

IFRS 2 Share-based payment

IFRS 3 Business combinations

IFRS 5 Non-current assets held for sale and discontinued operations

IFRS 6 Exploration for the evaluation of mineral resources

IFRS 7 Financial instruments: disclosures

IFRS 8 Operating segments

IFRS 9 Financial instruments

IFRS 10 Consolidated financial statements

IFRS 11 Joint arrangements

IFRS 12 Disclosure of interests in other entities

IFRS 13 Fair value measurement

IFRS 14 Regulatory deferral accounts

IFRS 15 Revenue from contracts with customers

IFRS 16 Leases

IFRS 17 Insurance contracts

IAS 1 Presentation of financial statements

IAS 2 Inventories

IAS 7 Statement of cash flows

IAS 8 Accounting policies, changes in accounting estimates and errors

IAS 10 Events after the reporting period

IAS 12 Income taxes

IAS 16 Property, plant and equipment

IAS 19 Employee benefits

IAS 20 Accounting for government grants and disclosure of government assistance

IAS 21 The effects of changes in foreign exchange rates

IAS 23 Borrowing costs

IAS 24 Related party disclosures

IAS 26 Accounting and reporting by retirement benefit plans

IAS 27 Separate financial statements

IAS 28 Investments in associates and joint ventures

IAS 29 Financial reporting in hyperinflationary economies

IAS 32 Financial instruments: presentation

IAS 33 Earnings per share

IAS 34 Interim financial reporting

IAS 36 Impairment of assets

IAS 37 Provisions, contingent liabilities and contingent assets

IAS 38 Intangible assets

IAS 40 Investment property

IAS 41 Agriculture

CHAPTER SUMMARY

You should now have learnt that:

- Very small businesses organise themselves as sole traders or partnerships that take on unlimited liability for the debts of their businesses
- Larger businesses organise themselves as limited liability companies whose investors (shareholders) have no obligation to meet the debts of their company beyond their investment in their company's share capital

- Accounting summarises numerical data relating to past events and presents this data as information to managers and other interested parties as a basis for both decision making and control purposes
- Accounting information is the bedrock upon which all business decisions are based
- Financial information should possess the two fundamental characteristics of relevance and faithful representation
- The qualitative characteristics of comparability, verifiability, timeliness and understandability will enhance the usefulness of information that is relevant and faithfully represented
- Financial accounting generates reports for users external to the business
- Financial accounting information is primarily aimed at existing and potential investors, lenders and other creditors who will find this information useful in making decisions about providing resources to the reporting entity
- Other user groups such as employees, customers, governments and the public may also find financial reporting information useful in making decisions and evaluating the performance of organisations
- Management accounting is prepared for internal users in a business to help them manage the business's activities
- Accounting does not measure, among other things, quality, pollution, social and environmental damage, human resources and the skills and knowledge base of organisations

 QUICK REVISION   Test your knowledge by attempting the activities in the **online workbook**, including flashcards on the key concepts, numerical exercises and Multiple choice questions. You can also try the further self-test questions which are available at www.oup.com/he/scott-i2a2e

END-OF-CHAPTER QUESTIONS

 Attempt the questions in the following sections and then look at the solutions which can be found in the **online workbook** to see whether there are areas that you need to revisit.

❯ RECALL AND REVIEW

❯**Question 1.1**

Which business format would be most suitable for the following businesses? Can you say why your chosen format would be most suited to each business?

- An oil exploration company
- A taxi driver
- A family-run knitwear manufacturing business
- Two friends setting up a dance school

> **Question 1.2**

What accounting and other information would the managers of the following organisations require in order to assess their performance and financial position?

- A charity
- A secondary school
- A university
- A manufacturing business

> **Question 1.3**

A premier league football club has received an offer for its star striker from Real Madrid. The star striker is eager to leave and join the Spanish team and the board of directors has reluctantly agreed to let him go for the transfer fee offered. The team now needs a new striker and the manager has been put in charge of identifying potential new centre forwards that the club could bid for. You have been asked by the manager to draw up a chart listing the numerical information about potential targets that the manager should take into account when evaluating possible replacements.

>> DEVELOP YOUR UNDERSTANDING

>> **Question 1.4**

Liam is an accounting student and his friend, Ela, is a management student. Both are required to take a basic accounting module in the first year of their studies. Ela is unsure why she needs to study accounting. How would you justify the claim that knowledge of accounting is helpful for a career in management? Explain how accounting information can be utilised by managers in the performance of their job.

>> **Question 1.5**

James has invested his savings of £200,000 in Aron plc. He is happy with his investment because at the end of the first year he has received £15,000 in dividends. A careful inspection of the accounting records by the auditors of Aron plc reveals that £250 of the company's assets has been lost. Further investigation indicates that £250 has been taken from the till by one of the top managers. James believes that this is a small amount of money compared to the cash he received from his investment. Do you agree with James? What would you advise?

>> **Question 1.6**

Accounting has two main branches, financial accounting and management accounting. Describe the differences between the two branches of accounting in terms of their:

- Objectives
- Main users
- Obligation to produce information
- Use of standards
- Type of information produced

1

》Question 1.7

Accounting is a profession. In the same way as other professions, accounting is regulated by professional accounting bodies. With regard to the accounting profession:

(a) Describe the types of services provided by qualified accountants.

(b) Describe the role played by professional accounting bodies.

(c) What will happen if a professional accounting body discovers a breach of the ethical rules of conduct by a qualified accountant?

》Question 1.8

Explain the main limitations of accounting and accounting information.

》》》TAKE IT FURTHER

》》Question 1.9

Jackson plc is a manufacturing company that produces car parts. The company was set up as a private limited company and financed entirely by Jamila Jackson in 2001. In 2020 the company decided to buy some key supplier companies in order to secure the supply of materials required in the production process. A large amount of investment was required to fulfil this ambitious expansion plan. The company successfully listed as a plc on the stock market and sold shares to the public to fund the expansion plan. The new shareholders require reassurance that their money is in safe hands and is working hard to increase their wealth.

Required

(a) Explain how accounting information can be used by the shareholders of Jackson plc to assess how the money they have invested in the company is being used.

(b) Explain what the shareholders can do if they think the company is not working to fulfil their expectations.

》》Question 1.10

Williamson Solutions is a software company currently operating in the United Kingdom. The company plans to expand its services to continental European countries. As this is a very important strategic decision, Maddie Barons, the CEO, calls for a meeting with the heads of all departments of the company including marketing, human resources, strategy, operations management and accounting. The head of the accounting department is on leave, so Maddie decides to postpone the meeting until her return.

Required

(a) Explain why Maddie insists on the presence at the meeting of the head of the accounting department.

(b) Describe how information provided by the accounting department can help the company make more informed and more effective business decisions in all its activities.

⟫ Question 1.11

The International Accounting Standards Board (IASB) develops, drafts and issues International Financial Reporting Standards (IFRS) that are applied globally to achieve consistent accounting practices at international level. The *Conceptual Framework for Financial Reporting* issued by the IASB is used in the development and drafting of IFRS. Briefly explain the following qualitative characteristics of accounting information as described by the IASB in its *Conceptual Framework for Financial Reporting*:

- Relevance
- Faithful representation
- Comparability
- Verifiability
- Timeliness
- Understandability

PART 1
FINANCIAL ACCOUNTING

CHAPTER 2   The statement of financial position

CHAPTER 3   The statement of profit or loss

CHAPTER 4   Double-entry bookkeeping 1: debits, credits,
             T accounts, the trial balance and the financial
             statements

CHAPTER 5   Double-entry bookkeeping 2: books of prime
             entry, accounting systems and other double-entry
             applications

CHAPTER 6   The statement of cash flows

CHAPTER 7   The financing of business

CHAPTER 8   Ratio analysis 1: profitability, efficiency and
             performance

CHAPTER 9   Ratio analysis 2: liquidity, working capital and
             long-term financial stability

THE STATEMENT OF FINANCIAL POSITION

2

LEARNING OUTCOMES

Once you have read this chapter and worked through the questions and examples in both this chapter and the online workbook, you should be able to:

- Define assets and liabilities

- Determine whether an entity should or should not recognise specific resources and obligations on its statement of financial position

- Distinguish between non-current and current assets and liabilities

- State the accounting equation

- Draw up a statement of financial position for organisations in compliance with the International Accounting Standards Board's requirements

- Explain how assets and liabilities are measured in monetary amounts at the statement of financial position date

- State what the statement of financial position does and does not show

- Understand how transactions affect two or more accounts on the statement of financial position (the duality principle)

- Correctly record the effect of transactions on assets, liabilities and equity in the statement of financial position

2

INTRODUCTION

Figure 2.1 summarises the elements that make up the statement of financial position. All financial statements present a statement of financial position. This is a summary, in money terms, of the assets an organisation controls and the liabilities an organisation owes to outside parties. To enable you to see how this statement is presented in full before we look at the detail, Illustration 2.1 shows the statement of financial position of Bunns the Bakers plc, a regional baker with a bakery and 20 shops in the East Midlands. At first glance, this might look confusing as there are all kinds of seemingly complex words and jargon. However, don't worry as, after working your way through this chapter and the materials in the online workbook, you will soon have a much clearer idea of what the words and jargon mean.

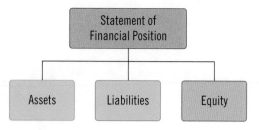

Figure 2.1 The statement of financial position

Notice that there are various headings provided and that these headings contain the words 'assets', 'liabilities' and 'equity'. In this chapter we will be looking at what constitutes an asset and a liability and how equity is calculated. We shall also review the criteria for recognising assets and liabilities and how those assets and liabilities are classified as current or non-current. Just as assets and liabilities can be recognised in an organisation's statement of financial position so, once assets have been used up or liabilities discharged, they are derecognised. This just means that they are removed from the statement of financial position as they are no longer controlled or owed by the entity.

Once the definitions are clear, we shall move on to constructing simple statements of financial position from given data. We shall then consider what the statement of financial position shows us and, equally importantly, what it does not show us. There are many misconceptions about what a statement of financial position represents. This chapter will dispel these misconceptions and provide you with a very precise idea of what the statement of financial position provides by way of information and what it does not.

Finally, at the end of the chapter, we will have a quick look at how new transactions affect the statement of financial position. Double-entry bookkeeping will be dealt with in much greater depth and detail in Chapters 4 and 5, but an early appreciation of how double entry works will give you an insight into the logic of accounting and how new transactions have a two-fold effect on figures in the financial statements of an organisation.

Illustration 2.1 Bunns the Bakers plc: statement of financial position at 31 March 2021

	2021 £000	2020 £000
ASSETS		
Non-current assets		
Intangible assets	50	55
Property, plant and equipment	11,750	11,241
Investments	65	59
	11,865	11,355
Current assets		
Inventories	60	55
Trade and other receivables	62	75
Cash and cash equivalents	212	189
	334	319
Total assets	12,199	11,674
LIABILITIES		
Current liabilities		
Current portion of long-term borrowings	300	300
Trade and other payables	390	281
Current tax liabilities	150	126
	840	707
Non-current liabilities		
Long-term borrowings	2,700	3,000
Long-term provisions	200	200
	2,900	3,200
Total liabilities	3,740	3,907
Net assets	8,459	7,767
EQUITY		
Called up share capital (£1 ordinary shares)	2,500	2,400
Share premium	1,315	1,180
Retained earnings	4,644	4,187
Total equity	8,459	7,767

GO BACK OVER THIS AGAIN!   A copy of this statement of financial position is available in the **online workbook**: you might like to keep this on screen or print off a copy for easy reference while you work your way through the material in this chapter. There is also an annotated copy of this statement of financial position at the back of the book to help you go over the relevant points again to reinforce your knowledge and learning.

TERMINOLOGY: STATEMENT OF FINANCIAL POSITION/BALANCE SHEET

International Financial Reporting Standards use the term 'statement of financial position' for what has traditionally been called the balance sheet. In keeping with the international focus of this book, the term 'statement of financial position' will be used throughout. However, you will find the two terms used interchangeably in your wider reading, so you should understand that the terms balance sheet and statement of financial position refer to the same summary statement of assets, liabilities and equity.

ASSETS

Illustration 2.1 presents the statement of financial position for Bunns the Bakers plc. As noted in the introduction, the first part of this statement of financial position shows you the assets that an entity controls. However, the first questions to ask are: 'What is an asset?' and 'What does an asset represent?'

The International Accounting Standards Board's *Conceptual Framework for Financial Reporting* provides the following definition of an asset:

> A present economic resource controlled by the entity as a result of past events.
> An economic resource is a right that has the potential to produce economic benefits.
>
> Source: IASB *Conceptual Framework for Financial Reporting*, paragraphs 4.3 and 4.4

This sounds complicated. However, once we consider the words carefully and analyse what they mean, we will find that this definition is actually very simple and presents a very clear set of criteria to determine whether an asset exists or not. So what does this definition tell us? Let's look at the key points:

- Control: 'an entity controls an economic resource if it has the present ability to direct the use of the economic resource and obtain the economic benefits that flow from it' (IASB *Conceptual Framework*, paragraph 4.20). A resource is controlled if it is owned or leased (rented) by an organisation which can enforce its legal rights over that resource. Control is therefore established if an entity can legally prevent anyone else from using that resource and obtaining the economic benefits from it.

- As a result of past events: to gain control of a resource it is likely that a contract has been signed transferring or granting the right to use that resource to the current owner and money has been paid to other parties in exchange for the transfer or rights to use that resource. Contractual rights gained over the resource mean that an entity can enforce its legal rights over that resource.

- Present: firstly, the economic resource must be under the control of an entity at the statement of financial position date. Any economic resource that is not under the control of the entity at the statement of financial position date cannot be included in the entity's statement of financial position. Secondly, the economic resource must have the potential to produce economic benefits at the statement of financial position date. If the economic resource does not have this potential then it cannot be recognised as an asset on the statement of financial position.

- Economic benefits: the economic resource will be used within an organisation to generate cash and profit from the sale of goods or services to other persons.

From this definition it follows that an asset represents a store of potential economic benefits, the ability to use the asset within an organisation to generate cash and profit. Let's see how this definition works in practice in Example 2.1.

EXAMPLE 2.1

Let us take the example of Bunns the Bakers. The company bought a city centre shop from a property developer 10 years ago for £500,000, with both the seller and the buyer of the shop signing a contract transferring legal title in the shop to Bunns the Bakers. The shop sells bread, cakes, hot and cold snacks, drinks and sandwiches. Does this constitute an asset of the business? Applying our criteria above:

- Do Bunns the Bakers *control* the shop (the resource)? Yes: the company *owns* the shop and, by virtue of the contract signed at the time the shop was purchased from the property developer, Bunns the Bakers can go to court to assert their legal rights to the shop and to prevent anyone else from using that shop for their own purposes. The company thus has the ability at the statement of financial position date (the present ability) to direct the use of this economic resource (the shop) and to obtain the economic benefits that flow from it.
- Is there *a past event*? Yes: Bunns the Bakers' representatives signed the contract and paid £500,000 to acquire the shop, so this is the *past event* giving rise to control of the economic resource.
- Does the economic resource (the shop) have the potential to produce economic benefits? Yes: Bunns the Bakers is using the shop to sell goods produced by the company and bought in from suppliers to customers in order to generate cash and profits from those sales. You can also view the shop as a store of potential economic benefits for Bunns the Bakers. The company can continue to use the shop to make sales, profits and cash into the future. Alternatively, that store of potential economic benefits could be realised by selling the shop to another company. This would still generate economic benefits as the sale of the shop would release the cash (= the economic benefits) tied up in that shop. Even if Bunns the Bakers did not sell the shop but chose to rent it out to another party, this would still represent potential economic benefits as monthly rental payments would be received in cash from the person or organisation renting the shop.

Thus, the shop represents an asset to the business as it meets the IASB criteria for recognition of an asset.

Assets: faithful representation

Our definition of what constitutes an asset now seems very clear. However, there is one further test to satisfy before an asset (or liability) can be recognised in the statement of financial position.

As we saw in Chapter 1 (What qualities should accounting information possess?), the IASB requires financial information to be relevant and faithfully represented. Faithful representation requires the presentation of information that is complete, neutral and free from error. Since the elements (assets, liabilities and equity) that make up the statement of financial position must be quantified in money terms (IASB, *Conceptual Framework*, paragraph 6.1), these elements must be measured at a monetary value before they can be recognised. While an accurate monetary value for many assets and liabilities can be determined easily from the accounting records of an entity, there will be times when estimates have to be used. When monetary values are estimated, they are subject to measurement uncertainty. In cases where the level of measurement uncertainty is so high that the faithful representation of the monetary value of an asset or liability is in doubt, then no asset or liability is recognised (IASB, *Conceptual Framework*, paragraphs 5.19–5.22). Thus, when the possible range of monetary values for an asset or liability is very wide or when measurement is based on very subjective measures, then the completeness, neutrality and freedom from error required for a faithful representation cannot be achieved and no asset or liability is recognised in the statement of financial position.

Can the cost of the shop be quantified in monetary terms in such a way that it is faithfully represented in the statement of financial position? Yes, as the cost of the shop was £500,000 this is a complete, neutral and error-free measurement so the shop can be recognised in Bunns the Bakers' statement of financial position as an asset.

Asset recognition: summary of the steps to follow

Diagrammatically, the steps to follow to determine whether an asset can be recognised on the statement of financial position are shown in Figure 2.2.

WHY IS THIS RELEVANT TO ME?   Definitions: assets

To provide you as a business professional with:

- An understanding of what assets on the statement of financial position actually represent

- An awareness of the strict criteria that must be met before an asset can be recognised on the statement of financial position

- The necessary tools to determine whether an asset should be recognised on the statement of financial position or not

---

SUMMARY OF KEY CONCEPTS   Are you quite convinced that you can define an asset? Go to the **online workbook** to revise this definition with Summary of key concepts 2.1 to reinforce your knowledge.

GO BACK OVER THIS AGAIN!   Are you sure that you have grasped the asset recognition criteria? Go to the **online workbook** Exercises 2.1 to make sure you understand how the asset recognition criteria are used in practice.

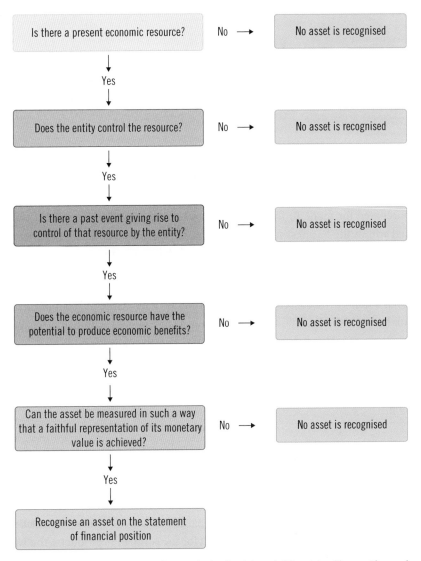

Figure 2.2 Steps in determining whether an asset can be recognised on the statement of financial position or not in accordance with the IASB *Conceptual Framework for Financial Reporting*

ASSETS IN THE STATEMENT OF FINANCIAL POSITION

Now we have found out what assets are and the criteria for their recognition, let's look again at the statement of financial position of Bunns the Bakers plc to see what sort of assets a company might own and recognise.

Illustration 2.1 shows that Bunns the Bakers has two types of assets, non-current assets and current assets. Non-current assets are split into intangible assets, property plant and equipment and investments. Current assets are split into inventories, trade and other receivables and cash and cash equivalents. Total assets are calculated by adding together non-current and current assets as shown in Figure 2.3. What is the distinction between current and non-current assets? Let us look in more detail at these two types of assets and then the categorisation of assets as non-current or current will readily become apparent.

Figure 2.3 The composition of total assets

Non-current assets

Non-current assets are those assets that are:

- Not purchased for resale in the normal course of business: this means that the assets are retained within the business for periods of more than one year and are not acquired with the intention of reselling them immediately or in the near future.

- Held for long-term use in the business to produce goods or services.

An example of a non-current asset would be the shop we considered in Example 2.1. This shop was not purchased with the intention of reselling it, but is held within the business for the long-term purpose of selling bakery goods to customers over many years.

 SUMMARY OF KEY CONCEPTS   Are you totally confident that you can define non-current assets? Go to the **online workbook** to revise this definition with Summary of key concepts 2.2 to check your understanding.

Intangible assets are those assets that have no material substance (you cannot touch them). Examples of such assets would be purchased goodwill, patents, trademarks and intellectual property rights. Tangible assets are those assets that do have a material substance (you can touch them) and examples of these would be land and buildings, machinery, vehicles and fixtures and fittings.

Intangible assets are represented on Bunns the Bakers' statement of financial position in Illustration 2.1 and these probably relate to trademarks for the company's products. You would, however, need to consult the notes to the accounts to find out precisely what assets were represented by these figures, as shown in Give me an example 2.1.

GIVE ME AN EXAMPLE 2.1   Intangible assets

Premier Foods plc is the owner of some of the best known grocery brands in the UK, with Mr Kipling, Sharwoods and Oxo among them. On its statement of financial position at 28 March 2020 the company records an amount of £341.3 million under the heading 'Other intangible assets'. The reader of the report and accounts is then referred to Note 12

in the notes to the financial statements for further information. Note 12 shows that the intangible assets recognised are Software at £15.3 million, Brands, Trademarks and Licences at £322.7 million and Assets under Construction at £3.3 million.

Source: Premier Foods annual report and accounts for the 52 weeks ended 28 March 2020 www.premierfoods.co.uk

The property, plant and equipment heading represents the tangible assets of the business. As this is a bakery retail business, these tangible assets will consist of shops, bakeries, delivery vans, counters, tills and display cabinets in the shops and any other non-current, long-term assets that the company requires to conduct its business.

Investments are just that: holdings of shares or other financial assets (such as loans to other entities) in other companies. These investments represent long-term investments in other companies or operations that are held in order to realise a long-term capital gain when they are eventually sold.

Give me an example 2.2 presents the non-current assets from the statement of financial position of Taylor Wimpey plc.

GO BACK OVER THIS AGAIN!   Do you think you can distinguish between intangible non-current assets, property, plant and equipment and investments? Go to the **online workbook** and complete Exercises 2.2 to make sure you can make these distinctions.

Current assets

Current assets, by contrast, are short-term assets that are constantly changing. On Bunns the Bakers' statement of financial position the following items are found:

- Inventory: inventory is another word for stock of goods. Inventory represents goods held for production or sale. As Bunns the Bakers is a baker, inventories held for production will consist of raw materials such as flour, sugar, eggs and other bakery ingredients. As such raw materials deteriorate rapidly, these inventories will be used and replaced on a regular basis as bakery activity takes place, goods are produced, delivered to the shops and sold to the public. Inventory goods for sale might be bread and cakes produced today and held in cool storage ready for next-day delivery to the shops. All inventories thus represent potential cash that will be generated from the production and sales of goods.

- Trade and other receivables: where organisations make their sales on credit terms to customers, customers are given time in which to pay so that the money due from these customers is recognised as money receivable. A moment's thought will convince you that, as Bunns the Bakers sells food products to the public for cash, there will be very few trade receivables. Any trade receivables that there are might arise from a business-to-business contract to supply large quantities of goods to another retailer such as a supermarket chain. As well as small amounts of trade receivables from such contracts, the company will also have other amounts receivable such as tax refunds or amounts paid in advance for services that have yet to be provided (these are called prepayments—see Chapter 3, Prepayments and accruals: recording transactions in the statement of profit or loss and statement of financial position for a detailed discussion of prepayments). While trade and other receivables represent the right to receive cash in the future, they are not cash yet and so are recognised in this separate category of current assets. You will find some sets of accounts that refer to trade and other receivables as debtors.

- Cash and cash equivalents: this category of current assets comprises of amounts of cash held in tills at the end of the year, cash held in the company's current account at the bank

GIVE ME AN EXAMPLE 2.2   Non-current assets

We have thought about intangible non-current assets, property, plant and equipment and investments, but what other categories of non-current assets do companies present in their financial statements? The consolidated balance sheet (= statement of financial position) at 31 December 2019 for Taylor Wimpey plc, a large UK residential housing developer, shows the following non-current assets.

Taylor Wimpey's statement of financial position records the share of the joint ventures' net assets attributable to the company. The other companies involved in the joint ventures will record their share of the net assets of the joint ventures in their statements of financial position. It may seem odd to see trade receivables recorded as a non-current asset when Bunns the Bakers shows this

	31 December	
	2019	2018
Non-current assets	£m	£m
Intangible assets	7.0	3.2
Property, plant and equipment	25.6	21.6
Right of use assets	27.4	27.1
Interests in joint ventures	55.3	48.3
Trade and other receivables	43.7	55.7
Deferred tax assets	29.8	40.7
	188.8	**196.6**

Source: Taylor Wimpey plc annual report and accounts 2019 www.taylorwimpey.co.uk

Intangible assets are made up of software development costs, while property, plant and equipment consists of land and buildings, plant, equipment and leasehold improvements. Right of use assets are assets leased but not owned by the group: IFRS 16 now requires that these leased assets (made up of office premises and equipment) be recognised as non-current assets and a corresponding liability to record all the assets used within the group and all the liabilities owed by the group. Joint ventures are entered into with other companies and

as a current asset. However, Taylor Wimpey has provided mortgages to customers to assist them with the purchase of their homes. Mortgages are long-term assets which will be repayable more than 12 months after the statement of financial position date so these mortgages are recorded as non-current trade and other receivables. Deferred tax is a very complex subject which you will consider at a later stage of your studies and can be either an asset (reduced future tax payments) or a liability (increased future tax payments).

and cash held in short-term deposit accounts with bankers and other financial institutions (for more detail on the components of cash and cash equivalents, see Chapter 6, Cash and cash equivalents).

Give me an example 2.3 presents the current assets on the statement of financial position of Nichols plc.

GIVE ME AN EXAMPLE 2.3   Current assets

When looking at the published financial statements of companies, you will find the same categories of current assets presented on the statement of financial position. The statement of financial position of Nichols plc, an international soft drinks business, at 31 December 2019 shows the same current assets as Bunns the Bakers.

	Years ended 31 December	
	2019	2018
Current assets	£000	£000
Inventories	8,361	7,164
Trade and other receivables	38,363	38,153
Cash and cash equivalents	40,944	38,896
Total current assets	**87,668**	**84,213**

Source: Nichols plc financial statements 2019 www.nicholsplc.co.uk

---

MULTIPLE CHOICE QUESTIONS   Are you confident that you can distinguish between different types of current assets? Go to the **online workbook** and have a go at Multiple choice questions 2.1 to make sure you can make these distinctions.

The distinction between non-current and current assets

The distinction between non-current and current assets comes down to one of time. As we have seen, non-current assets are held by businesses to provide benefits in accounting periods exceeding one year. On the other hand, current assets are held only for a short time in order to produce goods to be sold to convert into cash which can then be used to buy in more raw materials to produce more goods to convert into more cash in a short but constantly repeating trading cycle.

However, to decide whether a resource is a non-current or current asset it is also important to determine the business in which an entity is engaged. For example, you might think that a car would be a non-current asset in any business, an asset to be used for the long term. But if that car is parked on the premises of a motor trader, is this car an item of inventory, held in stock for resale, a car owned by the motor trading business for long-term use in the business or the property of a member of staff who drives to work each day (and so not a business asset at all)? Further enquiries would have to be made to determine whether the car is a business asset and, if it is, the exact statement of financial position classification of this vehicle.

WHY IS THIS RELEVANT TO ME?   Non-current and current assets

To enable you as a business professional to:

- Develop a clear understanding of the different types of assets entities recognise on their statement of financial position
- Distinguish effectively between the two types of assets
- Understand how the different types of assets can be used in evaluating entities' efficiency and working capital management (discussed in detail in Chapters 8 and 9)

GO BACK OVER THIS AGAIN!   How easily do you think you can distinguish between current and non-current assets? Go to the **online workbook** Exercises 2.3 to make sure you can make this distinction.

LIABILITIES

As shown in Illustration 2.1, liabilities appear lower down the statement of financial position and represent amounts that are owed to parties outside the business. As with assets, the first questions to ask are: 'What is a liability?' and 'What does a liability represent?'

The International Accounting Standards Board's *Conceptual Framework for Financial Reporting* provides the following definition of a liability:

> A present obligation of the entity to transfer an economic resource as a result of past events.
>
> Source: IASB *Conceptual Framework for Financial Reporting*, paragraph 4.26

While this definition again might seem complex, your experience gained in unravelling the meaning of the definition of assets earlier will certainly help you in understanding the various terms employed here. To put it simply, liabilities are the contractual or legal claims of outside parties against an entity. These contractual or legal claims may be short-term (current liabilities) or long-term (non-current liabilities). Again, let's break down this definition into its constituent parts in order to enable us to apply it in determining whether an entity has a liability or not:

- Present obligation: the obligation must exist at the statement of financial position date in order for any liability arising under that obligation to be recognised in the statement of financial position. Therefore, entities cannot recognise just any liability that they think they might incur at any time in the future. The event giving rise to the obligation must have taken place by the statement of financial position date to enable the entity to recognise that liability.

- As a result of past events: to give rise to an obligation, it is likely that a contract has been signed agreeing to pay for goods delivered but not yet paid for from a supplier or to take out a loan or an overdraft at the bank that will have to be repaid at some point in the future.

- Economic resource: the obligation will result in the entity transferring cash to an outside party in order to settle the liability or, possibly, transferring other assets by way of settlement. The term economic resource has exactly the same definition as that provided under Assets (this chapter).

Importantly, the obligation must be unavoidable: if the entity can avoid transferring cash or other economic resources then there is no obligation and no liability exists.

The IASB *Conceptual Framework* also requires that liabilities measured and presented in the statement of financial position meet the same standards of faithful representation as required for assets (this chapter, Assets: faithful representation). Where these standards of faithful representation are not met, no liability is recognised in the statement of financial position. Example 2.2 shows how liability recognition works in practice.

EXAMPLE 2.2

Let us take the earlier example of Bunns the Bakers in Example 2.1. When the company bought the city centre shop from the property developer 10 years ago, the purchase was financed by a loan from the bank of £500,000. This loan is currently repayable in full in eight years' time. Does this loan constitute a liability of the business? Applying our criteria:

- Does Bunns the Bakers have a present obligation at the statement of financial position date? Yes: the loan exists and is outstanding at the current year end. The obligating event (taking out the loan) had taken place by the statement of financial position date.

- Is the obligation to repay the loan unavoidable? Yes: the bank will hold signed documentation from the company agreeing that the loan was taken out and there will be entries in the relevant account at the bank and in bank statements to show the loan being received by the company. Should the company try to avoid repaying the loan, the bank will be able to enforce its legal rights against the company for repayment of the loan.

- Does the obligation arise as a result of past events? Yes: a loan agreement was signed by Bunns the Bakers at the time the loan was taken out and the money transferred to the company with which to buy the shop.

- Will Bunns the Bakers transfer an economic resource? Yes: the company will have to transfer cash to settle the obligation. If the company is unable to meet the obligation in cash, the bank will accept the shop as a suitable substitute for repayment of the loan. The shop embodies the potential to produce economic benefits as we saw in Example 2.1, so taking the shop instead of repayment will still be a transfer of an economic resource.

- Does the measurement of the liability in money terms result in a faithful representation? Yes: the loan is measured at £500,000 as a result of the cash transferred. This measurement is complete, neutral and free from error and so is a faithful representation of the amount of the obligation due to the bank.

Thus, the loan represents a liability of the business as it meets the IASB criteria for recognition of a liability.

Liability recognition: summary of the steps to follow

Diagrammatically, the steps to follow to determine whether a liability should be recognised on the statement of financial position are shown in Figure 2.4.

2

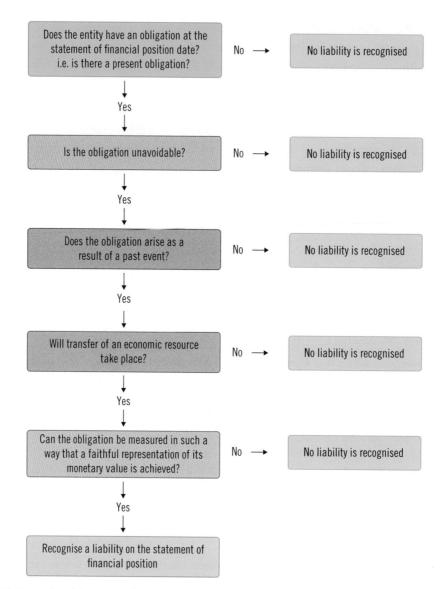

Figure 2.4 Steps in determining whether a liability should be recognised on the statement of financial position or not in accordance with the IASB *Conceptual Framework for Financial Reporting*

WHY IS THIS RELEVANT TO ME?   Liabilities

To provide you as a business professional with:

- An understanding of what liabilities on the statement of financial position actually represent

- An awareness of the strict criteria that must be met before a liability can be recognised on the statement of financial position

- The necessary tools to determine whether a liability should be recognised on the statement of financial position or not

SUMMARY OF KEY CONCEPTS   Are you sure that you can define a liability? Go to the **online workbook**
to revise this definition with Summary of key concepts 2.3 to reinforce your knowledge.

GO BACK OVER THIS AGAIN!   How well have you grasped the liability recognition criteria? Go to
the **online workbook** Exercises 2.4 to make sure you understand how the liability recognition criteria
are used in practice.

LIABILITIES IN THE STATEMENT OF FINANCIAL POSITION

Now that we have considered what the term 'liabilities' means and the criteria for liability recognition in the statement of financial position, let us look again at the statement of financial position of Bunns the Bakers plc in Illustration 2.1 to consider what sort of liabilities a company might recognise.

Liabilities, just as in the case of assets, are split into non-current and current. Total liabilities are calculated by adding current and non-current liabilities together, as shown in Figure 2.5.

Non-current liabilities are long-term liabilities that the entity will only have to meet in more than one year's time while current liabilities will have to be paid within the course of the next year. Current liabilities are not due on the day immediately after the statement of financial position date but they will be due for settlement over the course of the next 12 months.

Figure 2.5 The composition of total liabilities

Current liabilities

Just as with current assets, current liabilities are short-term liabilities that are constantly changing. Looking at Bunns the Bakers' statement of financial position the following liabilities are shown:

- Current portion of long-term borrowings: these are the loan instalments due to be repaid to lenders within the next 12 months.

- Trade and other payables: any organisation that is involved in business will trade on credit with their suppliers, consuming services and ordering goods that are both delivered but not paid for immediately. Customers then either use the goods received to produce more goods to sell to the public and businesses or just resell those goods. Suppliers are paid from the proceeds of the sales of goods produced or resold. Normal trading terms are that suppliers

2

are (usually) paid within 30 days of receipt of goods or services by the customer. Clearly, suppliers will not wait a long time for payment for goods delivered as they have their own suppliers and employees to pay. Therefore, suppliers will expect their cash to be returned to them quickly so trade and other payables are short-term, current liabilities. In the case of Bunns the Bakers, trade payables will consist of amounts of money owed to suppliers for flour, eggs, sugar, salt and other bakery ingredients as well as for services provided by, for example, their legal advisers or their accountants.

- Current tax liabilities: Bunns the Bakers plc has made a profit over the course of the year. This profit is subject to tax and the tax liability on this year's profit is recognised as an obligation on the statement of financial position. The government will want the tax due reasonably quickly so that it can meet its own obligations to provide services to the public and contribute to the running of government departments so this, too, is a short-term, current liability.

Non-current liabilities

On Bunns the Bakers' statement of financial position, the following non-current liabilities are represented:

- Long-term borrowings: these are loans and other forms of finance provided by lenders to finance the long-term non-current assets of the business. In the case of Bunns the Bakers, these could be loans used to finance the acquisition of shops (as in Example 2.2 in this chapter), the building of a new state-of-the-art bakery or the purchase of new plant and equipment with which to produce goods. Other companies may take out loans to finance the acquisition of other companies. Long-term borrowings are repayable in accounting periods beyond the next 12 months.

- Long-term provisions: these are liabilities that the entity knows it must meet but which will not be due for payment in the next accounting period but in accounting periods beyond the next 12 months. Examples of such long-term provisions would be deferred taxation and pensions, two highly technical accounting issues that you will consider in depth at a later stage of your studies.

Give me an example 2.4 presents the current and non-current liabilities on the statement of financial position of Experian plc.

GIVE ME AN EXAMPLE 2.4   Non-current and current liabilities

The group balance sheet (= statement of financial position) at 31 March 2020 of Experian, the credit services, decision analytics, marketing services and consumer services group illustrates the presentation of current and non-current liabilities in practice.

	31 March	
	2020	2019
Current liabilities	US$m	US$m
Trade and other payables	1,430	1,464
Borrowings	498	869
Current tax liabilities	225	313
Provisions	48	41
Other financial liabilities	23	152
	2,224	**2,839**
Non-current liabilities	US$m	US$m
Trade and other payables	121	99
Borrowings	3,916	2,455
Deferred tax liabilities	202	132
Post-employment benefit obligations	48	55
Other financial liabilities	107	13
	4,394	**2,754**

Source: Experian annual report 2020 www.experianplc.com

As in the case of Bunns the Bakers, Experian's current and non-current liabilities present trade and other payables, borrowings, current tax liabilities and provisions for deferred tax and pension liabilities (post-employment benefit obligations). Other financial liabilities refer to derivative transactions, another complex accounting topic that will be covered at a later stage of your studies.

WHY IS THIS RELEVANT TO ME?   Current and non-current liabilities

To enable you as a business professional to:

- Understand the different types of liabilities an entity recognises on its statement of financial position
- Distinguish between the two types of liabilities
- Use the different types of liabilities in assessing an entity's financial position, short-term liquidity and long-term financial stability (discussed in further detail in Chapter 9)

GO BACK OVER THIS AGAIN!   Are you convinced that you can distinguish between current and non-current liabilities? Go to the **online workbook** Exercises 2.5 to make sure you can make this distinction.

2

THE ACCOUNTING EQUATION

Before we discuss the third element on Bunns the Bakers' statement of financial position, equity, we need to think about the accounting equation. Looking at the statement of financial position, we notice that the net assets (total assets – total liabilities) and the total equity are the same figure. What does this tell us about the relationship between the assets, liabilities and equity in an entity? From this observation, we can draw up the following equations that express the link between the three elements in the statement of financial position:

Either

Total assets = total liabilities + equity

Or:

Total assets – total liabilities = equity

Equity is thus the difference between the total assets (the sum of the current and non-current assets) and the total liabilities (the sum of the current and non-current liabilities). As the two equations add to the same figure, the statement of financial position is said to balance. We shall see in Chapter 4, Double entry and the accounting equation, how this accounting equation forms the foundation upon which double entry and the duality principle are built.

WHY IS THIS RELEVANT TO ME?   The accounting equation

To enable you as a business professional to:

- Appreciate how the two halves of the statement of financial position balance
- Balance your own statements of financial position when you draw these up in the future
- Provide the framework within which to understand double-entry bookkeeping

---

 SUMMARY OF KEY CONCEPTS   Can you state the accounting equation? Go to the **online workbook** to revise this equation with Summary of key concepts 2.4.

EQUITY

The International Accounting Standards Board defines equity as:

> The residual interest in the assets of the entity after deducting all its liabilities.
>
> Source: IASB *Conceptual Framework for Financial Reporting*, paragraph 4.63

This is exactly the same as the accounting equation given earlier that says assets – liabilities = equity. In theory, equity represents the amount that owners of the entity should receive if the assets were all sold and the liabilities were all settled at their statement of financial position amounts. The cash received from these asset sales less payments made to discharge liabilities would belong to the owners and they would receive this cash on the winding up of the business. As well as the term equity, you will often find the term capital being used to describe this difference between assets and liabilities.

The components of equity

Different forms of business entity present the equity part of the statement of financial position in different ways. We discussed the characteristics of different types of business entity in detail in Chapter 1. The two ways in which to present the equity section of the statement of financial position that we shall consider at this point are firstly the equity of limited companies and public limited companies (both incorporated businesses) and secondly the equity of sole traders and other unincorporated businesses.

1. The equity section of the statement of financial position: limited companies and public limited companies (plcs)

Bunns the Bakers' (which is a public limited company, a plc) equity is made up of the following elements:

(a) Called up share capital: this is the number of shares issued multiplied by the par value (face value or nominal value) of each share (Chapter 7, Share capital: share issues at par value).

(b) Share premium: where each share is issued for an amount greater than its par value, then any amount received in excess of par value is entered into the share premium account (Chapter 7, Share capital: shares issued at a premium).

(c) Retained earnings: these are profits that the business has earned in past accounting periods that have not been distributed to shareholders as dividends.

You will see many company statements of financial position in practice that have many different accounts (other reserves) under the equity heading (see Give me an example 2.5). Many of these accounts arise from statutory requirements governing transactions entered into by the company and you will look at these at later stages of your studies. The basic calculation of equity for limited companies and plcs is shown in Figure 2.6.

Figure 2.6 Limited companies and plcs: the components of equity

GIVE ME AN EXAMPLE 2.5   Equity

The consolidated balance sheet (= statement of financial position) of First Group plc at 31 March 2020 provides an illustration of the many different accounts that can make up equity. As in the case of Bunns the Bakers, First Group plc reports figures for share capital, share premium and retained earnings together with various other reserve accounts classified as equity.

	31 March	
	2020	**2019**
EQUITY	**£m**	**£m**
Share capital	61.0	60.7
Share premium	688.6	684.0
Hedging reserve	(28.3)	17.5
Other reserves	4.6	4.6
Own shares	(10.2)	(4.7)
Translation reserve	635.6	544.3
Retained earnings	(141.5)	248.1
	1,209.8	**1,554.5**

Source: First Group annual report and accounts for the year ended 31 March 2020 www.firstgroupplc.com

2. Sole traders and unincorporated entities

As we saw in Chapter 1, not all businesses are incorporated as limited companies. Such businesses do not, therefore, have issued share capital, but they still have an equity section. For sole traders and other unincorporated entities, this is called the capital account. This comprises of the following headings:

(a) Capital at the start of the year: this is the capital account balance at the end of the previous accounting period. At the beginning of the first accounting period, the first year in which the unincorporated entity starts trading, the balance at the start of the year is £Nil.

(b) Capital introduced: this is the owner's own money that has been introduced into the business during the current accounting period.

(c) Retained profits for the year: any profit retained in the business during the year is added to the capital account as this profit belongs to the business's owner. Where the business makes a loss during the year, then this loss is deducted from the capital account.

(d) Capital withdrawn: the business's owner will draw money out of the business to meet personal rather than business expenses during the year. This is treated as a repayment of part of the capital of the business to the owner. These withdrawals of capital are called drawings and are a deduction from the capital account. This is an application of the business entity convention (Chapter 3, Drawings and the business entity convention) that states that the business and its owner(s) are totally separate individuals. Only business transactions are included in the financial statements of the business with any non-business, personal transactions excluded.

Just as in the case of limited companies and plcs, the amount in the capital account is the amount that would, in theory, be paid out to the owner(s) of the business if all the assets of the business were sold at the amounts recorded in the statement of financial position and all the liabilities of the business were settled at their statement of financial position amounts. The components and calculation of the capital account (equity) balance for sole traders and unincorporated entities are shown in Figure 2.7.

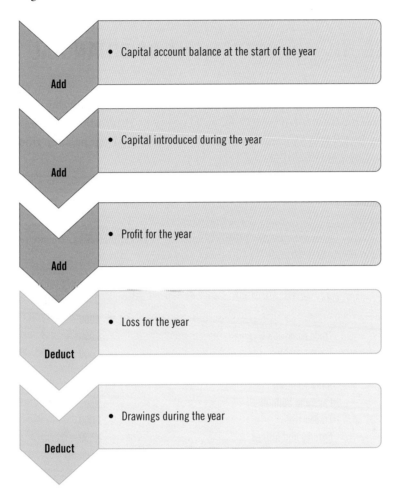

Figure 2.7 Sole traders and unincorporated entities: the components of equity (the capital account)

WHY IS THIS RELEVANT TO ME?   Equity and the components of equity

To enable you as a business professional to:

- Understand that equity is the difference between an entity's total assets and total liabilities
- Appreciate the different components of equity in incorporated and unincorporated businesses
- Distinguish elements of equity from assets and liabilities

MULTIPLE CHOICE QUESTIONS   Are you quite confident that you could calculate the equity of a business from a given set of information? Go to the **online workbook** and have a go at Multiple choice questions 2.2 to make sure you can make these calculations.

SUMMARY OF KEY CONCEPTS   Are you sure you can state the components of equity? Go to the **online workbook** to revise these components with Summary of key concepts 2.5 and 2.6.

2

DRAWING UP THE STATEMENT OF FINANCIAL POSITION

We now know what assets and liabilities are and how they relate to equity, but what steps should we follow in drawing up the statement of financial position? This section provides a step-by-step approach using Example 2.3 to preparing the statement of financial position from the account balances at the end of the financial year.

EXAMPLE 2.3

Illustration 2.2 shows a list of balances for Misfits Limited at 31 December 2021. You are required to draw up the statement of financial position from this list of balances.

Illustration 2.2 Misfits Limited: account balances at 31 December 2021

	£000
Trade receivables	2,000
Trade payables	1,500
Bank loan repayable in six years' time	10,000
Bank overdraft	200
Land and buildings	15,000
Trademarks	1,000
Fixtures and fittings	2,500
Share capital	1,800
Retained earnings	7,500
Share premium	2,300
Inventories	2,750
Cash in the tills	50

Guidelines on the approach to adopt in drawing up the statement of financial position

1. Decide whether each of the balances is an asset, a liability or an element of equity.

2. Once you have categorised the balances, think about whether the assets and liabilities are current or non-current.

3. Some of the balances might need adding together to produce one figure in the statement of financial position. For example, there might be cash in hand or in the safe, cash in the

bank current account and cash on deposit in a short-term investment account at the bank. All of these balances would be added together and shown as one figure for cash and cash equivalents.

4. Once you have made all your decisions, slot the figures into the relevant headings (use the headings in Illustration 2.1, adding any additional headings you might need and removing headings you do not need), add it all up and it should balance.

Illustration 2.3 presents the statement of financial position of Misfits Limited at 31 December 2021 using the figures from Illustration 2.2.

Illustration 2.3 Misfits Limited: statement of financial position at 31 December 2021

	£000	Note
ASSETS		
Non-current assets		
Intangible assets	1,000	1
Property, plant and equipment	17,500	2
	18,500	3
Current assets		
Inventories	2,750	4
Trade receivables	2,000	4
Cash and cash equivalents	50	4
	4,800	5
Total assets	**23,300**	6
LIABILITIES		
Current liabilities		
Bank overdraft (you could call this short-term borrowings)	200	7
Trade payables	1,500	7
	1,700	8
Non-current liabilities		
Bank loan (you could call this long-term borrowings)	10,000	7
Total liabilities	**11,700**	9
Net assets (total assets − total liabilities)	**11,600**	10
EQUITY		
Called up share capital	1,800	11
Share premium	2,300	11
Retained earnings	7,500	11
Total equity	**11,600**	12

2

Notes to the above statement of financial position for Misfits Limited:

1. Trademarks are intangible assets, as we noted earlier (this chapter, Non-current assets).

2. Land and buildings and fixtures and fittings are both classified under the heading 'Property, plant and equipment'. The land and buildings are property and the fixtures and fittings are plant and equipment. £15,000,000 for the land and buildings + £2,500,000 for the fixtures and fittings give the total figure of £17,500,000 for Property, plant and equipment.

3. This is the total of the two non-current asset headings £1,000,000 + £17,500,000 = £18,500,000.

4. These figures are as given in the list of balances.

5. £4,800,000 is the total of all the current assets added together.

6. £23,300,000 is the total non-current assets of £18,500,000 added to the total current assets of £4,800,000 to give the figure for total assets.

7. These figures are as given in the list of balances. If you were in any doubt that the loan is a non-current liability, look at the timing of repayment: the loan is due for repayment in six years' time so this liability is repayable more than 12 months after the statement of financial position date. Remember that current liabilities include all obligations payable within 12 months of the year-end date so that any liability payable after this is a non-current liability.

8. £1,700,000 is the total of the bank overdraft of £200,000 and of the trade payables of £1,500,000.

9. £11,700,000 is the total of the current liabilities of £1,700,000 and of the non-current liabilities of £10,000,000.

10. The figure for net assets is given by deducting the total liabilities figure of £11,700,000 from the total assets figure of £23,300,000 to give you net assets (total assets – total liabilities) of £11,600,000.

11. Called up share capital, Share premium and Retained earnings are all as given in the list of balances.

12. This is the total of the three elements of equity added together.

WHY IS THIS RELEVANT TO ME?   Drawing up the statement of financial position

To enable you as a business professional to:

● Understand how the statement of financial position is put together from the balances at the year-end date

● Draw up and present your own statements of financial position

---

SHOW ME HOW TO DO IT   Did you understand how Misfits Limited's statement of financial position was drawn up? View Video presentation 2.1 in the **online workbook** to see a practical demonstration of how this statement of financial position was put together.

NUMERICAL EXERCISES   Are you sure that you could draw up a statement of financial position from a list of year end balances? Go to the **online workbook** Numerical exercises 2.1 to practise this technique.

HOW ARE ASSETS AND LIABILITIES VALUED?
Historic cost v. fair value

How should we value assets and liabilities for inclusion in the statement of financial position? At their cost price? Selling price? Market value? Or some other amount?

Accounting has traditionally dictated that the monetary value of all assets and liabilities recognised in the statement of financial position should be based on their original cost: this is called the historic cost convention. Thus, for example, inventory is valued at its cost to the business, not its selling price or current market value, while trade payables are valued at their invoice amount and loans are valued at the amount borrowed less any repayments made.

However, this accounting convention has been relaxed over the past 60 years and entities can now choose to value different classes of assets either at their historic cost or at their fair value. Fair value is equivalent to market value, the amount at which an asset could be sold or a liability settled in the open market. However, although the cost or fair value option exists, organisations rarely choose the fair value alternative. The only class of assets that entities might wish to present at their fair value is land and buildings as these assets tend to rise in value over time. For all other assets and liabilities historic cost is preferred.

You will consider the arguments both in favour of and against valuing assets and liabilities at fair value or historic cost at a later stage of your studies. For now, you just need to be aware that these options exist.

A mixture of original cost and fair value: problems

So, users can be presented with a mixture of assets at cost and at fair value. Does this failure to present all assets and liabilities consistently at their fair values cause any problems for users of the statement of financial position?

Historic cost is seen as objective as it is verifiable by reference to a transaction at a fixed point in time. It is thus a reliable measure as it was determined by the market at the date of the transaction. With short-term current assets and liabilities this is not a problem as these assets and liabilities are, as we have seen, always changing and being replaced by new current assets and new current liabilities at more recent, up-to-date values. However, when long-term, non-current assets and liabilities are measured at historic cost these costs gradually become more and more out of date as time moves on. As a result, these costs become less and less relevant in decision making as the market moves forward and asset and loan values rise and fall in real terms with the onward march of the economy.

We will not consider this problem any further in this text, but it is a difficulty of which you should be aware. The cost v. fair/market value debate has been raging for well over a century and an acceptable solution is no nearer than it was when the problem was first pointed out. It is therefore going to be a continuing shortcoming of the statement of financial position for the indefinite future and a limitation that you will need to take into account whenever you are looking at sets of financial statements in your business career.

WHY IS THIS RELEVANT TO ME?   Historic cost, valuation and fair/market values

To enable you as a business professional to:

• Understand the basis upon which the figures in the statement of financial position are determined

• Gain an early awareness of the limitations of continuing to value non-current assets and non-current liabilities at historic cost

• Appreciate that there are alternative valuation bases for non-current assets and liabilities, but that companies rarely make use of these alternatives

---

WHAT DOES THE STATEMENT OF FINANCIAL POSITION SHOW?

This leads us neatly on to a discussion of what the statement of financial position shows and what it does not show.

Put simply, the statement of financial position shows the financial situation of an entity on the last day of its accounting year. However, it is important to remember that the statement of financial position just shows the financial situation on that one day in the year and it is thus a snapshot of the entity at this one point in time. A totally different view would be shown if the picture were taken on any other day in the year. It is true to say that, at this one point in time, the statement of financial position does show the financially measurable resources (assets) and financially measurable obligations (liabilities) of the business in money terms, but this might seem to present a rather limited view.

In order to gain a better understanding of what the statement of financial position represents, it is useful to consider what the statement of financial position does not show.

WHAT THE STATEMENT OF FINANCIAL POSITION DOES NOT SHOW

The statement of financial position does not show:

• All the assets of the organisation. The statement of financial position does not include or value the most valuable assets of an organisation. These comprise the skills and knowledge of the employees, goodwill, brands, traditions and all the other intangible but extremely difficult to value assets that make an organisation what it is. All entities are so much more than the sum of their financial assets and liabilities. Any attempted valuation of these assets would present monetary values that were so uncertain and subjective that the information presented would lack the relevance and faithful representation required by the IASB in its *Conceptual Framework* (this chapter, Assets: faithful representation).

- All the liabilities of a business. There might be liabilities for damage caused to the environment or to consumers as a result of product liability legislation, claims for damages or breaches of contract, none of which has come to light by the year-end date: as a result, these additional liabilities will not be reflected in the statement of financial position at the accounting year end.

- The market value of an entity. This is a common misconception about the statement of financial position. The monetary value of any entity is determined by the amount a third party would be willing to pay not only for all the known assets and liabilities but also for the unrecognised assets of the organisation noted previously. However, the amount an outside party would be willing to pay will change on a daily basis as more information comes to light about hidden liabilities or the true value of assets or as the economy moves from a boom to a recession or vice versa.

The IASB recognises these limitations of financial statements in full:

> General purpose financial reports are not designed to show the value of a reporting entity; but they provide information to help existing and potential investors, lenders and other creditors to estimate the value of the reporting entity … The *Conceptual Framework* does not allow the recognition in the statement of financial position of items that do not meet the definition of an asset, a liability or equity. Only items that meet the definition of an asset, a liability or equity are recognised in the statement of financial position.
>
> Source: IASB *Conceptual Framework for Financial Reporting*, paragraphs 1.7, 5.5 and 5.6

You should therefore remember that what the statement of financial position does not recognise is just as important as what it does include, or even more so. Let's see how these ideas are reflected in Example 2.4.

EXAMPLE 2.4

A moment's thought will show you that this is equally true of your own circumstances. You probably know the monetary value of the cash you hold in various bank and savings accounts and you might have a collection of various assets such as a tablet, a mobile phone, digital music and clothing, all of which you could value in money terms. But these assets are not the sum total of what represents you. There are your friends, family, memories and achievements, none of which can be valued or quantified in money terms, but which are just as important to you as those tangible items that can be given a monetary value, or even more so. Give me an example 2.6 demonstrates this further.

GIVE ME AN EXAMPLE 2.6   The statement of financial position does not show the true value of an entity

The published report and accounts for the year ended 31 December 2016 of Ablynx, the Belgian biotech group, showed a net assets (total assets less total liabilities) figure of €103m. In January 2018, Sanofi agreed to pay €3,900m to acquire Ablynx. Sanofi was bidding not for Ablynx's net assets but for its nanobody technology, its drugs in development, patented medicines and research, all of which represent value over and above the value of the net assets in the statement of financial position.

Sources: Ablynx annual report for the year ended 31 December 2016 www.ablynx.com; *The Financial Times* 30 January 2018 and Hargreaves Lansdown http://www.hl.co.uk/shares/stock-market-news/company--news/sanofi-to-buy-belgian-biotech-group-ablynx-for-3.9bn

2

To enable you as a business professional to:

- Appreciate the limitations of the monetary information presented in the statement of financial position

- Gain the necessary awareness of what the statement of financial position includes and what it does not include

- Be aware that the statement of financial position will not provide all the answers needed to evaluate an entity's financial and economic position

- Think outside the parameters of the statement of financial position when assessing an entity's standing in the business world

GO BACK OVER THIS AGAIN!   Do you think that you can say clearly what the statement of financial position does and does not show? Go to the **online workbook** Exercises 2.6 to test your knowledge of this area.

THE DUAL ASPECT CONCEPT

The statement of financial position for Misfits Limited was drawn up from a list of balances at a given point in time. But businesses are not static and new transactions will change the figures on the statement of financial position as they occur. These transactions have an effect on two or more accounts and may cause the balances on those accounts to rise or fall as new assets or liabilities are created or as assets are used up or liabilities settled. Accountants describe this dual aspect as double entry and the entries to the accounts affected by transactions as debits and credits. You might prefer to think of these transactions initially as pluses and minuses or increases and decreases in the various accounts in the following examples and in the online workbook. We will be looking at double entry in much greater depth and detail in Chapters 4 and 5. For the time being, Examples 2.5 and 2.6 together with the end-of-chapter exercises and the online workbook materials will provide you with a useful introduction to the dual effect that transactions have on the statement of financial position balances.

Firstly, think about how you would record the receipt of goods from a supplier that are to be paid for in 30 days' time. This receipt of goods will increase the inventory that is held by the business, but also increase the amounts owed to trade payables. If the goods were bought for cash, this would still increase the inventory but reduce the cash held in the bank if the company has a positive balance in their account. In both of these examples, two accounts were affected, inventory and trade payables or cash.

The following examples will show you how the dual aspect concept works and how the statement of financial position will still balance after each transaction is completed.

EXAMPLE 2.5

Misfits Limited's statement of financial position at 31 December 2021 is reproduced in Illustration 2.4 in the left hand column. On 2 January 2022 the company receives £50,000 from one of its trade receivables. This payment is paid into the bank account. How would this transaction be recorded in the statement of financial position? Trade receivables go down by £50,000 as this receivable has paid what was owed. The money has been paid into the bank so the bank overdraft (money owed to the bank) also goes down as less money is now owed to the bank. Recording the transactions as shown in Illustration 2.4 gives us the new statement of financial position at 2 January 2022:

Illustration 2.4 Misfits Limited: the effect on the statement of financial position of cash received from a trade receivable

Misfits Limited	Statement of financial position at 31 December 2021 £000	Increase (plus) £000	Decrease (minus) £000	Statement of financial position at 2 January 2022 £000
Non-current assets				
Intangible assets	1,000			1,000
Property, plant and equipment	17,500			17,500
	18,500			18,500
Current assets				
Inventories	2,750			2,750
Trade receivables	2,000		−50	1,950
Cash and cash equivalents	50			50
	4,800			4,750
Total assets	23,300			23,250
Current liabilities				
Bank overdraft	200		−50	150
Trade payables	1,500			1,500
	1,700			1,650
Non-current liabilities				
Bank loan	10,000			10,000
Total liabilities	11,700			11,650
Net assets	11,600			11,600
EQUITY				
Called up share capital	1,800			1,800
Share premium	2,300			2,300
Retained earnings	7,500			7,500
	11,600			11,600

Current assets have reduced by £50,000 and current liabilities have reduced by £50,000 so the statement of financial position still balances.

EXAMPLE 2.6

Let's try another example. On 3 January 2022, the company receives £100,000 of inventory from a supplier, the invoice to be paid in 30 days' time, and acquires a new piece of property, plant and equipment for £75,000 paid for from the bank. How will these transactions be shown in the statement of financial position? Illustration 2.5 shows the account headings affected.

Illustration 2.5 Misfits Limited: the effect on the statement of financial position of cash paid to buy new plant and equipment and inventory acquired on credit

Misfits Limited	Statement of financial position at 2 January 2022	Increase (plus)	Decrease (minus)	Statement of financial position at 3 January 2022
	£000	£000	£000	£000
Non-current assets				
Intangible assets	1,000			1,000
Property, plant and equipment	17,500	+75		17,575
	18,500			18,575
Current assets				
Inventories	2,750	+100		2,850
Trade receivables	1,950			1,950
Cash and cash equivalents	50			50
	4,750			4,850
Total assets	23,250			23,425
Current liabilities				
Bank overdraft	150	+75		225
Trade payables	1,500	+100		1,600
	1,650			1,824
Non-current liabilities				
Bank loan	10,000			10,000
Total liabilities	11,650			11,825
Net assets	11,600			11,600
EQUITY				
Called up share capital	1,800			1,800
Share premium	2,300			2,300
Retained earnings	7,500			7,500
	11,600			11,600

Non-current assets increase by £75,000 and the overdraft also increases by £75,000 as a result of the acquisition of the new piece of equipment paid for from the bank: assets have risen, but more is now owed to the bank as more money has been paid out so the bank overdraft goes up. Similarly, inventory has increased by £100,000, but more is now owed to trade payables so this figure has also risen by £100,000.

2

GO BACK OVER THIS AGAIN!   Are you sure you understand how the dual aspect concept applies to new transactions? Go to the **online workbook** Exercises 2.7 to look at further examples of the dual aspect and the effect of new transactions on the statement of financial position.

NUMERICAL EXERCISES   Are you quite convinced that you could record new transactions accurately in the statement of financial position? Go to the **online workbook** Numerical exercises 2.2 to test out your abilities in this area.

MULTIPLE CHOICE QUESTIONS   Are you confident that you could state the correct entries to record a new transaction in the statement of financial position? Go to the **online workbook** and have a go at Multiple choice questions 2.3 to test your knowledge in this area.

This is probably the first time you have come across the duality principle, so if you are finding this confusing this should not surprise you. Further practice at more examples will help to reduce this confusion and you will gradually appreciate how the duality principle works and how transactions affect two or more accounts on the statement of financial position. Chapters 4 and 5 together with the exercises in the online workbook and the extended case study will give you a wealth of practice in double entry and the dual effect of transactions. Working through these two chapters and the associated exercises will enable you to gain a very firm grasp of this essential technique for recording transactions.

CHAPTER SUMMARY

You should now have learnt that:

- An asset is a present economic resource controlled by the entity as a result of past events
- An economic resource is a right that has the potential to produce economic benefits
- A liability is a present obligation of the entity to transfer an economic resource as a result of past events
- Assets and liabilities are only recognised in the statement of financial position if their monetary values can be faithfully represented
- Non-current assets are resources not purchased for resale in the normal course of business and are held for long-term use in the business to produce goods or services
- Current assets consist of inventory, trade and other receivables and cash and cash equivalents whose economic benefits will be used up within 12 months of the statement of financial position date
- Current liabilities are obligations that will be settled within 12 months of the statement of financial position date, while non-current liabilities are obligations that will be settled in accounting periods beyond the next 12 months
- The accounting equation states that total assets − total liabilities = equity (capital)

2

- Some assets in the statement of financial position may be shown at historic cost, while some may be shown at fair (market) value

- The statement of financial position only presents figures for monetary resources (assets) whose economic benefits have not yet been consumed and figures for monetary obligations (liabilities) that have not yet been settled

- The statement of financial position does not show all the assets and liabilities of an entity nor does it give a market value for an entity

- Under the dual aspect concept (the duality principle), new accounting transactions affect two or more statement of financial position account headings

 QUICK REVISION   Test your knowledge by attempting the activities in the **online workbook**, including flashcards on the key concepts, numerical exercises and Multiple choice questions. You can also try the further self-test questions which are available at www.oup.com/he/scott-i2a2e

END-OF-CHAPTER QUESTIONS

 Attempt the questions in the following sections and then look at the solutions which can be found in the **online workbook** to see whether there are areas that you need to revisit.

❯ RECALL AND REVIEW

❯ Question 2.1

The statement of financial position includes three main elements: assets, liabilities and equity. Define these elements according to the International Accounting Standards Board's Conceptual Framework and explain the key points in those definitions.

❯ Question 2.2

Sophia owns and runs a shop as a sole trader. She started her business in February 2021 by paying £200,000 of her personal savings into her business bank account. In March 2021, she introduced one of her own properties valued at £100,000 into her business. In April she withdrew £5,000 from the till for her own personal use. The business had made a profit of £15,000 by the end of April 2021. Calculate the amount of equity at 30 April 2021 to be shown on the statement of financial position of the business.

❯❯ DEVELOP YOUR UNDERSTANDING

❯❯ Question 2.3

Using the criteria outlined in the summary in Figure 2.2, explain why the following items are assets that entities recognise on the statement of financial position:

(a)   Motor vehicles purchased by an entity.

(b)   Inventory received from suppliers.

(c)   Cash and cash equivalents.

Using the criteria outlined in the summary in Figure 2.2, explain why the following items are *not* assets and why they are not recognised on entities' statements of financial position:

(a) Redundant plant and machinery that has been replaced by faster, more technologically advanced machinery. This redundant plant and machinery is no longer used in the business or industry and has no resale or scrap value.

(b) A trade receivable from a customer who is bankrupt and from whom no payment is expected.

(c) A highly skilled workforce.

≫ Question 2.4

The directors of Oxford Academicals Football Club Limited are discussing whether player registrations can be recognised as assets on the club's statement of financial position. There are two groups of players. The first group consists of those players whose contracts have been bought by the club from other teams in the transfer market. The second group is made up of players who have come up through the youth scheme and who have been playing at various levels for the club since the age of 12. The accounts department has informed the directors that the transfer fees for the bought in contracts amount to £25 million. The directors, however, cannot agree on a valuation for the players that have been developed by the club. The managing director thinks these players should be valued at £30 million, while the finance director thinks this is far too high a figure and would value these players at £15 million. Various offers have been received from other clubs to sign the players developed by the club and the combined values of these offers have ranged from £10 million to £25 million. Advise the directors on whether any of the players' registrations can be recognised in the statement of financial position and, if they can be so recognised, the category of assets that these registrations would appear under and the value that can be recognised.

≫ Question 2.5

The following balances have been extracted from the books of the limited companies Alma, Bella, Carla, Deborah and Eloise at 30 April 2021. Using the statement of financial position format presented in this chapter, draw up the statements of financial position for the five companies at 30 April 2021.

	Alma £000	Bella £000	Carla £000	Deborah £000	Eloise £000
Share capital	1,000	5,000	2,500	3,000	4,500
Cash at bank	—	800	—	550	200
Goodwill	—	—	400	250	500
Inventory	1,000	700	800	750	900
Trade payables	1,450	4,000	1,750	5,600	5,800
Plant and machinery	2,000	9,500	3,750	4,250	5,000
Trade receivables	1,750	3,000	2,750	2,950	3,100
Bank overdraft	800	—	1,250	—	—
Loans due on 30 April 2028	1,000	10,000	1,500	—	—

2

	Alma £000	Bella £000	Carla £000	Deborah £000	Eloise £000
Loans due by 30 April 2022	200	400	300	—	—
Land and buildings	4,500	17,100	10,200	8,750	15,000
Taxation payable	540	1,100	800	—	—
Cash in hand	10	25	15	8	12
Trademarks	—	—	200	100	450
Motor vehicles	—	1,500	1,950	1,250	1,600
Tax repayment due	—	—	—	250	800
Retained earnings	2,770	4,625	7,465	5,508	8,262
Share premium	1,500	7,500	4,500	5,000	9,000

›› Question 2.6

Maria runs a small corner shop. Her statement of financial position at 31 October 2021 is shown below.

	£
Non-current assets	
Property, plant and equipment	15,000
Current assets	
Inventory	20,000
Other receivables	3,000
Cash and cash equivalents	500
	23,500
Total assets	38,500
Current liabilities	
Bank overdraft	7,000
Trade and other payables	8,000
Taxation	3,000
Total liabilities	18,000
Net assets	20,500
Capital account	
Balance at 31 October 2021	20,500

The following transactions took place in the first week of November 2021:

- Trade payables of £3,500 were paid from the bank account.
- Maria paid £10,000 of her own money into the bank account.
- Inventory of £1,200 was sold for £2,000 cash, a profit of £800 for the week.

- New inventory of £2,500 was purchased on credit from trade payables.
- Maria withdrew £300 from cash for her own personal expenses.

Required

Show how the above transactions would increase or decrease the various balances on the statement of financial position and draw up and balance the new statement of financial position at 7 November 2021.

» Question 2.7

Assets are categorised into current and non-current on the statement of financial position. Which of the following items are current assets and which are non-current assets? Explain your reasons for categorising each item as either a current or as a non-current asset.

(a) A building used by a service company for administration purposes.

(b) A car which is produced by a car manufacturer for sale.

(c) An amount owed by a customer arising from a credit sale transaction. Payment from this customer is due in 90 days' time.

(d) Patents.

(e) Production equipment.

(f) Wood to be used by a manufacturing company in making coffee tables.

»» TAKE IT FURTHER

»» Question 2.8

The statement of financial position for Andy Limited at 30 June 2021 is presented below. The following transactions took place in the first week of July 2021:

- 1 July 2021: paid a trade payable with a payment from the bank for £2,500 and received £3,000 from a trade receivable.
- 2 July 2021: took out a bank loan (full repayment is due on 30 June 2024) with which to buy a new vehicle costing £20,000. The vehicle purchase agreement was signed on 2 July 2021.
- 4 July 2021: sold goods which had cost Andy £7,500 to a customer on credit terms, the customer agreeing to pay for those goods on 3 August 2021. The selling price of the goods sold was £10,000.
- 5 July 2021: sold goods which had cost Andy £2,500 to a customer for £3,250. The customer paid cash for these goods.
- 6 July 2021: received new inventory from a supplier. The new inventory cost £15,000 and Andy Limited has agreed to pay for the inventory on 5 August 2021.
- 7 July 2021: paid tax of £3,000 and a trade payable of £7,000 from the bank account.

Required

Show how the above transactions would increase or decrease the various balances on the statement of financial position and draw up and balance the new statement of financial position at 7 July 2021.

Andy Limited	
Statement of financial position at 30 June 2021	
ASSETS	**£**
Non-current assets	
Property, plant and equipment	**320,000**
Current assets	
Inventories	50,000
Trade receivables	75,000
Cash and cash equivalents	20,000
	145,000
Total assets	**465,000**
LIABILITIES	
Current liabilities	
Trade payables	80,000
Taxation	20,000
	100,000
Non-current liabilities	
Bank loan (long-term borrowings)	250,000
Total liabilities	**350,000**
Net assets	**115,000**
EQUITY	
Called up share capital	20,000
Retained earnings	95,000
Total equity	**115,000**

>>> Question 2.9

(a) The following balances have been extracted from the books of Frankie Limited at 31 December 2021.

	£000
Cash at bank	600
Land and buildings	15,500
Loans due for repayment by 31 December 2022	850
Share premium	4,000
Loans due for repayment on 31 December 2030	8,500
Cash in hand	5
Share capital	2,000
Goodwill	1,000
Taxation payable	1,380
Fixtures and fittings	1,670
Trade receivables	4,910

Plant and machinery	10,630
Trade payables	6,720
Retained earnings	13,365
Inventory	2,500

Required

Using the statement of financial position format presented in this chapter, draw up the statement of financial position for Frankie Limited at 31 December 2021.

(b) During January 2022, the following transactions took place:

- Bought £12,200,000 of inventory on credit from suppliers.
- Made sales on credit to customers of £15,500,000. The inventory cost of the sales made was £11,450,000.
- Took out a loan of £2,500,000 with which to purchase new plant and machinery for £2,500,000. The new loan is due for repayment on 31 December 2026.
- Undertook a share issue, which raised cash of £1,500,000. £500,000 of the total amount raised represents share capital while the remaining £1,000,000 represents share premium.
- Made a tax payment from the bank account of £690,000.
- Received £6,450,000 from trade receivables.
- Paid trade payables £8,210,000.
- Sold a surplus piece of land that had cost £2,000,000 for £2,500,000.
- Made a short-term loan repayment of £200,000.

Required

Using the statement of financial position for Frankie Limited drawn up at 31 December 2021, show how the above transactions would increase or decrease the various balances on the statement of financial position and draw up and balance the new statement of financial position at the end of January 2022.

》》Question 2.10

In March 2021, Martina decided to open a book shop. The following transactions took place in the first month of its operation:

- 1 March 2021: paid £10,000 into the business bank account.
- 4 March 2021: bought books on credit from Alex for £4,300.
- 5 March 2021: bought shop fittings on credit from Mary for £1,000.
- 10 March 2021: sold goods which had cost £3,000 on credit to Alan for £4,500.
- 17 March 2021: paid Alex for the books bought on credit on 4 March 2021.
- 21 March 2021: sold goods which had cost £1,000 in cash to Filip for £1,500.
- 26 March 2021: received half of the amount owed by Alan from the sale on 10 March 2021.
- 30 March 2021: paid Mary for the shop fittings bought on 5 March 2021.

Required

Show how the above transactions would increase or decrease the relevant accounts on the statement of financial position and draw up Martina's statement of financial position at 31 March 2021.

3

THE STATEMENT OF PROFIT OR LOSS

LEARNING OUTCOMES

Once you have read this chapter and worked through the questions and examples in both this chapter and the online workbook, you should be able to:

- Define income and expenses

- Understand the different expense categories and profit figures that are presented in published financial statements

- Understand that revenue and costs in the statement of profit or loss represent income earned and expenditure incurred in an accounting period not just the cash received and cash paid in that period

- Apply the accruals basis of accounting in determining income earned and expenditure incurred in an accounting period

- Calculate prepayments and accruals at the end of an accounting period

- Define and calculate depreciation using both the straight line and reducing balance methods

- Make accounting adjustments to the statement of profit or loss to reflect the effect of irrecoverable debts, the allowance for receivables, sales returns, purchase returns, discounts allowed and discounts received

- Prepare a statement of profit or loss for an accounting period together with the statement of financial position at the end of that accounting period from a given set of information

3

INTRODUCTION

In the last chapter we looked at the statement of financial position. We noted that this statement just presents an entity's financial position on one day in the year, the financial year-end date. However, many users of financial information turn first of all not to the statement of financial position but to the main source of information about an entity's financial performance during an accounting period, the statement of profit or loss. This statement shows the income and expenditure of the entity for the year. The difference between total income and total expenditure represents the profit or loss that the entity has made during that financial year. It is this profit or loss figure that initially tends to be of most interest to financial statement users. A quick skim through the financial press on any day of the week will show you that profit or loss is one of the most discussed numbers in any set of financial statements. It is this figure, in many people's (and shareholders' and the stock market's) view, that determines whether a company has had a successful or unsuccessful year as shown by the two examples in Give me an example 3.1.

> **GIVE ME AN EXAMPLE 3.1   The importance of profits for businesses**
>
> Compare the stock market's reactions to these announcements from two different companies in May and October 2019.
>
> ### 14 May 2019: Greggs' shares rise 12.5%
>
> Greggs shares rose 12.5% to 2,014 pence when the company announced sales growth of 15.1% for the first 19 weeks of 2019. This was the first time that the shares had ever enjoyed a stock market valuation above 2,000 pence. The increase was based on both the rise in revenue and the expectation that profits for the year to December 2019 would be materially higher than previously forecast.
>
> Source: https://www.proactiveinvestors.co.uk/companies/news/220201/greggs-hits-all-time-high-after-fourth-profit-upgrade-in-five-months-220201.html
>
> ### 3 October 2019: Ted Baker bombs on yet another profit warning
>
> The announcement of first half profits that were worse than expected together with a warning that full year profits to January 2020 would be lower than expected resulted in a 31.4% fall in Ted Baker's share price to 635 pence.
>
> Source: https://www.sharesmagazine.co.uk/news/shares/ted-baker-bombs-on-yet-another-profit-warning

To enable you to see how the statement of profit or loss is presented in full before we consider the detail, Illustration 3.1 presents the statement of profit or loss for Bunns the Bakers plc for the years ended 31 March 2021 and 31 March 2020. This statement begins with income (revenue) and then deducts various categories of expenditure to arrive at the profit for the year. However, income and expenditure are not just simply cash received and cash spent during the year. There are various accounting conventions that have to be applied in the determination of income and costs for a period. How these conventions are applied to individual items of revenue and expenditure will determine the profit for each accounting period. The application of these conventions will form a large part of this chapter. Careful study of these applications will enable you to understand how income and expenditure are calculated and how, in turn, the profit or loss for a period is determined.

Illustration 3.1 Bunns the Bakers plc: statement of profit or loss for the years ended 31 March 2021 and 31 March 2020

	2021	2020	
	£000	£000	
Revenue	10,078	9,575	
Cost of sales	(4,535)	(4,596)	
Gross profit	5,543	4,979	The trading part of the statement of profit or loss
Distribution and selling costs	(3,398)	(3,057)	
Administration expenses	(1,250)	(1,155)	
Operating profit	895	767	
Finance income	15	12	The financing part of the statement of profit or loss
Finance expense	(150)	(165)	
Profit before tax	760	614	
Income tax	(213)	(172)	
Profit for the year	547	442	

GO BACK OVER THIS AGAIN!   A copy of this statement of profit or loss is available in the **online workbook:** you might like to keep this on screen or print off a copy for easy reference while you work your way through the material in this chapter. There is also an annotated copy of this statement of profit or loss at the end of the book to help you go over the relevant points again to reinforce your knowledge and learning.

TERMINOLOGY: STATEMENT OF PROFIT OR LOSS/ INCOME STATEMENT/STATEMENT OF FINANCIAL PERFORMANCE/PROFIT AND LOSS ACCOUNT

The statement of profit or loss is also known as the income statement or the profit and loss account. In keeping with the International Financial Reporting Standards approach adopted in this book, the term 'statement of profit or loss' is used throughout, but you will still find entities presenting an 'income statement' or a 'profit and loss account'. Under the IASB *Conceptual*

Framework for Financial Reporting, the statement of profit or loss is just one component of the statement of financial performance. This statement of financial performance includes both the statement of profit or loss and a statement of other comprehensive income which presents details of other gains and losses arising in an accounting period from, for example, the revaluation of assets or changes in the valuation of pension liabilities. Consideration of the statement of other comprehensive income is beyond the scope of this book. Our concern in this and subsequent chapters is with the income earned and expenditure incurred in the course of everyday trading operations of businesses that form the basis for the figures presented in the statement of profit or loss.

Note: in Illustration 3.1 income and profit figures are shown without brackets while items of expenditure are shown in brackets. This is to help you understand which items are subtracted and which items are added to determine the result (profit or loss) for the year. Taking revenue (= sales) and finance income as positive figures, subtract the expenses to ensure you understand the relationships between the figures and to make sure that:

- Revenue – cost of sales = gross profit
- Gross profit – distribution and selling costs – administration expenses = operating profit
- Operating profit + finance income – finance expense = profit before tax, and
- Profit before tax   income tax = profit for the year.

DEFINITIONS

Illustration 3.1 shows the statement of profit or loss for Bunns the Bakers plc. As noted in the introduction, the statement of profit or loss contains items of revenue (income) and expenditure (costs incurred in making goods and selling them and in running and financing the company). Before we look at these different items of income and expenditure in more detail, let's start with some definitions.

Income

The International Accounting Standards Board defines income as 'increases in assets, or decreases in liabilities, that result in increases in equity, other than those relating to contributions from holders of equity claims' (IASB *Conceptual Framework for Financial Reporting*, paragraph 4.68). Let's break this definition down to understand what it means. When you make a sale for cash you have increased your cash asset. At the same time, this cash sale transaction also increases the equity of the business. The £s of assets are now higher as a result of the cash generated by the sale made while the £s of liabilities have remained the same (remember that assets – liabilities = equity, Chapter 2, Equity). Similarly, making a sale on credit to a customer who will pay at some later date increases the trade receivables asset while having no effect on liabilities so this increase in assets also increases the equity of the business. Likewise, a reduction in the £s of liabilities while the £s of assets remain the same will also increase equity.

However, not every increase in assets or decrease in liabilities will result in an increase in equity. Taking out a loan increases the cash asset but the borrowings liability rises by an equal and opposite amount so that there is no change in the assets – liabilities figure and, consequently, no increase in equity. Simply paying a trade payable what is owed reduces liabilities but the cash asset also falls by an equal and opposite amount so, again, there is no increase in the equity of the business. To recognise income there must always be an increase in the £s of equity when the £s of liabilities are deducted from the £s of assets.

The IASB definition of income also refers to 'increases in equity, other than those relating to contributions from holders of equity claims'. What does this mean? When business owners pay money into their businesses or shareholders subscribe for new shares in companies, these transactions increase both the cash asset and equity (Chapter 2, The components of equity). Assets have increased but these receipts are not income as they are money received from business owners or investors, both holders of equity claims: these amounts are now owed to the business's owners and shareholders and thus do not meet the definition of income.

Expenses

As you might have expected, given the definition of income, the International Accounting Standards Board defines expenses as 'decreases in assets, or increases in liabilities, that result in decreases in equity, other than those relating to distributions to holders of equity claims' (IASB *Conceptual Framework for Financial Reporting*, paragraph 4.69).

Again, let's break this definition down to understand what it means.

When a business pays cash to meet an expense, the cash asset decreases. At the same time, this transaction also decreases the equity of the business. The £s of assets are now lower as a result of the cash paid while the £s of liabilities have remained the same (assets – liabilities = equity, Chapter 2, Equity). Similarly, buying goods or services on credit will increase the trade payables liability while having no effect on the assets of the business, so this increase in liabilities also decreases the equity of the business.

However, not every increase in liabilities or decrease in assets will result in a decrease in equity. Taking out a loan increases the borrowings liability but the cash asset rises by an equal and opposite amount so that there is no change in the equity (assets – liabilities) figure in the statement of financial position and, consequently, no decrease in equity. Likewise, paying cash to settle what is owed to a trade payable reduces the cash asset but it also reduces the trade payables liability by an equal and opposite amount so, again, there is no decrease in the equity of the business. To recognise an expense there must always be a decrease in the £s of equity when the £s of liabilities are deducted from the £s of assets.

The IASB definition of expenses also refers to 'decreases in equity, other than those relating to distributions to holders of equity claims'. What does this mean? When business owners take money out of their businesses or shareholders are paid a dividend, these transactions decrease both the cash asset and equity (Chapter 2, The components of equity). Assets have decreased but these payments are not an expense as they are cash paid out to business owners and shareholders, both holders of equity claims: these amounts have been paid out to the business's owners and shareholders in their capacity as holders of equity claims and thus do not meet the definition of expenses.

INCOME IN THE STATEMENT OF PROFIT OR LOSS

The first line in Illustration 3.1 refers to Revenue. Revenue represents sales income earned in an accounting period (usually one year) and may be referred to in some sets of accounts as sales or turnover as well as by the term revenue. These three terms all refer to the same type of income, income from trading goods or providing services.

Revenue appears as the first item in the statement of profit or loss and arises from sales made by an entity in the ordinary (everyday) course of business. For Bunns the Bakers plc this will mean selling bread, sandwiches, cakes, hot snacks, drinks and other products associated with their primary (everyday) activity, selling bakery and related goods. Were Bunns the Bakers to sell one of their shops, this would not be a transaction in the ordinary course of business and would not be recorded as part of revenue: selling shops is not what a bakery company would be expected to do on a regular basis. Instead, the profit or loss on the sale of the shop would be recorded in a separate line for exceptional income in the statement of profit or loss below operating profit. The way in which entities record exceptional income in their financial statements is illustrated in Give me an example 3.2.

The first six lines in the statement of profit or loss (from Revenue down to Operating profit) thus consist of items relating to the everyday trading activity of the organisation. Therefore, items of income and expense that do not relate to trading are excluded from the revenue, cost of sales, distribution and selling costs and administration expenses categories in the statement of profit or loss.

Not all income will arise from an entity's regular or trading activities. The other element of income shown in Bunns the Bakers plc's statement of profit or loss is Finance income. This will consist of interest income received and receivable from the company's bank on deposits of surplus cash held in Bunns' account(s) or dividends received and receivable from the company's investments. As Bunns the Bakers is not a bank, earning interest is not part of its everyday trading activities in the ordinary course of business, so any interest earned in the period is disclosed on a separate line. This income is disclosed outside the trading part of the statement of profit or loss in its own separate section. Figure 3.1 summarises the three different types of income in the statement of profit or loss.

GIVE ME AN EXAMPLE 3.2   Recording exceptional income in the statement of profit or loss

The following extract from the consolidated income statement (= statement of profit or loss) of Rolls-Royce Holdings plc for the year ended 31 December 2018 shows exceptional income recorded below the operating profit line.

Note that such exceptional income is not included in Revenue.

Source: Rolls-Royce Holdings annual report 2018
www.rolls-royce.com

	2018 £m	2017 £m
Operating (loss)/profit	(1,161)	366
Gain arising on the acquisition of ITP Aero	–	785
Gain arising on the disposal of L'Orange	358	–
(Loss)/profit before financing and taxation	**(803)**	**1,151**

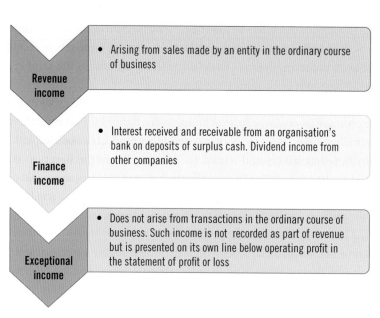

Figure 3.1 The different types of income in the statement of profit or loss

Revenue income
- Arising from sales made by an entity in the ordinary course of business

Finance income
- Interest received and receivable from an organisation's bank on deposits of surplus cash. Dividend income from other companies

Exceptional income
- Does not arise from transactions in the ordinary course of business. Such income is not recorded as part of revenue but is presented on its own line below operating profit in the statement of profit or loss

WHY IS THIS RELEVANT TO ME?   Income categorised under different headings

To enable you as a business professional to:

- Read a published statement of profit or loss and to understand what each category of income represents

- Appreciate that not all income arises from sales made in the ordinary course of business

---

GO BACK OVER THIS AGAIN!   Are you confident that you understand how revenue in the statement of profit or loss is split into income from sales made in the ordinary course of business, finance income and exceptional income? Go to the **online workbook** and complete Exercises 3.1 to make sure you can distinguish between these different types of income.

3

EXPENDITURE IN THE STATEMENT OF PROFIT OR LOSS

Expenditure in Bunns the Bakers' statement of profit or loss falls under various headings. Let's look at each of these in turn.

Cost of sales

This heading comprises those costs incurred directly in the making or buying in of products for sale. In the case of Bunns the Bakers, there will be the cost of the raw materials such as flour, fat, salt, cream, sugar and all the other ingredients that go into the bread, cakes, hot snacks and sandwiches, as well as goods bought in ready made from other manufacturers such as soft drinks and chocolate bars. In addition, the wages of the bakers, the electricity or gas used in heating the ovens and all the other associated costs of making or buying in the products will be included in cost of sales.

Determining the cost of making the products is important. The cost of the product is usually the starting point for setting a selling price at which customers will buy and to cover all the other costs of the operation so that a profit is made. In smaller entities, as we shall see shortly (this chapter, Statement of profit or loss by nature), cost of sales is usually calculated as: opening inventory of goods at the start of the accounting period + purchases during the accounting period – closing inventory of goods at the end of the accounting period.

Distribution and selling costs

These costs will comprise of all those costs incurred in the distribution and selling of the products. For Bunns the Bakers, advertising would fall under this heading, as would the transport of bakery goods produced from the main bakery to each of the individual shops. The wages of shop staff would be part of selling costs, too, as would the costs of running the shops, including shop expenditure on goods and services such as cleaning, repairs, electricity, maintenance, rent, rates and water.

Administration expenses

This category covers all the costs of running the trading operation that do not fall under any other heading. Examples of such costs for Bunns the Bakers (and many other entities) would be legal expenses, accountancy and audit costs, directors' salaries, accounting department costs, bank charges and human resource department expenditure. Such costs are essential in running the business, but they cannot be allocated to the costs of making and producing or distributing and selling the goods sold by the organisation. Figure 3.2 summarises the different types of trading expenditure incurred in running a business.

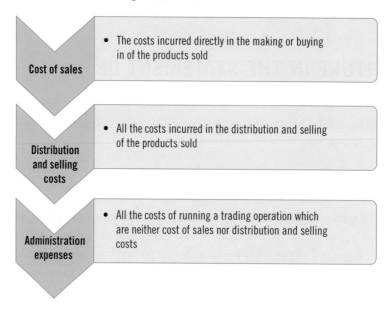

Figure 3.2 The different types of trading expenditure incurred in running a business

---

GO BACK OVER THIS AGAIN!   Are you convinced that you can distinguish between items that belong in the cost of sales, selling and distribution and administration sections of the statement of profit or loss? Go to the **online workbook** and complete Exercises 3.2 to make sure you can make these distinctions.

Finance expense

As with finance income, this expense is not incurred as part of trading activities. Finance expense is made up of interest paid on the borrowings used to finance the business. Look back at Illustration 2.1: Bunns the Bakers' statement of financial position shows that the company has borrowings under current and non-current liabilities. The finance expense will be the interest charged on these borrowings.

Income tax

The final expense to be deducted in Bunns the Bakers' statement of profit or loss is income tax. All commercial entities have to pay tax on their profits according to the tax law of the country in which they are resident and in which they operate. The income tax charge is based on the profits of the entity for the accounting period and the entity would expect to pay this tax at some point in the coming financial year. Figure 3.3 presents these five different categories of costs. As you will learn later on in your studies, UK companies pay corporation tax on their profits. However, the IASB presentation format in IAS 1 for the statement of profit or loss requires the heading income tax for all taxes paid on company profits.

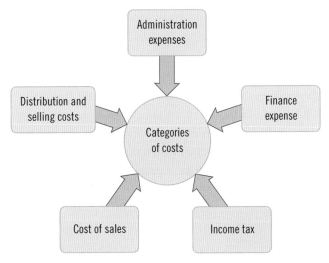

Figure 3.3 The different categories of costs (expenditure) in a typical statement of profit or loss

WHY IS THIS RELEVANT TO ME?   Expenditure categorised under different headings

To enable you as a business professional to:

● Appreciate that expenses are categorised according to different types of expenditure

● Read a published statement of profit or loss and understand what each category of expenditure represents

MULTIPLE CHOICE QUESTIONS   Are you certain that you can distinguish between items that belong in the various categories of income and expenditure in the statement of profit or loss? Go to the **online workbook** and complete Multiple choice questions 3.1 to make sure you can make these distinctions.

DIFFERENT CATEGORIES OF PROFIT

Bunns the Bakers' statement of profit or loss presents several different lines describing various different numbers as 'profit'. Why are there so many different figures for profit and what does each of them tell us about the profits of the company? The following observations can be made:

● Gross profit = revenue − cost of sales: this is the profit that arises when all the direct costs of production or purchase of the goods sold are deducted from the sales revenue earned in the accounting period.

● Operating profit = gross profit − distribution and selling costs − administration expenses: the profit remaining when all the other operating costs not directly associated with the

3

production or buying in of goods are deducted from the gross profit. Alternatively, this is the profit after all the costs of trading, direct (cost of sales) and indirect (distribution and selling costs and administration expenses), are deducted from sales revenue.

• Profit before tax = operating profit + finance income − finance expense: the profit that remains once the costs of financing operations have been deducted and any finance or other income has been added onto operating profit.

• Profit for the year = profit before tax − income tax (also called the profit after tax or the net profit): this is the profit that is left once the tax on the profits for the accounting period has been deducted from the profit before tax. Alternatively, this is the profit that remains once all the expenses have been deducted from the sales revenue and any other income for the accounting period added on. This profit is now available to the company to distribute to the shareholders as a dividend or to retain within the business to finance future expansion. Figure 3.4 presents the different categories of profit.

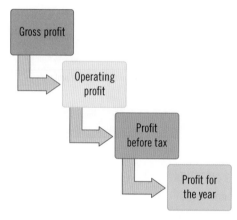

Figure 3.4 The different categories of profit in a typical company statement of profit or loss

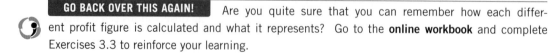

WHY IS THIS RELEVANT TO ME?   Different categories of profit

To enable you as a business professional to:

• Understand the accounting terminology describing the various categories of profit

• Understand how trading and financing activities have contributed to the results for the accounting period

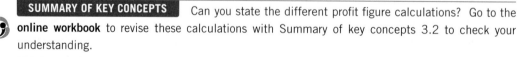

GO BACK OVER THIS AGAIN!   Are you quite sure that you can remember how each different profit figure is calculated and what it represents? Go to the **online workbook** and complete Exercises 3.3 to reinforce your learning.

SUMMARY OF KEY CONCEPTS   Can you state the different profit figure calculations? Go to the **online workbook** to revise these calculations with Summary of key concepts 3.2 to check your understanding.

STATEMENT OF PROFIT OR LOSS BY NATURE

The statement of profit or loss for Bunns the Bakers plc (Illustration 3.1) is presented in the format that you will find in published financial statements for limited and public limited companies which requires the classification of expenses by function (cost of sales, distribution and selling costs, administration expenses, finance expense). However, the rest of this chapter will use examples and exercises based on the statement of profit or loss format in Illustration 3.2, the format that is used every day by traders and companies as a simple way to present income and expenditure to determine whether a profit or loss has been made. Study this format now along with the notes below.

Illustration 3.2 A trader: statement of profit or loss by nature for the year ended 31 March 2021

	£	£
Sales		347,250
Opening inventory	13,600	
Purchases	158,320	
Closing inventory	(17,500)	
Cost of sales (opening inventory + purchases − closing inventory)		154,420
Gross profit (sales − cost of sales)		192,830
Expenses (can be listed in any order required)		
Heat and light	9,500	
Motor expenses	12,250	
Rent and rates	25,685	
Wages and salaries	48,345	
Administration expenses	10,050	
Accountancy	2,000	
Legal expenses	1,950	
Bank interest	6,000	
Depreciation of non-current assets	24,000	
Insurance	7,500	
Miscellaneous	1,890	
Total expenses (all expenses items added together)		149,170
Bank interest received		950
Net profit (gross profit − total expenses + bank interest received)		44,610

GO BACK OVER THIS AGAIN!   How would the income and expenditure in Illustration 3.2 be presented in the published financial statements format which presents expenses by function? Go to the **online workbook** Exercises 3.4 to see how the above information would be summarised ready for publication.

3

Notes to the statement of profit or loss in Illustration 3.2

- The statement of profit or loss by nature consists of three sections: sales, cost of sales and expenses.

- Just as in the case of published statements of profit or loss, sales are made up of all the revenue derived from the ordinary activities of the business.

- Cost of sales is the opening inventory of unsold goods at the start of the year, plus purchases of goods during the year, less the closing inventory of unsold goods at the end of the year.

- Expenses are listed in any order: there is no set order in which expenses have to be presented.

- Expenses would include finance expense if an entity has incurred any interest costs relating to money borrowed to finance the business (Bank interest in Illustration 3.2) while finance income (interest receivable) is shown on a separate line below total expenses (Bank interest received in Illustration 3.2).

- Note the format of the statement: the component parts of Cost of sales and Expenses are listed in the left hand column and then the figures for Cost of sales and Expenses are totalled in the right hand column and deducted from Sales and Gross profit, respectively.

- As in Bunns the Bakers' statement of profit or loss, sales − cost of sales = gross profit and gross profit − total expenses = net profit (profit for the year) for the accounting period.

WHY IS THIS RELEVANT TO ME?   Statement of profit or loss by nature

To enable you as a business professional to understand:

- That statements of profit or loss for internal use within businesses adopt a different format compared to published statements of profit or loss

- How to draw up statements of profit or loss by nature for presentation to interested parties

- What the income and two categories of expenditure represent

---

 NUMERICAL EXERCISES   Do you think that you could prepare statements of profit or loss by nature from a given set of information? Go to the **online workbook** and complete Numerical exercises 3.1 to test out your ability to prepare these statements.

 SUMMARY OF KEY CONCEPTS   Are you confident that you can state the calculation for cost of sales? Go to the **online workbook** to revise this calculation with Summary of key concepts 3.3 to check your knowledge.

Now that we have looked at the presentation of the statement of profit or loss and what it contains, it is time to find out how income and expense are determined in an accounting period.

DETERMINING THE AMOUNT OF INCOME OR EXPENSE

At the start of this chapter we noted that income and expenditure are not simply cash received and cash paid, although cash received and cash paid are the starting point when preparing any set of financial statements. Revenue for an accounting period consists of all the sales made during that period, whether the cash from those sales has been received or not. Where a sale has been made but payment has not been received the entity recognises both a sale and a trade receivable at the end of the accounting period. This trade receivable is money due to the entity from a customer to whom the entity has made a valid sale. Thus, the entity recognises this sale in the statement of profit or loss as part of sales for the period and as a trade receivable in the statement of financial position. Where a sale has been made and the cash received, the entity recognises the sale in the statement of profit or loss and the increase in cash in the statement of financial position.

Diagrammatically, the above transactions can be represented as shown in Table 3.1.

Table 3.1 Cash and credit sales: statement of profit or loss and statement of financial position effects

	Statement of profit or loss effect	Cash received?	Statement of financial position effect
Sale made for cash	Increase revenue	Yes	Increase cash
Sale made on credit, payment due in 30 days	Increase revenue	No	Increase trade receivables
Cash received from trade receivable	No effect: no new revenue	Yes	Increase cash, decrease trade receivables

Give me an example 3.3 illustrates Nestlé's revenue recognition policy which matches exactly the approach outlined in Table 3.1. As soon as goods are sent to a customer, Nestlé recognises the sale whether the cash has been received from the customer or not.

GIVE ME AN EXAMPLE 3.3   At what point in time do commercial organisations recognise revenue in their financial statements?

The following accounting policy regarding the timing of revenue recognition is taken from Nestlé's financial statements for the year ended 31 December 2019.

Revenue

Sales represent amounts received and receivable from third parties for goods supplied to the customers and for services rendered. Sales are recognised when control of the goods has been transferred to the customer which is mainly upon arrival at the customer.

Source: Nestlé financial statements 2019 www.nestle.com, p. 82

Note that revenue comprises both cash received ('amounts received') and cash receivable (amounts 'receivable'). Revenue is thus not just the cash received in an accounting period, it represents all the revenue that an entity has earned during an accounting period, whether the cash has been received or not.

Similarly, expenses are not just the cash paid during an accounting period for goods and services received but *all* the expenses incurred in that period whether they have been paid for or not. Where an entity has incurred an expense during an accounting period but not paid this amount by the statement of financial position date, then the entity records the expense along with a trade payable. This trade payable represents a present obligation of the entity to transfer an economic resource at the end of the accounting period for an expense validly incurred during that accounting period. If the expense has been paid then the expense is recognised along with a reduction in cash.

Diagrammatically, these transactions can be represented as shown in Table 3.2.

Table 3.2 Cash and credit expenses: statement of profit or loss and statement of financial position effects

	Statement of profit or loss effect	Cash paid?	Statement of financial position effect
Expense paid for with cash	Increase expenses	Yes	Decrease cash
Expense incurred on credit, payment due in 30 days	Increase expenses	No	Increase trade payables
Cash paid to trade payable	No effect: no new expense	Yes	Decrease cash, decrease trade payables

Give me an example 3.4 illustrates Nestlé's expenses recognition policy which matches exactly the approach outlined in Table 3.2. As soon as goods or services are received, Nestlé recognises the expense whether the cash has been paid by the company or not.

GIVE ME AN EXAMPLE 3.4   When do commercial organisations recognise costs and expenses in their financial statements?

The following accounting policy regarding the timing of expense recognition is taken from Nestlé's financial statements for the year ended 31 December 2019.

Expenses

Cost of goods sold is determined on the basis of the cost of production or of purchase, adjusted for the variation of inventories. All other expenses, including those in respect of advertising and promotions, are recognised when the Group receives the risks and rewards of ownership of the goods or when it receives the services.

Source: Nestlé financial statements 2019
www.nestle.com, p. 74

Note that expenses are recognised not when cash is paid but when goods and services are received and when the company has an obligation to pay for those goods and services (the point at which the risks and rewards of ownership are received, i.e. when the goods or services are delivered to the company).

 GO BACK OVER THIS AGAIN!   Are you convinced that you understand how to determine the correct amount of income or expense for a given period? Go to the **online workbook** and complete Exercises 3.5 to reinforce your learning.

THE ACCRUALS BASIS OF ACCOUNTING

The principle that all income earned and expenditure incurred in a period is recognised in that period is referred to as the accruals basis of accounting. Under this basis, the timing of cash payments and receipts is irrelevant as transactions are matched (allocated) to the time period in which they occur not to the time periods in which they are paid for or in which cash is received.

Why is the accruals basis of accounting applied to financial statements? If the accruals basis of accounting did not exist, entities could time their cash receipts and payments to manipulate their cash-based statements of profit or loss to show the picture they wanted to show rather than the portrait of the income actually earned and the expenses actually incurred during an accounting period. Thus, some accounting periods would show high sales receipts, low expense payments and high profits, while other accounting periods would show low sales receipts, high expense payments and low profits or even losses. Results would depend upon money received and money paid out rather than reflecting all the business activity that had actually taken place within a given period of time.

An ability to manipulate the accounts in this way would lead to a lack of comparability between different accounting periods and between different organisations. We saw in Chapter 1 that comparability is an enhancing qualitative characteristic of accounting information. Lack of comparability would make it very difficult for users to gain an understanding of how the entity is making (or failing to make) progress in terms of profits earned or increases in sales made due to the fluctuating nature of cash inflows and outflows. The International Accounting Standards Board recognises the importance of accruals accounting and how this approach to accounting for transactions provides much more useful information relating to an entity's financial performance and financial position to users:

> Accrual accounting depicts the effects of transactions and other events and circumstances on a reporting entity's economic resources and claims in the periods in which those effects occur, even if the resulting cash receipts and payments occur in a different period. This is important because information about a reporting entity's economic resources and claims and changes in its economic resources and claims during a period provides a better basis for assessing the entity's past and future performance than information solely about cash receipts and payments during that period.
>
> Source: IASB *Conceptual Framework for Financial Reporting*, paragraph 1.17

WHY IS THIS RELEVANT TO ME?   The accruals basis of accounting

To enable you as a business professional to appreciate that:

- The timing of cash received and cash paid is irrelevant in the preparation of financial statements

- Transactions are reflected in financial statements on the basis of when they take place not on the basis of when cash is received or paid

---

SUMMARY OF KEY CONCEPTS   Can you say what the accruals basis of accounting means? Go to the **online workbook** to revise this definition with Summary of key concepts 3.4 to check your learning.

The accruals basis of accounting looks like a difficult concept to grasp, but with practice you will soon be able to apply this concept readily to accounting problems. Let's look at some examples to show how the accruals basis of accounting works in practice. Think about the outcomes you would expect and compare your expectations to the actual answers. Remember that income and expenditure are allocated to an accounting period on the basis of income earned and expenditure incurred in that accounting period not on the timing of cash receipts and payments. Let's see how the accruals basis of accounting is applied in practice in Examples 3.1 and 3.2.

EXAMPLE 3.1

The Traditional Toy Company has an accounting year end of 30 June. On 1 January 2020, the company paid its annual insurance premium of £1,000, giving the company and its activities cover up to 31 December 2020. On 1 January 2021, the company paid its annual insurance premium of £1,200, which covers the company and its activities up to 31 December 2021. What expense should the Traditional Toy Company recognise for insurance for its accounting year 1 July 2020 to 30 June 2021?

The answer is £1,100. How did we arrive at this figure?

The premium paid on 1 January 2020 relates to the 12 months to 31 December 2020. Six of the months for the accounting period 1 July 2020 to 30 June 2021 are covered by this insurance premium, namely July, August, September, October, November and December 2020. Therefore 6/12 of the £1,000 belong in the accounting year to 30 June 2021; the other 6/12 of this payment (January to June 2020) belong in the accounting year 1 July 2019 to 30 June 2020.

Similarly, the premium paid on 1 January 2021 covers the whole calendar year to 31 December 2021. However, as the Traditional Toy Company's accounting year ends on 30 June 2021, only six months of this insurance premium belong in the financial year ended on that date, namely January, February, March, April, May and June 2021. Therefore 6/12 of £1,200 belong in the accounting year to 30 June 2021; the other 6/12 of this payment (July to December 2021) belong to the accounting year 1 July 2021 to 30 June 2022.

The total insurance expense recognised in the statement of profit or loss for the 12 months accounting year to 30 June 2021 is thus:

$$£1,000 \times 6/12 + £1,200 \times 6/12 - £1,100$$

While £1,200 was paid for insurance in the accounting year 1 July 2020 to 30 June 2021, the accruals basis of accounting requires that an expense of £1,100 for insurance is recognised in this financial year as this was the actual cost of insurance during this time period. Figure 3.5 will help you understand how the amounts paid in the above example have been allocated to the different accounting periods.

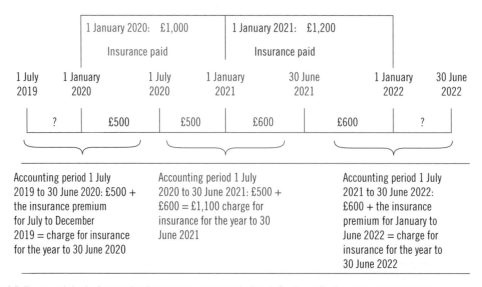

Figure 3.5 The accruals basis of accounting: insurance expense recognised in the Traditional Toy Company's accounting year 1 July 2020 to 30 June 2021

EXAMPLE 3.2

Hand Made Mirrors Limited has an accounting year end of 30 September. On 1 July 2020, the company paid its annual rates bill of £3,000 covering the period 1 July 2020 to 30 June 2021. On 1 July 2021, Hand Made Mirrors Limited received its annual rates bill for £3,600 covering the year to 30 June 2022 but did not pay this bill until 30 November 2021. What expense should the company recognise for rates for its accounting year 1 October 2020 to 30 September 2021?

The answer is £3,150. How did we arrive at this figure?

The rates paid on 1 July 2020 relate to the 12 months 1 July 2020 to 30 June 2021. Nine of the months for the accounting period 1 October 2020 to 30 September 2021 are covered by this rates bill, namely October, November and December of 2020 and January, February, March, April, May and June of 2021. Therefore 9/12 of this £3,000 belong in the accounting year to 30 September 2021.

Similarly, the rates paid on 30 November 2021 cover the whole year from 1 July 2021 to 30 June 2022. However, as Hand Made Mirrors Limited's accounting year ends on 30 September 2021, only three months of this rates bill belong in the accounting year ended on that date, namely July, August and September 2021. Therefore 3/12 of £3,600 belong in the accounting year to 30 September 2021.

The total rates expense recognised in the statement of profit or loss for the year to 30 September 2021 is thus:

£3,000 × 9/12 + £3,600 × 3/12 = £3,150

No rates have been paid in the financial year 1 October 2020 to 30 September 2021, but the accruals basis of accounting requires a cost of £3,150 to be recognised as the rates expense during the year. Again, a diagram as shown in Figure 3.6 will help you understand how the amounts paid in the above example have been allocated to the different accounting periods.

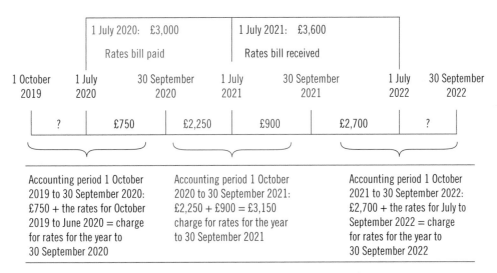

Figure 3.6 The accruals basis of accounting: Hand Made Mirrors Limited's rates expense recognised in the accounting year 1 October 2020 to 30 September 2021

MULTIPLE CHOICE QUESTIONS   Do you think you can allocate costs to accounting periods on an expense incurred basis under the accruals basis of accounting? Go to the **online workbook** and have a go at Multiple choice questions 3.2 to make sure you can make these allocations.

3

PREPAYMENTS AND ACCRUALS: RECORDING TRANSACTIONS IN THE STATEMENT OF PROFIT OR LOSS AND STATEMENT OF FINANCIAL POSITION

The two scenarios discussed provide us with one example of a prepayment and one example of an accrual at the end of an accounting period.

Prepayments

A prepayment is an expense paid in advance of the accounting period to which it relates. As this expense has been paid in advance, it is an asset of the entity. At 30 June 2021, in the case of the Traditional Toy Company, there is a prepaid insurance premium of £1,200 × 6/12 = £600. This prepayment is an asset as it is a present economic resource controlled by the entity as a result of past events (the payment of the insurance premium) and confers on the company a right that has the potential to produce economic benefits (the right to enjoy the protection provided by payment of the insurance premium in the next six months). While recognising the insurance expense of £1,100 for the accounting year to 30 June 2021, the entity also recognises a prepayment of £600 at the statement of financial position date of 30 June 2021.

At the end of the previous accounting period, at 30 June 2020, the Traditional Toy Company also had an insurance prepayment amounting to £1,000 × 6/12 = £500 (covering the months of July to December 2020 and paid in advance at 30 June 2020) so the insurance expense charge for the year is the £500 prepayment at the end of last year plus the £1,200 paid in the year less the prepayment at the end of the year of £600, thus:

£500 (prepayment at the end of last year) + £1,200 (payment in the year) − £600 (prepayment at the end of this year) = £1,100 insurance expense charge for the year

When attempting the multiple choice questions and exercises in the online workbook (and in real life situations), you can apply the rule presented in Figure 3.7 when you have an expense prepayment at the start and at the end of the financial year.

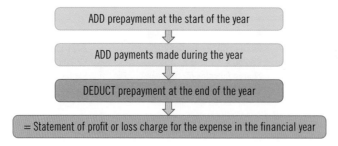

Figure 3.7 Calculating the statement of profit or loss expense for the financial year when there is a prepayment at the start and at the end of the accounting period

Accruals

An accrual is an expense owing at the end of the financial year for goods and services received but not yet paid for. As this expense is owed at the end of the year it represents a liability.

At 30 September 2021, Hand Made Mirrors Limited has a liability for unpaid rates of £3,600 × 3/12 = £900. This is a liability of the company at 30 September 2021 as it is a present obligation of the entity to transfer an economic resource (in the form of a cash payment to the local council on 30 November 2021) as a result of past events (the consumption of services). While recognising the total expense of £3,150 in the statement of profit or loss, Hand Made Mirrors Limited also recognises a £900 liability under trade and other payables in its statement of financial position at 30 September 2021. Remember that this is an expense incurred but not yet paid for, so you should increase the expense and increase the trade payables.

There was no accrual at the end of the previous accounting year. Had there been such an accrual this would have been treated as a deduction in arriving at the expense charge for the current accounting year. This is because an accrual at the end of the previous accounting period is a liability for a cost that was incurred in the previous accounting period but which will be paid in the current accounting period. The payment to discharge this liability has no bearing on the current accounting period's charge for this expense, so it is a deduction from the total payments made in the current accounting period.

When attempting the multiple choice questions and exercises in the online workbook (and in real life situations), you can apply the rule presented in Figure 3.8 when you have an expense accrual at the start and at the end of the financial year to find the amount you should recognise in the statement of profit or loss for that particular expense in the current financial year.

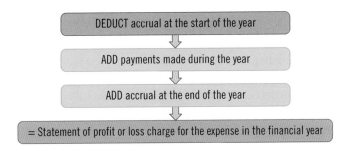

Figure 3.8 Calculating the statement of profit or loss expense for the financial year when there is an accrual at the start and at the end of the accounting period

WHY IS THIS RELEVANT TO ME?   Prepayments and accruals

To enable you as a business professional to understand how:

- Costs are allocated to accounting periods in which they are incurred
- To calculate simple accruals and prepayments at the end of an accounting period
- Assets and liabilities arise as a result of prepaid and accrued expenses

MULTIPLE CHOICE QUESTIONS   Are you confident that you can calculate statement of profit or loss expenses when there are prepayments and accruals at the start and end of the financial year? Go to the **online workbook** and have a go at Multiple choice questions 3.3 to test your ability to make these calculations.

DEPRECIATION

When we looked at the statement of financial position in Chapter 2, we noted that there are various types of non-current assets such as property, plant and equipment, patents and copyrights, among others. These assets are purchased by business organisations with a view to their long-term employment within the business to generate revenue, profits and cash. Businesses pay money for these assets when they buy them and then place these assets initially on the statement of financial position at their cost to the business.

A problem then arises. How should the cost of these non-current assets be allocated against income generated from those assets? The total cost of these assets is not allocated immediately against the income and profits made from those assets. Instead, the total cost is posted to the statement of financial position when the non-current asset is first acquired. Should we then allocate the cost of the asset to the statement of profit or loss at the end of the asset's life when the asset is worn out and of no further use to the business? Again, this will not happen. Setting the total cost of the asset against profit at the start or at the end of the asset's life would result in a very large one-off expense against profit in the year in which the asset is either bought or scrapped, so there has to be a better way to allocate the cost of non-current assets to accounting periods benefiting from their use. This is where depreciation comes in. Depreciation allocates the cost of a non-current asset to all those accounting periods benefiting from its use. Let's see how depreciation works in practice in Example 3.3.

EXAMPLE 3.3

Pento Printing Press buys a printing machine for £100,000 and expects this non-current asset to be used within the business for the next five years. By simply dividing the asset's cost by the number of years over which the asset will be used in the business, this will give us an annual allocation of the cost of this asset of £100,000 ÷ 5 years = £20,000 per annum. This means that there will be a charge in Pento's statement of profit or loss in year 1 of £20,000 for use of the asset in the business, a charge in the statement of profit or loss of £20,000 in year 2 for use of the asset and so on until the end of the five years when the asset is scrapped and a replacement asset is purchased.

The allocation of depreciation in this way has a dual effect: part of the cost of the asset is charged to the statement of profit or loss each year and at the same time the unallocated cost of the asset on the statement of financial position reduces each year. Table 3.3 shows how the annual depreciation is allocated to each accounting period benefiting from the printing machine's use and the effect that this will have on Pento's statement of financial position figure for this asset at the end of each financial year. In accounting terminology, this is expressed as follows: the original cost of the asset − the accumulated depreciation charged to the statement of profit or loss = the carrying amount of the asset shown on the statement of financial position at the end of each financial year.

The £20,000 depreciation on the asset is charged as an expense in the statement of profit or loss of each annual accounting period in which the asset is used within the business.

The accumulated depreciation charged rises each year as the printing machine ages. At the end of the first year, the accumulated depreciation is the same as the annual depreciation charge. By the end of the second year the accumulated depreciation of £40,000 is made up of the first year's charge of £20,000 plus the second year's charge of £20,000. Then, by the end of year 3, the accumulated depreciation of £60,000 is made up of three years' charges of £20,000 each year and so on until the end of the printing machine's useful life. At the end of year 5, the accumulated depreciation of £100,000 is the same as the original cost of £100,000. As each year progresses, the carrying amount of the printing machine (cost – the accumulated depreciation) gradually falls. Thus, the carrying amount reduces as more of the original cost is allocated against profit each year.

Table 3.3 Straight line depreciation on Pento Printing Press' printing machine costing £100,000 with £Nil value at the end of five years

Year	Statement of profit or loss: annual charge for depreciation on printing machine	Accumulated depreciation	Statement of financial position: carrying amount of printing machine at the end of each financial year
	£	£	£
1	20,000	20,000	80,000
2	20,000	40,000	60,000
3	20,000	60,000	40,000
4	20,000	80,000	20,000
5	20,000	100,000	Nil

WHY IS THIS RELEVANT TO ME?   Depreciation

To enable you as a business professional to understand how:

• The use of non-current assets within a business results in an annual depreciation expense in the statement of profit or loss

• The cost of non-current assets is allocated to the statement of profit or loss each year

• The carrying amount of non-current assets is calculated at the end of each financial year

MULTIPLE CHOICE QUESTIONS   How well do you understand the calculation of accumulated depreciation and carrying amount? Go to the **online workbook** and have a go at Multiple choice questions 3.4 to test your understanding of how to make these calculations.

RESIDUAL VALUE AND THE ANNUAL DEPRECIATION CHARGE

In Example 3.3 we assumed that all of the cost of the printing machine would be consumed over the five-year period and that it would have no value at the end of its projected five-year life. This might be a realistic scenario in the case of assets such as computers, which will be completely superseded by advancing technology and so have no value at the end of their useful lives within a business. However, it is just as likely that assets could be sold on to another buyer when the business wishes to dispose of them. A car, for example, will usually have some resale value when a company comes to dispose of it and, in the same way, second-hand machinery will find willing buyers.

It is thus normal practice, at the time of acquisition, to estimate a residual value for each non-current asset. Residual value is the amount that the original purchaser thinks that the asset could

3

be sold for when the time comes to dispose of it. When calculating the annual depreciation charge, the residual value is deducted from the original cost so that the asset is depreciated down to this value. If the residual value is estimated at £Nil, then the full cost of the asset is depreciated over its useful life. Example 3.4 illustrates the effect of residual value on the annual depreciation charge, on the accumulated depreciation and on the carrying amount of an asset at the end of each year in which the asset is used within a business.

EXAMPLE 3.4

The directors of Pento Printing Press now decide that their new printing machine will have an estimated residual value of £10,000 at the end of its five-year life. The annual depreciation charge will now fall to (£100,000 original cost − £10,000 residual value)/5 years = £18,000. Charging £18,000 depreciation each year will depreciate the asset down to its residual value as shown in Table 3.4.

Table 3.4 Pento Printing Press: straight line depreciation of a printing machine costing £100,000 with a £10,000 residual value

Year	Statement of profit or loss: annual charge for depreciation on printing machine	Accumulated depreciation	Statement of financial position: carrying amount of printing machine at the end of each financial year
	£	£	£
1	18,000	18,000	82,000
2	18,000	36,000	64,000
3	18,000	54,000	46,000
4	18,000	72,000	28,000
5	18,000	90,000	10,000

WHY IS THIS RELEVANT TO ME?   Residual value

To enable you as a business professional to understand that:

- The estimated residual value of an asset at the end of its useful life will result in a reduction in the annual depreciation charge
- Residual value is just an estimate of expected resale value at the end of a non-current asset's useful life

PROFITS AND LOSSES ON DISPOSAL OF NON-CURRENT ASSETS

You might now wonder what will happen if Pento Printing Press does not sell the asset at the end of the five years for £10,000. If the asset were to be sold for £8,000, £2,000 less than its carrying amount at the end of year 5, then Pento Printing Press would just record a loss (an additional expense) of £2,000 on the disposal of the printing machine in the statement of profit or loss. Profits would be reduced by that additional expense of £2,000. If, on the other hand, the asset were to be sold for £11,000, £1,000 more than the carrying amount at the end of the five years, Pento Printing Press would recognise a profit (a surplus) on the disposal of that asset in the statement of profit or loss. Profits on disposal of non-current assets are recorded as a deduction from expenses and are not recorded as additional revenue in the statement of profit or loss. Where the gain or loss on the disposal is a material amount, this gain or loss would be disclosed separately on the face of the statement of profit or loss as an exceptional item (this chapter, Income in the statement of profit or loss).

There would be no need for Pento Printing Press to go back and recalculate the depreciation for each of the five years in either of these cases as companies accept that the estimation of residual value is just that, a best guess at the time of acquisition of the asset of what the asset might be sold for at the end of its useful life within the business. It is quite normal for companies to recognise small gains and losses on the disposal of assets when they are sold on or scrapped either at the end of their useful lives or during the time that they are being used within the business.

WHY IS THIS RELEVANT TO ME?   Profits and losses on disposal of non-current assets

To enable you as a business professional to understand that:

- Profits on the disposal of non-current assets are recognised as income (a deduction from expenses) in the statement of profit or loss in the year of the asset's disposal

- Losses on the disposal of non-current assets are recognised as an expense in the statement of profit or loss in the year of the asset's disposal

- The profit or loss on disposal is calculated as the difference between the sale proceeds and the carrying amount of the asset at the date of disposal

---

MULTIPLE CHOICE QUESTIONS   Are you confident that you can calculate profits and losses arising on the disposal of non-current assets? Go to the **online workbook** and have a go at Multiple choice questions 3.5 to test your ability to make these calculations.

METHODS OF DEPRECIATION: STRAIGHT LINE AND REDUCING BALANCE

The approach used in the Pento Printing Press examples (Examples 3.3 and 3.4) to calculate depreciation resulted in the same depreciation charge for each year of the printing machine's useful life. This is the straight line basis of depreciation as it allocates an equal amount of depreciation to each year that the asset is used within the business.

An alternative method of depreciation that is also used is the reducing balance basis. This approach uses a fixed percentage of the cost in year 1 and the same fixed percentage of the carrying amount in subsequent years to calculate the annual depreciation charge. When using the reducing balance basis, residual value is ignored as the percentage used will depreciate the original cost down to residual value over the number of years in which the asset is used within the business. Example 3.5 illustrates how reducing balance depreciation is applied in practice.

EXAMPLE 3.5

Continuing with the Pento Printing Press example, a suitable percentage at which to depreciate the new printing machine on a reducing balance basis would be 36.90%. Let's see how this will work in Table 3.5.

The annual depreciation figures in Table 3.5 were calculated as follows:

- In year 1, depreciation is calculated on cost. This gives a figure of £100,000 × 36.90% = £36,900. This depreciation is then deducted from the original cost of £100,000 to leave a carrying amount at the end of year 1 of £100,000 − £36,900 = £63,100.

- In years 2 and onwards, depreciation is calculated on the carrying amount at the end of the preceding financial year. Carrying amount at the end of year 1 is £63,100, so depreciation for year 2 is £63,100 × 36.90% = £23,284 (rounding to the nearest £). This then gives a carrying amount at the end of year 2 of £63,100 − £23,284 (or £100,000 − £36,900 − £23,284) = £39,816.

- In year 3, depreciation is calculated on the carrying amount at the end of year 2. This gives an annual depreciation charge of £39,816 × 36.90% = £14,692 and a carrying amount at the end of year 3 of £39,816 − £14,692 = £25,124.

Work through the figures for years 4 and 5 to make sure that you understand how reducing balance depreciation works and to reinforce your learning.

Table 3.5 Pento Printing Press: reducing balance depreciation of a printing machine costing £100,000 with a £10,000 residual value

Year	Statement of profit or loss: annual charge for depreciation on printing machine	Accumulated depreciation	Statement of financial position: carrying amount of printing machine at the end of each financial year
	£	£	£
1	36,900	36,900	63,100
2	23,284	60,184	39,816
3	14,692	74,876	25,124
4	9,271	84,147	15,853
5	5,850	89,997	10,003

Figure 3.9 visually represents the annual depreciation charge under both the reducing balance (the blue line) and the straight line (the red line) methods. The straight line method of depreciation charges exactly the same depreciation each year, £18,000 (Table 3.4), so this is a straight line drawn across the graph through the £18,000 mark on the y axis. Reducing balance depreciation charges a high level of depreciation in the first year of the asset's life and this then gradually reduces each year, thereby producing the curved blue line on the graph.

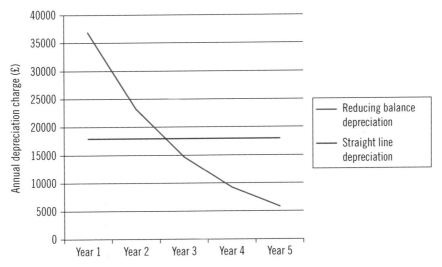

Figure 3.9 Graph representing the annual depreciation charges under both the reducing balance and straight line methods of depreciation for Pento Printing Press' printing machine costing £100,000 with a residual value of £10,000

WHICH DEPRECIATION METHOD IS MOST APPROPRIATE IN PRACTICE?

When selecting a method of depreciation, entities should always ask themselves how the economic benefits of each asset will be consumed. If most of the economic benefits that the asset represents will be used up in the early years of an asset's life, then reducing balance depreciation would be the most suitable method to use. Reducing balance would charge a higher proportion of the cost to the early years of the asset's life, thereby reflecting the higher proportion of economic benefits used up in these early years. Where benefits from the asset's use will be used up evenly over the asset's life, then straight line depreciation is the most appropriate method to use. Straight line and reducing balance depreciation are just two of the methods of depreciation that entities can use in allocating the costs of non-current assets to the accounting periods benefiting from their use. You will come across other methods of depreciation at later stages of your studies.

WHY IS THIS RELEVANT TO ME?   Methods of depreciation: straight line and reducing balance

To enable you as a business professional to understand:

- The two main methods of depreciation that are applied in practice
- How to undertake depreciation calculations to assess the impact of depreciation upon profits in the statement of profit or loss and upon the carrying amounts of assets in the statement of financial position
- The criteria to be used in the selection of the most appropriate depreciation method for non-current assets

3

What depreciation methods do entities use in practice? Give me an example 3.5 presents the depreciation accounting policy for Finsbury Food Group plc.

GIVE ME AN EXAMPLE 3.5   Depreciation

What sort of depreciation rates and methods do companies use in practice? The following extract from the accounting policies detailed in the report and accounts of Finsbury Food Group plc for the 52 weeks ended 29 June 2019 gives different depreciation rates for different classes of property, plant and equipment assets. Can you decide whether Finsbury Food Group plc uses the straight line or the reducing balance basis to calculate the annual depreciation charge?

Depreciation

Depreciation is provided to write off the cost, less estimated residual value, of the property, plant and equipment by equal instalments over their estimated useful economic lives to the Consolidated Statement of Comprehensive Income [= Statement of Profit or Loss]. When parts of an item of property, plant and equipment have different useful lives, they are accounted for as separate items (major components) of property, plant and equipment.

The depreciation rates used are as follows:

Freehold buildings 2% – 20%	Plant and equipment 10% – 33%
Leasehold property Up to the remaining life of the lease	Assets under construction Nil
Fixtures and fittings 10% – 33%	Motor vehicles 25% – 33%

Source: Finsbury Food Group plc annual report and accounts 2019 www.finsburyfoods.co.uk

Did you notice the words 'equal instalments' in the extract? Equal instalments means that Finsbury Food Group plc uses the straight line basis of depreciation when allocating the cost of non-current assets to the consolidated statement of profit and loss. Equal instalments = the same charge each year, i.e. the straight line basis.

MULTIPLE CHOICE QUESTIONS   Are you totally confident you can calculate depreciation charges on both the straight line and the reducing balance bases? Go to the **online workbook** and have a go at Multiple choice questions 3.6 to test your ability to make these calculations.

WHAT DEPRECIATION IS AND WHAT DEPRECIATION IS NOT

There are many misconceptions about what depreciation is and what it represents. The following notes and Example 3.6 will help you to distinguish between what depreciation is and what it is not:

- Depreciation is a deduction from the cost of a non-current asset that is charged as an expense in the statement of profit or loss each year.

- This depreciation charge represents an allocation of the cost of each non-current asset to the accounting periods expected to benefit from that asset's use by an organisation.

- Depreciation is another application of the accruals basis of accounting. Just as the accruals basis of accounting matches income and expenditure to the periods in which they occurred, so depreciation matches the cost of non-current assets to the periods benefiting from their use.

- Depreciation is NOT a method of saving up for a replacement asset.

- Depreciation does NOT represent a loss in value of a non-current asset.

- Depreciation does NOT represent an attempt to provide a current value for non-current assets at each statement of financial position date.

EXAMPLE 3.6

Think about these last two points. Suppose you were to buy a car today for £15,000 and expect to use that car for five years before buying a replacement. The resale value of that car the next day would not be £15,000 less one day's depreciation, the original cost less a very small charge for the asset's economic benefits used up by one day's travelling. The showroom that sold you the car the day before would probably offer you half of the original cost of £15,000. The car is now second-hand and so worth much less on the open market than you paid for it the day before even if it only has five miles on the clock and is still in immaculate condition. Thus, the carrying amount of non-current assets on a company's statement of financial position is just the original cost of those assets less the depreciation charged to date. This carrying amount represents the store of potential economic benefits that will be consumed by the entity over the remaining useful lives of those assets rather than presenting the current market value of those non-current assets.

WHY IS THIS RELEVANT TO ME?   What depreciation is and what depreciation is not

To enable you as a business professional to understand:

- The function of depreciation in accounting statements
- What depreciation does and does not represent

GO BACK OVER THIS AGAIN!   How firmly have you grasped the ideas of what depreciation is and what it is not? Go to the **online workbook** and complete Exercises 3.6 to reinforce your understanding.

FURTHER ADJUSTMENTS TO THE STATEMENT OF PROFIT OR LOSS

We have now looked at how the statement of profit or loss reflects the actual income earned and expenditure incurred in an accounting period rather than just the receipts and payments of cash during that accounting period together with the subject of depreciation. There are some further adjustments that are made to figures in the statement of profit or loss and statement of financial position that you should be aware of before we work through a comprehensive example.

Irrecoverable debts

Where entities trade with their customers on credit, providing customers with goods now and allowing them a period of time in which to pay, there will inevitably be times when some customers are unable or refuse to pay for whatever reason. When this situation arises, an administrative expense is recognised for the amount of the trade receivable that cannot be collected and trade receivables reduced by the same amount. Note that these irrecoverable debts are not deducted from sales (revenue) but are treated as an expense of the business.

Irrecoverable debts are recognised as an expense and a deduction from trade receivables when there is objective proof that the customer will not pay. Usually, this objective proof is in the form of a letter from the customer's administrator advising the company that no further cash will be forthcoming to settle the trade receivable owed.

The allowance for receivables

As well as known irrecoverable debts, organisations will also calculate an allowance for receivables, trade receivables that may not be collected rather than irrecoverable debts, receivables that will definitely not pay. An allowance for receivables is an application of the prudence principle, being cautious and avoiding over optimistic expectations, making a provision for a potential loss just in case. An allowance for receivables thus builds up a cushion against future irrecoverable debts, charging an expense now rather than in the future.

Allowances for receivables are calculated as a percentage of trade receivables after deducting known irrecoverable debts. The allowance for receivables is deducted in its entirety from trade receivables in the statement of financial position while only the increase or decrease in the allowance over the year is charged or credited to administrative expenses (not sales) in the statement of profit or loss. Example 3.7 will help you understand how an allowance for receivables is calculated and the accounting entries required.

EXAMPLE 3.7

Gemma runs a recruitment agency. She has year-end trade receivables at 30 September 2021 of £300,000. She knows that one trade receivable owing £6,000 will not pay as that company is now in liquidation. Gemma's experience tells her that 5% of the remaining trade receivables will not pay. Her allowance for receivables at 30 September 2020 was £12,000. What is the total amount that she should recognise in her statement of profit or loss for the year to 30 September 2021 for irrecoverable debts and the allowance for receivables? What figure for net trade receivables will appear in her statement of financial position at that date?

Irrecoverable debts and allowance for receivables charge in the statement of profit or loss

	£	£
Irrecoverable debts charged directly to the statement of profit or loss		6,000
Movement in the allowance for receivables:		
Year-end trade receivables (total)	300,000	
Less: known irrecoverable debts charged directly to the statement of profit or loss	(6,000)	
Net trade receivables on which allowance is to be based	**294,000**	
Allowance for receivables on £294,000 at 5%	14,700	
Less: allowance for receivables at 30 September 2020	(12,000)	
Increase in allowance charged to the statement of profit or loss this year		2,700
Total statement of profit or loss charge for irrecoverable debts and allowance for receivables for the year ended 30 September 2021		**8,700**

Trade receivables in the statement of financial position

	£
Total trade receivables at 30 September 2021	300,000
Less: known irrecoverable debts charged directly to the statement of profit or loss	(6,000)
	294,000
Less: allowance for receivables at the start of the year	(12,000)
Less: increase in the allowance for receivables during the year	(2,700)
Net trade receivables at 30 September 2021	**279,300**

The total allowance for receivables is made up of the allowance at the end of last year and the increase (or decrease) during the current year. The total allowance of £14,700 is deducted from trade receivables at the end of the year. The allowance for receivables charge (or credit) for the year in the statement of profit or loss, however, is just the increase (or decrease) during the year.

MULTIPLE CHOICE QUESTIONS   Are you confident that you can calculate allowances for receivables and the amounts to charge or credit to the statement of profit or loss? Go to the **online workbook** and have a go at Multiple choice questions 3.7 to test your ability to make these calculations.

Discounts allowed (early settlement discounts)

To encourage trade receivables to pay what they owe early, companies will offer a discount. As an example, a trade receivable is allowed 30 days in which to pay for goods supplied. However, the seller might offer a discount of, say, 2% if payment is made within 10 days of receipt of the goods. The seller of the goods does not know whether the trade receivable will take up this discount or not. Therefore, the invoice for the goods supplied will present two prices: the first price is after allowing for the early settlement discount, the second is the price if the early settlement discount is not taken up. Thus, if a customer is sold goods with a selling price of £3,000 but offered a 2.5% discount for payment within 10 days, the seller of the goods records a sale and a trade receivable of £3,000 x (100% − 2.5%) = £2,925. If the customer pays within ten days then the seller's cash increases by £2,925 and trade receivables decrease by £2,925. However, should the customer not take up the early settlement discount but pay £3,000 after 30 days, then cash will increase by £3,000, trade receivables will decrease by £2,925 and the additional £75 will be added to sales revenue. Discounts allowed are thus not treated as an expense but are deducted from the initial selling price and then added to sales if the discounts are not taken up.

Discounts received (quantity discounts)

Suppliers may reward their customers with a retrospective discount for buying a certain quantity of goods over a specified period of time (discounts received). These quantity discounts are a source of income in the statement of profit or loss, a deduction from cost of sales and a deduction from trade payables. All other discounts received from suppliers for early settlement or for bulk discounts allowed on each purchase will be included in the price of each invoice and so will be charged as a net expense in the statement of profit or loss with the same amount added to trade receivables as a current liability.

Sales returns

Sometimes, goods are just not suitable, are not of the requisite quality or they are faulty. In this case, customers will return these goods to the supplier (sales returns). These returns are treated as a deduction from sales, as the return of goods amounts to the cancellation of a sale, and a deduction from trade receivables.

Purchase returns

Similarly, when entities return goods to their suppliers (purchase returns), suppliers will reduce the amount that is owed to them by the issue of a credit note. As this is the cancellation of a purchase, the purchases part of cost of goods sold and trade payables are reduced.

Closing inventory

At the end of the financial year, entities count up the goods in stock and value them in accordance with the requirements of IAS 2 Inventory. This accounting standard requires inventory to be valued at the lower of cost and net realisable value. What do these terms mean?

Cost means the acquisition cost of the inventory, how much it cost the business to acquire or produce the items in stock at the end of the year. For retailers, cost is the purchase price of each product plus, for example, delivery costs and less any bulk or quantity discounts received. In manufacturing organisations, cost will be made up of the cost of inputs to a product or process such as materials, labour and other associated costs.

Inventory is valued at net realisable value when goods can only be sold at a price that is lower than the product's original purchase or production cost. In rapidly changing markets, today's must-have product will be superseded very quickly by new, more advanced products and any left-over goods will have to be discounted heavily in order to sell them. When goods can be sold for more than their purchase or production price, closing inventory is not valued at selling price as such a valuation would anticipate profit. This would contravene the realisation principle of accounting which says that profits should not be anticipated until they have been earned through a sale. However, valuing goods at selling price when this is lower than purchase price recognises the losses that will be made on the sale of these goods immediately.

The value of year-end inventory is carried forward to the next accounting period by deducting the cost of this inventory in the statement of profit or loss and recognising an asset in the statement of financial position. This is a further application of the accruals basis of accounting, carrying forward the cost of unsold goods to a future accounting period to match that cost against sales of those goods when these arise. Three methods of calculating the cost of closing inventory are presented in the Appendix to this chapter.

WHY IS THIS RELEVANT TO ME?   Further adjustments to the statement of profit or loss

To provide you as a business professional with:

- Knowledge of additional transactions that affect both income and expenditure and the statement of financial position
- Details of how these adjustments are treated in practice
- An ability to apply these adjustments in practical situations

---

We will look at how these adjustments are applied in practice in our comprehensive example and in Numerical exercises 3.2 in the **online workbook**.

PREPARING THE STATEMENT OF PROFIT OR LOSS

We have now considered all the building blocks for the statement of profit or loss. It is time to look at a comprehensive example (Example 3.8) to see how the statement of profit or loss is put together from the accounting records and how it relates to the statement of financial position. You will need to work through this comprehensive example several times to understand fully how all the figures are derived, but this is quite normal. Even those at the top of the accountancy profession today would have struggled with this type of problem when they first started out on their accounting studies. It is just a case of practice and familiarising yourself with the techniques involved in putting a set of accounts together. We shall return to this comprehensive example in demonstrating double-entry bookkeeping in Chapter 4 (Comprehensive example: double entry and the trial balance) so time spent on this example now will make you very familiar with the accounting entries and help you in understanding how double-entry bookkeeping works.

The following list of points is a quick summary of how to prepare a statement of profit or loss and the statement of financial position, starting with a simple list of receipts and payments presented by a business:

- First, summarise the receipts into and payments out of the entity's bank account: this will give you the basic sales receipts and expenses as well as any non-current assets that the entity may have purchased.

- Once you have completed the bank account you will have a difference between the receipts and payments in the period: if receipts are greater than payments, you have a positive cash balance in the bank account, a current asset. If the payments are greater than the receipts, you have a negative balance in the bank account, an overdraft, and this will be recorded as a current liability.

3

- Using the cash received and cash paid you should then adjust income and expenditure for the accruals basis of accounting. Add to sales any income earned in the accounting period for which cash has not yet been received and recognise a trade receivable for the outstanding balance due. For expenses, determine what the expense should be based on the time period involved and then add additional expenditure where a particular cost is too low (and add to current liabilities as an accrual, an obligation incurred but not yet paid for) and deduct expenditure where a particular cost is too high (and add to current assets as a prepayment of future expenditure that relates to a later accounting period).

- Remember to depreciate any non-current assets at the rates given, provide for any irrecoverable debts that might have been incurred, make an adjustment for the increase or decrease in the allowance for receivables, adjust sales and purchases for returns and deduct quantity discounts received from purchases.

EXAMPLE 3.8

Your friend Julia started a business on 1 April 2021 buying and selling sports equipment from a shop on the high street. It is now 30 June 2021 and Julia is curious to know how well or badly she is doing in her first three months of trading. She has no idea about accounts and presents you with the list of balances in Illustration 3.3 of the amounts received and paid out of her bank account.

Illustration 3.3 Julia's bank account receipts and payments summary

Date		Receipts £	Payments £
1 April 2021	Cash introduced by Julia	30,000	
1 April 2021	Three months' rent paid on shop to 30 June 2021		5,000
1 April 2021	Cash register paid for		1,000
1 April 2021	Shelving and shop fittings paid for		12,000
30 April 2021	Receipts from sales in April 2021	20,000	
5 May 2021	Sports equipment supplied in April paid for		15,000
12 May 2021	Rates for period 1 April 2021 to 30 September 2021 paid		800
19 May 2021	Cash withdrawn for Julia's own expenses		2,000
30 May 2021	Receipts from sales in May 2021	25,000	
5 June 2021	Sports equipment supplied in May paid for		20,000
10 June 2021	Shop water rates for the year 1 April 2021 to 31 March 2022 paid		400
30 June 2021	Receipts from sales in June 2021	30,000	
30 June 2021	Balance in bank at 30 June 2021		48,800
		105,000	105,000

Julia is very pleased with her first three months' trading and regards the additional £18,800 cash in the bank as her profit for the three months. Is she right? Has she really made £18,800 profit in the three months since she started trading? Her argument is that she started with £30,000 and now has £48,800 so she must have made a profit of £18,800, the difference between her opening and closing cash figures. Let us have a look and see how her business has really performed in its first three months of operations.

Our first job is to split the receipts and payments down into trading receipts and payments and statement of financial position (capital) receipts and payments. Have a go at this on your own before you look at the answer presented in Illustrations 3.4 and 3.5. You will need to add up the receipts for sales and the payments for purchases and other expenses: make a list of these individual totals.

You should now have the totals shown in Illustrations 3.4 and 3.5.

Illustration 3.4 Julia's receipts and payments account for the three months ended 30 June 2021

	£	£
Sales £20,000 (April) + £25,000 (May) + £30,000 (June)		75,000
Purchases £15,000 (May) + £20,000 (June)		35,000
Gross surplus (sales – purchases)		**40,000**
Expenses		
Rent £5,000 (April)	5,000	
Rates £800 (May)	800	
Water rates £400 (June)	400	
Total expenses		6,200
Net surplus for the three months		**33,800**

Illustration 3.5 Julia's statement of financial position based on her receipts and payments for her first three months of trading at 30 June 2021

	£
Non-current assets	
Cash register	1,000
Shelves and shop fittings	12,000
	13,000
Bank balance at 30 June 2021	48,800
Total assets	**61,800**
Equity	
Capital introduced by Julia	30,000
Drawings (cash withdrawn from the business for personal expenses)	(2,000)
Surplus for the three months	33,800
	61,800

All we have done in Illustrations 3.4 and 3.5 is to restate the figures from Julia's bank account, splitting them into statement of profit or loss and statement of financial position items on a purely receipts and payments basis. Sales and expenses have been entered into the statement of profit or loss, while non-current assets (the cash register and the shelving and shop fittings: those assets that are used long term in the business) have been entered into the statement of financial position. The statement of financial position also shows the cash in the bank, the asset remaining at the end of the financial period, along with the capital introduced by Julia less her drawings in the three-month period plus the surplus the business has made during that period.

SHOW ME HOW TO DO IT   Are you completely happy with the way in which Julia's bank receipts and payments were allocated to the receipts and payments account and the related statement of financial position? View Video presentation 3.1 in the **online workbook** to see a practical demonstration of how these allocations were made.

However, there is a problem with receipts and payments accounts. As we have seen in the earlier part of this chapter, what we need to do now is adjust these receipts and payments for the accruals basis of accounting, matching all the income and expenses to the three months in which they were earned and incurred rather than just allocating them to the three-month period on the basis of when cash was received or paid. By doing this we can then determine the actual sales made during the period and what it actually cost Julia to make those sales. This will give her a much clearer idea of the profits she has actually earned in her first three months of trading.

You mention this problem to Julia, who provides you with the following additional information:

- She counted up and valued the inventory at the close of business on 30 June 2021: the cost of this inventory at that date was £10,000.

- At 30 June 2021, Julia owed £25,000 for sports equipment she had purchased from her suppliers on credit in June. She paid this £25,000 on 5 July 2021.

- While her main business is selling sports equipment for cash, Julia has also made sales to two local tennis clubs in June on credit. At 30 June 2021, the two clubs owed £2,500, although one club disputes £50 of the amount outstanding, saying that the goods were never delivered. Julia has no proof that these goods were ever received by the club and has reluctantly agreed that she will never receive this £50.

- During the month of June, Julia employed a part-time sales assistant who was owed £300 in wages at the end of June 2021. These wages were paid on 8 July 2021.

- On 5 July 2021, Julia received a telephone bill for £250 covering the three months 1 April 2021 to 30 June 2021 together with an electricity bill for £200 covering the same period.

- Julia expects the cash register and shelving and shop fittings to last for five years before they need replacement. The level of usage of these assets will be the same in each of the next five years. She also expects that the assets will have no residual value at the end of their useful lives and that they will just be scrapped rather than being sold on.

- The cash register contained £500 in cash at 30 June 2021 representing sales receipts that had not yet been banked.

- On 29 June 2021, one of the tennis clubs she trades with on credit returned goods with a sales value of £400. These goods were faulty. Julia returned these goods to her supplier: the goods had originally cost Julia £250.

Taking into account the additional information, together with the transactions through the bank account and our receipts and payments account, Julia's statement of profit or loss and statement of financial position are shown in Illustrations 3.6 and 3.7.

Illustration 3.6 Julia's statement of profit or loss for the three months ended 30 June 2021

	£	£	Note
Sales £75,000 (cash received) + £2,500 (sales invoiced but cash not yet received) − £400 (goods returned: no sale or trade receivable recognised) + £500 (cash in till representing unrecorded sales)		77,600	1
Purchases £35,000 (cash paid) + £25,000 (goods received not yet paid for) − £250 (faulty goods returned to supplier: no cost or liability recognised)	59,750		2
Less: closing inventory (inventory of goods not yet sold at 30 June 2021)	(10,000)		3
Cost of sales (purchases − closing inventory)		49,750	4
Gross profit (sales − cost of sales)		**27,850**	5
Expenses			
Rent	5,000		6
Rates £800 − (£800 × 3/6) (payment is for a 6-month period, therefore three months out of six are prepaid)	400		7
Water rates £400 − (£400 × 9/12) (payment is for a 12-month period, so 9 months out of 12 are prepaid)	100		8
Irrecoverable debt £50 (sale made but no cash will be received)	50		9
Wages £300 (work performed for wages in June but paid in July)	300		10
Telephone £250 (service received but paid in July)	250		11
Electricity £200 (electricity received but paid in July)	200		12
Cash register depreciation (£1,000/5 years × 3/12 months)	50		13
Shelving and fittings depreciation (£12,000/5 years × 3/12 months)	600		14
Total expenses		6,950	15
Net profit for the three months		**20,900**	16

Illustration 3.7 Julia's statement of financial position at 30 June 2021

	£	Notes
Non-current assets		
Cash register £1,000 – (£1,000/5 years × 3/12 months)	950	13
Shelving and shop fittings £12,000 – (£12,000/5 years × 3/12 months)	11,400	14
	12,350	
Current assets		
Inventory (inventory of goods not yet sold at 30 June 2021)	10,000	3
Trade receivables £2,500 (sales invoiced but cash not yet received) – £50 (sale made but no cash will be received) – £400 (goods returned: no sale or trade receivable recognised)	2,050	1, 9
Rates prepayment £800 × 3/6 (6-month period, therefore 3/6 prepaid)	400	7
Water rates prepayment £400 × 9/12 (12-month period, 9 months prepaid)	300	8
Bank balance at 30 June 2021	48,800	
Cash in cash register at 30 June 2021 (£500 cash in till representing unrecorded sales, increase sales and increase cash)	500	1
	62,050	
Total assets (£12,350 non-current assets + £62,050 current assets)	74,400	

	£	Notes
Current liabilities		
Trade payables £25,000 (goods received not yet paid for) – £250 (goods returned to supplier: no cost or liability recognised)	24,750	2
Wages accrual	300	10
Telephone accrual	250	11
Electricity accrual	200	12
Total liabilities	25,500	
Net assets (total assets (£74,400) – total liabilities (£25,500))	48,900	
Equity (capital account)		
Capital introduced by Julia	30,000	
Drawings (cash paid from the business for personal expenses)	(2,000)	
Net profit for the three months	20,900	
Capital account at 30 June 2021	48,900	

Notes to Julia's statement of profit or loss and statement of financial position:

1. This figure consists of the sales represented by cash banked (£75,000) + the additional sales made on credit of £2,500 + the unrecorded cash of £500 representing sales made on 30 June 2021. The £2,500 credit sales are recognised now as they are sales that occurred in

the three-month period to 30 June 2021 and so are matched to this accounting period even though the cash from these sales will not be received until after the end of the three-month period. Similarly, the £400 goods returned are recognised as a deduction from the sales total as this sale was cancelled during the three-month period. Money owed by trade receivables is £2,100 (£2,500 credit sales made – £400 selling price of goods returned) while cash rises by £500 as these sales had already been realised in cash. Note that the irrecoverable debt of £50 is not deducted from sales but is disclosed as a separate expense in the statement of profit or loss.

2. Goods purchased on credit in the period and not paid for are likewise matched to the period in which the transaction occurred. Failure to recognise this expense in the period would incorrectly increase the profit for the period and give a completely false picture of how well the business is performing. The receipts and payments account initially showed purchases of £35,000. Once we have added in the additional purchases in the period and deducted the £250 of faulty goods returned to the supplier, the purchases figure has risen to £59,750, a significant increase on the original figure, but one that is required by the accruals basis of accounting. Just as the purchases expense has risen by £24,750 (£25,000 – £250), trade payables have risen by the same amount to reflect the amount owed by the business at 30 June 2021.

3. Closing inventory of goods is treated as a deduction in the statement of profit or loss as the cost of these unsold goods is carried forward to match against future sales of these goods. While cost of sales is thus reduced by £10,000, the statement of financial position reflects the same amount as an asset, a present economic resource the business owns which it can sell in future periods to generate economic benefits for the organisation.

4. Cost of sales, as we noted earlier in the chapter, is calculated as opening inventory (= last year's closing inventory) + purchases during the period – closing inventory. In Julia's case, there is no opening inventory as this is her first trading period, so opening inventory is £Nil.

5. Gross profit is calculated as: sales – cost of sales, income earned less the costs incurred in generating that income. Gross profit is an important figure in assessing the performance of an entity as we shall see in Chapter 8.

6. Rent is one figure that does not need adjusting. As stated in the bank receipts and payments, the rent paid is for the months of April, May and June 2021 and is paid right up to 30 June, so there is no prepayment (money paid in advance for services still to be received) or accrual (unpaid amount for services already received) of rent at the end of the three-month accounting period.

7. The rates are for the half year from 1 April 2021 to 30 September 2021. The whole amount due for the six months has been paid during the period. At 30 June 2021, the payment for July, August and September 2021 has been made in advance so half the £800 is a prepayment at 30 June 2021. The true cost of rates for the three months to 30 June 2021 is 3/6 of £800, so that only £400 is matched as an expense for the quarter.

8. Similarly, the water rates are paid for the whole year from 1 April 2021 to 31 March 2022, so that only three of the twelve months represented by this payment have been used up by 30 June 2021 (April, May and June 2021) leaving the nine months 1 July 2021 to 31 March 2022 prepaid. Again, the water rates expense for the period is only 3/12 of the total paid and this is the expense to match to the three-month period to the end of June 2021. The remainder of this expense is carried forward at the end of the three-month period to match against water usage in future accounting periods.

9. The irrecoverable debt is recognised as an expense and not as a deduction from sales. As well as being charged as an expense in the period to which it relates, it is also deducted from trade receivables. As this £50 will not be received, it no longer represents a present economic resource with the potential to generate economic benefits so it is deducted from trade receivables in the statement of financial position and charged as an expense in the statement of profit or loss.

10. The £300 wages cost has been incurred by 30 June 2021 and, while this amount is not paid until after the end of the three-month period, it is matched with the income that those wages helped to generate during June 2021. Expenses increase by £300 and, as this amount has not been paid by the period end, it is recognised as a liability.

11. Similarly, the telephone service has been received over the three-month accounting period so there is a liability at the end of the period together with an expense of £300 matched to the period in which it was incurred.

12. Again, the electricity has been consumed during the three-month period to 30 June 2021, so that a liability exists at the period end for this amount and this, too, is recognised as an expense matched to the accounting period in which it was incurred.

13. As we saw earlier in this chapter, depreciation is charged on non-current assets to reflect the economic benefits of those assets consumed during each accounting period. Julia expects the same level of usage each year from the cash register and the shelving and shop fittings, so this implies the straight line basis of depreciation, an equal amount charged to the periods benefiting from their use. As there is no residual value, the total cost is used to calculate the depreciation charge for the three-month period. In the case of the cash register, £1,000 divided by five years gives an annual depreciation charge of £200. However, as the accounting period is less than a year, the depreciation charge is spread out over the relevant months to give an expense of £200 × 3/12 = £50.

14. In the same way, the straight line basis of depreciation gives an annual charge of £12,000/5 = £2,400 on the shelving and shop fittings. As the accounting period is only three months long, only 3/12 of this annual depreciation is matched to the current accounting period, so that £2,400 × 3/12 = £600 charged to reflect the economic benefit of these assets used up in the accounting period.

15. Total expenses are the sum of all the expenses from rent down to shelving and fittings depreciation.

16. Net profit for the period is given by the gross profit – total expenses.

Drawings and the business entity convention

Julia's drawings for her personal expenditure have been deducted from equity. Why are these costs not treated as part of the business's expenditure? Firstly, the business's affairs and the owner's affairs must be kept entirely separate as the business and the owner are treated as two separate entities. Where the owner takes money out of the business for non-business personal expenditure, any such personal expenditure is deducted from the owner's interest in the business as it is not expenditure incurred on behalf of the business. Secondly, in accordance with the IASB *Conceptual Framework*, while the payment of cash to Julia represents a decrease in assets and a decrease in equity, this is not an expense but a decrease in equity resulting from a distribution to holders of equity claims (this chapter, Expenses). The owner's interest in the business is represented by the amounts in the capital account, as we saw in Chapter 2 (The components of equity). Any amounts for personal expenditure withdrawn from the business's bank account are treated as repayments of the capital owed to the owner and are thus not charged as an expense of the business.

SHOW ME HOW TO DO IT   Are you certain you understand how Julia's statement of profit or loss and statement of financial position were put together? View Video presentation 3.2 in the **online workbook** to see a practical demonstration of how these two statements were drawn up.

WHY IS THIS RELEVANT TO ME?   Comprehensive example: statement of profit or loss and statement of financial position

To enable you as a business professional to appreciate:

• How the statement of profit or loss and statement of financial position are drawn up from the receipts and payments for an accounting period together with the application of the accruals basis of accounting

• How you can approach statement of profit or loss and statement of financial position preparation problems

• The principles of accounts preparation before we consider double-entry bookkeeping in Chapter 4

NUMERICAL EXERCISES   Are you totally confident that you could prepare statements of profit or loss and statements of financial position from a given set of information? Go to the **online workbook** and complete Numerical exercises 3.2 to test out your ability to prepare these two statements.

APPENDIX: METHODS OF CALCULATING THE COST OF CLOSING INVENTORY

As we have seen (this chapter, Closing inventory), the inventory of goods at each accounting period end is valued at cost to the business. However, there are various ways in which the cost of closing inventory can be determined. Each of these different methods of determining cost will give a different valuation for closing inventory, for cost of sales and for gross profit. Inventory cost can be determined on the following three bases:

1. First in, first out (FIFO): this method of costing inventory assumes that the goods bought first are the first to be sold. As the goods acquired first are sold first, then the closing inventory at the end of an accounting period must consist of the goods that were acquired most recently. Goods acquired most recently are thus valued at the most recent invoice price.

2. Last in, first out (LIFO): this method of costing inventory assumes that the goods bought first are the last to be sold, with goods acquired more recently the first to be sold. As the goods acquired most recently are sold first, then the closing inventory at the end of an accounting period must consist of the goods that were acquired first. Goods acquired at this earliest date are valued at the earliest invoice price.

3. Weighted average cost (AVCO): this method pools all the costs of acquiring goods over an accounting period and divides this total cost by the total number of units acquired to give the average cost of each item during that accounting period. Closing inventory is valued by multiplying the number of items in stock by the weighted average cost of acquiring that inventory.

Let's illustrate these different methods of valuing inventory through Example 3.9.

EXAMPLE 3.9

During the month of June, Nissota Car Spares acquired engine part C3576 in the following quantities and at the following purchase prices:

> 300 at £210 each
>
> 500 at £240 each
>
> 700 at £270 each

There were no opening inventories of engine part C3576 at 1 June. During the month of June, the company sold 1,250 C3576 engine parts for £425 each. How would the closing inventory of 250 C3576 engine parts be valued using each of the three different inventory valuation methods?

First in, first out

Sales of 1,250 units are made up of the 300 units acquired at £210 each, the 500 units acquired at £240 each and 450 of the 700 units acquired at £270 each. Closing inventory thus consists of 250 units of inventory valued at the latest invoice price of £270, giving an inventory cost of £67,500. The goods sold are those acquired first and the engine parts in closing inventory are those that were acquired most recently valued at the most recent invoice price.

Last in, first out

Sales of 1,250 units are made up of the 700 units acquired at £270 each, the 500 units acquired at £240 each and 50 of the 300 units acquired at £210 each. There are thus 250 units of inventory valued at the earliest invoice price of £210, giving an inventory cost of £52,500. The goods sold are those acquired most recently and the engine parts in closing inventory are those that were acquired at the earliest point in the accounting period valued at the earliest invoice price.

Weighted average cost

The total cost of engine parts acquired during June was £372,000 ((300 × £210) + (500 × £240) + (700 × £270) = £372,000). 1,500 (300 + 500 + 700 = 1,500) engine parts were acquired for this £372,000. The average cost per engine part is thus £372,000 ÷ 1,500 = £248. As there are 250 C3576 engine parts in stock at 30 June, the weighted average cost of this closing inventory is 250 units x £248 = £62,000.

What effect does each different basis for determining the cost of closing inventory have upon the profit reported by the business? Each engine part sold for £425 during June, giving a total sales figure for the month of £425 × 1,250 = £531,250. We can draw up three simplified statements of profit or loss as shown in Illustration 3.8 to enable us to see the effect of costing inventory using the three different bases.

Illustration 3.8 The effect of different inventory valuation methods on gross profit

	First in, first out		Last in, first out		Weighted average cost	
	£	£	£	£	£	£
Sales		531,250		531,250		531,250
Purchases	372,000		372,000		372,000	
Closing inventory	(67,500)		(52,500)		(62,000)	
Cost of sales		304,500		319,500		310,000
Gross profit		226,750		211,750		221,250

What conclusions can we draw from these different results? We can make the following observations:

- The first in, first out method of valuing inventory gives the highest gross profit as well as the highest inventory valuation on the statement of financial position whereas the last in, first out method gives the lowest gross profit and closing inventory figures.

- However, this is only true when the purchase price of goods is rising: when purchase prices are falling, then last in, first out will give the highest valuation for both gross profit and inventory valuation on the statement of financial position.

- The first in, first out method provides the most up-to-date figure for inventory in the statement of financial position. We noted in Chapter 2 (A mixture of original cost and fair value: problems) that current assets are constantly being replaced by new assets with more recent, more up-to-date values to enable users of financial statements to assess the current fair value of current assets and liabilities. In this respect, the first in, first out inventory valuation method provides users of financial statements with more up-to-date information on the current value of inventories and their replacement cost to the business. Using a last in, first out inventory valuation basis will give users less relevant and less timely financial information as the last in, first out valuation basis presents out-of-date values for inventory.

- Higher profits do mean higher taxes on those profits. However, accounting policies must be applied consistently across different accounting periods. Therefore, a higher closing

3

inventory valuation using the first in, first out valuation basis will mean a higher cost at the start of the next accounting period when this inventory is sold so the profits and the taxes on those profits will even out over time.

It is worth noting, too, that IAS 2 Inventory only permits the valuation of closing inventory using either the first in, first out or weighted average cost bases: the last in, first out valuation is not permitted under the International Financial Reporting Framework.

GO BACK OVER THIS AGAIN!   Are you quite sure that you can distinguish between the three different inventory valuation methods? Go to the **online workbook** and complete Exercises 3.7 to test your ability to make these distinctions.

MULTIPLE CHOICE QUESTIONS   Are you confident that you could calculate the cost of inventory using the three valuation bases? Go to the **online workbook** and have a go at Multiple choice questions 3.8 to test your ability to make these calculations.

CHAPTER SUMMARY

You should now have learnt that:

- Statements of profit or loss and statements of financial position are drawn up on the accruals basis of accounting
- Statement of profit or loss income and expenditure represent all income earned and all expenditure incurred during an accounting period
- Statement of profit or loss income and expenditure do not just represent cash received and cash paid during an accounting period
- Accruals are expenses incurred in an accounting period but not yet paid
- Accruals give rise to additional expenditure in the statement of profit or loss and a current liability in the statement of financial position
- Prepayments are expenses paid in advance of the accounting period to which they relate
- Prepayments reduce current period expenditure and represent a current asset on the statement of financial position
- Depreciation is the allocation of the cost of non-current assets to the accounting periods benefiting from their use
- Depreciation does not represent a loss in value of non-current assets
- Depreciation is not a way of presenting non-current assets at market values

QUICK REVISION   Test your knowledge by attempting the activities in the **online workbook**, including flashcards on the key concepts, numerical exercises and Multiple choice questions. You can also try the further self-test questions which are available at www.oup.com/he/scott-i2a2e

END-OF-CHAPTER QUESTIONS

Attempt the questions in the following sections and then look at the solutions which can be found in the **online workbook** to see whether there are areas that you need to revisit.

❯ RECALL AND REVIEW

❯ Question 3.1

Forbes is a sole trader. Most of the business's transactions are made on credit. Forbes believes he does not need to keep accounting records because it only complicates the job. All he needs to do is to keep a record of his business receipts and payments and, in order to assess the performance of the company in any given period, he just needs to calculate the difference between the receipts and payments to determine his profit for that period.

Required

(a) Advise Forbes why he needs to keep accounting records.

(b) Explain what is meant by the accruals basis of accounting and why it is important.

❯ Question 3.2

In 2020, Johnson Limited signed a contract with a local newspaper to place an advertisement for the business and its products on the front page. The amount paid to the newspaper during 2021 was £3,200, of which £1,400 was for advertisements to be placed in the newspaper in 2022. At 1 January 2021, there was a prepaid advertising balance of £800 (the amount that Johnson Limited paid in 2020 for advertisements to be published in 2021).

Required

(a) What is the figure for advertising expenditure for 2021 on the statement of profit or loss of Johnson Limited?

(b) What is the figure for advertising to be reported on the statement of financial position of Johnson Limited at 31 December 2021?

❯❯ DEVELOP YOUR UNDERSTANDING

❯❯ Question 3.3

Abi runs a market stall selling fashion clothing for cash. Her business bank account balance at 1 September 2020, the start of her most recent trading year, was £7,342. She also had inventory of £2,382 and trade payables of £3,445 on that date. She rents her market stall at an annual cost of £6,000 payable quarterly in advance from 1 September each trading year. Abi paid all the rent that was due during the year to 31 August 2021. Her cash receipts from sales to customers for the year to 31 August 2021 totalled up to £157,689, but she also gave refunds to customers for returned goods of £3,789. She paid the outstanding trade payables at 1 September 2020 on 5 September 2020. Her purchases for the year totalled up to £120,465, of which she paid £116,328 during the year to 31 August 2021. At 31 August 2021 Abi valued her inventory of clothing at a cost of £4,638. From 1 September 2020 she employed a part-time assistant, Kate, agreeing to pay her

£100 a week for the year. At the end of August 2021, while Abi had paid Kate all the amounts due for the first 50 weeks of the year, she still owed her £200 for the last two weeks of August 2021. To improve the presentation of her fashion clothing ranges, Abi paid £600 to buy some display stands on 1 September 2020. Abi reckons that these display stands will last her for three years and that they will have a scrap value of £30. On 31 August 2021, Abi had £650 in cash representing sales that had not yet been banked. Abi withdrew £1,500 a month for her own personal expenses from the business bank account.

Required

1. Calculate Abi's opening capital account (equity) balance (remember the accounting equation) at 1 September 2020.

2. Draw up Abi's bank account for the year to 31 August 2021.

3. Prepare Abi's statement of profit or loss by nature for the year ended 31 August 2021 together with a statement of financial position at that date.

›› Question 3.4

Alison runs an online gift shop, trading for cash with individual customers and offering trading on credit terms to businesses. She presents you with the following figures from her accounting records for the year ended 31 December 2021:

	£
Purchases of goods for resale	225,368
Accumulated depreciation on racks, shelving and office furniture at 31 December 2021	14,650
Trade receivables	27,400
Administration expenses	15,265
Racks, shelving and office furniture at cost	33,600
Telephone expenses	5,622
Capital account at 1 January 2021	52,710
Sales	437,990
Accumulated depreciation on computers at 31 December 2021	13,850
Inventory at 1 January 2021	27,647
Purchase returns (already deducted from trade payables)	5,724
Bank balance (asset)	52,315
Trade payables	24,962
Rent on warehouse and office unit	15,000
Business rates	9,325
Computer equipment at cost	20,775
Quantity discounts received (already deducted from trade payables)	2,324
Delivery costs	36,970
Electricity and gas	8,736
Insurance	3,250
Drawings	40,000
Depreciation charge for the year on non-current assets	13,255
Sales returns (already deducted from trade receivables)	17,682

Alison provides you with the following additional information:

- She valued the inventory at 31 December 2021 at a cost of £22,600.
- All depreciation charges on non-current assets for the year to 31 December 2021 are included in the depreciation figures above.
- Rent on the trading unit prepaid at 31 December 2021 amounted to £3,000.
- Rates prepaid at 31 December 2021 amounted to £1,865.
- Accountancy costs of £1,250 had not been paid by the year end and are not included in the figures above.
- There were no other prepaid or accrued expenses at the year end.
- Alison would like to include an allowance for receivables of 10% of year-end trade receivables. There was no allowance for receivables at 31 December 2020.

Required

Using the list of figures and the additional information provided prepare Alison's statement of profit or loss by nature for the year ended 31 December 2021 together with a statement of financial position at that date.

>> **Question 3.5**

The following figures have been extracted from the accounting records of Volumes Limited, a book binder, at 30 September 2021:

	Assets and expenses £000	Income, liabilities and equity £000
Plant and machinery: cost	2,000	
Plant and machinery: accumulated depreciation at 30 September 2021		800
Sales		4,750
Trade receivables	430	
Administration expenses	300	
Selling and distribution costs	200	
Production costs	2,600	
Finance expense	100	
Cash at bank	175	
Loan (due 30 September 2030)		500
Trade payables		300
Finance income		25
Called up share capital		250
Share premium		125
Retained earnings at 30 September 2020		155
Inventory at 1 October 2020	100	
Production wages	1,000	
	6,905	**6,905**

3

Additional information

- Inventory at 30 September 2021 was valued at a cost of £150,000.
- Taxation on the profit for the year has been estimated to be £250,000.
- All depreciation charges for the year to 30 September 2021 have been calculated in the balances above.

Required

Using the list of balances and the additional information prepare the statement of profit or loss and statement of financial position for Volumes Limited in a form suitable for publication.

You will need to produce a working to calculate cost of sales.

You may find that consulting Illustrations 2.1 and 3.1 will assist you in the preparation of the statement of profit or loss and statement of financial position.

》 Question 3.6

The following balances have been extracted from the books of Guimaraes Limited and Porto Limited for the financial year ended 31 December 2021.

	Guimaraes Limited £000	Porto Limited £000
Insurance	500	–
Selling and administration expenses	1,600	12,800
Sales	14,500	99,400
Tax	840	9,000
Closing inventory	5,000	31,000
Depreciation of non-current assets	1,000	6,500
Bank interest paid	400	3,600
Opening inventory	4,000	21,000
Wages and salaries	1,200	7,300
Purchases	8,000	54,200
Other income	–	5,000

Required

Using the statement of profit or loss by nature format presented in this chapter, draw up the statements of profit or loss for the two companies for the year ended 31 December 2021 showing the different categories of profit.

》 Question 3.7

David plc purchased a piece of production machinery for £160,000. The expected useful life of this asset is five years. At the end of its useful life it is estimated that the asset will be sold for £10,000. Darius, the company's accountant, needs to decide which basis of depreciation is more appropriate for this asset.

(a) Calculate the annual depreciation charge for the asset using the straight line basis.

(b) Calculate the annual depreciation charge for the asset using the reducing balance basis at a rate of 40%.

(c) Advise Darius on how to choose the most appropriate basis of depreciation for this asset.

>>> TAKE IT FURTHER

>>> Question 3.8

The following figures have been extracted from the accounting records of Aaron Limited at 31 December 2021.

	£000
Bank (asset)	170
Trade receivables	250
Inventory at 1 January 2021	400
Purchases	1,300
Sales	2,500
Trade payables	175
Equipment at cost	2,400
Equipment accumulated depreciation at 1 January 2021	200
Equity at 1 January 2021	2,600
Selling and administrative expenses	330
Insurance	500
Power and heating	125

Additional information

- Closing inventory at 31 December 2021 is valued at £375,000.
- Equipment is depreciated on the straight line basis. The useful life of equipment is estimated to be 10 years with a residual value of £400,000 at the end of its useful life.
- £50,000 of the trade receivables is due from a customer who became insolvent in December 2021. Aaron Limited does not expect to receive any cash from this trade receivable.
- Half of the insurance was prepaid at 31 December 2021.
- At 31 December 2021, there is an unpaid bill of £45,000 for power and heating.

Required

Prepare the statement of profit or loss and statement of financial position for Aaron Limited for the year ended 31 December 2021.

>>> Question 3.9

The following figures have been extracted from the accounting records of Textiles Limited, a cloth manufacturer and wholesaler, at 30 June 2021:

	Assets and expenses £000	Income, liabilities and equity £000
Plant and machinery: cost	3,000	
Plant and machinery: accumulated depreciation at 30 June 2020		1,200
Motor vehicles: cost	800	
Motor vehicles: accumulated depreciation at 30 June 2020		400
Trade receivables	1,050	
Cost of sales	4,550	
Sales returns (already deducted from trade receivables)	150	
Issued share capital		200
Trade payables		300
Finance expense	110	
Purchase returns (already deducted from trade payables)		80
Administration expenses	700	
Bank overdraft		200
Selling and distribution costs	1,000	
Sales		7,550
Quantity discounts received (already deducted from trade payables)		125
Loan (due for repayment on 30 June 2030)		1,000
Retained earnings at 30 June 2020		545
Inventory at 30 June 2021	300	
Allowance for receivables at 30 June 2020		60
	11,660	**11,660**

Additional information

- Audit and accountancy fees (to be charged to administration expenses) of £10,000 have not been taken into account at 30 June 2021.

- Administration expenses include payments for insurance premiums of £30,000 for the 12 months to 31 December 2021.

- Since the year end, a customer of Textiles Limited has gone into liquidation owing £50,000. Textiles Limited does not expect to receive any cash from this trade receivable.

- The allowance for receivables is to be adjusted to 4% of trade receivables after deducting known irrecoverable debts. All irrecoverable debts and the change in the allowance for receivables are to be allocated to administration expenses.

- Depreciation for the year to 30 June 2021 still has to be calculated. Plant and machinery is to be depreciated at 20% straight line and motor vehicles are to be depreciated at 25% reducing balance. Plant and machinery depreciation should be charged to cost of sales and motor vehicle depreciation should be charged to distribution and selling expenses.

- Taxation on the profit for the year is to be calculated as 25% of the profit before tax.

Required

Prepare the statement of profit or loss and statement of financial position in a form suitable for publication in accordance with International Financial Reporting Standards.

⋙ Question 3.10

Laura was made redundant on 1 July 2020 and received £50,000 in redundancy pay. With this money, she opened a business bank account and set up a small building company undertaking household and small industrial construction work. She started trading on 1 September 2020 and she has now reached her year end of 31 August 2021. She has produced a summary of payments and receipts into her business bank account along with additional information that she thinks will be useful in preparing her statement of profit or loss and statement of financial position for her first year of trading. The details she has presented you with are as follows:

1. Laura's customers usually pay cash at the end of each job. Cash received and banked from these sales totals up to £112,000. However, her small industrial clients keep her waiting for payment. Her invoices to her small industrial customers add up to a total of £48,000 for work done during the year, but she had only collected £36,000 of this amount by 31 August 2021.

2. Laura buys her construction materials on credit from a local wholesaler. Her total spending on materials this year has been £45,000 of which she had paid £38,000 by 31 August 2021. Her annual trading summary from the wholesaler received on 5 September 2021 tells her that she has qualified for a quantity discount of £1,000 on all her purchases up to 31 August 2021. She will deduct this amount from her next payment to her supplier in September 2021.

3. Since 31 August 2021, a small industrial customer has gone into liquidation, owing Laura £2,500. The liquidator has told Laura that no payment towards this trade receivable will be made. The liquidation of her customer has made Laura think about the solvency of her other trade receivables. She decides that she would like to create an allowance for receivables of 10% of her remaining trade receivables at 31 August 2021.

4. Laura bought a second-hand van for £6,000 on 1 September 2020. She reckons this van will last for three years before she has to replace it. She anticipates that the trade-in value of this van will be £600 in three years' time. Laura expects the van to travel 5,000 miles each year on journeys for business purposes.

5. Van running expenses and insurance for the year amounted to £4,000. All of these expenses were paid from the business bank account. No van running expenses were outstanding or prepaid at 31 August 2021.

6. On 1 September 2020, Laura paid £5,000 for various items of second-hand construction equipment. These assets should last for four years and fetch £60 as scrap when they are replaced. Laura expects to make the same use of these assets in each of the four years of their expected useful life.

3

7. Two part-time helpers were employed for 13 weeks during June, July and August 2021. By 31 August 2021, Laura had paid both these helpers 12 weeks of their wages amounting to £9,600 out of the business bank account.

8. Comprehensive business insurance was taken out and paid for on 1 September 2020. As a new business customer, Laura took advantage of the insurance company's discount scheme to pay £1,800 for 18 months' cover.

9. Laura counted up and valued her inventory of building materials at 31 August 2021. She valued all these items at a cost to the business of £4,500.

10. Bank charges of £400 were deducted from Laura's bank account during the year. The bank manager has told her that accrued charges to the end of August 2021 amount to an additional £75. These accrued charges will be deducted from her business bank account during September 2021.

11. Laura's bank account was overdrawn in the early part of her first year of trading. The bank charged her £200 interest on this overdraft. Since then, her bank account has shown a positive balance and she has earned £250 in interest up to 31 July 2021. The bank manager has told her that in August 2021 her interest receivable is a further £50 and this will be added to her account in October 2021.

12. Laura withdrew £2,500 each month from the bank for her personal expenses. As she had so much cash in the bank in August 2021, on 31 August 2021 she used £90,000 from her business bank account to repay half of the mortgage on her house.

Required

1. Prepare Laura's bank account for the year ended 31 August 2021.

2. Prepare a statement of profit or loss by nature for Laura's business for the year to 31 August 2021 and a statement of financial position at that date.

DOUBLE-ENTRY BOOKKEEPING 1: DEBITS, CREDITS, ACCOUNTS, THE TRIAL BALANCE AND THE FINANCIAL STATEMENTS

4

LEARNING OUTCOMES

Once you have read this chapter and worked through the questions and examples in both this chapter and the online workbook, you should be able to:

- Define debits and credits

- Understand how double entry is a logical extension of the accounting equation

- Post transactions to T accounts using double entry

- State the double entry to record recurring business transactions and events

- Extract a trial balance from the T accounts at the end of an accounting period

- Use the trial balance to draw up the statement of profit or loss and statement of financial position

- Close off the T accounts, transfer income and expenditure balances to the statement of profit or loss and bring forward asset, liability and capital balances to the new financial period

INTRODUCTION

We considered in Chapter 2 (The dual aspect concept) how transactions have an effect on two or more accounts and how a business's transactions change the figures in the statement of financial position on a day-to-day or even on a minute-to-minute basis. It is now time to look in much more detail at this dual aspect concept and to show how transactions are recorded in the double-entry bookkeeping system. This approach to recording transactions will seem strange at first but skills built up through continual practice and experience will enable you to become so familiar with the double-entry approach that it will become as natural as breathing. Double entry is not a subject you will just study in the first year of your Accounting degree and then forget. Double entry will form the bedrock of your professional career in accountancy so you will have to understand how double entry works now and maintain and develop that understanding into the far distant future.

This chapter presents the terminology used in double-entry bookkeeping, debits and credits, together with the T account which is used to record transactions as they occur. We will then see how, once all the transactions and period-end adjustments have been recorded in the T accounts, the balances on all the T accounts at the end of the accounting period are used to compile the trial balance which is then used as the foundation from which to produce the statement of profit or loss and the statement of financial position of an organisation. Figure 4.1 summarises the stages in the recording and processing of accounting transactions into the final financial statements.

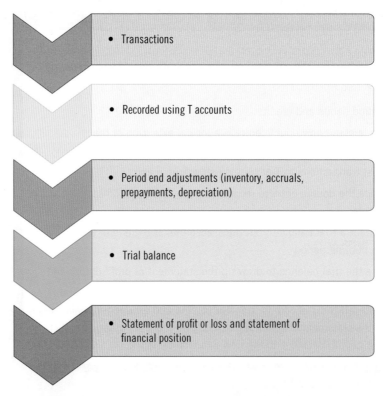

- Transactions

- Recorded using T accounts

- Period end adjustments (inventory, accruals, prepayments, depreciation)

- Trial balance

- Statement of profit or loss and statement of financial position

Figure 4.1 Stages in the recording and processing of transactions into the final financial statements

THE T ACCOUNT

In the double-entry bookkeeping system, a T account is set up for every asset and liability, for every source of income and expense and for every element of capital. The T account is the basic building block for recording accounting transactions and each T account will follow exactly the same pattern as shown in Figure 4.2.

Figure 4.2 The T account

Each and every T account has a title and two sides, one for debit entries and one for credit entries. What do these terms, debits and credits, signify?

Debits

Debit accounts represent assets and expenses. When the monetary amount of an asset or expense increases an entry is made to the debit side of the asset or expense T account. Conversely, when the monetary amount of an asset or expense decreases, then an entry is made to the credit side of the asset or expense T account. These debit and credit entries for asset and expense accounts are presented in Figure 4.3.

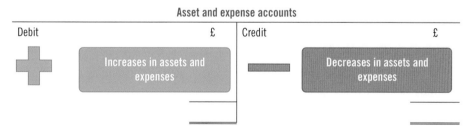

Figure 4.3 Asset and expense entries in the T account

Credits

Credit accounts represent liabilities, income and capital (equity). When there is an increase in the monetary amount of a liability, income or capital, an entry is made to the credit side of the liability, income or capital T account. Conversely, when there is a decrease in the monetary amount of a liability, income or capital, then an entry is made to the debit side of the liability, income or capital T account. These debit and credit entries for liability, income and capital accounts are presented in Figure 4.4.

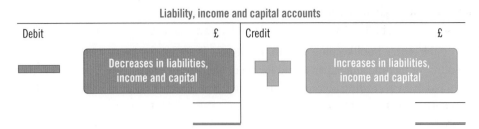

Figure 4.4 Liability, income and capital entries in the T account

We shall see how accounting transactions and events are recorded using T accounts and the debit and credit entry rules shortly. However, the golden rule for double entry states that every debit entry must have a corresponding and equal credit entry. Thus there cannot be two debit entries or two credit entries to record a monetary transaction, there must be a debit entry and a credit entry of equal value otherwise the accounts will not balance. The double-entry rule reflects the dual nature of business transactions and events. Therefore, when one account increases or decreases, another account also increases or decreases as we saw in Chapter 2 (The dual aspect concept) and as we shall also see in this chapter and the next.

WHY IS THIS RELEVANT TO ME?   Recording transactions in T accounts

To enable you as a business professional to understand:

• The way in which monetary transactions are recorded in T accounts

• That each and every debit entry must have an equal and opposite credit entry to ensure that the accounts balance

GO BACK OVER THIS AGAIN!   Are you quite sure you understand what debits and credits mean and how entries to debit and credit accounts increase or decrease the balance on those accounts? Go to the **online workbook** and have a go at Exercises 4.1 to test your understanding.

SUMMARY OF KEY CONCEPTS   Are you quite certain you can define debit and credit accounts and entries correctly? Go to the **online workbook** to check your understanding of debit and credit accounts with Summary of key concepts 4.1.

DOUBLE ENTRY AND THE ACCOUNTING EQUATION

Double entry is inextricably linked to the accounting equation. Our accounting equation (Figure 4.5 and refer back to Chapter 2, The accounting equation) states that:

Figure 4.5 The accounting equation

However, you might be wondering how income and expenses fit into the accounting equation. We can see assets, liabilities and capital, all of which we have considered as part of the double-entry system, but there is currently no sign of the income and expenses that also form part of the double-entry accounting records. As we saw in Chapter 2 (The components of equity), the capital of a business is made up of the capital introduced by the owner + the profit for the year − any drawings made by the business's owner. Capital introduced by the owner − drawings = equity while profit for the year is calculated by deducting expenses from income. On this basis we can rewrite our accounting equation as shown in Figure 4.6:

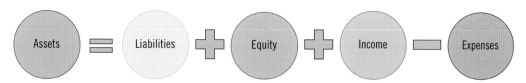

Figure 4.6 The accounting equation rewritten to include income and expenses

Moving expenses to the left hand side will then give us our double-entry equation shown in Figure 4.7:

Figure 4.7 The accounting equation rewritten so that debits = credits

WHY IS THIS RELEVANT TO ME?   The accounting equation and the duality principle

To enable you as a business professional to understand:

• How the accounting equation reflects the duality principle
• How all the debit entries will be equal to all the credit entries

GO BACK OVER THIS AGAIN!   Are you completely convinced that you can state the expanded accounting equation? Go to the **online workbook** and have a go at Exercises 4.2 to test your understanding.

SUMMARY OF KEY CONCEPTS   Are you certain that you have understood the expanded accounting equation? Go to the **online workbook** to revise this accounting equation with Summary of key concepts 4.2.

POSTING ACCOUNTING TRANSACTIONS TO T ACCOUNTS

Now that we have considered the basis upon which debits and credits work and how the accounts should always be in balance, let's see how accounting transactions and events are posted to the T accounts. We shall do this through a series of examples, Examples 4.1 to 4.6.

EXAMPLE 4.1

Arthur is starting up his own legal practice. He opens a business bank account on 1 June 2021 and pays in £5,000 of his own money to provide him with cash with which to finance transactions in the first few weeks of operations. How should Arthur record this transaction in the T accounts of his legal practice?

Firstly, we have to decide what this £5,000 represents. Is the £5,000 received by the business an asset or an expense (the debit entry)? Is the £5,000 a liability, income or capital (the credit entry)? Once we have made these decisions, then we can post the cash received to the correct T accounts.

As we saw in Chapter 2 (Current assets), cash is a business asset. Cash has been paid into the bank which means that the asset has increased. Therefore, there will be a debit entry to the bank account, an increase in the amount of an asset. Cash introduced by the owner of a business is part of equity (Chapter 2, The components of equity), money owed by the business to the owner, so this will result in a credit entry to the owner's capital account. Cash is not an expense as it is used to buy things for the business, so it is recorded as an asset. The £5,000 that Arthur has paid into the business does not represent a sale by the business or a gift to the business, so it is not income. It is money that Arthur has lent to the business with a view to increasing it so that he can take out a greater amount of money at a later date. Arthur will thus record the transaction as shown in Illustration 4.1. He will debit the bank account (increase the asset) with £5,000 and he will credit the capital account (an increase in capital) with £5,000.

Illustration 4.1 Posting the £5,000 capital introduced to Arthur's books of account

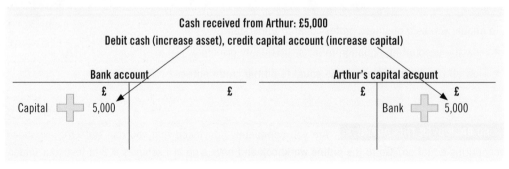

Both assets and capital increase, so both accounts record a plus entry.

Note the way in which the entries are recorded: Arthur notes down the name of the opposite account in each T account to enable him to trace the entries again at a future date.

Thus 'capital' is recorded as the opposing entry in the bank account while capital records 'bank' as the other side of the entry. When completing T accounts, you should also follow this approach to enable you to correct entries or to find out where an entry has been posted.

Do the accounts balance? Does the accounting equation still hold true? There is a debit of £5,000 and a credit of £5,000 so the accounts balance. By using the accounting equation, we can check to see if the accounts are in balance. Assets in this case are the cash of £5,000 + £0 expenses = £0 liabilities + £5,000 capital account + £0 income so we can conclude that we have completed the double entry correctly as the accounts balance at £5,000 on each side. Let's try another example, Example 4.2.

EXAMPLE 4.2

Arthur uses £1,000 of the cash in the bank to pay rent on the office lease he has taken out to provide him with a place from which to run his operations. How should Arthur record this transaction in the T accounts of his business? Again, we have to think about how this transaction will be recorded and which accounts will be affected. The amount of money in the bank account reduces by £1,000, which has now been spent. Thus this reduction in the asset account results in a credit entry to the bank account. Rent is an expense and this expense has increased by £1,000 so the rent account is debited with £1,000 to reflect this increase in the expense account. The double entry for the payment of rent is shown in Illustration 4.2.

Illustration 4.2 Posting the £1,000 payment for rent to Arthur's books of account

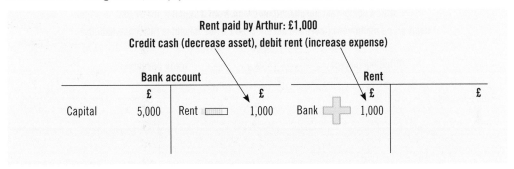

Here there is a reduction in the asset and an increase in the expense.

Do the accounts still balance? A cash asset of £4,000 (£5,000 debit − £1,000 credit) + rent expense of £1,000 = £5,000 capital account + £0 liabilities + £0 income so the accounts are still in balance at £5,000 on each side. Do note that the transactions on each account build up throughout the accounting period: the original cash received in the bank has not disappeared just because we have now moved on to record another transaction.

Let's keep going with more transactions to build up your knowledge and appreciation of how double entry works. These additional transactions are presented in Examples 4.3 to 4.6.

EXAMPLE 4.3

Arthur now buys some computers, desks and chairs from his local office equipment supplier. The cost of the computers, desks and chairs is £2,000. Arthur does not pay for these items of office equipment immediately, but buys them on credit from his supplier. This means that he will pay for these goods at a later date. You might think that Arthur does not need to record this transaction in his books yet as no cash has left the business. However, as we noted in Chapter 3 (The accruals basis of accounting) you must still record the transaction even if the cash has not been paid or received. If this transaction were not recorded immediately, then the debit and credit sides of the accounting equation would both be £2,000 lower than they should be. Think about the double entry for this transaction on credit. What do the computers, desks and chairs represent in accounting terms? These are non-current assets which will be used long-term in the business. Therefore, they will be recorded as assets. The assets increase so this is a debit entry to the office equipment account. We now need to think about the credit entry. No cash has changed hands, so we cannot reduce the asset in the bank account. Careful thought will enable you to realise that Arthur now has a liability, a present obligation to transfer an economic resource (a future payment of cash to settle what is owed to his supplier) as a result of past events (taking delivery of the office equipment). Therefore, Arthur must record a trade payable balance in his books of account. As there is a £2,000 liability, Arthur must credit the trade payables account because liabilities have increased by this amount. The double entry for this transaction is shown in Illustration 4.3.

Illustration 4.3 Purchase of office equipment on credit posted to Arthur's books of account

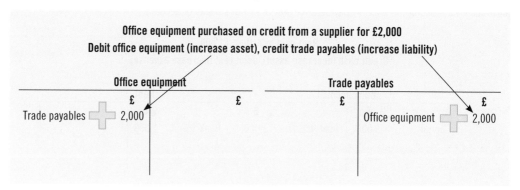

Arthur's assets have increased, but this increase in assets has also given rise to an increase in liabilities so both accounts increase.

Do the accounts still balance? £2,000 office equipment + £4,000 cash at the bank + £1,000 rent expense = £5,000 capital account + £2,000 trade payables + £0 income, so the accounts are still in balance with £7,000 on both the debit and credit sides.

EXAMPLE 4.4

Arthur now goes back to his office equipment supplier to buy £200 of paper and ink cartridges to enable him to print letters and documents. Again, he buys these supplies on credit. Your experience built up in Example 4.3 should enable you to state the double entry for this transaction straight away. Stationery supplies are not a non-current asset, but an expense. These office supplies will be used up quickly in the business so they will have only a short not a long life and so are recognised as an expense. The increase in expenditure gives rise to an increase in liabilities as more is owed to suppliers who will be paid the amounts owed at a later date. Thus the double entry will be debit stationery with £200 and credit trade payables with £200 as shown in Illustration 4.4.

Illustration 4.4 Purchase of stationery on credit posted to Arthur's books of account

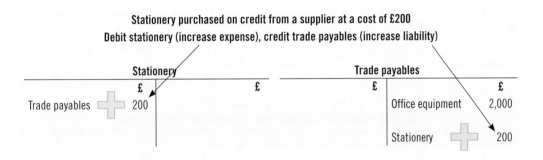

Do the accounts still balance? £200 stationery expense + £2,000 office equipment + £4,000 cash at the bank + £1,000 rent expense = £5,000 capital account + £2,200 trade payables + £0 income, so the accounts are still in balance with £7,200 on the debit side and £7,200 on the credit side of the equation.

EXAMPLE 4.5

Arthur provides legal services to a client. The client pays Arthur's fee of £500 which Arthur pays into the bank account. Cash paid into the bank account is clearly an increase in an asset, so there is a debit to the bank account. But what is the credit entry? Arthur has generated income for his practice, so he has increased his income. Therefore, he will credit his revenue account with £500. The double entry for this transaction is shown in Illustration 4.5.

Illustration 4.5 Revenue received of £500 posted to Arthur's books of account

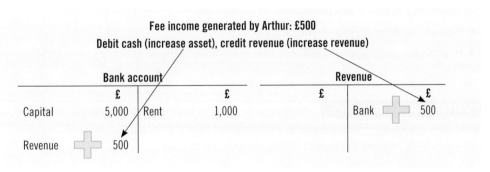

Do the accounts still balance? Let's check. £200 stationery expense + £2,000 office equipment + £4,500 cash at the bank (£5,000 + £500 − £1,000) + £1,000 rent expense = £5,000 capital account + £2,200 trade payables + £500 income, so the accounts are still in balance at £7,700 on each side after the completion of all the double entries.

4

EXAMPLE 4.6

Arthur now decides to pay £800 off the amounts he owes his trade payables. He uses cash from the bank to make the payment. As we have seen, a payment out of the bank represents a decrease in an asset balance, so there will be a credit entry to the bank of £800 thereby reducing the balance in the bank. What is the debit entry? Arthur is paying off part of what he owes to his trade payables. This means that the amounts owed to trade payables will decrease, so the debit entry will be made in the trade payables account, reducing the amounts owed by £800. The double entry for this transaction is shown in Illustration 4.6.

Illustration 4.6 Trade payable payment of £800 posted to Arthur's books of account

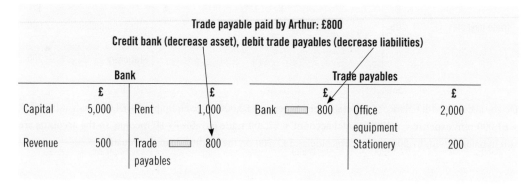

Do the accounts still balance? Let's check. £200 stationery expense + £2,000 office equipment + £3,700 cash at the bank (£5,000 + £500 – £1,000 – £800) + £1,000 rent expense = £5,000 capital account + £1,400 trade payables (£2,000 + £200 – £800) + £500 income, so the accounts are still in balance at £6,900 on each side after all the double entries have been completed.

WHY IS THIS RELEVANT TO ME?   Using double entry to post transactions to T accounts

To enable you as a business professional to understand:

• How double entry works in practical situations
• How the accounts remain in balance after completion of the double entry for each transaction

---

MULTIPLE CHOICE QUESTIONS   Are you quite sure you have understood the double entry required to record transactions? Go to the **online workbook** and have a go at Multiple choice questions 4.1 to test your ability to make the correct double entry in the accounts.

SHOW ME HOW TO DO IT   Are you completely certain you understood how double entry was used to post the transactions to Arthur's accounts? View Video presentation 4.1 in the **online workbook** to see a practical demonstration of how these entries were made.

THE TRIAL BALANCE

It is hard work balancing the accounts after each transaction has been entered. To make the job of checking whether all the double entry has been completed in full much easier, a trial balance is produced at regular intervals. A trial balance is a listing of all the debit and all the credit balances on the T accounts at any given point in time. If there is a difference on the trial balance then investigations can take place and corrective action can be taken to make the required adjustments to bring everything back into balance.

How is this trial balance drawn up? Firstly, we need to look at all our T accounts and determine what the balance is on each account. Arthur's T accounts after all the transactions have been posted are shown in Illustration 4.7.

Illustration 4.7 Arthur's T accounts after posting his transactions

Arthur's capital account				Bank account			
	£		£		£		£
		Bank	5,000	Capital	5,000	Rent	1,000
Debits =	0	Credits =	5,000	Revenue	500	Trade payables	800
				Debits =	5,500	Credits =	1,800

Office equipment				Rent			
	£		£		£		£
Trade payables	2,000			Bank	1,000		
Debits =	2,000	Credits =	0	Debits =	1,000	Credits =	0

Revenue				Stationery			
	£		£		£		£
		Bank	500	Trade payables	200		
Debits =	0	Credits =	500	Debits =	200	Credits =	0

Trade payables			
	£		£
Bank	800	Office equipment	2,000
		Stationery	200
Debits =	800	Credits =	2,200

The balance on each account is calculated by adding up the two sides of each account to determine the difference. If there are more debits than credits on the account, then there is a debit balance on that account. If there are more credits than debits on the account, then there is a credit balance on that account. Let's use Arthur's T accounts to illustrate how these rules are applied.

Arthur's capital account has credits of £5,000 and debits of £Nil so there is a credit balance (more credits than debits) of £5,000 on this account (£5,000 credits – £Nil debits). This credit balance is allocated to the credit side of the trial balance as shown in Illustration 4.8.

The bank account has debits of £5,000 and £500 and credits of £1,000 and £800. There is therefore a debit balance (more debits than credits) of £3,700 on the bank account (£5,000 + £500 – £1,000 – £800 = £3,700) and this is added to the debit side of the trial balance as shown in Illustration 4.8.

Office equipment has a debit balance (more debits than credits) of £2,000 as there are debits of £2,000 and credits of £Nil. Similarly, the rent account has a debit balance (more debits than credits) of £1,000, being made up of £1,000 of debits and £Nil credits. Illustration 4.8 shows both of these balances added to the debit side of the trial balance.

The credit balance (more credits than debits) on the revenue account is £500, as there are £500 of credits and £Nil debits so the resulting credit balance is allocated to the credit side of the trial balance (Illustration 4.8).

Stationery is showing a debit balance (more debits than credits) of £200 (£200 of debits – £Nil credits) and appears on the debit side of the trial balance (Illustration 4.8).

Finally, the trade payables account has credit entries of £2,000 and £200 and a debit entry of £800. The credit balance (more credits than debits) on this account is thus £1,400 (£2,000 + £200 – £800) and this balance is added to the credit side of the trial balance (Illustration 4.8).

Illustration 4.8 Arthur's trial balance

Arthur: trial balance at [Date]

	Debit £	Credit £
Arthur's capital account		5,000
Bank account	3,700	
Office equipment	2,000	
Rent	1,000	
Revenue		500
Stationery	200	
Trade payables		1,400
	6,900	**6,900**

The debit and credit columns in Arthur's trial balance are added up and both total up to £6,900. This is what would be expected as all the debits should equal all the credits. The trial balance (as we shall see in this chapter, Comprehensive example: double entry and the trial balance) is then used to draw up the statement of profit or loss and statement of financial position for organisations.

Work through the above trial balance again to ensure you have grasped how the trial balance is put together.

WHY IS THIS RELEVANT TO ME?   The trial balance

To enable you as a business professional to:

• Understand how the trial balance is compiled from the balances on the T accounts

• Appreciate that the trial balance must balance if all the double entry has been completed in full

• Draw up your own trial balance from a set of T accounts

GO BACK OVER THIS AGAIN!   Are you quite convinced that you understand how the trial balance works? Go to the **online workbook** and have a go at Exercises 4.3 to test your understanding.

NUMERICAL EXERCISES   Are you quite sure you could draw up a trial balance from a given set of information? Go to the **online workbook** and have a go at Numerical exercises 4.1 to test your ability and understanding of how to put a trial balance together.

SHOW ME HOW TO DO IT   Are you completely certain you understood how Arthur's trial balance was put together? View Video presentation 4.2 in the **online workbook** to see a practical demonstration of how Arthur's trial balance was compiled from his T accounts.

COMPREHENSIVE EXAMPLE: DOUBLE ENTRY AND THE TRIAL BALANCE

In Chapter 3 (Example 3.8) we put together Julia's statement of profit or loss and statement of financial position from Julia's bank receipts and payments account and the additional information that Julia provided. We will now use the same information to post the entries to T accounts. From these T accounts we will extract the trial balance and we will use this trial balance to prepare Julia's statement of profit or loss for the three months to 30 June 2021 together with a statement of financial position at that date.

Julia's bank receipts and payments for the three-month period are presented in Illustration 4.9.

Illustration 4.9 Julia's bank account receipts and payments summary (= Illustration 3.3)

		Receipts £	Payments £
1 April 2021	Cash introduced by Julia	30,000	
1 April 2021	Three months' rent paid on shop to 30 June 2021		5,000
1 April 2021	Cash register paid for		1,000
1 April 2021	Shelving and shop fittings paid for		12,000
30 April 2021	Receipts from sales in April 2021	20,000	
5 May 2021	Sports equipment supplied in April 2021 paid for		15,000
12 May 2021	Rates for period 1 April 2021 to 30 September 2021 paid		800
19 May 2021	Cash withdrawn for Julia's own expenses		2,000
31 May 2021	Receipts from sales in May 2021	25,000	
5 June 2021	Sports equipment supplied in May 2021 paid for		20,000
10 June 2021	Shop water rates for the year 1 April 2021 to 31 March 2022 paid		400
30 June 2021	Receipts from sales in June 2021	30,000	
30 June 2021	Balance in bank at 30 June 2021		48,800
		105,000	**105,000**

Julia's receipts and payments summary is already very much in the T account format with receipts on the left hand side (debit entries) increasing the balance on the bank asset account and payments on the right hand side (credit entries) reducing the balance on the bank asset account. We can rewrite Julia's receipts and payments summary in a T account format. Julia's bank account is shown in Illustration 4.10.

Illustration 4.10 Julia's bank account receipts and payments in T account format

	Bank Account				
Debit (increases the asset)		£	Credit (decreases the asset)		£
2021			2021		
1 April	Capital account	30,000	1 April	Rent	5,000
30 April	Sales (April)	20,000	1 April	Cash register cost	1,000
31 May	Sales (May)	25,000	1 April	Shelving and fittings cost	12,000
30 June	Sales (June)	30,000	5 May	Cost of sales (April)	15,000
			12 May	Rates	800
			19 May	Drawings	2,000
			5 June	Cost of sales (May)	20,000
			10 June	Water rates	400

The receipts of cash from capital and sales (income) increase the cash asset in the bank (debits) and the payments out of the bank (credits) reduce the cash asset in the bank. Note that, as well as including the corresponding account in each entry, the date has also been added to each transaction to make the job of tracing transactions through the accounts even easier.

The next step involves deciding which accounts will be credited and which accounts will be debited in order to complete the double entry. We will need the following T accounts to enable us to complete the entries into the accounting records:

- Capital account
- Sales account
- Rent account
- Cash register cost account
- Shelving and fittings cost account
- Cost of sales (opening inventory + purchases – closing inventory) account
- Rates account
- Water rates account

Draw these T accounts up for yourself now and have a go at posting the entries from the bank account into these accounts before you look at the answers presented in Illustrations 4.11 to 4.18. Remember that for every debit entry there must be a credit entry and for every credit entry there must be a debit entry.

Julia has paid £30,000 into the business, so the business owes Julia £30,000. Therefore, this £30,000 increases the capital of the business as shown in Illustration 4.11. If you were in any doubt as to whether this was a debit or credit entry to the capital account, you just had to follow the double-entry logic: as £30,000 has been debited to the bank account, the other side of the entry must be to the credit side of the capital account. Assets rise by £30,000 and capital rises by £30,000 so the accounts still balance (£30,000 asset + £0 expenses = £30,000 capital + £0 liability + £0 income).

Illustration 4.11 Julia's capital T account showing the posting of £30,000 capital introduced

Julia's capital account

Debit (decreases the capital)	£	Credit (increases the capital)	£
2021		2021	
		1 April Bank	30,000

Our next three receipts of cash are for sales. Sales = income so the three receipts of cash from sales are credited to the sales account (Illustration 4.12).

Illustration 4.12 Julia's sales T account showing the cash income from sales in the months of April, May and June 2021

Sales account				
Debit (decreases the income)	**£**	**Credit (increases the income)**		**£**
2021		**2021**		
		30 April	Bank (Sales April)	20,000
		31 May	Bank (Sales May)	25,000
		30 June	Bank (Sales June)	30,000

Again, if you were in any doubt as to whether the sales account should record a debit or a credit entry, you just had to follow the double-entry logic: as £20,000, £25,000 and £30,000 have been debited to the bank account, the other side of the entries must be to the credit side of the sales account. Assets rise by £75,000 and sales rise by the same amount so the accounts still balance (£30,000 + £75,000 assets + £0 expenses = £30,000 capital + £75,000 income + £0 liability).

Now that the debit entries in the bank account have been credited to the relevant income and capital accounts, it is time to turn our attention to the credit entries in the bank. As these are credit entries in the bank, they must be debit entries in their corresponding asset and expense accounts (Illustrations 4.13 to 4.18).

Illustration 4.13 Julia's rent T account showing the cash payment made for rent on 1 April 2021

Rent account				
Debit (increases the expense)	**£**	**Credit (decreases the expense)**		**£**
2021		**2021**		
1 April Bank	5,000			

Illustration 4.14 Julia's cash register cost T account showing the cash spent on the cash register on 1 April 2021

Cash register cost account				
Debit (increases the asset)	**£**	**Credit (decreases the asset)**		**£**
2021		**2021**		
1 April Bank	1,000			

Illustration 4.15 Julia's shelving and fittings cost T account showing the cash spent on shelving and fittings on 1 April 2021

Shelving and fittings cost account

Debit (increases the asset)	£	Credit (decreases the asset)	£
2021		2021	
1 April Bank	12,000		

Illustration 4.16 Julia's cost of sales T account showing the cash paid for purchases in May and June 2021

Cost of sales (opening inventory + purchases − closing inventory)

Debit (increases the expense)	£	Credit (decreases the expense)	£
2021		2021	
5 May Bank (purchases April)	15,000		
5 June Bank (purchases May)	20,000		

Illustration 4.17 Julia's rates T account showing the cash spent on rates in the three-month period April to June 2021

Rates account

Debit (increases the expense)	£	Credit (decreases the expense)	£
2021		2021	
12 May Bank	800		

Illustration 4.18 Julia's water rates T account showing the cash spent on water rates in the three-month period April to June 2021

Water rates account

Debit (increases the expense)	£	Credit (decreases the expense)	£
2021		2021	
19 May Bank	400		

These accounts show the recording of the assets and expenses in Julia's T accounts. Assets and expenses increase so the entries are all to the debit side of the T accounts. However, there is one more credit in the bank account that still has to be posted to the accounting records. On 19 May, Julia withdrew £2,000 from the business bank account to pay her personal expenses. This is not an asset (there is no economic resource with the potential to produce economic benefits) and is not a business expense as the payment was to Julia herself (Chapter 3, Drawings and the business entity convention). In which T account should this £2,000 be recorded? A little thought should enable you to realise that this £2,000 is a repayment of Julia's capital. Any repayment of capital reduces the amount in the capital account so this £2,000 will be debited to Julia's capital account as shown in Illustration 4.19.

Illustration 4.19 Julia's capital T account showing the £30,000 capital introduced and the £2,000 of capital repaid

Julia's capital account

Debit (decreases the capital)	£	Credit (increases the capital)	£
2021		2021	
19 May Bank (Drawings)	2,000	1 April Bank	30,000

Instead of deducting drawings directly from the capital account as we have done, a separate T account can be maintained for drawings. This T account would be headed up Drawings and any drawings made during the accounting period would be debited to this account in the same way. At the end of the accounting period, the balance on the drawings account would be transferred to the capital account (debit capital account, credit drawings account) to reduce the balance on the drawings account to zero.

SHOW ME HOW TO DO IT   Are you quite happy with the double entry for the figures in Julia's receipts and payments summary? View Video presentation 4.3 in the **online workbook** to see a practical demonstration of how the relevant debit and credit entries were made.

Do the accounts still balance? Let's add up all the debits and credits. Debits = £30,000 (bank) + £75,000 (bank) + £5,000 (rent) + £1,000 (cash register) + £12,000 (shelving and fixtures) + £15,000 (cost of sales) + £20,000 (cost of sales) + £800 (rates) + £400 (water rates) = £159,200. Credits = £56,200 paid out of the bank (add up the credit side of the bank account to make sure this is correct) + £30,000 (capital) − £2,000 (drawings) + £75,000 (sales) = £159,200. Therefore, all the debits are equal to all the credits and the accounts balance.

Can we now use the T accounts to draw up Julia's statement of profit or loss and statement of financial position? Not yet. As we saw in Chapter 3 (The accruals basis of accounting and Example 3.8), we must apply the accruals basis of accounting when producing financial statements. Using the T accounts as they currently stand as the basis for Julia's financial statements would mean preparing the figures on a receipts and payments basis, not on the accruals basis as required by accounting principles.

Firstly, let's look at the additional information Julia provided us with in Chapter 3 (Example 3.8):

- She counted up and valued the inventory at the close of business on 30 June 2021: the cost of this inventory at that date was £10,000.

- At 30 June 2021, Julia owed £25,000 for sports equipment she had purchased from her suppliers on credit in June. She paid this £25,000 on 5 July 2021.

- While her main business is selling sports equipment for cash, Julia has made sales to two local tennis clubs in June on credit. At 30 June 2021, the two clubs owed £2,500, although one club disputes £50 of the amount outstanding, saying that the goods were never delivered. Julia has no proof that these goods were ever received by the club and has reluctantly agreed that she will never receive this £50.

- During the month of June, Julia employed a part-time sales assistant who was owed £300 in wages at the end of June. These wages were paid on 8 July 2021.

- On 5 July 2021, Julia received a telephone bill for £250 covering the three months 1 April 2021 to 30 June 2021 together with an electricity bill for £200 covering the same period.

- Julia expects the cash register and shelving and shop fittings to last for five years before they need replacement. The level of usage of these assets will be the same in each of the next five years. She also expects that the assets will have no residual value at the end of their useful lives and that they will just be scrapped rather than being sold on.

- The cash register contained £500 in cash at 30 June 2021 representing sales receipts that had not yet been banked.

- On 29 June 2021, one of the tennis clubs that she trades with on credit returned goods with a sales value of £400. These goods were faulty. Julia returned these goods to her supplier: the goods had originally cost Julia £250.

To satisfy the accruals basis of accounting, all of these transactions must be reflected in Julia's accounting records up to 30 June 2021. But how should the above transactions be recorded in Julia's T accounts? To help you follow the double entry, the debit and credit entries in the following illustrations have been made in **red**.

- She counted up and valued the inventory at the close of business on 30 June 2021: the cost of this inventory at that date was £10,000.

Closing inventory is a deduction from cost of sales. This deduction will decrease the cost of sales expense. A decrease in an expense requires a credit entry to the expense account. But closing inventory is also an asset at the end of June 2021 as the resource has the potential to produce economic benefits for Julia from sales of this inventory in the next accounting period. Therefore there will be a debit to the inventory account. The required double entry is thus debit inventory, credit cost of sales (Illustration 4.20).

Illustration 4.20 T account double entry to record closing inventory in Julia's books at 30 June 2021

Cost of sales (opening inventory + purchases − closing inventory)					
Debit (increases the expense)		**£**	**Credit (decreases the expense)**		**£**
2021			**2021**		
5 May	Bank (purchases April)	15,000	30 June	Inventory	10,000
5 June	Bank (purchases May)	20,000			

Inventory					
Debit (increases the asset)		**£**	**Credit (decreases the asset)**		**£**
2021			**2021**		
30 June	Cost of sales	10,000			

- At 30 June 2021, Julia owed £25,000 for sports equipment she had purchased from her suppliers on credit in June. She paid this £25,000 on 5 July 2021.

Julia currently has an unrecognised expense and an unrecognised liability at 30 June. She must recognise both the liability and the expense that this liability represents. At 30 June 2021 she has a present obligation to transfer an economic resource (cash) to pay for the sports goods delivered to her in June. This obligation gives rise to a liability for the amount owed and a corresponding expense. Both expenses and liabilities must increase. Therefore she will debit her cost of sales account with £25,000 (a debit to an expense account will increase the balance on the expense account) and credit her trade payables account (this is a new account that needs setting up) with £25,000. A credit to a liability account will increase the balance on the liability account to record the amount owed at the end of the accounting period. These accounting entries are shown in Illustration 4.21.

Illustration 4.21 T account double entry to record the liability for purchases and cost of sales expense for June 2021

Cost of sales (opening inventory + purchases − closing inventory)					
Debit (increases the expense)		**£**	**Credit (decreases the expense)**		**£**
2021			**2021**		
5 May	Bank (purchases April)	15,000	30 June	Inventory	10,000
5 June	Bank (purchases May)	20,000			
30 June	Trade payables (June)	25,000			

Trade payables					
Debit (decreases the liability)		**£**	**Credit (increases the liability)**		**£**
2021			**2021**		
			30 June	Cost of sales (June)	25,000

- While her main business is selling sports equipment for cash, Julia has made sales to two local tennis clubs in June on credit. At 30 June 2021, the two clubs owed £2,500, although one club disputes £50 of the amount outstanding, saying that the goods were never delivered. Julia has no proof that these goods were ever received by the club and has reluctantly agreed that she will never receive this £50.

In this case, there are two transactions that must be reflected in Julia's books: the trade receivables and the sales that gave rise to those trade receivables and the irrecoverable debt that will result in a reduction in trade receivables and an increase in the irrecoverable debts expense. Let's deal with these two transactions one at a time.

Firstly, recognising the trade receivables (money due to Julia as a result of trading with her customers on credit) will result in an increase (debit) in the asset. The corresponding credit is to the sales account as income also increases (credit) as more sales have been made that require recognition in the three-month accounting period (Illustration 4.22). The double entry to record a sale made on credit is thus debit trade receivables, credit sales.

Secondly, there is a known irrecoverable debt of £50, money which Julia will not receive from her customer. This known irrecoverable debt will decrease the trade receivables asset (a credit to the asset account) by £50 as this asset is derecognised. The asset no longer exists so it is removed (derecognised) from the T account and from the statement of financial position. The known irrecoverable debt represents an expense so the irrecoverable debt expense account will show a debit to reflect this increase (a debit increases the balance on an expense account). The double entry for this event is shown in Illustration 4.23.

Illustration 4.22 T account double entry to record the trade receivables asset and sales income at 30 June 2021

Trade receivables

Debit (increases the asset)	£	Credit (decreases the asset)	£
2021		2021	
30 June Sales	2,500		

Sales account

Debit (decreases the income)	£	Credit (increases the income)	£
2021		2021	
		30 April Bank (Sales April)	20,000
		31 May Bank (Sales May)	25,000
		30 June Bank (Sales June)	30,000
		30 June Trade receivables	2,500

Illustration 4.23 T account double entry to derecognise a trade receivable asset and to charge the derecognised receivable as an irrecoverable debt expense

Trade receivables

Debit (increases the asset)		£	Credit (decreases the asset)		£
2021			2021		
30 June	Sales	2,500	June 30	Irrecoverable debts	50

Irrecoverable debts

Debit (increases the expense)		£	Credit (decreases the expense)	£
2021			2021	
30 June	Trade receivables	50		

- During the month of June, Julia employed a part-time sales assistant who was owed £300 in wages at the end of June. These wages were paid on 8 July 2021.

At 30 June, Julia has a liability for wages owed to her part-time sales assistant. At that date, there is a present obligation to transfer an economic resource as a result of past events (the work undertaken by the sales assistant and Julia's agreement to pay for this work) which will give rise to the outflow of cash (an economic resource) from the business (the payment of the wages on 8 July). Therefore, Julia will recognise a liability for the wages owed, an accrual. To recognise the increase in the liability, she will credit the wages accrual account. The wages payable is an expense so Julia will debit the wages account with this increase in expenses (Illustration 4.24).

Illustration 4.24 T account double entry to recognise a liability to pay wages at 30 June 2021 and the corresponding wages expense

Wages

Debit (increases the expense)		£	Credit (decreases the expense)	£
2021			2021	
30 June	Wages accrual	300		

Wages accrual

Debit (decreases the liability)	£	Credit (increases the liability)		£
2021		2021		
		30 June	Wages	300

- On 5 July 2021, Julia received a telephone bill for £250 covering the three months 1 April 2021 to 30 June 2021 together with an electricity bill for £200 covering the same period.

In the same way as for the wages payable, Julia has liabilities for both telephone expenses owed to the telephone company and for electricity owed to the electric company. Using the same logic as before, there are two present obligations to transfer an economic resource as a result of past events (the usage of the telephone to make business calls and the use of the electricity to light the shop) which will give rise to the outflow of cash (an economic resource) from the business to settle the telephone and electricity bills at a later date. Therefore, Julia will recognise a liability for the amounts owed to the telephone and electric companies, two accruals, crediting the telephone accrual and electricity accrual accounts to increase the liabilities of the business at 30 June 2021. The telephone and electricity bills payable are expenses, so Julia will debit the telephone and electricity accounts with these increases in expenses (Illustrations 4.25 and 4.26).

- Julia expects the cash register and shelving and shop fittings to last for five years before they need replacement. The level of usage of these assets will be the same in each of the next five years. She also expects that the assets will have no residual value at the end of their useful lives and that they will just be scrapped rather than being sold on.

We saw in Chapter 3 (Illustration 3.6) that the depreciation on the cash register for the three months was £50 (£1,000/5 years × 3/12 months) while the depreciation on the shelving and fittings was £600 (£12,000/5 years × 3/12 months). Depreciation charges are debited to the depreciation expense account (an increase in an expense) and credited to the accumulated depreciation account (Illustrations 4.27 and 4.28). Netting off the credit balance on the accumulated depreciation account and the debit balance on the non-current assets cost account gives the carrying amount of the non-current assets in the statement of financial position as we shall see (Illustration 4.43). The accumulated depreciation accounts are set up and used to maintain a record of depreciation charged to the statement of profit or loss in different accounting periods. The depreciation charged each year builds up on the accumulated depreciation account and increases each year as more depreciation is charged on the assets, thereby reducing the carrying amount of the non-current assets in the statement of financial position over their estimated useful lives.

Illustration 4.25 T account double entry to recognise the telephone liability and the corresponding telephone expense at 30 June 2021

Telephone

Debit (increases the expense)	£	Credit (decreases the expense)	£
2021		2021	
30 June Telephone accrual	250		

Telephone accrual

Debit (decreases the liability)	£	Credit (increases the liability)	£
2021		2021	
		30 June Telephone	250

Illustration 4.26 T account double entry to recognise the electricity liability and the corresponding electricity expense at 30 June 2021

Electricity

Debit (increases the expense)	£	Credit (decreases the expense)	£
2021		2021	
30 June Electricity accrual	200		

Electricity accrual

Debit (decreases the liability)	£	Credit (increases the liability)	£
2021		2021	
		30 June Electricity	200

Illustration 4.27 T account double entry to recognise the cash register depreciation charge and the accumulated depreciation on the cash register at 30 June 2021

Cash register depreciation charge

Debit (increases the expense)	£	Credit (decreases the expense)	£
2021		2021	
30 June Cash register accumulated depreciation	50		

Cash register accumulated depreciation

Debit (decreases the accumulated depreciation)	£	Credit (increases the accumulated depreciation)	£
2021		2021	
		30 June Cash register depreciation charge	50

Illustration 4.28 T account double entry to recognise the shelving and fittings depreciation charge and accumulated depreciation on shelving and fittings at 30 June 2021

Shelving and fittings depreciation charge

Debit (increases the expense)	£	Credit (decreases the expense)	£
2021		2021	
30 June Shelving and fittings accumulated depreciation	600		

Shelving and fittings accumulated depreciation

Debit (decreases the accumulated depreciation)	£	Credit (increases the accumulated depreciation)	£
2021		2021	
		30 June Shelving and fittings depreciation charge	600

- The cash register contained £500 in cash at 30 June 2021 representing sales receipts that had not yet been banked.

There is an unrecorded asset of £500 cash together with an unrecorded sale of the same amount. Therefore, assets rise by £500 with £500 debited to the cash account (this amount cannot be recorded in the bank account as the cash has not yet been paid into the bank. The cash is therefore maintained in a separate cash account) while income increases by £500, resulting in a credit to the sales account as shown in Illustration 4.29.

Illustration 4.29 T account double entry to recognise the cash asset and additional sales at 30 June 2021

Cash account

Debit (increases the asset)	£	Credit (decreases the asset)	£
2021		2021	
30 June Sales	500		

Sales account

Debit (decreases the income)	£	Credit (increases the income)	£
2021		2021	
		30 April Bank (Sales April)	20,000
		31 May Bank (Sales May)	25,000
		30 June Bank (Sales June)	30,000
		30 June Trade receivables	2,500
		30 June Cash	500

- On 29 June 2021, one of the tennis clubs that she trades with on credit returned goods with a sales value of £400. These goods were faulty. Julia returned these goods to her supplier: the goods had originally cost Julia £250.

There are two transactions represented in this note. Firstly, the trade receivables asset decreases by £400 as a result of the cancelled sale. Therefore, there is a credit entry to the trade receivables account to reflect this reduction in the asset (cash, an economic resource, will no longer be realised from this sale). As the sale has been cancelled, there is a reduction in the sales account, so sales are debited with £400 to reflect the decrease in the sales income as a result of this cancelled sale (Illustration 4.30).

Illustration 4.30 T account double entry to record a reduction in trade receivables and sales arising from a cancelled sale

Sales account

Debit (decreases the income)		£	Credit (increases the income)		£
2021			2021		
30 June	Trade receivables	400	30 April	Bank (Sales April)	20,000
			31 May	Bank (Sales May)	25,000
			30 June	Bank (Sales June)	30,000
			30 June	Trade receivables	2,500
			30 June	Cash	500

Trade receivables

Debit (increases the asset)		£	Credit (decreases the asset)		£
2021			2021		
30 June	Sales	2,500	June 30	Irrecoverable debts	50
			June 30	Sales	400

The second transaction in this note represents a decrease in the amounts owed by Julia to her suppliers: goods to the value of £250 have been returned to the supplier so trade payables will be debited with £250 to reflect this decrease in the liability, the amount that no longer needs to be paid. This return of goods, a cancellation of a present obligation, will also have an effect on the cost of sales. £250 less has been spent on purchases, so cost of sales will be credited with this decrease in expenditure (Illustration 4.31).

Illustration 4.31 T account double entry to record the reduction in the trade payables and cost of sales arising from the return of faulty goods to a supplier

Cost of sales (purchases account)

Debit (increases the expense)		£	Credit (decreases the expense)		£
2021			2021		
5 May	Bank (purchases April)	15,000	30 June	Inventory	10,000
5 June	Bank (purchases May)	20,000	**30 June**	**Trade payables**	**250**
30 June	Trade payables (June)	25,000			

Trade payables

Debit (decreases the liability)		£	Credit (increases the liability)		£
2021			2021		
30 June	**Cost of sales**	**250**	30 June	Cost of sales	25,000

We have now made all the entries to the T accounts required by the additional information provided by Julia. However, there are still two more entries to complete before our T accounts fully reflect all the transactions that have occurred in Julia's first three months of operation. Look back at Illustration 4.9, Julia's summary of bank receipts and payments. The rates payment of £800 on 12 May represents the rates expense for the six months April to September 2021. As our accounts are for the first three months of trading, April to June 2021, this means that three months (July, August and September 2021) have been paid in advance and represent a prepayment of rates. Therefore, £400 (£800 × 3/6) will be deducted from the rates account (a credit) and added to the rates prepayment account (debit). The credit to the rates account represents the decrease in the expense for the accounting period while the increase in the rates prepayment account represents an increase in the assets at the end of the three months. Illustration 4.32 shows the double entry required to reflect this prepayment.

Illustration 4.32 T account double entry to recognise a rates prepayment and the consequent reduction in the rates expense at 30 June 2021

Rates account

Debit (increases the expense)		£	Credit (decreases the expense)		£
2021			2021		
12 May	Bank	800	**30 June**	**Rates prepayment**	**400**

Rates prepayment account

Debit (increases the asset)		£	Credit (decreases the asset)		£
2021			2021		
30 June	**Rates**	**400**			

In the same way, the water rates of £400 were paid for the whole year April 2021 to March 2022. As we are only dealing with the first three months of trading, this means that £300 of water rates have been paid in advance (£400 × 9/12 = £300). Therefore, the prepayment is deducted from the water rates account to reflect the decrease in the expense (credit) and added to the water rates prepayment account to represent the increase in the asset at the end of June 2021 as shown in Illustration 4.33.

Illustration 4.33 T account double entry to recognise a water rates prepayment asset and the consequent reduction in the water rates expense at 30 June 2021

Water rates account

Debit (increases the expense)		£	Credit (decreases the expense)		£
2021			2021		
19 May	Bank	400	30 June	Water rates prepayment	300

Water rates prepayment account

Debit (increases the asset)		£	Credit (decreases the asset)		£
2021			2021		
30 June	Water rates	300			

MULTIPLE CHOICE QUESTIONS   Convinced you could state the double entry for any given transaction? Go to the **online workbook** and have a go at Multiple choice questions 4.2 to test your ability to identify the correct double entry required to record accounting transactions.

JULIA'S TRIAL BALANCE

We have now completed all the entries to the T accounts. Our next step is to check whether all the debits and all the credits have been included by extracting a trial balance. We saw how this worked in the case of Arthur (Illustrations 4.7 and 4.8) and the principles are exactly the same for Julia. The balance on each account is calculated by adding up the two sides of each account to determine the difference. If there are more debits than credits on the account, then there is a debit balance on that account. Whereas more credits than debits on the account means there is a credit balance on that account. Debit balances are posted to the debit side of the trial balance and credit balances are posted to the credit side.

The first account to consider is Julia's bank account, presented in Illustration 4.34.

The debit side of the bank account adds up to £105,000 while the credit side totals up to £56,200. £105,000 has been paid into the bank and only £56,200 has been taken out to acquire assets and pay expenses. There are more debits than credits on the bank account so there is a debit balance of £48,800 (£105,000 debits − £56,200 credits). This debit balance is allocated to the debit side of the trial balance in Illustration 4.41.

Illustration 4.34 (= Illustration 4.10) Julia's bank account

Bank Account

Debit (increases the asset)		£	Credit (decreases the asset)		£
2021			**2021**		
1 April	Capital account	30,000	1 April	Rent	5,000
30 April	Sales: April	20,000	1 April	Cash register	1,000
31 May	Sales: May	25,000	1 April	Shelving and fittings	12,000
30 June	Sales: June	30,000	5 May	Cost of sales	15,000
			12 May	Rates	800
			19 May	Drawings	2,000
			5 June	Cost of sales	20,000
			10 June	Water rates	400

Debit side total:
£30,000 + £20,000 +
£25,000 + £30,000 =
£105,000

Credit side total:
£5,000 + £1,000 +
£12,000 +£15,000 +
£800 + £2,000 +
£20,000 + £400 =
£56,200

Our next account is Julia's capital account (Illustration 4.35). Repeating the same approach on this account as for the bank account we can see that the capital account has £30,000 of credits and £2,000 of debits so there are more credits than debits. The £28,000 (£30,000 − £2,000) credit balance is added to the credit side of the trial balance in Illustration 4.41.

Illustration 4.35 (= Illustration 4.19) Julia's capital account

Julia's capital account

Debit (decreases the capital)		£	Credit (increases the capital)		£
2021			**2021**		
19 May	Bank (Drawings)	2,000	1 April	Bank	30,000

Illustration 4.36 (= Illustration 4.30) Julia's sales account

Sales account

Debit (decreases the income)		£	Credit (increases the income)		£
2021			**2021**		
30 June	Trade receivables	400	30 April	Bank (Sales April)	20,000
			31 May	Bank (Sales May)	25,000
			30 June	Bank (Sales June)	30,000
			30 June	Trade receivables	2,500
			30 June	Cash	500

Julia's sales account (Illustration 4.36) has £78,000 of entries on the credit side of the account and £400 of entries on the debit side of the account. There is therefore a £77,600 credit balance on the sales account (£78,000 of credits – £400 of debits) which is posted to the credit side of the trial balance (Illustration 4.41).

Illustration 4.37 (= Illustration 4.13) Julia's rent account

Rent account

Debit (increases the expense)		£	Credit (decreases the expense)		£
2021			**2021**		
1 April	Bank	5,000			

Our next three accounts (Illustrations 4.37 to 4.39) are debit accounts with only one entry in each on the debit side and no credit entries. The balances on the rent, cash register cost and shelving and fittings cost accounts show debit balances of £5,000, £1,000 and £12,000 respectively and these balances are added to the debit side of the trial balance in Illustration 4.41.

Illustration 4.38 (= Illustration 4.14) Julia's cash register cost account

Cash register cost account

Debit (increases the asset)		£	Credit (decreases the asset)		£
2021			**2021**		
1 April	Bank	1,000			

Illustration 4.39 (= Illustration 4.15) Julia's shelving and fittings cost account

Shelving and fittings cost account

Debit (increases the asset)		£	Credit (decreases the asset)		£
2021			2021		
1 April	Bank	12,000			

Julia's cost of sales account at the end of June 2021 is shown in Illustration 4.40. The cost of sales account shows debits of £60,000 (increases in the expense) and credits of £10,250 (decreases in the expense) so there is a debit (more debits than credits) balance of £49,750 to add to the debit side of the trial balance (Illustration 4.41).

Illustration 4.40 (= Illustration 4.31) Julia's cost of sales account

Cost of sales (purchases account)

Debit (increases the expense)		£	Credit (decreases the expense)		£
2021			2021		
5 May	Bank (purchases April)	15,000	30 June	Inventory	10,000
5 June	Bank (purchases May)	20,000	30 June	Trade payables	250
30 June	Trade payables (purchases June)	25,000			

NUMERICAL EXERCISES   You should now have gained an appreciation of how to determine whether there is a debit or credit balance on each T account and how to calculate that debit or credit balance for inclusion in the trial balance. Look back at our workings in Illustrations 4.20 to 4.33 to pick up the following balances to include in Julia's trial balance at 30 June 2021:

Rates (Illustration 4.32)	Electricity (Illustration 4.26)
Water rates (Illustration 4.33)	Electricity accrual (Illustration 4.26)
Inventory (Illustration 4.20)	Cash register depreciation charge (Illustration 4.27)
Trade payables (Illustration 4.31)	Cash register accumulated depreciation (Illustration 4.27)
Trade receivables (Illustration 4.30)	Shelving and fittings depreciation charge (Illustration 4.28)
Irrecoverable debts (Illustration 4.23)	Shelving and fittings accumulated depreciation (Illustration 4.28)
Wages (Illustration 4.24)	Cash (Illustration 4.29)
Wages accrual (Illustration 4.24)	Rates prepayment (Illustration 4.32)
Telephone (Illustration 4.25)	Water rates prepayment (Illustration 4.33)
Telephone accrual (Illustration 4.25)	

Have a go at constructing and balancing Julia's trial balance at 30 June 2021 before you have a look at Illustration 4.41 to see if you have all the correct answers. To help you construct the trial balance, the grid for completion is given in the **online workbook** in Numerical exercises 4.2.

Once you have completed your summary of the balances on each of Julia's accounts, you should have the trial balance shown in Illustration 4.41. The totals of the debits and credits are equal, so we can be confident that the double entry has been fully and accurately completed.

Illustration 4.41 Julia's trial balance at 30 June 2021

	Debit £	Credit £
Bank account	48,800	
Julia's capital account		28,000
Sales		77,600
Rent	5,000	
Cash register cost	1,000	
Shelving and fittings cost	12,000	
Cost of sales	49,750	
Rates	400	
Water rates	100	
Inventory	10,000	
Trade payables		24,750
Trade receivables	2,050	
Irrecoverable debts	50	
Wages	300	
Wages accrual		300
Telephone	250	
Telephone accrual		250
Electricity	200	
Electricity accrual		200
Cash register depreciation charge	50	
Cash register accumulated depreciation		50
Shelving and fittings depreciation charge	600	
Shelving and fittings accumulated depreciation		600
Cash	500	
Rates prepayment	400	
Water rates prepayment	300	
Totals (must be equal)	**131,750**	**131,750**

MULTIPLE CHOICE QUESTIONS Are you quite sure you could calculate the debit or credit balance on a T account to add to the trial balance? Go to the **online workbook** and have a go at Multiple choice questions 4.3 to test your ability to calculate the debit or credit balance on a T account.

NUMERICAL EXERCISES   Do you think you could put together a trial balance from a given set of T accounts? Go to the **online workbook** and have a go at Numerical exercises 4.3 to test your ability at drawing up a trial balance.

We can now use the figures from the trial balance to produce Julia's statement of profit or loss for the three months to 30 June 2021 together with a statement of financial position at that date. These financial statements are presented in Illustrations 4.42 and 4.43.

Illustration 4.42 Julia's statement of profit or loss for the three months ended 30 June 2021

	£	£
Sales		77,600
Cost of sales		49,750
Gross profit (sales – cost of sales)		**27,850**
Expenses		
Rent	5,000	
Rates	400	
Water rates	100	
Irrecoverable debt	50	
Wages	300	
Telephone	250	
Electricity	200	
Cash register depreciation	50	
Shelving and fittings depreciation	600	
Total expenses		6,950
Net profit for the three months		**20,900**

Compare Julia's statement of profit or loss and statement of financial position in Illustrations 4.42 and 4.43 with her statement of profit or loss and statement of financial position in Illustrations 3.6 and 3.7. The results are exactly the same. This is completely in line with what we would expect as the financial statements have been produced from exactly the same set of cash receipts and payments and exactly the same set of additional information. However, because all of the entries have been made in the T accounts, the figures can be transferred directly into the statement of profit or loss and the statement of financial position without any need for the additional calculations, narrative and notes that were presented in Illustrations 3.6 and 3.7.

Illustration 4.43 Julia's statement of financial position at 30 June 2021

	£
Non-current assets	
Cash register (£1,000 cost – £50 accumulated depreciation)	950
Shelves and shop fittings (£12,000 – £600 accumulated depreciation)	11,400
	12,350
Current assets	
Inventory	10,000
Trade receivables	2,050
Rates prepayment	400
Water rates prepayment	300
Bank balance	48,800
Cash	500
	62,050
Total assets (£12,350 non-current assets + £62,050 current assets)	**74,400**
Current liabilities	
Trade payables	24,750
Wages accrual	300
Telephone accrual	250
Electricity accrual	200
Total liabilities	**25,500**
Net assets (total assets (£74,400) – total liabilities (£25,500))	**48,900**
Equity (capital account)	
Capital introduced by Julia	30,000
Drawings (cash paid from the business for personal expenses)	(2,000)
Net profit for the three months	20,900
Capital account at 30 June 2021	**48,900**

CLOSING OFF THE T ACCOUNTS AT THE END OF AN ACCOUNTING PERIOD

At the end of each accounting period, each T account is closed off. Where the differences on the T accounts represent assets, liabilities or capital, these differences are carried forward to the next accounting period. Where the differences on the T accounts represent income or expenses, then these differences are transferred to the statement of profit or loss for the accounting period. Income and expenses balances are therefore *not* carried forward to future accounting periods. The difference between the income and the expenses for each accounting period is added to the owner's capital balance as the profit for the year (or deducted from the owner's capital if a loss has been made). This makes sense since the accounting equation states that assets = liabilities +

capital + income − expenses. Income − expenses = profit or loss so the net difference between income and expenses is added to the capital balance in the statement of financial position and carried forward to the next accounting period. Let's see how Julia's accounts are closed off at the end of June 2021.

Our first account is the bank account (Illustration 4.44). The entries on the debit side of the bank account add up to £105,000 while the credit side totals up to £56,200. As we have already seen (this chapter, Illustration 4.34), there are more debits than credits on the bank account so there is a debit balance of £48,800 (£105,000 debits − £56,200 credits). Is the bank account an asset or an expense? Cash is an asset so the debit balance on the bank account is carried forward to the next accounting period. The bank account is closed off as shown in red in Illustration 4.44.

Illustration 4.44 Julia's bank account closed off at 30 June 2021 and the carried forward balance brought forward at the start of the new accounting period

Bank Account					
Debit (increases the asset)		**£**	**Credit (decreases the asset)**		**£**
2021			**2021**		
1 April	Capital account	30,000	1 April	Rent	5,000
30 April	Sales: April	20,000	1 April	Cash register	1,000
31 May	Sales: May	25,000	1 April	Shelving and fittings	12,000
30 June	Sales: June	30,000	5 May	Cost of sales	15,000
			12 May	Rates	800
			19 May	Drawings	2,000
			5 June	Cost of sales	20,000
			10 June	Water rates	400
			30 June	**Balance c/f**	**48,800**
		105,000			**105,000**
1 July	**Balance b/f**	**48,800**			

Points to note about closing off T accounts:

- The accounts are balanced by adding in the debit or credit balance to the side of the account that is lower than the other. In Illustration 4.44 the credit side of the bank account is lower so £48,800 is added to the credit side of the account so that both sides total up to £105,000.
- The totals on both the debit and credit sides of each T account must be equal at the end of each accounting period.
- As both sides now equal £105,000, the account is said to balance.
- The abbreviation c/f means carried forward, a balance transferred to the next accounting period.
- The abbreviation b/f means brought forward, a balance transferred from the end of the previous accounting period.

- The brought forward balance appears in the bank account on the opposite side to the balance carried forward. This is logical: the bank balance is an asset so it must appear on the debit side of the bank account at the start of the next accounting period. This balance is an asset because more cash has been paid into the bank than has been paid out. Assets, as we have seen, are debits.

- Asset, liability and capital accounts will have balances carried forward at the end of the accounting period. These balances are then brought forward on the first day of the next accounting period on either the debit side (assets) or the credit side (liabilities and capital) ready for the next set of entries to be made to the accounts in the next accounting period.

Think about these points as we work our way through the remaining accounts.

Our next account is Julia's capital account. This account is balanced off as shown in Illustration 4.45.

Illustration 4.45 Julia's capital account closed off at 30 June 2021 and the carried forward balance brought forward at the start of the next accounting period

Julia's capital account					
Debit (decreases the capital)		**£**	**Credit (increases the capital)**		**£**
2021			**2021**		
19 May	Bank (Drawings)	2,000	1 April	Bank	30,000
30 June	Balance c/f	48,900	30 June	Profit for 3 months	20,900
		50,900			50,900
			1 July	Balance b/f	48,900

Before we can close off Julia's capital account, we must add in the profit for the three months. As we saw in Illustrations 4.42 and 4.43 this profit was £20,900. £20,900 is debited to the statement of profit or loss and credited to Julia's capital account as the business now owes Julia an additional £20,900. Julia's capital account has £50,900 of credits and £2,000 of debits. The credits are greater than the debits, so there is a £48,900 (£50,900 − £2,000) credit balance on Julia's capital account. This is posted to the debit side of the account so that both sides total up to £50,900. The brought forward balance appears on the credit side of the account. £48,900 is owed to Julia in her capacity as owner of the business so you would expect this to be a credit balance as it is the capital owed to the owner.

Our next account is the sales account. This account is balanced off as shown in Illustration 4.46.

The sales account has £78,000 of credits and £400 of debits so there is a £77,600 (£78,000 − £400) credit balance on this account. All of this income has been earned in the three-month accounting period so the £77,600 balance on the sales account is recognised as income for the three-month accounting period and transferred to the statement of profit or loss. There is thus no balance carried forward or brought forward on the sales account.

Illustration 4.46 Julia's sales account closed off at 30 June 2021 and the balance transferred to the statement of profit or loss for the period

Sales account

Debit (decreases the income)		£	Credit (increases the income)		£
2021			2021		
30 June	Trade receivables	400	30 April	Bank	20,000
30 June	Statement of profit or loss	77,600	31 May	Bank	25,000
			30 June	Bank	30,000
			30 June	Trade receivables	2,500
			30 June	Cash	500
		78,000			**78,000**

NUMERICAL EXERCISES   At this point, you might like to have a go at balancing off all the remaining T accounts before you check your answers against the T accounts presented in Illustrations 4.47 to 4.69. To help you in making this attempt, the **online workbook** Numerical exercises 4.4 presents the T accounts as they stand at 30 June 2021 after posting all the transactions up to that date but before the accounts are closed off and the balances either carried forward or transferred to the statement of profit or loss.

Julia's rent account is balanced and closed off as shown in Illustration 4.47.

Illustration 4.47 Julia's rent account closed off at 30 June 2021 and the balance transferred to the statement of profit or loss for the period

Rent account

Debit (increases the expense)		£	Credit (decreases the expense)		£
2021			2021		
1 April	Bank	5,000	30 June	Statement of profit or loss	5,000
		5,000			**5,000**

There is a debit balance on the account of £5,000, £5,000 of debits – £0 credits. The rent paid covered the three months of April, May and June 2021 so all the economic benefits of this payment have been consumed during the three-month period. This expense is transferred to the statement of profit or loss to be matched against the income generated from this expenditure to determine the net profit or loss for the accounting period.

Our next two accounts are the cash register cost and the shelving and fittings cost accounts, shown in Illustrations 4.48 and 4.49.

Illustration 4.48 Julia's cash register cost account closed off at 30 June 2021 and the carried forward balance brought forward at the start of the new accounting period

Cash register cost account					
Debit (increases the asset)		**£**	**Credit (decreases the asset)**		**£**
2021			**2021**		
1 April	Bank	1,000	30 June	Balance c/f	1,000
		1,000			1,000
1 July	Balance b/f	1,000			

Illustration 4.49 Julia's shelving and fittings cost account closed off at 30 June 2021 and the carried forward balance brought forward at the start of the new accounting period

Shelving and fittings cost account					
Debit (increases the asset)		**£**	**Credit (decreases the asset)**		**£**
2021			**2021**		
1 April	Bank	12,000	30 June	Balance c/f	12,000
		12,000			12,000
1 July	Balance b/f	12,000			

The cash register and shelving and fittings have a useful life of five years. Therefore, these are non-current assets which have the potential to produce economic benefits for more than one year. Both accounts show debit balances with debits of £1,000 and £12,000 and zero credits. These represent debit balances which are carried forward at the period end (30 June) and brought forward on the first day of the next accounting period 1 July.

The next three T accounts (Illustrations 4.50, 4,51 and 4.52) are debit accounts with more debits than credits. Cost of sales, rates and water rates are expense accounts whose balances are transferred to the statement of profit or loss. In this way the revenue generated is matched with the costs incurred to produce that revenue.

Illustration 4.50 Julia's cost of sales account closed off at 30 June 2021 and the balance transferred to the statement of profit or loss for the period

Cost of sales (opening inventory + purchases – closing inventory)					
Debit (increases the expense)		**£**	**Credit (decreases the expense)**		**£**
2021			**2021**		
5 May	Bank	15,000	30 June	Inventory	10,000
5 June	Bank	20,000	30 June	Trade payables	250
30 June	Trade payables	25,000	30 June	Statement of profit or loss	49,750
		60,000			60,000

Illustration 4.51 Julia's rates account closed off at 30 June 2021 and the balance transferred to the statement of profit or loss for the period

Rates account				
Debit (increases the expense)	**£**	**Credit (decreases the expense)**		**£**
2021		**2021**		
12 May Bank	800	30 June	Rates prepayment	400
		30 June	Statement of profit or loss	400
	800			800

Illustration 4.52 Julia's water rates account closed off at 30 June 2021 and the balance transferred to the statement of profit or loss for the period

Water rates account				
Debit (increases the expense)	**£**	**Credit (decreases the expense)**		**£**
2021		**2021**		
19 May Bank	400	30 June	Water rates prepayment	300
		30 June	Statement of profit or loss	100
	400			400

Inventory at the end of the three months is an asset which is carried forward to the next accounting period to match against the revenue that Julia expects to generate from the sale of that inventory. The entries required to close off the inventory account are shown in Illustration 4.53.

Illustration 4.53 Julia's inventory account closed off at 30 June 2021 and the carried forward balance brought forward at the start of the new accounting period

Inventory				
Debit (increases the asset)	**£**	**Credit (decreases the asset)**		**£**
2021		**2021**		
30 June Cost of sales	10,000	30 June	Balance c/f	10,000
	10,000			10,000
1 July Balance b/f	10,000			

The balance on the trade payables account is a credit balance as there are more credits than debits on this account. Trade payables are a liability, a present obligation for Julia which has arisen from trading with her suppliers on credit. This balance is carried forward to the next accounting period as shown in Illustration 4.54.

4

Illustration 4.54 Julia's trade payables account closed off at 30 June 2021 and the carried forward balance brought forward at the start of the new accounting period

Trade payables

Debit (decreases the liability)		£	Credit (increases the liability)		£
2021			2021		
30 June	Cost of sales	250	30 June	Cost of sales	25,000
30 June	Balance c/f	24,750			
		25,000			25,000
			1 July	Balance b/f	24,750

Trade receivables are the opposite of trade payables, money owed to the business rather than money owed by the business. The debit side of the account totals up to £2,500 while the credit side reflects reductions in the asset of £450 as a result of irrecoverable debts and sales returns. Therefore, the debit balance on the account is £2,050 (£2,500 − £50 − £400) which is carried forward to the next accounting period as an asset to be realised in the following months (Illustration 4.55) when customers pay what is owed.

Illustration 4.55 Julia's trade receivables account closed off at 30 June 2021 and the carried forward balance brought forward at the start of the new accounting period

Trade receivables

Debit (increases the asset)		£	Credit (decreases the asset)		£
2021			2021		
30 June	Sales	2,500	June 30	Irrecoverable debts	50
			June 30	Sales	400
			June 30	Balance c/f	2,050
		2,500			2,500
1 July	Balance b/f	2,050			

Julia's irrecoverable debts account (Illustration 4.56) is a debit account with more debits than credits. Irrecoverable debts are an expense account whose balances are transferred to the statement of profit or loss so that revenue generated is matched with the costs incurred to produce that revenue.

Illustration 4.56 Julia's irrecoverable debts account closed off at 30 June 2021 and the balance transferred to the statement of profit or loss for the period

Irrecoverable debts

Debit (increases the expense)		£	Credit (decreases the expense)		£
2021			2021		
30 June	Trade receivables	50	30 June	Statement of profit or loss	50
		50			50

Illustrations 4.57 to 4.62 show three expense accounts (Illustrations 4.57, 4.59 and 4.61) with debit balances that are transferred to the statement of profit or loss for the three months to match against the revenue generated. There are also three liability accounts for accrued expenses, costs incurred but not yet paid, which show more credits than debits. The balances on these three liability accounts (Illustrations 4.58, 4.60 and 4.62) are carried forward to match against the cash payments that will be made in the next accounting period to extinguish these liabilities.

Illustration 4.57 Julia's wages account closed off at 30 June 2021 and the balance transferred to the statement of profit or loss for the period

Wages

Debit (increases the expense)	£	Credit (decreases the expense)	£
2021		2021	
30 June Wages accrual	300	30 June Statement of profit or loss	300
	300		300

Illustration 4.58 Julia's wages accrual account closed off at 30 June 2021 and the carried forward balance brought forward at the start of the new accounting period

Wages accrual

Debit (decreases the liability)	£	Credit (increases the liability)	£
2021		2021	
30 June Balance c/f	300	30 June Wages	300
	300		300
		1 July Balance b/f	300

Illustration 4.59 Julia's telephone account closed off at 30 June 2021 and the balance transferred to the statement of profit or loss for the period

Telephone

Debit (increases the expense)	£	Credit (decreases the expense)	£
2021		2021	
30 June Telephone accrual	250	30 June Statement of profit or loss	250
	250		250

Illustration 4.60 Julia's telephone accrual account closed off at 30 June 2021 and the carried forward balance brought forward at the start of the new accounting period

Telephone accrual					
Debit (decreases the liability)		**£**	**Credit (increases the liability)**		**£**
2021			**2021**		
30 June	Balance c/f	250	30 June	Telephone	250
		250			250
			1 July	**Balance b/f**	**250**

Illustration 4.61 Julia's electricity account closed off at 30 June 2021 and the balance transferred to the statement of profit or loss for the period

Electricity					
Debit (increases the expense)		**£**	**Credit (decreases the expense)**		**£**
2021			**2021**		
30 June	Electricity accrual	200	**30 June**	**Statement of profit or loss**	**200**
		200			200

Illustration 4.62 Julia's electricity accrual account closed off at 30 June 2021 and the carried forward balance brought forward at the start of the new accounting period

Electricity accrual					
Debit (decreases the liability)		**£**	**Credit (increases the liability)**		**£**
2021			**2021**		
30 June	Balance c/f	200	30 June	Electricity	200
		200			200
			1 July	**Balance b/f**	**200**

Illustrations 4.63 to 4.66 present the two depreciation charge and the two accumulated depreciation accounts. Illustrations 4.63 and 4.65 show debit balances as there are more debits than credits on these accounts so these expense balances are charged to the statement of profit or loss, matching this expenditure with sales to determine the profit for the three months. Illustrations 4.64 and 4.66 present accounts with credit balances, more credits than debits, and these accumulated depreciation balances are carried forward to the next accounting period to set off against the cost of the associated non-current assets.

Illustration 4.63 Julia's cash register depreciation charge account closed off at 30 June 2021 and the balance transferred to the statement of profit or loss for the period

Cash register depreciation charge

Debit (increases the expense)	£	Credit (decreases the expense)	£
2021		2021	
30 June Cash register accumulated depreciation	50	30 June Statement of profit or loss	50
	50		50

Illustration 4.64 Julia's cash register accumulated depreciation account closed off at 30 June 2021 and the carried forward balance brought forward at the start of the new accounting period

Cash register accumulated depreciation

Debit (decreases the accumulated depreciation)	£	Credit (increases the accumulated depreciation)	£
2021		2021	
30 June Balance c/f	50	30 June Cash register depreciation charge	50
	50		50
		1 July Balance b/f	50

Illustration 4.65 Julia's shelving and fittings depreciation charge account closed off at 30 June 2021 and the balance transferred to the statement of profit or loss for the period

Shelving and fittings depreciation charge

Debit (increases the expense)	£	Credit (decreases the expense)	£
2021		2021	
30 June Shelving and fittings accumulated depreciation	600	30 June Statement of profit or loss	600
	600		600

Illustration 4.66 Julia's shelving and fittings accumulated depreciation account closed off at 30 June 2021 and the carried forward balance brought forward at the start of the new accounting period

Shelving and fittings accumulate depreciation

Debit (decreases the accumulated depreciation)	£	Credit (increases the accumulated depreciation)	£
2021		2021	
30 June Balance c/f	600	30 June Shelving and fittings depreciation charge	600
	600		600
		1 July Balance b/f	600

There is a debit balance on the cash account (Illustration 4.67). Cash is an asset which is carried forward to the next accounting period.

Illustration 4.67 Julia's cash account closed off at 30 June 2021 and the carried forward balance brought forward at the start of the new accounting period

	Cash account		
Debit (increases the asset)	**£**	**Credit (decreases the asset)**	**£**
2021		**2021**	
30 June Sales	500	**30 June** Balance c/f	500
	500		500
1 July Balance b/f	500		

Illustrations 4.68 and 4.69 are prepayment accounts. There are debit balances on these accounts, more debits than credits. Prepayments are expenditure paid in advance and are treated as assets at the end of each accounting period so these balances are carried forward at 30 June 2021.

Illustration 4.68 Julia's rates prepayment account closed off at 30 June 2021 and the carried forward balance brought forward at the start of the new accounting period

	Rates prepayment account		
Debit (increases the asset)	**£**	**Credit (decreases the asset)**	**£**
2021		**2021**	
30 June Rates	400	**30 June** Balance c/f	400
	400		400
1 July Balance b/f	400		

Illustration 4.69 Julia's water rates prepayment account closed off at 30 June 2021 and the carried forward balance brought forward at the start of the new accounting period

	Water rates prepayment account		
Debit (increases the asset)	**£**	**Credit (decreases the asset)**	**£**
2021		**2021**	
30 June Water rates	300	**30 June** Balance c/f	300
	300		300
1 July Balance b/f	300		

To enable you as a business professional to understand:

- How the asset, liability, capital, income and expense balances are treated at the end of each accounting period
- How the opening balances for each new accounting period arise

All our accounts have now been closed off, the income and expenditure balances transferred to the statement of profit or loss and the asset, liability and capital balances carried forward to the next accounting period. Extracting a trial balance at 1 July will enable Julia to make sure that her accounting records are still in balance and that no errors have crept into her books of account during the closing off process.

NUMERICAL EXERCISES   Make sure that the opening balances on Julia's accounts do balance by attempting Numerical exercises 4.5 in the **online workbook**.

APPENDIX: SEPARATE T ACCOUNTS FOR INVENTORY AND PURCHASES

In this chapter, we have posted transactions relating to inventory and to purchases to the same cost of sales account. This has enabled us to produce one single cost of sales account, adding opening inventory to purchases and deducting closing inventory from the total of opening inventory + purchases. However, two separate T accounts can be set up, one for inventory and one for purchases, to record the same transactions.

Purchases are recorded in the purchases T account as normal by debiting purchase invoices or cash payments to the purchases account and crediting goods returned to suppliers to the same account.

The double entry for inventory follows three steps.

Step 1 opening inventory at the start of the accounting period

Opening inventory is the figure brought forward from the end of the previous accounting period. This is recorded on the debit side of the inventory account to reflect the inventory asset at the start of the new financial period. This opening inventory is shown in Illustration 4.70 (note that the figure of £35,000 is used purely as an example and does not refer to any previous example in this chapter).

Illustration 4.70 The inventory T account showing inventory at the start of the accounting period

		Inventory		
Debit (increases the asset)	**£**	**Credit (decreases the asset)**		**£**
2021		2021		
1 Jan Balance b/f	35,000			

Step 2 opening inventory at the end of the accounting period

As we saw in Chapter 3 (Statement of profit or loss by nature), cost of sales = opening inventory + purchases – closing inventory. The purchases figure is the purchases – purchase returns figure on the purchases T account. At the end of the accounting period, opening inventory is no longer an asset and so is charged to cost of sales at the end of the accounting period by debiting the statement of profit or loss and crediting inventory with the opening inventory figure as shown in Illustration 4.71.

Illustration 4.71 The inventory T account showing opening inventory charged to the statement of profit or loss at the end of the accounting period

		Inventory		
Debit (increases the asset)	**£**	**Credit (decreases the asset)**		**£**
2021		2021		
1 Jan Balance b/f	35,000	31 Dec Statement of profit or loss		35,000

Step 3 closing inventory at the end of the accounting period

Closing inventory is a credit in the statement of profit or loss (a deduction from cost of sales) and a debit in the statement of financial position (an asset). The double entry required to record closing inventory is:

Debit inventory account, credit statement of profit or loss to record the removal of closing inventory from cost of sales for the accounting period.

This leaves a debit balance on the inventory account which is the closing inventory asset carried forward at the end of the accounting period.

The double entry for these transactions is shown in the inventory account in Illustration 4.72.

Illustration 4.72 The inventory T account showing the recording of closing inventory at the end of the accounting period

Inventory

Debit (increases the asset)		£	Credit (decreases the asset)		£
2021			**2021**		
1 Jan	Balance b/f	35,000	31 Dec	Statement of profit or loss	35,000
31 Dec	Statement of profit or loss	42,500	31 Dec	Balance c/f	42,500
		77,500			77,500
2022			**2022**		
1 Jan	Balance b/f	42,500			

Using a cost of sales T account or separate purchases and inventory T accounts will produce exactly the same cost of sales figure in the statement of profit or loss and inventory asset in the statement of financial position.

CHAPTER SUMMARY

You should now have learnt that:

- Accounting transactions and events are recorded in T accounts using the double-entry system
- The double-entry system uses debits and credits in the posting of transactions and events
- For every debit entry there must be an opposite credit entry of equal value to ensure that the accounts remain in balance
- Increases in assets and expenses are entered on the debit side of the T account
- Decreases in assets and expenses are entered on the credit side of the T account
- Increases in liabilities, income and capital are entered on the credit side of the T account
- Decreases in liabilities, income and capital are entered on the debit side of the T account
- Where the monetary value of the debits is greater than the monetary value of the credits on a T account, then there is a debit balance on that account
- Where the monetary value of the credits is greater than the monetary value of the debits on a T account, then there is a credit balance on that account
- Debit and credit balances on an entity's accounts are summarised in the trial balance at the end of each accounting period
- The sum of all the debit balances and the sum of all the credit balances on the trial balance will be equal if the double entry has been completed in full
- T accounts are closed off and balanced at the end of each accounting period
- At the end of each accounting period, income and expense account balances are transferred to the statement of profit or loss and are not carried forward to future accounting periods
- At the end of each accounting period, assets, liabilities and capital account balances are carried forward to the next accounting period

END-OF-CHAPTER QUESTIONS

4

 Attempt the questions in the following sections and then look at the solutions which can be found in the **online workbook** to see whether there are areas that you need to revisit.

❯ RECALL AND REVIEW

❯ Question 4.1

How does each of the following transactions affect the accounting equation? In addition, state the double entry to record each of these transactions:

(a) Paid power bills from the business bank account.

(b) The business owner introduces a building she owns into the business.

(c) Bought a van on credit.

(d) Purchase of inventory with cash.

(e) Received cash from a customer to pay for a credit sale made last month.

(f) Bank transfer to a supplier's bank account to pay for inventory purchased 10 days ago.

❯ Question 4.2

The following information is extracted from the financial statements of a company:

Expenses	£12,800
Current liabilities	£20,000
Income	£34,700
Capital	£65,300
Non-current liabilities	£34,000
Current assets	£41,200

Using the accounting equation, calculate non-current assets.

≫ DEVELOP YOUR UNDERSTANDING

≫ Question 4.3

State the double entry for the following transactions made by the TC Company Limited during September:

1. Cash sales of £35,225.

2. Credit sales of £125,750.

3. Received goods from suppliers on credit. The goods received had a cost of £62,894.

4. Insurance premium of £6,000 paid from the bank account.

5. Cash received from credit customers of £140,362.

6. Cash paid to suppliers for purchases made on credit of £55,574.

7. New plant and machinery purchased with a cash payment from the bank. The new plant and machinery cost £150,000.

8. Taxation paid of £27,450.

9. Loan instalment paid of £5,500.

10. Bank interest received of £250.

You are not required to produce T accounts to reflect the above transactions. Your answer should state which account will be debited and which account will be credited with the stated amounts.

≫ Question 4.4

Primrose is a market trader selling fabrics. She rents her market stall on a monthly basis from the local council. At 1 September 2021 she has inventory at a cost of £3,540. Her only other assets are cash in hand of £200 and a business bank account with a balance of £6,825. At 1 September 2021, Primrose owed her fabric suppliers £4,690. Her transactions during September were as follows:

1. She made total sales of £25,642. All sales made were for cash.

2. She paid £23,057 of her cash receipts into her bank account.

3. Her fabric suppliers delivered fabrics at a cost to Primrose of £12,300.

4. She paid her fabric suppliers a total of £13,460 during the month. All payments to the fabric suppliers were made from the business bank account.

5. She paid rent on her market stall to the local council of £250 in cash.

6. She made cash refunds to her customers of £1,985.

7. Her inventory at 30 September 2021 was counted up. The cost of this inventory at the end of the month was £2,695.

8. During the month, Primrose withdrew £1,200 from the business bank account and £300 from cash to pay her personal expenses.

Required

1. Calculate Primrose's capital account balance at 1 September 2021.

2. Enter the opening balances at 1 September 2021 into T accounts.

3. Enter the transactions for the month of September 2021 into the T accounts. You will need T accounts for cash, bank account, trade payables, cost of sales, capital account, sales, rent and inventory.

4. Extract a trial balance from the T accounts you have prepared.

5. Draw up Primrose's statement of profit or loss and statement of financial position at 30 September 2021 from the trial balance you have extracted.

6. Enter the profit for the month into Primrose's capital account and close off the T accounts at 30 September 2021.

7. Bring forward the balances on the T accounts at 1 October 2021.

» Question 4.5

Presented below are the first parts of the double entry to record a transaction. Complete the double entry in each situation. Note: there may be more than one possible entry to complete the double entry in each case.

1. Debit cash

2. Debit trade receivables

3. Debit non-current assets

4. Debit capital

5. Debit trade payables

6. Debit sales

7. Credit cash

8. Credit trade receivables

9. Credit trade payables

10. Credit capital

11. Credit sales

» Question 4.6

State the double entry required to record each of the transactions listed below:

(a) A business owner pays her own money into the business bank account.

(b) Sales made on credit terms to a customer.

(c) Income tax paid from the bank account.

(d) The introduction to the market of a new product by a company.

(e) Equipment bought on credit terms.

(f) Cash paid to buy goods from a supplier.

(g) Goods withdrawn by the owner of a business from the warehouse for personal use.

(h) Money in the till is paid into the business bank account.

(i)   Money received from a customer for goods sold last month.

(j)   Bank loan taken out paid into the business bank account.

(k)   Cash paid to a supplier for a credit purchase made two weeks ago.

» Question 4.7

The table below presents the account balances at 1 April 2021 together with a list of transactions made during April 2021. Complete the table to show the changes in each balance as a result of the transactions undertaken and calculate the balances at 30 April. Check that the accounting equation still holds true after completing each transaction line. The first transaction has been completed to show you how to complete the table.

	Bank £000	Receivables £000	Building £000	Expenses £000	Payables £000	Capital £000	Revenue £000
01/04: balances b/f	100	20	200	30	50	220	80
03/04: provided services for £25,000 on credit		+25					+25
05/04: paid £30,000 wages							
08/04: £40,000 cash received for services provided							
15/04: received £25,000 from a credit customer							
20/04: £80,000 paid into the business bank account by the owner							
25/04: paid gas and electricity bills of £2,000							
30/04: £30,000 cash received for services supplied							
30/04: balances c/f							

»»TAKE IT FURTHER

»» Question 4.8

Laura was made redundant on 1 July 2020 and received £50,000 in redundancy pay. With this money, she opened a business bank account on 1 September 2020 and set up a small building company undertaking household and small industrial construction work. She started trading on 1 September 2020 and she has now reached her year end of 31 August 2021. She has produced a summary of payments and receipts into her business bank account along with additional information that she thinks will be useful in preparing her statement of profit or loss and statement of financial position for her first year of trading. The details she has presented you with are as follows:

1. Laura's customers usually pay cash at the end of each job. Cash received and banked from these sales totals up to £112,000. However, her small industrial clients keep her waiting for payment. Her invoices to her small industrial customers add up to a total of £48,000 for work done during the year, but she has only collected £36,000 of this amount by 31 August 2021.

2. Laura buys her construction materials on credit from a local wholesaler. Her total spending on materials this year has been £45,000 of which she had paid £38,000 by 31 August 2021. Her annual trading summary from the wholesaler received on 5 September 2021 tells her that she has qualified for a quantity purchase discount of £1,000 on all her purchases up to 31 August 2021. She will deduct this amount from her next payment to her supplier in September 2021.

3. Since 31 August 2021, a small industrial customer has gone into liquidation, owing Laura £2,500. The liquidator has told Laura that no payment towards this trade receivable will be made. The liquidation of her customer has made Laura think about the solvency of her other trade receivables. She decides that she would like to create an allowance for receivables of 10% of her remaining trade receivables at 31 August 2021.

4. Laura bought a second-hand van for £6,000 on 1 September 2020. She reckons this van will last for three years before she has to replace it. She anticipates that the trade-in value of this van will be £600 in three years' time. Laura expects to use the van to travel 5,000 miles each year on journeys for business purposes.

5. Van running expenses and insurance for the year amounted to £4,000. All of these expenses were paid from the business bank account. No van running expenses were outstanding or prepaid at 31 August 2021.

6. On 1 September 2020, Laura paid £5,000 for various items of second hand construction equipment. These assets should last for four years and fetch £60 as scrap when they are replaced. Laura expects to make the same use of these assets in each of the four years of their expected useful life.

7. Two part-time helpers were employed for 13 weeks during June, July and August 2021. By 31 August 2021, Laura had paid both these helpers 12 weeks of their wages amounting to £9,600 out of the business bank account.

8. Comprehensive business insurance was taken out and paid for on 1 September 2020. As a new business customer, Laura took advantage of the insurance company's discount scheme to pay £1,800 for 18 months' cover.

9. Laura counted up and valued her inventory of building materials at 31 August 2021. She valued all these items at a cost to the business of £4,500.

10. Bank charges of £400 were deducted from Laura's bank account during the year. The bank manager has told her that accrued charges to the end of August 2021 amount to an additional £75. These accrued charges will be deducted from her business bank account during September 2021.

11. Laura's bank account was overdrawn in the early part of her first year of trading. The bank charged her £200 interest on this overdraft. Since then, her bank account has shown a debit balance and she has earned £250 in interest up to 31 July 2021. The bank manager has told her that in August 2021 her interest receivable is a further £50 and this will be added to her account in October 2021.

12. Laura withdrew £2,500 each month from the bank for her personal expenses. As she had so much cash in the bank in August 2021, on 31 August 2021 she used £90,000 from her business bank account to repay half the mortgage on her house.

Required

1. Open as many T accounts as you require and post all the above transactions into the T accounts you have opened.

2. Extract a trial balance from the T accounts you have produced.

3. Produce Laura's statement of profit or loss and statement of financial position for the year ended 31 August 2021.

4. Compare your statement of profit or loss and statement of financial position with Answer 3.10 to make sure that you have the same results.

5. Add the profit for the year to Laura's capital account and close off the T accounts for the year ended 31 August 2021. Income and expenditure balances are written off to the statement of profit or loss for the year whereas asset, liability and capital balances are carried forward at 31 August 2021. Bring forward the asset, liability and capital account balances at 1 September 2021.

6. Extract a trial balance at 1 September 2021 to ensure that Laura's accounts are in balance at the start of the new financial year.

⟩⟩⟩ Question 4.9

The following balances have been extracted from the books of Logan Limited as at 30 September 2021.

	£000s		£000s
Capital	2,200	Trade receivables	400
Retained profit	250	Insurance	200
Property, plant and equipment at cost	3,000	General and selling expenses	1,100
Loan	300	Loan interest	15
Property, plant and equipment: accumulated depreciation	600	Sales	4,400
Purchases	2,545	Inventory at 1 October 2020	600
Trade and other payables	110		

Additional information

1.   Inventory at 30 September 2021 is valued at £450,000.

2.   The insurance payment on 1 July was for 12 months' cover.

3.   Selling and general expenses of £40,000 remain unpaid at the year end.

4.   Property, plant and equipment are depreciated using the straight line method. The directors are assuming that property, plant and equipment will have no residual value and that the assets will have a useful life of 10 years. No depreciation has yet been charged on property, plant and equipment for the year to 30 September 2021.

5.   The company is liable to a charge for income tax of £60,000 on the profits for the year.

6.   Transfer the £2,545,000 balance on the purchases account and the £600,000 opening inventory on the inventory account to the cost of sales account.

Required

(a)   Enter the balances into T accounts.

(b)   Post the year-end adjustments to the relevant accounts.

(c)   Extract a trial balance at 30 September 2021.

(d)   Draw up Logan Limited's statement of profit or loss for the year ended 30 September 2021 and a statement of financial position at that date.

(e)   Close off the T accounts at 30 September 2021.

(f)   Bring forward the balances on the T accounts at 1 October 2021.

≫≫ Question 4.10

The following balances have been extracted from the accounting records of Emma Limited at 30 June 2021:

	£
Bank	6,000
Trade receivables	2,000
Inventory	5,200
Machinery cost	20,000
Trade and other payables	2,000
Loan	15,800
Capital	15,400

The following transactions were undertaken by Emma Limited during July and August 2021:

1.   £23,000 of cash sales were made.

2.   £2,400 of credit sales were made. £1,000 of the cash due from these credit sales had been received by the end of August.

3. £9,800 of cash was paid for purchases.

4. £3,300 of goods were purchased on credit. Of this amount, £2,300 had been paid by the end of August.

5. Rent is £1,600 per month. This amount was paid in full in July and August.

6. A power and heating bill for July was received. This bill, totalling up to £600, was paid in August.

7. £620 was paid in each month to staff for their wages and salaries.

8. Interest was paid on the bank loan. The interest rate on the loan is 6% per annum.

9. The cost of inventory at the end of August was £2,800.

10. Machinery is depreciated on the straight line basis. Machinery is estimated to have a 10-year useful life and a residual value of £2,000.

Required

(a) Enter the balances at 30 June 2021 into the T accounts.

(b) Record all the transactions made in July and August in the T accounts.

(c) Extract a trial balance at 31 August 2021 from the T accounts.

(d) Draw up Emma Limited's statement of profit or loss for July and August 2021 and statement of financial position at the end of August 2021.

5

DOUBLE-ENTRY BOOKKEEPING 2: BOOKS OF PRIME ENTRY, ACCOUNTING SYSTEMS AND OTHER DOUBLE-ENTRY APPLICATIONS

LEARNING OUTCOMES

Once you have read this chapter and worked through the questions and examples in both this chapter and the online workbook, you should be able to:

- Outline the transactions generated by the sales, purchases and payroll systems

- Describe the functions of and the details presented in the books of prime entry, the sales day book, the sales returns day book, the purchase day book, the purchase returns day book, the payroll, the cash book and the petty cash book

- Make the double entry from the books of prime entry into the T accounts in the nominal ledger

- Understand how the sales ledger records sales transactions with and cash received from individual credit customers

- Understand how the purchase ledger records purchases of goods and services from and payments to individual suppliers providing goods on credit

- Appreciate the effect of value added tax and payroll taxes on transactions undertaken by businesses and other organisations

- Understand how the trade receivables and trade payables control accounts help to ensure that trade receivables and trade payables figures are correct at the end of each financial period
- Undertake bank reconciliations to prove that the bank account and the cash book are in agreement
- Make the double entry required to record the disposal of non-current assets
- Use the logic of the double-entry system to reconstruct T accounts to find missing figures required to produce the financial statements
- Use journal entries to make corrections in the nominal ledger when transactions are recorded incorrectly or are omitted completely from the accounting records

INTRODUCTION

In the last chapter, we looked at the way in which double-entry bookkeeping works by recording Julia's accounting transactions in the relevant T accounts. The number of transactions was limited and it was easy to make these postings either on a monthly or three-monthly basis into the books of account. Julia's sales were made almost entirely for cash and her suppliers paid monthly.

However, many businesses buy and sell goods and services on credit many times each day, receive and pay out large sums of cash on a daily basis and trade frequently with large numbers of customers and suppliers of goods and services. Such businesses require much more detailed accounting records to ensure that each and every business transaction is captured and summarised. Transactions are initially captured and summarised in daily listings of sales, purchases, wages and salaries and cash. These daily listings (summaries of transactions) are then used to make the relevant double entries in the books of account, the nominal ledger.

While even the smallest businesses now use computers which complete the double entry automatically, it is very important for you to understand how these records are compiled and the ways in which the software packages in use summarise the accounting transactions to post to the books of account. Auditors test the logic of clients' computer systems to ensure that all transactions have been posted correctly and in full. As a result of this testing auditors can be confident that the financial statements present a true and fair view of the income and expenditure for the financial period and that the assets, liabilities and capital present a true and fair view of the financial position of an entity at the end of each and every accounting period. Without a detailed knowledge of double-entry bookkeeping and how it works, auditors would be unable to follow transactions through the computer systems to determine whether they had been correctly accounted for or not. As an accountant or business professional in practice, in industry, in the public or in the charitable sector, you, too, will want to be certain that the information you are working with has been correctly compiled from the source data to enable you to make valid decisions. Therefore, an understanding of double-entry principles and practice will be essential to your future career in accounting. Careful study to understand double entry now will make you a much more valuable accountant in the future.

In this chapter we will look at accounting systems. These accounting systems use day books or listings to record transactions on a daily basis. These daily listings are referred to as the books of prime entry, the first point at which transactions are recorded in the accounting system. These books of prime entry are then used to complete the double entry to the accounting records which form the basis for the preparation of the financial statements. This process is illustrated in Figure 5.1.

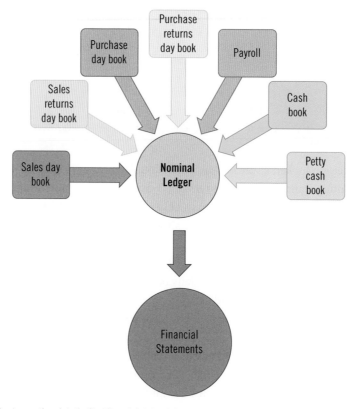

Figure 5.1 Processing transactions into the final financial statements

TRANSACTIONS AND TRANSACTION SYSTEMS

As we saw in Chapter 1 (What is accounting?), accounting involves the recording of transactions in money terms. All businesses use the following three systems which generate transactions that require recording in the books of account:

- The sales system: this system covers the selling of goods and services to customers and the collection of cash from those customers for the goods and services supplied.

- The purchases system: this system covers the buying in of goods and services from suppliers and the payment of cash to those suppliers for the goods and services provided.
- The payroll system: this system covers payments to employees for the time they have spent working for their organisations. In addition, organisations act as tax collection agencies for the state and they pay the income tax and national insurance deducted from employees' pay over to the tax authorities on a regular basis.

WHY IS THIS RELEVANT TO ME?   Transactions and transaction systems

To enable you as a business professional to:

- Appreciate that all organisations operate three main transaction systems: sales, purchases and wages
- Understand what each of these three main transaction systems involves
- Appreciate that these three transaction systems collect and record the information that builds up into the income and expenditure and the assets, liabilities and capital recorded in the financial statements

5

THE SALES AND CASH RECEIVED SYSTEM

All accounting systems generate records as evidence that transactions have taken place. These records can be in either paper or electronic form. The sales and cash received system has four transactions that require recording. The transactions in the sales system are presented in Figure 5.2.

Sales

When a sale occurs, a sales invoice is raised, recording the value of the goods or services supplied, any sales taxes such as value added tax (abbreviated henceforth to VAT) and the total amount owed by the customer (value of the sale made + the sales taxes). Illustration 5.1 shows an example of a sales invoice. Most businesses trade with their business customers on credit, so the cash due from each business customer for goods and services supplied will be received at a later date. The most common credit terms expect business customers to pay their invoices within 30 days of the invoice date. Where businesses make sales for cash, sales invoices are still produced to provide evidence that a transaction has occurred. Without evidence that a transaction has occurred, these cash sales might not be recorded in the accounting records and thus be omitted from the financial statements.

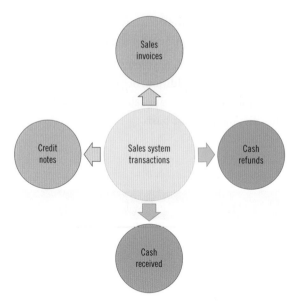

Figure 5.2 Transactions in the sales system

Illustration 5.1 An example of a sales invoice

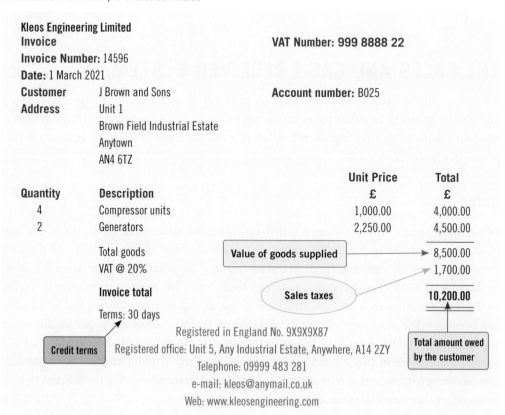

Credit notes

Credit notes are a negative sale. Goods supplied may be damaged on arrival, they may not meet the customer's requirements or there may just be an error on the invoice that requires correction. Damaged goods or goods that are not required are returned to the seller and a credit note issued to cancel the sales transaction either in part or in full. Credit notes record the value of the cancelled sale together with any cancelled sales taxes and show the total amount that is no longer owed by the customer (value of sale cancelled + the sales taxes). Illustration 5.2 shows an example of a credit note. Credit notes represent sales returns (Chapter 3, Sales returns).

Illustration 5.2 An example of a credit note

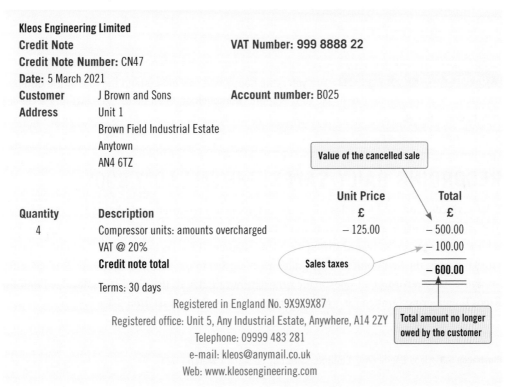

Cash received

When a customer pays what is owed, the receiving company receives cash either as physical cash or more commonly as a cheque or as a direct payment into the company's bank account. A payment from a credit customer relates to one or more invoices for goods or services supplied at an earlier date. Cash customers pay what is owed immediately with the cash received being recorded in the till.

Cash refunds

When customers return goods that they have already paid for, then they receive a cash refund. These refunds are made through cash taken from the till, by cheque sent to the customer or as a direct credit to the customer's bank account.

WHY IS THIS RELEVANT TO ME?   The sales and cash received system

To enable you as a business professional to:

- Familiarise yourself with the transactions in the sales and cash received system
- Understand how each transaction works in the sales and cash received system
- Understand the flow of transactions in the sales and cash received system

---

GO BACK OVER THIS AGAIN!   Are you quite happy that you understand the role of the different transactions in the sales system? Go to the **online workbook** and complete Exercises 5.1 to check your understanding.

RECORDING DAILY SALES: THE SALES DAY BOOK

Sales invoices produced for sales made to customers are recorded each day in the sales day book. The sales day book is also known as the sales listing but we shall use the term sales day book to refer to this transaction record throughout this chapter. The sales day book is the book of prime entry for sales, the first point at which sales are recorded in the accounting system. The sales day book is a daily record of all sales made on each trading day of the year. The sales day book for Kleos Engineering Limited for 1 March 2021 is presented in Illustration 5.3.

Illustration 5.3 Kleos Engineering Limited: sales day book for 1 March 2021

Date	Invoice number	Customer	Total £	VAT £	Net sales £
1 3 2021	14596	J Brown and Sons	10,200.00	1,700.00	8,500.00
1 3 2021	14597	Vivanti plc	4,346.40	724.40	3,622.00
1 3 2021	14598	Vodravid Limited	6,553.62	1,092.27	5,461.35
1 3 2021	14599	Mangonese plc	682.50	113.75	568.75
1 3 2021	14600	Tiddle and Toddle	375.36	62.56	312.80
1 3 2021	14601	F Smith and Co	9,300.00	1,550.00	7,750.00
Totals for day			**31,457.88**	**5,242.98**	**26,214.90**

As you can see, the sales day book is just a list of sales invoices categorised by customer with totals for net sales, VAT and the total value of each invoice. Each sales invoice has a date and is given a unique sequential number (Illustrations 5.1 and 5.3, Invoice number column) to enable companies to ensure that all their sales invoices have been recorded and to enable each invoice to be traced quickly and efficiently if a question or query relating to the invoice ever arises. The sales day book is not part of the double-entry system, but is used to make the double entry into the accounting records (this chapter, The double entry to record sales listed in the sales day book).

WHY IS THIS RELEVANT TO ME?   Recording daily sales: The sales day book

To ensure you as a business professional understand:

- The function of the sales day book as the book of prime entry for sales, the first point at which an organisation records details of the sales made in the accounting system
- The information that is recorded in the sales day book

GO BACK OVER THIS AGAIN!   Are you convinced that you can say what is included in the sales day book? Go to the **online workbook** and complete Exercises 5.2 to test your knowledge.

Where organisations sell more than one type of product, the sales day book may analyse the sales further into different categories of sales. Give me an example 5.1 shows the categories that Rolls Royce plc analyses its sales into in its annual report and accounts. Such an analysis helps organisations determine the performance of each division and whether divisional objectives and targets are being achieved.

GIVE ME AN EXAMPLE 5.1   **Different categories of sale**

Rolls Royce plc categorises sales as follows in its annual report and accounts for the year ended 31 December 2018:

Civil Aerospace—development, manufacture, marketing and sales of commercial aero engines and aftermarket services.

Power Systems—development, manufacture, marketing and sales of reciprocating engines,

power systems and nuclear systems for civil power generation.

Defence—development, manufacture, marketing and sales of military aero engines, naval engines, submarines and aftermarket services.

ITP Aero—design, research and development, manufacture and casting, assembly and test of aeronautical engines and gas turbines

Source: www.rolls-royce.com

5

VALUE ADDED TAX (VAT)

Value Added Tax is a tax on the value of sales. It is a very complex tax which you will learn much more about later on in your studies and throughout your professional career. For now, all you need to know is that VAT is charged on the value of each sale made by entities that are liable to registration for VAT (which is nearly all business organisations in the UK). The current standard rate of VAT in the UK is 20%. The sales value of the goods sold to J Brown and Sons (Illustrations 5.1 and 5.3) is £8,500.00. Value Added Tax on £8,500.00 at the rate of 20% is £1,700.00 (£8,500.00 × 20%). The sales value of £8,500.00 + the VAT of £1,700.00 results in a total invoice value of £10,200.00 (Illustrations 5.1 and 5.3). £10,200 is the amount that John Brown and Sons will pay to Kleos Engineering Limited to settle the invoice. Value Added Tax is collected on behalf of the government and paid over to HM Revenue and Customs every three months. The amount paid over at the end of each three-monthly period is the difference between the VAT charged and collected on sales and the VAT paid on purchases from other VAT registered businesses. A purchase from another business is a sale by that business, so VAT has to be charged on that sale. We shall see later on in this chapter how the VAT account summarises VAT on sales and purchases to generate a net amount payable at the end of each quarter.

> **WHY IS THIS RELEVANT TO ME?**   Value added tax
>
> To provide you as a business professional with:
>
> - A very brief introduction to Value Added Tax
>
> - An appreciation of how Value Added Tax is calculated on sales of goods and services
>
> - An understanding of how the net amounts due to HM Revenue and Customs are calculated

 MULTIPLE CHOICE QUESTIONS   Do you think you understand how VAT works and how it is calculated? Go to the **online workbook** and have a go at Multiple choice questions 5.1 to test your understanding.

THE DOUBLE ENTRY TO RECORD SALES LISTED IN THE SALES DAY BOOK

Given that the sales day book is not part of the double-entry system, how are the sales, VAT and total figures posted into the accounting records? What are the debit and what are the credit entries required to record these sales transactions? You should apply your knowledge of double-entry bookkeeping gained in Chapter 4 to determine the answers to these questions.

Making a sale generates an asset, either cash from sales made for cash or trade receivables if sales are made to customers on credit terms. Therefore, the cash or trade receivables account (we shall henceforth refer to the trade receivables account as the trade receivables control account) are debited with the daily sales day book total thereby increasing the balance on the asset account: the sales day book total for each day is the amount of economic benefits that will be received by the organisation. Sales are income so the sales value net of VAT or any other sales taxes is credited to the sales account. Value Added Tax, on the other hand, is a liability, the tax collected on sales which has to be paid over to the tax authorities. Therefore, the VAT liability account is credited with the VAT payable. Value Added Tax is not classified as revenue as it will never belong to the entity making the sale, it belongs to HM Revenue and Customs. Value Added Tax is therefore not an increase in assets or a decrease in liabilities that results in an increase in equity (the IASB definition of income, see Chapter 3, Income) so it is not revenue; it is an obligation to transfer an economic resource (cash) as a result of past events (the act of making each sale). The double entry for each daily sales day book total is shown in Illustration 5.4: in this illustration, it is assumed that all the sales in the sales day book have been made on credit to customers. Only credit sales are debited to the trade receivables control account. Cash sales are debited to the cash or bank account.

Do the double-entry postings balance? Yes. There is a debit of £31,457.88 and two credits totalling to £31,457.88 (£5,242.98 VAT + £26,214.90 net sales = £31,457.88). All the debits are equal to all the credits so the accounts are in perfect balance.

WHY IS THIS RELEVANT TO ME?   Double entry from the sales day book

To enable you as a business professional to:

- Understand how the daily sales day book totals are posted to the accounting records
- Make the required double entry to the accounting records to reflect the daily sales transactions in full

---

SUMMARY OF KEY CONCEPTS   Are you quite sure you can make the double entry to record daily sales day book totals in the books of account? Go to the **online workbook** to revise the required double entry in Summary of key concepts 5.1.

MULTIPLE CHOICE QUESTIONS   Are you completely confident you understand what the entries in the sales day book represent and how to make the required entries into the accounting records from the sales day book? Go to the **online workbook** and attempt Multiple choice questions 5.2 to test your abilities in this area.

Illustration 5.4 The double entry to record the daily sales day book totals in the books of account of Kleos Engineering Limited

Date	Invoice Number	Customer	Total £	VAT £	Net Sales £
1 3 2021	14596	J Brown and Sons	10,200.00	1,700.00	8,500.00
1 3 2021	14597	Vivanti plc	4,346.40	724.40	3,622.00
1 3 2021	14598	Vodravid Limited	6,553.62	1,092.27	5,461.35
1 3 2021	14599	Mangonese plc	682.50	113.75	568.75
1 3 2021	14600	Tiddle and Toddle	375.36	62.56	312.80
1 3 2021	14601	F Smith and Co	9,300.00	1,550.00	7,750.00
Totals for day			**31,457.88**	**5,242.98**	**26,214.90**

Trade receivables control account

2021		£	2021		£
1 March	Sales day book	31,457.88			

Debit trade receivables, increase the asset with monies owed by customers

VAT account

2021		£	2021		£
			1 March	Sales day book	5,242.98

Credit VAT, increase the liability for monies owed to HM Revenue and Customs

Sales account

2021		£	2021		£
			1 March	Sales day book	26,214.90

Credit sales, increase the revenue earned by the entity

SALES RETURNS DAY BOOK

The sales returns day book is also known as the sales returns listing but we shall use the term sales returns day book to refer to this transaction record throughout this chapter. The sales returns day book uses exactly the same headings as the sales day book. As there are fewer returns than sales, the sales returns day book is a much shorter record of daily transactions. The sales returns day book for Kleos Engineering Limited for 5 March 2021 and the illustration of how the entries from this record are recorded in the double-entry system are shown in Illustration 5.5.

Illustration 5.5 Sales returns day book for Kleos Engineering Limited for 5 March 2021 and the double entry to record the daily sales returns day book totals in the company's books of account

Date	Credit Note Number	Customer	Total £	VAT £	Net Credit £
5 3 2021	CN47	J Brown and Sons	600.00	100.00	500.00
5 3 2021	CN48	Vodravid Limited	410.70	68.45	342.25
Totals for day			**1,010.70**	**168.45**	**842.25**

VAT account

2021		£	2021		£
5 March	Sales returns	168.45	1 March	Sales day book	5,242.98

Debit VAT, decrease the liability as less money is now owed to HM Revenue and Customs

Sales account

2021		£	2021		£
5 March	Sales returns	842.25	1 March	Sales day book	26,214.90

Debit sales, decrease the revenue earned by the entity as a result of returns

Trade receivables control account

2021		£	2021		£
1 March	Sales day book	31,457.88	5 March	Sales returns	1,010.70

Credit trade receivables, decrease the asset as less is now owed by customers

THE DOUBLE ENTRY TO RECORD SALES RETURNS LISTED IN THE SALES RETURNS DAY BOOK

The double entries from the sales returns day book are the reverse of the double entry used to record sales. The sales returns reduce both assets and equity, so the sales (income) account is debited (decrease in income) as a result of these cancelled sales. A smaller amount of VAT is now owed to the tax authorities due to the cancellation of a sale so the liability is debited (a decrease) to reflect this reduction in the obligation. Less money is now owed by trade receivables so the trade receivables control account is credited (a decrease in an asset) by the total in the sales returns day book. Do the totals balance? Yes. There is a debit of £1,010.70 (£168.45 + £842.25 = £1,010.70) and a credit of £1,010.70 so the double entry is complete and the accounts continue to be in perfect balance.

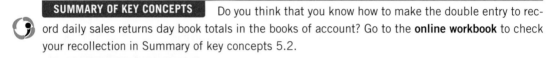

WHY IS THIS RELEVANT TO ME?   Sales returns day book

To enable you as a business professional to:

- Understand how the sales returns day book totals are posted to the accounting records
- Make the required double entry to the accounting records to reflect the daily sales returns transactions in full

SUMMARY OF KEY CONCEPTS   Do you think that you know how to make the double entry to record daily sales returns day book totals in the books of account? Go to the **online workbook** to check your recollection in Summary of key concepts 5.2.

GO BACK OVER THIS AGAIN!   Are you convinced that you understand what sales returns represent and how to make the required entries into the accounting records from the sales returns day book? Go to the **online workbook** and attempt Exercises 5.3 to test your abilities in this area.

SHOW ME HOW TO DO IT   Did you completely understand how the double entry was made from the sales day book and from the sales returns day book into the books of account? View Video presentation 5.1 in the **online workbook** to see a practical demonstration of how the double entry was completed in the trade receivables, VAT and sales accounts.

THE SALES LEDGER

As we have seen, the total value of daily sales is recorded in the trade receivables control account. However, with only one total figure for trade receivables, how will entities know what each trade receivable owes and whether individual customers are paying for the goods or services they have received? Control must be maintained over each and every trade receivable on an individual basis to ensure that sales are being paid for regularly and that certain customers are not building up an excessively large debt that they might not be able to pay in the future. In order to keep track of the activity on each customer's account, a sales ledger (trade receivable) account is maintained for each customer. The total balance on each customer's sales ledger account will be calculated at the end of each month. The total on each of these individual sales ledger accounts added together will be equal to the total on the trade receivables control account. Each individual customer's sales ledger account is debited with the total sales invoice value for each invoice raised and credited with any credit notes issued and any cash received (see this chapter, The sales ledger and cash receipts). Using our examples from Illustrations 5.3 and 5.5 for sales invoices and sales returns, the sales ledger accounts for the six customers of Kleos Engineering Limited are shown in Illustration 5.6. Note that the sales ledger accounts are listed in alphabetical order not invoice order so that each account can be found quickly and easily.

Illustration 5.6 Kleos Engineering Limited: individual sales ledger balances

J Brown and Sons sales ledger account

2021		£	2021		£
1 March	14596	10,200.00	5 March	CN47	600.00

Mangonese plc sales ledger account

2021		£	2021		£
1 March	14599	682.50			

F Smith and Co sales ledger account

2021		£	2021		£
1 March	14601	9,300.00			

Tiddle and Toddle sales ledger account

2021		£	2021		£
1 March	14600	375.36			

Vivanti plc sales ledger account

2021		£	2021		£
1 March	14597	4,346.40			

Vodravid Limited sales ledger account

2021		£	2021		£
1 March	14598	6,553.62	5 March	CN48	410.70

Adding up the balances on each sales ledger account gives us the following totals:

- Total debit balances on the individual sales ledger accounts: £10,200.00 + £682.50 + £9,300.00 + £375.36 + £4,346.40 + £6,553.62 = £31,457.88.
- Credit balances: £600.00 + £410.70 = £1,010.70.

Do these equal the totals on the trade receivables control account? Yes, they do, as shown in Illustration 5.7.

Illustration 5.7 (= Illustration 5.5) Trade receivables control account for Kleos Engineering Limited

Trade receivables control account

2021		£	2021		£
1 March	Sales day book	31,457.88	5 March	Sales returns day book	1,010.70

The sales ledger is maintained as a separate record of what each customer owes the business. Note that each sale and credit note transaction is recorded using the invoice number and the credit note number from the sales day book and the sales returns day book. Reference can thus be made quickly and easily to the source documents for each transaction should a query arise at a later date.

5

NUMERICAL EXERCISES Are you confident that you could complete the sales ledger accounts for a company's trade receivables and post the sales invoices and sales returns accurately and in full? Go to the **online workbook** and complete Numerical exercises 5.1 to test your abilities in this area.

CASH RECEIVED

Businesses use a cash book to record transactions made through the bank account, namely cash received and cash paid. The cash book is another book of prime entry, the first point at which an entity records individual amounts of cash received and cash paid. The cash book is in effect one large T account with cash received on the left hand side (debit, increase the cash asset) and cash paid on the right (credit, decrease the cash asset). Cash received and cash paid is analysed into various headings to reflect the different categories of cash received and cash paid out by a business. An example of the cash received side of the cash book for Kleos Engineering Limited is shown in Illustration 5.8. The main column in the cash received side will be the cash received (in the form of cheques or direct payments into the bank account) from trade receivables with other columns for cash from sources such as interest received and cash sales. When a business makes cash sales, the cash received from these cash sales is split into sales revenue and the liability to pay VAT on those cash sales to HM Revenue and Customs. In Illustration 5.8, the total cash receipt of £432.00 from cash sales is split into £360.00 for cash sales and £72.00 owed for VAT on those sales. The net sales and VAT on cash received from trade receivables do not require splitting in the same way as the net sales and VAT have already been recorded in the sales day book (Illustration 5.3) and in the sales returns day book (Illustration 5.5).

Illustration 5.8 Kleos Engineering Limited: cash book: cash received

Date	Detail	Total	Trade receivables	Cash sales	Interest received	VAT
2021		£	£	£	£	£
1 April	Interest received	26.21			26.21	
1 April	J Brown and Sons	8,400.00	8,400.00			
1 April	Tiddle and Toddle	375.36	375.36			
1 April	Cash sales	432.00		360.00		72.00
1 April	Vivanti plc	4,346.40	4,346.40			
Totals		**13,579.97**	**13,121.76**	**360.00**	**26.21**	**72.00**

How are these cash receipts recorded in the double-entry system? As we saw in Chapter 4, cash received is an increase in an asset, so any cash received is debited to the bank account. To complete the double entry, there has to be a credit to various other accounts as shown in Illustration 5.9. The credits represent increases in income (cash sales and interest received), an increase in liabilities (VAT) and a decrease in an asset (trade receivables).

Illustration 5.9 The double entry to record cash receipts in the books of account of Kleos Engineering Limited

	Total	Trade receivables	Cash sales	Interest received	VAT
Cash receipts totals	13,579.97	13,121.76	360.00	26.21	72.00

Bank account

2021		£	2021		£
1 April	Cash book	13,579.97			

Debit bank, increase asset with cash received

Trade receivables control account

2021		£	2021		£
1 March	Sales day book	31,457.88	5 March	Sales returns	1,010.70
			1 April	Cash book	13,121.76

Credit trade receivables, decrease the asset as less is now owed by customers

Sales account

2021		£	2021		£
5 March	Sales returns	842.25	1 March	Sales day book	26,214.90
			1 April	Cash book	360.00

Credit sales, increase the revenue earned by the entity

Interest received account

2021		£	2021		£
			1 April	Cash book	26.21

Credit interest received, increase the income earned by the entity

VAT account

2021		£	2021		£
5 March	Sales returns	168.45	1 March	Sales day book	5,242.98
			1 April	Cash book	72.00

Credit VAT, increase the liability for monies owed to HM Revenue and Customs

---

WHY IS THIS RELEVANT TO ME?   Cash received

To enable you as a business professional to:

- Understand how the cash received is posted to the accounting records
- Make the required double entry to the accounting records to record the cash received transactions in full

---

SUMMARY OF KEY CONCEPTS   Are you certain you know what the double entry to record cash received in the books of account is? Go to the **online workbook** to check your recollection in Summary of key concepts 5.3.

GO BACK OVER THIS AGAIN!   Are you convinced you understand how to make the required entries into the accounting records from the cash received records? Go to the **online workbook** and attempt Exercises 5.4 to test your understanding.

THE SALES LEDGER AND CASH RECEIPTS

The individual sales ledger accounts are also updated for the cash received from individual trade receivables. Each trade receivable is an asset, so the receipt of cash reduces the amounts owed by each trade receivable as shown in Illustration 5.10 while increasing the cash asset (debit cash, increase the cash asset, credit trade receivables, reduce the trade receivable asset).

Illustration 5.10 Kleos Engineering Limited: individual sales ledger balances showing the posting of trade receivables cash received on 1 April 2021

J Brown and Sons sales ledger account

2021		£	2021		£
1 March	14596	10,200.00	5 March	CN47	600.00
			1 April	Cash book	8,400.00

Tiddle and Toddle sales ledger account

2021		£	2021		£
1 March	14600	375.36	1 April	Cash book	375.36

Vivanti plc sales ledger account

2021		£	2021		£
1 March	14597	4,346.40	1 April	Cash book	4,346.40

J Brown and Sons have not paid the full amount of their invoice less the credit note, so company staff might want to contact this customer to find out whether there is a problem. Tiddle and Toddle and Vivanti plc have paid what is owed in full, but there are three other trade receivables that have not yet paid their March 1 invoices. The company can now start to chase these trade receivables for payments which are overdue (more than 30 days since the invoice date). Maintaining individual sales ledger accounts for each customer makes it much easier for the company to know who has and who has not paid and to control the amounts owed by individual trade receivables.

WHY IS THIS RELEVANT TO ME?   The sales ledger and cash receipts

To enable you as a business professional to:

• Understand how the cash received from trade receivables is posted to the individual sales ledger accounts

• Appreciate how maintaining individual sales ledger accounts for each customer enables entities to identify customers who are not paying so that action to recover outstanding debts can be taken

---

NUMERICAL EXERCISES   Do you think that you could complete the sales ledger accounts to reflect cash received from trade receivables? Go to the **online workbook** and complete Numerical exercises 5.2 to test your ability to make these entries.

SHOW ME HOW TO DO IT   Did you completely follow how the double entry was made from the cash book to the accounting records and to the individual sales ledger accounts? View Video presentation 5.2 in the **online workbook** to see a practical demonstration of how the double entry was completed in the relevant T accounts and the individual sales ledger accounts.

EXERCISING CONTROL: THE TRADE RECEIVABLES CONTROL ACCOUNT

The trade receivables control account summarises the transactions in the sales system for sales made on credit. As we have seen, total credit sales are debited to this account as the trade receivables asset increases while cash or sales returns are credited as trade receivables pay what is owed or sales are cancelled thereby reducing the asset. What other entries are made in the trade receivables control account? Illustration 5.11 presents all the entries that you would expect to find in this account (figures given are for illustration purposes only).

Illustration 5.11 The trade receivables control account

Trade receivables control account					
2021		**£**	**2021**		**£**
1 Jan	Balance b/f	52,867	31 Dec	Sales returns day book	15,742
31 Dec	Sales day book	408,383	31 Dec	Cash book	382,621
			31 Dec	Irrecoverable debts	2,600
			31 Dec	Balance c/f	60,287
		461,250			**461,250**

5

The left hand side of the account represents increases in the asset. The balance brought forward at the start of the year is made up of the trade receivables at the end of the previous accounting period. This balance represents money still owed by customers as a result of accepting goods and services from the organisation up to the end of the previous financial year. On the right hand side of the account, we find transactions and events that will reduce the trade receivables asset. As well as sales returns and cash received from trade receivables, irrecoverable debts (cash that will never be collected from trade receivables who cannot or will not pay, Chapter 3, Irrecoverable debts) will also reduce the amount of the trade receivables asset while increasing the corresponding expense account. Do note that the allowance for receivables does not form part of the trade receivables control account. The allowance for receivables is made for those trade receivables that might not pay what they owe rather than being trade receivables which will never pay the amounts due (Chapter 3, The allowance for receivables). As a result, the allowance for receivables is carried forward as a balance on a separate account which is netted off against the trade receivables carried forward at the end of the accounting period in the statement of financial position.

The balance brought forward + the sales − the sales returns − the cash received − the irrecoverable debts should then give us the trade receivables balance at the end of the accounting period. The trade receivables control account provides a quick summary of transactions and a total balance for amounts owed to the business at the end of the accounting period. As we have seen, the total transactions (sales, cash received, sales returns and irrecoverable debts) should be equal to the totals on each of the individual sales ledger accounts. At the end of the accounting period, the trade receivables balance carried forward at the end of the period should be equal to the total of all the individual sales ledger balances. Time will be spent making sure that this is the case. If it is not and there is a difference between the balance on the trade receivables control account and the total of all the individual balances on each of the sales ledger accounts, then there is an error and time will have to be devoted to finding and correcting this error. As the trade receivables control account balances carried forward and the total of the individual sales ledger balances should be the same, control is exercised through the two sets of figures which enables organisations to track down and correct errors as they arise. An irrecoverable debt may have been recorded in the individual sales ledger account which has not been added to the trade receivables control account or cash, sales returns or sales may have been missed out of the individual sales ledger accounts. Whatever the cause of the error, the comparison of the two independent records will ensure that the trade receivables figure at the end of the accounting period is correct.

WHY IS THIS RELEVANT TO ME?   Exercising control: The trade receivables control account

As a business professional you will be expected to be able to:

- Understand which entries are made in the trade receivables control account
- Compile the trade receivables control account from the available data on sales, sales returns, cash received and irrecoverable debts
- Reconcile the trade receivables control account balance at the end of an accounting period with the total of the individual trade receivable balances on the sales ledger

SUMMARY OF KEY CONCEPTS   Are you completely certain that you can say what the entries in the trade receivables control account are? Go to the **online workbook** to check your recollection with Summary of key concepts 5.4.

GO BACK OVER THIS AGAIN!   Are you quite sure you understand how the trade receivables control account works? Go to the **online workbook** and have a go at Exercises 5.5 to check your understanding.

THE PURCHASES AND CASH PAID SYSTEM

As well as selling goods and services, organisations buy in goods and services from other entities. As in the case of the sales system, the purchases and cash paid system has four transactions that require recording. These transactions are shown in Figure 5.3.

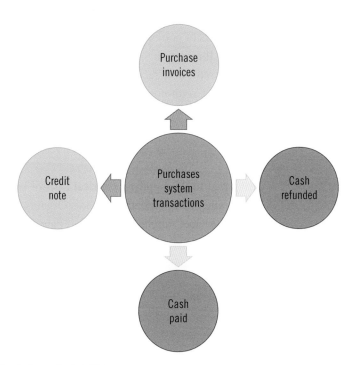

Figure 5.3 Transactions in the purchases system

5

Purchases

When an entity buys in goods or services, a purchase invoice is received from the supplier of those goods or services. This purchase invoice shows the value of goods or services supplied, any VAT charged on that supply of goods and services and the total amount owed by the entity (value of the goods or services supplied + the VAT). Purchase invoices will follow the same format as Illustration 5.1, the only difference being that the name and address of each supplier will be different on each purchase invoice while the customer's name, the buying company and address will always be the same. Most businesses trade with their suppliers on credit, so the cash due to each supplier for goods and services supplied will be paid at a later date.

Credit notes

Credit notes received from suppliers represent negative purchases. When goods supplied are damaged on arrival, do not meet the buying entity's requirements or there is just an error on the invoice from the supplier, a credit note will be issued. Damaged or unsuitable goods are returned to the supplier and a credit note issued to cancel the purchase transaction either in part or in full. Credit notes record the value of the cancelled purchase together with any VAT and show the total amount that is no longer owed by the organisation (value of purchase cancelled + VAT). Credit notes from suppliers of goods and services will follow the same format as the example of a credit note shown in Illustration 5.2 with the name and address of the supplier being different on each and every credit note received while the name and address of the buying company will always be the same. Credit notes represent purchase returns (Chapter 3, Purchase returns).

Cash paid

When an organisation pays what is owed to its suppliers, physical cash or more commonly a cheque or a direct payment into the supplier's bank account is made. Organisations will pay one or more purchase invoices for goods or services supplied at an earlier date.

Cash refunds

When an organisation returns goods that they have already paid for, then they receive a cash refund. These refunds are made by the supplier and will be recorded as a receipt of cash in the buying entity's books as this is cash coming in to the business. Cash refunds from suppliers are rare but you should be aware that they can arise.

WHY IS THIS RELEVANT TO ME?   The purchases and cash paid system

To enable you as a business professional to:

- Familiarise yourself with the transactions in the purchases and cash paid system
- Understand how each transaction works in the purchases system
- Understand the flow of transactions in the purchases system

---

GO BACK OVER THIS AGAIN!   Are you quite happy that you understand the role of the different transactions in the purchases system? Go to the **online workbook** and complete Exercises 5.6 to check your understanding.

RECORDING DAILY PURCHASES: THE PURCHASE DAY BOOK

Purchases made each day are recorded in the purchase day book. The purchase day book may also be called the purchase listing but we shall use the term purchase day book to refer to this transaction record throughout this chapter. The purchase day book is the book of prime entry for purchases and is a daily record of all purchases made on each trading day of the year. The purchase day book of Kleos Engineering Limited for 1 March 2021 is presented in Illustration 5.12.

Illustration 5.12 Kleos Engineering Limited's purchase day book for 1 March 2021

Date	Internal invoice number	Supplier	Total £	VAT £	Raw materials £	Office supplies £	Legal fees £
1 3 2021	2460	Optimo Ltd	6,900.00	1,150.00	5,750.00		
1 3 2021	2461	Fuzzy Ltd	1,200.00	200.00	1,000.00		
1 3 2021	2462	Doric plc	210.24	35.04		175.20	
1 3 2021	2463	Ionic Ltd	477.00	79.50	397.50		
1 3 2021	2464	Legal Bee	825.00	137.50			687.50
Totals for day			**9,612.24**	**1,602.04**	**7,147.50**	**175.20**	**687.50**

As was the case with the sales day book, the purchase day book is not part of the double-entry system, it is just a list of purchases made analysed by supplier and by expenditure type. While there may be a limited number of categories for sales, the classification of purchase expenditure is much wider. The purchase day book will therefore analyse purchase invoices into the categories of expenditure most frequently made by the entity. On receipt, each purchase invoice is given a unique internally generated sequential number (Illustration 5.12, Internal invoice number column) to enable companies to ensure that all their purchase invoices have been recorded and to enable each invoice to be traced quickly and efficiently if ever a query or a question about an invoice arises.

WHY IS THIS RELEVANT TO ME?　Recording daily purchases: The purchase day book

To ensure that you as a business professional understand:

- The function of the purchase day book as the book of prime entry for purchases, the first point at which each purchase is recorded by an organisation in the accounting system
- The information that is recorded in the purchase day book

GO BACK OVER THIS AGAIN!　Do you think that you can say what is included in the purchase day book? Go to the **online workbook** and complete Exercises 5.7 to test your knowledge.

THE DOUBLE ENTRY TO RECORD PURCHASES LISTED IN THE PURCHASE DAY BOOK

As the purchase day book is not part of the double-entry system, how are the purchases, VAT and figures for each category of expenditure posted into the accounting records? Making a purchase on credit from a supplier creates a liability, an obligation to transfer an economic resource (cash) to settle the liability. Therefore, the trade payables control account (we have called this account the trade payables account up to this point but will henceforth refer to it as the trade payables control account) is credited with the daily total as the liability, the amount owed to suppliers, increases. Purchases represent an increase in expenditure so the various totals on each category of purchases are debited to the various expenditure accounts. Value Added Tax on purchases is recoverable as a deduction from the VAT payable on sales, so the VAT liability account is debited with the reduction in the VAT payable. Value Added Tax incurred on expenditure is not classified as an expense as it is not a cost to a business. Value Added Tax on purchases is not a decrease in assets or an increase in liabilities that results in a decrease in equity (Chapter 3, Expenses). Value Added Tax on purchases is a reduction in a liability which is debited to the VAT account. As noted previously (this chapter, Value Added Tax (VAT)), the difference between the VAT charged on sales and the VAT recovered on purchases is paid to HM Revenue and Customs at the end of every quarter (three-monthly period). The double entry for the daily totals in the purchase day book is shown in Illustration 5.13.

Illustration 5.13 The double entry to record the daily purchase day book totals in the books of account of Kleos Engineering Limited

Date	Internal invoice number	Supplier	Total £	VAT £	Raw materials £	Office supplies £	Legal fees £
1 3 2021	2460	Optimo Ltd	6,900.00	1,150.00	5,750.00		
1 3 2021	2461	Fuzzy Ltd	1,200.00	200.00	1,000.00		
1 3 2021	2462	Doric plc	210.24	35.04		175.20	
1 3 2021	2463	Ionic Ltd	477.00	79.50	397.50		
1 3 2021	2464	Legal Bee	825.00	137.50			687.50
Totals for day			**9,612.24**	**1,602.04**	**7,147.50**	**175.20**	**687.50**

Trade payables control account

2021		£	2021		£
			1 March	Purchase day book	9,612.24

Credit trade payables with the increase in liabilities

VAT account

2021		£	2021		£
5 March	Sales returns	168.45	1 March	Sales day book	5,242.98
1 March	Purchase day book	1,602.04	3 April	Cash book	72.00

Debit VAT, decrease the liability for monies owed to HM Revenue and Customs

Raw materials account

2021		£	2021		£
1 March	Purchase day book	7,147.50			

Debit expense accounts with the increases in costs

Office supplies account

2021		£	2021		£
1 March	Purchase day book	175.20			

Legal fees account

2021		£	2021		£
1 March	Purchase day book	687.50			

Do the double-entry postings balance? Yes. There is a credit of £9,612.24 and four debits totalling to £9,612.24 (£1,602.04 + £7,147.50 + £175.20 + £687.50 = £9,612.24). All the debits are equal to all the credits so the accounts are in perfect balance.

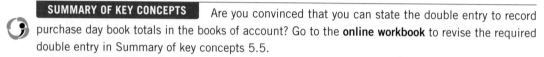

WHY IS THIS RELEVANT TO ME?　Double entry from the purchase day book

To enable you as a business professional to:

- Understand how the purchase day book totals are posted to the accounting records
- Make the required double entry to the accounting records to reflect the daily purchase transactions in full

SUMMARY OF KEY CONCEPTS　Are you convinced that you can state the double entry to record purchase day book totals in the books of account? Go to the **online workbook** to revise the required double entry in Summary of key concepts 5.5.

MULTIPLE CHOICE QUESTIONS　Are you completely confident you understand what the entries in the purchase day book represent and how to make the double entry into the accounting records from the purchase day book? Go to the **online workbook** and have a go at Multiple choice questions 5.3 to test your abilities in this area.

PURCHASE RETURNS DAY BOOK

The purchase returns day book is also known as the purchase returns listing but we shall use the term purchase returns day book to refer to this transaction record throughout this chapter. The purchase returns day book uses exactly the same headings as the purchase day book. As there are fewer returns than purchases, the purchase returns day book is a much shorter record of daily transactions. The purchase returns day book for Kleos Engineering Limited for 5 March 2021 and the illustration of how the entries from this record are recorded in the double-entry system are shown in Illustration 5.14.

Illustration 5.14 The purchase returns day book of Kleos Engineering Limited for 5 March 2021 and the double entry to record the daily purchase returns day book totals in the books of account of the company

Date	Purchase returns number	Supplier	Total £	VAT £	Raw materials £	Office supplies £	Legal fees £
5 3 2021	PR79	Optimo Ltd	510.00	85.00	425.00		
5 3 2021	PR80	Doric plc	30.30	5.05		25.25	
5 3 2021	PR81	Ionic Ltd	23.88	3.98	19.90		
Totals for day			**564.18**	**94.03**	**444.90**	**25.25**	—

Trade payables control account

2021		£	2021		£
5 March	**Purchase returns**	**564.18**	1 March	Purchase day book	9,612.24

Debit trade payables with the decrease in liabilities

Raw materials account

2021		£	2021		£
1 March	Purchase day book	7,147.50	5 March	Purchase returns	444.90

Credit expense accounts with the decrease in costs

Office supplies account

2021		£	2021		£
1 March	Purchase day book	175.20	5 March	Purchase returns	25.25

VAT account

2021		£	2021		£
5 March	Sales returns	168.45	1 March	Sales day book	5,242.98
1 March	Purchase day book	1,602.04	3 April	Cash book	72.00
			5 March	Purchase returns	94.03

Credit VAT, increase the liability for monies owed to HM Revenue and Customs

THE DOUBLE ENTRY TO RECORD PURCHASE RETURNS LISTED IN THE PURCHASE RETURNS DAY BOOK

The double entries from the purchase returns day book are the opposite of the double entry used to record purchases. The purchase returns decrease liabilities and so increase equity as expenditure is reduced, so the purchase (expense) accounts are credited (decrease in expense) as a result of these cancelled purchases. A smaller amount of VAT is reclaimed from the tax authorities so the liability is credited (an increase) to reflect this additional obligation. Less money is now owed to trade payables so the trade payables control account is debited (a decrease in a liability) with the total in the purchase returns day book. Do the totals balance? Yes. There is a debit of £564.18 and credits of £564.18 (£94.03 + £444.90 + £25.25 = £564.18) so the double entry is complete and the accounts continue to balance perfectly.

> ### WHY IS THIS RELEVANT TO ME?   Purchase returns day book
>
> To enable you as a business professional to:
>
> - Understand how the purchase returns day book totals are posted to the accounting records
> - Make the required double entry to the accounting records to reflect the daily purchase returns transactions in full

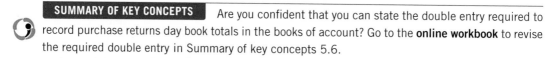

SUMMARY OF KEY CONCEPTS   Are you confident that you can state the double entry required to record purchase returns day book totals in the books of account? Go to the **online workbook** to revise the required double entry in Summary of key concepts 5.6.

GO BACK OVER THIS AGAIN!   Are you convinced that you understand what purchase returns represent and how to make the required entries into the accounting records from the purchase returns day book? Go to the **online workbook** and attempt Exercises 5.8 to test your understanding.

SHOW ME HOW TO DO IT   Did you completely appreciate how the double entry was made from the purchase day book and from the purchase returns day book? View Video presentation 5.3 in the **online workbook** to see a practical demonstration of how the double entry was completed in the trade payables, VAT and expense accounts.

THE PURCHASE LEDGER

As we have seen, the total value of purchases is recorded in the trade payables control account. However, with only one total figure for trade payables, how will entities know what is owed to each trade payable, whether the correct amounts are being paid to each supplier and that the entity is not paying more than once for goods and services supplied? In order to keep track of the activity on each supplier's account, a purchase ledger account is maintained for each provider of goods and services. The total balance on each supplier's purchase ledger account will be calculated at the end of each month. The total on each of the individual purchase ledger accounts added together will be equal to the total on the trade payables control account. Each supplier's purchase ledger account is credited with the total value of each purchase invoice received and debited with any credit notes received and any cash paid (see this chapter, The purchase ledger and cash payments). Using our examples from Illustrations 5.12 and 5.14 for the purchase day book and the purchase returns day book, the purchase ledger accounts for the five suppliers of Kleos Engineering Limited are shown in Illustration 5.15. Note that the purchase ledger accounts, just like the sales ledger accounts, are listed in alphabetical order rather than invoice order so that each account can be found quickly and easily should any queries or questions arise.

5

Illustration 5.15 Kleos Engineering Limited's individual purchase ledger accounts for suppliers

Doric plc purchase ledger account

2021		£	2021		£
5 March	PR80	30.30	1 March	2462	210.24

Fuzzy Limited purchase ledger account

2021		£	2021		£
			1 March	2461	1,200.00

Ionic purchase ledger account

2021		£	2021		£
5 March	PR81	23.88	1 March	2463	477.00

Legal Bee purchase ledger account

2021		£	2021		£
			1 March	2464	825.00

Optimo Limited purchase ledger account

2021		£	2021		£
5 March	PR79	510.00	1 March	2460	6,900.00

5

Adding up the balances on each purchase ledger account gives us the following totals:

- Total credit balances on the individual purchase ledger accounts: £210.24 + £1,200.00 + £477.00 + £825.00 + £6,900.00 = £9,612.24.

- Total debit balances on the individual purchase ledger accounts: £30.30 + £23.88 + £510.00 = £564.18.

Do these equal the totals on the trade payables control account? Yes, they do, as shown in Illustration 5.16.

Illustration 5.16 (= Illustration 5.14) Trade payables control account for Kleos Engineering Limited

Trade payables control account					
2021		**£**	**2021**		**£**
5 March	Purchase returns	564.18	1 March	Purchase day book	9,612.24

The purchase ledger is maintained as a separate record of what a business owes each supplier. Note that each purchase invoice and purchase returns transaction is recorded using the internal invoice number and the internal purchase returns number from the purchase day book and the purchase returns day book. Reference can thus readily be made to the source documents for each transaction should any questions or queries arise.

WHY IS THIS RELEVANT TO ME?   The purchase ledger

To enable you as a business professional to:

- Appreciate the control exercised over purchases, purchase returns and cash payments through maintaining individual accounts for each supplier

- Understand how the totals of all the individual purchase ledger balances add up to the total on the trade payables control account

- Understand the need for a purchase ledger to record individual balances owed to each supplier

---

NUMERICAL EXERCISES   Do you think that you could complete the purchase ledger accounts for a company's trade payables and post the purchase invoices and purchases returns accurately and in full? Go to the **online workbook** and complete Numerical exercises 5.3 to make sure you can.

CASH PAYMENTS

As noted in this chapter, Cash received, the right hand side of the cash book, is used to record cash payments. These payments represent reductions in the cash asset. As in the case of cash received, cash paid is analysed into various headings to reflect the different categories of cash payments made by a business. An example of the cash paid side of the cash book for Kleos Engineering Limited is shown in Illustration 5.17. The main column in the cash paid side will be the cash paid to trade payables but there are other significant outgoings such as payments for wages and salaries, payments to HM Revenue and Customs for tax and national insurance (PAYE and NIC) as well as for VAT. Any cash purchases will be split into the net purchases figure and the VAT recoverable on those purchases. The purchases and VAT on cash paid to trade payables do not require splitting in the same way as the net purchases and VAT have already been recorded in the purchase day book (Illustration 5.12) and in the purchase returns day book (Illustration 5.14).

Illustration 5.17 Kleos Engineering Limited: cash book: cash payments

Date 2021	Detail	Total £	Trade payables £	Wages and salaries £	PAYE and NIC £	Petty cash £
29 March	Optimo Limited	6,390.00	6,390.00			
29 March	Week 51 wages	19,341.36		19,341.36		
29 March	Fuzzy Limited	1,200.00	1,200.00			
29 March	Legal Bee	825.00	825.00			
29 March	HMRC Week 51	8,220.08			8,220.08	
29 March	Petty cash	100.00				100.00
Totals		36,076.44	8,415.00	19,341.36	8,220.08	100.00

How are these cash payments recorded in the double-entry system? As we saw in Chapter 4 (Posting accounting transactions to T accounts), cash paid is a decrease in an asset, so any cash paid is credited to the bank account. To complete the double entry, there has to be a debit to various other accounts as shown in Illustration 5.18. The debits represent increases in expenses (for example, bank charges or interest, which are not illustrated here), increases in other assets (petty cash) or decreases in liabilities (trade payables, wages control account and PAYE and NIC control).

Illustration 5.18 The double entry to record cash payments in the books of account of Kleos Engineering Limited

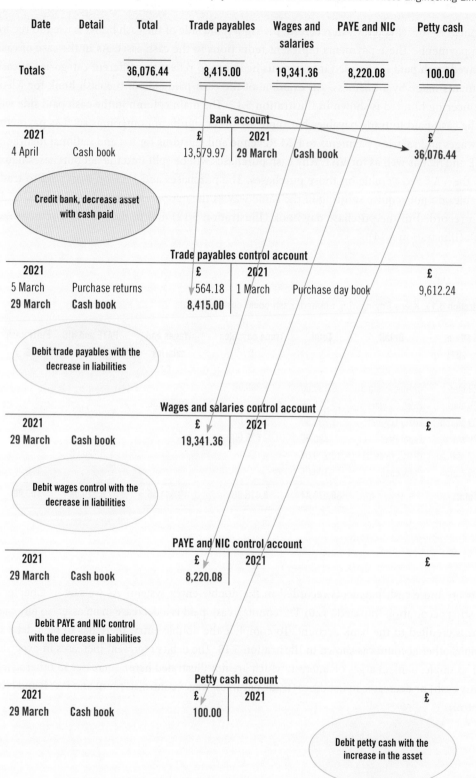

Date	Detail	Total	Trade payables	Wages and salaries	PAYE and NIC	Petty cash
Totals		36,076.44	8,415.00	19,341.36	8,220.08	100.00

Bank account

2021		£	2021		£
4 April	Cash book	13,579.97	29 March	Cash book	36,076.44

Credit bank, decrease asset with cash paid

Trade payables control account

2021		£	2021		£
5 March	Purchase returns	564.18	1 March	Purchase day book	9,612.24
29 March	Cash book	8,415.00			

Debit trade payables with the decrease in liabilities

Wages and salaries control account

2021		£	2021		£
29 March	Cash book	19,341.36			

Debit wages control with the decrease in liabilities

PAYE and NIC control account

2021		£	2021		£
29 March	Cash book	8,220.08			

Debit PAYE and NIC control with the decrease in liabilities

Petty cash account

2021		£	2021		£
29 March	Cash book	100.00			

Debit petty cash with the increase in the asset

WHY IS THIS RELEVANT TO ME?   Cash payments

To enable you as a business professional to:

• Understand how the cash paid is posted to the accounting records

• Make the required double entry to the accounting records to reflect the cash paid transactions in full

SUMMARY OF KEY CONCEPTS   Are you totally sure you can state the double entry to record cash payments in the books of account? Go to the **online workbook** to revise the required double entry in Summary of key concepts 5.7.

GO BACK OVER THIS AGAIN!   Convinced you understand how to make the required entries into the accounting records from the cash paid records? Go to the **online workbook** and attempt Exercises 5.9 to test your understanding.

THE PURCHASE LEDGER AND CASH PAYMENTS

The individual purchase ledger accounts are also updated for the cash paid to individual trade payables. Each trade payable is a liability, so the payment of cash reduces the amounts owed to each trade payable as shown in Illustration 5.19 (credit cash, decrease the cash asset, debit trade payables, decrease the trade payable liability).

Illustration 5.19 Kleos Engineering Limited: individual purchase ledger balances reflecting cash paid in March 2021

Fuzzy Limited purchase ledger account

2021		£	2021		£
29 March	Cash book	1,200.00	1 March	2461	1,200.00

Legal Bee purchase ledger account

2021		£	2021		£
29 March	Cash book	825.00	1 March	2464	825.00

Optimo Limited purchase ledger account

2021		£	2021		£
5 March	PR79	510.00	1 March	2460	6,900.00
29 March	Cash book	6,390.00			

Everything owed to the three trade payables in Illustration 5.19 has been paid. When reviewing the trade payables for unpaid amounts, the company's staff will see that these accounts have been paid in full and so will not pay these invoices again.

WHY IS THIS RELEVANT TO ME?   The purchase ledger and cash payments

To enable you as a business professional to:

- Understand how the cash paid to trade payables is posted to the individual purchase ledger accounts
- Appreciate how maintaining individual purchase ledger accounts for each supplier enables entities to identify suppliers who have and who have not been paid, thereby avoiding double payments to suppliers

---

NUMERICAL EXERCISES   Do you think you could complete the purchase ledger accounts to reflect cash paid to trade payables? Go to the **online workbook** and complete Numerical exercises 5.4 to test your ability to make these entries.

SHOW ME HOW TO DO IT   Did you completely follow how the double entry was made from the cash paid records to the accounting records and to the individual purchase ledger accounts? View Video presentation 5.4 in the **online workbook** to see a practical demonstration of how the double entry was completed in the relevant T accounts and the individual purchase ledger accounts.

EXERCISING CONTROL: THE TRADE PAYABLES CONTROL ACCOUNT

The trade payables control account summarises all the credit transactions in the purchases system. We have seen how total purchases are credited to the trade payables control account as the trade payables liability increases and how cash is debited to the account as trade payables are paid what is owed thereby reducing the liability. What other entries are made in the trade payables control account? Illustration 5.20 presents all the entries that you would expect to find in the trade payables control account with figures for illustration purposes only.

The right hand side of the account represents increases in the liability. The balance brought forward at the start of the year is the trade payables at the end of the previous accounting

Illustration 5.20 The trade payables control account

Trade payables control account

2021		£	2021		£
31 Dec	Purchase returns day book	1,998	1 Jan	Balance b/f	47,789
31 Dec	Discounts received	2,765	31 Dec	Purchase day book	344,622
31 Dec	Cash paid	339,325			
31 Dec	Balance c/f	48,323			
		392,411			**392,411**

period representing money still owed to suppliers as a result of trading on credit with these suppliers up to the end of the previous accounting period. On the left hand side of the account, we find transactions and events that will reduce the trade payables liability. As well as cash paid to suppliers, purchase returns and quantity discounts received from suppliers (Chapter 3, Discounts received) will also reduce the amount of the trade payables liability while decreasing the corresponding expense accounts and increasing the corresponding income account.

The balance brought forward + purchases – cash paid – discounts received – purchase returns should then give us the trade payables balance at the end of the accounting period. The trade payables control account provides a quick summary of transactions and a total balance for amounts owed by the business at the end of the accounting period. As we have seen, the total transactions (purchases, cash paid, purchase returns and discounts received) should be equal to the totals on each of the individual purchase ledger accounts. At the end of the accounting period, the trade payables balance carried forward at the end of the period should be equal to the total of all the individual purchase ledger balances. Time will be spent making sure that this is the case. If it is not and there is a difference between the balance on the trade payables control account and the total of all the individual balances on each of the purchase ledger accounts, then there is an error and time will have to be allocated to finding and correcting this error. As the trade payables control account balances carried forward and the total of the individual purchase ledger balances should be the same, control is exercised through the two sets of figures which enables organisations to track down and correct errors as they arise. A discount received may have been recorded in the individual purchase ledger account which has not been added to the trade payables control account or cash or purchases may have been missed out of the individual purchase ledger accounts. Whatever the cause of the error, the comparison of the two independent records will ensure that the trade payables figure at the end of the accounting period is correct.

WHY IS THIS RELEVANT TO ME?   Exercising control: The trade payables control account

As a business professional you will be expected to be able to:

• Understand which entries are made in the trade payables control account

• Compile the trade payables control account from the available data on purchases, purchase returns, cash paid and discounts received

• Reconcile the trade payables control account balance at the end of an accounting period with the total of the individual trade payable balances on the purchase ledger

SUMMARY OF KEY CONCEPTS   Are you convinced that you can say what the entries in the trade payables control account are? Go to the **online workbook** to check your recollection with Summary of key concepts 5.8.

GO BACK OVER THIS AGAIN!   Are you quite sure you understand how the trade payables control account works? Go to the **online workbook** and have a go at Exercises 5.10 to check your understanding.

EXERCISING CONTROL: THE BANK RECONCILIATION

We have considered how the sales and purchase ledger control accounts enable entities to ensure that their sales and purchase records are correct and to make corrections where they are not. Control over the cash book (= the bank account) is exercised through checking cash book receipts and payments with the bank statements provided regularly by the bank. Sometimes, there is no entry in the cash book for items such as bank charges, bank interest or trade receivables that may have made direct payments into an organisation's bank account which are not recorded in the cash book. Additional entries are then made in the cash book to ensure that the cash book and the bank account are in full agreement with each other and that the cash book presents a true and complete record of transactions through the bank account. At the end of every financial period, the cash book balance and the bank account balance are compared to ensure that they agree. However, there will also be entries in the cash book for cash received and cash paid that are not included in the bank statement at the end of an accounting period. This is because receipts paid in at the month end have not yet been cleared by the bank (this usually takes around three days) and payments to suppliers have been sent and recorded in the cash book but they have not yet cleared through the company's bank account. At the end of each period of account, therefore, organisations have to complete a bank reconciliation to ensure that the cash book balance (opening balance + receipts − payments) and the bank balance are in complete agreement after taking into account any uncleared or unrecorded items. Let's look at an example to see how the bank reconciliation works.

Illustration 5.21 shows the cash book Receipts and Payments total columns for Kleos Engineering Limited for the last week of June 2021.

Illustration 5.21 The cash book for the final week of June 2021 for Kleos Engineering Limited

	Receipts: June 2021			Payments: June 2021	
Date	Detail	Total £	Date	Detail	Total £
25 June	J Brown and Sons 110670	10,800.00	25 June	Optimo 005995	6,240.00
28 June	Tiddle and Toddle 110671	499.20	25 June	Wages and salaries BACS	32,462.10
28 June	Cash sales 110672	458.64	28 June	HMRC BACS	36,880.42
29 June	Vivanti plc 110673	632.64	29 June	Doric plc 005996	1,320.78
30 June	Vodravid 110674	2,429.80	30 June	Fuzzy Limited 005997	6,480.72
			30 June	Bodgitt and Leggott 005998	480.00

The balance in the bank, according to the cash book, is £25,200.42. Illustration 5.22 shows the bank statement for Kleos Engineering Limited for the final week of June 2021.

Illustration 5.22 Bank statement for the final week of June 2021 for Kleos Engineering Limited

Covetous Bank plc
Sort code: 99-99-99
Account number: 11112222

Kleos Engineering Limited
Unit 5
Any Industrial Estate
Anywhere
A14 2ZY

	Date 2021	Withdrawn	Paid in	Balance
Balance forward				94,244.16
DD BPower	25 June	400.00		93,884.16
BACS F Smith and Co	25 June		750.00	94,594.16
BACS	25 June	32,462.10		62,132.06
BACS HMRC	28 June	36,880.42		25,251.64
110672	28 June		458.64	25,710.28
110670	28 June		10,800.00	36,510.28
005995	30 June	6,240.00		30,270.28
110671	30 June		499.20	30,769.48

There is clearly a difference between the cash book balance of £25,200.42 and the bank statement balance of £30,769.48. How do these two figures reconcile with each other? Firstly we have to tick off those items that appear in both the cash book and in the bank statement to find out where the differences arise. The items that appear in both the cash book and in the bank statement are ticked and highlighted in **red** in Illustration 5.23.

Illustration 5.23 Highlighted items appearing in both the cash book and the bank statement for Kleos Engineering Limited for the final week of June 2021

Receipts: June 2021			Payments: June 2021		
Date	Detail	Total £	Date	Detail	Total £
25 June	J Brown and Sons 110670	✓10,800.00	25 June	Optimo 005995	✓6,240.00
28 June	Tiddle and Toddle 110671	✓499.20	25 June	Wages and salaries BACS	✓32,462.10
28 June	Cash sales 110672	✓458.64	28 June	HMRC BACS	✓36,880.42
29 June	Vivanti plc 110673	632.64	29 June	Doric plc 005996	1,320.78
30 June	Vodravid 110674	2,429.80	30 June	Fuzzy Limited 005997	6,480.72
			30 June	Bodgitt and Leggott 005998	480.00

	Date 2021	Withdrawn	Paid in	Balance
Balance forward				94,244.16
DD BPower	25 June	400.00		93,884.16
BACS F Smith and Co	25 June		750.00	94,594.16
BACS	25 June	✓32,462.10		62,132.06
BACS HMRC	28 June	✓36,880.42		25,251.64
110672	28 June		✓458.64	25,710.28
110670	28 June		✓10,800.00	36,510.28
005995	30 June	✓6,240.00		30,270.28
110671	30 June		✓499.20	30,769.48

The items that only appear in one of the two records are the reconciling items: these remain in black in the bank statement and in the cash book in Illustration 5.23. The first step in the bank reconciliation is to update the cash book balance for amounts paid in and withdrawn from the bank that do not appear in the cash book. This will produce the correct cash book balance to compare to the balance in the bank statement. In the bank statement, there is the receipt from F Smith and Co for £750 to add on to the cash book balance and the £400 direct debit to BPower to deduct. Illustration 5.24 shows the corrected cash book balance at 30 June 2021.

Illustration 5.24 Corrected cash book balance for Kleos Engineering Limited at 30 June 2021

	£
Cash book balance at 30 June 2021	25,200.42
Add: direct credit not in the cash book (25 June)	750.00
Deduct: direct debit to BPower (25 June)	(400.00)
Corrected cash book balance at 30 June 2021	**25,550.42**

Now that the cash book balance takes into account all the receipts and payments for the period, the cash book balance and the bank balance can be reconciled. The bank reconciliation starts with the balance in the bank statement. Receipts in the cash book that do not appear in the bank statement are then listed, totalled and added on to the bank account balance. Payments in the cash book that do not appear in the bank statement are listed, totalled and deducted from the bank statement balance. The final figure should be the balance as shown in the cash book. The bank reconciliation is presented in Illustration 5.25.

Illustration 5.25 Bank reconciliation for Kleos Engineering Limited at 30 June 2021

	£	£
Balance per bank statement (Illustration 5.22)		30,769.48
Add: cash book receipts not in the bank statement (Illustration 5.23)		
110673 29 June Vivanti plc	632.64	
110674 30 June Vodravid	2,429.80	
		3,062.44
Deduct: cash book payments not in the bank statement (Illustration 5.23)		
005996 29 June Doric plc	1,320.78	
005997 30 June Fuzzy Limited	6,480.72	
005998 30 June Bodgitt and Leggott	480.00	
		(8,281.50)
Balance per the cash book (Illustration 5.24)		**25,550.42**

Through regular checking of the cash book records to the bank statement, entities ensure that their bank balance is accurate and reflects the actual cash available for investment or making payments to clear liabilities. The bank reconciliation is another example of the ways in which organisations operate controls to ensure their financial figures are correct and up to date.

WHY IS THIS RELEVANT TO ME?   Exercising control: The bank reconciliation

As a business professional you will be expected to be able to:

- Understand how bank reconciliations are put together
- Compare the cash book and bank statements to identify unrecorded and reconciling items
- Produce and present bank reconciliation statements for the organisations you work for

SUMMARY OF KEY CONCEPTS   Are you quite sure you know what steps to follow to put the bank reconciliation together? Go to the **online workbook** to check your recollection with Summary of key concepts 5.9.

NUMERICAL EXERCISES   Do you think that you could reconcile the cash book balance and the bank statement balance? Go to the **online workbook** and complete Numerical exercises 5.5 to test your ability to make these entries.

SHOW ME HOW TO DO IT   Did you completely understand how the bank reconciliation was put together? View Video presentation 5.5 in the **online workbook** to see a practical demonstration of how the bank reconciliation was compiled.

PETTY CASH

As well as the main cash book which tracks the cash received and cash paid from the bank account, entities will also maintain a petty cash book. The petty cash book is another book of prime entry which makes the first record of small sums of cash paid out of the business on a day-to-day basis. Petty cash is a store of actual cash with which to meet small day-to-day expenses such as the purchase of, for example, tea and coffee for the office, postage stamps, items of stationery and so on. Suppliers would be unwilling to supply such small items on credit terms, so businesses use cash to make these purchases directly. The petty cash is topped up on a regular basis with money from the bank (Illustration 5.18) and this cash is then used to pay for small purchases in cash on a daily basis. Just like the bank account, the petty cash book is already a double-entry record with receipts of cash from the bank on the left hand side and payments of cash on the right. At any point in time, total receipts – total payments should be equal to the amount left in the petty cash box. Illustration 5.26 presents the petty cash book of Kleos Engineering Limited and the record of the double entry for the cash paid. Cash received is debited to the petty cash as the petty cash asset increases while the bank account is credited as the bank account asset decreases (Illustration 5.18). Cash paid out is credited to petty cash as the cash asset decreases and debited to expenditure as expenses increase (Illustration 5.26).

Illustration 5.26 The petty cash book of Kleos Engineering Limited for April 2021 and the double entry to record petty cash payments in the books of account of the company

Date	Supplier	Total £	VAT £	Tea and Coffee £	Postage £	Petrol £
6 4 2021	J and J Stores	10.20		10.20		
7 4 2021	Samoco plc	15.00	2.50			12.50
8 4 2021	Post office	12.60			12.60	
		37.80	2.50	10.20	12.60	12.50

Petty cash account

2021		£	2021		£
29 March	Cash book	100.00	8 April	Petty cash expenses	37.80

Credit petty cash, decrease asset with cash paid

VAT account

2021		£	2021		£
5 March	Sales returns	168.45	1 March	Sales day book	5,242.98
1 March	Purchase day book	1,602.04	6 April	Cash book	72.00
7 April	**Petty cash**	**2.50**	5 March	Purchase returns	94.03

Debit VAT, decrease the liability for monies owed to HM Revenue and Customs

Tea and coffee account

2021		£	2021		£
6 April	Petty cash	10.20			

Debit tea and coffee, increase the expense with cash paid

Postage account

2021		£	2021		£
8 April	Petty cash	12.60			

Debit postage, increase the expense with cash paid

Petrol account

2021		£	2021		£
8 April	Petty cash	12.50			

Debit petrol, increase the expense with cash paid

To enable you as a business professional to:

- Understand how petty cash is used to pay for small day-to-day expenses
- Make the relevant double entries in the accounting records to record receipts into petty cash
- Make the relevant double entries in the accounting records to record payments from petty cash
- Understand how the balance on the petty cash account at any point in time is calculated by deducting total payments from total receipts

MULTIPLE CHOICE QUESTIONS   Are you confident that you understand accounting for petty cash? Go to the **online workbook** and have a go at Multiple choice questions 5.4 to test your understanding.

THE PAYROLL SYSTEM

Employees provide their time in return for payment in the form of wages and salaries. Wages and salaries can be paid weekly or monthly. The rate of pay is agreed with employers in each employee's contract of employment, but employees do not receive this amount of money each week or each month. This is because employees' remuneration is subject to deductions for income tax and national insurance as well as other deductions for items such as pension contributions, trade union subscriptions and student loan repayments among others. The weekly payroll for Kleos Engineering Limited for week 51 is shown in Illustration 5.27.

Illustration 5.27 The weekly payroll for Kleos Engineering Limited

Employee name	Works number	Gross pay	PAYE (Income tax)	Employee's national insurance	Pension	Net	Employer's national insurance
		£	£	£	£	£	£
Afzal	167	700.00	86.85	65.40	35.00	512.75	74.52
Barrow	145	550.00	58.35	46.80	27.50	417.35	53.82
Begum	109	606.00	68.99	53.52	30.30	453.19	61.55
Carr	135	724.00	91.41	67.68	36.20	528.71	77.83
Desai	121	688.00	84.57	63.36	34.40	505.67	72.86
...	...	...	...	...	...	...	...
Totals for week 51		**26,144.00**	**3,121.36**	**2,374.08**	**1,307.20**	**19,341.36**	**2,724.64**

How does the payroll work? As Illustration 5.27 shows, there are various numbers that need to be considered and explained. Let's think about each of the headings and numbers in the payroll and what each of these represents.

Gross pay

Gross pay for employees with an annual salary is calculated by dividing the annual salary by 12. For example, the monthly gross pay of an employee with an annual salary of £30,000 will be £30,000 ÷ 12 = £2,500.00. Gross pay for weekly paid employees is the number of hours worked multiplied by the agreed hourly rate. Thus, for Afzal (Illustration 5.27), if she worked for 40 hours at an hourly rate of £17.50 this would give gross pay for the week of £700.00. Alternatively, £700.00 would be the gross pay for working 35 hours during the week at a rate of £20 per hour. The starting point for any payroll is the gross pay for each employee.

Income tax (PAYE)

Each employee's weekly or monthly gross pay is subject to income tax. This is often referred to as PAYE which is an abbreviation for pay-as-you-earn: employers make a deduction from each employee's gross pay for the tax that is due on their earnings each week or each month. This enables each employee to meet their obligation to pay the income tax on what they earn each year rather than being asked to pay all of the tax due for the year at the end of the tax year. The deductions for tax made by employers are paid over to HM Revenue and Customs on a regular basis throughout the financial year. Your future studies will show you how each employee's annual tax liability is calculated and how this translates into a weekly or monthly tax deduction. For now, you just need to be aware of the deduction that is made for tax and how this is accounted for each week or each month in the weekly or monthly payroll.

Employee's national insurance

As well as a weekly or monthly deduction for income tax, employees' gross pay is also subject to a deduction for national insurance contributions. These national insurance contributions are the basis for determining an individual's future rights to various state benefits such as a state pension. You will frequently see the abbreviation NIC, which is commonly used to refer to national insurance contributions. National insurance contribution deductions are made by employers and paid over to HM Revenue and Customs on a regular basis along with the deductions made for PAYE. Again, your future studies will explain how national insurance contributions are calculated and how much each individual pays on their earnings. For now, just be aware of the deductions made for national insurance and how these are accounted for on a weekly or monthly basis.

Pension contributions

Employees are not limited to just the state pension when they retire. Employers set up company pension schemes for their workforce and invite each employee to join the entity's own pension scheme when they take up employment with the organisation. Employees then make weekly or monthly contributions to the pension scheme from their wages and salaries. These contributions build up into a retirement fund for each employee over a number of

5

years which is then used to pay each employee a pension on their retirement. The contributions made by employees are deducted from their gross pay and paid over to the pension scheme on a regular basis. You will cover pension schemes and pension accounting in much greater detail in your later studies. For now you just need to understand that these deductions are made from the payroll and the way in which they are accounted for in the books of account.

Net pay

Net pay is what is left after all the deductions have been made from gross pay. For Afzal (Illustration 5.27), the gross pay of £700.00 – £86.85 (PAYE: income tax) – £65.40 (NIC) – £35.00 (pension contribution) = the net pay of £512.75. £512.75 is the amount of money that Afzal will receive for week 51. As noted above, the tax, national insurance and pension contributions are collected by the employing company and paid over to HM Revenue and Customs (tax and national insurance) and to the pension scheme (pension contribution) on Afzal's behalf.

Employer's national insurance

As well as each employee paying their own national insurance contribution each week or each month, employers also have to pay a national insurance contribution on the basis of what each employee earns each week or each month. These employer's national insurance contributions are an additional expense for the company over and above the gross pay that is paid to each employee. The employer's national insurance contributions are calculated each week or each month and paid over regularly to HM Revenue and Customs along with the PAYE and NIC deducted from employees' gross pay. You will, again, learn much more about these employer's national insurance contributions in your later studies. You should just understand for now how these employer national insurance contributions are accounted for.

> **WHY IS THIS RELEVANT TO ME?**   The payroll system
>
> To ensure you as a business professional understand:
>
> • How gross and net pay are calculated
>
> • What the various deductions from gross pay mean
>
> • How employer's national insurance is an additional expense for each employing entity

GO BACK OVER THIS AGAIN!   Are you completely certain that you understand the various parts of the payroll system? Go to the **online workbook** and complete Exercises 5.11 to check your grasp of these different elements in the payroll system.

THE DOUBLE ENTRY TO RECORD THE WEEKLY/ MONTHLY PAYROLL

Just as in the case of the sales day book, the sale returns day book, the purchase day book, the purchase returns day book, the cash book and the petty cash book, the weekly and monthly payroll is not part of the double-entry system. The weekly and monthly payroll is the book of prime entry for wages and salaries, the first point of recording expenditure made on remunerating employees for work undertaken. Therefore, the double entry still has to be completed from each weekly and monthly payroll. Three sets of double entries are required to record the payroll expenses and the additional obligations that are created when paying wages and salaries to employees.

The first double entry records the liability for gross pay and the expense that arises from the payment of wages and salaries. The liability for gross wages and salaries is credited to the wages control account as shown in Illustration 5.28. Employees have given their time in exchange for their earnings, so the giving of employees' time in the service of the entity creates a liability to pay wages and salaries. The gross wages and salaries expense is debited to the wages (expense) account (Illustration 5.28) to reflect the total expenditure incurred by the employing entity in paying their employees for the work they have undertaken.

Illustration 5.28 The double entry to record gross wages and salaries cost in the books of account of Kleos Engineering Limited

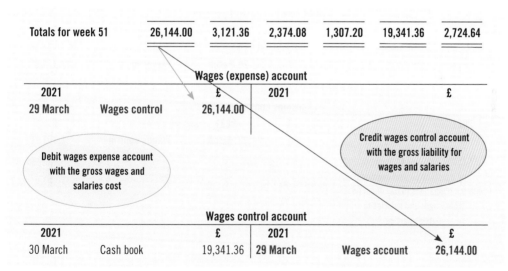

Once the double entry to record gross wages and salaries figures is complete, entries can be made to record the deductions for PAYE, employees' NIC and pensions. These deductions are debited to the wages control account as these deductions decrease the obligation to pay wages and salaries to the employees (Illustration 5.29): only the net amount (gross wages and salaries – deductions) is paid to employees. However, while these deductions from gross wages and salaries decrease the obligation to make payments to employees, they in turn create new obligations. The amounts deducted must be paid over to HM Revenue and Customs and to the pension scheme. Therefore the PAYE and employee NIC deductions are credited to the PAYE and NIC control account and the pension deductions are credited to the pensions control account to reflect this increase in liabilities (Illustration 5.29).

Illustration 5.29 The double entry to record deductions from gross wages and salaries in the books of account of Kleos Engineering Limited

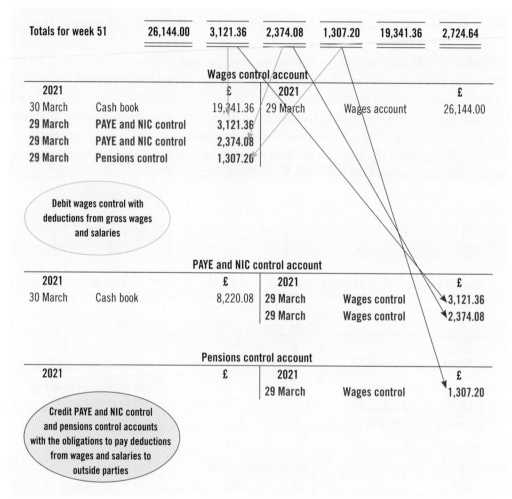

Totals for week 51	26,144.00	3,121.36	2,374.08	1,307.20	19,341.36	2,724.64

Wages control account

2021		£	2021		£
30 March	Cash book	19,341.36	29 March	Wages account	26,144.00
29 March	PAYE and NIC control	3,121.36			
29 March	PAYE and NIC control	2,374.08			
29 March	Pensions control	1,307.20			

Debit wages control with deductions from gross wages and salaries

PAYE and NIC control account

2021		£	2021		£
30 March	Cash book	8,220.08	29 March	Wages control	3,121.36
			29 March	Wages control	2,374.08

Pensions control account

2021		£	2021		£
			29 March	Wages control	1,307.20

Credit PAYE and NIC control and pensions control accounts with the obligations to pay deductions from wages and salaries to outside parties

The final double entry records the additional obligation and expense arising from the requirement to pay employer's national insurance on the gross wages and salaries of each employee. As we have seen, employer's national insurance is an expense over and above the expenditure on gross wages and salaries. This obligation creates a liability to pay more money to HM Revenue and Customs so this liability is credited to the PAYE and NIC control account. The increase in the liability is reflected as an expense which is debited to the employer's national insurance account. These entries are shown in Illustration 5.30.

Illustration 5.30 The double entry to record employer's national insurance contributions in the books of account of Kleos Engineering Limited

Totals for week 51	26,144.00	3,121.36	2,374.08	1,307.20	19,341.36	2,724.64

Employer's NIC (expense) account

2021		£	2021		£
29 March	PAYE and NIC control	2,724.64			

Debit employer's NIC expense account with the additional cost incurred

Credit PAYE and NIC account with the additional liability incurred but not yet paid

PAYE and NIC control account

2021		£	2021		£
30 March	Cash book	8,220.08	29 March	Wages control	3,121.36
			29 March	Wages control	2,374.08
			29 March	**Employer's NIC**	**2,724.64**

WHY IS THIS RELEVANT TO ME?   The double entry to record the weekly/monthly payroll

To ensure you as a business professional can:

- Make the required double entries to record the payroll expense in the books of account
- Recognise how the various expenses and liabilities associated with the payroll arise and how they are recorded in the books of account

SUMMARY OF KEY CONCEPTS   Are you quite certain that you can state the double entry to record payroll expenses and liabilities in the books of account? Go to the **online workbook** to revise the required double entry in Summary of key concepts 5.10.

GO BACK OVER THIS AGAIN!   Are you convinced that you can make the required double entry to record the payroll in the books of account? Go to the **online workbook** and complete Exercises 5.12 to make sure that you can.

SHOW ME HOW TO DO IT   Did you completely follow how the double entry was made from the payroll to the accounting records? View Video presentation 5.6 in the **online workbook** to see a practical demonstration of how the double entry was completed in the relevant T accounts.

THE NOMINAL LEDGER

Throughout both Chapters 4 and 5 we have referred frequently to the books of account to describe the various T accounts that make up the total of the accounting records of an organisation. All these accounts in their entirety make up what is called the nominal ledger (you will also find the nominal ledger referred to as the general ledger). The nominal ledger is a list of all the double-entry transactions in all the asset, liability, capital, income and expenditure T accounts of an organisation. The nominal ledger lists each account in alphabetical order and represents the books of account of the organisation. When a trial balance is extracted, this trial balance presents the balances on all the accounts in the nominal ledger. As the nominal ledger only records all the double entries made to record an organisation's transactions, it does not include the books of prime entry (which are not part of the double-entry system) or the sales and purchase ledgers (a record of individual amounts owed by customers and owed to suppliers that operate outside the double-entry system). You will find many references throughout your studies and your professional career to the nominal ledger, the record of all the double entries made by an organisation to record each and every transaction during the financial period which provide the foundation upon which the financial statements are built.

WHY IS THIS RELEVANT TO ME?   The nominal ledger

To ensure that you as a business professional understand that:

● The nominal ledger presents all the books of account of an organisation

● The nominal ledger records all the double-entry transactions of an organisation during a financial period

● The trial balance is extracted from the balances in the nominal ledger

● The books of prime entry and the sales and purchase ledgers are records separate from the nominal ledger

● The balances in the nominal ledger represent the figures that appear in the financial statements

---

SUMMARY OF KEY CONCEPTS   Are you quite certain that you understand the function and purpose of the nominal ledger? Go to the **online workbook** to check your understanding with Summary of key concepts 5.11.

GO BACK OVER THIS AGAIN!   Are you totally sure that you can describe the nominal ledger, its function and contents? Go to the **online workbook** and complete Exercises 5.13 to check your knowledge.

THE DOUBLE ENTRY TO RECORD DISPOSALS OF NON-CURRENT ASSETS

In Chapter 4 (Comprehensive example: double entry and the trial balance), we saw how Julia recorded her purchase of non-current assets (debit non-current assets with the cost of each asset, credit cash with the payment made) and the way in which depreciation of non-current assets is recorded (debit depreciation expense, credit accumulated depreciation). As we saw in Chapter 3 (Profits and losses on disposal of non-current assets), non-current assets can be sold, generating a profit or a loss on their sale if they are sold for more or less than their carrying amount. What is the double entry required when there is a disposal of non-current assets? The asset disposed of is no longer owned by the company, so the asset must be derecognised in the books of account. This derecognition must be made in both the asset cost account and the accumulated depreciation account so that the carrying amount of the asset is completely removed from the accounting records in the nominal ledger. The carrying amount of the asset disposed of is compared to the sale proceeds (if any) to determine whether there is a profit or loss on disposal. This profit or loss on disposal is recorded as either income (profit) or expense (loss) in the statement of profit or loss in the accounting period in which the disposal takes place. Let's have a look at the entries required to record an asset disposal in the books of account in Example 5.1.

EXAMPLE 5.1

Kleos Engineering Limited sells a piece of machinery on 26 February 2021 for £20,000. The machinery had originally cost £75,000. Depreciation of £60,000 had been charged on this piece of machinery up to the date of disposal.

There are three entries that have to be made on the disposal of any non-current asset. The first is to record any cash received from the disposal. The double entry to record this cash is to:

- Debit the cash asset as the cash asset has now increased (Illustration 5.31).

- Credit the non-current asset disposal account (Illustration 5.31). Cash has been received so the credit balance on this income account increases. Note that cash received from the sale of non-current assets is not recorded in sales as this is not a sale made in the ordinary course of business (Chapter 3, Income in the statement of profit or loss).

Illustration 5.31 Double entry to record the receipt of cash from the disposal of a non-current asset

Bank account

2021		£	2021		£
26 Feb	Non-current asset disposals	20,000			

Non-current asset disposals

2021		£	2021		£
			26 Feb	Bank	20,000

Step 2 is to derecognise the cost of the asset in the non-current assets cost account. The double entry to record the derecognition of cost is:

- Debit the non-current asset disposals account with the original cost of the asset (Illustration 5.32). The carrying amount of the asset at the date of disposal is compared with the cash received to determine the profit or loss on disposal. As we saw in Chapter 3, Depreciation, carrying amount = the cost of an asset – the accumulated depreciation charged on that asset. Therefore, moving the cost of the asset disposed of to the non-current asset disposals account is the first step in determining the carrying amount of the asset at the date of disposal.

- Credit the non-current asset cost account (Illustration 5.32) with the original cost of the asset. The cost of the assets still in use in the business has now decreased as a result of the disposal, so the credit to the cost account reduces the cost of the assets still employed within the business.

Illustration 5.32 Double entry to record the derecognition of the cost of a non-current asset disposed of

Non-current asset disposals

2021		£	2021		£
26 Feb	Machinery	75,000	26 Feb	Bank	20,000

Machinery account

2021		£	2021		£
			26 Feb	Non-current asset disposals	75,000

Step 3 then removes the accumulated depreciation on the asset disposed of from the accumulated depreciation account. The double entry required to remove this accumulated depreciation is to:

- Debit accumulated depreciation with the depreciation on the asset to the date of disposal (Illustration 5.33). Accumulated depreciation is a credit balance. Debiting this account will reduce the accumulated depreciation. The accumulated depreciation left on this account is then just the accumulated depreciation on assets that are still employed within the business.

- Credit the non-current asset disposal account (Illustration 5.33) with the accumulated depreciation on the asset to the date of disposal.

Illustration 5.33 Double entry to record the derecognition of the accumulated depreciation on a non-current asset disposed of

Non-current asset disposals

2021		£	2021		£
26 Feb	Machinery	75,000	26 Feb	Bank	20,000
			26 Feb	Machinery accumulated depreciation	60,000

Machinery accumulated depreciation account

2021		£	2021		£
26 Feb	Non-current asset disposals	60,000			

Is there a profit or loss on this disposal? Illustration 5.33 shows that the credit side of the non-current asset disposals account totals up to £80,000 (£20,000 cash received + £60,000 accumulated depreciation) while the debit side totals up to £75,000 (machinery cost). The total of the credits on the account is higher than the total of the debits, so the non-current asset disposals account has a credit balance of £5,000 (£80,000 − £75,000). A credit balance on an income or expense account means that this is a profit of £5,000 on disposal and this £5,000 will be recorded as a non-trading income in the statement of profit or loss in the year of disposal. Had the balance on the non-current asset disposals account been a debit balance (a higher total on the debit side of the account than on the credit side), then this would have been a loss not a profit on disposal, an additional expense in the statement of profit or loss.

Does this result make sense? You can look at this disposal from a different point of view to check that the conclusion of a profit is correct. The carrying amount of the asset disposed of is £15,000 (£75,000 cost − £60,000 accumulated depreciation). The cash received for this asset was £20,000. Therefore, a receipt of £20,000 for an asset with a carrying amount of £15,000 gives a profit of £5,000, indicating that our profit on disposal from the T account is correct.

At the end of the financial period (30 June 2021), the non-current asset disposals account is closed off as shown in Illustration 5.34.

Illustration 5.34 Closing off the non-current asset disposals account at the end of the financial period

Non-current asset disposals

2021		£	2021		£
26 Feb	Machinery	75,000	26 Feb	Bank	20,000
30 June	Statement of profit or loss	5,000	26 Feb	Machinery accumulated depreciation	60,000
		80,000			**80,000**

WHY IS THIS RELEVANT TO ME? The double entry to record disposals of non-current assets

To make sure you as a business professional can:

• Make the required double entries to record the disposal of non-current assets

• Understand why these entries are required when non-current assets are disposed of

SUMMARY OF KEY CONCEPTS Are you totally sure that you can state the double entry to record the disposal of non-current assets in the books of account? Go to the **online workbook** to revise the required double entry in Summary of key concepts 5.12.

MULTIPLE CHOICE QUESTIONS Are you confident that you can make the required double entry to record the disposal of non-current assets in the books of account and calculate profits and losses on disposal? Go to the **online workbook** and have a go at Multiple choice questions 5.5 to test your ability in this area.

FINDING MISSING FIGURES BY USING T ACCOUNTS: INCOMPLETE RECORDS

Sometimes, certain figures required to produce a set of accounts are not available as they have not been recorded. This is a common situation when preparing financial statements for cash-based businesses. However, we can find a missing figure by using the logic of T accounts as shown in Example 5.2.

EXAMPLE 5.2

Madge is a market trader selling fruit and vegetables for cash. She provides you with the following information:

- Cash in the till counted up at 31 December 2020: £529.

- Cash in the till counted up at 31 December 2021: £380.

- Cash paid into her business bank account during the year: £85,242. This figure can be verified by totalling up the receipts for the year in her business bank statements.

- Cash used to pay suppliers for goods received during the year: £50,647. This figure can be verified by reference to her purchase invoices stamped 'paid in cash' or 'cash received'.

- Total sales during the year to 31 December 2021: no records have been kept of daily cash takings on the market stall.

To complete Madge's accounts, we need to find the sales figure. As she has not kept any records of her daily cash takings, we will have to reconstruct her sales figure using the information we already have and which we can verify from other independent sources. How can we do this?

Using a T account, we can reconstruct the cash account as shown in Illustration 5.35.

Illustration 5.35 Using a T account to find an unknown or missing figure

Madge: cash account

2021		£	2021		£
1 Jan	Balance b/f	529	31 Dec	Bank account	85,242
31 Dec	Balancing figure = sales	135,740	31 Dec	Purchases	50,647
			31 Dec	Balance c/f	380
		136,269			136,269

How was the cash account shown in Illustration 5.35 reconstructed to determine the sales figure?

- The £529 cash in hand at 31 December 2020 is the closing balance of cash for that year and forms the opening cash balance at the start of the current financial year. Cash is an asset, so the opening balance of £529 will be brought down on the debit side of the cash account.

- Money paid into the bank is an increase in the bank asset (debit bank) but a decrease in the cash asset. Decreases in assets are posted to the credit side of asset accounts, so £85,242 of payments out of cash into the bank are credited to the cash account to reflect this reduction in the cash balance.

- Similarly, payments to suppliers represent a decrease in cash as money is paid out of the cash account to pay for purchases. Therefore, £50,647 is posted to the credit side of the cash account and debited to the purchases account, a reduction (credit) in cash and an increase (debit) in expenses (cost of sales).

- The balance left in the cash account at the end of the financial year is an asset, a debit balance: for a debit balance to arise on the cash account, the total on the debit side of the account has to be greater than the total on the credit side of the account. Total cash received – total cash paid out = the balance on the cash account at the end of the financial year. This cash at the end of the year is added to the credit side of the account to balance the account for the year and is carried forward as an asset transferred from the current financial year into the next financial year.

- The total on the credit side of the account is £136,269 (£85,242 of cash paid into the bank out of cash + £50,647 of cash paid for purchases from cash + £380 remaining at the end of the year to transfer to the next financial year). The only figure on the debit side of the account is the cash at the start of the year, a figure of £529. This cash existed at the start of the year, so cannot be part of cash receipts from sales for the current year. To balance the account at £136,269, a figure of £135,740 is added to the debit side. If there are £136,269 of credits, then sales of £135,740 (£136,269 – £529) must have been made to increase (debit) the cash account in order to meet the actual payments out of cash during the year and still have £380 left over at 31 December 2021.

You can use this technique to find other missing figures when putting accounting statements together. In Illustration 5.35 we found the figure for sales by using the logic of T accounts. We could also use the same logic to find missing figures for purchases or drawings among others. We shall return to this technique in Chapter 6 (Using T accounts to calculate cash flows and Appendix) to see how missing figures for cash received from sales, cash paid to suppliers and other figures can be determined from numbers given in the financial statements in order to prepare statements of cash flows.

WHY IS THIS RELEVANT TO ME?   Finding missing figures by using t accounts: incomplete records

To provide you as a business professional with:

- A way to use the logic and discipline of T accounts to reconstruct accounting figures
- A method to use in examinations to calculate figures that are not given in a question
- An awareness of the techniques you can use in practice to find missing figures

---

MULTIPLE CHOICE QUESTIONS   Do you think that you can use T accounts to determine missing numbers required to complete a set of financial statements? Go to the **online workbook** and have a go at Multiple choice questions 5.6 to make sure you can apply this technique in practice.

POTENTIAL ERRORS

Once all the double entries have been made, the trial balance is extracted from the nominal ledger accounts. If the trial balance balances, then it is tempting to assume that all the double entry has been completed correctly and that the financial statements drawn up from the nominal ledger accounts are totally accurate. However, you should be aware that various errors might arise that will require correction, even if the trial balance balances perfectly. These errors fall into six categories. These six categories are presented in Table 5.1. Think about the double entry that would be required to correct these errors.

Table 5.1 Potential double-entry errors

Category of error	Description
Error of omission	A transaction is completely missed out. For example, omitting sales for a day would understate sales income, the VAT liability and the trade receivables or cash asset. The trial balance will still balance as the debits and the credits will both be understated by exactly the same figure. Once any omissions are discovered, then the double entry must be completed with debits and credits to the relevant accounts to make the correction and to ensure that all transactions are recorded accurately and in full.
Error of commission	A transaction is posted to the correct type of account (income, expense, asset, liability or capital) but the wrong account is debited or credited. For example, recording rent as motor expenses records the rent in the correct type of account, an expense account, but in the wrong account: rent is not a motor expense. In this case, the motor expenses account would be credited and the rent account debited to record the expense in the correct account. Again, the trial balance will balance but the amounts recorded on the two expense accounts will be incorrect.
Error of principle	This is where a transaction is posted to the wrong type of account. For example, a sale is recorded as a credit to an expense account instead of a credit to the sales account. Correcting this entry would require a debit to the expense account and a credit to the sales account. The trial balance will still balance but both sales and expenses will be understated by the same amount.
Error of original entry	The correct accounts are debited and credited, but the wrong amount is recorded. For example, sales of £17,280 are recorded instead of the correct amount of £17,820. These errors are also called transposition errors as the wrong figures are entered due to two figures in the transaction total being transposed. When a transposition error occurs, the difference is divisible exactly by 9: £17,820 − £17,280 = £540 ÷ 9 = £60. Where both double entries record the incorrect figure, then the trial balance will still balance. However, where one figure is recorded correctly while the other is subject to a transposition error, then the trial balance will not balance. Should the difference on your trial balance divide by 9, then look out for a transposition error in the double entry in your T accounts. This will require methodical checking of all the double entries made to find and correct the source of the error.
Compensating error	These arise when two or more errors cancel each other out. Thus, the property, plant and equipment account might be incorrectly added up, resulting in an understatement of £1,000. An expense account is then also incorrectly added up and produces an overstatement of £1,000. These two errors will cancel each other out as one debit is £1,000 too high and another debit is £1,000 too low.
Complete reversal of entries	Transactions are posted to the correct accounts, but the debit and credit entries are reversed. For example, sales are debited with £10,000 while cash is credited with £10,000. To correct this error, the sales will be credited with £20,000 and the bank account will be debited with £20,000. The first £10,000 adjustment on both accounts will reverse the incorrect entry to bring the balances back to zero and the second £10,000 on both accounts will enter the correct amounts on the correct sides of each account.

THE TRIAL BALANCE DOES NOT BALANCE

If all the double entry has been completed correctly, then the trial balance will balance. However, when the trial balance does not balance, then there is a problem with the double entry. The trial balance may not balance for the following reasons:

- A transaction has been entered as two debits or two credits instead of one debit and one credit.

- Only the debit or the credit entry to record the transaction has been made and the double entry is incomplete.

When the trial balance fails to balance, then the difference is recorded in a suspense account. If the debits in the trial balance are lower than the credits, then the balance on the suspense account is a debit balance. If the credits in the trial balance are lower than the debits, then a credit balance is recorded in the suspense account. The T accounts are then subjected to detailed scrutiny to find and correct the trial balance difference and to reduce the balance on the suspense account to zero.

EXAMPLE 5.3

The trial balance of Kleos Engineering Limited at 30 June 2021 shows total debits of £34,491,950 and total credits of £34,500,650, a difference of £8,700. The total credits are larger than the total debits, so the difference is recorded on the debit side of the suspense account as shown in Illustration 5.36.

Illustration 5.36 Kleos Engineering Limited: the suspense account used to record the difference on the trial balance

Suspense account				
2021		**£**	**2021**	**£**
30 June	Trial balance difference	8,700		

A detailed review of the nominal ledger shows that a payment for rates in the cash book of £5,850 on 1 April was credited correctly to the bank account and credited (instead of being debited) to the rates account. Rates of £5,850 are paid quarterly in advance on 1 July, 1 October, 1 January and 1 April. The total rates charge for the year should be £23,400 (£5,850 × 4 = £23,400), but the rates account currently shows a balance of £11,700 (£17,550 debits − £5,850 credits) as presented in Illustration 5.37.

Illustration 5.37 Kleos Engineering Limited's rates account at 30 June 2021 before any corrections have been made

Rates account					
2020		**£**	**2021**		**£**
1 July	Cash book	5,850	1 April	Cash book	5,850
1 Oct	Cash book	5,850			
2021					
1 Jan	Cash book	5,850			

In addition, a further error was uncovered. Cash sales of £3,000 (including VAT of £500) had been correctly debited to the bank account but not credited to the sales account or to the VAT account. How should these errors be corrected?

The current rates expense account balance is £11,700 lower than it should be (£23,400 − the current balance of £11,700). Therefore, the rates account is debited with £11,700 and the suspense account credited with £11,700 to correct this error (Illustration 5.38). The first £5,850 of this correction eliminates the credit entry to the account and the remaining £5,850 adds the expense on to the correct side of the account. The balance on the rates account is now £23,400 (£29,250 on the debit side − £5,850 on the credit side). This leaves a balance of £3,000 credit on the suspense account (£8,700 debit balances − £11,700 credit balances). As the double entry relating to sales and VAT has been omitted from the sales and VAT account, then completing the credit entries to these accounts while debiting the suspense account will reduce the suspense account balance to zero (Illustration 5.38). There should always be a zero balance on the suspense account at the end of every financial period so that the financial statements present a complete and accurate picture of the results and financial position of an entity with no unresolved differences.

Illustration 5.38 Kleos Engineering Limited: correction of the errors on the rates, sales and VAT accounts and the cancellation of the suspense account balance

Suspense account

2021		£	2021		£
30 June	Trial balance difference	8,700	30 June	Rates (correction)	11,700
30 June	Sales (correction)	2,500			
30 June	VAT (correction)	500			
		11,700			11,700

Rates account

2020		£	2021		£
1 July	Cash book	5,850	1 April	Cash book	5,850
1 Oct	Cash book	5,850	30 June	Statement of profit or loss	23,400
2021					
1 Jan	Cash book	5,850			
30 June	Suspense (correction)	11,700			
		29,250			29,250

Sales account

2021		£	2021		£
			30 June	Suspense (correction)	2,500

VAT account

2021		£	2021		£
			30 June	Suspense (correction)	500

WHY IS THIS RELEVANT TO ME?   The trial balance does not balance

To enable you as a business professional to:

- Understand how a balance on the suspense account arises
- Make corrections to eliminate the suspense account balance
- Understand that the balance on the suspense account must be reduced to zero at the end of each financial period

---

MULTIPLE CHOICE QUESTIONS   Are you confident that you can state the required double entry to eliminate the balance on the suspense account? Go to the **online workbook** and have a go at Multiple choice questions 5.8 to test your understanding.

JOURNALS

Corrections and changes to the books of account in the nominal ledger must be recorded to provide a record of all the changes made. These changes are recorded through entries called journals. Each journal consists of details of the account or accounts to be debited and credited together with a brief explanation of the changes made by the journal entries. Journal entries are given a unique sequential number and a date to enable other users of the accounting system and books of account to trace any changes made and to ensure that all journals are recorded and that they are recorded in the correct accounting period. The journal for the corrections made in Example 5.3 would be as follows:

Journal number: 1	Debit	Credit
Date: 30 June 2021	£	£
Rates account	11,700	
Suspense account		11,700
Suspense account	2,500	
Suspense account	500	
Sales account		2,500
VAT account		500
Journal totals (must be equal)	14,700	14,700

Being entries to correct the suspense account balance on the trial balance.

WHY IS THIS RELEVANT TO ME?   Journals

To provide you as a business professional with:

• Knowledge of how corrections and changes to accounts in the nominal ledger are recorded

• A suitable journal format to use in practice now and in your future career

CHAPTER SUMMARY

You should now have learnt that:

• There are three transaction streams that give rise to financial data that require recording, sales, purchases and payroll

• Day books are the books of prime entry which are used to make the first record of accounting transactions

• Double entries are made into the nominal ledger from the books of prime entry

• Control is exercised over the sales ledger and purchase ledger through the use of control accounts reconciled to the totals on the individual sales and purchase ledger balances

- Control is exercised over the bank account through regular reconciliations between the cash book and the bank statements
- Sales and purchase transactions give rise to a net liability to pay VAT to HM Revenue and Customs
- Employing staff gives rise to liabilities to pay income tax and national insurance to HM Revenue and Customs
- Disposals of non-current assets require the cost and accumulated depreciation on those assets to be removed from the nominal ledger cost and accumulated depreciation accounts
- T accounts can be used to reconstruct accounting records to discover missing financial information
- Accountants cannot assume that nominal ledger accounts are correct as errors can arise in the preparation of accounting records

QUICK REVISION   Test your knowledge by attempting the activities in the **online workbook**, including flashcards on the key concepts, numerical exercises and Multiple choice questions. You can also try the further self-test questions which are available at www.oup.com/he/scott-i2a2e

END-OF-CHAPTER QUESTIONS

Attempt the questions in the following sections and then look at the solutions which can be found in the **online workbook** to see whether there are areas that you need to revisit.

❯ RECALL AND REVIEW

❯ Question 5.1

The following is a summary of purchases and sales made by Joanna and Co, a UK retail company, during February 2021. All transactions were made in cash. All figures given include VAT at the rate of 20%.

- Bought goods: £1,500,000.
- Sold goods which had cost £1,800,000 for £2,400,000.

Required

(a) Record the above transactions in the relevant T accounts.

(b) Calculate the net VAT payable to HMRC at 28 February 2021.

❯ Question 5.2

John Holland runs a small business. He suspects that some items of inventory have been stolen in the financial year to 31 October 2021. The company made sales with a selling price of £120,000 and purchased goods with a cost of £95,000 during the financial year to 31 October 2021.

Inventory was counted and valued at £15,000 at 31 October 2020 and at £3,000 at 31 October 2021. The mark-up on goods sold is set at 20%.

Required
Determine whether or not any inventory is missing and, if so, the cost of the inventory lost.

≫ DEVELOP YOUR UNDERSTANDING

≫ Question 5.3

Maria sets up in business on 1 April 2021 as a provider of plumbing services. She employs three members of staff. Her firm carries out work for the following customers in April, May and June:

Date 2021	Invoice number	Customer	Sales value £
16 April	0001	Benzo Limited	5,000
23 April	0002	Zorro	8,000
30 April	0003	Cotoneaster Limited	3,500
8 May	0004	Tramp Limited	2,750
11 May	0005	Dingdongbell plc	9,500
15 May	0006	Jerry Builders Limited	6,100
21 May	0007	Benzo Limited	3,400
30 May	0008	Cotoneaster Limited	5,000
6 June	0009	D-Day Builders Limited	1,300
14 June	0010	Zorro	18,000
18 June	0011	Jerry Builders Limited	9,200
26 June	0012	Dingdongbell plc	8,300
29 June	0013	Monzo plc	2,350

Maria invoiced all the above customers, adding on 20% VAT to the sales value on each invoice. In addition, she issued the following credit notes (adding 20% VAT on to each credit note) to reflect amounts overcharged on invoices:

Date 2021	Credit note number	Customer	Credit note value £
28 May	CN001	Benzo Limited	500
15 June	CN002	Zorro	1,000
20 June	CN003	Jerry Builders Limited	800
28 June	CN004	Dingdongbell plc	750

Maria trades on credit with her customers, allowing them 30 days in which to pay what is owed. During April, May and June, she received the following amounts from her trade receivables:

Date 2021	Customer	Cash Received £
16 May	Benzo Limited	6,000
23 May	Zorro	9,000
31 May	Cotoneaster Limited	4,200
12 June	Dingdongbell plc	11,400
13 June	Jerry Builders Limited	7,320
18 June	Tramp Limited	3,000
29 June	Benzo Limited	3,480

In addition, there were cash receipts from cash sales to domestic customers of £720 on 29 April, £900 on 30 May and £840 on 28 June. The amounts received from these cash sales include VAT at 20%.

Maria paid £20,000 of her own money into her business bank account on 3 April 2021.

Required

1. Write up the sales day book, the sales returns day book and the cash book for April, May and June 2021.

2. Post the entries from the sales day book, the sales returns day book and the cash book into the nominal ledger accounts, using as many T accounts as you require.

3. Post the relevant entries from the sales day book, the sales returns day book and the cash book into individual sales ledger accounts for each customer.

4. Extract the balance on each sales ledger account (total debits – total credits), add up the individual balances and agree the total of the individual balances to the trade receivables control account.

5. Without closing off the T accounts for the three months, extract a trial balance at 30 June 2021.

≫ Question 5.4

Maria's plumbing services business makes the following purchase transactions on credit with the suppliers listed below in April, May and June 2021:

Date 2021	Internal invoice number	Supplier	Plumbing materials £	Stationery £	Other £
1 April	P001	Such a Wrench Limited			1,440
5 April	P002	Honest Autos Limited			2,736
7 April	P003	Tapz n Pipez Limited	6,000		
8 April	P004	Washerz plc	1,182		
8 April	P005	Pens and Paper		300	
30 April	P006	Tapz n Pipez Limited	4,500		
4 May	P007	Washerz plc	3,000		

Date 2021	Internal invoice number	Supplier	Plumbing materials £	Stationery £	Other £
8 May	P008	Tapz n Pipez Limited	3,840		
23 May	P009	Tapz n Pipez Limited	5,250		
1 June	P010	PCUK			5/6
8 June	P011	Washerz plc	1,314		
14 June	P012	Tapz n Pipez Limited	5,400		
18 June	P013	Washerz plc	5,250		
20 June	P014	Tapz n Pipez Limited	3,906		

All the above purchase invoices include VAT at 20%. The other purchases are as follows:

- P001: tools and tool boxes with an estimated useful life of four years.
- P002: second hand van with an estimated useful life of three years.
- P010: a laptop for recording business information which has an estimated useful life of two years.

Maria made returns of goods only once during the three months and received the following credit note from her supplier:

Date 2021	Credit note number	Supplier	Credit note value £
15 June	PR01	Tapz n Pipez Limited	204

This credit note from Tapz n Pipez Limited includes VAT at 20%.

During April, May and June, Maria made the following payments to her trade payables from her bank account:

Date 2021	Supplier	Cash paid £
20 April	Such a Wrench Limited	1,440
30 April	Honest Autos Limited	2,736
8 May	Washerz plc	1,182
10 May	Pens and Paper	300
25 May	Tapz n Pipez Limited	10,500
4 June	Washerz plc	3,000
20 June	Tapz n Pipez Limited	9,090
29 June	PC UK	576

In addition, there were payments from the bank for plumbing materials of £480 on 25 April, £360 on 18 May and £540 on 22 June: all these payments include VAT at 20%.

Cash withdrawn from the bank for petty cash was £200 on 10 April, £250 on 16 May and £300 on 14 June. Petty cash payments for petrol for the van were £180 for April, £240 for May and £312 for June. The payments for petrol include VAT at 20%.

Maria paid the VAT due to HM Revenue and Customs on 30 June 2021 (use the balance on the VAT account (total credits – total debits) to calculate Maria's payment on 30 June).

Payments to her employees for wages were £7,036 on 30 April, £7,172 on 31 May and £6,560 on 29 June. Pay as you earn and NIC payments of £3,030 were made on 15 May and £3,122 on 18 June.

Required

1. Write up the purchase day book, the purchase returns day book, the cash book and the petty cash book for April, May and June 2021.

2. Post the entries from the purchase day book, the purchase returns day book, the cash book and the petty cash book into the nominal ledger accounts, adding as many new T accounts as you require. You should use the relevant accounts you set up in your answers to Question 5.3 and add in additional entries where required.

3. Post the relevant entries from the purchase day book, the purchase returns day book and the cash book into individual purchase ledger accounts for each supplier.

4. Extract the balance on each purchase ledger account (total credits – total debits), add up the individual balances and agree the total of the individual balances to the trade payables control account.

5. Without closing off the T accounts for the three months, extract a trial balance at 30 June 2021. You should include the T accounts relating to sales transactions from Question 5.3 in your trial balance.

›› Question 5.5

Maria pays her employees monthly and presents you with the following payroll information for April, May and June 2021:

Month	Gross	PAYE	Employee's NIC	Net	Employer's NIC
	£	£	£	£	£
April	9,100	1,221	843	7,036	966
May	9,300	1,261	867	7,172	994
June	8,400	1,081	759	6,560	869

Required

1. Post the entries from the monthly payroll into the nominal ledger accounts, adding as many new T accounts as you require. You should use the relevant accounts you set up in your answers to Question 5.4 and add in additional entries where required.

2. Using the information on non-current assets and their expected useful lives given in Question 5.4, calculate depreciation on the non-current assets for the three months to 30 June 2021. Opening as many new T accounts as you require, post the depreciation charges to the relevant accounts.

3. Without closing off the accounts, extract Maria's trial balance at 30 June 2021.

4. Using the trial balance, prepare Maria's statement of profit or loss for the three months ended 30 June 2021 together with a statement of financial position at that date. Maria had no inventory at 30 June 2021 and there was no prepaid expenditure and no accrued expenditure at 30 June 2021.

>> Question 5.6

Alex runs a small shop. At 31 October 2021 the shop's cash book showed a debit balance of £4,550. On checking the business's bank statement, Alex found the following differences between the bank statement and the shop's cash book:

- A cheque for £2,300 received from Jack had been returned unpaid as there were insufficient funds in Jack's account.

- A cheque for £900 paid to Alana, a supplier, has not yet been presented for payment to Alex's bank.

- Alex deposited £780 on 30 October 2021 which is not shown in the bank statement.

- Bank charges of £65 have not yet been recorded in the cash book.

- £370 was paid directly into the bank by Arthur, a customer. This amount does not appear in the shop's cash book at 31 October 2021.

Required

Using the above information, calculate the balance per the bank statement at 31 October 2021.

>> Question 5.7

Brianna Limited bought a piece of equipment on 1 July 2019 for £250,000. It is expected that the equipment will be in use for five years and have a residual value of £30,000 at the end of its useful life. The company may use the straight line basis of depreciation or the reducing balance basis at 35%.

Required

(a) Compute the annual depreciation charges on the equipment using the straight line and reducing balance bases.

(b) The company sells the equipment for £150,000 on 30 June 2021. How much is the gain or loss on disposal if the straight line basis is used?

(c) What is the double entry for the sale of the asset described in part (b)?

(d) Recalculate your answer for part (b) using the reducing-balance basis.

Explain the difference arising between the gain or loss on the sale of the asset calculated in parts (b) and (d).

>>> TAKE IT FURTHER

The cashier of the Wright Company has completed the entries in the cash book for April 2021. The bank statement received on 30 April 2021 shows a bank balance that does not agree with the bank balance shown in the cash book. The cash book and bank statement for April 2021 are presented below.

Cash book

Date	Description	Debit £	Credit £	Balance £
01/04/2021	Balance b/f			3,500
05/04/2021	Deposit	800		4,300
06/04/2021	Cheque 315		450	3,850
15/04/2021	Cheque 316		340	3,510
19/04/2021	Cheque 317		230	3,280
23/04/2021	Deposit	760		4,040
24/04/2021	Cheque 318		550	3,490
29/04/2021	Deposit	290		3,780

Bank statement

Date	Description	Withdrawn £	Paid in £	Balance £
01/04/2021	Balance b/f			3,500
06/04/2021	Deposit		800	4,300
13/04/2021	Cheque 315	450		3,850
17/04/2021	Cheque 316	340		3,510
19/04/2021	Cheque 2216 – NFS	370		3,140
20/04/2021	Bank charges	15		3,125
25/04/2021	Deposit		760	3,885
28/04/2021	Cheque 318	550		3,335
29/04/2021	Transfer by Watson Limited		490	3,825
29/04/2021	Interest		60	3,885

Required

(a) Prepare a bank reconciliation statement showing how the difference between the cash book balance and the bank statement arises.

(b) Adjust the balance in the cash book.

>>> **Question 5.9**

Shortly after graduation, Sarah decided to start her own business, Sarah's Plants, a flower shop. The following transactions were undertaken by Sarah's Plants during February 2021:

- 1 February: Transferred £20,000 from Sarah's personal savings account into the business bank account.
- 4 February: Took out a bank loan of £10,000.
- 7 February: Paid the first month's shop rent of £800.
- 8 February: Bought a delivery van for £5,000 with a cheque.
- 9 February: Paid £2,000 to a local newspaper for advertising.
- 10 February: Purchased flowers for £2,500 on credit.
- 11 February: Made cash sales of £600.
- 13 February: Purchased flowers by bank card for £700.
- 15 February: Made credit sales of £900.
- 18 February: Paid the amount owed for the flowers purchased on 10 February.
- 23 February: Paid £320 for electricity and gas.
- 25 February: Made sales of £1,600. The customer paid by bank transfer.
- 27 February: Made credit sales of £1,400.
- 28 February: Sarah withdrew £1,000 from the business bank account for her own personal expenditure.

On 28 February 2021 Sarah downloaded a bank statement and compared it to the business bank account transactions recorded in her books. She found the following differences:

- Bank charges of £25 were recorded in the Withdrawn column of the bank statement.
- Interest of £10 was recorded in the Paid in column of the bank statement.
- £900 was recorded in the Paid in column of the statement.

You are also provided with the following additional information:

- The delivery van is to be depreciated using the reducing balance basis. The depreciation rate to be applied is 30%.
- Flowers with a cost of £800 remained unsold at 28 February 2021.
- The amount paid for advertising covers adverts in the local newspaper for 10 months.

Required

(a) Record Sarah's Plants' transactions in T accounts.

(b) Post the necessary adjustments to the relevant T accounts at the end of February 2021.

(c) Make any additional entries required to adjust the bank account based on the transactions recorded in the bank statement.

(d) Extract a trial balance at 28 February 2021.

(e) Prepare a statement of profit or loss for the month to 28 February 2021 and a statement of financial position at that date.

>>> Question 5.10

Question 5.10 is an extended case study, building up a full set of T accounts and final financial statements. After attempting each task, you should check your answer with the solutions presented in the **online workbook** to make sure that your answers are correct before moving on to the next task.

ABC Limited is a manufacturing company which produces and sells Bodgets. Opening balances at 1 May 2020 are as follows:

	Debit £	Credit £
Factory cost	650,000	
Factory accumulated depreciation		78,000
Motor vehicles cost	220,000	
Motor vehicles accumulated depreciation		88,000
Plant and machinery cost	275,000	
Plant and machinery accumulated depreciation		137,500
Inventory at 1 May 2020	112,280	
Trade receivables control account	2,056,918	
Allowance for receivables		30,854
Prepayments: insurance	1,000	
rates	1,600	
equipment hire	1,850	
Bank account	132,158	
Petty cash	290	
Trade payables control account		1,222,955
Accruals: audit fee		3,000
bank charges		180
rent		4,500
wages		3,000
PAYE and NIC control account		31,216
VAT		378,599
Taxation payable		199,800
Share capital		600,000
Share premium		90,000
Retained earnings at 1 May 2020		583,492
	3,451,096	**3,451,096**

Task 1

Set up nominal ledger T accounts and post the opening balances to these nominal ledger T accounts.

You should post opening inventory to the cost of sales account.

***

An analysis of the books of prime entry for the year to 30 April 2021 shows the following details:

Sales day book	£
Sales (net of VAT)	9,435,600
VAT	1,887,120
Sales day book total	**11,322,720**

Sales returns day book	£
Sales returns (net of VAT)	385,600
VAT	77,120
Sales returns day book total	**462,720**

Purchase day book	£
Raw materials	4,451,920
Motor expenses	39,200
Plant and machinery	70,000
Motor vehicle	25,000
Audit and accountancy	9,000
Legal expenses	5,000
Printing and stationery	12,000
Postage	5,400
VAT	922,424
Purchase day book total	**5,539,944**

Purchase returns day book	£
Raw materials	111,300
Motor expenses	450
VAT	22,350
Purchase returns day book total	**134,100**

Petty cash book payments	£
Postage	1,875
Office refreshments	4,214
Entertaining customers	2,632
Stationery	1,642
Petrol	8,600
VAT	3,410
Total petty cash expenditure	**22,373**

Petty cash receipts	£
From bank	22,500
Stamps sold	20
Total petty cash receipts	**22,520**

Cash book receipts	£
Trade receivables	10,994,382
Receipt from sale of motor vehicle	5,500
Receipt from sale of plant and machinery	4,800
VAT on asset sales	960
Bank interest	800
Total cash book receipts	**11,006,442**

Cash book payments	£
Trade payables	5,524,932
Wages payments	2,163,488
Salaries payments	434,976
PAYE and NIC	1,063,732
VAT	1,059,206
Pension payments	161,750
Petty cash	22,500
Taxation	199,800
Dividends	60,000
Bank charges	1,988
Total cash book payments	**10,692,372**

Wages and salaries	Wages	Salaries
	£	£
Gross wages	2,929,100	600,000
PAYE	352,529	78,000
Employees NIC	266,628	57,024
Pension	146,455	30,000
Net wages and salaries paid to employees	**2,163,488**	**434,976**
Employers NIC	**306,622**	**65,578**

The bank statement shows the following items not in the cash book at the year end:

	£
Bank charges	50
BACS receipt from a trade receivable customer	750

Task 2

Post all the transactions from the books of prime entry to the nominal ledger T Accounts. In addition to the T accounts already set up with the opening balances, you will need to open T accounts with the following headings:

- Bank interest
- Dividends
- Employers' NIC salaries
- Employers' NIC wages
- Entertaining customers
- Legal expenses
- Motor expenses
- Non-current asset disposals
- Office refreshments
- Pension control
- Postage
- Printing and stationery
- Salaries
- Sales
- Wages control

Raw materials figures should be posted to the cost of sales T account.

***

Task 3

Adjustments

1 Non-current asset disposals

The non-current assets sold during the year had an original cost of £20,000 (plant and machinery) and £19,000 (motor vehicle). The plant and machinery had been purchased four years ago and had been depreciated at the rate of 20% per annum straight line. The motor vehicle had been purchased three years ago and had been depreciated at the rate of 30% per annum reducing balance. Adjustments to remove these assets have not yet been made in the books of the company.

2 Depreciation

Depreciation is to be provided at the following rates:

Plant and machinery	20% per annum straight line on cost at the end of the financial year
Motor vehicles	30% per annum reducing balance on carrying amount at the end of the financial year
Factory	2% per annum straight line on cost

Land is not depreciated.

The factory buildings have a cost of £490,000 and land a cost of £160,000.

3 Prepayments

Prepayments at 30 April 2021 were as follows:

	£
Insurance	750
Rates	500

You should set up a prepayments account in which to record all the prepayments at 30 April 2021.

4 Accruals

Accruals for the following expenses are required:

	£
Audit and accountancy	5,000
Bank charges	100
Legal expenses	750
Rent	2,750
Wages	2,500

You should set up an accruals account in which to record all the accruals at 30 April 2021.

5 Irrecoverable debts and allowance for receivables

The allowance for receivables is to be adjusted to 1.50% of trade receivables at 30 April 2021 after allowing for specific irrecoverable debts at the year end of £17,786. You should set up a combined irrecoverable debts and allowance for receivables expense account in which to record both irrecoverable debts and changes in the allowance for receivables balance.

6 Inventory

Inventory at the year end was counted and had a cost of £125,228.

7 Taxation

A provision for taxation on the profit for the year of £118,285 is to be made in the accounts.

8 Errors/mispostings

The following expenditure has been posted to raw materials (cost of sales) and requires reallocating to the correct expenditure heading:

Insurance: £20,000

Rates: £15,000

Rent: £11,000

Post the above adjustments to the nominal ledger T accounts, opening any new T accounts required.

***

5

Task 4

Extract the trial balance at 30 April 2021.

***

Task 5

Prepare a statement of profit or loss for the year ended 30 April 2021 and a statement of financial position for the company at that date. Expenditure in the statement of profit or loss should be allocated to the following headings:

Cost of sales

- Cost of sales
- Employer's NIC wages
- Equipment hire
- Factory annual depreciation charge
- Plant and machinery annual depreciation charge
- Rates
- Rent
- Wages

Distribution and selling costs

- Employer's NIC salaries (50%)
- Entertaining customers
- Motor expenses
- Motor vehicle annual depreciation charge
- Salaries (50%)

Administration expenses

- Audit and accountancy
- Bank charges
- Employer's NIC salaries (50%)
- Insurance
- Irrecoverable debts and allowance for receivables expense
- Legal expenses
- Profit or loss on non-current asset disposals
- Office refreshments
- Postage
- Printing and stationery
- Salaries (50%)

Finance income

- Bank interest

***

Task 6

Close off all the T accounts and bring down the opening balances at 1 May 2021.

***

THE STATEMENT OF CASH FLOWS

6

LEARNING OUTCOMES

Once you have read this chapter and worked through the questions and examples in both this chapter and the online workbook, you should be able to:

- Understand that profit does not equal cash

- Appreciate that without a steady cash inflow from operations an entity will not be able to survive

- Describe the make up of operating, investing and financing cash flows

- Prepare statements of cash flows using both the direct and indirect methods

- Use T accounts to calculate figures for use in preparing statements of cash flows

- Explain the importance of statements of cash flows as the third key accounting statement alongside the statement of profit or loss and statement of financial position

- Understand why statements of cash flows on their own would be insufficient to present a clear picture of an entity's performance and financial position

- Summarise and describe the conventions upon which accounting is based

INTRODUCTION

Chapters 2 and 3 considered two of the three main accounting statements that entities publish relating to each accounting period. The statement of financial position gives us a snapshot of an entity's assets and liabilities at the end of each accounting period, while the statement of profit or loss shows us the profit or loss based on the income generated and expenditure incurred within each accounting period. This chapter will consider the third key accounting statement, the statement of cash flows, which presents users of financial information with details of cash inflows and outflows for an accounting period. As we shall see, the statement of cash flows links together the statement of profit or loss and statement of financial position to demonstrate changes in an entity's financial position over each accounting period arising from operating, investing and financing activities.

Without a steady inflow of cash, businesses cannot survive. Thus, if cash is not generated from sales, there will be no money with which to pay liabilities owed, to pay wages to employees to produce or sell goods, to pay rent on facilities hired, to pay returns to investors or to finance growth and expansion. Over time, cash inflows must exceed cash outflows in order for an entity to remain a going concern, a business that will continue into the foreseeable future. The ability of a business to generate cash is thus critical to its survival as, without a steady inflow of cash, the business cannot carry on, no matter how profitable. It is hugely important to appreciate that profit does not represent cash. To illustrate this fact, Give me an example 6.1 presents the case of Salesforce.com which generates a modest profit while enjoying very strong cash inflows from its daily operations.

GIVE ME AN EXAMPLE 6.1   Salesforce.com

In the financial year to 31 January 2019, Salesforce.com, the customer relationship management software business, reported a net profit of $1,110m. However, cash generated from operations amounted to $3,398m, a difference of $2,288m. How does this difference arise? Many if not all customers pay in full for the services they buy when they sign the contract. However, the sales income and profit from each contract are recognised over the life of that contract which may extend for several months or even years. Cash is thus received far in advance of the point in time at which services are provided.

Source: https://investor.salesforce.com/financials/default.aspx

WHY IS THIS RELEVANT TO ME?   The importance of cash

To enable you as a business professional to understand that:

• Profit is not equivalent to cash

• Turning profits into cash is a most important task for businesses

• Without cash, businesses will not be able to meet their commitments or fund their expansion plans and will fail

GO BACK OVER THIS AGAIN!   Do you really appreciate how important cash and cash inflow are? Go to the **online workbook** Exercises 6.1 to make sure you have grasped this critical lesson.

STATEMENT OF CASH FLOWS: THE IAS 7 PRESENTATION FORMAT

What format does the statement of cash flows take? International Accounting Standard 7 (IAS 7) sets out the format in which the statement of cash flows should be presented. Illustration 6.1 shows the statement of cash flows for Bunns the Bakers plc for the years ended 31 March 2021 and 31 March 2020 in the IAS 7 required format. As with the statement of financial position and the statement of profit or loss, we shall look at the statement of cash flows in its entirety before considering how each part of the statement is constructed and what the terminology means.

Note: cash inflows (money coming in) are shown without brackets while cash outflows (money going out) are shown in brackets. Work through the statement of cash flows, adding the figures without brackets and deducting the figures in brackets to help you understand how the cash inflows and outflows add up to the subtotals given.

The net increase in cash and cash equivalents for the year ended 31 March 2021 of £23,000 is given by adding the net cash inflow from operating activities (+ £1,219,000) and then subtracting the net cash outflow from investing activities (− £891,000) and subtracting the net cash outflow from financing activities (− £305,000). Check back to the statement of financial position for Bunns the Bakers plc (Chapter 2, Illustration 2.1) to make sure that the figure given for cash and cash equivalents at 31 March 2021 is £212,000. Repeat the calculations for 2020 to make sure you understand how the figures in the statement of cash flows are derived.

SUMMARY OF KEY CONCEPTS   Are you certain that you know how to calculate the net increase/ (decrease) in cash and cash equivalents? Go to the **online workbook** to check your knowledge with Summary of key concepts 6.1.

GO BACK OVER THIS AGAIN!   A copy of this statement of cash flows (Illustration 6.1) is available in the **online workbook**. You might like to keep this on screen or print off a copy for easy reference while you work your way through the material in this chapter. There is also an annotated copy of this statement of cash flows available at the end of the book to help you go over the relevant points again to reinforce your knowledge and learning.

Illustration 6.1 Bunns the Bakers plc statement of cash flows for the years ended 31 March 2021 and 31 March 2020

6

	2021 £000	2020 £000
Cash flows from operating activities		
Profit for the year	547	442
Income tax expense	213	172
Finance expense	150	165
Finance income	(15)	(12)
(Increase)/decrease in inventories	(5)	8
Decrease in trade and other receivables	13	9
Increase/(decrease) in trade and other payables	109	(15)
Amortisation of intangible non-current assets	5	7
Depreciation of property, plant and equipment	394	362
(Profit)/loss on the disposal of property, plant and equipment	(3)	4
Cash generated from operations	1,408	1,142
Taxation paid	(189)	(154)
Net cash inflow from operating activities	1,219	988
Cash flows from investing activities		
Acquisition of property, plant and equipment	(910)	(600)
Acquisition of investments	(6)	(11)
Proceeds from the sale of property, plant and equipment	10	47
Interest received	15	12
Net cash ouflow from investing activities	(891)	(552)
Cash flows from financing activities		
Proceeds from the issue of ordinary share capital	235	148
Dividends paid	(90)	(72)
Repayment of the current portion of long-term borrowings	(300)	(300)
Interest paid	(150)	(165)
Net cash ouflow from financing activities	(305)	(389)
Net increase in cash and cash equivalents	23	47
Cash and cash equivalents at the start of the year	189	142
Cash and cash equivalents at the end of the year	212	189

CONSTRUCTING THE STATEMENT OF CASH FLOWS

Illustration 6.1 shows that Bunns the Bakers' statement of cash flows consists of three sections:

- Cash flows from operating activities
- Cash flows from investing activities
- Cash flows from financing activities.

These three sections represent the inflows and outflows of cash for all entities. Let us look at each of these categories in turn.

Cash flows from operating activities

All entities operate with a view to generating cash with which to finance their day-to-day operations, their operating activities, and with the intention and expectation of generating surplus cash for future investment and expansion. This cash generated will consist of the cash from sales less the cash spent in both generating those sales and in running the organisation.

As we have already seen, Bunns the Bakers produces bakery goods and buys in other goods for resale in the shops. Operating cash inflows will thus consist of money received from sales in the shops while operating cash outflows will be made up of the money spent on:

- Producing the goods
- Buying goods in for resale
- Distributing the goods to shops
- Selling those goods in the shops
- Administration expenses incurred in the running of the business.

The difference between the trading and operating cash flowing into the business and the trading and operating cash flowing out of the business will give the net operating cash inflows or outflows for each accounting period, the cash generated from operations. Any taxation paid by the entity will also be deducted from operating cash flows as shown in Illustration 6.1. Tax arises as a consequence of profits made from operating activities, so any tax paid in an accounting period will be deducted from the cash generated from operations.

Bunns the Bakers' statement of cash flows is an example of the indirect method of cash flow preparation. This approach requires that the profit for the year is subjected to certain adjustments: these adjustments are presented in the Cash flows from operating activities calculation in the first part of Illustration 6.1. These adjustments to the profit firstly add back the income tax expense, finance expense and finance income to arrive at the operating profit line in the statement of profit or loss. Further adjustments then represent the effect of non-cash income and expenses in the statement of profit or loss alongside movements in working capital (changes in inventory, trade and other receivables and trade and other payables over the course of the accounting period) and are made in order to work back to the actual cash generated from operating activities. These adjustments and how they are derived are explained in more detail later in this chapter, The indirect method. Give me an example 6.2 presents the Cash flows from operating activities for Greggs plc to illustrate many of the adjustments made to the profit for the year to determine the cash flows from operating activities that you will come across in practice.

GIVE ME AN EXAMPLE 6.2 Cash flows from operating activities

What sort of cash flows from operating activities do companies present in their annual reports and accounts? The following extract is taken from the statements of cash flows of Greggs plc for the 52 weeks ended 28 December 2019 and the 52 weeks ended 29 December 2018.

Cash flow statement—cash generated from operations

	2019 £m	2018 £m
Profit for the financial year	87.0	65.7
Amortisation	3.8	3.0
Depreciation – property, plant and equipment	56.1	52.9
Depreciation – right-of-use assets	50.8	–
Impairment – property, plant and equipment	0.3	0.3
Impairment – right-of-use assets	0.5	–
Loss on sale of property, plant and equipment	1.2	1.6
Release of government grants	(0.5)	(0.5)
Share-based payment expenses	4.4	2.0
Finance expense	6.5	–
Income tax expense	21.3	16.9
(Increase) in inventories	(3.1)	(2.1)
Decrease in receivables	4.5	1.8
Increase in payables	19.9	12.9
Decrease in provisions	(1.7)	(4.0)
(Decrease)/ increase in pension liability	(5.0)	1.7
Cash from operating activities	**246.0**	**152.2**

Source: Greggs plc annual report and accounts 2019 https://corporate.greggs.co.uk/investors/results-centre

Just as in the case of Bunns the Bakers, Greggs plc presents the movements in working capital (changes in inventory, receivables, trade payables and provisions as well as increases or decreases in the pension liability), adds back amortisation and depreciation charged on non-current assets together with losses on the sale of non-current assets and adds back the income tax and finance expenses deducted from operating profit in calculating the profit for the year. In addition, Greggs makes an entry for the impairment of non-current assets: this is a loss in the carrying value of non-current assets over and above the regular charge for depreciation that is added to the statement of profit or loss as an expense as soon as it is known: charges for (or reversals of) impairment are an expense (income) in the statement of profit or loss which do not involve any cash inflow or outflow. Companies that receive government grants record the cash received in the year of receipt as a cash inflow from financing activities but release a portion of each grant to the statement of profit or loss each year: as this allocation to the statement of profit or loss is not a cash flow, the income is deducted from operating profit to arrive at cash flows from operating activities. Payments in shares are an expense but do not involve cash as shares are used to make the payments, so these share-based payment expenses are also added back to profit for the year in calculating cash flows from operating activities.

GO BACK OVER THIS AGAIN!   Are you convinced that you can distinguish between cash inflows and cash outflows from operating activities? Go to the **online workbook** and complete Exercises 6.2 to make sure you can make these distinctions.

Cash flows from investing activities

In order to expand a business, entities must invest in new capacity in the form of non-current assets. Any cash paid out to buy new property, plant and equipment or intangible assets such as trademarks will appear under this heading as this represents investment of cash into new long-term assets with which to generate new income by expanding and improving the business. Where an entity has surplus funds that cannot currently be used to invest in such assets, it will place those funds in long-term investments to generate interest or dividend income that will increase the profits of the organisation. Thus, any investment in non-current asset investments will also appear under this heading. Note that both of these uses of cash represent outflows of cash as cash is leaving the business in exchange for new property, plant and equipment or new long-term investments.

In addition to these outflows of cash, investing activities also give rise to inflows of cash. When buying new property, plant and equipment, it is quite likely that some other non-current assets will be sold or scrapped at the same time, as these are now worn out or surplus to requirements. Selling or scrapping these assets will result in a cash inflow and any cash raised in this way will be classified under investing activities. Likewise, any interest or dividends received from investing surplus funds in current or non-current asset investments are also cash inflows under investing activities: the investments were made with a view to generating investment income, so such cash inflows are logically included under this heading. Cash inflows and outflows from investing activities are summarised in Figure 6.1 while Give me an example 6.3 presents the Cash flows from investing activities for Greggs plc to provide a real life illustration of these cash inflows and outflows.

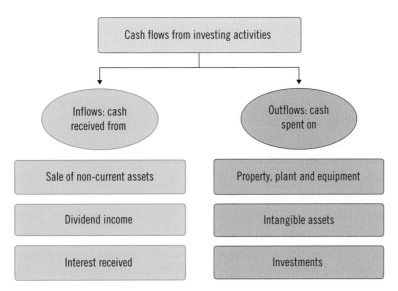

Figure 6.1 Cash inflows and outflows from investing activities

6

GIVE ME AN EXAMPLE 6.3   Cash flows from investing activities

What sort of cash flows from investing activities do companies present in their annual reports and accounts? The following extract is taken from the statements of cash flows of Greggs plc for the 52 weeks ended 28 December 2019 and the 52 weeks ended 29 December 2018.

Investing activities

	2019 £m	2018 £m
Acquisition of property, plant and equipment	(85.4)	(61.4)
Acquisition of intangible assets	(3.7)	(5.2)
Proceeds from sale of property, plant and equipment	1.4	1.7
Interest received	0.3	0.2
Net cash outflow from investing activities	**(87.4)**	**(64.7)**

Source: Greggs plc annual report and accounts 2019 https://corporate.greggs.co.uk/investors/results-centre

All the above entries should be familiar to you from the statement of cash flows of Bunns the Bakers.

GO BACK OVER THIS AGAIN!   Are you quite sure that you could say whether a transaction is a cash inflow or cash outflow from investing activities? Go to the **online workbook** and complete Exercises 6.3 to make sure you can make these decisions correctly.

Cash flows from financing activities

There are three main sources of finance for a business. The first of these is cash generated from operations. This source of cash has already been dealt with earlier under 'Cash flows from operating activities'.

The second source of finance for business is from the issue of share capital. Bunns the Bakers have issued shares during the year for cash and so this is recorded as a cash inflow to the business: money has been paid into the company in return for new shares. Shareholders expect a return on their investment in the company: the cash outflows related to share capital are the dividends paid out to shareholders (Chapter 7, Dividends). The payment of dividends is an outflow of cash and is recorded under financing activities as it relates to the cost of financing the business through share capital.

The third source of finance is provided by lenders, money borrowed from banks or the money markets to finance expansion and the acquisition of new non-current assets. As the expansion/new non-current assets generate cash from their operation, these cash inflows are used to repay the borrowings over the following years, much as a taxi driver might borrow money to buy a taxi and then repay that loan from monthly fares earned. This is the case for Bunns the Bakers this year. While no new borrowings have been taken out (this would be an inflow of cash) part of the money previously borrowed has now been repaid from cash generated from operations in the current year. Repayments of borrowings are an outflow of cash. Any interest paid that arises from borrowing money is recorded as an outflow of cash under financing activities. Just as dividends are the cost of financing operations or expansion through the issue of share capital, interest is the cost of financing operations or expansion through borrowing and so is matched to the financing activities section of the statement of cash flows. Figure 6.2 summarises the cash inflows and outflows from financing activities while Give me an example 6.4 presents the Cash flows from financing activities for Greggs plc to provide a real life example of these cash inflows and outflows.

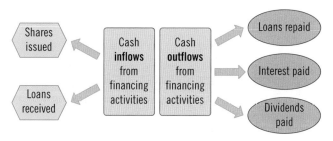

Figure 6.2 Cash inflows and cash outflows from financing activities

---

GIVE ME AN EXAMPLE 6.4   Cash flows from financing activities

What sort of cash flows from financing activities do companies present in their annual reports and accounts? The following extract is taken from the statements of cash flows of Greggs plc for the 52 weeks ended 28 December 2019 and the 52 weeks ended 29 December 2018.

Financing activities

	2019 £m	2018 £m
Sale of own shares	4.9	5.2
Purchase of own shares	(11.8)	(9.9)
Dividends paid	(72.1)	(33.0)
Repayment of principal of lease liabilities	(49.6)	–
Net cash outflow from financing activities	**(128.6)**	**(37.7)**

Source: Greggs plc annual report and accounts 2019 https://corporate.greggs.co.uk/investors/results-centre

Just as in the case of Bunns the Bakers, cash from the sale of shares is an inflow of cash to the business while dividends paid are an outflow. Why would Greggs buy its own shares? As noted under Give me an example 6.2, Cash flows from operating activities, Greggs incurs share-based payment expenses. The company buys shares in the stock market and then uses these shares to make the share-based payments. As we noted in Give me an example 6.2, share-based payments do not involve a cash outflow. Instead, the cash outflow occurs when the company buys its shares with which to meet the share-based payments. As we saw in Chapter 2 (Non-current assets, Give me an example 2.2) IFRS 16 now requires organisations to recognise all assets leased but not owned by an entity as both non-current assets and as a corresponding liability. As payments are made to landlords and other owners of these leased assets, these payments represent both a repayment of the principal (the amount 'borrowed' under these lease agreements) of these lease liabilities and a payment of interest on the amounts 'borrowed' under the leases. Greggs plc records a cash outflow for interest paid of £6.6m on these lease liabilities as a deduction from cash generated from operating activities, an alternative presentation permitted by IAS 7.

GO BACK OVER THIS AGAIN! How easily can you distinguish between cash inflows and cash outflows from financing activities? Go to the **online workbook** and complete Exercises 6.4 to make sure you can make these distinctions.

Cash and cash equivalents

The sum of all three cash flow sections will equal the movement in cash and cash equivalents during the accounting period. The meaning of cash is quite clear, but you might be puzzled by the phrase cash equivalents. Is there really an equivalent to cash?

What this means is anything that is close to cash, a source of cash that could be called upon immediately if required. Such a source might be a bank deposit account rather than money held in the current account for immediate use. Where money held in bank deposit accounts is readily convertible into cash then this is a cash equivalent. Thus, cash held in a deposit account requiring 30 days' notice would be a cash equivalent as the cash can easily be converted into a fixed sum of cash in a maximum of 30 days. However, cash currently held in a bond with a maturity date in two years' time would not be a cash equivalent as it cannot be converted easily to cash now or in the very near future. The International Accounting Standards Board allows any deposit of cash with a notice term of 90 days or less to be classified as a cash equivalent alongside money held in current accounts and held as cash on the business premises.

WHY IS THIS RELEVANT TO ME?   Cash flows from operating activities, investing activities and financing activities

To enable you as a business professional to:

• Understand the different sources from which cash flows into and out of an entity

• Read statements of cash flows and understand what the various cash inflows and outflows of an organisation represent, along with the transactions behind them

---

MULTIPLE CHOICE QUESTIONS   Do you think that you can say to which category of cash flows a cash inflow or outflow belongs? Go to the **online workbook** and complete Multiple choice questions 6.1 to make sure you can identify these accurately.

GO BACK OVER THIS AGAIN!   Are you confident you can categorise cash inflows and outflows correctly? Go to the **online workbook** and complete Exercises 6.5 to check your understanding.

SUMMARY OF KEY CONCEPTS   Are you quite sure that you can say how cash flows from operating activities, investing activities and financing activities are made up? Go to the **online workbook** to revise these categories with Summary of key concepts 6.2–6.4.

PROFIT ≠ CASH

We have already touched upon the idea—both in the Julia example in Chapter 3 (Preparing the statement of profit or loss) and at the start of this chapter—that profit does not equal cash. It is now time to show how true this statement is with the detailed example presented in Example 6.1.

EXAMPLE 6.1

Start Up begins a wholesale trading business on 1 January and makes sales of £20,000 in January, £30,000 in February and £40,000 in March. The cost of purchases is £15,000 in January, £22,500 in February and £30,000 in March. All goods purchased each month are sold in that month so that cost of sales equals cost of purchases.

The statement of profit or loss for Start Up for each month and in total for the three months will be as follows:

	January £	February £	March £	Total £
Sales	20,000	30,000	40,000	90,000
Cost of sales	15,000	22,500	30,000	67,500
Gross profit	**5,000**	**7,500**	**10,000**	**22,500**

Start Up makes a profit each month. Profit is rising so the owners of Start Up will be pleased. However, to show that profit is not cash, let's look at two alternative scenarios for the way in which Start Up collects its cash from customers and pays cash to its suppliers.

Start Up's cash flow: scenario 1

Start Up is unable to gain credit from its suppliers and so pays for goods in the month of purchase. In order to build up trade with its customers, Start Up offers generous credit terms and allows its customers to pay for goods delivered two months after sales are made. There is no cash in the bank on 1 January and each month that the company is overdrawn a charge of 1% of the closing overdraft is incurred on the first day of the following month. Each month that the company is in credit (has a surplus in its account) the bank pays interest of 0.5% on the credit balance at the end of the month on the first day of the following month. The cash flow for the three months ended 31 March will be as follows:

	January £	February £	March £	Total £
Opening cash balance	—	(15,000)	(37,650)	—
Cash receipts from sales	—	—	20,000	20,000
Cash paid to suppliers	(15,000)	(22,500)	(30,000)	(67,500)
Interest received	—	—	—	—
Overdraft charges (1%)	—	(150)	*(377)	(527)
Closing cash balance	**(15,000)**	**(37,650)**	**(48,027)**	**(48,027)**

*Rounded to the nearest whole £.

Despite the profit made according to the statement of profit or loss, look how poorly trading has turned out from a cash flow point of view. All the purchases have been paid for in the month in which they were made, but the company is still owed £70,000 by customers (£30,000 for February + £40,000 for March: might any of these trade receivables become irrecoverable debts?) at the end of March. In addition, Start Up has incurred overdraft charges of £527 in February and March with the prospect of another £480 to pay in April (£48,027 × 1%).

Clearly, the £22,500 gross profit for the three months has not translated into surplus cash at the end of the three-month period. Start Up's bank manager might begin to worry about the increasing overdraft and put pressure on the company to reduce this. But, with cash being paid out up front to suppliers while customers enjoy a two-month credit period in which to pay, a reduction in the overdraft in the near future looks highly unlikely. Many small businesses when they start up offer generous credit terms to customers while being forced to pay quickly by their suppliers, so it should come as no surprise that many small businesses collapse within a year of starting to trade as their cash flow dries up and banks close them down to recover what they are owed.

Start Up's cash flow: scenario 2

Facts are as in Scenario 1, except that this time Start Up pays for its supplies one month after the month of purchase and collects cash from its customers in the month in which sales are made. The three-month cash flow will now be as shown in the table below.

	January £	February £	March £	Total £
Opening cash balance	—	20,000	35,100	—
Cash receipts from sales	20,000	30,000	40,000	90,000
Cash paid to suppliers	—	(15,000)	(22,500)	(37,500)
Interest received	—	100	*176	276
Overdraft charges	—	—	—	—
Closing cash balance	**20,000**	**35,100**	**52,776**	**52,776**

*Rounded to the nearest whole £.

What a difference a change in the terms of trade makes! By requiring customers to pay immediately for goods received and deferring payments to suppliers for a month, the cash flow has remained positive throughout the three months and additional interest income has been received from the bank by keeping cash balances positive. Suppliers are still owed £30,000, but there is more than enough cash in the bank to meet this liability and still have money available with which to keep trading.

Notably, the cash in the bank again bears no relationship to the gross profit of £22,500, so, once again, this example illustrates the key point that profit does not equal cash. The lesson to learn here is clear: if you can make sure that your customers pay before cash has to be paid to suppliers, the business will survive. In situations in which customers pay what is owed after suppliers have been paid, then the business will struggle to maintain cash inflows and be in danger of being closed down by the banks to which the business owes money.

WHY IS THIS RELEVANT TO ME?   Profit ≠ cash

To enable you as a business professional to:

- Appreciate that profit does not equal cash in an accounting period
- Realise that the timing of cash inflows and cash outflows has to be finely balanced to ensure that positive cash inflows are achieved
- Understand that positive cash inflows are critical to a business's ability to survive

NUMERICAL EXERCISES   Are you quite convinced that you could calculate cash flows from given terms of trade? Go to Numerical exercises 6.1 in the **online workbook** to test out your abilities in this area.

CASH IS CASH IS CASH: THE VALUE OF STATEMENTS OF CASH FLOWS

The statement of profit or loss and the two cash flows for Start Up in Example 6.1 also illustrate the advantages and the true value of the statement of cash flows when making comparisons between entities. If two companies presented exactly the same statement of profit or loss figures, it would be very difficult, if not impossible, to choose between the two and to say which company enjoyed the more stable, cash generative financial position. However, by looking at the statements of cash flows, we could say instantly that the company that presented the cash flow shown in scenario 2 was in a much better position financially compared to the company presenting the cash flow in scenario 1. Without the statement of cash flows we would not see that one company is doing very well from a cash management point of view while the other is doing very poorly. Hence the value of the statement of cash flows in enabling users to determine the financial position of an entity, information that is not available from just the statement of profit or loss.

However, the two statements of cash flows above illustrate further advantages of this statement. As we saw in Chapter 3 (The accruals basis of accounting and Preparing the statement of profit or loss), the statement of profit or loss is drawn up on the accruals basis of accounting, which requires income and expenditure to be recognised in the period in which it was earned and incurred. The statement of cash flows just presents the cash inflows and outflows relating to that period. As we have seen, profit, the difference between income earned and expenditure incurred, does not equate to cash. Therefore, the provision of a statement of cash flows enables users to see much more clearly how quickly profit is turned into cash: in scenario 2 cash is clearly being generated very effectively whereas in scenario 1 the company looks as though it is about to collapse. While the accrual of expenses and income into an accounting period can produce the impression of an excellent result from a profit point of view, since cash is cash is cash it does not suffer from any distortion that might arise in the timing of income and expenditure recognition.

6

WHY IS THIS RELEVANT TO ME?   The value of statements of cash flows

To enable you as a business professional to appreciate how statements of cash flows:

- Enable users to discriminate between different entities with the same levels of profit
- Are not distorted by the effect of the accrual of income and expenditure into different accounting periods

---

 GO BACK OVER THIS AGAIN!   Are you quite sure that you appreciate why statements of cash flows are so valuable? Go to the **online workbook** and have a go at Exercises 6.6 to test your grasp of their value.

IS THE STATEMENT OF CASH FLOWS ENOUGH ON ITS OWN?

If statements of cash flows are so useful, why do entities have to present the statement of profit or loss and the statement of financial position as well? Why not just require all organisations to produce the statement of cash flows only? This is a valid question and it leads us into thinking about why the statement of cash flows in isolation does not actually tell us very much beyond the cash generated and spent during an accounting period. Let's think first about how useful the statement of financial position and the statement of profit or loss are.

In Chapter 2 we saw that the statement of financial position provides us with details of:

- Liabilities to be paid
- Assets employed within the organisation.

Users of financial statements can look at an entity's assets and make an assessment of whether they will be able to generate the cash necessary to meet the liabilities as they fall due. If only a statement of cash flows were to be presented, then there would be no details of either assets or liabilities and so no assessment of an entity's cash generating potential would be possible.

In Chapter 3 we saw that the statement of profit or loss presents details of:

- Income earned
- Expenditure incurred.

Users of financial statements can then assess how profitable an organisation is and, in conjunction with the statement of cash flows, how effectively it can turn profits into cash with which to meet operating expenses and liabilities as they fall due. Without a statement of profit or loss, the statement of cash flows cannot tell us how profitable an organisation is or how quickly profits are being turned into cash.

A statement of cash flows on its own could be subject to manipulation. Entity owners or directors could time their cash inflows and outflows to present the most flattering picture of their organisation (Chapter 3, The accruals basis of accounting). Therefore, just as a statement of profit or loss or statement of financial position in isolation does not tell us very much, so a statement of cash flows presented as the sole portrait of performance would also be much less informative without its fellow financial statements.

The IASB's Conceptual Framework recognises that all three statements are essential in providing information to users about the cash generating potential of businesses and that a statement of cash flows on its own is insufficient:

> Accrual accounting [in the statement of profit or loss and statement of financial position] depicts the effects of transactions and other events and circumstances on a reporting entity's economic resources and claims in the periods in which those effects occur, even if the resulting cash receipts and payments occur in a different period. This is important because information about a reporting entity's economic resources and claims [the statement of financial position] and changes in its economic resources and claims during a period [the statement of profit or loss] provides a better basis for assessing the entity's past and future performance than information solely about cash receipts and payments during that period. Information about a reporting entity's financial performance during a period [the statement of profit or loss], reflected by changes in its economic resources and claims . . . is useful in assessing the entity's past and future ability to generate net cash inflows. That information indicates the extent to which the reporting entity has increased its available economic resources, and thus its capacity for generating net cash inflows through its operations . . . Information about a reporting entity's cash flows during a period also helps users to assess the entity's ability to generate future net cash inflows . . . It [the statement of cash flows] indicates how the reporting entity obtains and spends cash, including information about its borrowing and repayment of debt, cash dividends or other cash distributions to investors, and other factors that may affect the entity's liquidity or solvency. Information about cash flows helps users understand a reporting entity's operations, evaluate its financing and investing activities, assess its liquidity or solvency and interpret other information about financial performance.

> Source: IASB *Conceptual Framework for Financial Reporting*, paragraphs 1.17, 1.18 and 1.20

Thus, any one (and indeed any two) of the three financial statements on their own will not provide all the information that users require to make the necessary evaluations. Figure 6.3 summarises the interactions between and the interconnected nature of the three main financial statements.

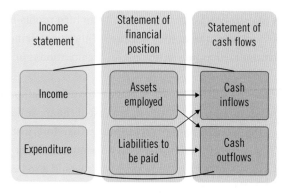

Figure 6.3 The three main financial statements and the ways in which they interact

---

WHY IS THIS RELEVANT TO ME?   Is the statement of cash flows enough on its own?

To enable you as a business professional to appreciate how:

• Statements of cash flows would not on their own provide sufficient useful information about an entity's financial position and performance

• The three main financial statements work together to provide useful information to users

---

GO BACK OVER THIS AGAIN!   Are you convinced that you understand how statements of cash flows work in conjunction with the other two financial statements? Go to the **online workbook** and have a go at Exercises 6.7 to test your grasp of the value of cash flow statements.

GO BACK OVER THIS AGAIN!   Can you see how the statement of cash flows explains the changes in the financial position of an entity? Go to the **online workbook** and attempt Exercises 6.8 to see how the one statement explains the changes in the other.

PREPARING THE STATEMENT OF CASH FLOWS: THE DIRECT METHOD

We shall illustrate the direct method of preparation of the statement of cash flows through Illustration 6.2 and Example 6.2.

Illustration 6.2 Julia's bank account receipts and payments summary (= Illustration 3.3)

Date		Receipts £	Payments £
1 April 2021	Cash introduced by Julia	30,000	
1 April 2021	Three months' rent paid on shop to 30 June 2021		5,000
1 April 2021	Cash register paid for		1,000
1 April 2021	Shelving and shop fittings paid for		12,000
30 April 2021	Receipts from sales in April 2021	20,000	
5 May 2021	Sports equipment supplied in April paid for		15,000
12 May 2021	Rates for period 1 April 2021 to 30 September 2021 paid		800
19 May 2021	Cash withdrawn for Julia's own expenses		2,000
30 May 2021	Receipts from sales in May 2021	25,000	
5 June 2021	Sports equipment supplied in May paid for		20,000
10 June 2021	Shop water rates for the year 1 April 2021 to 31 March 2022 paid		400
30 June 2021	Receipts from sales in June 2021	30,000	
30 June 2021	Balance in bank at 30 June 2021		48,800
		105,000	105,000

EXAMPLE 6.2

There are two approaches to preparing the statement of cash flows, the direct and indirect methods. We will use the example of Julia from Chapter 3 (Preparing the statement of profit or loss) to illustrate both methods. Julia's bank summary for the three months ended 30 June 2021 from Chapter 3 (Example 3.8, Illustration 3.3) is shown again in Illustration 6.2.

While Illustration 6.2 is already almost a complete statement of cash flows, showing cash received and cash paid out, all these transactions (together with the cash not yet banked from sales on 30 June 2021) would be presented in the required format as shown in Illustration 6.3.

Illustration 6.3 Julia: statement of cash flows for the three months ended 30 June 2021 using the direct method

	£	£
Cash flows from operating activities		
Receipts from sales banked 20,000 + 25,000 + 30,000	75,000	
Cash sales not yet banked	500	
Payments to trade payables for sports equipment 15,000 + 20,000	(35,000)	
Payments for expenses 5,000 (rent) + 800 (rates) + 400 (water)	(6,200)	
Net cash inflow from operating activities		34,300
Cash flows from investing activities		
Payments to acquire shop fittings and shelving	(12,000)	
Payments to acquire cash register	(1,000)	
Net cash outflow from investing activities		(13,000)
Cash flows from financing activities		
Cash introduced by Julia	30,000	
Cash withdrawn by Julia	(2,000)	
Net cash inflow from financing activities		28,000
Net increase in cash and cash equivalents		49,300
Cash and cash equivalents at the start of the period		—
Cash and cash equivalents at the end of the period		**49,300**

The figure for cash and cash equivalents at the end of the period is exactly the same as the bank balance plus the cash in the till at 30 June 2021 as shown in Julia's statement of financial position in Chapter 3, Illustration 3.7.

NUMERICAL EXERCISES   Are you certain that you could prepare statements of cash flows using the direct method? Go to Numerical exercises 6.2 in the **online workbook** to test out your ability to prepare these statements.

Using T accounts to calculate cash flows

Under normal circumstances, users of financial statements will not have access to the cash books of the entities they are assessing. Without an organisation's cash book, how can users work out the cash inflows generated by sales and the cash outflows arising from payments to suppliers and providers of services in order to produce the statement of cash flows using the direct method? By using T accounts, these cash flows can be calculated from the information provided in the statement of profit or loss and the statement of financial position. Suppose that we just have Julia's statement of profit or loss and statement of financial position as shown in Illustrations 6.4 and 6.5 (= Illustrations 3.6 and 3.7).

Illustration 6.4 (= Illustration 3.6) Julia's statement of profit or loss for the three months ended 30 June 2021

	£	£
Sales		77,600
Purchases	59,750	
Less: closing inventory	(10,000)	
Cost of sales (purchases − closing inventory)		49,750
Gross profit (sales − cost of sales)		**27,850**
Expenses		
Rent	5,000	
Rates	400	
Water rates	100	
Irrecoverable debt	50	
Wages	300	
Telephone	250	
Electricity	200	
Cash register depreciation	50	
Shelving and fittings depreciation	600	
Total expenses		6,950
Net profit for the three months		**20,900**

Illustration 6.5 (= Illustration 3.7) Julia's statement of financial position at 30 June 2021

	£
Non-current assets	
Cash register	950
Shelves and shop fittings	11,400
	12,350
Current assets	
Inventory	10,000
Trade receivables	2,050
Rates prepayment	400
Water rates prepayment	300
Bank balance	48,800
Cash	500
	62,050
Total assets	**74,400**

	£
Current liabilities	
Trade payables	24,750
Wages accrual	300
Telephone accrual	250
Electricity accrual	200
Total liabilities	**25,500**
Net assets	**48,900**
Equity (capital account)	
Capital introduced by Julia	30,000
Drawings	(2,000)
Net profit for the three months	20,900
Capital account at 30 June 2021	**48,900**

In the statement of profit or loss and the statement of financial position we have sufficient information from which to reconstruct the trade receivables control account, the trade payables control account and the expenses account so that we can calculate the cash received from customers, the cash paid to suppliers and the cash paid for expenses. By adding in the known numbers, the missing number, the balancing figure, in each account will be the cash received or paid.

Calculating cash received from the trade receivables control account

The trade receivables control account, as we saw in Chapter 5 (Exercising control: the trade receivables control account and Illustration 5.3), is made up as shown in Illustration 6.6.

Illustration 6.6 The trade receivables control account

Trade receivables control account

	£		£
Trade receivables brought forward	x	Cash received	x
Sales	x	Irrecoverable debts	x
		Sales returns	x
		Trade receivables carried forward	x
	xx		**xx**

Which of these figures are already available in the statement of profit or loss and the statement of financial position? As this is Julia's first year of trading, trade receivables brought forward are £Nil. Trade receivables carried forward are £2,050 while irrecoverable debts are £50. Sales in the statement of profit or loss amount to £77,600. After entering these figures into the trade receivables control account, we now have the position shown in Illustration 6.7.

Illustration 6.7 Julia's trade receivables control account for the three months ended 30 June 2021 showing the figures available in the statement of profit or loss and the statement of financial position

Trade receivables control account

	£		£
Trade receivables brought forward	0	Cash received	?
Sales	*78,000	Irrecoverable debts	50
		Sales returns	*400
		Trade receivables carried forward	2,050
	78,000		**78,000**

*Illustration 3.6 shows gross sales of £78,000 – £400 sales returns = sales of £77,600. Net sales of £77,600 can be used instead of £78,000 debits – £400 credits.

The total on both sides of the trade receivables control account must be £78,000 so that the account balances. Therefore, cash received, the missing number, is £78,000 – £50 irrecoverable debt – £400 sales returns – £2,050 trade receivables carried forward = £75,500. Is this figure correct? Illustration 6.3 shows cash received from sales of £75,000 banked + £500 cash in the till but not yet banked = £75,500.

WHY IS THIS RELEVANT TO ME?   Calculating cash received from the trade receivables control account

To enable you as a business professional to:

● Understand how the trade receivables control account can be used to calculate the missing figure for cash received from sales

● Use the trade receivables control account to reconstruct cash flows from sales when preparing the statement of cash flows using the direct method

---

SHOW ME HOW TO DO IT   Quite sure you understand how Julia's cash received from sales was calculated using the trade receivables T account? View Video presentation 6.1 in the **online workbook** to see a practical demonstration of how this calculation was made from the information presented in the statement of profit or loss and statement of financial position.

MULTIPLE CHOICE QUESTIONS   Do you think you can use the trade receivables control account to calculate missing figures for use in the statement of cash flows? Go to the **online workbook** and complete Multiple choice questions 6.2 to test your ability to apply these calculations.

Calculating cash paid to suppliers from the trade payables control account

The trade payables control account, as we saw in Chapter 5 (Exercising control: the trade payables control account), is made up as shown in Illustration 6.8.

Illustration 6.8 The trade payables control account

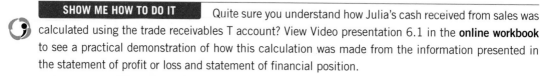

Trade payables control account

	£		£
Purchase returns	X	Trade payables brought forward	X
Cash paid	X	Purchases	X
Discounts received	X		
Trade payables carried forward	X		
	XX		XX

Unlike the sales figure, the purchases figure is not instantly available from the statement of profit or loss. Our first step therefore is to calculate the figure for purchases. Illustration 6.4 shows purchases before deducting closing inventory, so we could just use the figure of £59,750 as our purchases in Julia's case. However, most sets of accounts will only show a single figure for cost of sales. How, then, can we calculate purchases from this cost of sales number? Cost of sales, as we saw in Chapter 3 (Statement of profit or loss by nature), is calculated by adding opening inventory to purchases and deducting closing inventory (cost of sales = opening inventory + purchases – closing inventory). Rearranging this equation will enable us to calculate purchases as follows:

Purchases = cost of sales + closing inventory – opening inventory

If we take Julia's cost of sales figure from the statement of profit or loss of £49,750 and the closing inventory of £10,000 from the statement of financial position, this gives us a figure for purchases of £59,750:

£49,750 (cost of sales) + £10,000 (closing inventory) – £Nil (opening inventory—this is Julia's first period of trading so there is no opening inventory) = £59,750 purchases

Trade payables brought forward are also £Nil as this is Julia's first period of trading while trade payables carried forward are £24,750. Entering these figures into the trade payables control account gives us the account shown in Illustration 6.9.

Illustration 6.9 Julia's trade payables control account for the three months ended 30 June 2021 showing the known numbers derived from the statement of profit or loss and the statement of financial position

Trade payables control account

	£		£
Purchase returns	*250	Trade payables brought forward	0
Cash paid	?	Purchases	*60,000
Trade payables carried forward	24,750		
	60,000		**60,000**

*Illustration 3.6 shows gross purchases of £60,000 – £250 purchase returns = purchases of £59,750. Net purchases of £59,750 can be used instead of £60,000 credits – £250 debits.

The total on both sides of the trade payables control account must be £60,000 so that the account balances. Therefore, cash received, the missing number, is £60,000 purchases – £250 purchase returns – £24,750 trade payables carried forward = £35,000. Is this figure correct? Illustration 6.3 shows cash paid to suppliers of £35,000 so our calculation is correct.

WHY IS THIS RELEVANT TO ME?   Calculating cash paid to suppliers from the trade payables control account

To enable you as a business professional to:

• Understand how the trade payables control account can be used to calculate the missing figure for cash paid to suppliers

• Use the cost of sales calculation and the trade payables control account to reconstruct cash outflows when preparing the statement of cash flows under the direct method

SHOW ME HOW TO DO IT   Quite sure you understand how Julia's cash paid to suppliers was calculated using the trade payables control account? View Video presentation 6.2 in the **online workbook** to see a practical demonstration of how this calculation was made from the information presented in the statement of profit or loss and statement of financial position.

MULTIPLE CHOICE QUESTIONS   Are you quite sure that you could use the cost of sales calculation and the trade payables control account to calculate missing figures for use in the statement of cash flows? Go to the **online workbook** and complete Multiple choice questions 6.3 to test your ability to make these calculations.

Calculating cash paid for expenses using the expenses T account

The final step in calculating cash inflows under the direct method is to determine how much cash has been paid out as expenses. This calculation is also made using a T account, but one that we have not come across before. This T account will consider the different elements of expenses, some of which involve cash flows and some which do not, and summarise these into one account. Illustration 6.10 presents the expenses T account.

Illustration 6.10 The expenses T account

Expenses account

	£		£
Prepayments brought forward	X	Accruals brought forward	X
Depreciation	X	Statement of profit or loss expenses total	X
Increase in allowance for receivables	X	Decrease in allowance for receivables	X
Irrecoverable debts	X	Prepayments carried forward	X
Discounts allowed	X		
Cash paid (balancing figure)	X		
Accruals carried forward	X		
	XX		**XX**

The debit side of this account builds up those expenses which do not result in a cash outflow during the current financial period. Prepayments brought forward from the previous accounting period are expenses for the current period which arose from cash outflows in the previous period. There is therefore no cash outflow associated with these brought forward prepayments in the current accounting period. Depreciation is not a cash outflow so this is also posted to the debit side of the account as an addition to expenditure that does not generate any cash outflows. Likewise, an irrecoverable debt and an increase in the allowance for receivables are expenses that do not arise from cash outflows. Finally, accruals at the end of an accounting period are expenses that have not resulted in a cash outflow in the period under review but which will generate an outflow of cash in the following accounting period.

The credit side of the expenses account on the other hand presents those items increasing cash outflows in the current accounting period. Accruals at the start of the year will result in a cash outflow as these expenses charged in a previous period are paid in the current period. Prepayments carried forward at the end of the current period represent costs that belong to a future accounting period but which have been paid in the current accounting period. A decrease in the allowance for receivables represents a reduction in an expense that does not relate to an inflow of cash from expenses but to an inflow of cash from sales.

Entering the known figures from Julia's statement of profit or loss and statement of financial position in Illustrations 6.4 and 6.5 results in the expenses T account shown in Illustration 6.11.

Illustration 6.11 Julia's expenses account for the three months ended 30 June 2021 showing the known numbers derived from the statement of profit or loss and the statement of financial position

Expenses account

	£		£
Prepayments brought forward	0	Accruals brought forward	0
Depreciation (£600 + £50)	650	Statement of profit or loss expenses	6,950
Irrecoverable debts	50	Prepayments c/f (£400 + £300)	700
Cash paid (balancing figure)	?		
Accruals c/f (£300 + £250 + £200)	750		
	7,650		**7,650**

As this is Julia's first year of trading, there are no prepayments or accruals brought forward at the start of the year. The irrecoverable debt expense of £50, the two depreciation charges of £600 (shelving and fittings) and £50 (the cash register) and the total expenses of £6,950 for the three months are given in Julia's statement of profit or loss. The accruals and prepayments carried forward are shown under current assets and current liabilities in the statement of financial position. The total expenses of £6,950 are made up of all the charges to the statement of profit or loss on each of the expense accounts in Chapter 4 (Closing off the T accounts at the end of an accounting period). Check that the individual expenses charged to the statement of profit or loss on these T accounts do total up to £6,950 as shown in Illustration 6.4.

The cash outflow from expenses is thus £6,950 (statement of profit or loss expenses) + £700 (prepayments carried forward) − £650 (depreciation) − £50 (irrecoverable debts) − £750 (accruals carried forward) = £6,200. Is this correct? Yes, Illustration 6.3 shows payments for expenses of £6,200.

Further applications of T accounts to calculate missing figures for inclusion in the statement of cash flows are presented in the appendix to this chapter.

WHY IS THIS RELEVANT TO ME?   Calculating cash paid for expenses using T accounts

To enable you as a business professional to:

• Understand how the expenses T account can be used to calculate the missing figure for cash paid for expenses

• Use the expenses T account to reconstruct cash outflows when preparing the statement of cash flows under the direct method

---

SHOW ME HOW TO DO IT   Convinced that you followed how Julia's cash paid for expenses was calculated using the expenses T account? View Video presentation 6.3 in the **online workbook** to see a practical demonstration of how this calculation was made from the information presented in Julia's statement of profit or loss and statement of financial position.

MULTIPLE CHOICE QUESTIONS   Are you convinced that you could use the expenses T account to calculate missing figures for use in the statement of cash flows? Go to the **online workbook** and complete Multiple choice questions 6.4 to test your ability to make these calculations.

PREPARING THE STATEMENT OF CASH FLOWS:
THE INDIRECT METHOD

The statement of cash flows for Julia in Illustration 6.3 represents an example of the direct method of cash flow preparation: this takes all the cash inflows and outflows from operations and summarises them to produce the net cash inflow from operating activities. Thus, receipts from sales are totalled up to give the cash inflow from sales and payments to suppliers and payments for expenses are totalled up to give a figure for payments to trade payables and other suppliers of goods and services in the period. The difference between the inflows of cash from sales and the outflows of cash for expenses represents the operating cash inflows for the three months.

However, as we noted in this chapter in the Cash flows from operating activities section, the example of Bunns the Bakers' statement of cash flows in Illustration 6.1 represents an example of the indirect method of cash flow preparation. Under this method, the total inflows and out-flows from operations are ignored and the operating profit for a period is adjusted for increases or decreases in inventory, receivables, prepayments, payables and accruals and for the effect of non-cash items such as depreciation. As we saw in Chapter 3 (Depreciation), depreciation is an accounting adjustment that allocates the cost of non-current assets to the accounting periods benefiting from their use. The actual cash flows associated with non-current assets are the cash paid to acquire the assets in the first place and the cash received on disposal of those assets when they are sold or scrapped at the end of their useful lives.

Illustration 6.12 Julia: statement of cash flows for the three months ended 30 June 2021 using the indirect method

	£	£
Cash flows from operating activities		
Net profit for the 3 months to 30 June 2021 (Illustrations 3.6 and 6.4)		20,900
Add: depreciation on shelving and fittings (Illustrations 3.6 and 6.4)		600
Add: depreciation on the cash register (Illustrations 3.6 and 6.4)		50
Deduct: increase in inventory		(10,000)
Deduct: increase in receivables		(2,050)
Deduct: increase in prepayments		(700)
Add: increase in payables		24,750
Add: increase in accruals		750
Net cash inflow from operating activities (= Illustration 6.3)		34,300
Cash flows from investing activities		
Payments to acquire shop fittings and shelving	(12,000)	
Payments to acquire cash register	(1,000)	
Net cash outflow from investing activities (= Illustration 6.3)		(13,000)
Cash flows from financing activities		
Cash introduced by Julia	30,000	
Cash withdrawn by Julia	(2,000)	
Net cash inflow from financing activities (= Illustration 6.3)		28,000
Net increase in cash and cash equivalents		49,300
Cash and cash equivalents at the start of the period		—
Cash and cash equivalents at the end of the period		**49,300**

6

Let's look at how using the indirect method would affect the preparation of Julia's statement of cash flows. While the direct method of cash flow preparation is very easy to understand and put together from summaries of cash receipts and payments, most entities use the indirect method. For Julia, the cash flow for the three months ended 30 June 2021 under the indirect method would be as shown in the accounting statement in Illustration 6.12.

Not surprisingly, both the direct and the indirect method give the same answer for net cash inflow for the three months, £49,300. The only differences between the two cash flows are in the calculation of the cash flow from operating activities.

In the cash flow from operating activities section, depreciation on the shelving and fittings and on the cash register is exactly the same as the depreciation charged in the statement of profit or loss for the three months ended 30 June 2021 (Chapter 3, Illustration 3.6 = this chapter, Illustration 6.4). The changes in the amounts for inventory, receivables, prepayments, payables and accruals are usually the difference between the current period end's figures and the figures at the end of the previous accounting period. As this is Julia's first trading period, the figures for the changes in these amounts are exactly the same as the figures from her statement of financial position (Chapter 3, Illustration 3.7 = this chapter, Illustration 6.5). The figures at the start of the business were all £Nil. Thus, for example, in the case of inventory £10,000 – £Nil = an increase of £10,000.

WHY IS THIS RELEVANT TO ME? Preparing the statement of cash flows: direct and indirect methods

To enable you as a business professional to:

- Prepare cash flow statements for a given period using either the direct or indirect method
- Understand that the two different methods used to prepare statements of cash flows produce the same results

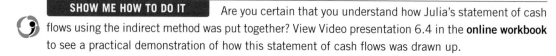

SHOW ME HOW TO DO IT   Are you certain that you understand how Julia's statement of cash flows using the indirect method was put together? View Video presentation 6.4 in the **online workbook** to see a practical demonstration of how this statement of cash flows was drawn up.

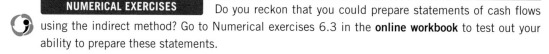

NUMERICAL EXERCISES   Do you reckon that you could prepare statements of cash flows using the indirect method? Go to Numerical exercises 6.3 in the **online workbook** to test out your ability to prepare these statements.

THE INDIRECT METHOD: CASH FLOWS FROM OPERATING ACTIVITIES: INFLOWS OR OUTFLOWS?

Why are the cash flows associated with Julia's inventory, receivables and prepayments treated as outflows of cash (appearing in brackets) while the cash flows associated with payables and accruals are all inflows of cash (appearing without brackets)? The answer lies in the fact that the statement of profit or loss is prepared on the accruals basis of accounting, recognising income and expenses in the period in which they are earned or incurred rather than in the periods in which cash is received or paid. Some income has thus been recognised in the statement of profit or loss that has not yet resulted in a cash inflow. Similarly, some expenses have been recognised in the statement of profit or loss without the corresponding cash outflow. Therefore, adjustments for these 'non-cash' figures have to be made to operating profit to determine the actual cash flows from operating activities under the indirect method. Let's look at each of these adjustments in turn.

Inventory

An increase in inventory is an increase in an asset. This represents an outflow of cash as more money will have been spent on acquiring this additional inventory. Hence the deduction from operating profit. On the other hand, if the cost of inventory decreases over the year, this would mean that more inventory had been sold, resulting in larger cash inflows. Such a fall in inventory would result in an inflow of cash and be added to operating profit.

Receivables

An increase in receivables means additional sales have been recognised in the statement of profit or loss, but that cash has not yet been received from this additional income. As no cash inflow relating to these additional sales has occurred yet, the increase in receivables is treated as a deduction from operating profit to reflect this reduction in cash inflows. As in the case of inventory, if the amount of receivables falls, this means more money has been generated from receivables so this is treated as an increase in cash inflows and is added to cash flows from operating activities.

Trade payables

On the other hand, if trade payables have increased, you have spent less money on paying your suppliers. An increase in trade payables means that cash has not flowed out of the business, so this reduction in payments is added to operating profit. Where trade payables have decreased, this means more cash has been spent on reducing liabilities, so this is treated as a decrease in cash and a deduction is made from operating profit to reflect this outflow of cash.

Prepayments and accruals

Prepayments represent expenses paid in advance so an increase in prepayments means that more cash has flowed out of the business due to an increase in payments made in the current year. This increase is deducted from operating profit. An increase in accruals on the other hand, as with the increase in payables, means that while an expense has been recognised no cash has yet been paid out so this increase is added to operating profit. Where prepayments fall, this is treated as an increase in operating cash flows as less cash has been spent on paying expenses in advance, while a decrease in accruals would represent increased cash outflows as more money would have been spent on reducing these liabilities.

Initially these rules will seem confusing, but practice will enable you to become familiar with them and to apply them confidently in the preparation of statements of cash flows. To assist you in applying these rules, Table 6.1 shows which adjustments should be added to and which adjustments should be deducted from profit for the year in arriving at the cash flows from operating activities when applying the indirect method. Keep this table handy when you are working through the online examples and the questions at the end of this chapter.

Table 6.1 Figures to add to and figures to deduct from profit for the year to determine the cash flow from operating activities when preparing statements of cash flows using the indirect method

Starting point: profit for the year in the statement of profit or loss	
Add	**Deduct**
Income tax charge	
Finance expense	Finance income
Depreciation of non-current assets	
Amortisation of intangible non-current assets	
Loss on disposal of non-current assets	Profit on disposal of non-current assets
Decrease in inventory	Increase in inventory
Decrease in receivables	Increase in receivables
Decrease in prepayments	Increase in prepayments
Increase in payables	Decrease in payables
Increase in accruals	Decrease in accruals
Increase in provisions	Decrease in provisions

 GO BACK OVER THIS AGAIN!   How well can you remember Table 6.1? Go to the **online workbook** and complete Exercises 6.9 to check your recollection.

The only items in Table 6.1 that we have not dealt with in our cash flow studies to date are the profits and losses on the disposal of non-current assets. The actual cash flow associated with the disposal of non-current assets is the actual cash received. Just as depreciation, which was treated as an expense in arriving at operating profit, is added back to operating profit to determine the cash flows from operating activities, so losses on disposal are added as they, too, have been treated as an additional expense in arriving at operating profit. Profits on disposal, on the other hand, have been treated as income in determining operating profit and so have to be deducted in arriving at the cash flows from operating activities.

WHY IS THIS RELEVANT TO ME?   The indirect method: cash flows from operating activities: inflows or outflows?

To enable you as a business professional to understand how:

- Adjustments under the indirect method of preparing the statement of cash flows have been calculated
- Movements in the working capital (inventory, receivables and payables) impact upon the cash flows from operating activities

---

MULTIPLE CHOICE QUESTIONS   Could you calculate profits and losses on the disposal of non-current assets? Say what the cash inflow was on a non-current asset disposal? Go to the **online workbook** and complete Multiple choice questions 6.5 to make sure you can make these calculations correctly.

ACCOUNTING PRINCIPLES AND CONVENTIONS

We have now worked through the three key accounting statements, the statement of profit or loss, the statement of financial position and the statement of cash flows, and shown how double-entry bookkeeping is used to record all the transactions that form the basis of the figures in the financial statements. On our journey this far, we have noted various accounting principles and conventions that apply in the preparation of the three key financial statements. These principles and conventions are summarised below:

Accruals (also known as matching)

The accruals basis of accounting was covered in Chapter 3 (The accruals basis of accounting). This principle states that all income earned and all expenditure incurred in an accounting period is recognised in that period irrespective of when cash is received or paid.

Business entity

Under the business entity principle, the affairs of the business and the affairs of the owner are kept entirely separate. The business and the owner are thus treated as two separate entities. This principle requires that personal and business transactions are not mixed together so that the financial statements of the business present just the results and financial position of the business (Chapter 3, Drawings and the business entity convention).

Consistency

Presentation and measurement in the financial statements of the same items in the same way from year to year will assist users in understanding the information presented and in making comparisons between different accounting periods and between different business entities. Consistency in presentation and measurement will help achieve comparability (Chapter 1, What qualities should accounting information possess?).

Dual aspect

This principle states that every transaction has a dual effect on the financial statements. As assets are created, this gives rise to an increase in liabilities, income or capital. Similarly, as liabilities are assumed this causes assets or expenditure to increase. An increase in one asset can cause a reduction in another asset or both assets and liabilities can decrease. (Chapter 2, The dual aspect concept, Chapter 4, Double entry and the accounting equation).

Going concern

The financial statements of an entity are drawn up on the basis that the entity will continue in existence for the foreseeable future. In preparing the financial statements for publication, it is assumed that an entity does not intend to cease trading and that it will not be entering into liquidation. If an organisation does intend to cease trading or enter into liquidation, it is not a going concern and the financial statements will be drawn up on an entirely different basis.

Historic cost

The historic cost convention dictates that the assets and liabilities of a business should be valued at their original (historic) cost to the organisation. This convention has been relaxed over the years and the IASB now allows (and sometimes requires) the recognition of assets and liabilities at their fair value (Chapter 2, How are assets and liabilities valued?).

Materiality

Information is material if its omission or misstatement could influence the decisions of users based on the financial information provided by an entity. Information can be material by virtue of its size, its nature or both its size and nature (Chapter 1, Materiality).

Money measurement

Money is the unit of measurement in financial statements. Figures presented in the statement of profit or loss, statement of financial position and statement of cash flows must be measured in money terms.

Periodicity

Entities report their financial performance and their financial position at regular intervals. The usual reporting period for business organisations is at yearly intervals to allow users to assess how well the organisation is performing and to enable the tax authorities to tax each entity on the basis of its financial performance.

Prudence

'Prudence is the exercise of caution when making judgements under conditions of uncertainty' (IASB *Conceptual Framework for Financial Reporting*, paragraph 2.16). This means that preparers of financial statements should take care to ensure that assets, expenses, liabilities and income are neither overstated nor understated. The exercise of excessive prudence in the valuation of items in financial statements should be avoided as this will introduce bias into financial reporting and mean that the financial information presented is no longer faithfully represented or relevant. Note that prudence only applies to judgements made under conditions of uncertainty: when there is no uncertainty, there is no requirement to exercise prudence.

Realisation

Profits should not be anticipated until they have been earned through a sale (Chapter 3, Closing inventory). Until a sale has been completed through the delivery of goods to and the acceptance of those goods by a customer no sale or profit should be recognised as the customer can change their mind up until that point. Once goods have been delivered to and accepted by a customer then the sale and the associated profit can be recognised by an entity.

WHY IS THIS RELEVANT TO ME?   Accounting principles and conventions

To enable you as a business professional to understand the principles and conventions:

- Upon which financial statements are based
- Which you will have to apply when you are required to produce sets of financial statements

---

GO BACK OVER THIS AGAIN!   How well have you remembered what these principles and conventions state and how they are applied? Go to the **online workbook** and complete Exercises 6.10 to check your recollection.

MULTIPLE CHOICE QUESTIONS   Do you think that you can distinguish between different accounting principles and conventions? Go to the **online workbook** and complete Multiple choice questions 6.6 to test your ability to make these distinctions.

APPENDIX: FURTHER USES FOR T ACCOUNTS IN THE CALCULATION OF FIGURES TO INCLUDE IN THE STATEMENT OF CASH FLOWS

As we noted earlier (this chapter, Calculating cash paid for expenses using the expenses 'T' account), T accounts can be used in various other situations to calculate missing numbers for inclusion in the statement of cash flows. While the detail provided in this appendix may be beyond the scope of your current studies, you will find these notes helpful when preparing statements of cash flows in the future.

1 Property, plant and equipment

Figures may need to be calculated in three situations:

- Cash paid to acquire property, plant and equipment
- Depreciation charged during the accounting period on property, plant and equipment
- The carrying amount of disposals of property, plant and equipment

To calculate any one of these figures, the property, plant and equipment T account in Illustration 6.13 will be used.

Illustration 6.13 The property, plant and equipment T account

Property, plant and equipment account

	£		£
Carrying amount brought forward	x	Disposals at carrying amount	x
Additions at cost	x	Depreciation charged in year	x
		Carrying amount carried forward	x
	xx		**xx**

The carrying amounts brought forward and carried forward will be presented in the statements of financial position provided in the question. Information given about the sale of property, plant and equipment will require some thought to work out the carrying amount of the property, plant and equipment disposed of. Details of either additions at cost or depreciation will then be provided, leaving you to calculate the missing figure using the framework shown in the T account in Illustration 6.13. The left hand side of the T account shows transactions that will result in increases in the carrying amount of the asset (additions), while the right hand side shows transactions that will result in decreases in the carrying amount of the asset (disposals and depreciation charged in the year).

To show how these calculations work in practice, let's look at the financial statements of Bunns the Bakers. Illustration 2.1 shows property, plant and equipment with a carrying amount at 31 March 2020 of £11,241,000 and of £11,750,000 at 31 March 2021. There is a difference of £509,000 between the figures at the two dates. But how much of this difference is due to cash spent on new property, plant and equipment, how much is due to the depreciation charge for the year and how much is due to disposals of property, plant and equipment assets during the year? The statement of cash flows for the company (Illustration 6.1) provides us with the following relevant information:

- Depreciation of property, plant and equipment in the year to 31 March 2021 amounted to £394,000.

- The profit on disposal of property, plant and equipment during the year was £3,000.

- Acquisition costs of property, plant and equipment in the year to 31 March 2021 amounted to £910,000.

- The proceeds from the sale of property, plant and equipment were £10,000.

We now have all the information required to draw up our property, plant and equipment T account. This T account is presented in Illustration 6.14.

Illustration 6.14 Bunns the Bakers' property, plant and equipment T account

Property, plant and equipment account

	£000		£000
Carrying amount brought forward at 1 April 2020	11,241	Disposals at carrying amount	7
Additions at cost	910	Depreciation charged in year	394
		Carrying amount carried forward at 31 March 2021	11,750
	12,151		12,151

The carrying amount of the disposals is £7,000. How was this figure calculated? £10,000 was received for the assets disposed of and this resulted in a profit of £3,000. To generate a £3,000 profit from a selling price of £10,000 means that the item sold must have had a carrying amount of £7,000 (£10,000 selling price – £3,000 profit = £7,000 carrying amount). £910,000 additions at cost – £7,000 carrying amount of disposals – £394,000 depreciation = £509,000, the difference between the opening and closing carrying amounts calculated above. When tackling questions that require the preparation of a statement of cash flows, you will be provided with information to calculate four of the numbers shown in Illustrations 6.13 and 6.14. The missing number will then be the balancing figure for additions at cost, depreciation charged for the year or the carrying amount of disposals. Work through the figures in Illustration 6.14, omitting one of the figures each time to prove to yourself that the missing figure is the balancing figure.

MULTIPLE CHOICE QUESTIONS   Are you convinced that you can calculate property, plant and equipment figures for inclusion in the statement of cash flows? Go to the **online workbook** and complete Multiple choice questions 6.7 to test your ability to calculate these figures correctly.

---

2 Tax paid during the year

When preparing the statement of cash flows, there is only one question with respect to taxation that requires answering: how much tax was paid during the year? This question is answered by preparing the T account shown in Illustration 6.15.

Illustration 6.15 The taxation T account

Taxation account

	£		£
Balancing figure = cash paid	x	Taxation liability brought forward	x
Taxation liability carried forward	x	Statement of profit or loss income tax charge	x
	XX		XX

Taxation is a liability so the balance brought forward appears on the credit side of the T account. The balance on the T account once payments have been made and the taxation liability to carry forward has been calculated is charged to the statement of profit or loss as the income tax charge. Questions will provide the balances brought forward and carried forward in the statement of financial position and the income tax charge for the year in the statement of profit or loss. Entering these figures into the taxation T account will then provide the cash paid figure for taxation. Again, let's illustrate this process using the statement of financial position and statement of profit or loss of Bunns the Bakers (Illustrations 2.1 and 3.1). Illustration 6.16 presents the relevant figures from Bunns the Bakers' statement of financial position and statement of profit or loss.

Illustration 6.16 Bunns the Bakers' taxation T account showing the figures known from the statement of financial position (Illustration 2.1) and the statement of profit or loss (Illustration 3.1)

Taxation account

	£000		£000
Balancing figure = cash paid	?	Taxation liability brought forward at 1 April 2020 (Illustration 2.1)	126
Taxation liability carried forward at 31 March 2021 (Illustration 2.1)	150	Statement of profit or loss income tax charge (Illustration 3.1)	213
	339		**339**

The credit side of the account adds up to £339,000 while the debit side shows only the liability carried forward at the end of the year of £150,000. To balance the account, the cash paid figure of £189,000 (£339,000 – £150,000) is debited to the taxation account. How can we be sure that cash paid is a debit figure in this account? A payment from the bank account is a credit to the bank account, so to complete the double entry there must be a debit figure. As the payment of tax is the reduction of a liability, the tax paid is debited to the taxation account to reflect this reduction in the taxation liability. The completed taxation account is shown in Illustration 6.17.

Illustration 6.17 Bunns the Bakers' taxation T account showing the cash paid as the balancing figure

Taxation account

	£000		£000
Balancing figure = cash paid	189	Taxation liability brought forward at 1 April 2020 (Illustration 2.1)	126
Taxation liability carried forward at 31 March 2021 (Illustration 2.1)	150	Statement of profit or loss income tax charge (Illustration 3.1)	213
	339		**339**

The taxation paid figure of £189,000 is added to Bunns the Bakers' statement of cash flows (Illustration 6.1).

MULTIPLE CHOICE QUESTIONS   Do you think that you can calculate the taxation paid figure for inclusion in the statement of cash flows? Go to the **online workbook** and complete Multiple choice questions 6.8 to test your ability to calculate this figure correctly.

3 Dividends paid

Dividends paid are deducted directly from retained earnings. Retained earnings fall and the bank balance also falls with the reduction in the asset as a result of the payment made. The double entry for the payment of dividends is debit retained earnings, credit bank account. The retained earnings T account is shown in Illustration 6.18.

Illustration 6.18 The retained earnings T account

Retained earnings account

	£		£
Balancing figure = dividends paid	x	Retained earnings brought forward	x
Retained earnings carried forward	x	Profit for the year (statement of profit or loss)	x
	—		—
	xx		xx

Using the retained earnings figures from Bunns the Bakers' statement of financial position (Illustration 2.1) and the profit for the year in the statement of profit or loss (Illustration 3.1), the retained earnings account is presented in Illustration 6.19.

Illustration 6.19 Bunns the Bakers' retained earnings T account showing the figures known from the statement of financial position (Illustration 2.1) and the statement of profit or loss (Illustration 3.1)

Retained earnings account

	£000		£000
Balancing figure = dividends paid	90	Retained earnings brought forward at 1 April 2020 (Illustration 2.1)	4,187
Retained earnings carried forward at 31 March 2021 (Illustration 2.1)	4,644	Statement of profit or loss profit for the year (Illustration 3.1)	547
	4,734		4,734

The balancing figure of £90,000 (£4,734,000 − £4,644,000) represents the dividends paid during the year. Again, looking at the statement of cash flows for the company (Illustration 6.1), cash flows from financing activities shows a figure of £90,000 for dividends paid.

MULTIPLE CHOICE QUESTIONS   Do you think that you can calculate the dividends paid figure for inclusion in the statement of cash flows? Go to the **online workbook** and complete Multiple choice questions 6.9 to test your ability to calculate this figure correctly.

---

4 Interest received (finance income)

Bunns the Bakers' statement of profit or loss (Illustration 3.1) and statement of cash flows (Illustration 6.1) both show finance income/interest of £15,000. There is thus no difference between the income recognised in the statement of profit or loss and actual cash inflow from this interest received during the year. However, for most entities the receipt of cash from interest does not coincide exactly with the accounting period end. As a result of the accruals basis of accounting, organisations record a receivable at each year end for finance income that has accrued since the last cash receipt from this source of income. To calculate the cash actually received from finance income during the year, the T account presented in Illustration 6.20 is used.

Illustration 6.20 The interest receivable T account

Interest receivable account

	£		£
Interest receivable brought forward	x	Balancing figure = cash received	x
Finance income in the statement of profit or loss	x	Interest receivable carried forward	x
	xx		**xx**

Let's see how the cash received from interest receivable would be calculated in Example 6.3.

EXAMPLE 6.3

At 30 April 2020 CHY Limited had interest receivable of £24,000. At 30 April 2021, interest receivable was £27,000 and the statement of profit or loss showed finance income (all from interest) for the year to 30 April 2021 of £92,000. How much cash was received from interest during the year to 30 April 2021? We can use our T account in Illustration 6.20 to calculate the cash received from interest during the year. The results of these calculations are shown in Illustration 6.21.

Illustration 6.21 CHY Limited interest receivable T account

Interest receivable account

	£000		£000
Interest receivable brought forward at 1 May 2020	24	Balancing figure = cash received	89
Finance income in statement of profit or loss	92	Interest receivable carried forward at 30 April 2021	27
	116		**116**

MULTIPLE CHOICE QUESTIONS   Are you quite sure that you can calculate the cash received from finance income figure for inclusion in the statement of cash flows? Go to the **online workbook** and complete Multiple choice questions 6.10 to test your ability to calculate this figure correctly.

5 Interest paid (finance expense)

The same approach applies to interest paid. Bunns the Bakers' statement of profit or loss (Illustration 3.1) and statement of cash flows (Illustration 6.1) both show finance expense/interest paid of £150,000. There is thus no difference between the expense recognised in the statement of profit or loss and actual cash outflow to lenders during the year. Again, most entities find that they have an accrual for interest at the end of each accounting period, an interest cost that has been incurred but not paid by the accounting period end. Organisations thus record a payable (a liability) at each year end for interest that has accrued since the last payment. To calculate the finance expense cash actually paid during the year, the T account presented in Illustration 6.22 is used.

Illustration 6.22 The interest payable T account

Interest payable account

	£		£
Balancing figure = cash paid	x	Interest payable brought forward	x
Interest payable carried forward	x	Finance expense in the statement of profit or loss	x
	XX		XX

Example 6.4 shows how this interest paid T account is used in practice to determine the cash paid during an accounting period.

EXAMPLE 6.4

At 30 April 2020 CHY Limited had an interest payable liability of £35,000. At 30 April 2021, the interest payable liability stood at £32,000 and the statement of profit or loss showed finance expense (all interest paid) for the year to 30 April 2021 of £160,000. How much cash was paid in interest during the year to 30 April 2021? We can use our T account in Illustration 6.22 to calculate the cash paid in interest during the year. The results of these calculations are shown in Illustration 6.23.

Illustration 6.23 CHY Limited interest payable T account

Interest payable account

	£000		£000
Balancing figure = cash paid	163	Interest payable brought forward	35
Interest payable carried forward	32	Finance expense in the statement of profit or loss	160
	195		195

MULTIPLE CHOICE QUESTIONS   Are you convinced that you can calculate the finance expense (interest) cash paid figure for inclusion in the statement of cash flows? Go to the **online workbook** and complete Multiple choice questions 6.11 to test your ability to calculate this figure correctly.

CHAPTER SUMMARY

You should now have learnt that:

- Organisations' cash flows are made up of cash flows from operating activities, cash flows from investing activities and cash flows from financing activities
- Cash generated during an accounting period is not the same as profit
- Cash flow is critical to the survival of an organisation
- Statements of cash flows can be prepared using both the direct and indirect methods
- A statement of cash flows is not sufficient on its own to provide users of financial statements with all the information they will need to assess an entity's financial position, performance and changes in financial position
- T accounts can be used to calculate missing figures for inclusion in the statement of cash flows
- Various accounting principles and conventions apply in the preparation of financial statements

QUICK REVISION   Test your knowledge by attempting the activities in the **online workbook**, including flashcards on the key concepts, numerical exercises and Multiple choice questions. You can also try the further self-test questions which are available at www.oup.com/he/scott-i2a2e

END-OF-CHAPTER QUESTIONS

Attempt the questions in the following sections and then look at the solutions which can be found in the **online workbook** to see whether there are areas that you need to revisit.

❯ RECALL AND REVIEW

> ❯Question 6.1

State the section in the statement of cash flows in which each of the following items will be reported:

(a)   Cash received from the sale of a property

(b)   Cash received from customers

(c) Cash received from the sale of inventory

(d) Income tax paid to HMRC

(e) Dividend received from an investment in another company

(f) Interest paid on a bank loan

(g) Interest received

(h) Cash paid to suppliers for goods purchased

(i) Depreciation of equipment

(j) Proceeds from the issue of preference shares

> **Question 6.2**

The following information is extracted from the statement of cash flows of the Maison Company for the year ended 30 June 2021:

- Cash and cash equivalents at 1 July 2020: £105,300
- Cash and cash equivalents at 30 June 2021: £115,800
- Cash outflow from investing activities for the year ended 30 June 2021: £2,400
- Cash inflow from financing activities for the year ended 30 June 2021: £1,300

Required

Calculate the cash flow from operating activities for the year ended 30 June 2021.

>> DEVELOP YOUR UNDERSTANDING

>> **Question 6.3**

Look up the answer to End-of-chapter question 3.3. Using details of Abi's assets and liabilities at the start of the trading year, her statement of profit or loss, her statement of financial position and her bank account summary for the year, present Abi's statement of cash flows using both the direct and the indirect method for the year ended 31 August 2021.

>> **Question 6.4**

Alison runs an online gift shop, trading for cash with individual customers and offering trading on credit terms to businesses. Alison provides you with the following list of statement of financial position balances at 31 December 2020:

	£
Non-current assets	
Computer equipment at cost	12,775
Less: accumulated depreciation on computer equipment at 31 December 2020	(7,245)
Racks, shelving and office furniture at cost	24,000
Less: accumulated depreciation on racks, shelving and office furniture at 31 December 2020	(8,000)
	21,530
Current assets	
Inventory	27,647
Trade receivables	27,200
Rent prepayment	2,500
Rates prepayment	1,965
Cash and cash equivalents	3,682
	62,994
Total assets	84,524
Current liabilities	
Trade payables	30,314
Telephone, electricity and gas accruals	1,500
Total liabilities	31,814
Net assets	52,710
Capital account	52,710

Alison provides you with the following additional information:

- During the year to 31 December 2021, Alison spent £8,000 on buying new computer equipment and £9,600 on new racks, shelving and office equipment as her business expanded.

- There were no disposals of non-current assets during the year.

Required

Using the statement of financial position at 31 December 2020 and the additional information above, together with the answer to Question 3.4, prepare Alison's statement of cash flows for the year ended 31 December 2021 using both the direct and the indirect method. For your calculation of cash flows from operating activities under the direct method you will need to prepare the trade receivables control account (Illustration 6.6), the trade payables control account (Illustration 6.8) and the expenses T account (Illustration 6.10).

>> Question 6.5

Look up the answer to End of chapter question 3.10. Using the statement of profit or loss, the statement of financial position and the bank account, present the statement of cash flows for Laura for the year ended 31 August 2021 using both the indirect and direct method.

≫ Question 6.6

Donald's business made a profit of £20,000 in 2021. Donald decided to withdraw £10,000 from the business. He believes that this will not affect the business as this is half the surplus made by the business in 2021. His accountant advises him that the company does not have that amount of money in the bank account. The bank statement shows there is only £4,000 in the bank.

Required

(a) Explain why there is insufficient cash in the bank account to cover the amount Donald intends to withdraw even though the business has made a profit much larger than that amount.

(b) Explain why profit and cash are different.

(c) Explain the different bases on which the statement of profit or loss and the statement of cash flows are prepared.

≫ Question 6.7

The following information is extracted from the statement of profit or loss and the statement of financial position of the Palace Company for 2021:

	£000
Cash at 1 January 2021	3,300
Cash at 31 December 2021	11,400
Operating profit	45,500
Dividends paid	19,500
Increase in trade and other receivables	7,800
Decrease in trade and other payables	8,200
Receipts from bond issue	13,200
Dividends received	1,020
Proceeds from the sale of machinery	2,130
Decrease in inventory	2,900
Depreciation expense	3,800
Income tax paid	24,950

Required

Prepare a statement of cash flows for the Palace Company for the year ended 31 December 2021 using the indirect method.

≫≫≫ TAKE IT FURTHER

≫≫≫ Question 6.8

The statements of financial position for Potters Limited, together with relevant notes, are given below. Potters Limited produces crockery for sale to shops and through its site on the Internet.

Potters Limited: statements of financial position at 30 June 2021 and 30 June 2020

	2021 £000	2020 £000
ASSETS		
Non-current assets		
Intangible assets: trademarks	100	120
Property, plant and equipment	10,200	8,600
	10,300	8,720
Current assets		
Inventories	1,000	1,100
Trade and other receivables	1,800	1,550
Cash and cash equivalents	200	310
	3,000	2,960
Total assets	13,300	11,680
LIABILITIES		
Current liabilities		
Trade and other payables	1,200	1,000
Current tax liabilities	300	250
	1,500	1,250
Non-current liabilities		
Long-term borrowings	3,200	2,600
Total liabilities	4,700	3,850
Net assets	8,600	7,830
EQUITY		
Called up share capital (£1 ordinary shares)	1,000	800
Share premium	2,500	2,150
Retained earnings	5,100	4,880
Total equity	8,600	7,830

During the year to 30 June 2021:

- Potters Limited paid £2,500,000 to acquire new property, plant and equipment
- Depreciation of £800,000 was charged on property, plant and equipment
- Plant and equipment with a carrying amount of £100,000 was sold for £150,000
- Amortisation of £20,000 was charged on the trademarks
- Dividends of £100,000 were paid
- Taxation of £275,000 was paid
- £200,000 interest was paid on the long-term borrowings
- Operating profit for the year was £845,000
- 200,000 new ordinary shares were issued for cash at a price of £2.75 each
- Potters Limited received no interest during the year to 30 June 2021

Required

Prepare the statement of cash flows for Potters Limited for the year ended 30 June 2021 using the indirect method.

>>> Question 6.9

Statements of financial position for Metal Bashers plc, together with the statement of profit or loss for the current year and relevant notes, are given below. Metal Bashers plc produces machine tools for industrial use.

Metal Bashers plc: statements of financial position at 30 September 2021 and 30 September 2020

	2021 £000	2020 £000
ASSETS		
Non-current assets		
Intangible assets: patents	200	150
Property, plant and equipment	21,800	18,850
	22,000	19,000
Current assets		
Inventories	1,400	1,200
Trade receivables	2,000	2,100
Prepayments	350	300
Cash and cash equivalents	750	400
	4,500	4,000
Total assets	26,500	23,000
LIABILITIES		
Current liabilities		
Current portion of long-term borrowings	500	500
Trade payables	1,800	2,050
Accruals	200	250
Current tax liabilities	400	350
	2,900	3,150
Non-current liabilities		
Long-term borrowings	6,500	7,000
Total liabilities	9,400	10,150
Net assets	17,100	12,850
EQUITY		
Called up share capital (£1 ordinary shares)	3,600	2,000
Share premium	5,600	2,400
Retained earnings	7,900	8,450
Total equity	17,100	12,850

Metal Bashers plc: statement of profit or loss for the year ended 30 September 2021

	2021 £000
Revenue	12,196
Cost of sales	9,147
Gross profit	3,049
Distribution and selling costs	425
Administration expenses	899
Operating profit	**1,725**
Finance income	100
Finance expense	870
Profit before taxation	**955**
Income tax	425
Profit for the year	**530**

During the year to 30 September 2021:

- Metal Bashers plc paid total dividends of £1,080,000
- New patents costing £70,000 were acquired
- Amortisation charged on patents was £20,000. This amortisation was charged to administration expenses
- 1.6 million new shares were issued during the year for cash at a price of £3 each
- Finance income and finance expense represent the actual cash received and paid during the year
- Income tax of £375,000 was paid during the year
- New property, plant and equipment costing £5,000,000 was purchased during the year for cash
- Redundant property, plant and equipment with a carrying amount of £250,000 was sold for £175,000. Profits and losses on disposal of non-current assets are credited or charged to administration expenses
- Depreciation of £1,800,000 was charged on property, plant and equipment during the year. This depreciation was charged to cost of sales
- Administration expenses include a charge for an irrecoverable debt of £125,000

Required

Prepare the statement of cash flows for Metal Bashers plc for the year ended 30 June 2021 using both the direct and indirect method. For your calculation of cash flows from operating activities under the direct method you will need to prepare the trade receivables control account (Illustration 6.6), the trade payables control account (Illustration 6.8) and the expenses T account (Illustration 6.10).

⟩⟩⟩ Question 6.10

Watson Limited sells medical equipment. The statement of financial position of Watson Limited at 31 December 2021 is presented overleaf together with the statement of profit or loss for the year ended 31 December 2021.

Watson Limited: statement of profit or loss for the year ended 31 December 2021

	£
Revenue	52,640
Cost of sales	27,090
Gross profit	25,550
Other income: dividends received	1,540
General expenses	10,850
Depreciation	4,900
Interest expense	1,260
Income tax	2,310
Profit for the year	7,770

Watson Limited: statements of financial position at 31 December 2021 and 31 December 2020

	2021 £	2020 £
ASSETS		
Non-current assets		
Property, plant and equipment	34,160	32,900
Investments	17,500	17,500
	51,660	50,400
Current assets		
Inventory	16,170	14,840
Trade and other receivables	9,800	10,990
Cash and cash equivalents	1,050	50
	27,020	25,880
Total assets	78,680	76,280
LIABILITIES		
Current liabilities		
Current portion of long-term borrowings	4,460	4,460
Trade and other payables	12,740	12,320
Interest payable	210	–
Taxation payable	2,310	3,850
	19,720	20,630
Non-current liabilities		
Borrowings	1,840	6,300
Total liabilities	21,560	26,930
Net assets	57,120	49,350
Equity		
Share capital	20,300	18,200
Retained earnings	36,820	31,150
Total equity	57,120	49,350

During the financial year ended 31 December 2021 Watson Limited paid a dividend of £2,100.

Required

Prepare the statement of cash flows for Watson Limited for the year ended 31 December 2021 using the indirect method.

7 THE FINANCING OF BUSINESS

INTRODUCTION

We looked at the different types of business organisations in Chapter 1 (Types of business organisation). The two business organisations we have looked at so far in Chapters 2, 3 and 6 adopted different methods through which to finance their operations. Julia introduced her own money into her sports equipment retailing business and was allocated all the profit from that activity at the end of the accounting year. Bunns the Bakers is financed by share capital, but how is the profit from that business allocated to its investors? In this chapter we will be looking at how different businesses raise the monetary resources with which to finance their operations and the requirements that each different financing method imposes upon each different business format.

FINANCING BUSINESS

All businesses have to raise finance at the start of their lives and at regular intervals as they expand. Providers of finance to businesses require some form of reward for providing that finance. So what sort of finance is raised by different businesses and what are the payments made to each type of finance?

Capital introduced: sole traders and partnerships

We have already looked briefly at this method of financing for sole traders in Chapter 2 (The components of equity). When a sole trader or a partnership is set up, the owners pay money into the new venture. It will take a little time for trading income to begin to flow into the business so this start-up capital is needed to buy non-current assets with which to set up the operations of the business and to provide cash to ensure the continuity of trading in the early stages of the business's life.

As an example, look back to Chapter 3, Illustration 3.3. Julia paid £30,000 into her business bank account and then used this cash to pay the initial rent of £5,000 and to buy the cash register and the shelves and fittings for her shop for £11,000 on the same day. No trading had taken place at this point so Julia had made no cash profits from which to pay for these non-current assets. Without her initial payment into the business, Julia would not have had the cash with which to make these necessary investments to run her retail operation. Many businesses start up in the same way with the owners paying in cash to buy assets and meet initial expenses from their own resources.

Sole traders and partners do not charge their businesses interest on this capital introduced. Instead, they draw on this capital and the profits made by the business as their source of income from which to meet their personal expenses and to finance their lifestyles. Chapter 2 (The components of equity) noted that the term for these withdrawals is 'drawings', money taken out of the business by the owner(s) for their own personal use.

As sole traders and partners are considered to be an extension of their businesses, withdrawing money in this way from their businesses is perfectly acceptable. However, it is not possible for shareholders in limited companies to withdraw money from their companies in the same way as limited companies have a separate legal identity (Chapter 1, Limited companies: separate legal identity) and are regarded as completely distinct from their owners.

> **WHY IS THIS RELEVANT TO ME?**   Capital introduced: sole traders and partnerships
>
> To enable you as a business professional to:
>
> ● Revise capital introduced from earlier chapters
>
> ● Understand how sole traders and partnerships finance their start-up capital
>
> ● Remind yourself how the owner's capital account for sole traders and partnerships works

GO BACK OVER THIS AGAIN!   Are you sure that you understand capital introduced? Go to the **online workbook** and have a go at Exercises 7.1 to make sure you can describe capital introduced.

Bank finance: all businesses

Banks provide short- and medium-term finance to businesses in the form of overdrafts and loans. In Chapter 2 we noted that such overdrafts and loans are described as borrowings under current and non-current liabilities in the statement of financial position. The cost of both these sources of finance is interest that the bank charges on the amounts borrowed.

Bank overdrafts have the following features (these features are summarised in Figure 7.1):

- Overdrafts are short-term finance.

- The overdraft amount varies each month depending on cash inflows and outflows during each month. The more cash received and the lower the amounts of cash paid out, the lower the overdraft will be and vice versa.

- There is usually a limit on the amount of the overdraft allowed by the bank. When customers reach or exceed this overdraft limit, the bank is entitled to refuse any further credit on that account.

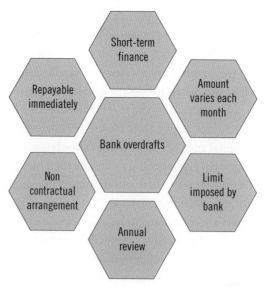

Figure 7.1 Features of bank overdrafts

- Overdrafts are subject to an annual review by the bank to determine whether the overdraft limit should remain the same, increase or decrease.

- Overdrafts are not contractual arrangements and banks can ask for overdrafts to be repaid immediately.

Give me an example 7.1 provides a real life example of bank overdraft facilities offered by Lloyds Bank plc.

GIVE ME AN EXAMPLE 7.1   **Bank overdrafts**

Details of overdrafts offered by Lloyds Bank on 20 January 2020:

Business Overdraft

With our Business Overdrafts, you can make sure that extra funds are available for when you need them. Apply for an amount that suits you, and only pay interest on the funds you use.

Features and Benefits

- Get a quote online in minutes (your credit rating will not be affected).

- Make sure extra funds are there when you need them.

- Only pay interest on the funds you use.

- Apply for a limit that suits your business.

- The interest rate you will pay on your overdraft is linked to the Bank of England Bank rate, which may change from time to time.

- Tailored interest rates based on your business status. (Rates are linked to Bank of England Bank rate, which may vary from time to time.)

- 8.35% EAR representative (varies with Bank of England Bank rate) applies only to unsecured overdrafts up to £25,000

Rates and Charges

	Unsecured overdrafts up to £25,000	Unsecured overdrafts over £25,000 and all secured overdrafts
Representative Interest Rate	8.35% EAR representative (varies with Bank of England Bank Rate)	Rates will be discussed on application
Overdraft Term	Up to 12 months	
Overdraft Amount	£500+	
Fees	Please be aware that charges apply. You will pay an arrangement fee of up to 1.5% on the amount of your overdraft, subject to a minimum fee of £250*. Subsequent renewals will include an arrangement fee of 1%, subject to a minimum fee of £200*. We will discuss full terms with you before any overdraft is taken out. *The minimum fee is applicable in order to cover the administration cost of arranging smaller overdrafts.	
Important Information	EAR stands for equivalent annual rate. It is the rate you would pay if you go overdrawn to the full limit of your facility for the entire year. It takes into account the interest rate you are charged as a result and how often it's charged—in this case interest is calculated daily and charged monthly. It then takes into account the effect of compounding—charging interest on interest—on your debt. Charges for unarranged overdrafts are charged separately.	

Tell us about your business's plans and needs. We will then agree on an interest rate and let you know if we require any security. We'll discuss the terms with you before any overdraft is taken out.

Source: https://www.lloydsbank.com/business/commercial-banking/loans-and-financing/loans/business-overdraft.asp

Notes to the above table: terms with which you may not be familiar

Bank of England Bank Rate: the Bank of England sets the interest rate (the base rate) it will pay to the commercial banks for the amounts of cash they deposit with the Bank of England. If the Bank lowers this base rate then interest rates charged by banks on loans to customers will fall. If the Bank raises this rate, then interest rates charged by banks on loans to customers will rise.

Security: when banks lend money to their customers, they want to be sure that they will receive the money back in the future. Banks can ask for security for loans taken out. Borrowers offer security in the form of assets such as land and buildings or other assets of the business: if the borrower is unable to repay the amounts borrowed, then the assets pledged as security to the bank will be taken by the bank and sold. The borrowings taken out are repaid from the sale proceeds from the sale of the assets. Where banks are confident that businesses will be able to repay what is borrowed, they will not request security. In these cases, the lending is said to be unsecured.

Bank loans operate as follows (the features of bank loans are summarised in Figure 7.2):

- A fixed amount is borrowed for a fixed term, usually a period of 5–10 years.
- Repayments are made on a regular basis, either monthly or quarterly.
- Each monthly repayment consists of an interest element and a repayment of part of the sum originally borrowed.
- Loans are contractual arrangements. Banks can only demand immediate repayment of loans when the borrower has failed to meet a contractual repayment or a payment of interest by the due date.

How do bank loans work in practice? Give me an example 7.2 and Table 7.1 present the features of the different types of business loans offered by Lloyds Bank.

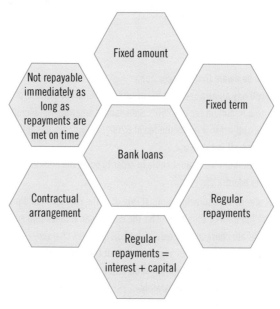

Figure 7.2 Features of bank loans

GIVE ME AN EXAMPLE 7.2   **Bank loans**

Table 7.1 Details of business loans offered by Lloyds Bank on 20 January 2020

Base Rate Loan	• Borrow from £1,000 over 1 to 25 years • Interest rate varies with Bank of England Bank Rate • No arrangement fees on loans up to £25,000 • No early repayment costs • 9.3% APR Representative Representative example: 9.3% APR based on an assumed unsecured loan amount of £8,000 with 60 monthly repayments of £165.68 at an annual interest rate of 8.90% (variable). Total amount payable £9,940.80.
Fixed Rate Loan	• Borrow from £1,000 to £50,000 over 1 to 10 years • No arrangement fees on loans up to £25,000 • No early repayment costs • 9.3% APR Representative Representative example: 9.3% APR based on an assumed unsecured loan amount of £8,000 with 60 monthly repayments of £165.68 at an annual interest rate of 8.90% (fixed). Total amount payable £9,940.80.
Commercial Fixed Rate Loan	• Borrow from £50,001 to £500,000 over 1 to 25 years • An arrangement fee will apply and is related to the amount you borrow • Capital repayment holidays • Interest rate can be fixed from 1 year to the full term of the loan Any early payment made during the fixed rate period will incur a defined break cost. Break costs are defined at the outset of your loan, giving you certainty around the costs involved.

Annual Percentage Rate (APR) is the total cost of the credit expressed as an annual percentage of the total amount of credit. It represents the actual yearly cost of credit over the loan term and includes not only the interest but also any other charges you have to pay, for example, an arrangement fee. The APR will vary depending on the loan amount and term.

Source: http://www.lloydsbank.com/business/retail-business/loans-and-finance.asp

Notes to the above table: terms with which you may not be familiar

Bank of England Bank Rate: the Bank of England sets the interest rate (the base rate) it will pay to the commercial banks for the amounts of cash they deposit with the Bank of England. If the Bank lowers this base rate then interest rates charged by banks on loans to customers will fall. If the Bank raises this rate, then interest rates charged by banks on loans to customers will rise.

Unsecured: when banks lend money to their customers, they want to be sure that they will receive the money back in the future. Banks can ask for security for loans taken out. Borrowers offer security in the form of assets such as land and buildings or other assets of the business: if the borrower is unable to repay the amounts borrowed, then the assets pledged as security to the bank will be taken by the bank and sold. The borrowings taken out are repaid from the sale proceeds from the sale of the assets. Where banks are confident that businesses will be able to repay what is borrowed, they will not request security. In these cases, the lending is said to be unsecured.

Capital repayment holidays: the amount borrowed is called the capital element of the loan. The capital element is distinct from the interest element of the loan. For example, if a borrower borrows £25,000 at an interest rate of 5%, the capital amount of the loan is £25,000 and the annual interest on the loan is £25,000 × 5% = £1,250. Each loan instalment repaid by a borrower consists of a repayment of part of the capital of the loan and a payment of interest. Should borrowers find that cash inflows are temporarily insufficient to repay both the capital and the interest elements in each instalment on a loan, then they can stop repaying the capital part of the instalments for a set period of time, just paying the interest element. This period is called a capital repayment holiday, a break from repaying the capital element of the loan. The outstanding capital balance of what is still owed does not fall, but it does not rise either. Once the capital repayment holiday finishes, then the borrower recommences payments of both the capital and the interest elements of the loan.

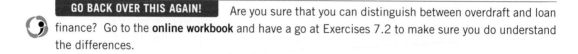

WHY IS THIS RELEVANT TO ME? Bank finance

To enable you as a business professional to:

● Understand the difference between bank overdrafts and bank loans

● Appreciate the key features of overdraft and loan finance

GO BACK OVER THIS AGAIN! Are you sure that you can distinguish between overdraft and loan finance? Go to the **online workbook** and have a go at Exercises 7.2 to make sure you do understand the differences.

SUMMARY OF KEY CONCEPTS Are you confident that you can describe the main features of overdraft and loan finance? Go to the **online workbook** to revise these main features using Summary of key concepts 7.1.

7

Other types of long-term finance: public limited companies

Debenture loans/bonds/loan notes

Public limited companies can issue debentures, bonds or loan notes to the public. Debentures, bonds and loan notes are long-term loans with a fixed rate of interest and a fixed repayment date. Thus a plc might issue a £500 million loan note with an interest rate of 5.25% and a repayment date of 31 January 2029. Lenders would then receive an interest payment of £26.25 million (£500m × 5.25%) every year on the anniversary of the loan note's issue and full repayment of the £500 million plus any interest outstanding up to the date of repayment on 31 January 2029. An example of corporate bonds issued by a plc is presented in Give me an example 7.3.

Debentures, bonds and loan notes are traded on stock exchanges around the world so lenders can sell their holdings in these long-term loans without waiting for the repayment date.

GIVE ME AN EXAMPLE 7.3 Bonds

Next plc records the following corporate bond liabilities together with their associated interest rates and maturity dates in note 19 to the annual report and accounts for the financial year ended 25 January 2020.

Corporate bonds

	Balance sheet value	
	2020	2019
	£m	£m
Corporate bond 5.375% repayable 2021	327.0	327.5
Corporate bond 3.000% repayable 2025	250.0	–
Corporate bond 4.375% repayable 2026	286.7	277.7
Corporate bond 3.625% repayable 2028	300.0	300.0
	1,163.7	**905.2**

Source: www.nextplc.co.uk

WHY IS THIS RELEVANT TO ME?   Bond and debenture finance

To provide you as a business professional with:

- An awareness of bonds, loan notes and debentures as a means of raising finance for large companies
- A brief overview of the features of bonds and debentures

GO BACK OVER THIS AGAIN!   Are you convinced that you understand bonds, loan notes and debentures? Go to the **online workbook** and have a go at Exercises 7.3 to make sure you can describe these sources of finance.

SUMMARY OF KEY CONCEPTS   Do you think that you can describe the main features of bond, loan note and debenture financing? Go to the **online workbook** to revise these main features with Summary of key concepts 7.2.

Share capital: limited companies

All limited companies, whether public or private, issue share capital. Share capital is a source of indefinite long-term finance for a company. Shares subscribed by shareholders will be in issue for as long as the company exists. Share capital financing is not available to sole traders or partnerships unless they choose to transfer their operations to a limited company set up for this purpose. As well as issues of ordinary share capital, some companies also issue preference share capital.

Companies distribute dividends to their shareholders. Dividends are a share of the profit earned in a financial period (usually one year) paid out to the shareholders. Whereas interest on loans and overdrafts has to be paid no matter what the circumstances of the business are, companies do not have to distribute a dividend if the directors decide that it is not in the company's best interests to do so. For example, if the company were about to make a large investment in new non-current assets, it would make more sense for the company to hold onto its cash to make this investment rather than paying a dividend.

Before we consider dividends further and how these are calculated, let's look at the two types of share capital that companies issue.

Preference share capital

Preference shares are so called because holders of preference shares receive preferential treatment from the issuing company in the following ways:

- Preference shareholders must receive their dividends from the company before any distribution of profit is made to ordinary shareholders.

- Thus, if there are no profits left over for distribution after the preference dividends have been paid then the ordinary shareholders receive no dividend for that year.

- On the winding up/liquidation of a company, once all the claims of a company's creditors have been settled, any money left over and available to shareholders is repaid to preference shareholders before any payment is made to ordinary shareholders.

However, preference shareholders also suffer various restrictions as a result of this preferential treatment:

- The rate of dividend on preference shares is fixed. Thus, preference shareholders are not entitled to any further share of the profits available for distribution once their fixed rate of dividend has been paid.

- Preference shareholders have no right to vote in general meetings.

Preference shareholders' rights are restricted in the above ways as they take on a lower level of risk when compared to ordinary shareholders. Although the companies in which preference shareholders invest might still fail or not earn much profit, the fact that they are paid their dividends first and receive their money back in a liquidation before the ordinary shareholders means that they are taking less risk than ordinary shareholders who stand to lose everything. The advantages and limitations of preference shares are summarised in Figure 7.3.

Ordinary share capital

Ordinary share capital is the name given to the most common form of share capital issued by companies. You will often see ordinary share capital referred to as equity share capital. Ordinary shareholders take on the highest risks when they buy shares in a company. Investors in ordinary shares might receive all of a company's profits as dividends (after the payment of any preference dividend) and see the value of their shares rise many times above what they originally paid for them or they could receive no dividends and nothing when the company goes into liquidation, losing all of their investment. All limited companies must issue ordinary share capital. Ordinary shares are the only shares that carry voting rights at company general meetings. The positive and negative aspects of ordinary shares are summarised in Figure 7.4.

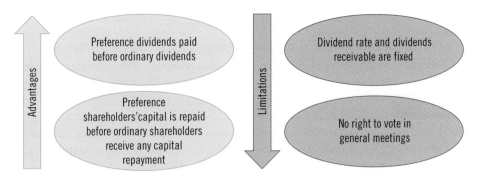

Figure 7.3 The characteristics of preference shares

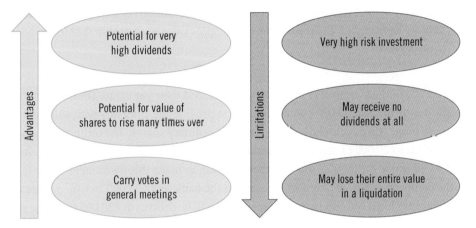

Figure 7.4 The characteristics of ordinary shares

WHY IS THIS RELEVANT TO ME? Share capital: preference and ordinary shares

To enable you as a business professional to:

- Develop a clear awareness of the different types of share capital that companies issue
- Understand the characteristics of the two different types of share capital

---

GO BACK OVER THIS AGAIN! Are you certain you understand how ordinary and preference shares differ? Go to the **online workbook** and have a go at Exercises 7.4 to make sure you can distinguish between these two types of share capital.

SUMMARY OF KEY CONCEPTS Do you think that you could describe the main features of ordinary and preference shares? Go to the **online workbook** to revise these main features with Summary of key concepts 7.3.

Share capital: share issues at par value

Under the Companies Act 2006, every company can issue as many shares as it wishes. Share capital is increased simply by issuing more shares. Example 7.1 presents details of the par value of share capital.

EXAMPLE 7.1

Printers Limited has share capital made up of ordinary shares of £1 each and preference shares of 50 pence each. Printers can issue any number of shares it wishes. However, companies only issue shares as and when they need to raise funds rather than raising all the cash they can from shareholders immediately.

In this example, the ordinary shares have a par value of £1. The par value is the face value or nominal value of each share. Par values can be of any amount. As well as the ordinary shares with a par value of £1 each, Printers also has preference shares with a par value of 50 pence each. However, par values could be 1 pence or 12½ pence or 25 pence or any other amount that the founders of the company decide as indicated in Give me an example 7.4. The par value of a company's shares is stated in the Memorandum and Articles of Association.

At the start of a limited company's life, shares are issued at their par value. Thus, Printers' directors might decide to raise £20,000 on its first day to provide the company with sufficient capital to start operating. The directors decide to issue just ordinary shares. The ordinary shares have a par value of £1, so 20,000 £1 shares will need to be issued to raise the £20,000 required. Investors are said to subscribe for their shares and they pay cash to make this investment. After the share issue, the company will now have £20,000 cash in the bank and £20,000 in issued share capital. The double entry to record this issue of share capital will be debit cash £20,000 (increase the cash asset), credit ordinary share capital (increase the amount owed to the shareholders).

GIVE ME AN EXAMPLE 7.4   The par value of shares

As an example of par values of share capital, Balfour Beatty plc has ordinary shares with a par value of 50 pence each and preference shares with a par value of 1 penny each.

Source: Balfour Beatty annual report and accounts 2019 www.balfourbeatty.com

---

 MULTIPLE CHOICE QUESTIONS   Are you confident that you can calculate the sums raised from a share issue? Go to the **online workbook** and have a go at Multiple choice questions 7.1 to make sure you can calculate these amounts.

Share capital: shares issued at a premium

As companies grow, their shares increase in value. Therefore, when companies want to issue shares at a later stage of their lives, these new shares are issued at par value plus a premium to reflect this increase in value. Example 7.2 presents details of the issue of shares at a premium.

EXAMPLE 7.2

Printers' directors decide to issue a further 30,000 £1 ordinary shares after one year of trading, but they now set the issue price for these additional shares at £1.25. The issue price for each share is made up of the £1 par value and a 25 pence premium. How much cash will be raised and how will this be recorded in Printers' financial statements?

The cash raised is calculated by multiplying the 30,000 shares by the £1.25 issue price for each share. This gives total cash raised of 30,000 × £1.25 = £37,500. This £37,500 comprises £30,000 of ordinary share capital (the par value of £1 × 30,000 shares) and a share premium of £7,500 (30,000 shares issued × 25 pence). The £30,000 is credited to share capital and the £7,500 is credited to the share premium account in the statement of financial position with the whole £37,500 raised being debited to cash in the bank.

Example 7.2 tells us that the share premium is any amount raised from an issue of shares over and above the par value of the shares issued. Give me an example 7.5 presents an example of an issue of shares at a premium.

GIVE ME AN EXAMPLE 7.5   Shares issued at a premium to the par value

As an example of shares issued at a premium, note 24 in the Thrive Renewables 2018 annual report presents the following information: '45,779 Ordinary shares of 0.50 each were allotted, issued and fully paid at a premium of £1.85 per share during the year. This allotment is part of a SCRIP scheme whereby shareholders can receive new shares instead of cash dividends.'

Source: Thrive Renewables annual report 2018 www.thriverenewables.co.uk

WHY IS THIS RELEVANT TO ME?   Share issues at par value and share issues at a premium

To enable you as a business professional to understand:

• How limited companies raise cash from share issues

• The financial effect of issuing shares at a premium

• The double entry required to record the cash raised through the issue of share capital in the accounting records

MULTIPLE CHOICE QUESTIONS   Could you calculate the sums raised from a share issue when shares are issued at a premium? Go to the **online workbook** and have a go at Multiple choice questions 7.2 to see if you can make these calculations correctly.

SUMMARY OF KEY CONCEPTS   Can you define share premium? Go to the **online workbook** to revise this definition with Summary of key concepts 7.4.

Share capital: bonus issues

As well as issuing shares for cash, limited companies also make what are called bonus issues of shares. Bonus issues are made when a company has a large surplus on its retained earnings on the statement of financial position. These retained earnings have not yet been distributed to shareholders as dividends and the company wants to keep these earnings within the business as share capital. This process is known as capitalising reserves, turning distributable retained earnings into new non-distributable share capital. No cash is raised in a bonus issue, but the number of shares in issue increases while the retained earnings reduce by a corresponding amount. Bonus issues are only made to existing ordinary shareholders and the amount capitalised as share capital is the par value of the shares issued.

A bonus issue is always expressed as a certain number of bonus shares for a certain number of shares already held by ordinary shareholders. Thus, a one-for-four bonus issue means that one new bonus share is issued to ordinary shareholders for every four shares they already hold. A two-for-five bonus issue means that two bonus shares are issued for every five shares currently held. Let's see how a bonus issue works with Example 7.3.

7

EXAMPLE 7.3

James plc currently has 12 million ordinary shares of £1 each in issue. The balance on retained earnings is currently £25 million. The directors propose a four-for-three bonus issue.

In this example, four bonus shares are issued for every three shares currently held. This means that 12m × 4 new shares ÷ 3 shares currently in issue = 16m new shares of £1 each are issued to ordinary shareholders. This transaction would be presented as shown in Illustration 7.1: £16 million is added (credited) to ordinary share capital and £16 million is deducted (debited) from retained earnings.

Illustration 7.1 James plc: bonus issue of four £1 shares for every three £1 shares already held by ordinary shareholders

	Before bonus issue	Debit	Credit	After bonus issue
Equity (credit balances)	£m	£	£	£m
Ordinary share capital	12,000,000		16,000,000	28,000,000
Retained earnings	25,000,000	16,000,000		9,000,000
	37,000,000			**37,000,000**

James plc now has 28 million ordinary £1 shares in issue compared to the original 12 million before the bonus issue. These newly issued bonus shares will receive dividends in the future just as the ordinary shares currently do. Issuing bonus shares is a good way of increasing the number of shares in issue and strengthening the fixed capital base of a company. Once the bonus shares have been issued the retained earnings balance falls and this limits the retained earnings that can be paid out in future as dividends.

Share capital: rights issues

From time to time, limited companies make new issues of shares to raise funds. However, companies cannot just issue new shares to anyone they want. The Companies Act 2006 prevents companies from issuing new shares to outside parties until those new shares have first been offered to current shareholders. Only when existing shareholders have turned down the opportunity to buy these new shares can the shares be offered to investors who are not currently shareholders of the company. These rights to subscribe for new issues of shares are known as pre-emption rights, the right to be offered first refusal on any new issue of shares.

Why does the Companies Act 2006 protect shareholders' rights in this way? Pre-emption rights prevent the dilution of existing shareholders' interests in a company. What this means and how pre-emption rights protect existing shareholders are illustrated in Example 7.4.

EXAMPLE 7.4

Joe and Bill each hold 50,000 ordinary shares in Painters Limited. Painters Limited has a total of 100,000 ordinary shares in issue, so Joe and Bill each own a 50% interest in the company. The directors decide that Painters needs to issue another 100,000 shares. If the directors were able to offer the shares to external investors, then Joe's and Bill's interest in Painters would fall to 25% each (50,000 shares ÷ (100,000 shares currently in issue + 100,000 new shares being issued)). They would thus suffer a 50% reduction in their interest in the company as a result of new shareholders being brought in. Whereas before they each controlled 50% of Painters, they now control only 25% each as a result of this new issue of shares to new investors. The Companies Act 2006 thus requires the directors to offer the new shares to Joe and Bill first so that they can take up the new shares in proportion to their current holdings and each maintain their 50% holding in the company. Only when Joe and Bill have declined the right to buy these new shares can the shares be offered to outside parties.

Rights issues: pricing

Rights issues are priced at a discount to the current market price to encourage shareholders to take up the issue. An example of a rights issue and how rights issues work is presented in Example 7.5.

EXAMPLE 7.5

If the current market value of one James plc £1 ordinary share is £3, then the directors will price the rights issue at, for example, £2.20 to encourage shareholders to take up their rights. £2.20 is an 80 pence discount to the current market price (£3.00 – £2.20). The number of shares will rise when the rights issue is complete. As you will know from studying economics, when supply increases, price goes down. Since there will be more James plc shares in issue after the rights issue the market price will fall. The discount to the current market price of the ordinary shares thus compensates James plc's shareholders for this anticipated fall in the market value of their shares.

Do note that the pricing of a rights issue at a discount to the market price is not the same as issuing shares at a discount. Issuing shares at a discount is illegal under the Companies Act 2006 and would involve, for example, selling shares with a par value of £1 for 99 pence or less. This is not allowed under company law.

How does a rights issue work? James plc's directors decide to make a rights issue of £1 ordinary shares, one for every four currently held. There are 28 million shares in issue after the bonus issue and the rights issue price is set at £2.20.

Your first task is to determine how many new shares will be issued. One new ordinary share is being issued for every four in issue, so this will give us 28,000,000 ÷ 4 = 7,000,000 new ordinary shares to issue.

How much money will this raise? Each share is being issued at £2.20, so an issue of seven million shares will raise 7,000,000 × £2.20 = £15,400,000.

You know from our earlier discussions (this chapter, Share capital: shares issued at a premium) that, with the par value of the shares being £1, there is a share premium to account for as well as the new addition to share capital. How much is this premium? Issuing £1 par value shares at £2.20 means that the premium on each share issued is £2.20 − £1.00 = £1.20. The total premium on the issue of seven million shares is then 7,000,000 × £1.20 = £8,400,000. Cash is thus debited with the £15,400,000 raised from the rights issue, ordinary share capital is credited with £7,000,000 and the share premium account is credited with £8,400,000. Give me an example 7.6 presents details of a rights issue recently undertaken by a listed company, Marks and Spencer plc.

GIVE ME AN EXAMPLE 7.6   Rights issues of shares

On 22 May 2019, Marks and Spencer plc, the food and clothing retail group, announced a one-for-five rights issue of 325.1 million new shares at 185 pence per share. The closing price of the company's shares was 259.38 pence on the day before the rights issue was announced. The par value of each ordinary share is 25 pence, so the rights issue price of 185 pence per share was a large discount to the current market price but not a discount to the par value of the shares. The aim of the rights issue was to raise £601.3m to help to finance a joint venture with Ocado. On the day after the announcement of the rights issue, the share price of Marks and Spencer plc fell to 235.09 pence and on 13 June 2019, the day after the rights issue offer closed, the share price fell to 216.00 pence.

Source: https://corporate.marksandspencer.com/investors/shareholder-information/corporate-actions/2019

WHY IS THIS RELEVANT TO ME?   Bonus and rights issues

To enable you as a business professional to understand:

- How bonus and rights issues work

- The financial effect of bonus and rights issues

- The double entry required to record share capital issued under bonus and rights issues in the accounting records

---

MULTIPLE CHOICE QUESTIONS   Are you convinced that you understand how bonus and rights issues work? Go to the **online workbook** and have a go at Multiple choice questions 7.3 to make sure you can calculate the entries to make to the relevant accounts for bonus and rights issues.

SUMMARY OF KEY CONCEPTS   Are you sure that you can define bonus and rights issues? Go to the **online workbook** to revise these definitions with Summary of key concepts 7.5 and 7.6.

DIVIDENDS

We have already discussed the subject of dividends. It is now time to see how dividends for the year are calculated.

Dividends are distributions of profit to shareholders. They are not an expense of the distributing company in the way that wages, rent or electricity are expenses (Chapter 3, Expenses). Dividends are deducted directly from retained earnings in the statement of financial position and do not appear in the statement of profit or loss. The double entry to record a payment of a dividend is: debit retained earnings (retained earnings are reduced by the distribution to shareholders), credit the bank account (the cash asset is reduced by the payment out of the bank).

When a company decides to pay a dividend to the shareholders, a figure of pence per share is quoted. Dividends are always paid on the number of shares in issue. How does a dividend distribution work? Let's look at how the total dividend distribution is calculated through two examples, Example 7.6 and Example 7.7.

EXAMPLE 7.6

James plc declares a dividend of 12 pence per ordinary share. How much dividend will be paid out? There are 35 million shares in issue after the rights issue (Example 7.5). This means that holders of the 35 million £1 ordinary shares will receive 12 pence for each share that they hold. The total dividend payment will thus be 35,000,000 × £0.12 = £4,200,000. When this dividend is paid, cash at the bank will fall by £4,200,000 (credit the bank account) and retained earnings will be reduced by £4,200,000 (debit retained earnings).

EXAMPLE 7.7

When calculating preference dividends, the par value of the preference shares is simply multiplied by the dividend rate. Remember that preference dividends are paid at a fixed rate and preference shareholders receive nothing more than their contractually agreed preference dividend. James plc also has 10,000,000, 50 pence, 5% preference shares in issue. This tells us that every 50 pence preference share receives a dividend of 2.5 pence (£0.50 × 5%). The total preference dividend for the year will thus be £250,000 (10,000,000 shares × £0.025).

Public limited companies paying dividends usually make two distributions in each financial year. These are known as the interim dividend, paid part way through the financial year, and a final dividend based on the profits for the financial year.

DISTRIBUTABLE AND NON-DISTRIBUTABLE RESERVES

Dividends are paid from distributable reserves only. Ordinary share capital, preference share capital, share premium and revaluation reserves are all capital reserves and the funds in these capital reserves are not distributable to shareholders. To make a dividend distribution from any of these reserves would be illegal under the Companies Act 2006.

For our purposes, the only distributable reserve, the one that represents realised profits of the company, is retained earnings. Retained earnings are a revenue reserve and it is this reserve from which dividends can be paid. However, if a company has retained losses and a negative balance on retained earnings, no dividends, either ordinary or preference, can be paid. Only when a company has a positive balance showing that the company has made profits can a distribution be made from the retained earnings reserve.

WHY IS THIS RELEVANT TO ME?   Dividends

To enable you as a business professional to:

● Understand how dividends are calculated

● Distinguish between capital reserves and revenue reserves

 MULTIPLE CHOICE QUESTIONS   Are you confident that you could calculate dividends correctly? Go to the **online workbook** and have a go at Multiple choice questions 7.4 to make sure you can calculate dividend distributions accurately.

CHAPTER SUMMARY

You should now have learnt that:

● Sole traders and partnerships raise money to finance their operations from their own capital resources, from the profits of their businesses, from bank loans and from bank overdrafts

● Limited liability companies raise money to finance their operations from the issue of ordinary and preference share capital and by borrowing from banks in the form of loans or overdrafts and by issuing bonds, loan notes and debentures

● The par value of a share is the face value or nominal value of that share

● A bonus issue involves the reduction of retained earnings and an increase in the issued share capital

● A rights issue is the issue of shares to shareholders at a discount to the current market price

● Dividends can only be distributed from retained earnings

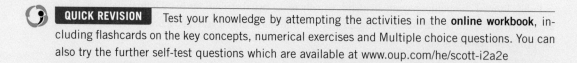 **QUICK REVISION**   Test your knowledge by attempting the activities in the **online workbook**, including flashcards on the key concepts, numerical exercises and Multiple choice questions. You can also try the further self-test questions which are available at www.oup.com/he/scott-i2a2e

END-OF-CHAPTER QUESTIONS

 Attempt the questions in the following sections and then look at the solutions which can be found in the **online workbook** to see whether there are areas that you need to revisit.

❯ RECALL AND REVIEW

❯Question 7.1

Anne intends to invest in the Rainbow Company. The company offers two types of shares, ordinary shares and 5% preference shares. Anne wonders which type of shares she should invest in. She requires a steady income to help cover her mortgage.

(a)   Advise Anne which type of shares would be better suited to her needs.

(b)   Outline the benefits and drawbacks of ordinary and preference shares.

> **Question 7.2**

Goldberg Limited is a private limited company. The directors (who are also the shareholders) have developed an expansion plan which requires a large investment. One option is to convert the company into a public limited company and sell shares to the public to raise the required funds. The alternative is to take out a bank loan. Advise the directors on the factors they should consider when making this decision. The advantages and disadvantages of each of the two financing options should be included in your discussion.

>> DEVELOP YOUR UNDERSTANDING

>> **Question 7.3**

An investor has £200,000 to invest and has to choose between three different investments:

- An investment in a £200,000 bond paying 5% interest per annum
- An investment in a new issue of preference shares with a par value issue price of 50 pence paying an annual dividend of 3 pence per share
- An investment in a new issue of ordinary shares with a par value issue price of 25 pence paying an annual dividend of 2 pence per share.

How much will each investment return to the investor? Which investment would be preferable on the assumption that the investor wishes to maximise income from investing the £200,000?

>> **Question 7.4**

A printing company wishes to raise £3,000,000 to finance its expansion. It can do this in one of three ways: borrowing from the bank at an annual interest rate of 5%, by issuing ordinary shares at their par value of 40 pence, which will require an annual dividend payment of 1.9 pence per share, or by issuing preference shares with a par value of 60 pence, which requires a fixed dividend of 3.15 pence per share. Which financing option will require the lowest cash outlay for the printing company?

>> **Question 7.5**

The equity section of the statement of financial position of Robin plc at 20 September 2021 presents the following figures:

	£000
Ordinary shares (800,000 shares with a par value of £1.50)	1,200
Share premium	600
Retained earnings	900
Total equity	2,700

On 20 September 2021, the company's board of directors decided to make a rights issue of shares. Shareholders will be offered the right to buy one new ordinary share for every two ordinary shares currently held. The new shares will be offered at a price of £1.80. The current market

price of one ordinary share in Robin plc is £2.00. By the end of September 2021, half of the shares have been taken up under the rights issue.

Required

After calculating the relevant figures, redraft the equity section of Robin plc's statement of financial position at 30 September 2021 to show the effect of the issue of shares under the rights issue.

»Question 7.6

At 1 July 2021, Thomson plc had 4,000,000 ordinary shares in issue (with a par value of £0.20 each), a share premium account with a balance of £50,000 and retained earnings of £650,000. The company undertakes the following transactions:

- 15 July 2021: Thomson plc's board of directors decides to issue a further 500,000 ordinary shares to fund the company's research and development projects. The issue price for each share is set at £0.30. All the shares are sold.
- 20 July 2021: the directors propose a one-for-five bonus issue.
- 10 August 2021: the company raises cash from the issue of 200,000 4% preference shares with a par value of £1 each.
- 24 December 2021: the company pays a dividend of 5 pence per ordinary share. The preference dividend for the six months to 10 February 2022 is also paid on this day.

Required

Show how the components of equity of Thomson plc change over the period 1 July to 24 December 2021.

»»»TAKE IT FURTHER

»»»Question 7.7

Plants Limited runs a garden centre business selling garden plants and products to the public from its busy edge of town site. In the year to 31 October 2021, Plants Limited's issued share capital consists of 100,000 ordinary shares of 50 pence each and 100,000 preference shares of £1 each. The preference share dividend rate is 6%. Preference dividends are payable on 31 October each year. An interim dividend of 10 pence per share was paid on the ordinary share capital on 15 May 2021 and the directors paid a final ordinary dividend of 20 pence per ordinary share on 15 October 2021.

Required

(a) Calculate the preference dividend that Plants Limited will pay for the year ended 31 October 2021.

(b) Calculate the total ordinary dividend for the year ended 31 October 2021.

(c) If retained earnings at 1 November 2020 were £45,000 and profit for the year to 31 October 2021 was £50,000, what is the balance on retained earnings after all the dividends for the year have been paid at 31 October 2021?

>>> Question 7.8

Plants Limited is looking to expand its operations in the year to 31 October 2022, but needs to raise additional finance to do so. The company proposes raising £500,000 by the issue of 200,000 ordinary shares on 1 May 2022. Profits for the year to 31 October 2022 are expected to be £90,000. An interim ordinary dividend of 15 pence per share will be paid on 15 April 2022 and a final ordinary dividend of 25 pence per share will be paid on 15 October 2022.

Required

Using the information above, the information from Question 7.7 and the answer to Question 7.7:

(a) Calculate the amounts to be credited to ordinary share capital and share premium in the equity section of the statement of financial position in respect of the new issue of ordinary shares on 1 May 2022.

(b) Calculate the total dividends, both ordinary and preference, to be paid in the year to 31 October 2022.

(c) Calculate the expected balance on retained earnings at 31 October 2022 after dividends for the year have been paid.

>>> Question 7.9

At 1 July 2021 Halyson plc had 500,000 ordinary shares of 25 pence each in issue together with 300,000 7½% preference shares of £1 each. The balance on Halyson's retained earnings at 1 July 2021 is £5,200,000.

Halyson plc is proposing a bonus issue of seven new ordinary shares for every two ordinary shares currently held. Once this bonus issue is complete, a rights issue will be made of five new ordinary shares for every three ordinary shares held at a price of £0.95. These transactions will take place on 1 April 2022.

On 28 June 2022, Halyson plc will pay the preference dividend for the year and a total ordinary dividend for the year of 30 pence per share. The loss for the year to 30 June 2022 is expected to be £1,500,000.

Required

Calculate for Halyson plc:

(a) The number of bonus shares to be issued

(b) The par value of the bonus shares to be added to ordinary share capital

(c) The number of ordinary shares to be issued in the rights issue

(d) The amount to be credited to ordinary share capital and share premium as a result of the rights issue

(e) The preference dividend for the year to 30 June 2022

(f) The ordinary dividend for the year to 30 June 2022

(g) The balance on the ordinary share capital account at 30 June 2022

(h) The expected balance on retained earnings at 30 June 2022

8 RATIO ANALYSIS 1: PROFITABILITY, EFFICIENCY AND PERFORMANCE

LEARNING OUTCOMES

Once you have read this chapter and worked through the questions and examples in both this chapter and the online workbook, you should be able to:

- Understand the importance and advantages of using ratios to evaluate the profitability, efficiency, performance, liquidity and long-term financial stability of entities

- Understand how the financial statements and ratios interact in the interpretation of the profitability, efficiency, performance, liquidity and long-term financial stability of organisations

- Calculate profitability ratios for gross profit percentage, operating profit percentage, profit before tax percentage and profit after tax percentage

- Suggest economic reasons for the changes in profitability ratios year on year

- Calculate efficiency ratios for non-current asset turnover, revenue per employee and profit per employee
- Show how efficiency ratios help to explain changes in the profitability ratios
- Understand how increasing the revenue from each unit of fixed resource employed in the business will increase an entity's profits
- Calculate performance ratios for earnings per share, price/earnings ratio, dividends per share, dividend yield and dividend cover
- Explain what the performance ratios you have calculated mean from a shareholder's point of view
- Compare an entity's profitability, efficiency and performance ratios with the profitability, efficiency and performance ratios of other companies as a way of benchmarking an entity's financial outcomes

INTRODUCTION

In Chapters 2, 3 and 6 we looked at the three major accounting statements, how they are put together, how they integrate with each other and what they tell us individually about the profits and cash generated in each accounting period and the financial position of the entity at the end of each accounting period. However, the real skill in accounting lies not in an ability to produce these statements but in analysing and interpreting the information they contain. Such analysis and interpretation enable users to draw conclusions about how well an entity is performing and the strength of its financial position. Financial information as presented in the three major statements has to be analysed to determine the profitability of an entity, how efficiently its assets are being used, how well an organisation is performing to meet the expectations of its investors and how secure its future cash flows and financial stability are. These aspects are analysed under the headings of profitability, efficiency, performance, liquidity and long-term financial stability and we will consider each of these measures in turn in this and the next chapter.

When reading the business and financial pages, the importance of these indicators will readily become apparent as we see in Give me an example 8.1.

What these terms mean and how they are used in evaluating entities' profitability, efficiency, performance, liquidity and long-term financial stability will become clear as you work through this chapter and the next. To appreciate how common the above terms are and how relevant they continue to be in assessing companies' performance and financial position, quickly read through the Companies and Markets section in today's *Financial Times* and see how many of these terms, among others, continue to appear.

8

GIVE ME AN EXAMPLE 8.1   A selection of terms linked to the analysis of companies' results and position

- Profitability
- Earnings
- Dividend cover
- Dividend yield
- Dividend per share
- Operating profit growth
- Market value
- Earnings per share
- Gross margins
- Revenue growth

- Cost cutting
- Liquidity
- Market capitalisation
- Net cash
- Price/earnings ratio
- Insolvency
- Liquidation

Source: taken from a quick skim read of the *Financial Times* Companies and Markets section on 27 September 2019.

EVALUATING FINANCIAL STATEMENTS: RATIO ANALYSIS

How do users evaluate and assess financial statements? The technique most commonly used is ratio analysis. A ratio in its simplest form expresses the relationship between two different figures. The calculation of the same ratio over several different time periods enables comparisons to be made between those different time periods to determine whether that ratio is rising, falling or staying the same. In this way, the performance and position of entities can be evaluated by analysing the trends that emerge over time. Ratio analysis, however, is not just confined to financial information but can be applied to any sets of numbers where relationships can be established. Consider Example 8.1.

EXAMPLE 8.1

When grocery shopping you might be evaluating two different sizes of a particular product: one costs £1.50 for 100g and the other costs £4.00 for 250g: which one offers the better value? By calculating the per gram price, the ratio of cost for one unit of weight, you can determine that the 100g product costs 1.50 pence per gram, while the 250g product costs 1.60 pence per gram. Therefore, the smaller sized product offers better value. Bigger is not always cheaper!

GO BACK OVER THIS AGAIN!   Are you sure that you understand how ratios can be used to simplify the relationship between two figures to enable comparisons to be made? Go to the **online workbook** and look at Exercises 8.1 to see how ratios can be used in this way.

As a business professional you will:

- Understand how ratios simplify the relationships between two figures to enable meaningful comparisons to be made
- Appreciate the role of ratios in evaluating information used for making economic decisions

WHY IS RATIO ANALYSIS NEEDED?

Example 8.1 shows the value of ratios, expressing one figure in relation to another to highlight information critical to making an economic decision. However, why is ratio analysis needed in the interpretation and evaluation of financial statements? Again, a simple example will help to explain why ratios are such a useful tool in analysing financial performance and position. Consider the information presented in Example 8.2 and how this information is used to assess changes in profitability year on year.

EXAMPLE 8.2

A pottery company has sales of £110,376 in the year to 31 December 2020 and sales of £150,826 in the year to 31 December 2021. The company owners will see the year to 31 December 2021 as a great success in terms of the increase in sales achieved. Profit for the year to 31 December 2020 was £27,594 and £34,690 for the year to 31 December 2021. Again, you might say that the company has been successful in the most recent financial year as it has generated more profit than it did in the previous year. While it is true that profit has risen, the figures alone do not tell us whether the company is now more *profitable*. The figures for sales and profits have both increased, but is each sale in the year to 31 December 2021 generating as much, less or more profit as each sale in the year to 31 December 2020? A simple comparison, as shown in Table 8.1, of the profit to the sales in each year will tell us the answer to this question.

Table 8.1 Comparison of profit to sales in each year

	2021 Calculation	Ratio	2020 Calculation	Ratio
$\dfrac{\text{Profit}}{\text{Sales}} \times 100\%$	$\dfrac{\pounds 34,690}{\pounds 150,826} \times 100\%$	23%	$\dfrac{\pounds 27,594}{\pounds 110,376} \times 100\%$	25%

Calculating these two profitability ratios shows us that despite the rise in both sales and profits in 2021, each sale has generated less profit than sales in 2020. For every £1 of sales, 23 pence is profit in 2021 compared to 25 pence of profit per £1 of sales in 2020. Ratios thus provide a relative measure from which to determine simple relationships between the financial figures. Calculating the ratio for the two time periods has enabled us to highlight a variance in profitability that was not at all apparent from the raw figures as presented in the accounts.

GO BACK OVER THIS AGAIN!   Are you certain you could calculate ratios from a given set of data and draw valid conclusions? Go to the **online workbook** and have a go at Exercises 8.2 to check your understanding.

> **WHY IS THIS RELEVANT TO ME?**   Why is ratio analysis needed?
>
> As a business professional you will:
>
> • Appreciate that larger numbers do not necessarily indicate greater success or an improvement in relative terms
>
> • Understand how ratios can be used to determine changes relative to other figures
>
> • Carry out ratio analysis on sets of financial statements in order to evaluate the profitability, performance and financial position of different entities

Now that we have this information showing reduced profitability in 2021 we can ask questions to determine why the pottery company's profitability has fallen this year. If the company had sold exactly the same goods at exactly the same prices to exactly the same customers in both years, then the profitability percentage, the pence of profit from each £1 of sales, should have been exactly the same. As the profitability percentage has fallen, financial statement users will want to know the reasons for the change and will ask questions with a view to identifying these reasons. Questions asked will focus on changes in the business and the economic climate with a view to explaining this fall. Examples of such questions (among others) might be as follows:

- Has the pottery business reduced selling prices to increase sales in an attempt to increase the company's share of the local pottery sales market?

- Has there been an increase in the price of clay used to make the pottery or has there been a rise in the potters' wages which the owner has chosen not to pass on to customers?

- Has the pottery business offered discounted prices to bulk buyers of its goods?

- Has a rival business opened in the area forcing selling prices down through increased competition?

- Is an economic recession forcing the owner to reduce prices to attract customers?

GO BACK OVER THIS AGAIN!   Are you sure that you understand how profitability would fall in the circumstances outlined in the questions above? Visit the **online workbook** to take a look at Exercises 8.3 to see how profitability would fall as a result of the reasons suggested.

Ratios are thus a starting point in the interpretation and evaluation of financial information. Calculating the ratios gives us information about which relationships have changed. We can then seek out explanations for these changes to assist us in understanding the business and how it operates and then use this information in making decisions about the future prospects of the business.

As a business professional you will:

- Calculate ratios for businesses and compare these ratios to ratios from earlier accounting periods
- Use ratios to evaluate the performance of different parts of an organisation
- Use ratios to determine aspects of a business in which improvements could be made
- Evaluate the effect of internal and external changes on a business and how these changes have affected the financial statement figures and the ratios derived from them

RATIOS, FIGURES OR BOTH?

Given that ratios are so useful in interpreting an organisation's results, should we just ignore the financial statement figures once we have calculated the ratios? While ratios are an excellent interpretative tool, it is important to realise that the interpretation of financial statements relies on both the figures presented in the statement of profit or loss, the statement of financial position and the statement of cash flows *and* the ratios derived from these figures. Just taking the figures or the ratios on their own would be insufficient to enable users to form a full understanding of what the financial statements are telling them about the profitability, performance, efficiency and liquidity of an entity. Thus, an evaluation of an entity should look at both the figures presented in the financial statements and the ratios derived from those numbers. To understand why both the figures and the ratios are used together, consider Examples 8.3 and 8.4.

EXAMPLE 8.3

An entity has a profitability percentage of 20% compared to its competitor with a profitability percentage of 10%. Logically, based on just this ratio, users will prefer the company with a profitability percentage of 20% as this is higher. However, the entity with the 20% profitability has a profit of £50,000 and sales of £250,000 while its competitor has a profit of £10,000,000 and sales of £100,000,000. Which is the preferable company now? Clearly the company with sales of £100 million and profit of £10 million will attract greater attention. This is a much larger company, probably very well established and with higher profits (if not higher profitability) from which to pay regular dividends to shareholders and with a longer, more stable and more firmly grounded trading record. Hence it is vital to look at the financial statement figures as well as the ratios when evaluating an organisation's financial performance and position.

EXAMPLE 8.4

A profit of £1 million sounds impressive. However, the £1 million figure has no context. If the profit of £1 million was generated from sales of £10 million, this would give a profitability percentage of 10% (£1m/£10m × 100%). Yet if the £1 million profit was generated from sales of £100 million this would give a profitability percentage of just 1% (£1m/£100m × 100%). Profitability of 10% is definitely preferable to 1% profitability. Hence, it is vital to look at the ratios as well as the financial statement figures when evaluating an organisation's financial performance and position.

Even more useful would be information comparing the profitability percentage achieved in prior years: if the entity generating 10% profitability this year had achieved 20% profitability in each of the previous five years, the 10% profitability in the current year would be seen as a very poor performance, but might be understandable if those profits had been generated during a period of contraction in the economy. However, if the profitability percentage in the previous five years had been 5%, then doubling the profitability percentage to 10% would be seen as a very worthwhile achievement indeed.

WHY IS THIS RELEVANT TO ME?   Ratios, figures or both?

As a business professional you will appreciate:

- That the figures and the ratios based on them are both equally valuable in analysing and interpreting financial statements

- The interlinking nature of both ratios and figures in the analysis and interpretation of financial results

- The different perspectives that both ratios and financial statement figures bring to the analysis and interpretation of financial results

---

GO BACK OVER THIS AGAIN!   Do you understand how ratios and financial statement figures interact? Go to the **online workbook** and have a go at Exercises 8.4 to check your understanding.

THE ADVANTAGES OF RATIOS: SUMMARY

The preceding pages have presented a lot of arguments and ideas, so let's just pause for a moment to summarise how ratios and ratio analysis are advantageous in the evaluation of financial statements:

- Ratios are easy to calculate and to understand.

- Ratios highlight trends and variances by simplifying data into key indicators.

- Ratios help to express relationships between different figures in the financial statements.

- Calculating ratios across different time periods helps us to build up a picture of the trend in a particular indicator.

- Because ratios are a proportion calculated on a consistent basis across different time periods, this helps to overcome the problem of figures changing from year to year.

- Ratios, of course, are not the final answer: changes in ratios over different accounting periods will just indicate that we need to investigate why those ratios have changed and to rationalise the changes by reference to different economic conditions prevailing in each accounting period, different product mixes or the strategy the organisation is pursuing in relation to its goals.

- Ratios are thus not an end in themselves; they are an indicator of change or movement that prompts further questions and further action to correct unfavourable movements or to take further actions to maintain the positive trend.

REFER BACK   To illustrate the ratios discussed below and in the next chapter we will use the statement of financial position, statement of profit or loss and statement of cash flows for Bunns the Bakers presented in Chapters 2, 3 and 6. You should refer to Illustrations 2.1, 3.1 and 6.1 in these chapters or refer to the copies available in the **online workbook** as you work through the rest of this chapter and the next.

PROFITABILITY RATIOS

Now that we have considered the role of ratios in conjunction with the financial statement figures, it is time to look at the specific ratios used in analysing organisations' profitability. While we have already looked at a simple example of a profitability ratio earlier in this chapter (Example 8.2), we will now think about profitability ratios in much more depth and detail and consider the ratios presented in Figure 8.1.

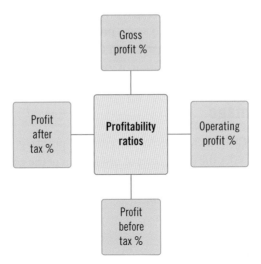

Figure 8.1 Profitability ratios

As we noted in Chapter 3 (Chapter 3, Introduction), profit is one of the most discussed numbers in any set of financial statements. However, to put profit into context, we have to know whether profits are higher or lower and how these profits compare with results from previous accounting periods. In money terms: is the profit of an organisation rising or falling? In relative terms: is the entity making more or less profit per pound of sales than in previous years? Profitability ratios compare the various profit figures shown in the statement of profit or loss to the revenue for the year in order to make this assessment.

Bunns the Bakers' statement of profit or loss (Illustration 8.1) shows the revenue and profit figures for the years ended 31 March 2021 and 31 March 2020.

Illustration 8.1 Bunns the Bakers: revenue and profit figures for the years ended 31 March 2021 and 31 March 2020

	2021	2020
	£000	**£000**
Revenue	10,078	9,575
Gross profit	5,543	4,979
Operating profit	895	767
Profit before tax	760	614
Profit for the year	547	442

Following the principle discussed earlier that we must consider ratios and the absolute figures together, we should first highlight the trends in the revenue and profits in Illustration 8.1 before we calculate any ratios. All the figures given for the revenue and the different profits for 2021 are higher than the revenue and profits in 2020. This looks good: in money terms, revenue and profits are rising. However, as we have already noted, these raw figures only tell us that Bunns the Bakers has made more profit on the back of higher revenue in the current year, but do not tell us whether the company is more *profitable*. To assess profitability, we need to compare the various profit figures to the sales made by the organisation to see whether more or less profit is being generated per £ of sales through the calculation of various ratios.

Gross profit percentage

As we saw in Chapter 3 (Chapter 3, Different categories of profit), gross profit is the profit left over after deducting from sales the direct costs of production of the goods sold or, in Julia's case, after deducting the costs of buying in goods for resale. This ratio is very useful when assessing how effectively the organisation is controlling its costs of production or costs of buying in goods for resale. This ratio is calculated as follows:

$$\text{Gross profit}\% = \frac{\text{Gross profit}}{\text{Revenue}} \times 100\%$$

Looking at Illustration 8.1, the company has made a gross profit in the year to 31 March 2021 of £5,543,000 from revenue of £10,078,000. This gives the organisation a gross profit percentage for 2021 of:

$$\frac{£5,543,000}{£10,078,000} \times 100\% = 55.00\%$$

Conventionally, ratios are calculated to two decimal places.

Have Bunns the Bakers achieved a higher ratio in 2021 compared with 2020? Let's calculate the gross profit ratio for 2020 to see whether 2021's gross profit percentage is higher or lower than 2020's. Gross profit in the statement of profit or loss (Illustration 8.1) for the year ended

31 March 2020 is £4,979,000 from revenue of £9,575,000, so this gives a gross profit percentage for 2020 of:

$$\frac{£4,979,000}{£9,575,000} \times 100\% = 52.00\%$$

WHY IS THIS RELEVANT TO ME?   Gross profit percentage

As a business professional you will:

• Find information relevant to the gross profit percentage calculation in the financial statements

• Know and apply the gross profit percentage calculation

• Calculate your own gross profit percentage figures from any given statement of profit or loss

MULTIPLE CHOICE QUESTIONS   Are you confident that you can calculate a gross profit percentage from a given set of financial information? Go to the **online workbook** and have a go at Multiple choice questions 8.1 to test out your ability to calculate this ratio.

Interpretation of the results

The increase in gross profit percentage is encouraging. Bunns the Bakers are making 55 pence of gross profit from each £1 of sales in 2021 compared to a gross profit of 52 pence from each £1 of sales in 2020. However, as we noted earlier, just calculating the ratios is not enough: in your role as a business professional, you will be expected to investigate in order to determine the reasons why ratios have changed when compared with the previous year. The way to do this is to consider and enquire into possible reasons for the changes or to rationalise these changes by reference to the economic factors affecting the organisation both locally and nationally.

Why might Bunns the Bakers be generating a higher gross profit percentage in the current year compared to the previous year? It is important to explain this change as it might be expected that each sale less the cost of sales will generate the same gross profit percentage every time (for this idea, see Chapter 12, Relevant costs, marginal costing and decision making: assumptions and the assumption that contribution (sales – variable costs) from each extra unit of production sold will be the same as for all other units of sales).

There are two aspects to the gross profit of an organisation, the revenue and the cost of sales, so either or both of these figures might have been subject to certain changes to give a higher gross profit percentage. Therefore, possible reasons for the increase in 2021 might be as follows:

• An increase in selling prices that is higher than the rise in costs incurred in producing or buying in the goods for sale.

• A change in the types of sales made from lower profitability products such as bread to higher profitability goods such as pies, pastries and ready-made sandwiches.

• A fall in the price of input materials thereby lowering the cost of sales while maintaining selling prices at the same level.

- An increase in the productivity of the workforce, producing more goods per hour or selling more goods per shop than in the previous year.
- The company might have benefited from bulk discounts from suppliers: when goods are ordered in larger quantities, suppliers often give their customers a discount for placing larger orders. Bulk discounts received reduce the cost of raw materials in the production process thereby lowering the cost of sales and increasing the gross profit.

These are just some of the possible reasons for the change in the gross profit percentage and you can probably think of other perfectly valid reasons to explain this improvement. As a business professional you will be expected to calculate the ratios and then think about and offer reasons why ratios are changing in order to understand and explain the economic trends underlying the movements in these figures.

WHY IS THIS RELEVANT TO ME?   Interpretation of the results

As a business professional you should appreciate that:

- You will be expected to think about changes in ratios and present reasons why those ratios are changing
- Senior managers and other users of accounting information will want to know why the gross profit percentage is changing: they will not just accept the changes without any explanation
- Business leaders and other users of accounting information do not have to be told that ratios are changing, they want to know *why* they are changing so that action can be taken to extend favourable or to correct unfavourable movements

---

GO BACK OVER THIS AGAIN!   How certain are you that you could determine the causes of rises and falls in the gross profit percentage? Go to the **online workbook** and have a go at Exercises 8.5 to make sure you can distinguish between factors that will cause the gross profit percentage to rise and factors that will cause it to fall.

MULTIPLE CHOICE QUESTIONS   Are you confident that you could determine factors affecting the gross profit percentage? Go to the **online workbook** and have a go at Multiple choice questions 8.2 to test out your ability to determine these factors.

Other profitability ratios

As well as the gross profit figure, Illustration 8.1 gives statement of profit or loss figures for operating profit, profit before tax and profit for the year (= profit after tax). Profitability ratios can be calculated for these figures as shown in Table 8.2.

Using the figures for revenue and for profits in Illustration 8.1, we can calculate the other profitability percentages for Bunns the Bakers for the two years ending 31 March 2021 and 31 March 2020. These figures are shown in Table 8.3.

Table 8.2 Profitability ratios for operating profit, profit before tax and profit for the year

Ratio	Calculation	What does this ratio tell us?
Operating profit %	$\dfrac{\text{Operating profit}}{\text{Revenue}} \times 100\%$	Determines profitability on the basis of revenue less all operating costs, before taking into account the effects of finance income, finance expense and taxation
Profit before tax %	$\dfrac{\text{Profit before tax}}{\text{Revenue}} \times 100\%$	Bases the profitability calculation on profit before taxation to eliminate the distorting effect of changes in tax rates. The profit before tax percentage is the profitability of the entity after deducting all costs incurred and taking into account income earned from all sources, both trading and investment
Profit after tax %	$\dfrac{\text{Profit for the year}}{\text{Revenue}} \times 100\%$	Calculates profitability for the period after adding all income and deducting all expenses and charges for the period under review

8

Table 8.3 Other profitability percentages for Bunns the Bakers for the two years ending 31 March 2021 and 31 March 2020

	2021 Calculation	Ratio	2020 Calculation	Ratio
Operating profit %	$\dfrac{£895,000}{£10,078,000} \times 100\%$	8.88%	$\dfrac{£767,000}{£9,575,000} \times 100\%$	8.01%
Profit before tax %	$\dfrac{£760,000}{£10,078,000} \times 100\%$	7.54%	$\dfrac{£614,000}{£9,575,000} \times 100\%$	6.41%
Profit after tax %	$\dfrac{£547,000}{£10,078,000} \times 100\%$	5.43%	$\dfrac{£442,000}{£9,575,000} \times 100\%$	4.62%

These profitability ratios have risen, too, so it is quite clear that Bunns the Bakers is more profitable in 2021 than it was in 2020 as shown in Figure 8.2. The rise in gross profit is part of the explanation for the increase in the above ratios. There is now more gross profit from which to pay all the other operating and finance expenses and still leave a larger profit for the year. Cost control will also be a factor and we can investigate which costs are lower or higher than in the previous year and determine how these rises and falls have affected profits and profitability in the current year. However, we can also investigate the efficiency with which assets are being used within the business. The greater the efficiency and productivity of these assets, the higher the revenue and profits will be.

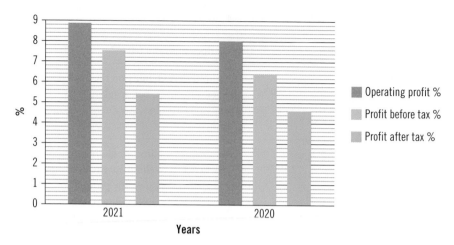

Figure 8.2 Bunns the Bakers' operating profit, profit before tax and profit after tax percentages

WHY IS THIS RELEVANT TO ME?   Profitability ratios

As a business professional you will:

• Understand how ratios relevant to assessing profitability are calculated

• Calculate those profitability ratios yourself

• Use the calculated profitability ratios as a foundation on which to build explanations for changes in the ratios in comparison to previous years

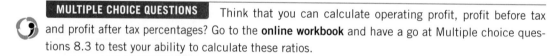

MULTIPLE CHOICE QUESTIONS   Think that you can calculate operating profit, profit before tax and profit after tax percentages? Go to the **online workbook** and have a go at Multiple choice questions 8.3 to test your ability to calculate these ratios.

SUMMARY OF KEY CONCEPTS   How well have you grasped the formulae for gross profit percentage, operating profit percentage, profit before tax percentage and profit after tax percentage? Go to the **online workbook** to take a look at Summary of key concepts 8.1–8.4 to reinforce your understanding.

EFFICIENCY RATIOS

Efficiency ratios consider how effectively and productively the resources of the organisation are being used to create both revenue and profit. An organisation's resources fall into two categories. First, non-current assets used in the production and sale of goods and services and, second, the employees engaged within the business as illustrated in Figure 8.3. Various ratios can be calculated to demonstrate how efficiently these resources are being used within an organisation and these ratios should also help to explain the improved profitability of Bunns the Bakers in the year to 31 March 2021.

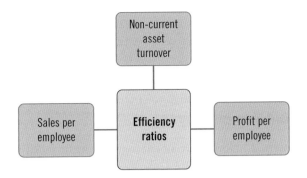

Figure 8.3 Efficiency ratios

Non-current asset turnover

This ratio compares the sales achieved by an organisation with the non-current assets in use in that organisation to determine how many £s of sales are produced by each £ of non-current assets. Ideally, this ratio will rise over time as non-current assets are used more efficiently to generate increased revenue.

This ratio is calculated as follows:

$$\text{Non-current asset turnover} = \frac{\text{Revenue}}{\text{Non-current assets}}$$

We have already seen that Bunns the Bakers has revenue of £10,078,000 for the year ended 31 March 2021 and revenue of £9,575,000 for the previous financial year. From the statement of financial position in Illustration 2.1, total non-current assets at 31 March 2021 and 31 March 2020 are £11,865,000 and £11,355,000 respectively. This gives the following figures for non-current asset turnover:

$$2021:\text{Non-current asset turnover}:\frac{£10,078,000}{£11,865,000}=£0.85$$

$$2020:\text{Non-current asset turnover}:\frac{£9,575,000}{£11,355,000}=£0.84$$

The figures show a slight improvement over the year. In 2020 each £1 of non-current assets generated revenue of 84 pence and in 2021 this has improved to 85 pence. Our conclusion from this ratio would be that non-current assets are being used more efficiently to generate revenue for the business as more revenue is being produced per £ of non-current assets.

However, a word of caution is needed at this point. As we saw in Chapter 2 (How are assets and liabilities valued?), users have to be careful when using information on assets employed within an organisation. The carrying amount at which assets are recorded in the statement of financial position may be increased by restating these assets to current values. Conversely, this amount may be too low because assets bought many years ago are still being used within the business. When such assets are still recorded at their original cost less any depreciation charged, these figures will now be seriously out of date and produce much less meaningful comparisons. Despite this shortcoming in this ratio, the non-current asset turnover figure does present users with relevant information on how effectively the organisation is using its long-term assets to generate revenue.

MULTIPLE CHOICE QUESTIONS Are you sure that you can calculate non-current asset turnover ratios? Go to the **online workbook** and have a go at Multiple choice questions 8.4 to test your ability to calculate this ratio.

Revenue and profit per employee

Unlike non-current assets, employees are not recognised in financial statements due to the very high level of measurement uncertainty associated with their valuation (Chapter 2, Assets). However, employees are a vital part of every organisation and how they perform during their working hours will determine how successful and how profitable organisations are. Increased productivity on the part of employees, generating more output or selling more goods during the hours worked each week, will have a significant impact upon both revenue and profitability. Employees are usually paid a fixed weekly wage, so the more they produce for that fixed weekly wage, the more profit entities will make. As an example of this, think about Bunns the Bakers' shop employees. They will be paid the same amount each week for selling 10 sandwiches or 400 sandwiches, but the latter sales figure will lead to much higher profits in each shop. Increasing sales while keeping input costs the same inevitably leads to higher profits. This principle holds where any cost is fixed: the more production or the more sales that can be generated from this fixed cost, the more profitable organisations will be.

NUMERICAL EXERCISES Are you convinced you understand how increasing output while keeping input costs the same can lead to higher profits? Visit the **online workbook** to take a look at Numerical exercises 8.1 to reinforce your understanding of how this is true.

If employees are not given a monetary value within financial statements, how can we assess whether they have been more or less productive during each accounting period? In many jurisdictions, organisations must disclose the average number of employees during each financial reporting period in the annual report and financial statements. You may have to search for this information in the notes to the financial statements, but it will be there and you will be able to use this information to make meaningful comparisons of the revenue and profit per employee across different years. The higher the revenue and profit per employee, the more efficiently organisations are working to generate returns to satisfy the business's objectives of profit and revenue growth. Where these ratios are falling, management can look into the reasons for declining revenue and profit per employee. Are operations overstaffed and is there scope to reduce employee numbers to improve the efficiency, productivity and profitability of operations?

These measures of employee efficiency are calculated as follows. While operating profit per employee is calculated, you could just as easily calculate per employee figures for gross profit, profit before tax or profit after tax (= profit for the year). Whichever measure you use, you must be consistent in your calculation of the ratio so that you are comparing like with like across different accounting periods. Similarly, the measure calculated below is based on all employees, but the ratios could be calculated using just production employees or production plus retail employees or any other combination of employee numbers deemed suitable, provided that the calculation continues to be consistently applied.

$$\text{Revenue per employee} = \frac{\text{Total revenue}}{\text{Total number of employees}}$$

$$\text{Profit per employee} = \frac{\text{Operating profit}}{\text{Total number of employees}}$$

From the notes to Bunns the Bakers' accounts, it can be determined that the average number of employees in the year to 31 March 2021 was 120 and 112 in the year to 31 March 2020. Using these figures and the figures for revenue and operating profit in Illustration 8.1, the following efficiency ratios can be calculated:

$$2021: \text{Revenue per employee} = \frac{\pounds10,078,000}{120} = \pounds83,983$$

$$2020: \text{Revenue per employee} = \frac{\pounds9,575,000}{112} = \pounds85,491$$

$$2021: \text{Operating profit per employee} = \frac{\pounds895,000}{120} = \pounds7,458$$

$$2020: \text{Operating profit per employee} = \frac{\pounds767,000}{112} = \pounds6,848$$

While revenue per employee has fallen in 2021, operating profit per employee has risen by £610, a rise of 8.91% ((£7,458 − £6,848)/£6,848 × 100%). This increase suggests that costs have been well controlled this year and that the company's employees are working effectively to generate increased profit for the business. This increase in profit per employee might also go some way to explaining the increased profitability noted earlier in this chapter: more profit has been generated per unit of resource employed, possibly due to higher productivity, and, as a result, a higher profit and higher profitability percentages have been produced.

WHY IS THIS RELEVANT TO ME?   Efficiency ratios

To enable you as a business professional to:

- Understand ratios that are relevant to determining the effectiveness of asset utilisation
- Calculate and apply these ratios yourself
- Appreciate that the more revenue and profit that can be generated from a fixed cost resource, the more profitable and successful an organisation will be

---

MULTIPLE CHOICE QUESTIONS   Do you reckon you can calculate revenue and profit per employee ratios? Go to the **online workbook** and have a go at Multiple choice questions 8.5 to test your ability to calculate these ratios.

Sales and profit per unit of input resource

One further aspect of efficiency merits our attention at this point. It is common practice in the retail sector to measure sales and profits per square metre or square foot of selling space (where shops differ greatly in size from superstores down to small high street outlets) or per shop (where shop size does not vary significantly). When these figures rise year on year, then more has been produced from the same unit of resource: input resources have been used more effectively and efficiently to produce more sales and hence more profits. Let's see if Bunns the Bakers are producing more sales and profits from their resources by calculating asset utilisation ratios (Figure 8.4).

Bunns the Bakers had 19 shops all of similar size open to the public in the year to 31 March 2020. During the year to 31 March 2021 an additional shop was opened on 1 October 2020, exactly six months into the current year. During the year to 31 March 2021, then, Bunns the Bakers had 19 + $(1 \times 6/12) = 19.5$ shops selling the company's goods and products. Dividing the figures for the number of shops into the revenue for each year will give us the following results for revenue per shop:

$$2021 : \text{Revenue per shop} : \frac{£10,078,000}{19.5} = £516,821$$

$$2020 : \text{Revenue per shop} : \frac{£9,575,000}{19} = £503,947$$

These figures tell us that Bunns the Bakers has achieved higher sales per shop and so is using the company's resources much more efficiently, squeezing more output from the same unit of

Figure 8.4 Asset utilisation ratios

resource. A similar calculation can be undertaken to find out whether more profit has been generated from the resources used. The focus of our attention here will be the operating profit per shop, the sales less all the operating costs of the business.

$$2021 : \text{Operating profit per shop} : \frac{£895,000}{19.5} = £45,897$$

$$2020 : \text{Operating profit per shop} : \frac{£767,000}{19} = £40,368$$

Again, just as in the case of the employees, the shops have generated higher profits per shop in 2021 compared to 2020. More revenue and more profit have been generated from the same resources and so the business is more profitable in comparison to the previous year.

GO BACK OVER THIS AGAIN!   Are you sure you understand how increasing income per unit of input resource leads to higher profits? Visit the **online workbook** and look at Exercises 8.6 to prove to yourself that this is true.

A real life example is presented in Give me an example 8.2. Selling space has increased, but has this resulted in higher sales and profits from each unit of input resource?

8

GIVE ME AN EXAMPLE 8.2   Ted Baker's annual report and accounts for the 52 weeks to 26 January 2019 presents the following figures:

	52 weeks ended 26 January 2019	52 weeks ended 27 January 2018
Retail revenue	£461.0 million	£442.5 million
Operating profit	£59.2 million	£71.0 million
Average square footage of retail space	431,646 square feet	410,190 square feet

Retail revenue has certainly increased in the year to January 2019 while operating profit has declined. But is the retail space being used more efficiently and productively to generate higher revenue from each unit of input resource? Using the figures presented, we can calculate the retail revenue per square foot of retail space. In the 52 weeks to 26 January 2019, the sales per square foot of retail space were £1,068.00 (£461,000,000 ÷ 431,646 square feet) while in the 52 weeks to 27 January 2018 sales generated per square foot of retail space were £1,078.77 (£442,500,000 ÷ 410,190 square feet). Thus fewer sales per unit of resource have been achieved in the 52 weeks to January 2019 when compared to the 52 weeks to January 2018. The available retail space has not been used as effectively and efficiently to produce higher sales per unit of input resource despite the expansion of the available resource. This reduction in revenue per square foot of input resource together with the steep fall in operating profits in the year to January 2019 reflect both external economic difficulties and problems arising within the business itself. Expansion has occurred, but this expansion has not yet resulted in improved revenue and profit for the company.

WHY IS THIS RELEVANT TO ME?   Sales and profit per unit of input resource

To enable you as a business professional to:

• Appreciate that increasing sales per unit of input resource is often the key to improving an organisation's profitability

• Devise suitable efficiency ratios to measure output per unit of input resource to see if this is rising, falling or staying the same

---

GO BACK OVER THIS AGAIN!   Can you identify ways in which to increase sales and profit per unit of input resource? Go to the **online workbook** and have a go at Exercises 8.7 to test your understanding of how this works.

PERFORMANCE RATIOS

These ratios, illustrated in Figure 8.5, are of particular interest to an entity's shareholders as they measure the returns to the owners of shares in the business. Shareholders invest money into the shares of a business with a view to earning dividends from the profits made by that business. The various ratios considered under this heading first compare the profits generated to the number of shares in issue and then think about the dividends paid out on each share. Comparisons of dividends to the market price of each share tell shareholders what their return is on that share. In this way they can assess whether they could earn more by investing their money in alternative investments, while comparing dividends paid with profits generated helps investors to decide how safe their future dividend income will be.

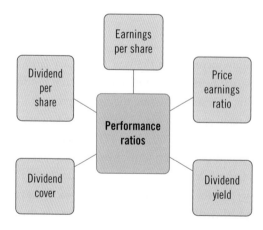

Figure 8.5 Performance ratios

Earnings per share (EPS)

The first performance ratio that shareholders consider is the earnings per share (this is frequently abbreviated to EPS). This figure is produced simply by dividing the profit for the year by the number of ordinary shares in issue. This figure represents the dividend that would result if all the profits for the period were paid out to ordinary shareholders as dividends. As we noted in Chapter 7, such a pay-out is most unlikely as the directors hold back some of the profits each year from which to finance future investment in the company.

EPS is calculated as follows:

$$\text{Earnings per share} = \frac{\text{Profit after taxation and after preference dividends}}{\text{Number of ordinary shares in issue}} \times 100 \text{ pence}$$

The profit after taxation is equivalent to the profit for the year. In situations in which an entity has preference shares in issue, any dividends paid on those preference shares will be paid out before any dividends are paid to ordinary shareholders. Therefore, this prior claim on the profits of an entity has to be deducted from profit for the year before the profits available for distribution to the ordinary shareholders can be determined. Note that EPS is always expressed in pence per share.

Looking at the figures for Bunns the Bakers, the profit after taxation (= profit for the year) for 2021 is £547,000 and £442,000 for 2020. The number of shares in issue can be observed in the statement of financial position. As shown in Illustration 2.1, Bunns the Bakers had 2,500,000 £1 shares in issue in the year to 31 March 2021, while in the previous year there were only 2,400,000 £1 ordinary shares. The increase in the number of shares indicates that additional shares have been issued during the year to 31 March 2021. The calculations for EPS for the two years under consideration are thus:

$$2021: \text{Earnings per share} = \frac{£547,000}{2,500,000} \times 100\text{p} = 21.88 \text{ pence}$$

$$2020: \text{Earnings per share} = \frac{£442,000}{2,400,000} \times 100\text{p} = 18.42 \text{ pence}$$

Bunns the Bakers has no preference shares in issue, so there are no preference dividends to deduct from the profit for the year before the EPS figures can be calculated. Therefore, the EPS calculation is simply based on the profit for the year divided by the number of ordinary shares in issue. Given the rise in EPS, shareholders will be pleased and the stock market will give the shares a higher valuation based on these increased returns.

MULTIPLE CHOICE QUESTIONS   Are you confident that you can calculate a figure for earnings per share? Go to the **online workbook** and have a go at Multiple choice questions 8.6 to test your ability to calculate this ratio.

EPS is a key figure in the evaluation of an entity's performance by the stock market and by stock brokers and traders. A review of the financial press will show you that where profits and thus EPS are expected to increase, the share price rises ahead of the announcement of earnings for the financial period under review. Similarly, where an entity's actual profits and EPS do not meet market expectations, share prices of that entity are marked down by the market. This reduction in the market price of the shares arises first from the fact that the results are a disappointment and second because the flows of cash to shareholders in the form of dividends from that entity are likely to be lower than expected. Ideally, the EPS figure should keep rising each year. Where this is the case, the share price will keep rising too and a rising share price is a source of happiness to shareholders as such rises indicate increasing wealth. In reality, EPS rise and fall in line with the economy: during periods when the economy surges, profits, and hence EPS, rise, but when the economy contracts and slows down, profits reduce, causing EPS and share prices to fall. Similarly, when companies' results and EPS are better than expected, share prices rise, but when they fall or are expected to fall, then the share price falls, too. Give me an example 8.3 provides two examples to illustrate these share price movements.

GIVE ME AN EXAMPLE 8.3   The effect of profits on share prices

The online fashion retailer Boohoo.com saw pre-tax profits for the year to 28 February 2017 rise 97% to £30.9m. Over the same time period, revenue rose 51% to £294.6m. The share price, which stood at 49.75 pence on 27 April 2016, rose almost 3.80 times to 188.75 pence over the course of the year to 26 April 2017.

Sources: *Financial Times*, 27 April 2017 and This is Money.co
.uk http://www.thisismoney.co.uk/money/markets/article-
4446616/Boohoo-s-profits-rise-97-year-amid-share-price-
hike.html

At the close of business on 24 April 2017, Whitbread plc's shares stood at 4,307 pence. At the start of business on 25 April 2017, the share price had fallen 6.66% to 4,020 pence as a result of slowing sales growth, profits that rose less strongly than expected and worries about reduced consumer spending. Profit before tax for the 52 weeks to 2 March 2017 was up 5.7% to £515.4m against a market expectation of £554m. The share price fall occurred despite an increase in the final dividend of 6% to 95.80 pence.

Source: *ShareCast News*, Whitbread warns of tough consumer outlook, 25 April 2017 http://sharecast.com/news/
whitbread-warns-of-tough-consumer-outlook/25844885.
html

WHY IS THIS RELEVANT TO ME?   Earnings per share

As a business professional you will be required to:

- Calculate the earnings per share ratio
- Be aware of the effects that profits or losses will have on the earnings per share of an entity
- Understand how the stock market values companies' shares on the basis of earnings per share

Price/earnings ratio (the P/E ratio)

The price/earnings ratio is linked to the EPS. This ratio divides the EPS into the current market price of that share. This gives a number that is an indicator of how many years of current period earnings are represented in the share price today. Alternatively, you can look at this ratio as the amount that a shareholder would be willing to pay today for every £1 of current earnings made by a company. A quick glance at the financial pages will show you that every listed company has a different P/E ratio (as shown in Give me an example 8.4), some higher and some lower than others. Typically, shares in companies with steady or rising profits have a higher P/E ratio as the earnings are perceived to be more secure and enduring than from other shares. On the other hand, shares in companies whose earnings are expected to be subject to lower or negative growth rates have lower P/E ratios as the earnings in these companies are expected to be much less secure and so P/E ratios for shares in these companies are lower. You might say that the P/E ratio is an indicator of the market's confidence in a particular company and its ability to maintain or grow its current earnings: the more likely it is that a company will continue to produce profits, earnings and dividends for shareholders, the higher the P/E ratio of that company will be.

GIVE ME AN EXAMPLE 8.4   **Differing price/earnings ratios**

A glance at Hargreaves Lansdown's website on Tuesday 31 March 2020 shows the following P/E ratio information for three companies:

Company	P/E ratio
Marks and Spencer	4.08
Next	8.39
Ted Baker	0.94

Source: https://www.hl.co.uk/shares

On 31 March 2020, following the outbreak of coronavirus in the UK, all non-essential retail operations had been suspended. Marks and Spencer's food retail outlets remained open, but general merchandise and homeware outlets had closed for the foreseeable future. In the view of the markets at this date, the partial ability to trade should have enabled Marks and Spencer to generate some sales and profits over the period of the outbreak, but the location of Marks and Spencer food outlets in railway stations, motorway service stations and other low footfall locations inevitably

lowered the expectations of investors. Both Ted Baker and Next sell non-essential fashion goods and accessories along with homewares so their stores were all closed, with trading taking place only online. Prior to the shutdown, Next had reported a 3.5% increase in sales and a 2% increase in operating profit for the 52 weeks ended 25 January 2020, together with a comprehensive risk assessment to show how it would withstand the impact of the coronavirus outbreak on both sales and cash flows. Ted Baker anticipates a profit of £5m–£10m for the 52 weeks to 25 January (compared to an operating profit in the 52 weeks to 26 January 2019 of £59.2m). In addition, the company announced on 23 March 2020 that the proceeds from the sale of its head office building in London would be used to pay down debt owed to lenders. As the market considered Next's survival prospects to be strong, the P/E ratio remains at a reasonably high level compared to the other two companies. Ted Baker's short-term prospects did not look encouraging at this time and the market responded accordingly by downgrading the company's share price, thereby lowering its P/E ratio to a very low level.

The price/earnings ratio is calculated in the following way:

$$\text{Price/earnings ratio} = \frac{\text{Market value of one ordinary share}}{\text{Earnings per share}}$$

Share prices for Bunns the Bakers, when their results were released for the years ended 31 March 2021 and 31 March 2020, were 310.7 pence and 254.2 pence respectively. These prices and the EPS calculated above give P/E ratios as follows:

$$2021: \text{Price/earnings ratio} = \frac{310.7}{21.88} = 14.2$$

$$2020: \text{Price/earnings ratio} = \frac{254.2}{18.42} = 13.8$$

The share price has risen as the EPS have increased in 2021. Given the rise in EPS in the current financial year, the stock market would expect future earnings to be more secure (and that a higher dividend will be paid from higher earnings) and so the price/earnings ratio has also risen. Given the nature of Bunns the Bakers' products, investors would also expect customers to continue buying such products in the foreseeable future. Indeed, they might even buy additional treats to cheer themselves up during a difficult economic period. A higher level of confidence in the shares to continue producing an enduring earnings and dividend stream is thus being shown by the higher P/E ratio.

GO BACK OVER THIS AGAIN!   Are you sure you understand the relationship between price and earnings in the price/earnings ratio? Go to the **online workbook** and have a go at Exercises 8.8 to test your understanding of this relationship.

MULTIPLE CHOICE QUESTIONS   How quickly do you think you can calculate price/earnings ratios? Go to the **online workbook** and have a go at Multiple choice questions 8.7 to make sure you can calculate this figure.

Dividend per share (DPS)

This ratio is used by shareholders to determine how much dividend is being paid on each share. As in the case of EPS, the ideal situation for shareholders is for the dividends to keep rising each year. Such increases indicate confidence in the company's ability to continue generating rising profits into the future. In addition, higher dividends result in rising share prices as expectations of future dividend increases feed into the market's valuation of the shares. The DPS can be compared to the EPS to calculate the pay-out ratio, the percentage of the EPS that have been distributed as dividend to the shareholders over the year.

The DPS figure is worked out in almost exactly the same way as EPS, but the total dividends paid out are substituted for the profits after taxation and after preference dividends. This ratio is calculated as follows:

$$\text{Dividend per share} = \frac{\text{Total ordinary dividends}}{\text{Number of ordinary shares in issue}} \times 100 \text{ pence}$$

From the statement of cash flows in Illustration 6.1, we can see that the dividends paid out in the year to 31 March 2021 were £90,000 compared with £72,000 in the year to 31 March 2020. This gives DPS figures for the two years as follows:

$$2021: \text{Dividend per share} = \frac{£90,000}{2,500,000} \times 100\text{p} = 3.60\text{ pence}$$

$$2020: \text{Dividend per share} = \frac{£72,000}{2,400,000} \times 100\text{p} = 3.00\text{ pence}$$

Comparing these figures to the EPS for the two years gives a pay-out ratio (dividend per share as a percentage of earnings per share for the year) of:

$$2021: \text{Payout ratio} = \frac{3.60\text{ pence}}{21.88\text{ pence}} \times 100\% = 16.45\%$$

$$2020: \text{Payout ratio} = \frac{3.00\text{ pence}}{18.42\text{ pence}} \times 100\% = 16.29\%$$

DPS has risen and this represents a higher pay-out ratio as well. The company has thus paid out more DPS this year as a percentage of EPS, but has still retained a significant proportion of the earnings (over 83% in both years under review) with a view to reinvesting these into the business to generate further expansion in the future and to increase both sales and profits.

Dividend yield

Shareholders invest in companies firstly to generate income in the form of dividends and secondly to increase their wealth through the capital appreciation (the increase in the market price of a share over the year) of their shares' value. These same shareholders could just as easily invest their cash in the safety of bank or building society accounts and earn interest on their deposits. Is the dividend and capital appreciation they are earning on their shares sufficient compensation for the risk they are taking by investing in the stock market?

The dividend earned by shareholders is compared with the market price of a share to give the dividend yield. This figure is calculated as follows:

$$\text{Dividend yield} = \frac{\text{Ordinary dividends per share}}{\text{Current market price of one ordinary share}} \times 100\%$$

For Bunns the Bakers, the dividend yield for the financial years ended 31 March 2021 and 31 March 2020 is as follows:

$$2021: \text{Dividend yield} = \frac{3.60\text{ pence}}{310.7\text{ pence}} \times 100\% = 1.16\%$$

$$2020: \text{Dividend yield} = \frac{3.00\text{ pence}}{254.2\text{ pence}} \times 100\% = 1.18\%$$

The dividend yield does not appear to be very high at present, though it compares well with the Bank of England base rate of 0.10%. By investing in a building society account with a more favourable interest rate, shareholders could gain a much better monetary return of around 1.00% to 1.50%. However, using this building society interest rate as a benchmark would ignore the fact that the share price has risen from 254.2 pence a year ago to 310.7 pence today, a rise of 22.23% ((310.7 − 254.2)/254.2 × 100%). This capital appreciation along with the dividends received represent the total return to shareholders over the year. When looking at the dividend yield, it is important to remember that a low return does not necessarily indicate a poorly performing share. Both the capital appreciation in the share price and the dividend actually received have to be taken into account.

Dividend cover

This ratio measures how many times the current year ordinary dividend could be paid from the profit for the year. Dividend cover looks at the profit after taxation and after any preference dividends that have to be paid first. This ratio is a measure of the security of the dividend that has been paid: the higher the ratio, the more secure the dividend. A dividend cover of 1.0 would indicate that all the EPS were being paid out as dividends with no retention of profits within the entity to finance future expansion and development. Whereas a dividend cover of 3.0 would indicate that the current year dividend could be paid out three times and that two-thirds of the profit for the year is being retained within the business.

The dividend cover ratio is calculated in the following way:

$$\text{Dividend cover} = \frac{\text{Profit after tax and after preference dividends}}{\text{Total ordinary dividends}}$$

Looking at Bunns the Bakers, the dividend cover ratio for the two financial years that concern us is:

$$2021 : \text{Dividend cover} = \frac{£547,000}{£90,000} = 6.08 \text{ times}$$

$$2020 : \text{Dividend cover} = \frac{£442,000}{£72,000} = 6.14 \text{ times}$$

As Bunns the Bakers have no preference shares in issue, the relevant number to use in this calculation is the profit for the year as given in the statement of profit or loss. From the results of the above calculations, the ratio has fallen slightly, but a dividend cover of over six times is very safe indeed and shareholders can anticipate that their dividend will continue to be paid for the foreseeable future.

WHY IS THIS RELEVANT TO ME?   Performance ratios

As a business professional you will be required to:

- Understand ratios relevant to investors and the stock market
- Understand how these ratios are calculated
- Calculate these ratios yourself
- Comment meaningfully on the ratios you have calculated

Are you certain that you can distinguish between the five performance ratios? Go to the **online workbook** and have a go at Exercises 8.9 to test your understanding of which ratio does what.

Are you convinced that you can calculate dividend per share, pay-out, dividend yield and dividend cover ratios? Go to the **online workbook** and have a go at Multiple choice questions 8.8 to make sure you can calculate these figures.

Can you remember the formulae for earnings per share, price/earnings ratio, dividend per share, pay-out ratio, dividend yield and dividend cover? Go to the **online workbook** and take a look at Summary of key concepts 8.8–8.13 to reinforce your understanding.

Will Bunns the Bakers' shareholders be happy with the company's performance?

How have Bunns the Bakers performed this year? Shareholders will consider the following factors:

- EPS and DPS are both higher than in 2020.
- The increase in the P/E ratio indicates the market's expectation that the company will continue producing rising earnings and dividends for shareholders into the foreseeable future.
- While the dividend yield fell very slightly from 1.18% to 1.16%, the increase in the share price over the year will have more than compensated for this reduction.
- Taken together, the dividend yield and the increase in the share price have comfortably exceeded the returns on what are perceived to be safer investments (bank and building society deposit accounts).
- Shareholders will therefore be happy with the dividends paid and the increase in the market value of their shares.
- The dividend cover indicates that future dividends should be easily affordable from profits.
- The low dividend pay-out ratio indicates that the company is keeping plenty of profit back with which to finance future growth and expansion.
- While shareholders might want profits, earnings, dividends and share price to be even higher, they can be satisfied with the company's performance in the year ended 31 March 2021 when comparing this performance with the previous year.

WHY IS THIS RELEVANT TO ME?   Evaluation of performance ratios

As a business professional you will be expected to:

- Appreciate what factors shareholders and the stock market will take into account when assessing an entity's performance
- Be able to make an objective assessment of an entity's performance yourself

RETURN ON CAPITAL EMPLOYED

A common ratio that you will find in other books on accounting is the return on capital employed (abbreviated to ROCE). This ratio is calculated as follows:

$$\frac{\text{Profit before interest and tax}}{\text{Capital employed}} \times 100\%$$

Capital employed is defined as the equity of an entity plus the long-term borrowings. Looking at the statements of financial position of Bunns the Bakers at 31 March 2021 and 31 March 2020 (Illustration 2.1) equity totals up to £8,459,000 and £7,767,000 respectively. Long-term borrowings (included in non-current liabilities) at the two accounting dates are £2,700,000 and £3,000,000. Profit before interest and tax is equivalent to the operating profit line in Illustration 8.1 and this amounts to £895,000 for the year to 31 March 2021 and £767,000 for the year to 31 March 2020. This gives us the following figures for return on capital employed for the two years as follows:

$$2021 : \text{ROCE} = \frac{£895,000}{(£8,459,000 + £2,700,000)} \times 100\% = 8.02\%$$

$$2020 : \text{ROCE} = \frac{£767,000}{(£7,767,000 + £3,000,000)} \times 100\% = 7.12\%$$

What is this ratio trying to do? ROCE is used to compare the different profits of different companies that have different capital structures. As we saw in Chapter 7, some companies raise their finance solely through share capital while others rely on loans and still others use a mixture of both share and loan capital to finance their businesses. In this way, the operating profits generated by these different capital structures can be compared to determine which entities produce the highest returns from their capital structures. Investors can then determine which entities they will invest their money into to produce the highest returns. Return on capital employed is often used to compare returns available from companies with interest rates available from banks and building societies to decide whether it would be safer to invest in these much less risky investments rather than in a particular company.

However, the ROCE ratio suffers from a number of problems. We saw in Chapter 2 that not all the assets of an entity are reflected in organisations' statements of financial position. Similarly, the figures presented on the statement of financial position are not necessarily as up to date as they might be. The equity of an entity is made up of share capital that may have been issued many years ago along with retained earnings that have been accumulated over many different accounting periods. These figures would need to be adjusted for changes in the purchasing power of the pound to bring all the pounds tied up in equity up to current day values for this ratio to be meaningful. After all, the profit before interest and tax has been earned in the current year, but this is being compared to share capital and retained earnings from previous years when the value of each pound was very different from what it is today. As noted in Give me an example 8.5 dealing with Ryanair, this is tantamount to comparing apples and pears so that the comparison loses its validity.

It should be possible to restate all the share capital and retained earnings figures to current values (for example by multiplying the market value of each share by the total number of shares in issue) to produce a suitable figure for equity. However, this is a time-consuming exercise and users of accounts might prefer to look at the total shareholder return as represented by the dividend yield and the increase in the market value of shares over the year as the best indicator of the returns available from each company. Users are completely free to use the ROCE ratio as they see fit, but they must be fully aware of the severe limitations that this ratio presents and how these limitations will affect their perceptions of the returns available from each entity.

WHY IS THIS RELEVANT TO ME?   Return on capital employed

To enable you as a business professional to understand:

- The way in which return on capital employed is used by entities and individuals
- The limitations of the return on capital employed ratio
- That total shareholder return represents a more effective way in which to distinguish between different investment opportunities

THE IMPORTANCE OF CALCULATING AND PRESENTING RATIOS CONSISTENTLY

Emphasis has been placed throughout this chapter on the need to calculate and present ratios consistently year on year. Why is this consistency so important? Failure to calculate and present ratios consistently from year to year will mean that comparisons are distorted and figures misleading rather than being accurate portrayals of the financial position compared to previous accounting periods. The dangers of trying to compare information that is not consistently presented and the distortions that this gives rise to are illustrated in Give me an example 8.5.

WHY IS THIS RELEVANT TO ME?   The importance of calculating and presenting ratios consistently

As a business professional you will be expected to:

- Present unbiased reports with consistent data that is not misleading
- Present data that has been compiled and calculated consistently in order to produce fair and valid comparisons between different reporting periods
- Be aware of the dangers of not comparing like with like

HOW WELL ARE WE DOING? COMPARISONS WITH OTHER COMPANIES

So far we have just looked at the financial statements and ratios of Bunns the Bakers. The company seems to be moving in the right direction with increased profits and profitability, improved efficiency leading to rising revenue and shareholders who should be content with the returns they are receiving. However, we have looked only at internal information with no benchmark against which

8

GIVE ME AN EXAMPLE 8.5   Ryanair's Stansted spin

Michael O'Leary's ability to spin a tale has reached a new level this week. Along with the gullibility of parts of the media in accepting it. Hook, line and sinker.

'Ryanair cuts Stansted winter capacity by 40 per cent,' claimed his press release. The assertion was patently rubbish. But it is almost universally already accepted as fact. On the most charitable assessment, he is planning to cut Stansted winter capacity by 14 per cent. The probability is that the year-on-year decline in Ryanair passenger numbers at Stansted will be much lower even than that. BAA, Stansted's owner, is forecasting a drop of 6–7 per cent.

To get to the claim of a drop of 40 per cent Mr O'Leary is comparing an apple with a pear. He is comparing the number of aircraft he is operating from Stansted, his biggest base, this summer (40) with the number he plans to deploy in the winter (24). But the airline industry is highly seasonal. Comparing Ryanair's summer capacity with its winter capacity at any airport is about as useful as saying 'ice-cream sales to fall by 40 per cent this winter' or 'temperature to fall by 40 per cent'. Shock horror.

Last winter Ryanair operated between 26 and 28 aircraft at Stansted. This year it is planning to operate 24, a decline of at most 14 per cent year on year and a long way from the claimed fall of 40 per cent. The decline will doubtless be even less in the number of flights operated year on year. Mr O'Leary chose to describe only the number of aircraft overnighting at Stansted. He gave no numbers for the volume of weekly flights that includes services operating in and out of Stansted from other Ryanair bases.

The summer/winter capacity comparison is about as silly as comparing profits/losses between different quarters of the year rather than year on year. Not even Ryanair has yet adopted that approach as a new accounting standard.

This week's spin was egregious even by Mr O'Leary's standards. A year ago, when he staged the same show over cutbacks at Stansted, at least he had the good grace to compare an apple with an apple. But the result was much less impressive.

Source: Brian Groom, 2009, *Ryanair's Stansted spin*, the Financial Times, 23 July. Used under licence from the Financial Times. All Rights Reserved.

---

to compare our company's results. Therefore, we cannot say how well Bunns the Bakers is doing in comparison with the market, whether it is doing better, worse or just as well as its peer companies.

To determine the company's relative success in comparison to other bakery sector companies, we need to compare Bunns the Bakers' figures and ratios with those of a competitor or a series of competitors. In this way, we can benchmark the financial performance of our company against a company in the same line of business to decide whether Bunns' ratios are in line with the sector or whether they are lower or higher. Ratios are a relative measure and, as such, they can be compared with other relative measures from other companies to highlight differences and trends. Such comparisons make ratios especially useful in understanding the profitability, efficiency, performance, liquidity and long-term financial stability of several organisations and in providing individual business entities with a target to aim for.

Ideally, when making inter-company comparisons of ratios and financial statement figures, we should only compare:

- similar businesses
- of similar size
- in a similar industry

- in a similar location
- over the same accounting period

in order to eliminate random variances arising from differences in activities, size, industry, geographical location and economic factors. All comparative data should be consistently prepared to avoid distortions and bias in the analysis. In addition, organisations can also compare:

- budgeted or planned performance data to see where the plan went well or went off course (see Chapters 13 and 14)
- industry data and averages for the same accounting period

when making assessments of their own profitability, efficiency and performance.

WHY IS THIS RELEVANT TO ME?   How well are we doing? Comparisons with other companies

As a business professional it is important for you to:

- Appreciate that a full evaluation of an entity's profitability, efficiency and performance cannot be made just from looking at data generated from internal sources
- Understand how comparative data from outside an entity can be used to assess and evaluate that entity's profitability, efficiency and performance
- Source comparative data to make assessments of an entity's profitability, efficiency and performance

---

Undertaking comparisons

One company that is in the same industry as Bunns the Bakers is Greggs plc. Greggs is engaged in bakery retail throughout the United Kingdom and has 2,050 shops supplied by the company's own bakeries and distribution centres (Greggs Annual Report for the 52 Weeks Ended 28 December 2019, page 2). To test your knowledge and your ability to calculate and interpret the ratios of another company, you will now need to turn to Numerical exercises 8.2, to undertake the analysis of the financial statements of Greggs plc and to compare Bunns the Bakers' 2020 results with this competitor company.

NUMERICAL EXERCISES   Do you think you can calculate profitability, efficiency and performance ratios for Greggs plc and interpret them in a meaningful way? Are you sure you can use the ratios you have calculated to draw conclusions about Bunns the Bakers' profitability, efficiency and performance in comparison to a competitor? Have a look at Numerical exercises 8.2 which presents extracts from the financial statements of Greggs plc and then have a go at the various exercises linked to the two companies in the **online workbook**.

APPENDIX: RATIOS CONSIDERED IN THIS CHAPTER

To assist your learning, the ratios we have considered in this chapter are summarised in Table 8.4.

Table 8.4 Calculations and descriptions for the profitability, efficiency and performance ratios covered in this chapter

	Calculation	What does this ratio tell us?
Profitability ratios		
Gross profit %	$\dfrac{\text{Gross profit}}{\text{Revenue}} \times 100\%$	Calculates profitability after deducting all the direct costs of goods sold from sales to determine how effectively an entity is controlling its costs of producing goods for sale or buying in goods for resale.
Operating profit %	$\dfrac{\text{Operating profit}}{\text{Revenue}} \times 100\%$	Determines profitability on the basis of revenue less all operating costs, before taking into account the effects of finance income, finance expense and taxation.
Profit before tax %	$\dfrac{\text{Profit before tax}}{\text{Revenue}} \times 100\%$	Bases the profitability calculation on profit before taxation to eliminate the distorting effect of changes in tax rates. The profit before tax percentage is the profitability of the entity after deducting all costs incurred and taking into account income earned from all sources, both trading and investment.
Profit after tax %	$\dfrac{\text{Profit for the year}}{\text{Revenue}} \times 100\%$	Calculates profitability for the period after adding all income and deducting all expenses and charges for the period under review.
Efficiency ratios		
Non-current asset turnover	$\dfrac{\text{Revenue}}{\text{Non-current assets}}$	Calculates the £s of sales from each £1 of non-current assets to determine how effectively and efficiently non-current assets are being used to generate revenue.
Revenue per employee	$\dfrac{\text{Revenue}}{\text{Total number of employees}}$	Determines how productively employees are working to generate sales for an entity: the higher the sales per employee figure, the higher the organisation's profitability will be.
Profit per employee	$\dfrac{\text{Operating profit}}{\text{Total number of employees}}$	Determines how much profit each employee generates during an accounting period. The higher the profit per employee, the more efficiently employees are working to fulfil the business's objectives of profit generation.

Ratio	Formula	Description
Sales per unit of input resource	$\dfrac{\text{Revenue}}{\text{Total units of input resource}}$	Focuses on the productivity of each unit of resource employed in generating sales for the business.
Profit per unit of input resource	$\dfrac{\text{Operating profit}}{\text{Total units of input resource}}$	Indicates how efficiently each unit of resource is employed to generate profits for the organisation.
Performance ratios		
Earnings per share	$\dfrac{\text{Profit after taxation and after preference dividends}}{\text{Number of ordinary shares in issue}} \times 100 \text{ pence}$	Represents the profit in pence attributable to each ordinary share in issue for a given accounting period.
Price/Earnings ratio	$\dfrac{\text{Market value of one ordinary share}}{\text{Earnings per share}}$	Indicates the price an investor is willing to pay for £1 of earnings in a company today or the number of years of profit represented in the current share price.
Dividend per share	$\dfrac{\text{Total ordinary dividends}}{\text{Number of ordinary shares in issue}} \times 100 \text{ pence}$	The dividend paid out on each ordinary share in issue.
Dividend payout ratio	$\dfrac{\text{Dividend per share}}{\text{Earnings per share}} \times 100\%$	Determines the percentage of earnings per share paid out as dividends together with the percentage of earnings held back for future investment in the business.
Dividend yield	$\dfrac{\text{Ordinary dividends per share}}{\text{Current market price of one ordinary share}} \times 100\%$	Expresses the dividend paid out on each share for an accounting period as a percentage of the current share price.
Dividend cover	$\dfrac{\text{Profit after tax and after preference dividends}}{\text{Total ordinary dividends}}$	Assesses how many times the total dividend could be paid out of current year profits after deducting all prior claims on those profits.
Return on capital employed	$\dfrac{\text{Profit before interest and tax}}{\text{Capital employed}} \times 100\%$	Capital employed = equity + long term borrowings. This ratio is used to determine the profitability of a business to facilitate comparisons with the return on capital employed of other businesses which have different capital structures.

8

CHAPTER SUMMARY

You should now have learnt that:

- Financial statement figures are an absolute performance measure while ratios are a relative performance measure

- Financial statement figures and ratios interact in the interpretation of profitability, efficiency and performance

- Ratios are a very good way in which to understand the changing relationship between two figures

- Managers use ratios to understand and improve the operations of a business

- Profitability ratios are calculated by dividing revenue into gross profit, operating profit, profit before tax and profit after tax

- Ratios are just a starting point in identifying the reasons for changes in financial statement figures year on year

- Efficiency ratios comprise of non-current asset turnover, revenue per employee and profit per employee

- Efficiency ratios can be used to understand changes in profitability

- Increasing the revenue from each unit of fixed resource employed in the business will increase an entity's profits

- Performance ratios are calculated for earnings per share, dividends per share, dividend yield and dividend cover

- The price/earnings ratio compares the current price of a share with the earnings per share

- Performance ratios are used by shareholders to assess how well an organisation has performed over an accounting period

- Assessments of an entity's profitability, efficiency and performance should never take place in a vacuum but should be compared with measures from other companies in the same industry to provide a better understanding of how an entity's results compare to those of peer companies in the market

 QUICK REVISION   Test your knowledge by attempting the activities in the **online workbook**, including flashcards on the key concepts, numerical exercises and Multiple choice questions. You can also try the further self-test questions which are available at www.oup.com/he/scott-i2a2e

END-OF-CHAPTER QUESTIONS

Attempt the questions in the following sections and then look at the solutions which can be found in the **online workbook** to see whether there are areas that you need to revisit.

❯ RECALL AND REVIEW

❯ Question 8.1

Balmoral plc has experienced an 8% decrease in its gross profit percentage in 2021 compared with 2020. The directors blame the operational managers for the poor results. The operational managers believe that they have done their job to the same standard as last year and that the decline in the gross profit percentage is not their fault. Outline possible reasons for the decline in the gross profit percentage of Balmoral plc.

❯ Question 8.2

John believes that profit is the key number in any set of financial statements and that the performance of any two companies can only be assessed on the basis of the profits they have generated. Discuss the factors that must be taken into account when the performance of the two companies is compared.

❯❯ DEVELOP YOUR UNDERSTANDING

❯❯ Question 8.3

Cuddles Limited produces teddy bears. The statements of profit or loss for the years ended 30 April 2021 and 30 April 2020 are presented below.

	2021 £000	2020 £000
Revenue	34,650	29,360
Cost of sales	15,939	14,093
Gross profit	18,711	15,267
Distribution and selling costs	5,355	4,550
Administration expenses	3,654	3,083
Operating profit	9,702	7,634
Finance income	150	75
Finance expense	750	650
Profit before tax	9,102	7,059
Income tax	2,182	1,694
Profit for the year	**6,920**	**5,365**

Other information for the two years 30 April 2021 and 30 April 2020:

	2021	**2020**
Total dividends paid for the year	£4,400,000	£3,700,000
Number of shares in issue during the year	20,000,000	18,500,000
Number of employees during the year	275	250
Non-current assets at the financial year end	£21,655,000	£18,820,000

Cuddles Limited had no preference shares in issue in either of the two years ended 30 April 2021 and 30 April 2020.

For Cuddles Limited calculate the following ratios for the years ended 30 April 2021 and 30 April 2020 (all calculations should be made to two decimal places):

- Gross profit percentage
- Operating profit percentage
- Profit before tax percentage
- Profit after tax percentage
- Non-current asset turnover
- Revenue per employee
- Operating profit per employee
- Earnings per share
- Dividends per share
- Dividend pay-out ratio
- Dividend cover

>> Question 8.4

The following information has been extracted from the financial statements of DD Limited for the years ended 30 June 2021 and 30 June 2020:

	2021	**2020**
Profit for the year	£8,622,350	£7,241,330
Number of ordinary shares in issue during the year	37,192,500	36,197,500
Number of preference shares in issue during the year	22,000,000	20,000,000
Ordinary dividend for the year	3,347,325	2,895,800

Further information for the two years 30 June 2021 and 30 June 2020:

- The preference shares have a par value of 50 pence each and a dividend rate of 4%.
- Market values of one ordinary share:

30 June 2019	220 pence
30 June 2020	260 pence
30 June 2021	325 pence

For DD plc calculate the following ratios for the years ended 30 June 2021 and 30 June 2020:

- Earnings per share
- Dividends per share
- Dividend pay-out ratio
- Dividend cover
- Dividend yield
- Growth in the share price over the course of each year

You should make all your calculations to two decimal places.

›› Question 8.5

The following information is available for Green plc and Blue plc:

	Profit for the year £	Preference dividend for the year £	Number of ordinary shares in issue	Share price at the year end £
Green plc	250,000	–	1,000,000	2.50
Blue plc	400,000	50,000	2,000,000	3.50

Required

(a) Calculate the earnings per share for the two companies.

(b) As an investor, explain whether you would consider the total profit figure or the earnings per share figure when evaluating a company's performance.

(c) Calculate the price/earnings ratio for the two companies.

In your opinion, which company has better growth prospects?

›› Question 8.6

Milner plc presents the following information in its annual financial statements. The board of directors is investigating the reasons why net profit has declined in 2021.

	2021 £m	2020 £m
Sales revenue	2,500	2,750
Gross profit	750	825
Operating profit	375	495
Profit before tax	175	275
Profit after tax	140	220

Required

Using ratio analysis, identify the reason(s) for the decline in net profit in 2021 compared with 2020.

>> **Question 8.7**

The following information is reported in the financial statements of Mendez plc.

	2021 £m	2020 £m
Interest expense	15	12
Income tax	35	30
Net profit	140	120
Total assets	920	985
Current liabilities	150	145

Required

(a) Calculate return on capital employed (ROCE) for 2021 and 2020.

(b) Compare the results for the two years and discuss possible reasons for any changes.

(c) Discuss the limitations of the ROCE.

>>> TAKE IT FURTHER

>>> **Question 8.8**

The following are extracts from the income statements (= statements of profit or loss), statements of financial position and notes to the financial statements for Taylor Wimpey plc (years ended 31 December 2019 and 31 December 2018, https://www.taylorwimpey.co.uk/corporate/investors/2019-annual-report), Persimmon plc (years ended 31 December 2019 and 31 December 2018, https://www.persimmonhomes.com/corporate/media/401786/persimmon_ar19-final.pdf) and Crest Nicholson plc (years ended 31 October 2019 and 31 October 2018, https://www.crestnicholson.com/-/media/investor%20relations/reports/2019/crest%20nicholson%20air%202019%20interactive.pdf?la=en). All three companies build residential housing in the UK.

	Taylor Wimpey plc		Persimmon plc		Crest Nicholson plc	
	2019 £m	2018 £m	2019 £m	2018 £m	2019 £m	2018 £m
Revenue	4,341.3	4,082.0	3,649.4	3,737.6	1,086.4	1,121.0
Cost of sales	3,297.2	3,007.5	2,518.7	2,557.7	902.9	874.1
Gross profit	1,044.1	1,074.5	1,130.7	1,179.9	183.5	246.9
Operating profit	856.8	828.8	1,029.4	1,082.7	114.6	182.0
Profit before tax	835.9	810.7	1,040.8	1,090.8	102.7	168.7
Profit for the year	673.9	656.6	848.8	886.4	82.5	136.6
Non-current assets	188.8	196.6	420.7	436.0	108.2	109.8
Dividends for the year (total)	*600.5	544.7	*749.5	746.3	*84.7	84.7

*The dividend for the year total figures for all three companies include final dividends for the 2019 financial year. These final dividends were declared by the companies when they each published their final results for the year. As a result of the coronavirus shutdown in March 2020 these final dividends were subsequently cancelled in order to conserve cash while building sites and all other operations remained closed.

| | Taylor Wimpey plc | | Persimmon plc | | Crest Nicholson plc | |
	2019	2018	2019	2018	2019	2018
	Number	Number	Number	Number	Number	Number
Employees: average during the year	5,883	5,442	5,097	4,809	1,005	1,016
Shares in issue (million)	3,283.108	3,278.055	318.902	317.560	256.921	256.921
Houses sold in the year	15,719	14,933	15,855	16,449	2,912	3,048

None of the three companies had any preference shares in issue in either of the accounting periods shown above.

Required

For the three companies for both 2019 and 2018 calculate:

- Gross profit percentage
- Operating profit percentage
- Profit before tax percentage
- Profit after tax percentage
- Non-current asset turnover
- Revenue per employee
- Operating profit per employee
- Earnings per share
- Dividends per share
- Dividend pay-out ratio
- Dividend cover

Make your calculations to two decimal places other than for revenue per employee and operating profit per employee, which should be made to the nearest whole £.

>>> **Question 8.9**

Using the ratios you have calculated in Question 8.8 for the three companies:

- Suggest reasons for the changes in profitability over the two years for all three companies. To assist you with your analysis you should consult the annual reports and accounts of the companies at the websites given at the start of Question 8.8 to see what factors have affected the profitability of each company this year.
- Evaluate the performance of the three companies from the point of view of the shareholders.

>>> **Question 8.10**

From the financial press or Internet, track the share price of the three companies in Question 8.8 for one week and calculate the average share price for each company.

Using your average share price, the earnings per share and the dividends per share from the answers to Question 8.8, calculate:

- Dividend yield
- Price/earnings ratio.

Using a share price tracker on the Internet, look back to the same week you have chosen a year ago and track the share price for that week. Average the share price for that week a year ago and then calculate the percentage increase in the share price over the past year. Which of the three companies has produced the best total return over the year?

8

RATIO ANALYSIS 2: LIQUIDITY, WORKING CAPITAL AND LONG-TERM FINANCIAL STABILITY

9

LEARNING OUTCOMES

Once you have read this chapter and worked through the questions and examples in both this chapter and the online workbook, you should be able to:

- Understand what is meant by the term 'liquidity'

- Appreciate that the length of the cash flow cycle varies for different types of business

- Calculate the current ratio and the quick ratio and explain what each of these ratios tells you about the short-term liquidity of an organisation

- Understand the shortcomings of current and quick ratios in the assessment of entities' short-term liquidity

- Define the term working capital and state its components

- Calculate ratios for inventory days, receivables days and payables days and discuss what these ratios tell you about the short-term liquidity of an entity

- Calculate the cash conversion cycle and explain what this means for a particular entity

- Show how organisations manage to meet their liabilities as they fall due from year-end cash and from future cash inflows from sales despite having current and quick ratios that fall well below the expected norms

- Calculate the gearing ratio, debt ratio and interest cover and explain what these ratios tell us about the long-term solvency and financial stability of an organisation

INTRODUCTION

The previous chapter considered profitability, efficiency and performance ratios in the interpretation and evaluation of the financial results of each accounting period's trading and operations. These ratios concentrated on the statement of profit or loss as the source of data on which to build these ratios and the evaluations based upon them. Chapter 6 discussed the importance of cash flows and how cash flows and their timing are the key to the survival of any entity. The cash flows of an organisation are extremely important in your evaluation of the liquidity of that organisation and you should quickly go over the lessons of Chapter 6 again before reading further in this chapter. This is to ensure that you fully appreciate the importance of cash flow information in the assessment of an entity's financial position and its financial stability.

This chapter will look at liquidity ratios and the related analysis provided by working capital ratios. Liquidity ratios and working capital ratio assessments are built upon the information contained in the statement of financial position. In addition, we will consider how an entity's capital structure contributes to an assessment of that entity's long-term financial stability. We saw in Chapter 7 that businesses issue shares and take on borrowings with which to finance their activities: the proportions in which share capital and borrowed funds finance an entity have a bearing on the ability of that entity to continue operating when economic conditions become less favourable. We will look at the key ratios in the assessment of entities' capital structures as well as evaluating organisations' ability to survive with high levels of borrowings.

The International Accounting Standards Board recognises the critical importance of information on an organisation's liquidity, solvency, cash flow generating capacity and its ability to raise additional funds to finance operations:

> Information about the nature and amounts of a reporting entity's economic resources and claims can help users to identify the reporting entity's financial strengths and weaknesses. That information can help users to assess the reporting entity's liquidity and solvency, its needs for additional financing and how successful it is likely to be in obtaining that financing . . . Information about priorities and payment requirements of existing claims helps users to predict how future cash flows will be distributed among those with a claim against the reporting entity.
>
> Source: IASB *Conceptual Framework for Financial Reporting*, paragraph 1.13

Analysis of these aspects is critical to any assessment of an entity's short- and long-term survival prospects. It is these aspects and the analysis of this information that will form the main subject of this chapter.

REFER BACK   To illustrate the ratios discussed later we will use the statement of financial position, statement of profit or loss and statement of cash flows for Bunns the Bakers presented in Chapters 2, 3 and 6. You should refer back to Illustrations 2.1, 3.1 and 6.1 in these chapters or look up the copies available in the **online workbook** as you work through this chapter.

LIQUIDITY AND THE CASH FLOW CYCLE

Liquidity refers to the ability of an entity to raise cash to pay off its liabilities as they become due for payment. Any company that is unable to generate this cash with which to meet its debts will be unable to survive and will file for bankruptcy; in this situation, an administrator is appointed to sell the company's assets and the cash raised from these asset sales is used to pay at least some of what is owed to the company's creditors. Insolvent companies have more liabilities than assets, so it is unlikely that the liabilities of such companies will be repaid in full as shown in Give me an example 9.1.

GIVE ME AN EXAMPLE 9.1   Insolvent companies failing to repay all their debts

When the construction group Carillion went into liquidation in January 2018 it was estimated that the group owed as much as £7bn to its various creditors. At 5 November 2019 the liquidators reported that just over £500m had been recovered from the group's assets with the prospect of another £10m becoming available to settle creditors' claims.

At that date, it was expected that creditors of 20 of Carillion's constituent firms would receive some of what they were owed while the creditors of the other 61 constituent firms in liquidation would receive nothing.

Source: https://www.constructionnews.co.uk/contractors/carillion/carillion-liquidation-recover-510m-13-11-2019/

How do business entities generate cash from their operations? Some businesses sell their goods for cash so they immediately have money with which to pay suppliers and other parties (such as employees or banks) what they are owed. Other entities sell goods to customers on credit, allowing their customers time in which to pay. In this case, organisations will have to wait for payment, but the cash will be expected to flow in eventually to meet the demands of creditors as they become due. What effect do these two different approaches to selling goods have on the length of the cash flow cycle? The cash flow cycle for retailers and manufacturers is illustrated in Figures 9.1 and 9.2.

Figure 9.1 The cash flow cycle for retailers

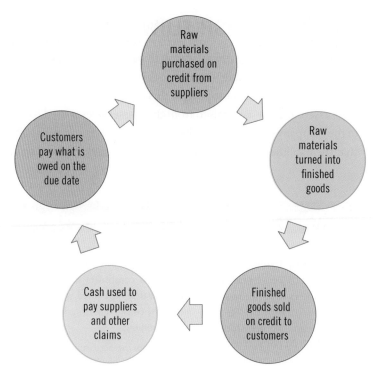

Figure 9.2 The cash flow cycle for manufacturers

9

Figure 9.1 shows that the retailing cash flow cycle is very short: goods are purchased on credit from suppliers, sold on for cash and are then paid for. Figure 9.2 shows that the manufacturing cycle is much longer. Raw materials bought on credit from suppliers first have to be converted into finished goods inventory. These finished goods are then sold to customers, but they demand time in which to pay. In the meantime, suppliers will be demanding payment and will most likely have to be paid before customers have settled what is owed. A store of cash will thus have to be retained within the business to meet the demands of suppliers and of other claims upon the business while waiting for customers to pay what is owed. There are thus many delays in the manufacturing cash flow cycle, first in producing the goods and then in waiting for the cash from customers. We shall consider the effect these different business cycles have on our assessment of a business's liquidity when we look at working capital management. However, you should appreciate at this early stage how the cash flow cycle operates and how it is vital for entities to have cash available to meet liabilities as they fall due.

WHY IS THIS RELEVANT TO ME?   Liquidity and the cash flow cycle

To enable you as a business professional to:

- Appreciate that different businesses have different cash flow cycles
- Evaluate the speed at which different types of business generate cash from their operations with which to pay their debts
- Understand that the faster an entity converts its sales into cash, the more liquid that business is

---

GO BACK OVER THIS AGAIN!   Are you quite sure you understand how vital the cash flow cycle is to businesses? Go to the **online workbook** and look at Exercises 9.1 to enable you to appreciate the need to ensure cash inflows from which to pay liabilities as they fall due.

LIQUIDITY RATIOS

Have a look at Bunns the Bakers' current assets (Illustration 2.1): these are made up of inventory, trade and other receivables and cash. Now look at the current liabilities, which show the current portion of long-term liabilities, that part of borrowings that is due for repayment within one year, trade and other payables (the amounts due to suppliers and for other liabilities such as rent, business rates and electricity among others) and current tax liabilities. Along with the cash and cash equivalents already available, the other current assets are used to generate cash from sales of inventory and receipts from receivables to pay off the current liabilities. Short-term assets are thus used to meet short-term liabilities: this is the liquidity, the availability of cash in the near future, referred to in the IASB's Conceptual Framework for Financial Reporting cited earlier (this chapter, Introduction). How is the ability of short-term assets to meet short-term liabilities assessed? Not surprisingly, the first step in this assessment will be through the calculation of ratios.

Current ratio

The first ratio that we will look at compares current assets to current liabilities in an attempt to determine whether an organisation has sufficient short-term assets from which to meet short-term liabilities. This ratio is called the current ratio and is calculated as follows:

$$\text{Current ratio} = \frac{\text{Current assets}}{\text{Current liabilities}}$$

This figure is expressed as a ratio and tells us how many £s of current assets there are for each £ of current liabilities. Calculating the current ratio for Bunns the Bakers at 31 March 2021 and 31 March 2020 gives us the following results:

$$2021: \text{Current ratio}: \frac{£334,000}{£840,000} = 0.40:1$$

$$2020: \text{Current ratio}: \frac{£319,000}{£707,000} = 0.45:1$$

What do these ratios mean? At 31 March 2021, Bunns the Bakers has 40 pence of current assets for each £1 of current liabilities, while at 31 March 2020 the company had 45 pence of current assets for each £1 of current liabilities. This might not sound very good as the company does not seem to have much in the way of current assets with which to meet liabilities as they fall due.

However, remember that the statement of financial position is just a snapshot of the financial position at one day in the year: the position will change tomorrow and the next day and the day after that as goods are produced, sales are made, cash flows in and liabilities are paid. The current ratio also ignores the timing of the receipt of cash and of the payment of liabilities.

9

How quickly is cash received by the business? If this is immediately at the point of sale then the entity will have a very positive cash inflow from which to meet its liabilities. If cash is received from trade receivables some time after the sales were made then a much more careful management of cash inflows and outflows will be required. The current ratio's logic assumes that all the liabilities will be due for payment on the day following the statement of financial position date; this is highly unlikely and we will investigate the likely payment pattern for liabilities later on in this chapter to show that, contrary to appearances, Bunns the Bakers is a very liquid, cash generative business indeed (this chapter, Current liabilities: the timing of payments).

WHY IS THIS RELEVANT TO ME?   Current ratio

To enable you as a business professional to:

- Understand what the current ratio represents and how it is used in the assessment of short-term liquidity
- Calculate current ratios for organisations
- Appreciate the shortcomings of the current ratio as a key measure in short-term liquidity assessment

---

GO BACK OVER THIS AGAIN!   Do you really understand what the current ratio is trying to do and what factors you have to take into account when using it? Go to the **online workbook** and have a go at Exercises 9.2 to check your understanding.

MULTIPLE CHOICE QUESTIONS   Are you convinced that you can calculate a current ratio from a given set of financial information? Go to the **online workbook** and have a go at Multiple choice questions 9.1 to test out your ability to calculate this ratio.

Quick (acid test) ratio

This ratio is a modification of the current ratio and ignores inventory in its assessment of an entity's ability to pay its short-term liabilities. Why is inventory taken out of the calculation? There is always a chance that inventory produced by an organisation will not be sold quickly, so that this inventory cannot be counted as convertible into cash in the near future. Therefore, the quick (acid test) ratio only takes account of current assets that are cash or that are readily realisable in cash: trade receivables are readily convertible into cash as the entity has a contractual right to receive the money due for sales already made to customers. The quick (acid test) ratio is calculated as follows:

$$\text{Quick (acid test) ratio} = \frac{(\text{Current assets} - \text{Inventory})}{\text{Current liabilities}}$$

Using Bunns the Bakers' statement of financial position at 31 March 2021 and 31 March 2020 the following quick ratios can be calculated:

$$2021: \text{Quick ratio} = \frac{(£334,000 - £60,000)}{840,000} = 0.33:1$$

$$2020: \text{Quick ratio} = \frac{(\pounds319,000 - \pounds55,000)}{\pounds707,000} = 0.37:1$$

These ratios are inevitably lower than the current ratios calculated earlier as inventory is taken out of the current assets with no corresponding decrease in current liabilities. Again, this paints a very gloomy picture of Bunns the Bakers' short-term liquidity as the company only has 33 pence of readily realisable current assets per £1 of current liabilities at 31 March 2021, a figure that has fallen from 37 pence per £1 of current liabilities at 31 March 2020.

How realistic is the assumption that inventory will not sell quickly? It all depends upon the particular activity in which an entity is engaged. A moment's thought should convince you that the quick ratio is completely irrelevant to any assessment of Bunns the Bakers' short-term liquidity. The company sells freshly baked goods from their shops in towns. People usually get up too late to make their own sandwiches or snacks to take to work (or are too lazy to do so!) and will go out at lunch time to buy the company's products, which will sell quickly rather than being stockpiled for several weeks or months before they are sold. Therefore, what is produced today is sold today and cash is received immediately from cash paying customers at the till. Even if there are sandwiches, pies and pastries left towards the end of the day, shop staff will discount the prices in order to tempt customers to buy up the left over inventory so only very small amounts of the goods produced will be wasted.

The quick ratio may be much more relevant in a manufacturing situation. The swift pace of change in markets and products means that any advance production might result in such goods becoming obsolete or out of fashion so that entities are unable to sell them to recover the costs of producing or buying them. As a result of this risk, many companies today only produce to order rather than manufacturing goods in the hope that they will sell. Such an approach removes the risk of goods becoming obsolete and the losses that disposal of such goods will incur as, first, discounts are given on the original selling price and then goods have to be scrapped as interest in them finally runs out. It is particularly important only to produce goods to order in the high-tech sector; new developments are taking place every few minutes so that products are being improved all the time and earlier models quickly become outdated. As a result, high-tech goods such as laptops, tablets, mobile phones and other electronic devices are produced as orders come in to avoid the losses that would arise if several months' advance sales of such goods were produced all at once.

Consider Give me an example 9.2, which presents the differing experiences of Next plc and Ted Baker plc with regard to the effect of old stock on their profit margins.

Where entities are subject to any kind of unpredictable pattern of demand that can suddenly be turned off or interrupted by, for example, an economic downturn, a change in consumer tastes or technological developments, your evaluation of liquidity will be much more cautious. If an organisation does not enjoy steady demand for its products then that organisation is at much higher risk of suffering liquidity problems and you would expect that entity to maintain much higher current and quick ratios as well as operating a very sophisticated forecasting system to stop production of its goods at the first sign of a decline in demand. In Bunns the Bakers' case, office workers will keep visiting their outlets at lunch time and shoppers will drop in throughout the day as they seek out the company's value for money products, so declines in demand will not be a problem for this organisation.

9

> ### GIVE ME AN EXAMPLE 9.2   Out-of-date goods and their effect on profit margins
>
> In the 52 weeks to 26 January 2019, Ted Baker plc reported a decrease in the gross profit margin from 61.00% to 58.30%. This decrease in gross profit margin was attributed to 'competitive discounting across the retail sector' and 'an increase in promotional activity in response to the challenging trading conditions'. This means that more goods were discounted in the sales, resulting in a reduction in goods sold at full price which generated a lower gross margin.
>
> Similarly, in the 52 weeks to 26 January 2019, Next plc reported a decrease in its retail profit mar-gin from 12.7% to 10.9%. However, this margin would have been low had discounted goods not reduced by 11% over the course of the year. Next notes that 'the combination of improved clearance rates and a higher participation of full price sales increased margin by +0.5%'. In this case, a reduction in goods discounted in the sales meant that more goods were sold at full price which contributed positively to the result for the year.
>
> Sources: Ted Baker's annual report and accounts: www.tedbakerplc.com; Next plc annual report and accounts: www.nextplc.co.uk.

> ### WHY IS THIS RELEVANT TO ME?   Quick ratio
>
> As a business professional you must:
>
> - Understand what the quick ratio represents and how it is used in the assessment of short-term liquidity
> - Understand the situations in which inventory obsolescence is a risk and those in which it is not
> - Calculate quick ratios for organisations
> - Appreciate the situations in which the quick ratio is applicable and not applicable in an assessment of short-term liquidity

GO BACK OVER THIS AGAIN!   How well have you grasped what the quick ratio is trying to do and what factors you have to take into account when using it? Go to the **online workbook** and have a go at Exercises 9.3 to check your understanding.

SUMMARY OF KEY CONCEPTS   Can you remember the formulae for current and quick ratios? Go to the **online workbook** to take a look at Summary of key concepts 9.1 and 9.2 to reinforce your understanding.

MULTIPLE CHOICE QUESTIONS   Are you confident that you can calculate a quick ratio from a given set of financial information? Go to the **online workbook** and have a go at Multiple choice questions 9.2 to test out your ability to calculate this ratio.

Current and quick ratios: the traditional view

Convention has it that a business entity needs a current ratio of 2:1, £2 of current assets for every £1 of current liabilities, and a quick ratio of 1:1, £1 of trade receivables and cash for every £1 of current liabilities, in order to be able to survive financially. On a conventional reading of the figures for Bunns the Bakers, then, the assessment would be that the company is heading into bankruptcy. Bunns the

Bakers has nowhere near current and quick ratios of 2:1 and 1:1, so the question must be asked how the company manages to survive quite happily on much lower ratios than convention dictates.

WORKING CAPITAL

A much more effective way in which to assess liquidity is to look at the working capital cycle, the time it takes for an entity to turn raw materials into goods for sale, sell these goods, collect the cash and then pay suppliers for goods and raw materials supplied. The length of this working capital cycle is determined through the use of the three working capital ratios presented in Figure 9.3. We looked at the cash flow cycle at the start of this chapter for both retailers and manufacturers, but it is now time to look in more detail at the components of working capital and how to use these as a guide to the liquidity and cash flow generating capability of an organisation.

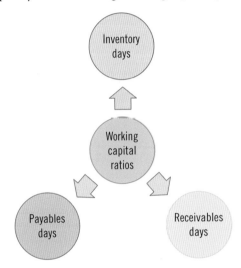

Figure 9.3 The three working capital ratios

First, though, what is working capital? The basic definition of working capital is as follows:

Working capital = current assets − current liabilities

Working capital thus comprises:

- Inventories of raw materials for use in production, of finished goods ready for sale or of goods purchased for resale to customers.
- Trade receivables from customers of the business who have been provided with a credit facility by the entity.
- Cash in the bank or in hand that is held to meet day-to-day needs.
- Trade payables of the business which require settlement on a daily basis. For the purposes of the working capital calculation, amounts due to lenders and money due to settle tax liabilities are ignored as these (as we shall see in this chapter, Current liabilities: the timing of payments) do not require payment on a day-to-day basis, being settled on a monthly or three-monthly basis.

WORKING CAPITAL RATIOS

In order to evaluate the efficiency of working capital management, the ratios in Table 9.1 are used.

Table 9.1 Working capital ratios, how they are calculated and what they tell users

Ratio	Calculation	What does this ratio tell us?
Inventory days (also known as stock days)	$\dfrac{\text{Inventory}}{\text{Cost of sales}} \times 365$	• This ratio measures the average stockholding period, how long an entity holds goods in inventory before they are sold • The more quickly inventory turns over the better, as inventory is turned into sales (and hence into cash) much more quickly while obsolete inventories and the risk of deterioration (and hence loss of future cash inflows from the sale of this inventory) are minimised • However, when calculating their optimum level of inventory holding, businesses should consider future demand (no inventory, no sale), any anticipated future shortages or price rises, discounts available for buying in bulk, storage, insurance and any other costs involved in holding inventory
Receivables days (also known as debtor days)	$\dfrac{\text{Trade receivables}}{\text{Credit sales}^1} \times 365$	• This ratio indicates the average credit period taken by customers, the length of time it takes for credit customers to pay what they owe • Evaluates the efficiency of the credit control system and the speed with which credit sales are turned into cash • Where this ratio is increasing, steps can be taken to speed up payments (e.g. by offering early settlement discounts) to minimise the funds tied up in receivables: it is better to have cash in our bank account than in our customers' bank account
Payables days (also known as creditor days)	$\dfrac{\text{Trade payables}}{\text{Cost of sales}^2} \times 365$	• This ratio measures how quickly the business is paying off its purchases made on credit • Ideally, the receivables days and payables days should be equal: as cash is received, it is used to pay off liabilities • Paying trade payables before trade receivables have paid usually has a negative impact upon cash flow: see the profit ≠ cash example for Start Up in Example 6.1 in Chapter 6

[1]Strictly this ratio should use only credit sales in the calculation of receivables days: sales made for cash have already been settled and thus no cash is outstanding from these transactions. Therefore, cash sales should be omitted in the determination of receivables days, the number of days of credit allowed to credit customers. However, in practice, companies do not disclose separate figures for their cash sales and their credit sales, so it is normal just to use total sales in this calculation.

[2]Again, while trade payables should be compared to purchases of goods on credit, entities do not publish details of their credit purchases, so cost of sales is used to approximate the cost of purchases. In reality, cost of sales may include the wages and salaries of production operatives in the manufacturing part of a business, which should not strictly be classified as purchases on credit, but the cost of sales is a useful substitute for the credit purchases of a business.

As long as you are consistent in your calculations (as noted in Chapter 8, The importance of calculating and presenting ratios consistently), the relationships and ratios produced should provide a suitable like-for-like basis on which to assess the working capital strengths or weaknesses of a business.

GO BACK OVER THIS AGAIN!   Are you certain you can distinguish between the three working capital ratios? Go to the **online workbook** and have a go at Exercises 9.4 to make sure you can make these distinctions.

The working capital ratios for Bunns the Bakers are as follows:

$$2021: \text{Inventory days}: \frac{£60,000}{£4,535,000} \times 365 = 4.83 \text{ days}$$

$$2020: \text{Inventory days}: \frac{£55,000}{£4,596,000} \times 365 = 4.37 \text{ days}$$

Trade and other receivables for Bunns the Bakers at 31 March 2021 and 31 March 2020 from the statement of financial position are £62,000 and £75,000 respectively. By looking at the notes to the financial statements we can determine that the actual trade receivables, as distinct from other receivables and prepayments, are £25,000 at 31 March 2021 and £35,000 at 31 March 2020. This will give us the following receivables days for the two accounting periods:

$$2021: \text{Receivables days}: \frac{£25,000}{£10,078,000} \times 365 = 0.90 \text{ days}$$

$$2020: \text{Receivables days}: \frac{£35,000}{£9,575,000} \times 365 = 1.33 \text{ days}$$

9

This ratio is very low, but, as most sales will be made for an immediate cash payment from customers in the shops, this is not at all surprising. As we noted in Chapter 2 (Current assets), credit sales will be limited to a small number of credit customers such as supermarkets.

The rest of the sales will be made for cash to customers as they come into the shops and make their purchases, so a very low receivables days ratio would be expected in such a situation.

Trade and other payables for Bunns the Bakers at 31 March 2021 and 31 March 2020 from the statement of financial position are £390,000 and £281,000 respectively. By looking at the notes to the financial statements we can determine that the actual trade payables, as distinct from other payables, are £300,000 at 31 March 2021 and £220,000 at 31 March 2020. This will give us the following payables days for the two accounting periods:

$$2021: \text{Payables days}: \frac{£300,000}{£4,535,000} \times 365 = 24.15 \text{ days}$$

$$2020: \text{Payables days}: \frac{£220,000}{£4,596,000} \times 365 = 17.47 \text{ days}$$

> ### WHY IS THIS RELEVANT TO ME?   Working capital ratios
>
> As a business professional you will be expected to:
>
> • Understand what working capital ratios are and what they represent
>
> • Be able to calculate working capital ratios for organisations
>
> • Use working capital ratios to assess the efficiency of working capital management in entities

SUMMARY OF KEY CONCEPTS   Do you think you can remember the formulae for the three
working capital ratios? Go to the **online workbook** to take a look at Summary of key concepts 9.3–9.5 to reinforce your understanding.

MULTIPLE CHOICE QUESTIONS   Are you certain you can calculate working capital ratios from
a given set of financial information? Go to the **online workbook** and have a go at Multiple choice questions 9.3 to test out your ability to calculate these ratios.

What do these figures tell us? First, that, in 2021, inventories are sold within 4.8 days, a very slight increase on the 4.4 days it took to sell inventory in 2020. Much of Bunns the Bakers' inventory will comprise raw materials ready for use in the production of bread, pies, pastries and other bakery goods. Finished goods themselves will probably represent only one day's production as goods are produced fresh and ready for delivery and sale the next day. Certain other inventories, such as soft drinks, which have a longer sell-by date, can be kept in storage for several weeks or months before they are out of date, but most of the company's raw materials will be delivered on a daily basis and turned into finished goods for sale on the same or the next day.

This is a very low inventory days ratio and indicates that stocks are turned into sales very quickly indeed. As most of these sales are for cash, the receivables days are also very low. However, trade payables are settled every 24 days in the year to 31 March 2021 (an increase on the previous year) so Bunns the Bakers is holding on to the cash received from customers before they pay this cash out to their suppliers. Money is received at the point of sale, but the company holds on to the cash until the time to pay their suppliers comes around.

The cash conversion cycle

The ratios shown in Figure 9.3 enable us to calculate the cash conversion cycle (sometimes referred to as the operating cycle or working capital cycle). The cash conversion cycle tells us how quickly inventory is turned into trade receivables and how quickly trade receivables are turned into cash with which to pay trade payables (Figure 9.4). The shorter this cycle, the better the working capital is being managed and the more readily cash is available with which to meet liabilities. Conversely, the longer this process, the higher the investment required in working capital and the higher the emergency sources of cash will need to be (for example, financing by an agreed short-term overdraft from the bank) to pay liabilities as they fall due.

The cash conversion cycle is calculated in the following way:

Inventory days + receivables days – payables days

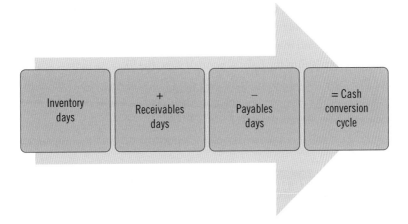

Figure 9.4 The cash conversion cycle

For Bunns the Bakers, the cash conversion cycle for the two years under consideration is as follows:

2021: Cash conversion cycle: 4.83 inventory days + 0.90 receivables days − 24.15 payables days
= −18.42 days

2020: Cash conversion cycle: 4.37 inventory days + 1.33 receivables days − 17.47 payables days
= −11.77 days

The figures above and Figure 9.5 show that the cash conversion cycle figures for both years are negative. This means that Bunns the Bakers are converting their sales into cash well before they have to pay their suppliers. The negative cash conversion cycles also mean that the company is holding onto this cash for several days before it is paid out and this will enable the company to use this cash to generate

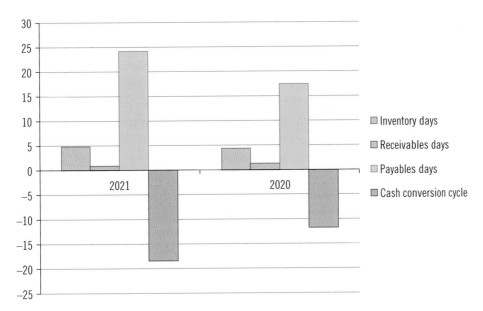

Figure 9.5 Bunns the Bakers' working capital ratios and cash conversion cycle

additional finance income (interest receivable) on their surplus bank deposits. This additional interest may not amount to much in total in the statement of profit or loss, but it is an important extra source of income for the company and this spare cash is being used effectively to generate additional profits for the shareholders. From Bunns the Bakers' point of view, the increase in the cash conversion cycle this year means that they are taking an extra 6.65 days (18.42 days − 11.77 days) in which to pay their suppliers, indicating that they are holding onto their cash for longer. By using the credit facilities provided by their suppliers, Bunns the Bakers do not have to rely on a short-term bank overdraft to finance their working capital: this finance is in effect being provided by the company's suppliers.

WHY IS THIS RELEVANT TO ME?   Working capital ratios and the cash conversion cycle

To equip you as a business professional with the ability to:

- Calculate additional ratios with which to evaluate short-term liquidity
- Calculate the length of the cash conversion cycle
- Interpret the results of the working capital ratio and the cash conversion cycle calculations
- Appreciate how working capital ratios and the cash conversion cycle help to supplement the current and quick ratios in liquidity analysis

---

GO BACK OVER THIS AGAIN!   Are you quite sure that you understand what the cash conversion cycle is telling you? Go to the **online workbook** and have a go at Exercises 9.5 to check your understanding.

MULTIPLE CHOICE QUESTIONS   How easily can you calculate the cash conversion cycle from a given set of financial information? Go to the **online workbook** and have a go at Multiple choice questions 9.4 to test out your ability to undertake the required calculations.

WHY IS WORKING CAPITAL SO IMPORTANT?

Organisations need short-term finance to enable them to buy raw materials with which to produce goods to sell to customers. As indicated in Figure 9.2, a firm's suppliers cannot wait for payment until the raw materials have been turned into finished goods, sold on credit and then paid for by that firm's customers. Such a period would be too lengthy and the supplier might well have gone bankrupt while waiting for payment. Therefore, manufacturers and their suppliers rely on short-term credit provided by banks in the form of overdrafts. These overdrafts are used to finance the purchase of materials and the payment of wages to workers to tide them over the short-term lack of funds that arises when waiting for products to be manufactured and sold and for customers to pay. Such short-term working capital allows organisations to build up momentum with this short-term finance being paid back when projects are up and running and cash inflows from customers are financing cash outflows to suppliers. As organisations expand, they receive more orders from customers which require more materials from suppliers and an increasing numbers of workers. Customers still want time in which to pay for the goods supplied so companies have to source ever-increasing amounts of working capital to finance their commitments to suppliers and to their workforces. Management of payables, receivables and inventory thus requires a very careful balancing act to ensure that working capital continues to flow into the company to finance all the obligations as they fall due.

> **WHY IS THIS RELEVANT TO ME?**   Why is working capital so important?
>
> To enable you as a business professional to appreciate that:
>
> - Entities need short-term finance with which to finance growth and to start up new projects
> - Short-term finance has to come either from cash saved within the entity or from outside sources such as bank overdrafts
> - The required short-term finance is not always readily available from outside sources

CURRENT LIABILITIES: THE TIMING OF PAYMENTS

Our calculations in the Current ratio section earlier showed that at 31 March 2021 Bunns the Bakers has only 40 pence of current assets for each £1 of current liabilities. At that point we also noted that the current and quick ratios take no account of when liabilities are actually due for payment and make the assumption that all liabilities might call in the money owed to them at the statement of financial position date. Let us now think about how much of Bunns the Bakers' current liabilities might actually be due for payment on the day after the statement of financial position date so that we can assess how liquid the company really is and how easily it can afford to pay its debts from the current assets it already owns.

Bunns the Bakers' statement of financial position shows the following current liabilities at 31 March 2021:

	£000
Current portion of long-term borrowings	300
Trade and other payables	390
Current tax liabilities	150
	840

At 31 March 2021, Bunns the Bakers has £212,000 of cash with which to meet these current liabilities. This does not appear to be a good position to be in, as current liabilities exceed the cash available with which to pay them. However, by thinking about when these liabilities will actually fall due we will be able to see that the company can meet its liabilities very easily from the cash it has at the year end together with all the cash generated from sales in the days and weeks after the year end.

First, let us think about when the current portion of long-term borrowings will be payable. When an entity borrows money from a bank under a formal loan agreement, the entity and the bank sign a contract. This contract governs the loan terms, the terms of repayment and the interest that is payable on the loan. As long as the borrower does not breach the terms of the contract (e.g. by failing to pay either any interest due or a loan instalment by the agreed date), then the bank cannot demand its money back immediately and has to wait for the borrower to meet each repayment as it becomes due. The £300,000 due at 31 March 2021 probably represents 12 monthly payments of £25,000 each so that the most that could be due on 1 April 2021 would be £25,000. The other monthly repayments would be due one month after this, two months after this and so on. This is a very pessimistic assumption: most loan instalments are payable at the end of the month rather than at the beginning, giving the company up to 30 days to save up for the next payment. But for now we will assume that loan repayments are due on the first day of each month so that £25,000 is repayable on 1 April 2021.

While bank loans are covered by contracts in this way, bank overdrafts are not. Should the entity you are evaluating have an overdraft with its bank, do remember that overdrafts are repayable on demand so that all of the overdraft should be added in to the calculation of immediate liquidity on the day after the statement of financial position date.

Turning now to what is owed to suppliers, we saw earlier that trade payables amount to £300,000 and that this represents 24.15 days of purchases. We noted that suppliers of raw materials will deliver to the company each day so that the ingredients going into the bread, sandwiches, pies and pastries are always fresh. Therefore, the total amount due to trade payables on 1 April 2021 would be £300,000/24.15 = £12,422, with £12,422 due on 2 April, £12,422 on 3 April and so on. In reality, these amounts will not be spread so evenly, but the £12,422 is a useful average to work with, based on the payables days we calculated earlier. The other payables of £90,000 (£390,000 − £300,000 trade payables) will probably be payable to a variety of different creditors at different times over the next two to three months. However, as we are cautious accountants, let us assume that one-quarter of this amount is due tomorrow, which represents £90,000/4 = £22,500 payable immediately.

Tax liabilities for limited liability companies in the UK are payable in quarterly instalments three months, six months, nine months and 12 months after the statement of financial position date, so the earliest that any of the £150,000 tax is due would be 30 June 2021, three months after 31 March 2021. Therefore, none of the tax liabilities will be due on 1 April 2021.

Summarising our results below tells us that we have only a fraction of the total current liabilities at 31 March 2021 to pay on 1 April 2021. The figures below may be seriously overestimated as the long-term borrowings are probably repayable at the end of April 2021 rather than at the beginning of the month and it is unlikely that 25% of the other payables is actually due one day after the year end:

	£
Current portion of long-term borrowings	25,000
Trade payables	12,422
Other payables	22,500
Current tax liabilities	—
Total payable on 1 April 2021	59,922
Cash available at 31 March 2021	212,000
Surplus cash available on 1 April 2021 (£212,000 − £59,922)	**152,078**

Thus, when it comes to determining how liquid a company is and how easily it can meet its current liabilities when they fall due, timing is critical. In addition, we should not forget that cash will be coming into the business on 1 April 2021 as sales are made at the tills. How much will this be? Given that annual sales are £10,078,000 and that there are, say, 300 trading days a year, this would give daily sales of £33,593. As this cash will come into the business on every trading day of the year, there is always going to be plenty of cash available from which to meet debts as they become payable. Therefore, the current and quick ratio, while giving a good idea of how many £s of current assets are available to meet each £ of liabilities, should not be used as the final indicator of how easily a company can meet its liabilities as they fall due. You must think about the timing of receipts and payments of cash and the way in which an entity manages its cash inflows and outflows to make a full evaluation of an entity's short-term liquidity.

To illustrate the truth of this approach, just think about your own situation for a moment. If we all drew up our own personal statement of financial position at the end of each calendar year and included everything that we had to pay for the next 12 months and compared this to what cash we had available at the start of the year, we would all be in despair. However, we know that all our liabilities for the next 12 months are not due immediately on 1 January and that we have monthly inflows of cash from our salaries that will gradually pay what we owe throughout the year. Cash outflows are matched by cash inflows and, with a bit of luck, we will be able to save some cash towards a holiday or towards some other treat for ourselves. We do not worry that we do not have enough cash now to pay off everything that is due in the next 12 months and neither do businesses.

WHY IS THIS RELEVANT TO ME?　The timing of payments and the shortcomings of the current and quick ratios

To enable you as a business professional to:

- Appreciate that an entity's current liabilities will never all be due for payment at the same time unless that entity is in liquidation
- Calculate the amounts due for payment on the day after the statement of financial position date as part of your assessment of an entity's liquidity
- Forecast monthly cash outgoings for the next year to determine whether entities can meet those monthly outgoings from current trading
- Appreciate how timing of payments analysis helps to overcome the shortcomings of the current and quick ratios in liquidity analysis

---

GO BACK OVER THIS AGAIN!　Are you sure you understand how the timing of payments is critical to an assessment of short-term liquidity? Go to the **online workbook** and look at Exercises 9.6 to enable you to appreciate that not all liabilities are due immediately and that the assumptions of the current and quick ratios are invalid when assessing an entity's ability to meet its short-term liabilities.

CAPITAL STRUCTURE RATIOS: LONG-TERM SOLVENCY AND FINANCIAL STABILITY ASSESSMENT

Working capital, cash conversion cycle and current and quick ratios measure short-term liquidity and the ability of entities to pay their debts on a short-term (within the next 12 months), day-to-day basis. But just as there are ratios with which to measure short-term liquidity, there are also ratios to determine long-term solvency and financial stability (Figure 9.6). As we saw in Chapter 7, companies have a choice of financing models through which to raise the capital required to finance their operations for the long term. They can either raise the necessary funds through an issue of share capital or they can raise the money from borrowings from the bank or the money markets. Many companies combine both share capital and borrowings in their long-term financing. The combination of the two will have implications for our assessment of how easily entities will be able to repay those borrowings while still servicing that long-term capital from profits either through the distribution of dividends to shareholders or the payment of interest on borrowings. This is the solvency, the availability of cash in the longer term, referred to in the IASB's Conceptual Framework quoted earlier in this chapter.

When assessing long-term solvency and financial stability, the ratios in Table 9.2 are used.

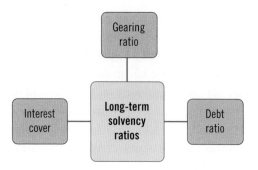

Figure 9.6 Long-term solvency and financial stability ratios

Table 9.2 Long-term solvency and financial stability ratios, how they are calculated and what they tell users

Ratio	What does this ratio tell us?
$\text{Gearing ratio} = \dfrac{\text{Long and short-term borrowings}}{\text{Equity}} \times 100\%$	• The gearing percentage is often seen as a measure of risk: companies with higher borrowings are supposedly more risky than those with lower borrowings
$\text{Debt ratio} = \dfrac{\text{Total liabilities}}{\text{Total assets}}$	• This ratio measures the £s of liabilities per £1 of total assets • The lower the ratio, the more secure the entity
$\text{Interest cover} = \dfrac{\text{Profit before interest and tax}}{\text{Interest}}$	• Assesses how many times interest payable on borrowings is covered by operating profits (in the same way that dividend cover measures how many times the ordinary dividend is covered by profit for the year) • The higher the figure, the better, as a high figure indicates an ability to continue meeting interest payments from profits in the future

WHY IS THIS RELEVANT TO ME? Capital structure ratios: long-term solvency and financial stability assessment

As a business professional you will be expected to:

• Understand what gearing, debt and interest cover ratios are telling you about an entity's long-term solvency and financial stability

• Calculate gearing, debt and interest cover ratios for organisations

• Evaluate the results of gearing, debt and interest cover ratio calculations to produce an assessment of an entity's long-term solvency and financial stability position

Gearing ratio

Looking at the statement of financial position for Bunns the Bakers (Illustration 2.1), the company has borrowings of £300,000 in current liabilities and borrowings of £2,700,000 in non-current liabilities, giving a total borrowings figure of £3,000,000 at 31 March 2021. At 31 March 2020, the figures are £300,000 and £3,000,000 giving total borrowings of £3,300,000. Equity in the statement of financial position in Illustration 2.1 is £8,459,000 at 31 March 2021 and £7,767,000 at 31 March 2020. Using these figures we can calculate gearing percentages as follows:

$$2021: \text{Gearing}\%: \frac{£3,000,000}{£8,459,000} \times 100\% = 35.47\%$$

$$2020: \text{Gearing}\%: \frac{£3,300,000}{£7,767,000} \times 100\% = 42.49\%$$

Gearing has fallen this year as borrowings represent a lower proportion of equity than in previous years. This fall is partly due to the repayment of £300,000 during the year to 31 March 2021 and partly due to the increase in equity as a result of the issue of new share capital and the profits retained for the current year. The statement of cash flows (Illustration 6.1) shows us that the company has repaid £300,000 of its borrowings over each of the past two years, so this debt seems to be very manageable. The percentage of borrowings to equity is low and, given the consistency of the trade in which Bunns the Bakers are engaged and the constant demand that their products enjoy, it would be perfectly logical to draw the conclusion that the company's long-term financing strategy is very stable and poses no solvency risk to the organisation.

MULTIPLE CHOICE QUESTIONS   How easily do you think you can calculate gearing from a given set of financial information? Go to the **online workbook** and have a go at Multiple choice questions 9.5 to test out your ability to calculate this ratio.

Debt ratio

Total assets and total liabilities just have to be read off the relevant lines of the statement of financial position (Illustration 2.1). The company has total assets of £12,199,000 at 31 March 2021 and total assets of £11,674,000 at 31 March 2020. Similarly, total liabilities at 31 March 2021 amount to £3,740,000 and £3,907,000 at 31 March 2020. Comparing the total liabilities with the total assets gives us the following results:

$$2021: \text{Debt ratio:} \frac{£3,740,000}{£12,199,000} = 0.31:1$$

$$2020: \text{Debt ratio:} \frac{£3,907,000}{£11,674,000} = 0.33:1$$

Bunns the Bakers has 31 pence of total liabilities for every £1 of total assets at 31 March 2021 compared to 33 pence of total liabilities for every £1 of total assets at 31 March 2020. This is not a high figure and it would be reasonable to conclude that the company is highly solvent and financially stable.

MULTIPLE CHOICE QUESTIONS   Are you quite confident that you can calculate the debt ratio from a given set of financial information? Go to the **online workbook** and have a go at Multiple choice questions 9.6 to test out your ability to calculate this figure.

Interest cover

The gearing percentages and debt ratios are not high, but how easily can the company meet its interest obligations? To determine the interest cover, we will need to turn to the statement of profit or loss in Illustration 3.1. This statement tells us that the finance expense (= interest payable) figures for the years to 31 March 2021 and 31 March 2020 were £150,000 and £165,000 respectively. This expense now needs matching to the operating profit (the profit before interest and tax) of £895,000 and £767,000 for the two years that concern us.

$$2021\text{: Interest cover: }\frac{£895{,}000}{£150{,}000} = 5.97 \text{ times}$$

$$2020\text{: Interest cover: }\frac{£767{,}000}{£165{,}000} = 4.65 \text{ times}$$

Increased profits and reduced finance expense in 2021 mean that this ratio has improved greatly this year. Given that interest is covered nearly six times by the operating profit, we can conclude that Bunns the Bakers is a very secure company indeed, with low gearing, low total liabilities to total assets and with a very strong interest cover ratio that indicates that the company will be able to keep servicing its long-term borrowings into the foreseeable future.

SUMMARY OF KEY CONCEPTS   Can you remember the formulae for the three long-term solvency and financial stability ratios? Go to the **online workbook** to take a look at Summary of key concepts 9.6–9.8 to reinforce your understanding.

MULTIPLE CHOICE QUESTIONS   Are you completely confident that you can calculate interest cover from a given set of financial information? Go to the **online workbook** and have a go at Multiple choice questions 9.7 to test out your ability to calculate this ratio.

WHEN ARE BORROWINGS RISKY?

How much borrowing is too much? The answer to this question is, 'it all depends'. Provided that an organisation has sufficiently strong cash inflows from operations and can afford to keep paying the interest as well as saving money towards repayment of borrowings, then that organisation will be able to borrow as much as it likes. Profitability, remember, is not enough: we saw in Chapter 6 that, without the associated inflows of cash from operations, profit means nothing. Many profitable companies have gone out of business because they were unable to generate the necessary cash flows from which to repay borrowings they had taken on.

Let's illustrate these issues with Give me an example 9.3 and 9.4.

What lessons can we draw from Give me an example 9.3 and 9.4? First, as with the current and quick ratios, you should never jump to conclusions based on isolated figures. An apparently

At the end of January 2020, Next plc had bank and bond borrowings of £1,237.4 million and equity of £441.5 million. The gearing ratio based on these figures is 280.27% (£1,237.4m/£441.5m × 100%). Looked at in isolation, this figure would suggest that Next plc has seriously over-borrowed and is in imminent danger of collapse. And yet, the company is still trading and lenders are falling over themselves to lend the company money: of the total borrowings of £1,237.4 million, £250.2 million was raised from a bond issue during the 52 weeks ended on 25 January 2020. Clearly, lenders would not continue to provide this amount of funding unless they had cast iron confidence in Next's ability to repay this debt. Therefore, several additional factors must be taken into consideration before we can draw a conclusion on the long-term solvency position of Next plc.

Affordability

Is this debt affordable? Next plc had an operating profit of £853.9 million and interest payable on bond and other borrowings of £43.6 million for the 52 weeks ended 25 January 2020, giving interest cover of 19.58 times (£853.9m/£43.6m). This level of interest is thus very affordable and sales and profits would have to collapse to very low levels before the interest on the borrowings could not be covered by profits from operations.

Repayment dates

When are the borrowings repayable? Of the total borrowings, only the bank overdraft of £33.7 million and the unsecured loans of £40.0 million are due for repayment in the next 12 months. The remainder of the borrowings is made up of bonds, of which £327.0 million is due in 2021, £250.0 million falls due in 2025, £286.7 million is repayable in 2026 and £300.0 million is due for repayment in 2028, so the company has plenty of time in which to save up the necessary cash to meet these repayment dates. The interest rates on the four bonds are fixed at 5.375%, 3.000%, 4.375% and 3.625% respectively, so the company would not suffer higher interest charges if there were to be a sudden increase in bank base rates.

Operating cash inflows

How easily can this debt be repaid? Cash inflows from operations amounted to £1,065.2 million for the financial year ended 25 January 2020. With annual cash inflows this strong, there is little doubt that the company has the operating cash inflows to meet these liabilities when they become due. In reality, the group's bankers will probably offer the company new loans with which to repay their existing loans when they are due for payment, fixing the interest rates on these new loans for a further five to 10 years. Much public company borrowing is rolled over in this way: borrowings are not actually repaid, they are just swapped for new borrowings at rates of interest fixed at a suitable level given the prevailing market rate of interest at the time the new borrowings are taken out.

Consistency of product demand

As a clothing retailer appealing to the 16–35 age group, Next has a consistency of demand for its goods ensuring a steady stream of profits and cash flows for the foreseeable future. There is nothing risky in its business and nothing to suggest that its products will suddenly go out of fashion. This would not be the case for a mobile phone manufacturer, for example, whose products might suddenly become obsolete if a revolutionary new technology were to be introduced to the market by a competitor.

Source: Next 2020 report and accounts www.next.co.uk

GIVE ME AN EXAMPLE 9.4   The dangers of borrowing too much

The private equity firm Terra Firma bought EMI plc in 2007 for £4.2 billion. Despite turning the ailing music business round and generating much improved profitability, with operating profit rising to nearly £300 million, by late 2010 it was clear that Terra Firma had paid far too much for EMI. Interest on the borrowings used to fund the acquisition could not be met from the improved operating cash inflows, resulting in Citigroup, Terra Firma's lender, taking control of EMI in February 2011. Organisations that do not keep within their borrowing capacity will not survive, so it is important for entities to borrow only as much as they can afford to service through interest payments and to repay when the debt becomes due. Contrast Terra Firma's situation with that of Next, whose interest cover of 19.58 times and operating cash inflows of £1,065.2 million from which to meet annual interest payments of around £44 million indicate that their borrowings are highly affordable.

Source: *Guardian* news 5 February 2010; *Financial Times* news 14 February 2010

unhealthy gearing ratio turns out to be perfectly sound when all the facts are taken into consideration. When evaluating long-term solvency and financial stability, you should look at:

- The interest cover to determine how affordable the borrowings are: does the business generate sufficiently high profits from which to meet interest payments?

- The dates on which repayments are to be made: the more distant the repayment date, the higher the chance the business has of meeting repayment by that date.

- The strength of the operating cash inflows from the statement of cash flows: high operating cash inflows indicate that there will be sufficient cash on hand both to repay borrowings when they become due for payment and to pay the annual interest payable on those borrowings.

- The consistency of demand for a company's products: the more consistent the demand, the less likely the company will be to face financial difficulties in the future and be unable to meet its liabilities when they become due. You should also think about the likelihood of new products from different firms replacing the current market leader's products: the more likely this is, the riskier the business will be and the higher the possibility that they could eventually default on their borrowings.

WHY IS THIS RELEVANT TO ME?   When are borrowings risky?

To enable you as a business professional to:

- Appreciate that apparently high levels of borrowings do not always indicate potential problems for an organisation in meeting repayments when these become due

- Evaluate the affordability of long-term borrowings and the ability of entities to repay those borrowings from current resources and cash inflows

- Consider the consistency of demand for a business's products and the impact that replacement products would have on a business's long-term solvency and financial stability

NUMERICAL EXERCISES   Do you think you can calculate long- and short-term solvency and financial stability ratios, working capital ratios and evaluate the cash conversion cycle and timing of payments for a real company? Can you interpret these ratios in a meaningful way? Have a look at Numerical exercises 9.1 dealing with the financial statements of Greggs plc and then have a go at the various exercises linked to this example in the **online workbook**.

APPENDIX: RATIOS CONSIDERED IN THIS CHAPTER

To assist your learning, the ratios we have considered in this chapter are summarised in Table 9.3.

Table 9.3 Calculations and descriptions for the liquidity, working capital and long-term financial stability ratios discussed in this chapter

	Calculation	What does this ratio tell us?
Liquidity ratios		
Current ratio	$\dfrac{\text{Current assets}}{\text{Current liabilities}}$	The current ratio presents the £s of current assets per £1 of current liabilities. The ratio shows us whether an organisation has sufficient short-term assets with which to meet short-term liabilities immediately.
Quick (acid test) ratio	$\dfrac{(\text{Current assets} - \text{inventory})}{\text{Current liabilities}}$	This ratio removes inventory from current assets and then compares the resulting figure with current liabilities. Inventory is removed from current assets on the assumption that it is not readily convertible into cash in the near future. The quick ratio compares current assets that are cash or that are readily realisable in cash (trade receivables) with current liabilities in an attempt to determine whether an entity is able to cover immediately its short-term commitments from readily realisable current assets.
Working capital ratios		
Inventory days	$\dfrac{\text{Inventory}}{\text{Cost of sales}} \times 365$	This ratio measures the average stockholding period, how long an entity holds goods in inventory before they are sold. The shorter the inventory holding period the better, as inventory is turned into sales (and hence into cash) much more quickly while obsolete inventories and the risk of deterioration (and hence loss of future cash inflows from the sale of this inventory) are minimised.

 →

	Calculation	What does this ratio tell us?
Receivables days	$\dfrac{\text{Trade receivables}}{\text{Credit sales}} \times 365$	This ratio indicates the average credit period taken by credit customers. This is the length of time it takes for credit customers to pay what they owe.
Payables days	$\dfrac{\text{Trade receivables}}{\text{Cost of sales}} \times 365$	This ratio measures how quickly the business is paying off its suppliers for purchases made on credit. Ideally, the receivables days and payables days should be equal: as cash is received, it is used to pay off liabilities.
Cash conversion cycle	Inventory days + receivables days − payables days	The cash conversion cycle tells us how quickly inventory is turned into trade receivables and how quickly trade receivables are turned into cash with which to pay trade payables. The shorter this cycle, the better the working capital is being managed and the more readily cash is available with which to meet liabilities as they fall due.
Long-term solvency (financial stability) ratios		
Gearing %	$\dfrac{\text{Long and short-term borrowings}}{\text{Equity}} \times 100\%$	The gearing percentage compares all borrowings to the equity of an entity. This ratio is often seen as a measure of risk: companies with higher borrowings are supposedly more risky than those with lower borrowings.
Debt ratio	$\dfrac{\text{Total liabilities}}{\text{Total assets}}$	This ratio measures the £s of liabilities per £1 of total assets. The lower the debt ratio, the more secure the entity.
Interest cover	$\dfrac{\text{Profit before interest and tax}}{\text{Interest (finance expense)}}$	Assesses how many times interest payable on borrowings is covered by operating profits to determine the affordability of monies borrowed. The higher the figure, the better, as a high figure indicates an ability to continue meeting interest payments from profits in the future.

CHAPTER SUMMARY

You should now have learnt that:

- An entity's liquidity depends upon how quickly goods purchased and traded are turned into cash

- Current and quick ratios express the relationship between current assets and current liabilities at an arbitrary point in time, the statement of financial position date

- Current and quick ratios make the misleading and unrealistic assumption that creditors will demand the payment of all monies owed on the day immediately following the accounting period end

- Careful working capital management is vital to an organisation's short-term liquidity

- Working capital ratios are used to determine the speed of an entity's cash conversion cycle

- A full appreciation of the short-term liquidity of an organisation must be based upon an assessment of the timing of cash receipts and cash payments

- Long-term solvency and financial stability depend upon an entity's ability to repay interest and borrowings from operating cash flows

QUICK REVISION   Test your knowledge by attempting the activities in the **online workbook**, including flashcards on the key concepts, numerical exercises and Multiple choice questions. You can also try the further self-test questions which are available at www.oup.com/he/scott i2a2e

END-OF-CHAPTER QUESTIONS

Attempt the questions in the following sections and then look at the solutions which can be found in the **online workbook** to see whether there are areas that you need to revisit.

❯ RECALL AND REVIEW

❯ **Question 9.1**

Define the following terms:

(a) Liquidity

(b) Cash flow cycle

(c) Acid test

(d) Working capital

(e) Cash conversion cycle

(f) Solvency

(g) Gearing

❯ **Question 9.2**

Maxim Limited has applied for a £500,000 loan which is repayable in 10 years' time. The bank manager is assessing the financial position and performance of Maxim Limited to decide whether to accept or reject the application. Advise the bank manager how she should carry out this assessment. Set out any relevant financial ratios that the bank manager needs to consider.

➤➤ DEVELOP YOUR UNDERSTANDING

➤➤ Question 9.3

Samoco plc operates a chain of in town grocery convenience stores and edge of town supermarkets across the UK. The company is expanding rapidly and is adding new stores every year. Below are the statements of profit or loss for the company for the years ended 31 May 2021 and 31 May 2020 together with statements of financial position at those dates.

Samoco plc: statements of profit or loss for the years ended 31 May 2021 and 31 May 2020

	2021 £m	2020 £m
Revenue	13,663	12,249
Cost of sales	12,570	11,330
Gross profit	1,093	919
Distribution and selling costs	121	108
Administration expenses	240	225
Operating profit	732	586
Finance income	20	15
Finance expense	104	84
Profit before tax	648	517
Income tax	162	129
Profit for the year	**486**	**388**

Samoco plc: statements of financial position at 31 May 2021 and 31 May 2020

	2021 £m	2020 £m
ASSETS		
Non-current assets		
Property, plant and equipment	**6,040**	**5,150**
Current assets		
Inventories	485	500
Other receivables	45	40
Cash and cash equivalents	122	99
	652	639
Total assets	**6,692**	**5,789**
LIABILITIES		
Current liabilities		
Current portion of long-term borrowings	240	216
Trade payables	830	790
Other payables	150	140
Dividends	200	180
Current tax	170	150
	1,590	1,476

→

	2021 £m	2020 £m
Non-current liabilities		
Long-term borrowings	2,230	2,024
Pension liabilities	756	524
	2,986	2,548
Total liabilities	4,576	4,024
Net assets	2,116	1,765
EQUITY		
Called up share capital	110	100
Share premium	145	140
Retained earnings	1,861	1,525
Total equity	2,116	1,765

Notes to the financial statements:

- Samoco plc's sales are made on an entirely cash basis, with no credit being allowed to customers at its convenience stores and supermarkets. Therefore, at 31 May 2021 and 31 May 2020 there were no monies owed by trade receivables.
- Finance expense is made up entirely of interest payable on the long-term borrowings.
- Samoco plc's long-term borrowings are repayable by equal annual instalments over the next 10 years.

Required

(a) Using the financial statements for Samoco plc calculate for both years:
- Current ratio
- Quick ratio
- Inventory days
- Payables days
- The cash conversion cycle
- Gearing %
- Debt ratio
- Interest cover

(b) Using the ratios you have calculated and the financial statements above, evaluate the liquidity, working capital and long-term solvency and financial stability of Samoco plc at 31 May 2021.

» Question 9.4

A colleague who has just started studying accounting on her business degree has read in another book that companies without current ratios of 2:1 and quick (acid test) ratios of 1:1 will find it difficult to meet their current liabilities as they fall due. She has just noticed your current and quick ratio calculations for Samoco plc in Question 9.3 and has concluded that the company is about to collapse. Using the information in Question 9.3, ratios that you have already calculated and details of when liabilities can be assumed to be due for payment presented below, calculate the maximum amount of the current liabilities of Samoco plc that could be due for repayment on the day after the statement of financial position date (1 June 2021 and 1 June 2020). Draw up arguments to put to your colleague to show her that a simple reliance on current and quick ratios as an indicator of short-term liquidity fails to address all the relevant issues.

For the purposes of this exercise you should assume that current liabilities are due for payment as follows:

- Bank loans: repayable in 12 monthly instalments
- Trade payables: repayable according to your payables days calculations in Question 9.1
- Current tax: due in four instalments: three months, six months, nine months and 12 months after the statement of financial position date
- Other payables: assume that 20% of this figure is payable immediately
- Dividends: due for payment in August 2021 and August 2020

You can assume that there are 360 days during the financial year on which Samoco plc's shops are open and trading.

» Question 9.5

The following information has been presented in the financial statements of Albert plc.

	2021 £000	2020 £000
Inventory	799	846
Cost of sales	6,326	6,438
Trade receivables	128	130
Credit sales	10,312	10,310
Trade payables	967	915

Required

(a) Calculate inventory days, receivables days and payables days ratios for Albert plc for 2020 and 2021.

(b) Calculate the cash conversion cycle for Albert plc for 2020 and 2021. Discuss any changes in the cash conversion cycle that have occurred between the two accounting periods and explain the causes of these changes.

(c) Which industry do the working capital ratios and cash conversion cycle suggest that Albert plc operates in? Explain your conclusion.

➤ Question 9.6

You are given the following information about three companies:

	Company A	Company B	Company C
Inventory days	20	25	35
Receivables days	48	45	40
Payables days	36	33	38
Gearing ratio	120%	70%	50%
Interest cover	4 x	6 x	8 x

Rank the companies from the most to least favourable from the point of view of the following parties, justifying your conclusions:

(a) Suppliers

(b) Credit customers

(c) Lenders

➤ Question 9.7

Alton plc's statement of financial position at 30 June 2021 shows the following:

	£000
Current liabilities	
Current portion of long term borrowings	570
Trade payables	270
Dividends payable	190
Tax payable	250
	1,280
Current assets	
Inventory	470
Trade receivables	310
Cash at bank	450
	1,230

Additional information

- The current portion of long-term borrowings is payable in monthly instalments over the next 12 months.
- Of the total trade payables, £70,000 is due in the first week of July 2021.
- The dividend is due for payment in full on 1 July 2021.
- Tax is payable in quarterly instalments starting on 30 September 2021.

Required

Assess the liquidity of Alton plc at 1 July 2021.

⟫⟫⟫ TAKE IT FURTHER

Banchory plc and Ballater plc are two manufacturing companies operating in the same industry and in the same geographical area. Below are the statements of profit or loss for the two companies for the year ended 31 December 2021 together with statements of financial position at that date.

Statements of profit or loss for the year ended 31 December 2021

	Banchory plc £000	Ballater plc £000
Revenue	15,400	17,100
Cost of sales	10,500	11,300
Gross profit	4,900	5,800
Operating expenses	1,950	2,750
Operating profit	2,950	3,050
Interest expense	140	950
Profit before tax	2,810	2,100
Income tax	560	420
Profit for the year	2,250	1,680

Statements of financial position at 31 December 2021

	Banchory plc £000	Ballater plc £000
ASSETS		
Non-current assets		
Property, plant and equipment: cost	13,600	20,000
Less: accumulated depreciation	(1,200)	(2,800)
	12,400	17,200
Current assets		
Inventory	1,400	2,400
Trade receivables	1,800	2,900
Cash	900	200
	4,100	5,500
Total assets	16,500	22,700
LIABILITIES		
Current liabilities		
Current portion of bank borrowings	850	600
Trade payables	1,200	3,100
	2,050	3,700

→

	Banchory plc £000	Ballater plc £000
Non-current liabilities		
Bank borrowings	1,300	9,300
Total liabilities	3,350	13,000
Net assets	13,150	9,700
EQUITY		
Share capital	5,000	6,000
Share premium	2,000	1,000
Retained earnings	6,150	2,700
Total equity	13,150	9,700

(a) Calculate for the two companies:

- Current ratio
- Quick ratio
- Inventory days
- Receivables days
- Payables days
- Gearing percentage
- Debt ratio
- Interest cover

(b) Using the ratios you have calculated, comment on the liquidity, working capital and long-term solvency of the two companies.

(c) You are a lender who has received loan applications from these two companies. Due to funding constraints you can only provide a loan to one of them. Which of the two companies is preferable from a lender's point of view? How would you justify your choice?

≫ Question 9.9

Listed below is information relating to four companies:

- Ibstock is a manufacturer of innovative clay and concrete building products.
- Nichols is a producer of still and carbonated soft drinks.
- The Weir Group is an engineering company which focuses mainly on the production and maintenance of pumps and valves for use in the mining, oil and gas industries.
- National Express is a leading public transport operator with bus, coach and rail services in the UK, Continental Europe, North Africa, North America and the Middle East.

	Ibstock	Nichols	Weir Group	National Express
Year ended	31/12/2019	31/12/2019	31/12/2019	31/12/2019
Income statement	£m	£m	£m	£m
(= statement of				
profit or loss)				
Revenue	409.3	147.0	2,661.9	2,744.4
Cost of sales	250.0	77.0	1,787.7	1,765.0
Operating profit	84.0	32.4	352.1	242.3
Finance expense	4.2	0.2	45.0	58.4
	Ibstock	**Nichols**	**Weir Group**	**National Express**
Year-end date	31/12/2019	31/12/2019	31/12/2019	31/12/2019
Statement of financial	£m	£m	£m	£m
position				
Total assets	771.1	156.3	3,852.2	4,408.3
Total liabilities	306.8	31.0	2,338.8	3,295.8
Current assets				
Inventory	84.3	8.4	642.9	29.4
Trade receivables	53.9	35.0	440.2	314.6
Other receivables	4.2	3.4	171.8	229.7
Cash and cash equivalents	19.5	40.9	273.8	478.3
Current assets (total)	**161.9**	**87.7**	**1,528.7**	**1,052.0**
Bank overdrafts	—	—	1.7	—
Bank loans	0.4	—	299.6	105.1
Other loans	6.6	1.0	232.8	534.9
Trade payables	56.0	7.6	306.7	342.6
Other current liabilities	39.2	17.3	372.5	830.7
Current liabilities (total)	**102.2**	**25.9**	**1,213.3**	**1,813.3**
Total equity	464.3	125.3	1,513.4	1,112.5
Total borrowings	134.7	3.6	1,430.3	1,744.9

Using the financial information, calculate for all four companies:

- Current ratio
- Quick ratio
- Inventory days
- Receivables days
- Payables days
- The cash conversion cycle
- Gearing percentage
- Debt ratio
- Interest cover

>>> Question 9.10

Given the activities of each company, comment on how you would expect each company to generate its cash inflows together with an assessment of the liquidity, solvency and long-term financial stability of each company. Your answers should address the following issues, among others:

- The current and quick ratios of the four companies.
- The cash conversion cycles of the four companies.
- Why do the inventory, receivables and payables days vary so much in the four companies?
- The gearing levels in the four companies and whether these are manageable.

9

PART 2
COST AND MANAGEMENT ACCOUNTING

CHAPTER 10   Cost and management accounting in context

CHAPTER 11   Product costing: absorption costing

CHAPTER 12   Relevant costs, marginal costing
             and short-term decision making

CHAPTER 13   Standard costing and variance analysis

CHAPTER 14   Budgeting

CHAPTER 15   Process costing

CHAPTER 16   Capital investment appraisal

CHAPTER 17   Corporate governance and sustainability

COST AND MANAGEMENT ACCOUNTING IN CONTEXT

10

LEARNING OUTCOMES

Once you have read this chapter and worked through the questions and examples in both this chapter and the online workbook, you should be able to:

- Define cost accounting and explain its role in organisations

- Define management accounting and explain its role in organisations

- Explain the differences between financial accounting and cost and management accounting

- Describe the overlaps between financial accounting and cost and management accounting information

- Understand how cost and management accounting is both internally and externally focused

- Describe the qualities that cost and management accounting information possesses

- Understand that all organisations use cost and management accounting information to make decisions, to plan and to control their operations

INTRODUCTION

As we have seen in the first part of this book, financial accounting records and reports economic outcomes to users external to the business. Behind these economic outcomes lie a host of internal organisational processes and decisions that go into shaping and determining the results achieved. Decisions are made about the products to make or the services to provide and organisations have to calculate the prices they will charge for the various products and services offered. How is the cost of each product or service determined? Do organisations just produce products and provide services and hope for the best or is there an underlying logic and plan to what they do? What role does accounting play in making these decisions and in costing and pricing these products? How is accounting information used to monitor and review outcomes as they happen? How do decisions made at the micro level impact upon the macro level strategy and aims of organisations? We briefly touched on the roles and functions of cost and management accounting in Chapter 1 (Accounting branch 2: cost and management accounting). It is now time to look in much greater detail at the ways in which cost and management accounting is used to inform all business decisions, both strategic and operational, to present the ways in which product and service costs are calculated with a view to determining a selling price which will fulfil an organisation's objectives and to show how cost and management accounting is used in the fundamental business cycle of decision making, planning and controlling activities (Figure 10.1).

Figure 10.1 The roles of cost and management accounting

COST ACCOUNTING AND COST OBJECTS: DEFINITIONS

Costing will take up a large part of the second half of this book. But what do we mean by costing and how is this term defined? Let's look at the definitions of cost accounting and cost objects provided by the Chartered Institute of Management Accountants (CIMA) in that body's *Official Terminology*:

> [The] gathering of cost information and its attachment to cost objects (for example a product, service, centre, activity, customer or distribution channel in relation to which costs are ascertained), the establishment of budgets, standard costs and actual costs of operations, processes, activities or products; and the analysis of variances, profitability or the social use of funds.
>
> Source: *CIMA Official Terminology*, The Chartered Institute of Management Accountants, 2005

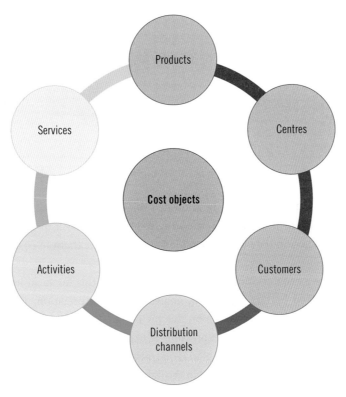

Figure 10.2 Examples of cost objects

From the definitions, it is clear that cost accounting embraces a very wide set of different approaches to gathering and allocating costs. Cost accounting revolves around the determination of the cost of cost objects as shown in Figure 10.2. These examples of cost objects are not exhaustive and costs can be accumulated for any clearly defined activity or event. The different levels of expenditure on module materials might be one example from your own experience or the varying costs of different social or sporting activities.

WHY IS THIS RELEVANT TO ME?   Cost accounting and cost objects: definitions

To enable you as a business professional to understand:

• The wide range of activities encompassed by cost accounting

• That organisations adopt the most appropriate and meaningful methods of gathering and allocating costs to cost objects

---

SUMMARY OF KEY CONCEPTS   Are you totally sure you can remember the definitions of cost accounting and cost objects? Go to the **online workbook** to check your recollection with Summary of key concepts 10.1 and 10.2.

GO BACK OVER THIS AGAIN!   Quite certain you appreciate what cost accounting involves and how it works? Go to the **online workbook** and have a look at Exercises 10.1 and 10.2 to clarify your understanding of cost accounting and how you are working with cost accounting data on a daily basis.

10

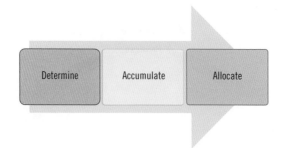

Figure 10.3 Steps in the cost allocation process

Costs can be allocated to cost objects in any way required, so organisations must first determine the most effective or most appropriate way in which they wish to gather costs and then decide how they will accumulate these costs in order to allocate them to cost objects as shown in Figure 10.3.

Once the costs have been accumulated and allocated, then this financial information can be distributed to interested parties for review, analysis and interpretation. Decisions will then be taken and plans will be made based upon this review, analysis and interpretation. Plans will be turned into budgets, the monetary expression of expected outcomes, which will be used to compare actual results to ensure that the plan is on track; where plans are not on track, corrective action can be proposed or the plans revised in the light of changed circumstances. Costing information can also be used to improve organisational efficiency and effectiveness through eliminating unnecessary costs or streamlining processes to improve profitability. Taking these decisions and making these plans is the role of management who use the cost and management accounting information gathered and presented to make decisions, to plan and to control operations.

MANAGEMENT ACCOUNTING: A DEFINITION

But what is management accounting and how does it differ from cost accounting? Cost accounting gathers costs and summarises them. These costs form the basic building blocks upon which management build and monitor their strategic and operational plans for an organisation. Costs are the foundation for the decisions that management take in running an entity and in planning its future direction with a view to fulfilling its objectives in the short, medium and long term. The Chartered Institute of Management Accountants defines management accounting as follows:

> Management accounting is the application of the principles of accounting and financial management to create, protect, preserve and increase value for the stakeholders of for-profit and not-for-profit enterprises in the public and private sectors. Management accounting is an integral part of management. It requires the identification, generation, presentation, interpretation and use of relevant information to:
>
> • Inform strategic decisions and formulate business strategy
>
> • Plan long, medium and short-run operations
>
> • Determine capital structure and fund that structure
>
> • Design reward strategies for executives and shareholders

- Inform operational decisions
- Control operations and ensure the efficient use of resources
- Measure and report financial and non-financial performance to management and other stakeholders
- Safeguard tangible and intangible assets
- Implement corporate governance procedures, risk management and internal controls

Source: *CIMA Official Terminology*, The Chartered Institute of Management Accountants, *2005*

The role of management accounting and management accountants is thus very widely drawn, but it is clear that accounting lies at the heart of the strategic and operational decision-making process whose aim is to create, preserve and improve value for stakeholders. Give me an example 10.1 illustrates the ways in which management use accounting information and techniques to make long-term business decisions.

In the following chapters we shall present a detailed review of the short-term operational planning and decision-making aspects of cost and management accounting together with the ways in which cost and management accounting information is used to control operations. Thus in Chapters 11 and 15, the accumulation and allocation of costs to products, activities and processes will assist in the calculation of a selling price that will enable an organisation to make a profit. The role of marginal costing in short-term management decisions will be considered in Chapter 12, while the measure of control exercised through standard costs, variance analysis and

---

GIVE ME AN EXAMPLE 10.1   The role of cost and management accounting in the strategic management of businesses

Rio Tinto plc is a mining company which is split into divisions mining and trading in iron ore, aluminium, copper and diamonds and energy and minerals. The group's risk report for 2018 describes the ways in which accounting information is used to manage the operations and the strategy of the business.

'Our business planning processes include preparing detailed financial plans for the next two years, as well as more strategic and higher level financial plans for the next five years. We develop our strategy and make capital investment decisions based on an assessment of cash flows over a multi-decade horizon. We also regularly test our investment capacity to make sure any capital commitments are in line with our capital allocation model. This multi-year approach to planning reflects our business model of investing in and running long-life assets, and selling into commodity markets over which we have limited influence. Our planning includes modelling a series of macroeconomic scenarios and using a range of assumptions, including:

- Projections of economic growth and commodity demand in major markets, primarily China.
- Commodity prices and exchange rates, which are often correlated.
- Potential new technology and productivity enhancements.
- Cost and supply parameters for our major inputs.
- The schedule and cost of organic and inorganic growth programmes.'

Source: Rio Tinto plc Risk management 2018 https://www. riotinto.com

10

budgets will be considered in Chapters 13 and 14. Chapter 16 will review the various techniques used to evaluate investments in long-term projects before Chapter 17 presents an overview of corporate governance and the ways in which control over the whole organisation and its operations is exercised. All of these practices and techniques will form the foundation of your later studies in both management accounting and strategy so careful and active consideration of these practices and techniques now will give you a very solid grounding upon which to build your second and final year studies.

WHY IS THIS RELEVANT TO ME?   Management accounting: a definition

As a business professional you should appreciate:

- The critical role that cost and management accounting plays in the planning and evaluation of business activities

- That no matter what your particular business specialism, a knowledge of the techniques and practice of management accounting will be crucial to your success in that specialist role

---

SUMMARY OF KEY CONCEPTS   Can you recall the CIMA definition of management accounting? Go to the **online workbook** to have a look at Summary of key concepts 10.3 to test your recollection.

GO BACK OVER THIS AGAIN!   Are you quite sure you appreciate how the definition of management accounting applies in practice? Have a look at Exercises 10.3 in the **online workbook** for a practical application of this definition.

10

COST AND MANAGEMENT ACCOUNTING V. FINANCIAL ACCOUNTING

The first part of this book looked in detail at financial accounting, how the three key financial accounting statements are put together, the recording system upon which they are based, the information they contain and their usefulness in understanding a business's past performance. As we have seen, financial accounting reports summarise accounting data, usually on an annual basis, for presentation to interested external parties. It is important to appreciate the historical aspect of these financial accounting statements, that they report on what has happened not on what might or is expected to happen in the future. They are thus not specifically designed to be used for planning purposes although users of these financial accounts might use them as a basis for making investment decisions, to buy, hold or sell shares in an entity. Financial accounts are prepared for parties outside the business and summarise all the transactions that have taken place, together with information relevant to a specific accounting period. The content of these financial statements is highly regulated by law and accounting standards. Annual financial statements are subject to audit to ensure that a true and fair view of the results, cash flows and financial position of the entity is presented. The rigidly specified content means that financial accounting reports tend to be inflexible and are general in nature rather than being shaped to the specific needs of individual users.

By contrast, cost and management accounting reports are produced as frequently as required by management: reports are most commonly provided on a monthly basis but weekly or even daily information can be generated in critical situations which require very careful and constant monitoring. There is no prescribed content or format and reports can be presented in the way that is most helpful in highlighting the required information in order for effective decisions to be made. Cost and management accounting reports often set out data that relates to past performance, but this past performance information is used to inform present decisions with a view to improving future outcomes to fulfil short- and long-term goals. These reports are thus forward rather than backward looking and the focus is very much on internal not external users. Instead of a summary of transactions, there is a detailed analysis of costs, selling prices and any other decision relevant financial and non-financial information. All of this cost and management accounting information is reported with a view to making decisions, planning for the future and guiding and controlling outcomes in the most effective and efficient way. Such careful attention to detail enables entities to work towards achieving their short- and long-term objectives. Without planning and decision making, no one, whether an individual or a business, will achieve anything. Without monitoring actual outcomes against the plan entities will be unable to determine whether their plans are reaching fulfilment or not. Figure 10.4 compares and contrasts the characteristics of both financial accounting and cost and management accounting.

Financial accounting reports	Cost and management accounting reports
Reports produced infrequently, usually annually	Reports produced as frequently as required for the effective management of the organisation
Decision usefulness is limited	Decision usefulness is very high
Backward looking	Forward looking
Reports on the past	Reports on the past and present to inform the future
External user focus	Internal user focus
Summary of transactions	Detailed analysis of costs, selling prices and any other information required for the management of the entity
Usually finanicial information only	Both financial and non-financial information
Content and presentation highly regulated	No regulation of content and presentation. Complete freedom to present information in the most decision-useful and effective way
High degree of comparability with current and previous reports for the same organisation	High degree of comparability with current and previous reports for the same organisation
High degree of comparability with present and past reports of other organisations	No comparability with reports of other organisations
Results are presented in a rigid format	Information is presented in a fluid format so that, for example, sensitivity analysis can be applied to forecast information

Figure 10.4 A comparison of financial accounting and cost and management accounting

To enable you as a business professional to appreciate:

• The differences between financial accounting and cost and management accounting

• The different purposes served by financial accounting and cost and management accounting

• The different audiences for financial and cost and management accounting information

---

GO BACK OVER THIS AGAIN!   Have you fully understood the differences between financial and cost and management accounting? Go to the **online workbook** and complete Exercises 10.4 to make sure you understand the distinctions.

SUMMARY OF KEY CONCEPTS   Are you quite sure you understand the differences between financial accounting and cost and management accounting? Go to the **online workbook** to take a look at Summary of key concepts 10.4 and 10.5 to reinforce your understanding.

FINANCIAL ACCOUNTING INFORMATION V. COST AND MANAGEMENT ACCOUNTING INFORMATION: A COMPARISON

What sources of information does cost and management accounting information use? Given that financial and cost and management accounting reports have such different functions, it might be expected that they would both derive their financial information from completely different sources. However, both financial accounting and cost and management accounting reports derive their numerical input from the same internal sources. In the financial accounting system, a purchase of raw materials on credit is debited to the raw materials account and credited to the trade payables control account (Chapter 5, The double entry to record purchases listed in the purchase day book and Illustration 5.13). In the cost and management accounting system, after the initial debit to the raw materials account and the initial credit to the trade payables account, the value of the raw materials is reallocated to each of the cost objects (jobs) using those raw materials as shown in Illustration 10.1. The double-entry system can thus also be used in the cost and management accounting system to take the total figures for the costs of materials, labour, overheads and other expenses and break these total costs down further to allocate them to the cost objects that consume those resources as required by cost accounting. A total for each resource is debited to the master account for that resource and as costs are consumed by cost objects, the master resource account is credited and each cost object account is debited with the costs reallocated. In this way it can be seen that the financial and cost and management accounting systems both rely on the same cost information for their reports: while financial accounting uses the total figures, cost and management accounting breaks those total figures down into their relevant sub-headings.

Illustration 10.1 Double entry for raw materials purchased on credit in both the financial and cost and management accounting systems

Financial and cost and management accounting systems

Raw materials					Trade payables			
Dr	**£**	**Cr**	**£**		**Dr**	**£**	**Cr**	**£**
Trade payables	24,000						Raw materials	24,000

Cost and management accounting system

Raw materials					Job 3620			
Dr	**£**	**Cr**	**£**		**Dr**	**£**	**Cr**	**£**
Trade payables	24,000	Job 3620	7,500		Raw materials	7,500		
		Job 3627	4,800					
		Job 3629	6,000					

Job 3627					Job 3629			
Dr	**£**	**Cr**	**£**		**Dr**	**£**	**Cr**	**£**
Raw materials	4,800				Raw materials	6,000		

While the same base internal financial figures are used to allocate costs to cost objects, management accounting also makes use of other external financial and non-financial information in the decision making, planning and controlling process. For example when deciding on a selling price for a product or service, that selling price cannot be set by reference to the internal financial costs alone. Attention must also be paid to the prices charged by other providers of the same or similar products and services so that the entity's own products and services remain competitive within the overall market. There is a very great deal of external financial and non-financial information that can be used by organisations in their decision-making and planning processes and cost and management accounting will make full use of this information to reach economically valid conclusions. Figure 10.5 illustrates the sources of information used in generating both financial accounting reports and cost and management accounting reports. Cost and management accounting reports have both an internal and an external focus whereas financial accounting reports present internal information to external parties.

In Chapter 1 (What qualities should accounting information possess?) we considered the distinct qualities of useful financial information. These characteristics are also applicable to cost and management accounting information. To be useful, cost and management accounting information must be relevant, timely, comparable and understandable. However, unlike financial accounting information, cost and management accounting information does not have to be verifiable and does not have to faithfully represent what it purports to represent. As long as management are confident that the accounting system is generating accurate information, there is no further need for verification of the details produced. Faithful representation is a quality of accounting information that is only required when reporting to third parties, individuals and organisations with no connection to the reporting entity: cost and management accounting information is reported within organisations for internal purposes only and does not purport to represent anything further to outside parties. Useful cost and management accounting information

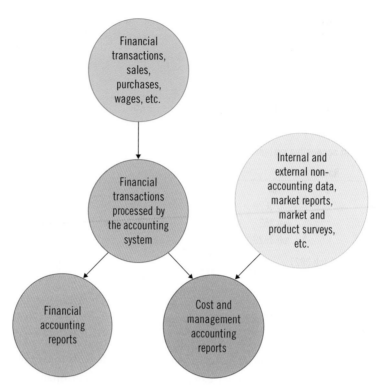

Figure 10.5 Sources of information used in financial accounting and cost and management accounting reports

is also subject to the cost-benefit rule: the cost of obtaining the information should always be lower than the benefit gained from that information. Where this is not the case, time and effort should not be wasted on acquiring the information. Likewise, immaterial information should not be included in cost and management accounting reports as this will only distract attention away from the critical details.

10

WHY IS THIS RELEVANT TO ME?   Financial accounting information v. cost and management accounting information: a comparison

To enable you as a business professional to appreciate:

• The ways in which financial accounting and cost and management accounting reports depend upon the same data

• That cost and management accounting reports increase their relevance and effectiveness by incorporating both internal and external data

• That the data in cost and management accounting reports should be relevant, timely, comparable and understandable but does not have to be verifiable or faithfully represent what it purports to represent

---

SUMMARY OF KEY CONCEPTS   How well do you remember the qualities of useful financial information? Go to the **online workbook** to check your recollection by referring back to Summary of key concepts 1.6–1.11.

GO BACK OVER THIS AGAIN!   Are you quite certain you can remember the definitions of relevance, comparability, timeliness and understandability? Go to the **online workbook** and complete Exercises 10.5 to make sure you can define these qualities of financial information accurately.

CHAPTER SUMMARY

You should now have learnt that:

● Cost accounting embraces a wide range of activities and includes the costing of products and services, the setting of budgets and standard costs, determining the actual costs of operations, processes and activities and the analysis of variances from expected outcomes

● Management accounting creates, preserves and increases value for stakeholders through the application of the principles of accounting and financial management to strategic and operational decision making, planning and control

● Financial accounting reports are backward looking summaries of past results produced annually and are presented to external users as a basis for assessing past performance

● Cost and management accounting reports are detailed, forward looking and presented as frequently as required to internal users as a basis for making decisions to improve present and future outcomes

● Financial accounting and cost and management accounting reports are based upon the same financial data which is presented in the most appropriate format to suit the purposes of each type of report

● Cost and management accounting reports are prepared using both internally focused and externally focused financial and non-financial data whereas financial accounting reports are based on just internal financial data

● Cost and management accounting information possesses the qualitative characteristics of relevance, timeliness, comparability and understandability, but does not have to be faithfully represented or verifiable

● Both financial and cost and management accounting information are subject to the same cost-benefit and materiality constraints

---

QUICK REVISION   Test your knowledge by attempting the activities in the **online workbook**, including flashcards on the key concepts, numerical exercises and Multiple choice questions. You can also try the further self-test questions which are available at www.oup.com/he/scott-i2a2e

---

10

END-OF-CHAPTER QUESTIONS

 Attempt the questions in the following sections and then look at the solutions which can be found in the **online workbook** to see whether there are areas that you need to revisit.

❯ RECALL AND REVIEW

❯ Question 10.1

Define a cost object and give examples of cost objects.

❯ Question 10.2

The terms 'cost accounting' and 'management accounting' are sometimes used interchangeably. Discuss what is meant by each term and describe the difference between the two.

❯❯ DEVELOP YOUR UNDERSTANDING

❯❯ Question 10.3

Your friend is an experienced cake maker who has worked for several baking companies in the past but he is now keen to branch out on his own and to open his own cake shop in his local town. He will bake all the cakes himself and offer a selection of regular cakes each day as well as making cakes to order for specific events such as birthdays, weddings and other special occasions. Your friend has applied to the local bank to open a business bank account. However, the bank has asked him to produce a business plan and present this to the bank for consideration before opening a business bank account can be considered. Your friend has identified a suitable shop and has asked for your help in putting his business plan together. List the information you will require to enable you to assist your friend in writing and completing his business plan.

❯❯ Question 10.4

Your friend runs a packaging business which makes flat-pack cardboard boxes in standard sizes. The boxes are sold to numerous online retailers who use the boxes to package up customers' orders, which are then delivered by parcel couriers. Your friend's business operates from a rented factory. The business now has more orders for flat-pack cardboard boxes than can be fulfilled from the current factory and your friend is considering expansion to a bigger factory with a much larger capacity in a different part of town. There are several local factory units to choose from with various different levels of rent. What factors would you advise your friend to take into account when making her decision about which factory to rent for her expanded business?

❯❯ Question 10.5

Describe the process of cost allocation and the steps involved. Explain how cost allocation can improve profitability.

❯❯ Question 10.6

Reports are generated by both management accountants and by financial accountants. Undertake a comparison of these two types of reports paying particular attention to:

(a)   The frequency of reporting

(b)   The decision-usefulness of each type of report

(c)   The main users

(d)   The type of information generated

(e)   The regulations governing each type of report

(f)   Comparability with the reports of other organisations

(g)   The level of detail in each type of report

›› Question 10.7

Financial accounting uses double-entry bookkeeping to record financial transactions and events. The output of financial accounting is a set of financial statements prepared according to the requirements of financial reporting standards and the Companies Act 2006. In comparison to financial accounting, describe the sources of management accounting information, how it is recorded and the output of management accounting.

››› TAKE IT FURTHER

››› Question 10.8

John runs a manufacturing company. He has recently hired an accounting graduate as a financial accountant to produce financial statements in accordance with the requirements of financial reporting standards and the Companies Act 2006. This accounting graduate advises him that they also need to recruit a management accounting expert to carry out cost and management accounting tasks. John disagrees with the accounting graduate, believing that hiring such a person would be unnecessary.

Required
Advise John why his business needs a cost and management accountant.

››› Question 10.9

'Management accounting is an integral part of management.' Explain how management accounting enables management to fulfil its various functions.

››› Question 10.10

The International Accounting Standards Board defines the qualitative characteristics of useful financial information. Describe these qualitative characteristics and determine whether they are as applicable to management accounting information as they are to financial reporting information.

11 PRODUCT COSTING: ABSORPTION COSTING

LEARNING OUTCOMES

Once you have read this chapter and worked through the questions and examples in both this chapter and the online workbook, you should be able to:

- Understand the importance of costing to business organisations in making pricing decisions

- Explain what is meant by the terms direct costs and indirect costs

- Explain the distinction between fixed costs and variable costs

- Construct simple costing statements to determine the total cost of products on an absorption (full) costing basis

- Draw simple graphs to illustrate fixed, variable and total cost behaviour in a business context

- Outline the limitations of absorption costing approaches in allocating overheads to products

- Apply activity-based costing to overhead allocation problems

- Discuss the assumptions on which costing is based

INTRODUCTION

In Chapter 10 we considered the role of cost and management accounting in organisations. Managers make decisions, they plan and they control their organisations' operations. The first aspect of a business that managers must understand is the costs of products and services produced. Without knowing the costs of an organisation and how these are incurred, managers will not be able to make decisions about selling prices or to know what they are controlling and they will not be able to plan for the future. But how are the costs of a product or service made up? What costs are incurred by a business and how can these costs all be allocated to the products and services provided by a business in order to determine a selling price? This chapter will look in detail at the different categories of costs incurred by organisations and consider the ways in which the cost of products and services can be determined.

WHY IS IT IMPORTANT TO KNOW ABOUT COSTS?

Businesses exist to make a profit. Without knowing what costs a business will incur in producing goods for sale or in providing a service, it will not be possible for that business to set a selling price higher than the costs incurred. When selling price exceeds the costs, a profit is made. Should selling price be lower than the costs, then a loss will be made and the business will soon be in financial trouble. We saw in Chapter 3 that revenue (income, sales) − costs = profit. All businesses will be seeking to increase their profits over time 'to create, protect, preserve and increase value for the stakeholders of for-profit and not-for-profit enterprises in the public and private sectors' (*CIMA Official Terminology, The Chartered Institute of Management Accountants, 2005*). There are two paths an entity can take when it wishes to increase profits: either revenue has to increase or costs must decrease. Let's prove this in Example 11.1.

EXAMPLE 11.1

Henry buys T-shirts for £5 and sells them for £10 each. Currently he sells 1,000 T-shirts a year on his market stall. He wishes to increase his profits.

Given his current level of sales, Henry now has a profit of:

	£
Sales 1,000 × £10	10,000
Cost of sales 1,000 × £5	5,000
Profit	**5,000**

If Henry could buy 1,000 T-shirts for £4 while still selling them for £10 his profit would be:

	£
Sales 1,000 × £10	10,000
Cost of sales 1,000 × £4	4,000
Profit	**6,000**

Henry has reduced the cost of the goods he sells without reducing his selling price and so his profit has increased from £5,000 to £6,000.

However, by increasing his sales to 2,000 T-shirts, while still buying them at £5 each, his profit will be:

	£
Sales 2,000 × £10	20,000
Cost of sales 2,000 × £5	10,000
Profit	**10,000**

Reducing costs or increasing sales are thus the two ways in which businesses can increase their profits.

WHY IS THIS RELEVANT TO ME?   Costs and pricing

- No matter what field of commercial or not-for-profit activity you are engaged in, as a business professional you must know about costs and income
- Knowing about your costs will enable you to determine a selling price to cover those costs and to generate a profit/surplus for your organisation
- Knowledge of an activity's costs will enable you as a business professional to devise strategies by which to increase profit, whether by reducing costs, increasing income or both

---

GO BACK OVER THIS AGAIN!   Are you quite sure that you understand the relationship between selling price, costs and profit? ? Go to the **online workbook** Exercises 11.1 to make sure you understand these relationships.

11

Give me an example 11.1 shows how cost increases reduce profits.

GIVE ME AN EXAMPLE 11.1   Taylor Wimpey plc's operating profit margin falls as costs increase

Taylor Wimpey plc, the housebuilder, reported a reduction in operating profit margin of 2% in the six months of trading to 30 June 2019. The operating profit margin fell from 20% in the first six months of 2018 to 18% in the first six months of 2019. While the average selling price of houses had risen by 2%, the costs of building those houses had risen by 4%.

This 'build cost inflation' arose as a result of increased prices for housebuilding materials imported from Europe. This increase in prices was caused by the falling value of the pound, which pushed up the cost of importing goods from overseas.

Source: Taylor Wimpey plc half year results – July 2019 https://www.taylorwimpey.co.uk

COSTS AND COSTING

We have seen that costs are important to businesses, but what costs will a business consider in making its decisions? The type and number of costs will depend upon the complexity of each business. Very simple businesses will have very simple costing systems and very few costs, while more complex businesses will have many costs and very complex costing systems to inform management decisions. Consider Example 11.2.

Anna is a self-employed carpenter working at home producing handmade wooden dining chairs. During the month of June, she produced 30 chairs. What price should she sell her chairs for? She provides you with invoices showing the costs of the materials she used in June:

	£
Wood	540
Glue	18
Screws	30
Sandpaper	12

Totalling up the costs above, Anna has spent £600 on making 30 chairs. Dividing the total costs by the 30 chairs made gives a cost of £20 per chair.

Setting a selling price

As long as Anna sells her chairs for more than £20 each, then she will make a profit on each sale. However, what other considerations should she bear in mind when setting her selling price? First, she will think about what a reasonable profit on each chair sold would be. If each chair takes her an hour to make, she would probably consider a profit of £30 to be a reasonable reward for the time and effort she has put into making each chair. The selling price for each chair would then be £50: £20 costs plus £30 profit. If each chair takes Anna five hours to make, then she would want significantly more profit and a significantly higher selling price to reflect the time spent on producing each chair.

While considering her own internal perspective, the profit she would like to make based on her time spent on making chairs, she will also need to consider the external market. She will thus take into account the prices her competitors are charging for the same type of chair. If she charges more than her competitors, she will not have many sales as buyers in the market like to buy goods as cheaply as possible. Alternatively, if she sets her selling price lower than her competitors, then she will expect to have a lot of orders from her customers, all of whom will want to buy her chairs at her lower price. However, can she fulfil all those orders? Does she have the time to produce as many chairs as her customers will demand?

Setting a selling price is thus a complex decision that needs to factor in many considerations. While cost is only one of those considerations it is now time to look in more detail at the types of cost that organisations incur in their operations.

11

DIRECT COSTS, VARIABLE COSTS AND MARGINAL COSTS

In our example, each one of Anna's costs can be attributed directly to each chair she produces. If she were to produce 31 chairs, we would expect her to incur costs of £600 ÷ 30 chairs × 31 chairs = £620. That is, for each additional chair she produces she will incur an additional £20 of materials cost. These costs are called the direct costs of production, the costs that are directly attributable to each unit of output. In Anna's case, these direct costs vary directly in line with each unit of output that is produced and are therefore her variable costs of production. Variable costs reflect the additional costs that are incurred by a business in producing one more unit of a product or service. Borrowing a term from economics, these variable costs are also known as the marginal cost of production, the costs that are incurred in producing one more unit of a product or service. However, as we shall see, not all direct costs of production are variable costs.

> **SUMMARY OF KEY CONCEPTS**   Are you quite sure you understand what direct cost, variable cost and marginal cost mean? Go to the **online workbook** Summary of key concepts 11.1 to 11.3 to check your understanding.

Direct costs can be of three types. The first direct cost is materials. In Example 11.2 the wood, glue, screws and sandpaper are all materials used in the production of each chair. The second direct cost is labour, the amount paid to workers for making products. Direct labour may be paid to workers on the basis of an agreed amount for each unit of product produced so that the more the workforce produces, the more they are paid. In this case, direct labour is a variable cost of production. Where production workers are paid a fixed salary that does not depend upon the number of goods produced, this is still a direct cost of production. However, it is not a variable cost as salary costs do not rise or fall in line with production. The final type of direct cost is direct expense, costs other than material and labour that can be traced directly to the production of each unit of product. An example of a direct expense would be the electricity required to power machinery to produce one unit of production: the total amount of electricity used by a piece of machinery can be measured precisely and the total cost of electricity divided by the number of units of production to determine a per unit expense for electricity. Example 11.3 presents examples of direct costs.

EXAMPLE 11.3

To illustrate the three types of direct cost, material, labour and expense, let us consider the costs incurred in the bread making section of Bunns the Bakers' central bakery. Think about each cost and decide whether it is an example of direct material, direct labour or direct expense.

Cost:

• Flour

• Gas used to heat the ovens

• Bakers' wages paid on the basis of the number of loaves of bread produced

• Ingredient mixing costs

- Equipment cleaning costs after each batch of loaves is produced
- Yeast
- Bakers' productivity bonus
- Olive oil
- Packaging for loaves
- Water

Which of these costs are direct material, direct labour and direct expense? We can allocate these costs to each heading as shown in Table 11.1.

Table 11.1 Cost allocation

Cost	Direct material	Direct labour	Direct expense
Flour	✓		
Gas used to heat the ovens			✓
Bakers' wages paid on the basis of the number of loaves of bread produced		✓	
Ingredient mixing costs			✓
Equipment cleaning costs after each batch of loaves is produced			✓
Yeast	✓		
Bakers' productivity bonus		✓	
Olive oil	✓		
Packaging for loaves	✓		
Water	✓		

Flour, yeast, olive oil, water and packaging are clearly materials used in each loaf, while the bakers' wages and productivity bonus are labour costs. The gas used to heat the ovens is a direct expense used in production of each loaf as, without the gas to heat the ovens to bake the loaves, there would be no product to sell. The gas is not a material as it is not part of the finished loaf. Similarly, the ingredient mixing costs (by machine rather than by hand) are expenses: the cost of mixing ingredients together is essential to the production of the loaves but is neither direct labour nor direct material. Cleaning the equipment after each batch of loaves is produced is another expense that has to be incurred in the production of bread. Each time a batch of loaves is produced, more cleaning costs are incurred so the cleaning costs are the direct result of production.

GO BACK OVER THIS AGAIN!   Are you confident you can distinguish between direct materials, direct labour and direct expenses? Go to the **online workbook** Exercises 11.2 to make sure you understand what types of cost fall into each category.

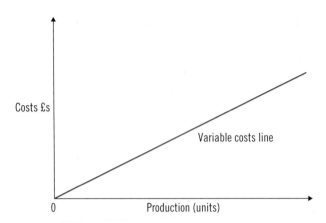

Figure 11.1 Graph showing the effect of production on variable costs

Variable cost behaviour: graphical presentation

In costing, the variable costs of production are assumed to behave in a linear fashion. This mathematical term just means that the variable costs of production rise precisely in line with the number of units produced. For each additional unit of production, the additional cost of producing that additional unit (the marginal cost) will be exactly the same as for all the previous units of production. In Example 11.2, the additional cost of producing one more chair is £20, which is exactly the same cost as all the other chairs Anna has produced.

The relationship between the variable costs of production and the number of units produced can be illustrated graphically as shown in Figure 11.1.

As production increases, variable costs rise in line with that production. Production of one chair costs Anna £20 in materials. Production of two chairs costs her £40 and so on. As each chair costs exactly the same to produce as the previous one, the total variable costs of production on the graph will rise in a straight line. If Anna produces no chairs, she will incur no variable costs and so the variable costs line starts at zero.

FIXED COSTS

However, not all costs incurred by a business are variable, marginal costs. There are also costs that are fixed, which do not vary in line with production. These costs are called fixed costs because, for a given period of time, they are assumed to remain the same whether zero units, 10 units or 1,000 units of product are produced. Fixed costs can be direct costs of production (such as the fixed salaries of production workers) or they may be general overheads incurred in the running of the business, costs that cannot be directly attributed to specific products or services. Fixed costs come in many forms, but let us start with the following simple example, Example 11.4.

EXAMPLE 11.4

Anna is so successful in her chair-making enterprise at home that she decides to expand and set up a workshop from which to produce her chairs. She starts renting a small workshop at an annual rental cost of £6,000. Business rates on the workshop amount to £1,000 per annum and the workshop heating and lighting bills amount to £800 for the year. In addition, she takes on two employees who are paid £25 for each chair that they make. Anna now concentrates on running the business rather than crafting chairs herself. How would you classify these additional costs? Which of these new costs do not vary directly in line with production and which will rise or fall precisely in line with the number of chairs produced?

Rent and business rates on the workshop are totally fixed as Anna has to pay these costs whether the employees make no chairs in the year or whether they make 10,000. Thus, her workshop can produce as few or as many chairs as she likes without incurring any additional rent or business rate costs. The rent and business rates are thus both fixed costs. They are also the indirect costs of production: the workshop is essential to the production of the chairs, but the rent and business rates cannot in any way be attributed directly to each chair produced.

By contrast, the employees are a direct cost of production as each additional chair that is made by each employee incurs a further cost of £25, this cost varying directly in line with production. Thus, £25 is a completely variable cost of production, the marginal labour cost of producing one more chair. This £25 will be added to the £20 material costs to give the total direct cost of one chair of £45.

The heating and lighting bills are a little trickier to classify. How much is paid for lighting will depend on how many days the workshop is open. If the workshop is closed, then the lights will not be turned on and no cost will be incurred. Similarly, if no one works in the workshop for the whole year, there will be no need to turn on the lights or the heating and the heating and lighting costs will be £Nil. However, even if the workshop is open and the lights are turned on, there is no guarantee that a consistent level of production will be achieved each day. The two employees might be able to produce eight chairs in a day between them, but if either of them is unwell and absent from work, then only four chairs will be produced, assuming that they each make four chairs a day. However, the lighting cost would still be the same for four chairs as it was for eight chairs. If the weather is hot, then the employees will work more slowly and only six chairs a day might be produced. In the same way, more lighting will be used in winter than in summer and this variability is also true of the heating costs: a very cold winter will mean a higher heating bill than when the winter weather is milder. Given this difficulty in allocating the costs of heating and lighting to individual units of production, it is safer to treat these costs as a fixed cost for the year.

Can we illustrate the relationship between fixed costs and production as we did for variable costs in Figure 11.1? Yes we can and this relationship is shown in Figure 11.2.

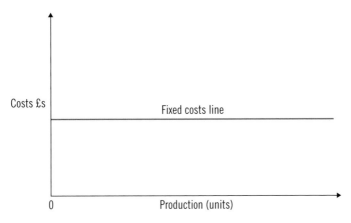

Figure 11.2 Graph showing the effect of production on fixed costs

The fixed costs line is a straight line just like the variable costs line. However, the fixed cost line shows that fixed costs are the same for all levels of production over a given period of time. As we noted earlier, the fixed costs are the same whether no chairs or 10,000 chairs are produced. Thus, the fixed cost line does not pass through zero but starts at the level of the fixed costs on the cost axis and continues as a straight line across the graph as there is no variation in the level of fixed costs. Even when no chairs are produced, the fixed costs are still incurred and have to be paid.

WHY IS THIS RELEVANT TO ME?   Direct costs and indirect costs

In your role as a business professional you will be expected to be able to:

- Identify those costs that are directly attributable to units of production or to services provided
- Identify those costs that vary in line with increased or decreased business activity
- Identify those costs that do not vary in line with increased or decreased business activity
- Possess the knowledge required to identify costs that are relevant in decision making (discussed further in Chapter 12)

GO BACK OVER THIS AGAIN!   Are you sure that you appreciate the difference between fixed and variable costs? Go to Exercises 11.3 in the **online workbook** to make sure you understand this distinction.

VARIABLE COSTS, FIXED COSTS AND TOTAL COSTS

Total costs for an accounting period are the total variable costs incurred in producing goods or services plus the total fixed costs incurred in that same time period. This is illustrated graphically in Figure 11.3.

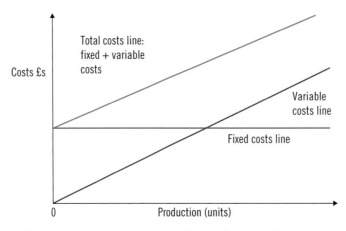

Figure 11.3 Graph showing the behaviour of production on variable costs, fixed costs and total costs

The variable cost and fixed cost lines are drawn on the graph as before in exactly the same positions. The total cost line adds together the variable and fixed costs for a period to give the total costs incurred by an organisation. At a zero level of production, variable costs are zero, so total costs are the same as fixed costs. However, as production takes place, variable costs are incurred and the total costs line rises as these variable costs are added to fixed costs. As production increases, the average total cost of each product produced will fall as the fixed costs are spread across more units of production. To prove that this is the case, consider Example 11.5.

EXAMPLE 11.5

Using the facts from Examples 11.2 and 11.4, let's work out the average cost per unit for levels of production of Anna's chairs at 100 units, 200 units, 300 units and 400 units. Remember that variable costs are materials (£20) + labour (£25) = £45 per chair while the fixed costs of the workshop are £6,000 (rent) + £1,000 (business rates) + £800 (heating and lighting) = £7,800.

As Table 11.2 shows, the average total cost per chair falls as production increases and the fixed costs are gradually spread over an increasing number of chairs.

Table 11.2 Anna's average cost per chair at different levels of production

(a) Units of production	(b) Variable cost per unit	(c) = (a) × (b) Total variable costs	(d) Fixed costs	(e) = (c) + (d) Total costs	(f) = (e) ÷ (a) Average total cost per chair
100	45	4,500	7,800	12,300	123.00
200	45	9,000	7,800	16,800	84.00
300	45	13,500	7,800	21,300	71.00
400	45	18,000	7,800	25,800	64.50

NUMERICAL EXERCISES   How well have you appreciated that higher levels of production mean a smaller average total cost for each product produced? Go to the **online workbook** and complete Numerical exercises 11.1 to prove to yourself that this is still true for higher levels of production in Anna's workshop.

11

ALLOCATING FIXED OVERHEAD COSTS TO PRODUCTS: ABSORPTION COSTING

We noted earlier in this chapter that organisations need to know the total cost of their products or services so that they can calculate a suitable selling price to enable them to make a profit on their activities. As we have seen, the costs involved are the direct and indirect costs of production and organisations will take both of these types of cost into account when setting their selling prices. Typically, a cost card will be drawn up for each product that shows the direct costs for one unit of production. Anna's cost card for one chair is shown in Example 11.6.

However, how should the indirect costs of production be allocated to products? Organisations have to take into account their indirect costs when setting a selling price for a product otherwise they might set the selling price too low and fail to cover their indirect as well as their direct costs. But different levels of production will result in different allocations of indirect costs to products and in different total costs for products. Anna has indirect costs of £7,800 for her rent, rates, heating and lighting. As we saw in Table 11.2, at different levels of production the average total cost for each product rises or falls depending on how many or how few products are produced. How can Anna set a selling price for her chairs if actual numbers of chairs produced are not known?

The answer to this problem is that entities will estimate the normal, expected level of production achievable within an accounting period and use this normal level of production as the basis for allocating indirect costs to products. Thus, an allocation of indirect costs is made to each unit of production on the basis of this expected production level so that the indirect costs are recovered with each unit of production sold. This technique is called absorption costing: indirect costs are absorbed into (allocated to) each unit of production to give a total cost for each product. At the same time, the indirect costs are recovered (essentially, paid for by the customer) as each unit of production is sold. Let us see how this will work in the case of Anna's chairs in Example 11.6.

EXAMPLE 11.6

Anna decides that her workshop will be capable of producing 1,000 chairs in the next year. She now needs to calculate the total cost for one chair based on the figures given in Examples 11.2 and 11.4 so that she can decide upon her selling price. Her cost card for one dining chair is shown here.

Cost card: wooden dining chair	£
Direct production costs	
Wood £540 ÷ 30 (Example 11.2)	18.00
Glue £18 ÷ 30 (Example 11.2)	0.60
Screws £30 ÷ 30 (Example 11.2)	1.00
Sandpaper £12 ÷ 30 (Example 11.2)	0.40
Direct labour (Example 11.4)	25.00
Prime cost (total direct cost of production	45.00
of one chair:	
direct material + direct labour + direct expenses)	
Indirect production costs (overheads)	
Rent £6,000 ÷ 1,000 (Example 11.4)	6.00
Business rates £1,000 ÷ 1,000 (Example 11.4)	1.00
Heating and lighting £800 ÷ 1,000 (Example 11.4)	0.80
Total production cost of one chair	**52.80**

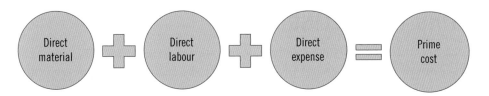

Figure 11.4 The components of prime cost

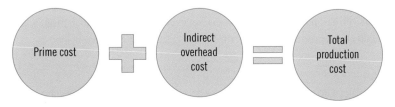

Figure 11.5 The total production cost of one unit of production

Direct costs of production are split into their component parts (direct material, direct labour and direct expense). The total direct production cost is called prime cost (Figure 11.4), the direct cost of producing one dining chair. Indirect (overhead) costs are then allocated to each item of production on the basis of what production is expected to be, the normal level of production. Thus, each element of indirect costs is divided by the total expected production of 1,000 units to give the overhead cost that should be allocated to each unit of production. Adding the indirect (overhead) costs per unit of production to the total direct cost (prime cost) gives the total production cost of one chair (Figure 11.5).

SUMMARY OF KEY CONCEPTS   Can you define prime cost and production cost? Go to Summary of key concepts 11.4 in the **online workbook** to reinforce your understanding.

WHY IS THIS RELEVANT TO ME?   Prime cost and production cost

As a business professional you should understand that:

- Setting a selling price to achieve a profit requires knowledge of all the costs incurred in the production of a good or service

- Indirect overhead costs as well as direct costs of production have to be taken into account when setting a selling price

- A suitable method of allocation of indirect overhead costs to products has to be found in order to build the indirect costs incurred into the cost of each product produced and sold

NUMERICAL EXERCISES   Are you convinced you can allocate direct and indirect costs to a product or service? Go to the **online workbook** and complete Numerical exercises 11.2 to make sure you can apply this technique.

SETTING THE SELLING PRICE

As management accounting is about informing operational decisions as well as costing, Anna will now consider (in Example 11.7) what selling price she ought to charge for each chair and how much profit she will make on the basis of her decision.

EXAMPLE 11.7

Given that each chair is expected to incur a total production (absorption) cost of £52.80, Anna decides that a selling price of £85 is reasonable and will meet market expectations. How much profit will she make if she sells all of the 1,000 chairs produced? The detailed profit calculation is shown below.

	£	£
Sales 1,000 × £85		85,000
Direct costs		
Wood 1,000 × £18	18,000	
Glue 1,000 × £0.60	600	
Screws 1,000 × £1	1,000	
Sandpaper 1,000 × £0.40	400	
Direct labour 1,000 × £25	25,000	
Prime cost (total direct cost for 1,000 chairs)		45,000
Rent 1,000 × £6	6,000	
Business rates 1,000 × £1	1,000	
Heating and lighting 1,000 × £0.80	800	
Indirect production costs		7,800
Total expected profit for the year		**32,200**

Rather than drawing up the detailed costing statement shown above, you might have taken a short cut to determine Anna's expected profit for next year. You could have taken the selling price of one chair of £85 and deducted the total production cost of one chair of £52.80 to give you a profit per chair of £32.20 (£85.00 − £52.80). Multiplying this profit per chair of £32.20 by 1,000 chairs produced and sold would give you the same answer of £32,200.

NUMERICAL EXERCISES   How well have you understood the calculation of profit from a given set of costing data? Go to the **online workbook** and complete Numerical exercises 11.3 to make sure you can apply this technique.

ABSORPTION COSTING AND INVENTORY VALUATION

At the end of each accounting period, most organisations will hold unsold items of production. The question that arises is how such inventory should be valued. In Chapter 3, Julia's retail business valued her inventory at the cost to the business, the costs charged by suppliers for goods sold to the business (Chapter 3, Closing inventory). This is an acceptable method of inventory valuation in a retail trading business as this is the cost of the inventory to the business. However, International Accounting Standards (IAS 2) require organisations to value their inventory on an absorption costing basis, the direct production costs of a product plus a proportion of the indirect production overheads incurred in each product's manufacture. Therefore, it is important for organisations to be able to calculate the costs associated with each item of production both in terms of its direct costs and the proportion of indirect production overhead costs attributable to each unit of product.

In Anna's case, any unsold chairs at the end of the accounting period would be valued at £52.80 each, the direct costs of £45 per chair plus the attributable overheads of £7.80 allocated to each chair. These costs would be carried forward under the accruals basis of accounting (Chapter 3, Closing inventory) to match against sales made in the following accounting period.

Give me an example 11.2 reproduces Rolls Royce Holdings plc's accounting policy on inventory valuation: note how direct materials, direct labour and overheads are included in the valuation of inventory.

GIVE ME AN EXAMPLE 11.2   Overheads included in inventory valuation

Inventories

Inventories and work in progress are valued at the lower of cost and net realisable value. Cost comprises direct materials and, where applicable, direct labour costs and those direct and indirect overheads, including depreciation of property, plant and equipment, that have been incurred in bringing the inventories to their present location and condition. Net realisable value represents the estimated selling prices less all estimated costs of completion and costs to be incurred in marketing, selling and distribution.

Source: www.rolls-royce.com

NUMERICAL EXERCISES   Are you happy that you know how to calculate the value of inventory at the end of an accounting period? Go to the **online workbook** and complete Numerical exercises 11.4 to make sure you can calculate an inventory valuation.

WHY IS THIS RELEVANT TO ME?   Inventory valuation

As a business professional you should understand that:

• Not all production will be sold by the end of an accounting period

• This inventory has to be valued to determine the profit for the accounting period and to match costs to products actually sold

• To comply with IAS 2 inventory should be valued at direct cost plus a proportion of the indirect production overheads incurred

---

Anna's business is simple, with just three indirect overhead costs to allocate to production units of one product. How would these indirect overhead costs be allocated in a more complex organisation in which more than one product is produced?

ABSORPTION COSTING: OVERHEAD ALLOCATION

In reality, manufacturing and service organisations have many indirect production overhead costs and many different products and services. Entities will seek to allocate these overheads to departments and then to products on the most appropriate basis. This will enable organisations to absorb these overheads into products or services on the way to determining a selling price for each product or service. Commonly, each overhead is determined in total and it is then apportioned to departments. The overhead total for each department is then divided up into an hourly rate on the basis of the number of labour hours or the number of machine hours used in each department (Figure 11.6).

Where labour is the key input to a production process, overheads will be allocated on the basis of the number of labour hours worked in a year. Service industries such as car maintenance, delivery services or catering will allocate overheads on the basis of labour hours as the provision of

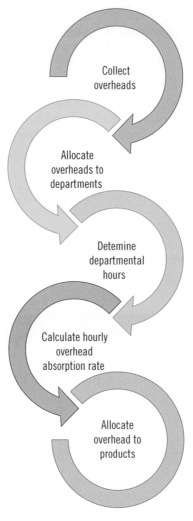

Figure 11.6 The overhead allocation process

the service is based on employees rather than on machines. Where a production process is highly mechanised, as is the case in most manufacturing industries, then machine hours will be used as the basis for overhead allocation.

How will the number of hours of labour or machine time be calculated? Businesses will first determine their operating capacity, the number of hours that production employees work or the number of hours that production machinery operates during a year. Once capacity has been determined, then overheads will be totalled up and divided by the number of hours of capacity to give an hourly overhead absorption rate.

As an example of this technique, suppose that a car maintenance operation has 10 employees who each work a 40-hour week for 48 weeks of the year (allowing for four weeks of holidays for each employee). The labour hour capacity of the business in one week is 10 employees × 40 hours = 400 hours. The labour hour capacity of the business for the year is then 400 hours in one week × 48 working weeks = 19,200 hours. Annual overheads incurred in the car maintenance operation will be totalled up and this total divided by the 19,200 available hours in the year to determine an overhead recovery rate for each job that the operation quotes for. If the total overheads of the business come to £288,000, then the hourly allocation rate will be £288,000 ÷ 19,200 labour hours = £15 per hour. If a job is expected to take five hours, then an overhead cost of £15 × 5 hours = £75 will be added to the direct cost estimate for that job when the customer is quoted a price. Remember that direct costs plus overhead costs give the total cost of providing a service and will be used as a basis on which to determine a selling price that will give a profit on each job.

The car maintenance operation is a simple example. In more complex situations, the stages in overhead allocation will be to:

1. Determine each overhead cost from invoices and payments.

2. Allocate overhead costs to departments on the most appropriate basis.

3. Total up overhead costs for each department.

4. Determine a labour hour or machine hour absorption rate for departmental overheads.

5. Allocate overheads to products or services on the basis of labour or machine hours used in the production of each product or provision of each service.

Think about how steps 1–5 are applied in Example 11.8.

EXAMPLE 11.8

Information relating to the overheads (indirect costs) of the Picture Frame Company is presented in Table 11.3. You have been asked to allocate the costs to two departments, machining and finishing. The directors of the Picture Frame Company want to absorb overheads in each department into products on the basis of machine hours used in each department, as they consider that this basis will best reflect the way in which departmental overheads are incurred. The Picture Frame Company sells its products at absorption cost plus 20%.

Table 11.3 The Picture Frame Company's annual overhead costs and machine hours

Annual Costs	Total £	Machining	Finishing
Rent	100,000	Floor area: 1,800 square metres	Floor area: 1,200 square metres
Business rates	25,000		
Depreciation	40,000	Machinery value: £160,000	Machinery value: £240,000
Heating	15,000	Departmental volume: 10,000 cubic metres	Departmental volume: 5,000 cubic metres
Directors' salaries	80,000	Percentage of directors' time spent in department: 37.5%	Percentage of directors' time spent in department: 62.5%
Machining department manager	29,000		
Finishing department manager	34,000		
Employee salaries	270,000	Number of employees in department: 9	Numbers of employees in department: 6
Repairs: machining	19,000		
Repairs: finishing	35,000		
Water rates	20,000	Departmental water usage: 1,800,000 litres	Departmental water usage: 1,200,000 litres
Lighting	18,000	Number of lights in department: 3,600	Number of lights in department: 1,800
Service department	50,000	Departmental usage: 20% of service department	Departmental usage: 80% of service department
	Total hours	**Machining**	**Finishing**
Machine hours	195,000	75,000	120,000

This mass of information might look daunting, but the application of common sense to how these overheads should be allocated to machining and finishing should enable you to determine the total overheads for each department. When allocating overheads, you should use any systematic basis that will result in a fair and equitable allocation of overheads to each department. Taking rent as an example in Table 11.3, the total floor area for the two departments is 3,000 square metres, 1,800 square metres in machining + 1,200 square metres in finishing. The total rent cost is £100,000 so £100,000 × 1,800/3,000 = £60,000 allocated to machining and 1,200/3,000 × £100,000 = £40,000 allocated to finishing.

Using the additional information on departmental usage of each particular production overhead cost and department specific details on particular production costs, overheads can be allocated to the machining and finishing departments as shown in Table 11.4.

Table 11.4 The Picture Frame Company's annual costs allocated to machining and finishing

Annual costs	Total £	Machining £	Finishing £	Notes
Rent	100,000	60,000	40,000	Total floor area: 3,000 sq metres, split both rent and rate costs 1,800:1,200
Business rates	25,000	15,000	10,000	Split on the basis of total floor area 1,800:1,200
Depreciation	40,000	16,000	24,000	Split according to machinery value, 160,000:240,000
Heating	15,000	10,000	5,000	Split according to volume heated, 10,000:5,000
Directors' salaries	80,000	30,000	50,000	£80,000 split according to usage, 37.5%:62.5%
Machining department manager	29,000	29,000	—	Actual departmental cost
Finishing department manager	34,000	—	34,000	Actual departmental cost
Employee salaries	270,000	162,000	108,000	£270,000 split 9:6 on the basis of the number of employees in each department
Repairs: machining	19,000	19,000	—	Actual departmental cost
Repairs: finishing	35,000	—	35,000	Actual departmental cost
Water rates	20,000	12,000	8,000	Split according to water usage, 1,800:1,200
Lighting	18,000	12,000	6,000	Split according to number of lights, 3,600:1,800
Service department	50,000	10,000	40,000	Split according to usage, 20%:80%
Totals	735,000	375,000	360,000	

SHOW ME HOW TO DO IT   Are you quite sure you understand how these allocations were calculated? View Video presentation 11.1 in the **online workbook** to see a practical demonstration to reinforce your understanding of how this overhead allocation between departments was carried out.

Now that overheads have been allocated to each department, we can work out an overhead absorption rate, the amount to be charged per hour of resource consumed within the department. As noted in Example 11.8, the directors have chosen to allocate overheads to products on the basis of machine hours as the most appropriate method of overhead allocation and absorption.

11

In the machining department, £5 of overhead will be allocated to products per machine hour (£375,000 ÷ 75,000 hours), while in finishing, products will absorb £3 of overhead per machine hour (£360,000 ÷ 120,000 hours).

Let us assume that the 50 × 60 centimetre gilt edged frame has a direct material, direct labour and direct expense cost of £56 and requires four hours of machining department time and eight hours of finishing department time. The total absorption cost for 50 × 60 centimetre gilt edged frames is then as follows:

	£
Direct material, direct labour and direct expense cost (prime cost)	56
Machining department overhead absorbed: 4 hours at £5/hour	20
Finishing department overhead absorbed: 8 hours at £3/hour	24
50 × 60 centimetre gilt edged frame total absorption cost	**100**

Selling price for 50 × 60 centimetre gilt edged frames will be £100 absorption cost × 120% (100% cost + 20% of the absorption cost) = £120.

WHY IS THIS RELEVANT TO ME?   Overhead allocation, overhead allocation rates

As a business professional you will be expected to be able to:

- Allocate total overheads between different operating departments with a view to determining overhead allocation rates for each department

- Use overhead allocation rates to determine the overhead absorbed by particular products or services

- Recommend a selling price on the basis of the total absorption cost of a product or service

---

NUMERICAL EXERCISES   Are you convinced you could carry out this kind of overhead allocation exercise for yourself? Go to the **online workbook** and complete Numerical exercises 11.5 to practise this technique.

Give me an example 11.3 illustrates the level of overhead allocation practices in businesses across the world.

GIVE ME AN EXAMPLE 11.3   The use of overhead allocation in business

The July 2009 CIMA report, *Management accounting tools for today and tomorrow*, surveyed the current and intended usage by business of more than 100 management accounting and related tools based on a questionnaire completed by 439 respondents from across the globe. The seventh most commonly used technique in practice was overhead allocation. When used as an operational tool, overhead allocation was undertaken by 66 per cent of respondents, the second most popular operational tool in use behind variance analysis on 73 per cent. The survey discovered that the larger the organisation, the more likely it was that overhead allocation would be in use in determining product cost.

Source: www.cimaglobal.com

11

ALLOCATING SERVICE DEPARTMENT OVERHEADS

Service departments do not produce products or make sales of services to outside parties, but they are an essential support activity in many business operations. Service department costs are allocated to production departments on the basis of each department's usage of each service department. In this way, service department costs are allocated to products and thus built into product selling prices to enable all costs incurred to be recovered through sales of products and services. In the example of the Picture Frame Company, the service department's overheads were allocated on the basis of usage by the two departments, machining and finishing. But what happens in cases where one service department provides services to another service department? In situations such as this, costs are apportioned between production departments and service departments until all the overheads have been allocated. Consider how this approach works in Example 11.9.

EXAMPLE 11.9

Alpha Manufacturing has three production departments, welding, sanding and painting, and three service departments, parts, set up and repairs. The costs and overheads of the six departments together with the usage made of each of the service departments by the production and service departments are given in Table 11.5.

Table 11.5 Alpha Manufacturing's production and service department costs and overheads and service department usage percentages

	Production departments			Service departments		
	Welding	Sanding	Painting	Parts	Set up	Repairs
Costs and overheads	£94,200	£86,200	£124,200	£40,000	£24,000	£26,400
Percentage usage of parts	25%	30%	25%		20%	
Percentage usage of set up	20%	40%	10%			30%
Percentage usage of repairs	40%	25%	35%			

You are required to reallocate the overheads for the three service departments to the welding, sanding and painting departments to determine the total costs and overheads for each of the three production departments.

Method

The parts department's overheads of £40,000 will be allocated to each of the three production departments in the proportions indicated in Table 11.5 (25% to welding, 30% to sanding and 25% to painting) and then 20% of the £40,000 overheads will be allocated to the set up department. This will now give overheads in the set up department of £24,000 + (£40,000 × 20%) = £32,000. The set up department's new overheads of £32,000 will now be allocated in the proportions given in the question to the production departments (20% to welding, 40% to sanding and 10% to painting) while 30% of the set up department's overheads will be allocated to the repairs department. The repairs department now has overheads of £26,400 + (£32,000 × 30%) = £36,000 to allocate to each of the three production departments in the proportions 40% to welding, 25% to sanding and 35% to painting.

These calculations are shown in Table 11.6.

All the service department costs and overheads have now been reallocated to production departments. The overhead recovery rates can be determined on the basis of labour or machine hours in those production departments and overheads allocated to products produced in the welding, sanding and painting departments.

Table 11.6 Alpha Manufacturing's service department overheads reallocated to production departments

	Production departments			Service departments		
	Welding £	Sanding £	Painting £	Parts £	Set up £	Repairs £
Costs and overheads	94,200	86,200	124,200	40,000	24,000	26,400
Parts costs reallocated	10,000	12,000	10,000	(40,000)	8,000	—
Set up costs reallocated	6,400	12,800	3,200	—	(32,000)	9,600
Repairs costs reallocated	14,400	9,000	12,600	—	—	(36,000)
Total costs and overheads	125,000	120,000	150,000	—	—	—

SHOW ME HOW TO DO IT   Are you sure that you understand how service department overheads are reallocated to production departments? View Video presentation 11.2 in the **online workbook** to see a practical demonstration of how this reallocation between service and production departments is carried out.

WHY IS THIS RELEVANT TO ME? ABSORPTION COSTING: overhead allocation, allocating service department overheads

As a business professional you will be expected to:

- Understand how costs relating to non-production service departments are allocated to production departments

- Appreciate that this reallocation process is necessary to ensure that all production overhead costs are absorbed into products and services to provide a solid basis on which to determine selling prices

NUMERICAL EXERCISES   Are you confident you could carry out this kind of overhead reallocation exercise for yourself? Go to the **online workbook** and complete Numerical exercises 11.6 to practise this technique.

ADMINISTRATION OVERHEADS, MARKETING OVERHEADS AND FINANCE OVERHEADS: PERIOD COSTS

So far, we have considered the costs of production, direct and indirect, fixed and variable. However, all business entities incur overhead costs through administration activities, marketing activities and the costs of financing their operations.

It is possible that marketing activities will incur certain costs that vary in line with sales: such costs might be the commission paid to sales representatives to reward them for the sales they generate, as higher sales would incur higher commission. However, most marketing costs such as advertising, brochures, product catalogues, the salaries of marketing staff, the costs of running delivery vehicles and of running sales representatives' cars will all count as fixed costs.

Administration, marketing and financing fixed costs are known as period costs and they relate only to the period in which they are incurred. Therefore, while these costs are not taken into account in the valuation of inventory, it is still important to set the production levels and selling prices of products and services in order to cover these costs. Thus, these additional period costs will be built into the cost price of products in the same way as indirect production costs are allocated to products.

> **GO BACK OVER THIS AGAIN!**   An example of a cost card for a product that includes all costs and the determination of a selling price is presented in Exercises 11.4 in the **online workbook**.

PROBLEMS WITH ABSORPTION COSTING

Absorption costing seems like an easy and effective way in which to build costs into products to determine first the total cost of the product and then its selling price. However, absorption costing has come in for criticism in recent years. The technique was originally developed as a way to cost products during the early part of the twentieth century. Each factory would turn out products that were all alike for undiscerning customers. Production runs were long and it was easy to spread fixed overheads over many products using the traditional absorption costing technique.

But times have changed. Modern manufacturers are no longer suppliers of goods to a passive market that accepts mass produced products lacking any individual distinction. Today's producers work assiduously to meet and fulfil customer demands and expectations. Production runs are now very short and products are individualised and tailored to each customer's specific requirements. Markets are not easily satisfied: customers have very specific requirements and, if their regular supplier is unable to meet those requirements, there are plenty of other businesses that will. Costs are thus no longer incurred in a steady, easy to allocate way. Lots of different organisational activities give rise to costs as businesses seek to fulfil each order's very specific requirements. As a result, the simplistic allocation of costs to particular products on an absorption costing basis may no longer be the most appropriate method with which to determine a product's total costs. A different approach has to be found to allocate overheads to products so that a more accurate cost and a more competitive selling price for each product can be determined.

Commentators have criticised absorption costing on the following grounds:

- The allocation of costs to products on either a labour or machine hour basis is too simplistic and does not reflect the actual costs incurred in the provision of specific goods and services.
- Traditional absorption costing fails to recognise the demands made by particular products on an entity's resources.
- Overheads arise not in proportion to direct labour and machine hours but as a result of the range and complexity of products and services offered.
- Selling prices calculated on the basis of absorption costs may be wrong in one of two ways:
  - overhead is either underallocated to products that consume more activities resulting in underpricing of these products, or
  - overhead is overallocated to products consuming lower levels of activity and so over-prices these products.
- As a result of these misallocations, some products are subsidised by others rather than making a profit in their own right.

WHY IS THIS RELEVANT TO ME?   Problems with absorption costing

To enable you as a business professional to appreciate that traditional absorption costing:

- Is not the only way in which costs can be allocated to products
- May not provide accurate product or selling prices
- May not be particularly well suited to allocating overhead costs to products in modern manufacturing environments

---

GO BACK OVER THIS AGAIN!   Are you confident that you understand the limitations of traditional absorption costing? Go to the **online workbook** and try Exercises 11.5 to make sure you appreciate these shortcomings.

SUMMARY OF KEY CONCEPTS   Are you quite sure that you can state the limitations of traditional absorption costing? Go to the **online workbook** to take a look at Summary of key concepts 11.5 to reinforce your knowledge.

OVERHEAD ALLOCATION: ACTIVITY-BASED COSTING

As we have seen, the aim of costing is to allocate costs to products and services to enable businesses to determine selling prices for those goods and services so that entities generate profits. Absorption costing works well in the case of mass produced, indistinguishable products, but modern manufacturing approaches require a more sophisticated cost allocation mechanism. Activity-based costing has been put forward as a way of providing this more sophisticated, more precise method of costing products and services to enable businesses to produce more accurate costs and hence more realistic selling prices.

How does activity-based costing work?

Traditional absorption costing adds together all the indirect production overheads incurred by a business and then allocates them across products on the basis of either labour or machine hours. Activity-based costing recognises that activities cause costs: the more activity that is undertaken, the higher the cost incurred. Under activity-based costing, costs are allocated to products on the basis of activities consumed: the more activities that are associated with a particular product, the more overhead is allocated to that product and so the higher its cost and selling price will be.

Activity-based costing allocates overheads to products using the following two-step approach.

Step 1: establish cost pools

- Rather than lumping all indirect production overheads into cost centres (departments), activity-based costs are allocated to cost pools.
- Cost pools reflect different activities incurred in the production of goods and services.
- Examples of cost pools might be design costs, set up costs, quality control costs, material ordering costs and production monitoring costs.
- The number of cost pools will depend upon the complexity or simplicity of an entity's operations: the more complex the operations, the more cost pools there will be.

Step 2: allocate costs to products and services

- Once cost pools have been established, a systematic basis on which to allocate those costs to products and services has to be found.
- The most logical method of allocating costs is on the basis of cost drivers: cost drivers reflect the level of activity associated with each cost pool.
- For example, if there were 50 machine set ups in a year, then the total cost in the machine set ups cost pool would be divided by 50 to give the cost per machine set up.
- Costs in the cost pools are then allocated to products on the basis of the activities consumed by those products. In our set up costs example, if a product used five machine set ups in the year, then the cost for five machine set ups would be allocated to that product.
- Where product costs turn out to be very high, management can take steps to reduce the activities consumed by those products as a way to lower costs and improve price competitiveness.

It is important to remember that activity-based costing is used to allocate overhead costs to products. Direct costs are still allocated to products in the usual way. Any costs directly linked to a product are still allocated to and form part of the prime cost of that product.

11

> **WHY IS THIS RELEVANT TO ME?**   Activity-based costing
>
> To enable you as a business professional to:
> - Understand how activity-based costing works
> - Appreciate the terminology used in activity-based costing and what each term means

GO BACK OVER THIS AGAIN!   Are you sure that you understand the differences between traditional absorption costing and activity-based costing? Go to the **online workbook** Exercises 11.6 to make sure you can distinguish between these two methods of overhead allocation.

SUMMARY OF KEY CONCEPTS   Do you think you can state the steps involved in activity-based costing? Go to the **online workbook** to take a look at Summary of key concepts 11.6 to reinforce your knowledge of these steps.

Having dealt with the theory and logic behind activity-based costing, let's look now at Example 11.10 to see how overheads allocated under both the traditional absorption costing and activity-based costing methods produce different results.

EXAMPLE 11.10

Cookers Limited assembles microwave ovens and traditional electric cookers from parts produced by various suppliers. The following information relates to the costs and production of the two products:

	Microwave ovens	Electric cookers
Direct materials	£30	£52
Direct labour	£24	£48
Direct labour hours	3	7
Annual production in units	5,000	15,000
Annual number of set ups	15	30
Number of parts suppliers	14	6

Overheads	£
Output related overheads	160,000
Quality control	60,000
Set up related overheads	90,000
Supplier related overheads	50,000
Total overheads	**360,000**

The directors of Cookers Limited have traditionally allocated overhead costs to the two products on an absorption costing basis based on total labour hours. They have heard of activity-based costing and are wondering whether this would make a difference to the costing of their products. Selling prices for the company's two products are set at cost plus 25%, rounded to the nearest whole £.

Absorption costing

On an absorption costing basis, the first task will be to determine the total labour hours as the basis on which to allocate overheads: 5,000 microwaves each take three hours while 15,000 cookers each take seven hours of labour time to produce. Total labour hours are thus 3 × 5,000 + 7 × 15,000 = 120,000 hours. The overhead absorption cost per labour hour is thus £360,000 ÷ 120,000 labour hours = £3 per labour hour.

Using this absorption cost rate gives us the following product costs on a traditional overhead absorption basis:

	Microwave ovens	Electric cookers
	£	£
Direct materials	30	52
Direct labour	24	48
Production overhead: 3 × £3/7 × £3	9	21
Total cost	63	121
Selling price (cost + 25%, rounded)	**79**	**151**

Activity-based costing

In this question, our overhead costs have already been allocated to cost pools for output, quality control, set up and supplier related overheads. In order to allocate the costs in these cost pools to products, we now need to determine the cost drivers of each particular overhead cost pool.

Output related and quality control overhead costs will most logically be driven by the number of production units. The more of a particular product that is produced, the more that product drives those particular categories of overhead costs as more output is achieved and more quality control inspections take place.

Production units total up to 20,000 units (5,000 microwaves + 15,000 electric cookers) so the output related overhead per unit of production is £8 (£160,000 ÷ 20,000 units of production). Here, 15,000 × £8 = £120,000 output related overhead will be allocated to electric cookers and 5,000 × £8 = £40,000 will be allocated to microwaves.

Similarly, quality control costs are allocated over 20,000 units of production. The quality control overhead per unit of production is £3 (£60,000 ÷ 20,000 units of production). In this case £45,000 of quality control costs will be allocated to electric cookers (15,000 × £3) and £15,000 to microwaves (5,000 × £3).

The unit cost for set up overheads will be based upon the number of set ups consumed by each product. Microwaves have 15 set ups in the year and electric cookers have 30, so the total set up related overhead of £90,000 is divided by 45 (15 + 30) set ups to determine the cost per set up of £2,000. Thus, 15 × £2,000 = £30,000 set up related costs are allocated to microwaves and 30 × £2,000 = £60,000 set up costs are allocated to electric cookers.

In the same way, supplier related overheads will be driven by the number of suppliers for each product. The more suppliers of parts there are for a particular product, the more overhead cost will be incurred in ordering, handling and processing those parts from the different suppliers. There are 14 parts suppliers for microwaves and six for electric cookers, a total of 20 suppliers. The total supplier related overhead of £50,000 is divided by 20 to determine the cost per supplier of £2,500 and then 14 × £2,500 = £35,000 of supplier related costs allocated to microwaves and 6 × £2,500 = £15,000 supplier related costs allocated to electric cookers.

Summarising the above calculations, the total overhead cost allocated to each product is as follows:

Overhead	Allocation basis	Unit cost £	Microwave ovens £	Electric cookers £
Output related	Production	8	40,000	120,000
Quality control	Production	3	15,000	45,000
Set up related	Set ups	2,000	30,000	60,000
Supplier related	Number of parts suppliers	2,500	35,000	15,000
			120,000	240,000

These total overhead costs are now divided by the number of units of production and allocated to product costs to determine the total cost price of each product. The 5,000 microwaves drive £120,000 of related costs, so £24 is added to the cost of each microwave (£120,000 ÷ 5,000); £240,000 of overhead cost is driven by electric cookers, so £240,000 ÷ 15,000 = £16 is added as the unit overhead to the cost of electric cookers. These overhead allocation rates now give the following costs and selling prices:

	Microwave ovens £	Electric cookers £
Direct materials	30	52
Direct labour	24	48
Production overhead	24	16
Total cost	78	116
Selling price (cost + 25%, rounded)	98	145

As the above calculations demonstrate, overheads have been underallocated to microwaves and overallocated to electric cookers under the traditional absorption costing approach. Under activity-based costing, microwaves carry a much greater load of overhead cost compared with electric cookers and should sell for a much higher price. Once management are aware of this overhead cost burden attaching to microwaves, they can begin to think about reducing these costs. Most obviously, they should start by sourcing parts for microwaves from fewer suppliers to reduce the supplier related overheads allocated to this product and so lower the cost and selling price.

WHY IS THIS RELEVANT TO ME? Traditional absorption costing v. activity-based costing overhead allocation

To enable you as a business professional to:

• Allocate overheads to products using both absorption costing and activity-based costing

• Make recommendations for ways in which product costs could be lowered to improve profitability and make product pricing more competitive

SHOW ME HOW TO DO IT Did you follow the overhead allocation process using the activity-based costing methodology? View Video presentation 11.3 in the **online workbook** to see a practical demonstration of how this allocation of overheads was carried out.

NUMERICAL EXERCISES Do you think you can allocate overheads using the activity-based costing methodology? Go to the **online workbook** and complete Numerical exercises 11.7 to test out your ability to apply your knowledge to activity-based costing problems.

What advantages does activity-based costing bring in practice? Give me an example 11.4 provides a summary of a case study that illustrates the benefits of adopting an activity-based costing approach to product costing.

GIVE ME AN EXAMPLE 11.4   The practical benefits of implementing activity-based costing

Dr Lana Yan Jun Liu of the University of Newcastle in the UK and Professor Fei Pan of the Shanghai University of Finance and Economics in China studied the implementation of activity-based costing (ABC) at Xu Ji Electric Co. Ltd, a large Chinese manufacturing company (*Activity Based Costing in China: Research executive summary series*, vol. 7(13), 2011, CIMA). An ABC pilot was implemented in one of the main production divisions in December 2001, with two further attempts to expand the use of ABC in a subsidiary and in its sales functions in 2005 and 2008. The subsidiary ran trials with the system in 2009 and then in 2010 reported a record annual sales increase of 50 per cent over 2009 together with a net profit margin increase of 13 per cent. Following the introduction and roll out of the ABC system, management expressed confidence in the accuracy of the company's product costs while the marketing department was able to compete more quickly and more effectively in its market as quotes could now be given instantly. The cost information presented by the new system made staff much more aware of cost savings and the ways in which to achieve them while top management were able to use the ABC information to exercise informed control over sales expenses.

Source: www.cimaglobal.com

THE LIMITATIONS AND ASSUMPTIONS OF COSTING

So far, we have taken it for granted in this chapter that fixed and variable costs are easily identifiable and that they behave in exactly the way we have described. Thus, it has been stated that variable costs vary directly in line with production and that fixed costs for a period (usually one year) are fixed and do not vary at all in that period. However, as we shall see, these assumptions should be challenged and it is important to understand the limitations of costing analysis when you are considering what price to charge for a product or service.

Assumption 1: fixed costs are fixed

In all of our examples so far we have assumed that fixed costs will remain at the same level for all levels of production over that period. However, this might not be the case. Once a certain level of

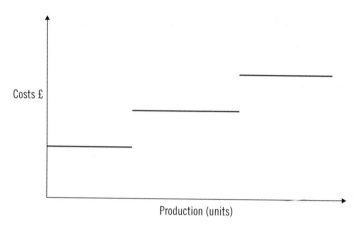

Figure 11.7 Stepped fixed costs behaviour

production is reached, additional fixed costs might have to be incurred to cope with the increase in capacity. Thus, once Anna's production reaches, say, 2,000 chairs in a year, she might have to rent additional workshop space in which to increase production to more than 2,000 chairs. This would entail more rent, more business rates and more heating and lighting costs causing her fixed costs to jump when production reaches 2,001 units. This increased level of fixed costs would stay the same until production reached 4,000 chairs, at which point Anna would need to rent even more workshop space to produce 4,001 chairs or more. Fixed costs thus rise in steps, staying the same up to a certain level of production and then rising to a new level once the limit of production capacity is reached.

Fixed costs might thus behave in a stepped fashion as shown in Figure 11.7. In this figure, costs remain fixed for a given range of production and then they rise to a new level once the original range of production is exceeded, remaining steady over the next range of production. Once this increased range of production is exceeded, the fixed costs rise again. Thus, it might not be true to say that fixed costs remain fixed for a given period of time; they might only be fixed for a given range of production.

GO BACK OVER THIS AGAIN!   Are you certain you understand how fixed costs might rise in steps? Visit the **online workbook** and work through Exercises 11.7 to see how fixed costs will rise in steps as production increases.

Assumption 2: variable costs remain the same for all units of production

Our analysis in this chapter has been based on the assumption that variable costs remain the same for all units of production. A moment's thought should enable you to see that this assumption will probably not be true in the real world. Increased purchases of materials from suppliers will earn quantity or bulk discounts from those suppliers. The higher the level of direct material purchases, the bigger the discounts and so the lower the average price of those materials will become.

Similarly, we have assumed that the unit cost of labour for each item produced will remain constant. However, this assumption, too, will not hold in the real world as increased productivity will earn productivity bonuses for employees, thereby pushing up the average cost of each unit of production.

GO BACK OVER THIS AGAIN!   Are you sure you understand how bulk discounts and productivity bonuses might affect the variable cost of materials and labour per unit of production? Try Exercises 11.8 in the **online workbook** to see how variable costs can change at different levels of production.

In situations in which production facilities use materials that fluctuate in price, such as metals and oil, the price of these direct materials can rise and fall during an accounting period. This makes forecasting very difficult but, again, it illustrates our point that variable costs will not necessarily remain the same for all units of production during an accounting period.

It is thus quite likely that the variable costs of production will not behave in the truly linear fashion we have assumed and that variable costs will not be represented by a sloping line of a perfectly even gradient as shown in Figures 11.1 and 11.3.

Assumption 3: costs can be determined with the required precision

An underlying assumption of all the discussions thus far has been that the costs of products and of activities in making those products can be determined with the necessary degree of accuracy in order to produce accurate selling prices. This is highly unlikely in practice as there are often under or over estimations of the time it will take to complete a given task, of the cost of materials used in the production of goods and of the amount of direct expenses used to make products. Material costs will vary in line with market prices or become cheaper or more expensive depending on the current supply of those materials to the market. Labour may become more expensive if the required skills are in short supply and so push up the direct labour cost of production.

In the same way, your estimate of how quickly you expected to work through this chapter and the online workbook may have proved completely wrong. Whatever your original estimate, it is likely to have been rather different from the actual time taken. Similarly, you may over or under estimate how much you will spend on a night out with your friends; again, though you have been out with them many times before, your expectations of what each evening out will cost will be very different from the costs in reality.

Cost accountants in industry may not achieve complete accuracy in their calculations and they may under or over estimate the cost of direct materials, the time that it will take direct labour to produce each unit of production and the overheads that will be incurred in a given period. Absolute accuracy is not going to be achieved and the best that can be done is a reasonably close estimate. As we shall see in Chapter 13, standard costing makes assumptions about what the costs of production should be and then uses variance analysis to explain the differences between what costs and income were expected to be and what they turned out to be.

11

WHY IS THIS RELEVANT TO ME?   The limitations and assumptions of costing

As a business professional you should:

• Appreciate that product costing is not an exact science

• Understand the bases of product costing and how these give rise to its limitations

• Be equipped with the tools to critique solutions that are produced by product costing analysis in a real world context

---

CHAPTER SUMMARY

You should now have learnt that:

• Direct costs are those costs directly attributable to products or services

• Direct costs of production may be variable or fixed

• Variable costs are assumed to vary directly in line with levels of activity

• Fixed costs are assumed to be fixed for a given period of time

• Product and service costing is used by business organisations in making pricing decisions

• A cost card for a product is drawn up by splitting product costs into direct and indirect production costs

• Indirect production costs (overheads) are apportioned to departments to determine total overhead costs for each production department

• Overhead recovery rates for products are calculated on the basis of total departmental overheads and expected (normal) levels of production

• Service department overheads are reapportioned to production departments as part of each production department's total overheads

• Simple graphs can be drawn up to illustrate fixed, variable and total cost behaviour in a business context

• Using traditional absorption costing to allocate overhead costs to products may no longer be relevant in modern manufacturing environments and may result in the mispricing of products

• Activity-based costing allocates overhead costs to products on the basis of resources consumed by each product

• Costing is based on the assumptions that:
    – Fixed costs are and remain fixed for a given period of time or range of production
    – Variable costs remain the same for all units of production
    – Costs can be determined with the required precision

 QUICK REVISION   Test your knowledge by attempting the activities in the **online workbook**, including flashcards on the key concepts, numerical exercises and Multiple choice questions. You can also try the further self-test questions which are available at www.oup.com/he/scott-i2a2e

END-OF-CHAPTER QUESTIONS

Attempt the questions in the following sections and then look at the solutions which can be found in the **online workbook** to see whether there are areas that you need to revisit.

❯ RECALL AND REVIEW

❯ Question 11.1

Summerfield Manufacturing produces dental equipment. The following information is extracted from its costing records:

- Direct material: £230 per unit
- Direct labour: £45 per unit
- Other direct costs: £18 per unit
- Rent and rates: £90,000 per annum

The normal production level is 1,500 units. The company's policy is to calculate selling price as production cost + 20%.

Required

For Summerfield Manufacturing calculate:

(a) The total prime cost and prime cost per unit.

(b) The total production cost and production cost per unit.

(c) The selling price of each unit.

❯ Question 11.2

Mr Sim, the management accountant of Marvell Limited, currently uses absorption costing to allocate overhead costs. A consultant has suggested that the company should switch to activity-based costing. Mr Sim thinks this is unnecessary and will only be a burden on the management accounting department. Discuss the advantages and disadvantages of the switch from the current absorption costing system to an activity-based costing system.

❯❯ DEVELOP YOUR UNDERSTANDING

❯❯ Question 11.3

Mantinea Limited manufactures various kitchenware products. The following direct costs are incurred in producing a batch of 2,000 food processors:

	£
Materials	22,500
Direct labour	16,500
Direct expenses	13,000

The factory overheads for the year are £3,000,000. Total machine hours for the year are 750,000 and each processor takes 4.5 hours of machine time to produce. The selling price of food processors is total absorption cost plus 50%.

Required

Calculate the total absorption cost of one food processor together with the selling price for each food processor produced by Mantinea Limited.

≫ Question 11.4

Printers Limited has been asked by the local university press to quote for the printing of a new book. The print run will be for 2,000 books of 400 pages each. The costing records of Printers Limited contain the following information:

- Paper is bought from a local supplier. The local supplier provides paper at a price of 2,500 sheets for £9.
- Printing ink costs £57.50 per gallon, which is sufficient to print 20,000 pages.
- Covers for each book will be bought in at a cost of 66 pence for each book.
- Finishing costs per book are 50 pence.
- Production workers are paid an hourly rate of £12.50. The costing records show that a print run of 2,000 books would require 200 hours of production labour time.
- Printers' total production overheads for the year are £500,000 and the normal production level of the business is 50 million pages per annum.
- Printers Limited's pricing policy is to set selling price at total absorption cost plus 25%.

Required

Calculate the price that Printers Limited should charge the local university press for the print run of 2,000 books.

≫ Question 11.5

Taylor Limited manufactures shirts. The following costs are incurred by Taylor Limited in its shirt production process.

Fabric	£9 per shirt
Thread and other direct materials	30p per shirt
Wages paid to sewing operators	£3 per shirt
Factory electricity and gas	£22,000 per annum
Packaging materials	20p per shirt
Wages paid to packaging workers	50p per shirt
Machinery repairs and maintenance	£20,000 per annum
Factory rent	£50,000 per annum

Required

(a) Determine which of the above costs are direct (direct material, direct labour, direct expense) and which are indirect costs of production.

(b) Calculate the total production cost per shirt if 20,000 shirts are normally produced and sold.

❯❯ Question 11.6

Using the information in Question 11.5:

(a) Calculate the total cost of production using absorption costing.

(b) Calculate the profit if 20,000 shirts are produced and sold for £20 each.

(c) Calculate how much Taylor Limited should charge for each shirt sold to make a total profit of £60,000.

❯❯ Question 11.7

Maxwell plc has three production lines and three support departments, human resources (HR), information technology (IT) and stores. The management accountant has gathered cost information for these production lines as well as the percentage usage of support departments by the production lines in the table below.

	Production lines			Support departments		
	Line 1	Line 2	Line 3	IT	HR	Stores
Costs	£183,000	£349,000	£155,000	£80,000	£52,000	£56,000
Usage of IT	25%	30%	30%	–	10%	5%
Usage of HR	20%	40%	25%	–	–	15%
Usage of stores	25%	45%	30%	–	–	–

Required
Reallocate the costs of support departments to the three production lines.

❯❯❯ TAKE IT FURTHER

❯❯❯ Question 11.8

Applokia Limited is a manufacturer of smart phones. The company has the following costs for the month of September:

	£000
Factory rent	100
Factory manager's salary	38
Administration salaries	85
Marketing costs	50
Plastic smart phone covers	250
Quality control staff salaries	75
Production line workers' salaries	500
Chip assemblies for smart phones produced	1,498
Administration office rent	25
Marketing office rent	20
Factory rates	47
Power for production machinery	50

Factory lighting and heating	43
Administration lighting and heating	5
Marketing lighting and heating	4
Marketing department salaries	51
Batteries	242
Production machinery depreciation	37

Required

(a) For the above costs, state whether they are:

- Fixed or variable.
- Direct production costs, production overheads or period costs.

(b) Draw up a table that summarises the above costs into prime cost, production cost and total cost.

(c) If Applokia produces 130,000 smart phones in a month and selling price is total cost + 25%, calculate the selling price for each smart phone produced in September.

(d) If rival companies are selling similar products for £27, what margin will Applokia make on its costs per smart phone if it sells its smart phones at the same price as its rivals?

⫸ Question 11.9

Folly Limited produces novelty products. The products are produced on machines in the manufacturing department and they are then hand painted and finished in the finishing department. Folly Limited has forecast the following indirect production overheads for the year ended 31 January 2022:

	£000
Machinery maintenance staff salaries (manufacturing department)	100
Employees' salaries (painting and finishing department)	300
Employers' national insurance contributions for both departments	40
Rent and rates	60
Heating (the manufacturing department is not heated)	25
Lighting	25
Machinery depreciation	75
Canteen expenses*	56
Electricity for machinery	50
Insurance: machinery	25

*The canteen is in a separate building. The canteen rent, rates, heating, lighting, insurance and staff costs are all included in the figure for canteen expenses.

The manufacturing department has a capacity of 96,000 machine hours and 2,000 labour hours. The painting and finishing department has a capacity of 4,000 machine hours and 80,000 labour hours.

Additional information:

Recovery/absorption bases	Manufacturing	Painting and finishing
Area (square metres)	4,800	1,200
Value of machinery	£360,000	£15,000
Number of employees	5	15

Required

(a) Using the information provided, calculate the total production overheads to be allocated to the manufacturing and painting and finishing departments.

(b) Calculate the most appropriate overhead recovery/absorption rate for the manufacturing and painting and finishing departments and justify your choice of machine or labour hours as an absorption basis for the two departments.

(c) Using the rates you have calculated in (b), calculate the cost of the following job:

Novelty Christmas pixies: 5,000 units	
Direct materials and packaging	£10,000
Direct labour	£1,000
Machine time: manufacturing department	500 hours
Labour time: manufacturing department	5 hours
Machine time: painting and finishing department	10 hours
Labour time: painting and finishing department	1,000 hours

≫≫ Question 11.10

Metal Bashers Limited produces steel fabrications for the construction industry. Steel girders and supports are cut to size and welded in the welding department and then painted in the paint shop before proceeding to the finishing department. Details of the overheads incurred by the three production departments are given below along with information on the two additional departments, the canteen and the service department. The canteen is used by all the employees of Metal Bashers Limited but the canteen staff are too busy to make use of the canteen facilities themselves. The service department repairs and cleans the machinery used in the three production departments. External catering equipment maintenance contractors service the canteen equipment.

	Welding	Painting	Finishing	Canteen	Service
Overheads	£100,000	£75,000	£43,000	£60,000	£42,000
Number of employees	15	5	6	2	4
Percentage usage of service department	40%	30%	30%		
Department labour hours	30,000	12,500	10,000		

Metal Bashers Limited is currently quoting for Job No 12359 which will require £1,500 of direct material, £2,000 of direct labour and £500 of direct expenses. It is estimated that job 12359 will use 120 hours of labour in the welding department, 50 hours in the painting department and 25 hours in the finishing department. Overheads are absorbed into jobs on the basis of direct labour hours in each department. The selling price for jobs is the total production cost of each job plus 40% of cost.

Required

(a) Calculate overhead recovery rates for the welding, painting and finishing departments.

(b) Calculate the production cost and selling price of job 12359.

▶▶▶ Question 11.11

Playthings Limited produces two dolls houses, the standard and the deluxe. The direct costs and overhead information relating to these two dolls houses are listed below.

	Standard	Deluxe
Direct materials	£50	£76
Direct labour	£30	£42
Labour hours	5	7
Annual production	2,500	1,000
Direct materials orders	400	600
Employees	5	10
Machine hours	10,000	5,000
Annual number of set ups	15	35

Overheads	£
Machining	45,000
Factory supervisor	30,000
Set up related overheads	50,000
Purchasing department costs	25,000
Total overheads	**150,000**

Playthings currently absorb their total overheads into their dolls houses on the basis of machine hours. The selling price of dolls houses is total production cost plus 50%. The directors are concerned about a build-up in the warehouse of standard dolls houses. Deluxe models are still selling well and the current price charged by Playthings is the most competitive in the market: their nearest rivals are selling the same type of dolls house for £300. Investigations have shown that competitors are selling comparable standard dolls houses for £165. You have been asked for your advice on the current costing system at Playthings and whether you can suggest a better way in which to allocate overheads to products together with any other suggestions you are able to provide.

Required

(a) Calculate the current total absorption cost and selling price for standard and deluxe dolls houses based on the absorption of total overheads on a machine hour basis.

(b) Determine suitable cost drivers for the four overhead cost pools.

(c) Calculate the activity-based cost of standard and deluxe dolls houses and determine the selling price of each based on activity-based cost plus 50%.

(d) Given your results in (a), advise the directors on how they might reduce the cost of deluxe dolls houses in order to compete more effectively in the market.

12 RELEVANT COSTS, MARGINAL COSTING AND SHORT-TERM DECISION MAKING

LEARNING OUTCOMES

Once you have read this chapter and worked through the questions and examples in both this chapter and the online workbook, you should be able to:

- Define contribution

- Use the distinction between fixed and variable costs to determine the costs that are relevant and those that are irrelevant in making short-term decisions

- Understand how analysis of contribution is used to make short-term decisions

- Undertake break-even analysis and determine the margin of safety

- Use marginal costing and contribution analysis to make a range of decisions aimed at maximising short-term profitability

- Understand the assumptions upon which marginal costing analysis is based

INTRODUCTION

The previous chapter discussed the various types of costs that organisations incur in their activities. These costs can be variable or fixed and can be categorised as direct costs of production, indirect costs of production and period costs. We also saw how fixed production overheads are absorbed into products to enable organisations to make pricing decisions to set the selling price at the right level so that an overall profit is generated from operations.

SUMMARY OF KEY CONCEPTS   Are you a little unsure about the terminology here? Go to the **online workbook** to revisit Summary of key concepts 11.1, 11.2 and 11.3 to revise direct, variable and marginal costs.

In this chapter, we will expand the analysis of costs to enable us to use this costing information in making decisions that will be valid in the short term (a period of one year or less). This analysis will be used to show which costs are relevant in short-term decision-making situations and which costs are not. In making these decisions, the profitability of the organisation will always be uppermost in our minds and we will be seeking to maximise the profits that can be made.

DECISION MAKING: NOT JUST SELLING PRICE

Our focus in Chapter 11 was on determining a product's costs to make just one decision: what our selling price should be to enable us to cover all our expenses and make a profit. However, there are other decisions that entities need to make. For example:

- What minimum level of production and sales is required to ensure that all costs are covered and that losses are not incurred?
- What level of production would be required to make a certain target profit?
- How profitable will our business be if the economy takes a downturn and sales and profits fall?
- If we lowered our selling price as a marketing strategy, would we make more or less profit?
- Will orders from new customers be profitable if these customers are looking to buy our products at a price lower than our usual selling price?
- Is it more profitable to make components for our products ourselves or to buy those components in the open market?
- If there are several products that could be made, but there are only sufficient resources to make some of them, which product(s) should be made in order to maximise the short-term profits of the organisation?

The first step on the road to using costing to help us make these additional decisions is to look at the calculation and definition of contribution, the surplus that arises from the production and sale of one unit of product or service. As we shall see, contribution is a highly relevant consideration in the decision-making process and is a crucial step in determining those costs that are relevant and those costs that are irrelevant in a short-term decision-making context.

CONTRIBUTION

Figure 12.1 The calculation of contribution per unit

We noted in the last chapter that fixed costs are assumed to be fixed over a given period of time and that variable costs vary with production or service delivery. Variable costs thus rise and fall directly in line with rises and falls in production as more or fewer goods or services are produced. However, no matter what the level of production is, fixed costs remain the same. Contribution for one unit of production and sales is the selling price less the variable costs of production (Figure 12.1). Our first practical example in this chapter is presented in Example 12.1.

EXAMPLE 12.1

Taking the example of Anna from Chapter 11 (Example 11.6), the contribution from selling one dining chair is given as follows:

	£	£
Selling price for one dining chair		85.00
Materials (wood, glue, screws and sandpaper) for one chair	20.00	
Direct labour cost to produce one chair	25.00	
Total variable cost for one chair		45.00
Selling price per unit – variable costs per unit = contribution per unit		**40.00**

So, with a selling price of £85 and a total variable cost of £45, Anna is making £40 contribution from each dining chair that she sells. Contribution is very similar to the gross profit that we considered in Chapter 3 (Different categories of profit), the selling price less the directly attributable costs of making each sale.

WHY IS THIS RELEVANT TO ME?   Contribution

- To provide you as a business professional with knowledge of the basic building blocks used in marginal cost decision making

- As a business professional, you will need to appreciate that contribution = selling price – the variable costs of production/service provision

---

SUMMARY OF KEY CONCEPTS   Go to the **online workbook** to use Summary of key concepts 12.1 to remind yourself of how contribution is calculated throughout your reading of this chapter.

MARGINAL V. ABSORPTION COSTING

But hold on, you might say. In Chapter 11, we used absorption costing and a production level of 1,000 dining chairs per annum to work out the total cost of one chair at £52.80, which would give a profit per chair of £85 − £52.80 = £32.20. This is different from the analysis undertaken above. Why is this?

The answer to this question lies in the distinction between fixed and variable costs. The variable costs rise and fall directly in line with production whereas the fixed costs do not. Remember that Anna set her production level at 1,000 chairs per annum and absorbed her fixed costs into each chair on this basis to enable her to set a selling price. However, the rate at which Anna absorbed her fixed costs into her production was based on a purely arbitrary assumption that production would be 1,000 chairs in a year. To illustrate the effect that this decision has had on the absorption cost of one chair, consider the following alternative scenarios in Example 12.2.

EXAMPLE 12.2

Anna's total fixed cost of £7,800 means that each of the 1,000 chairs was allocated a fixed cost element of £7,800 ÷ 1,000 chairs = £7.80. Anna could just as easily have set her production level at 2,000 dining chairs per annum and she would then have absorbed her fixed costs into production at the rate of £7,800 ÷ 2,000 chairs = £3.90 per chair. Alternatively, Anna might have been less optimistic about the level of production her workshop could achieve and set her expected production level at 500 chairs. In this case, her fixed costs would have been absorbed into production at the rate of £7,800 ÷ 500 chairs = £15.60 per chair.

The total fixed costs do not change, but the rate at which they are absorbed into the cost of products changes depending on the assumptions made about the normal level of production. The absorption rate adopted is a decision for management, a decision that is a matter of judgement completely dependent upon management's expectations of what represents a normal level of production over a given period of time.

Have a look now at Example 12.3. What are the differences between the two production and sales scenarios in this example? The fixed costs have not changed, but have remained the same for both the original and the increased levels of production and sales. Sales, however, have increased by the selling price of one additional dining chair (£85) and variable costs have increased by the cost of materials (£20) and the cost of direct labour (£25) for one additional dining chair. This has had the effect of both increasing contribution by £40 (selling price of £85 − materials cost of £20 − direct labour cost of £25) and increasing profit for the year by £40. Fixed costs have already been more than covered by the contribution generated by sales of 1,000 chairs per annum, so every additional unit of production and sales will add all of the contribution to the profit for the year.

EXAMPLE 12.3

While fixed costs in total are fixed, sales, variable costs and profits all change with each additional unit of production and sales. To prove that this is true, consider what the profit would be if Anna produced 1,001 chairs rather than 1,000 chairs in a year.

12

	Selling 1,000 chairs in a year		Selling 1,001 chairs in a year	
	£	£	£	£
Sales: 1,000 × £85/1,001 × £85		85,000		85,085
Materials 1,000 × £20/1,001 × £20	20,000		20,020	
Direct labour 1,000 × £25/1,001 × £25	25,000		25,025	
Total variable costs		45,000		45,045
Selling price – variable costs = contribution		40,000		40,040
Fixed costs (rent, rates, heating and lighting)		7,800		7,800
Profit for the year		**32,200**		**32,240**

This approach, as we saw in Chapter 11 (Direct costs, variable costs and marginal costs), is called marginal costing: the costs and revenues of producing and selling one more or one fewer unit of product or service and the contribution that results from this increased or decreased activity at the margin. The contribution from each unit of production and sales contributes towards meeting the fixed costs of the organisation. The higher the sales, the higher the contribution and the more easily a business can generate a net profit (sales less all fixed and variable costs) by covering its fixed costs and providing a profit on top.

WHY IS THIS RELEVANT TO ME? Marginal v. absorption costing

As a business professional you need to be aware:

• That a product's absorption cost depends upon the production level used to absorb fixed costs into products or services

• That fixed costs do not change in line with production and sales over a given period of time

• That variable costs and contribution vary directly in line with production and sales

• Of the distinction between contribution and the absorption cost profit per unit of production and sales

• That, once fixed costs are covered, the contribution from every additional unit of production and sales is pure profit

GO BACK OVER THIS AGAIN!   Are you confident that you can distinguish between fixed and variable costs? Go to the **online workbook** and complete Exercises 12.1 to make sure you understand the distinction.

SUMMARY OF KEY CONCEPTS   Have you fully grasped the ideas of contribution and marginal cost? Go to the **online workbook** to take a look at Summary of key concepts 12.1 and 12.2 to reinforce your understanding.

RELEVANT COSTS AND SUNK COSTS

Contribution and marginal costing analysis helps us to consider the short-term costs that are relevant and those that are irrelevant when a choice between two alternatives has to be made. Relevant costs are those costs that we will incur if we decide to follow a certain course of action. Relevant costs are the costs that influence our decision making.

Costs already incurred cannot influence future decision making as this money has already been spent and nothing you subsequently do will change those costs. Costs that have already been incurred and that do not influence future decisions are known as sunk costs. Sunk costs are past costs and have no further influence on decisions to be made for the future. To illustrate this idea of sunk costs, consider Example 12.4.

You are on holiday for a week in a seaside town. Your train fare has been paid and cost you £70 for a return ticket. Your hotel bill for the week is £500, which you have paid in advance. Now you have arrived you are free to decide what you want to do during your week. You have the option of going to the beach, going walking in the hills, visiting the local historical sites or travelling to another local town that is staging a sporting event you are keen to attend. You have £300 spending money for the week. What are the relevant costs and the sunk costs in this situation?

Your train fare and your hotel bill are now sunk costs, costs that have been paid and that have no further bearing on how you will spend your week. The only costs you will take into account now are the different costs of the four options in front of you and how much of your spending money each of these activities will use up. Going to the beach and going walking in the hills are likely to be less expensive alternatives compared with visiting the historical sites or attending the sporting event: both of the latter two options will require the purchase of entrance tickets whereas the former two options will not.

The past sunk costs will have no influence on your decisions about how to spend your time and money and so are disregarded when you consider your future options and actions. What counts now and what will influence your decisions are the costs and benefits that will be incurred enjoying any one of the four options available to you and the relative costs of each.

In the same way, costs that an entity incurs, whether any activity takes place or not, are irrelevant to its short-term decision making. Costs relevant in short-term decision making are those costs that will be incurred as a result of making decisions and implementing a particular course of action. In Anna's case, the relevant costs are the variable costs of producing a larger or smaller number of dining chairs. The rent, rates and heating and lighting costs are all fixed and will be incurred regardless of the number of chairs produced and sold. All Anna has to do is to decide what level of production she needs to achieve in order to cover her fixed costs and what additional revenue she will generate and what additional costs she will incur in doing so.

12

WHY IS THIS RELEVANT TO ME?   Relevant costs and sunk costs

As a business professional, knowledge of relevant and sunk costs will enable you to:

- Distinguish between those costs that are relevant and irrelevant in a decision-making context
- Appreciate that costs that do not change as a result of a decision have no bearing on that decision
- Understand that fixed costs are irrelevant in short-term decision making

GO BACK OVER THIS AGAIN!   Do you think you can identify sunk costs and costs relevant to a decision? Go to the **online workbook** and complete Exercises 12.2 to reinforce your understanding of this distinction.

SUMMARY OF KEY CONCEPTS   Are you confident that you understand what relevant costs and sunk costs represent? Go to the **online workbook** to take a look at Summary of key concepts 12.3 and 12.4 to reinforce your understanding.

RELEVANT COSTS: OPPORTUNITY COST

Another relevant cost that has to be taken into account is opportunity cost. This is the loss that is incurred by choosing one alternative course of action over another. Opportunity cost only applies when resources are limited: when there is no shortage of a resource, then there is no opportunity cost. This might seem like an academic exercise, but a moment's reflection will enable you to see that opportunity cost is involved in many everyday choices. See how the idea of opportunity cost works in Examples 12.5 and 12.6.

EXAMPLE 12.5

Before you started your university course, you were faced with a choice. You could spend three years gaining your degree or you could start work immediately and earn money straight away. Choosing to study for your degree involves the loss of income from employment for three years and the loss of being able to spend that money on whatever you wanted. However, by deciding to start work immediately, you faced the loss of three years studying a subject you enjoy and the improved personal and career prospects that such study would have brought to you. Time is limited and you can only make one of the two choices, so making either choice for your time involves an opportunity cost.

EXAMPLE 12.6

In a decision-making context in business, opportunity cost will be the next best alternative use for a resource. In a manufacturing business, raw materials can either be used for one project or another. That piece of steel that cost £100 could be used to produce a new steel fabrication to sell to a customer for £5,000 or it could be scrapped for £20. The opportunity cost of using the steel in the new fabrication is the next best alternative to using it, which is scrapping it. Therefore, the opportunity cost of using the steel in the fabrication is £20. The £100 purchase cost is irrelevant as this is a past cost, a sunk cost and a cost that has no further bearing on your decision. Your choice lies in using the steel in the fabrication to sell to a customer or scrapping it and receiving £20.

WHY IS THIS RELEVANT TO ME?   Relevant costs: opportunity costs

As a business professional:

- You should appreciate that the opportunity cost of a decision is the next best alternative use for the resource used in that decision
- You need to be able to identify the opportunity cost of a resource as a relevant cost in a decision-making context

---

GO BACK OVER THIS AGAIN!   Opportunity cost sounds like a difficult concept. Go to the **online workbook** and complete Exercises 12.3 to see if you can decide what the opportunity costs of various decisions are.

SUMMARY OF KEY CONCEPTS   Are you sure that you understand what opportunity cost represents? Go to the **online workbook** to take a look at Summary of key concepts 12.5 to reinforce your understanding.

As we have discovered earlier, relevant costs are those costs that affect short-term decision making. Let us now see how marginal costing and relevant costs are used in decision making by businesses.

CONTRIBUTION ANALYSIS AND DECISION MAKING
Break-even point

Anna's first concern when setting up her business was to determine the selling price of her dining chairs. Her second concern (and the concern of many new businesses when they start up) is to calculate the number of units of production she will need to sell to cover all her costs, both fixed and variable. The point at which the revenue from sales = the total costs (Figure 12.2) is known as the break-even point, the level of sales that produces neither a profit nor a loss. Contribution analysis is relevant in determining break-even point. As we have seen, each additional unit of production and sales adds contribution towards the fixed costs so each sale is a further step towards covering those fixed costs. This is very similar to walking up a hill: the hill does not move (fixed costs) and each step you take (contribution) brings you closer to the top of the hill. Just as all your steps take you to the top, so the contribution from each sale takes an entity closer and closer to the break-even point.

This knowledge enables us to calculate the break-even point as:

$$\frac{\text{Total fixed costs}}{\text{Contribution per unit of sales}} = \text{Break-even point in sales units}$$

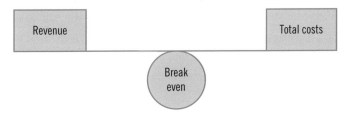

Figure 12.2 Break-even point: revenue = total costs

12

Anna's break-even point is calculated in Example 12.7.

EXAMPLE 12.7

How many dining chairs does Anna need to sell to break even? We know from our calculations in Example 12.1 that the contribution from the sale of one chair is £40. We also know from our examples in Chapter 11 that Anna's annual fixed costs for her workshop are £7,800 (annual rent of £6,000, annual business rates of £1,000 and heating and lighting costs of £800, see Example 11.4).

Using the break-even formula given previously, Anna's break-even point is thus:

$$\frac{£7,800}{£40} = 195 \text{ dining chairs}$$

Anna needs to sell 195 chairs in order to break even. Using this figure, let's prove that she does in fact break even if she sells 195 chairs in the year.

	£	£
Sales of 195 dining chairs at £85 each		16,575
Materials cost for 195 dining chairs at £20 each	3,900	
Direct labour cost for 195 dining chairs at £25 each	4,875	
Total variable cost		8,775
Selling price – variable costs = contribution		7,800
Fixed costs (rent, rates, heating and lighting)		7,800
Profit/loss for the year		—

The above calculations prove that our formula for break-even point works and gives us the correct answer. For Anna, at the break-even point, her sales of £16,575 are exactly equal to her variable costs for the break-even level of sales (£8,775) plus the fixed costs that she is incurring during the year (£7,800). She makes neither a profit nor a loss at this point. Once she sells 196 chairs, the additional £40 of contribution is pure profit as there are no further fixed costs that must be covered before a profit can be made.

WHY IS THIS RELEVANT TO ME?   Break-even point

As a business professional knowledge of break-even point analysis will enable you to:

• Appreciate that a business breaks even when all of its costs, both fixed and variable, are exactly covered by the revenue from sales

• Calculate the break-even point in sales units and sales value in £s for different products and services

• Determine break-even points for new products or services that your company intends to introduce

| **SUMMARY OF KEY CONCEPTS** | Are you certain that you can state the break-even formula and say what break-even represents? Go to the **online workbook** to take a look at Summary of key concepts 12.6 to test your knowledge.

| **MULTIPLE CHOICE QUESTIONS** | Are you confident that you can calculate a break-even point from a given set of data? Go to the **online workbook** and have a go at Multiple choice questions 12.1 to try out your new knowledge.

Break-even point: graphical illustration

Just as we drew graphs to illustrate the behaviour of fixed, variable and total costs in Chapter 11, so, too, can we draw a graph to show the break-even point. Break-even charts require three lines to be drawn: the line representing sales revenue, the line representing fixed costs and the line representing total costs (fixed costs + variable costs). Fixed costs remain the same throughout the period under review just as we saw in Chapter 11 (Fixed costs), but sales revenue and total costs both rise directly in line with the level of sales and production activity. The point at which the sales revenue line and total costs line intersect is the break-even point as shown in Figure 12.3. Beneath the break-even point losses will be made while above the break-even point profits are made.

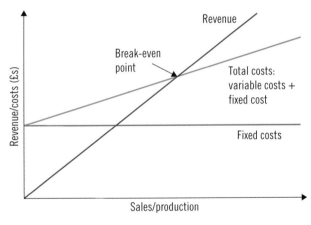

Figure 12.3 Graphical presentation of sales revenue, fixed costs, total costs and break-even point

The margin of safety

As we have seen, the break-even point in sales tells us how many units of production we have to sell in order to cover all our fixed costs and make neither a profit nor a loss. However, it also tells us how far our projected sales could fall before we reach a break-even position. In Anna's case, we found that she needs to sell 195 chairs before she breaks even. As her projected sales are 1,000 units for the year, she has a margin of safety of 1,000 − 195 = 805 chairs (Figure 12.4). This means that her projected sales could fall by 805 chairs before she reaches her break-even point. The higher the margin of safety, the less an organisation is exposed to the risk of a fall in sales

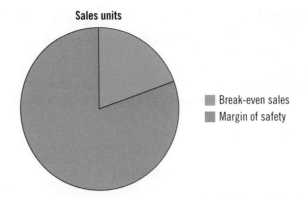

Figure 12.4 Anna's break-even sales units and margin of safety

that could result in a loss-making situation. In Anna's case, even if her projected sales fell to 500 units, she will still make a profit as sales of 500 chairs are still well above the break-even point of 195 chairs.

WHY IS THIS RELEVANT TO ME?   Margin of safety

To enable you as a business professional to:

- Calculate the margin of safety for a product or service
- Appreciate that the larger the margin of safety, the less likely it is that a business will make a loss

---

SUMMARY OF KEY CONCEPTS   Are you sure you can you say what the margin of safety represents? Go to the **online workbook** to take a look at Summary of key concepts 12.7 to test your knowledge.

MULTIPLE CHOICE QUESTIONS   Are you confident that you can calculate break-even point and the margin of safety? Complete Multiple choice questions 12.2 in the **online workbook** to reinforce your learning.

Sensitivity analysis

Knowledge of the break-even point enables us to determine the profit or loss from any given level of sales as illustrated in Example 12.8.

EXAMPLE 12.8

Anna knows that selling her chairs at £85 each will give her a contribution per chair of £40. Her break-even point is 195 chairs, so what will her profit or loss be if she sells 180 chairs or 300 chairs?

We could calculate individual profit and loss accounts for sales of 180 chairs and 300 chairs to determine profit or loss at the two sales levels. However, as we know that the break-even point is 195 chairs, we can calculate Anna's profit or loss by subtracting the break-even point from the projected sales units and then multiplying the difference by the contribution per unit of sales.

Thus, using our previous calculations, the loss at sales of 180 chairs will be $(180 - 195) \times £40 = £600$. Is this right? Contribution of £40 per chair will result in total contribution from sales of 180 chairs of $180 \times £40 = £7,200$. After deducting the fixed costs of £7,800, Anna's loss will be $£7,200 - £7,800 = £600$ so our calculation using the number of chairs from the break-even point is correct.

Similarly, at sales of 300 chairs, Anna's profit will be $(300 - 195) \times £40 = £4,200$. Proof: $300 \times £40 =$ a total contribution of £12,000. Deducting fixed costs of £7,800 gives a profit of $£12,000 - £7,800 = £4,200$.

WHY IS THIS RELEVANT TO ME?   Break-even point and sensitivity analysis

As a business professional knowledge of break-even point and sensitivity analysis will:

- Enable you to calculate the profit or loss at a given level of sales quickly
- Show you that the profit or loss depends on how far the level of sales differs from the break-even point
- Provide you with a useful analysis tool when evaluating the profit or loss from different levels of sales of products or services

---

SUMMARY OF KEY CONCEPTS   Are you certain that you can state the relationship between break-even point and the profit or loss at a given level of sales? Go to the **online workbook** to take a look at Summary of key concepts 12.8 to test your knowledge.

MULTIPLE CHOICE QUESTIONS   How accurately do you think you can you use break-even analysis to determine profits and losses at a given level of production? Complete Multiple choice questions 12.3 in the **online workbook** to reinforce your learning.

Target profit

Example 12.9 shows how break-even analysis can be used to calculate a target profit.

EXAMPLE 12.9

If Anna sells 1,000 chairs she will make a profit of £32,200 (Chapter 11, Example 11.7). However, she might consider that this profit does not compensate her sufficiently for the time and effort she has put into the business. She might decide that a profit of £40,000 is much more acceptable. How many chairs would she need to sell to achieve this target profit?

Break-even analysis will enable us to calculate the number of sales units required to achieve this target profit. Anna makes a contribution per chair sold of £40. Sales of her first 195 chairs will cover her fixed costs and enable her to break even. Therefore, she will need to sell a further $£40,000 \div £40 = 1,000$ chairs to make a net profit of £40,000. Adding these two figures together means that Anna will have to sell $1,000 + 195 = 1,195$ chairs to make a profit of £40,000.

12

Is this right? Let's check. 1,195 chairs produce a total contribution of 1,195 × £40 = £47,800. Deducting the fixed costs of £7,800 gives a net profit for the year of £47,800 − £7,800 = £40,000, so our calculations are correct.

WHY IS THIS RELEVANT TO ME?   Break-even point and target profit

As a business professional knowledge of break-even analysis will:

- Enable you to calculate a target profit
- Provide you with the technique to calculate the number of units of sales required to achieve a target profit

---

SUMMARY OF KEY CONCEPTS   Can you state the relationship between break-even point and the target profit? Go to the **online workbook** to take a look at Summary of key concepts 12.9 to test your knowledge.

MULTIPLE CHOICE QUESTIONS   Are you sure that you can use break-even analysis to determine a target profit? Complete Multiple choice questions 12.4 in the **online workbook** to reinforce your learning.

Cost-volume-profit analysis

The techniques we have considered so far in this chapter are examples of cost-volume-profit (CVP) analysis, which studies the relationship between costs, both fixed and variable, the level of activity, in terms of sales, and the profit generated. Do entities actually use these techniques in practice? Give me an example 12.1 describes the findings of a CIMA sponsored survey into the use of management accounting practices in small and medium sized entities in the UK.

12

GIVE ME AN EXAMPLE 12.1   Break-even point and cost-volume-profit analysis

Management Accounting Practices of UK Small-Medium-Sized Enterprises published in July 2013 investigated the management accounting techniques and practices used by a sample of small and medium sized enterprises in the UK. All of the small and medium sized enterprises used break-even analysis with managers having a rough idea of their fixed costs and the level of sales revenue required to cover these. However, while all of the medium sized entities surveyed used cost-volume-profit analysis, this technique was only used by a few of the small organisations in the survey: the view was taken that, as small entities are unable to exercise much control over the selling price that they can charge or the variable costs that they pay for inputs, respondents considered that they would gain little benefit from trying to evaluate alternative scenarios based on selling and cost prices.

Source: www.cimaglobal.com

High and low fixed costs

Anna has very low fixed costs and, consequently, a high margin of safety given that she aims to make sales of 1,000 units in a year. However, many businesses have very high fixed costs with very low levels of variable costs. Such businesses will have a very high break-even point and, as a result, a very low margin of safety. Such businesses are thus very vulnerable during a downturn in the economy and, if they do not collapse, they will incur very large losses before the recovery enables them to reach their break-even level of sales. Example 12.10 provides an example of a high fixed costs industry.

EXAMPLE 12.10

Premier League football clubs are an example of businesses with very high fixed costs. Players' wages are a very high proportion of each club's total costs. These wages are fixed and do not vary in line with the number of customers who pay to watch the team each week. Therefore, Premier League clubs need to fill their stadia for every match in order to cover these fixed costs and still make some sort of profit. Thus, their margin of safety is very low. Recent data, however, suggests that high attendances are resulting in Premier League football clubs making a profit despite increased costs, as shown in Give me an example 12.2.

GIVE ME AN EXAMPLE 12.2   19 out of 20 Premier League football clubs made a profit in 2017/2018

In the 2017/2018 season, stadium utilisation rates (attendances at matches) at Premier League football clubs in England reached 96% (compared to 90% in Germany's Bundesliga and 70% in Spain's La Liga). In that season, 19 out of 20 Premier League clubs generated an operating profit. This was down on the previous season when all 20 top flight clubs were profitable at the operating profit level. Aggregate operating profits at the 20 clubs dropped from £1,038m in 2016/2017 to £867m in 2017/2018. Total wages as a percentage of revenue increased from 55% in the previous season to 59% in 2017/2018, accounting for the fall in profits. The one club to record an operating loss, Everton, had a wages: revenue ratio of 85% in 2017/2018.

Source: Annual Review of Football Finance 2019 https://www2.deloitte.com/uk/en/pages/sports-business-group/articles/annual-review-of-football-finance.html

CONTRIBUTION ANALYSIS, RELEVANT COSTS AND DECISION MAKING

Marketing and selling price

Example 12.11 illustrates how contribution and relevant costs analysis can be used in making marketing and selling price decisions.

EXAMPLE 12.11

Anna is currently selling her chairs at £85 each. A friend who is in marketing and who knows the market well has looked at her chairs and has suggested that she should reduce the selling price to £70. Her friend estimates that this reduction in selling price will enable her to increase sales by 50 per cent. As the workshop has spare capacity, there would be no need to take on any additional workshop space and so fixed costs will not increase as a result of this decision. Similarly, the costs of materials and labour will not increase and will remain the same at £20 and £25 per chair respectively. Anna is now trying to decide whether this marketing strategy will increase her profits or not.

To help her make this decision, we can draw up two costing statements as follows to assess the profits produced by the two different strategies, one for the original level of sales of 1,000 chairs at £85 and one for the expected level of sales of 1,500 chairs (1,000 × 150 per cent) at £70.

	Selling 1,000 chairs at £85 each		Selling 1,500 chairs at £70 each	
	£	£	£	£
Sales 1,000 × £85/1,500 × £70		85,000		105,000
Materials 1,000 × £20/1,500 × £20	20,000		30,000	
Direct labour 1,000 × £25/1,500 × £25	25,000		37,500	
Total variable costs		45,000		67,500
Selling price − variable costs = contribution		40,000		37,500
Fixed costs (rent, rates, heating and lighting)		7,800		7,800
Profit for the year		**32,200**		**29,700**

However, if you have been following the argument so far, you will have realised that you could have used contribution analysis to solve this problem much more quickly. A selling price of £70 and a variable cost per chair of £45 gives a revised contribution of £70 − £45 = £25. Selling 1,500 chairs at £70 each would give a total contribution of 1,500 × £25 = £37,500. Fixed costs will not change, so the profit for the year after deducting fixed costs will be £37,500 − £7,800 = £29,700, lower than the current strategy of selling 1,000 chairs at £85.

How many chairs would Anna need to sell to make the new strategy as profitable as the current strategy? Again, contribution analysis will help us to determine the answer to this question. Current contribution from selling 1,000 chairs at £85 each is £40,000. The contribution per unit in the new strategy will be £70 − £45 = £25. To produce a total contribution of £40,000 from selling the chairs at £70 each would thus require sales of £40,000 ÷ £25 = 1,600 chairs. This is a large increase on current sales and Anna might well decide that she is quite happy selling 1,000 chairs at £85 each rather than taking the risk of trying to increase production by 60 per cent for no increase in the profit generated.

WHY IS THIS RELEVANT TO ME? Relevant costs and evaluating the profitability of different marketing strategies

- As a business professional you will be involved in making pricing decisions for products
- Knowledge of relevant costs and contribution will enable you to evaluate different marketing strategies in terms of their relative profitability and to choose the profit maximising pricing strategy

---

GO BACK OVER THIS AGAIN!   Are you convinced that you can use contribution analysis to determine the profit that will arise from different marketing strategies? Have a go at Exercises 12.4 in the **online workbook** to make sure you can use contribution analysis in analysing such decisions.

Special orders

Thus far, we have assumed that selling prices will remain the same for all customers and for all of an organisation's output. In reality, this is rather unrealistic and most organisations will have different selling prices for different customers. When a new customer approaches an entity with a price they would be willing to pay for goods or services, the organisation has to decide whether to accept the new order or not at the customer's offered price. Again, contribution analysis will enable us to determine whether the new order is worth taking and whether it will add to our profit or not. Examples 12.12 and 12.13 illustrate the steps involved in decisions such as these.

EXAMPLE 12.12

Anna receives an enquiry from a charity that wishes to place an order for 50 dining chairs. They have seen examples of Anna's chairs and are very impressed by the quality of the workmanship and the sturdiness of the chairs, but they have been put off by the £85 selling price. They can only afford to pay £50 for each dining chair and have asked Anna whether she would be willing to sell the chairs at this price or not. Anna looks at her cost card for one chair (see Chapter 11, Example 11.6) and discovers that her absorption cost price per chair is £52.80. Her first thoughts are that if she sells the chairs at £50 each, she will be making a loss of £2.80 per chair. The workshop has spare capacity and the order could be accommodated without incurring any additional costs other than the variable costs of producing each chair. This additional order will not affect Anna's current production of 1,000 chairs. As the price offered by the charity is £2.80 less than the absorption cost per chair, Anna is considering refusing the order. Is she right to do so?

Let's see what Anna's total profit will be if she accepts the new order for 50 chairs at £50 each.

	£	£
Current sales: 1,000 chairs at £85 each		85,000
Additional sales: 50 chairs at £50 each		2,500
Total sales		87,500
Variable costs of production		
Materials: 1,050 chairs at £20 each	21,000	
Direct labour: 1,050 chairs at £25 each	26,250	
Total variable costs		47,250
Total contribution		40,250
Fixed costs (rent, rates, lighting and heating)		7,800
Profit for the year		**32,450**

12

Anna's original production level of 1,000 chairs produced a profit of £32,200. Accepting the new order alongside the current production of 1,000 chairs increases profit by £250 to £32,450. Anna expected to make a loss of £2.80 per chair (£50.00 selling price – £52.80 absorption cost per chair) so why is her profit not lower if she accepts the new order?

The answer again lies in the fact that the fixed costs are irrelevant to this decision; fixed costs are fixed for a given period of time and do not change with increased levels of activity. The only relevant costs are those that do change with the increase in the level of activity. These are the variable costs relating to production and the selling price for each additional chair produced. The selling price of £50 is £5 higher than the variable costs of production which are £45. Each additional chair in the new order adds £5 of contribution (and a total additional contribution and profit of £5 × 50 chairs = £250), the selling price less the variable costs, so, as the new order generates more profit for Anna, she should accept.

EXAMPLE 12.13

The decision above was made on the basis that Anna has spare capacity in her workshop and can easily add the new order to her existing level of production. Would your advice have been different if the additional order for 50 dining chairs had meant giving up 50 chairs of current production? Again, let's look at the effects of this decision and consider the relevant costs of making this decision to decide whether accepting the new order would be worthwhile in terms of the overall effect on profit.

If the new order were to be accepted and 950 full price chairs and 50 special price chairs produced, Anna's profit for the year would be as follows.

	£	£
Full price sales: 950 chairs at £85 each		80,750
Discounted sales: 50 chairs at £50 each		2,500
Total sales		83,250
Variable costs of production		
Materials: 1,000 chairs at £20 each	20,000	
Direct labour: 1,000 chairs at £25 each	25,000	
Total variable costs		45,000
Total contribution		38,250
Fixed costs (rent, rates, lighting and heating)		7,800
Profit for the year		**30,450**

As we can see, the decision now would be to reject the new order as profits fall by £1,750 from £32,200 for 1,000 full price chairs to £30,450 for 950 full price chairs and 50 special price chairs. How has this fall occurred? Our 50 special price chairs generate a contribution of £5 each, but to generate this contribution of £5, a contribution of £40 has been given up on each of the 50 full price chairs that this order has replaced. This has led to the fall in profit of £1,750 as follows: (£40 (contribution per chair given up) – £5 (contribution per reduced price chair gained)) × 50 chairs = £1,750. Thus, from a profitability point of view, no additional contribution is generated and so the order should be declined. More profitable production would have to be given up to take in a less profitable order so the charity would be turned away if there were no spare capacity in the business.

WHY IS THIS RELEVANT TO ME?   Relevant costs and special orders

To enable you as a business professional to:

- Use contribution analysis to evaluate the profitability of new orders with a selling price lower than the normal selling price

- Appreciate that new orders should be accepted if they give rise to higher total contribution, add to total profits and make use of spare capacity

- Understand that where more profitable production is given up, orders at a special price should not be accepted

---

SUMMARY OF KEY CONCEPTS   Are you unsure whether to accept a special order or not? Go to the **online workbook** to take a look at Summary of key concepts 12.10 to review the criteria you should apply when evaluating such decisions.

NUMERICAL EXERCISES   Do you think you can use contribution analysis to determine whether a special order should be accepted? Have a go at Numerical exercises 12.1 in the **online workbook** to test your grasp of the principles.

Special orders: additional considerations

Other than additional income and costs and the effects on overall profit, what other considerations should be taken into account when making these special order decisions? First, as we have seen, entities faced with this choice should have spare capacity with which to fulfil orders at a lower selling price. Entities operating at full capacity have no idle resources with which to meet new orders at lower selling prices and so will not accept them. To do so would be to replace production generating higher contribution with production generating lower contribution. As a result, profits after fixed costs will fall.

Second, entities must also consider how easily information about a special price for a new customer could leak into the market. If existing customers found out that dining chairs are being supplied to a charity at £50 when they are paying £85, they are likely to demand a similar discount and this would have a very severe effect on Anna's profitability in the long run. Where information is likely to be available in the wider market, special orders should thus be declined as long-run profits will suffer as all customers will demand special prices.

In order to avoid rejected orders and hence lost profits, organisations can adopt a product differentiation strategy. Rather than producing and selling all their production under one label, producers have a quality label and an economy label to enable them to overcome the problem of all customers demanding the same reduced price. In the same way, supermarkets sell branded products from recognised manufacturers and they also sell goods with the supermarkets' own label at lower prices. Both quality and economy products might have been manufactured in the same production facility, but they are marketed in different ways.

On the positive side, should Anna accept the order from the charity, she might well receive some welcome publicity for her dining chairs as the charity recommends her business by word of mouth. This would amount to free advertising in return for her cutting the selling price for this special order and, in her attempts to expand her business, she might consider this short-term reduction in profits to be a worthwhile sacrifice for the longer-term growth of the business as a whole.

In such special order situations, after taking into account the additional considerations, the short-term decision will always be to accept the new order when this increases contribution and to reject the order when this results in a reduction in contribution.

WHY IS THIS RELEVANT TO ME?   Relevant costs and special orders: additional considerations

To enable you as a business professional to:

- Appreciate that additional profit is not the only consideration in deciding whether to accept a special order or not
- Understand the non-financial, business related considerations involved in making special order decisions
- Discuss and evaluate the non-financial aspects relating to special order decisions

---

Outsourcing (make or buy decisions)

Relevant costs can also be used in making decisions on whether it is more economical to buy goods and services from external parties or whether it will be more profitable to produce or provide these goods and services in-house. Again, when making this decision, only those costs that change with the level of activity will be considered. Think about this in Example 12.14.

EXAMPLE 12.14

Anna is expanding rapidly and has more orders for dining chairs than she can currently fulfil with two employees in her workshop. She has annual orders now for 1,500 dining chairs at a selling price of £85 each. She is considering whether to take on a third employee to help with these additional orders. Taking on this third employee will not increase her fixed costs as she has spare capacity in her workshop to accommodate another two workers and the new employee will be paid at the same rate for producing chairs as the existing employees. Another dining chair producer, Wooden Wonders, has offered to make the additional 500 dining chairs for Anna and to sell them to her at a cost of £49 each. Anna is delighted as this £49 cost is lower than her absorption cost per chair of £52.80, so she is expecting to make an additional profit of £1,900 (500 × (£52.80 −£49.00)) by buying in the chairs. She is ready to accept Wooden Wonders' offer, but, knowing how your advice has proved invaluable in the past, she has asked you whether it will be more profitable to take on the new employee or to contract out the manufacture of the dining chairs to Wooden Wonders.

Let us solve this problem in both a long and short way to show that both approaches give us the same answer and to provide you with a quick method of calculating the alternatives where profit maximisation is the objective. First, let us look at a comparison of Anna's sales, costs and profits if she either makes all of her production in-house or if she makes 1,000 chairs in her workshop and contracts out the additional 500 chairs to Wooden Wonders.

	Making and selling 1,500 chairs at £85 each		Making 1,000 chairs, buying in 500 chairs and selling 1,500 chairs at £85 each	
	£	£	£	£
Sales 1,500 × £85		127,500		127,500
Materials 1,500 × £20/1,000 × £20	30,000		20,000	
Direct labour 1,500 × £25/1,000 × £25	37,500		25,000	
Buying in 500 chairs at £49 each	—		24,500	
Total variable costs		67,500		69,500
Selling price − variable costs = contribution		60,000		58,000
Fixed costs (rent, rates, heating and lighting)		7,800		7,800
Profit for the year		**52,200**		**50,200**

Anna's expectation was of £1,900 more profit, gained by buying in 500 chairs at £49 each alongside the in-house production of 1,000 chairs. However, this option results in a profit for the year that is lower by £2,000 in comparison with making all the chairs in-house. How does this difference arise?

Using marginal costing and contribution analysis, you could have solved this problem much more quickly. Contribution from in-house production is £40 (£85 selling price less the £20 material costs less the £25 labour cost) whereas contribution from the bought in chairs is £36 (£85 selling price less the £49 purchase cost from Wooden Wonders). The difference in contribution per chair of £4 (£40 − £36) multiplied by the 500 chairs that are bought in from Wooden Wonders gives the £2,000 lower profit if the second alternative course of action is chosen.

Fixed costs are again irrelevant in making this decision as these do not change with the level of production: only those costs that change with the decision should be taken into account alongside the contribution that will be gained from each alternative. Anna had forgotten that the fixed costs had already been covered by the production of 1,000 chairs and that the only relevant costs in this decision were the additional variable costs that she would incur. These would either be £45 if she produces the chairs in her own workshop or £49 if she buys them in from an outside supplier. Given that the outside supplier charges more for the chairs than Anna's employees can make them for, Anna will engage the third employee in the workshop as this is the more profitable solution to her production problem.

WHY IS THIS RELEVANT TO ME?   Relevant costs and outsourcing (make or buy) decisions

To enable you as a business professional to:

- Use contribution analysis and relevant costs to determine whether outsourcing decisions are more or less profitable than in-house production

- Appreciate that where profit maximisation is the only consideration, products should be bought in when additional contribution is generated by outsourcing production

SUMMARY OF KEY CONCEPTS　Are you quite sure that you understand the relevant costs in making outsourcing decisions? Go to the **online workbook** to take a look at Summary of key concepts 12.11 to review the criteria you should apply when evaluating such decisions.

NUMERICAL EXERCISES　Are you convinced that you can use contribution analysis and relevant costs to determine whether production should be outsourced or not? Have a go at Numerical exercises 12.2 in the **online workbook** to test your grasp of the principles.

Outsourcing (make or buy decisions): additional considerations

While profit maximisation is a valid aim for many organisations, costs saved and additional profit will be only one of the considerations in an outsourcing (make or buy) situation. There are also various qualitative factors that have to be taken into account when making decisions of this nature as shown in Figure 12.5.

First, we will need to consider the products or services that the external provider will be offering us. Will these products or services meet our quality standards? Will the product or service be of the same quality or at the same level as our own in-house employees provide? Should the level of quality be lower, then further costs will arise. Products that use lower quality outsourced

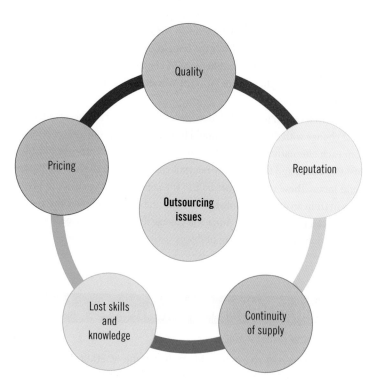

Figure 12.5 Factors to consider in outsourcing (make or buy) decisions

parts will break down more often and require more maintenance visits or refunds to dissatisfied customers. Services such as cleaning might not be carried out to the same exacting standards as the organisation sets for its own staff, leading to an increase in complaints and a loss of customers as they go to other product or service providers who are providing the quality that customers demand.

While the product or service might look cheaper to buy in now, there are longer-term hidden costs that have to be considered. These longer-term costs might be much more damaging for the organisation in terms of loss of reputation and they will often outweigh the benefit of saving a few pounds at the present time. In Anna's case, she would need to determine whether the chairs bought in from Wooden Wonders will be made to the same standards and with the same care and attention as that given by her own employees. Where the chairs are not made to the same standards, Anna will want to ensure that her own reputation for quality chairs is maintained by producing all her chairs in-house.

Second, the price might be cheaper now, but will it always be cheaper? Once our new supplier has captured our custom and we have closed down our own production facility, will the price rise and wipe out all the previous savings? Contracts for the supply of goods and services have to be drawn up very carefully to ensure that a short-term advantage is not suddenly eroded by a change in price.

Organisations will also need to consider their willingness to be reliant upon another entity. In this case, one organisation relies upon the other to maintain continuity of supply and continuity of quality. This may not always happen and disruptions at a supplier very soon affect production and sales to customers. Where components are produced in-house, there is a much greater level of control over production and, hence, sales. Organisations might prefer to maintain their self-reliance rather than handing over responsibility for their parts, sales and production to other businesses.

Similarly, handing over production to another organisation will lead to a loss of skills within the business and an inability to reintroduce production at a later date should the current supply contract prove inadequate. Entities will lack in-house knowledge of how their products work and be unable to provide customers with advice on these products. When an organisation closes down part of its production facility and makes workers redundant, there is a knock-on effect on other workers. Job losses weaken employee morale, job satisfaction and productivity. These knock-on effects also have an effect on profitability as the current workforce becomes demoralised and more concerned about their own job security than completing the work in hand. Anna's two employees might become concerned about the continuity of their employment with Anna if production is outsourced. Concerned employees are distracted employees and they will not be concentrating on the quality of what they are producing but on whether they will still be employed in a year's time.

However, with the appropriate attention to detail and close cooperation and collaboration between the contracting parties, outsourcing can work very well indeed. Give me an example 12.3 shows how Toyota overcomes the potential difficulties of outsourcing through very close relationships with its suppliers.

12

GIVE ME AN EXAMPLE 12.3   Outsourcing at Toyota

The Japanese car company, Toyota, prizes high quality at a low price. However, the company outsources 70% of the components for its cars to suppliers and produces just 30% of the components in its own production facilities. In order to ensure the quality of the products produced by its suppliers, Toyota adopts a policy of strong relationships and collaboration with its suppliers through the Toyota Production System. Toyota's high quality has been achieved as a result of the collaborative advantage it enjoys with its suppliers. Toyota regularly evaluates its suppliers' performance and provides suggestions on how they could improve their operations. However, this is not a one way relationship: the company also invites its suppliers to evaluate Toyota and to provide their suggestions for operational improvement. This continuous improvement approach enables the Toyota Production System to deliver the high quality products demanded by both Toyota and its customers despite the fact that most of its car parts are not manufactured in-house.

Source: www.scribd.com/doc/53016595/Vertical-Integration-or-Outsourcing-Nokia-Ford-Toyota-IBM-Intel-Toshiba-Matsushita#scribd

WHY IS THIS RELEVANT TO ME?   Relevant costs and outsourcing (make or buy) decisions: additional considerations

As a business professional you should:

- Appreciate the additional strategic factors that must be taken into account when an outsourcing decision is being made

- Understand that cost reduction and profit are not the only grounds on which to base make or buy/outsourcing decisions

- Be able to discuss and evaluate non-financial, business related considerations when undertaking make or buy/outsourcing decisions

12

Limiting factor (key factor) analysis

Contribution analysis can also be used in making decisions to maximise short-term profits where organisations are facing a shortage of direct material or direct labour. In this situation, contribution analysis can be used to determine which products generate the highest contribution per unit of material or labour input in order to maximise profits. Those products that generate the highest contribution per unit of limiting factor (key factor) will be produced, while those that produce a lower contribution per unit of limiting factor will be discontinued in the short term. Limiting factor analysis is only relevant where two or more products are produced. If only one product is produced, then there is no decision that has to be made, manufacturers will just produce their one product up to the maximum number that they can based upon the limitations imposed by the shortage of direct materials or direct labour. Let us consider how this would work and the steps that would be undertaken to determine which products produce the highest level of contribution per unit of limiting factor in Example 12.15.

EXAMPLE 12.15

Anna's business has grown and is now a very successful producer of wooden dining chairs, small wooden coffee tables and wooden kitchen cabinets. However, a new government has come to power in the country from which she sources her supplies of wood. This new government has introduced restrictions on the export of timber as new environmental policies are put in place to preserve rather than exploit the local forests. Anna is thus currently facing a shortage of wood from her suppliers because of these restrictions. While she investigates new production methods to enable her to use wood from other sources, Anna is looking to maximise her short-term profit and needs help in deciding which products she should make to achieve this.

The selling price and variable costs for her three products are as follows:

	Dining chairs	Coffee tables	Kitchen cabinets
	£	£	£
Selling price	85.00	50.00	80.00
Materials: wood	(18.00)	(12.60)	(10.80)
Materials: other	(2.00)	(5.40)	(9.20)
Direct labour	(25.00)	(18.00)	(30.00)
Contribution	**40.00**	**14.00**	**30.00**

All three products use the same type of wood at a cost of £1.80 per kg. The new government in the country of her supplier has allocated Anna a maximum of 12,600 kgs of wood for the next three months. Anna has thought about the figures above and is considering diverting all her production into dining chairs as these provide the highest total contribution of the three products and she thinks that producing just chairs will maximise her profit for the period. Is Anna right? If she is not right, which (or which combination) of the three products should she produce to maximise her profits in the next three months?

In problems of this nature you should work through the following three steps.

Step 1: calculate the quantity of limiting factor used in the production of each product

In order to maximise contribution when there is a limiting factor, the first step is to determine the usage that each unit of production makes of that limiting factor. Given that wood costs £1.80 per kg and using the product costing details above, each of the three products uses the following amounts of material:

Dining chairs: material usage: £18.00 ÷ £1.80 = 10 kilograms
Coffee tables: material usage: £12.60 ÷ £1.80 = 7 kilograms
Kitchen cabinets: material usage: £10.80 ÷ £1.80 = 6 kilograms

Step 2: calculate the contribution per unit of limiting factor delivered by each product

The next step is to determine how much contribution each product generates per unit of limiting factor. This calculation divides the total contribution for each product by the number of units of limiting factor used in the production of each product. The products are then given a ranking: the highest contribution per unit of limiting factor is placed first and the lowest contribution per unit of limiting factor comes last.

Using the information about Anna and our calculations in Step 1, the three products generate the following contributions per unit of limiting factor:

	Contribution per unit of limiting factor	Ranking
Dining chairs	£40/10 kg per unit = £4 of contribution per unit of material used	2
Coffee tables	£14/7 kg per unit = £2 of contribution per unit of material used	3
Kitchen cabinets	£30/6 kg per unit = £5 of contribution per unit of material used	1

As the above calculations show, the highest contribution per unit of limiting factor is delivered by kitchen cabinets. These use 6 kg of material in each finished unit and deliver a total contribution of £30 per product. Dining chairs are ranked second with the second highest contribution per unit of limiting factor, while coffee tables are ranked last out of the three products, with a contribution per unit of limiting factor of only £2.

Step 3: calculate the contribution maximising production schedule

If Anna wishes to maximise her contribution and profit, she will now need to determine how much of the limiting factor is available to use and the most profitable products to produce. In Anna's business, if demand for each product is not limited, then she would just produce kitchen cabinets as each kitchen cabinet delivers £5 per unit of limiting factor used. A more likely scenario would be that demand for each product would be limited and so the contribution maximising production schedule will involve producing all of the product delivering the highest contribution per unit of limiting factor first, then producing the product delivering the second highest contribution per unit of limiting factor next and so on until all of the limiting factor is used up.

Anna estimates that demand for each product for the next three months will be as follows:

Dining chairs:	580 units
Coffee tables:	500 units
Kitchen cabinets:	900 units

What will the profit maximising production schedule be? As we have seen, Anna should produce as many kitchen cabinets as she can, as this product gives her the highest contribution per unit of limiting factor. She should then produce as many dining chairs as possible and finally produce coffee tables up to the total amount of material available, the limiting factor. Her production schedule and contribution will look like this:

Product	(a) Kgs of material per unit	(b) Quantity produced	(c) ((a) × (b)) Kgs of material used	(d) (12,600 − (c)) Kgs of material remaining	(e) Contribution per unit	(f) ((b) × (e)) Total contribution
	kg	units	Kg	kg	£	£
Cabinets	6	900	5,400	7,200	30	27,000
Chairs	10	580	5,800	1,400	40	23,200
Tables	7	200	1,400	—	14	2,800
		Total material used (kg)	**12,600**		Total contribution	**53,000**

The above production schedule shows that demand for kitchen cabinets and chairs can be met in full as there is sufficient material to make the 900 kitchen cabinets and 580 chairs that customers require. However, there is only sufficient material remaining to produce 200 of the 500 coffee tables that customers are looking to buy, so production of these will be limited if Anna adopts a profit maximising strategy. This strategy will produce a total contribution of £53,000.

SHOW ME HOW TO DO IT!   Are you sure that you understand how the above allocation of limiting factor was made to the three products? View Video presentation 12.1 in the **online workbook** to see a practical demonstration of how this allocation between the three products is carried out.

What of Anna's intention to produce only chairs? How much contribution would this production scheme have produced? As there are 10 kgs of wood in each chair, 12,600 kgs of wood would have produced 1,260 chairs. The contribution from one chair is £40, so 1,260 chairs would produce a total contribution of 1,260 × £40 = £50,400. This is a good contribution, but it is not as high as the contribution forecast by using the contribution per unit of limiting factor calculated above. Given that demand for dining chairs is only 580 units, Anna will have a lot of chairs in stock at the end of the three months and these unsold chairs, too, will limit her profit for the three-month period.

The above production schedule shows what the maximum profit could be, given the limiting factor and the current maximum demand. However, in reality, it would be very difficult for Anna to stick to this schedule as her customers will be ordering her products in the expectation that she will fulfil all those orders. It would not be easy to refuse an order for coffee tables from a current customer on the grounds that she could not produce those products as they were not profitable enough. Such an excuse would lead to the loss of that customer, who would then source coffee tables from another supplier. In the longer term, the loss of customers could lead to a loss of reputation with all the attendant effects that this would have on sales and profits. Therefore, while the profit maximising schedule is a useful technique to determine what maximum profit could be in times of shortage, considerations other than cost and profit will tend to determine what is produced to meet customers' expectations of the organisation.

12

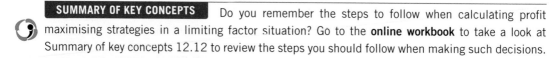

To enable you as a business professional to:

- Use contribution analysis and relevant costs to devise contribution and profit maximising strategies when resources are scarce

- Understand that this technique has certain limitations in the real world

SUMMARY OF KEY CONCEPTS   Do you remember the steps to follow when calculating profit maximising strategies in a limiting factor situation? Go to the **online workbook** to take a look at Summary of key concepts 12.12 to review the steps you should follow when making such decisions.

NUMERICAL EXERCISES   Do you think you could use contribution analysis and relevant costs to determine which products should be produced to maximise contribution when resources are scarce? Have a go at Numerical exercises 12.3 in the **online workbook** to test whether you have fully grasped the techniques involved.

RELEVANT COSTS, MARGINAL COSTING AND DECISION MAKING: ASSUMPTIONS

The decisions discussed and illustrated above all seem to be very straightforward and easy to apply. However, in practice, difficulties will be encountered. This is because of the assumptions upon which marginal costing analysis is based. These assumptions can be summarised as follows:

- First, it has been assumed that the variable costs of a product can be identified by a business with the required level of precision to enable accurate calculations to be made.

- Second, fixed costs for a period are assumed to be completely predictable and unchanging.

- Variable costs are assumed to be linear, that is, variable costs vary directly in line with production. In reality, the purchase of more materials will result in bulk discounts causing the average cost of materials used in each product to fall (see Chapter 11, Assumption 2: variable costs remain the same for all units of production). Similarly, additional units of production might well entail the payment of overtime premiums or bonuses to existing staff, causing the direct labour cost to jump when higher levels of production are reached.

- Prices have been assumed to be stable whereas, in reality, prices of materials change all the time depending on whether there is a shortage or an oversupply of those materials in the market. For example, in a delivery business, the price of fuel to run delivery vans changes on a daily basis.

- In break-even analysis, it is assumed that only one product is produced. Once two or more products are produced, the techniques behind break-even analysis are invalidated by the presence of two sets of variable costs and two contributions, making it impossible to determine the break-even point for one set of fixed costs.

12

Nevertheless, despite these limitations, relevant cost analysis does have some application in practice, as illustrated in Give me an example 12.4.

GIVE ME AN EXAMPLE 12.4   Relevant costing for decisions in practice

The July 2009 CIMA report, *Management accounting tools for today and tomorrow*, surveyed the current and intended usage by business of more than 100 management accounting and related tools based on a questionnaire completed by 439 respondents from across the globe. The findings indicated that relevant costing for decisions was used by small (43 per cent), medium (48 per cent), large (50 per cent) and very large (44 per cent) companies worldwide. However, product/service profitability analysis was the preferred profitability analysis tool across all companies surveyed. Of those intending to introduce relevant costing for decisions in the coming year, only a small percentage of UK respondents aimed to adopt this technique while much higher percentages of respondents across all regions were planning to introduce product/service profitability analysis.

Source: www.cimaglobal.com

WHY IS THIS RELEVANT TO ME?   Relevant costs, marginal costing and decision making: assumptions

To enable you as a business professional to:

- Appreciate the assumptions upon which marginal costing and decision-making analysis are based
- Develop an insight into the limitations posed by these assumptions

---

CHAPTER SUMMARY

You should now have learnt that:

- Contribution per unit = selling price per unit – variable costs per unit
- The concept of opportunity cost is used to determine the benefits lost by using a resource in one application rather than in another
- Fixed costs are not relevant when making short-term decisions as these costs do not vary with changes in the level of activity in the short term
- The only costs relevant in short-term decision making are those that change in line with levels of activity
- The break-even point is calculated by dividing fixed costs by the contribution per unit
- The margin of safety is the number of units of sales above the break-even point: the higher this number, the higher the margin of safety
- Knowledge of the break-even point enables entities to calculate the profit or loss from any given level of sales

12

- Contribution analysis enables entities to determine the effect of different pricing strategies on short-term profits

- Special orders should be accepted when they increase contribution

- Make or buy decisions can be made on the basis of the marginal costing technique

- Calculation of the contribution per unit of resource enables entities to devise profit maximising strategies when resources are limited

- Users of the costing techniques discussed in this chapter have to be aware of the advantages and limitations of marginal costing

QUICK REVISION   Test your knowledge by attempting the activities in the **online workbook**, including flashcards on the key concepts, numerical exercises and Multiple choice questions. You can also try the further self-test questions which are available at www.oup.com/he/scott-i2a2e

END-OF-CHAPTER QUESTIONS

Attempt the questions in the following sections and then look at the solutions which can be found in the **online workbook** to see whether there are areas that you need to revisit.

❯ RECALL AND REVIEW

❯ Question 12.1

Outsourcing decisions are made not only on the basis of quantitative factors. Short-term profit maximisation is not the only concern of managers. Discuss the non-financial factors that are considered in the make or buy decision.

❯ Question 12.2

The strength of marginal costing analysis depends upon its underlying assumptions. Briefly describe the underlying assumptions which must be taken into account when performing marginal costing analysis.

❯❯ DEVELOP YOUR UNDERSTANDING

❯❯ Question 12.3

Define the following terms

(a) Contribution

(b) Relevant costs

(c) Irrelevant costs

(d) Sunk costs

(e) Opportunity cost

(f) Break-even point

(g) Margin of safety

(h) Target profit

≫ Question 12.4

Podcaster University Press is a small publishing company producing a range of introductory text books on a variety of academic subjects for first year undergraduate students. The company's marketing department is considering reducing the selling price of text books to generate further sales and profit. The company's text books currently retail at £30 each. Variable production costs are £10 per book and Podcaster University Press has annual fixed costs of £3,000,000. Current sales of text books are 200,000 per annum. The marketing department has forecast that a £5 reduction in the selling price of each text book will boost annual sales to 275,000 books whereas decreasing the selling price to £21 would increase annual sales to 360,000 books.

Required

Using contribution analysis, evaluate the proposals of the marketing department and advise the company on whether the two proposals would be financially beneficial or not.

≫ Question 12.5

Whittington Limited produces tables. The cost of each table is made up of £37 of materials, £25 of wages and £13 of variable overhead costs. The selling price of each table is £90 and total fixed costs for the year are £120,000.

(a) How many tables should the company make in order to break even?

(b) Calculate the margin of safety given that the current level of sales is 10,000 units.

(c) How many tables would the company need to sell to make a profit of £150,000?

(d) Due to changes in market, the material cost of each table rises to £42 and the selling price falls to £85. Under these new conditions, how many tables would the company need to sell to make a profit of £150,000?

≫ Question 12.6

Marlin plc produces and sells beds. The breakdown of cost per bed is as follows:

	£
Direct material	30
Direct labour	35
Other variable costs	15

The normal level of production is 5,000 units. At the normal level of production annual fixed production overheads and general expenses are budgeted to be £180,000 and £60,000 respectively. The budget for these fixed production overheads and general expenses shows that they are expected to be incurred evenly over the year. In January 2022, the company produced and sold 350 beds at a selling price of £170 each.

Required

Calculate Marlin plc's profit for January 2022 using marginal costing.

>> Question 12.7

Spears Limited produces pipeline equipment. Currently, all parts for pipeline equipment are produced in-house by the company. The board of directors of Spears Limited is considering outsourcing production of pipeline equipment parts to outside producers. The marketing manager of Lakers plc has produced a proposal to produce and sell 8,500 units of part A7635 to Spears Limited. The total cost to buy in 8,500 units of part A7635 from Lakers plc would be £760,000.

The annual costs of producing 8,500 units of part A7635 in-house by Spears Limited is as follows:

	£000
Direct material	250
Direct labour	100
Fixed overhead	450
Total annual costs	800

If the part is bought in from Lakers plc, £280,000 of fixed overhead costs can be avoided and Spears Limited can also save a further £90,000 per annum on production equipment maintenance.

Required

(a) Determine the relevant costs of buying in part A7635.

(b) Advise the directors of Spears Limited on whether they should accept the offer to buy in the part from Lakers plc.

>>> TAKE IT FURTHER

>>> Question 12.8

Big Bucks University is planning to offer a series of professional accounting course classes. The fee payable for this professional accounting course is £400 per student per module. The university has already allocated lecturers currently employed at the university to each class and has determined that lecturers are being paid £60 per hour for the 60 hours required to deliver each module. The lecturers will be paid whether any students are enrolled on each module or not and they can be diverted to other classes if the professional accounting course modules do not run. Books and handouts are provided to each student at a cost of £100 per student per module. The university allocates £1,200 of central overhead costs for the year to the room used in the provision of each module. The university has asked for your help in deciding on the number of students that should be recruited to each module.

Required

(a) State which costs are relevant to the decision as to how many students to recruit to each module.

(b) Determine how many students the university should recruit to each module to ensure that each module breaks even.

(c) What is the margin of safety if the university recruits 25 students to each module?

(d) Calculate the profit or loss the university will make on each module if 14 students or 30 students are recruited to each module.

(e) What will the break-even point be if the university decides to charge £340 per module instead of £400?

>>> Question 12.9

Gurjit Limited produces and sells ink jet printers. The selling price and cost card for each printer are as follows:

	£	£
Selling price		40.00
Direct materials	9.50	
Direct labour	11.25	
Direct expenses	3.65	
Fixed overhead	5.60	
Total cost of one ink jet printer		30.00
Profit per ink jet printer sold		**10.00**

Currently, production and sales are running at 5,000 printers per annum. The fixed overhead allocated to each printer has been based on production and sales of 5,000 units. However, because of the popularity of the product and a strong advertising campaign, the directors of Gurjit Limited are expecting sales to rise to 10,000 units. The directors are currently reviewing the costs and profits made by printers along with their expectations of future profits from the increased sales. One option open to Gurjit Limited is to outsource production of their printers to another company. It is estimated that any outsourcing of production would lead to an increase in total fixed overheads of £40,000 to enable Gurjit Limited to ensure the quality of printers produced outside the company. The directors have a quote from Anand Limited to produce all 10,000 ink jet printers for £200,000. The directors of Gurjit Limited are considering whether to accept this offer and have asked for your advice.

In order to advise the directors of Gurjit Limited on whether to accept the offer from Anand Limited, you should:

(a) Calculate the current profit made at a level of sales and production of 5,000 ink jet printers per annum.

(b) Calculate the profit that will be made if production is retained in-house and sales rise to 10,000 printers per annum.

(c) Calculate the profit that will be made if sales and production rise to 10,000 printers and production of printers is outsourced to Anand Limited.

(d) Advise the directors of Gurjit Limited whether to outsource production to Anand Limited and what additional factors they should take into account in this decision other than costs and profit.

12

Diddle Limited produces ornamental statues for gardens whose selling price, costs and contribution per unit are as follows:

	Clio £	Diana £	Athena £
Selling price	81	58	115
Materials (clay)	(30)	(12)	(42)
Direct labour	(15)	(27)	(30)
Variable overheads	(6)	(3)	(8)
Contribution	30	16	35

The same specialised clay is used in all three statues and costs £6 per kg. The company faces a shortage of this clay, with only 3,000 kg available in the next month. The board of directors is therefore considering which statues should be produced in order to maximise contribution in the coming month. The sales director has suggested that production should concentrate on Athena as this statue has the highest contribution of the three products. Is the sales director right?

Maximum predicted demand for the three products for the coming month is as follows:

Clio: 198 units
Diana: 900 units
Athena: 200 units

12

STANDARD COSTING AND VARIANCE ANALYSIS

13

LEARNING OUTCOMES

Once you have read this chapter and worked through the questions and examples in both this chapter and the online workbook, you should be able to:

- Appreciate that a standard cost is an expected cost rather than an actual cost

- Determine how a standard cost is calculated

- Calculate direct material total, price and usage variances

- Calculate direct labour total, efficiency and rate variances

- Calculate sales volume and price variances

- Calculate fixed overhead expenditure variance

- Calculate variable overhead total, expenditure and efficiency variances

- Discuss the function of standard costing as an accounting control device

- Understand that variances are merely an indication of a problem that requires further management investigation to establish and rectify the causes

INTRODUCTION

In the last two chapters we have looked at the different types of cost that organisations incur in their operations and how the distinction between fixed and variable costs can be used to make decisions that aim to maximise the short-term profitability of an organisation. It is now time to turn to the second function of management accounting: planning. Initially, this involves the use of accounting data to make predictions and forecasts for the future. Once actual outcomes are known, then comparison of actual results with these forecasts is used as a means to control an organisation's operations. The next chapter will consider budgeting in much greater detail and look at how the use of budgets and the comparison of outcomes with expectations enable an entity to control its operations, to enhance positive trends and to take action to correct problems as they arise. In this chapter we will consider the use of the related technique of standard costing and how the analysis of divergences from the standard can be used to identify problems requiring management's attention.

WHAT IS STANDARD COSTING?

As we saw in Chapter 11, the product costing process takes up a lot of time as information is gathered about the inputs of direct material, direct labour, direct expenses and indirect production overheads and as costs are allocated to products and services. This information is then used to determine selling prices for products so that a profit is made. However, prices of inputs change rapidly. The cost of materials rises and falls as users demand more or less of a particular raw material, wages rise each year, electricity and gas prices go up and down as the weather warms or cools. To change all these prices on a daily or weekly basis would be time consuming in the extreme and the task would eventually overwhelm the individuals performing this role. What is needed is an efficient, predictive tool that provides a reasonably accurate estimate of what the cost of a product or service should be over a given period of time. Variations from this estimate can then be analysed to determine whether the estimate needs revising or not. This reasonably accurate estimate can be provided by standard costing.

A standard cost card will include all the direct materials, direct labour, direct expenses, variable overheads and an allocation of fixed overheads that go into a product or service. These standard costs are the expected costs of that product and the standard cost card will also include the expected selling price for each product, along with the standard profit. Standard costs are derived from numerous observations of an activity over time and represent an expectation of costs incurred by and income generated from mass produced products and services. As the number of observations increases, so the standard is revised and the accuracy of the estimate becomes much closer to the actual cost of each product.

Standard costs recognise that goods are made up of a fixed set of inputs, whether materials, labour or overheads. These inputs are measured and costed and then summarised to present the total costs of producing one item of output. As an example, consider this book. Variable costs will include the paper, the ink, the covers, the binding, the power to drive the printing machinery and the handling of each book as it comes off the press. Fixed costs to be allocated across each print run will include typesetting, editing, development, website construction and maintenance, advertising and marketing. All these costs can be readily determined as a result of Oxford University Press's vast experience of printing books and the staff's detailed knowledge of the costs of book production. All the costs involved can be summarised to calculate the cost of one book and this is then the standard cost of that book. Management will set an expected selling price based on the costs incurred and the anticipated market for the book and this becomes the standard selling price.

WHY IS THIS RELEVANT TO ME?   Standard costing

To provide you as a business professional with:

- A basic understanding of what standard costing involves and how it works
- A predictive accounting tool you can use in the future to forecast the costs and profits of mass produced products and services

---

GO BACK OVER THIS AGAIN!   Confident you can say what standard costing is? Go to the **online workbook** and complete Exercises 13.1 to make sure you understand the aims and objectives of standard costing.

VARIANCE ANALYSIS

Standard costs just represent expectations, the expected costs and revenues from each product produced and sold. What happens when the reality turns out to be different from the expectation? When the actual costs and revenues are known, then a comparison of the standard expected results and the actual results is undertaken. The differences between the standard costs and revenues and the actual figures are known as variances. These variances are calculated and then used to explain the difference between anticipated and actual outcomes. In the case of book production, the cost of materials might be more than expected as a shortage of the expected quality of paper might have resulted in more expensive paper being used. Ink prices might have been higher or lower than forecast, a rise or fall in power costs might have resulted in changes to the anticipated printing cost, the selling price might have been set higher to cover these additional costs and so on. Explanations for variances will be sought as a means of controlling operations. Where actual costs are significantly different from the standard, the standard can be updated to produce more accurate information in the future.

What use do organisations across the world make of variance analysis? Give me an example 13.1 describes the findings of a 2009 CIMA survey.

13

GIVE ME AN EXAMPLE 13.1   Variance analysis

The July 2009 CIMA report, *Management accounting tools for today and tomorrow*, surveyed the current and intended usage by business of more than 100 management accounting and related tools based on a questionnaire completed by 439 respondents from across the globe. The fourth most commonly used technique in practice was variance analysis. When used as a costing tool, variance analysis was undertaken by 73% of respondents, the most popular costing tool in use. Over 60% of small companies in the survey used variance analysis while more than 80% of large companies employed this technique.

Source: www.cimaglobal.com

WHY IS THIS RELEVANT TO ME?   Variance analysis

To enable you as a business professional to:

- Understand how expected and actual costs and revenues are compared to explain deviations from forecast performance

- Appreciate that variances between expected and actual costs and revenues can lead to improvements in standards

- Appreciate the roles that standard costing and variance analysis perform in the control of business operations

GO BACK OVER THIS AGAIN!   How clearly have you understood what variance analysis involves? Go to the **online workbook** and complete Exercises 13.2 to make sure you understand how variance analysis works and what it aims to achieve.

13

DIFFERENT STANDARDS

The different types of standards are shown in Figure 13.1. Setting standards requires thought about expectations and what you want to achieve through the use of standards. You might hope that your favourite sports team will win all its matches, win all the trophies for which they are competing and play perfectly in every match. This would be an ideal standard, the best that can be achieved. However, ideal standards are unrealistic and unachievable as they would only ever be attained in a perfect world. In the real world, your team will lose some matches and draw others, play poorly yet win and play well but still lose. Therefore, a degree of realism is required in setting standards. Attainable standards are those standards that can be achieved with effort and you might set your team the attainable standard of winning one trophy during the coming season: it

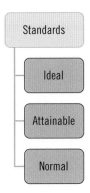

Figure 13.1 The hierarchy of different standards

can be done, but winning that trophy will require focus, concentration and special effort. Alternatively, you might just set a normal standard, which is what a business usually achieves. Your team might finish in the middle of the table each year, avoiding relegation yet not playing particularly well or winning any trophies and you might settle for this as this is what is normally achieved. Anything beyond this is a bonus!

In the same way, businesses will set standards based on what they consider to be achievable under normal circumstances, with anything beyond this basic level of achievement being seen as a bonus for the business. Alternatively, directors can set performance targets to encourage staff to put in more effort to generate higher levels of productivity. Staff will be incentivised with the prospect of additional rewards to work towards these attainable standards.

WHY IS THIS RELEVANT TO ME?   Different standards

To enable you as a business professional to appreciate the different performance standards that can be set by businesses and what these different performance standards involve.

GO BACK OVER THIS AGAIN!   Are you sure you can summarise what ideal, attainable and normal standards are? Go to the **online workbook** and complete Exercises 13.3 to make sure you understand the different standards of performance that can be set.

SETTING THE STANDARD

We have already considered Anna's cost card, the revenue and costs for one dining chair. This is reproduced on the next page. This cost card can be seen as an example of a standard cost card, the expected costs of each input into each chair along with the revenue that each chair is expected to generate.

Standard cost card: wooden dining chair	£
Variable costs	
Wood	18.00
Glue	0.60
Screws	1.00
Sandpaper	0.40
Direct labour	25.00
Prime cost (total variable cost)	45.00
Rent	6.00
Business rates	1.00
Heating and lighting	0.80
Total production cost of one chair	52.80
Standard selling price	85.00
Standard profit per dining chair	**32.20**

The standard cost card shows the direct inputs into a product, together with an allocation of fixed overhead to each product. Anna will use this standard cost card to measure actual outcomes and to analyse variances from her expectations. These variances could be positive (favourable variances) resulting in lower costs or more revenue than expected, or negative (unfavourable variances) arising from higher costs or lower revenue than anticipated. Unfavourable variances are sometimes called adverse variances but we will stick with the term unfavourable in this book.

To illustrate how standard costing and variance analysis work in practice, let us consider a comprehensive example (Example 13.1).

13

EXAMPLE 13.1

Anna has completed her first year of dining chair production. Things have gone well and her workshop has made and sold 1,100 chairs over the first 12 months of operations. While happy with her success, Anna is puzzled. She has used her original standard cost card to produce a forecast of the profit she should have made based on production and sales of 1,100 chairs. This calculation is shown in Illustration 13.1. However, her actual results are somewhat different from this forecast and these actual results are shown in Illustration 13.2.

Illustration 13.1 Anna: expected sales income, costs and profit for the first year of trading based on the standard cost card for sales and production of 1,100 dining chairs

	£	£
Sales 1,100 chairs at £85		93,500
Direct materials: wood 1,100 chairs at £18	19,800	
Direct materials: other 1,100 chairs at £2	2,200	
Direct labour 1,100 chairs at £25	27,500	
Total variable costs		49,500
Total contribution (sales – variable costs)		44,000
Fixed costs		
Rent	6,000	
Rates	1,000	
Heating and lighting	800	
Total fixed costs		7,800
Expected profit for the year		**36,200**

Illustration 13.2 Anna: actual sales income, costs and profit for the first year of trading from the production and sale of 1,100 dining chairs

	£	£
Sales		92,400
Direct materials: wood	19,720	
Direct materials: other	2,200	
Direct labour	28,644	
Total variable costs		50,564
Total contribution (sales – variable costs)		41,836
Fixed costs		
Rent	6,000	
Rates	1,000	
Heating and lighting	600	
Total fixed costs		7,600
Actual profit for the year		**34,236**

Given that her calculations show that she should have made a profit of £36,200 from the sale of 1,100 dining chairs, Anna is disappointed that her actual sales income and costs statement above shows a profit of only £34,236, a difference of £1,964. She has asked you to investigate how this difference has arisen.

A comparison of the two statements will enable us to determine where the differences between expected and actual profit lie. A comparison table can be drawn up as shown in Illustration 13.3. What is this comparison telling us? We can summarise our conclusions as follows:

13

Illustration 13.3 Anna: comparison of actual and expected sales, expenses and profit for the first year of trading from the production and sale of 1,100 dining chairs

	Actual for 1,100 chairs £	Expected for 1,100 chairs £	Total variance £
Sales	92,400	93,500	(1,100)
Less:			
Direct materials: wood	19,720	19,800	80
Direct materials: other	2,200	2,200	—
Direct labour	28,644	27,500	(1,144)
Rent	6,000	6,000	—
Rates	1,000	1,000	—
Heating and lighting	600	800	200
Profit for the year	**34,236**	**36,200**	**(1,964)**

- Sales revenue from the sale of the 1,100 chairs is £1,100 lower than it should have been had Anna sold all her output at £85 per chair.

- The wood for chairs cost £80 less than it should have done based on a wood cost per chair of £18.

- Direct labour cost Anna £1,144 more than it should have done for the production of 1,100 chairs.

- Heating and lighting cost £200 less than expected.

- All other expenses (direct materials: other, rent and rates) cost exactly what Anna had expected them to.

- The positive reductions in spending on wood and heat and light are deducted from the lower sales income and the overspend on direct labour to give the net difference between the two profits of £1,964.

13

WHY IS THIS RELEVANT TO ME?   Expected costs v. actual costs and calculation of total variances

As a business professional you will be expected to understand:

- How standard costs can be used to calculate a statement of expected revenue and costs at any given level of production and sales

- How to compare actual revenue and costs with expected revenue and costs

- How to produce a variance statement comparing actual and expected outcomes

- That each total variance is the difference between the expected revenue and costs of actual production and sales and the actual revenue and costs of actual production and sales

Are you completely confident that you could use a standard cost card to:

- Produce a statement of expected costs and revenue
- Compare this to a statement of actual costs and revenue and
- Calculate total variances from this comparison?

Go to the **online workbook** and attempt Numerical exercises 13.1 to make sure you can undertake these tasks.

You explain these differences to Anna, but she is still not satisfied. Why has sales revenue fallen from what she expected it to be and why has so much more been spent on labour than she expected? You ask Anna for her accounting records for the year in order to investigate these differences. Once you have undertaken your investigations, you make the following discoveries:

- The average selling price for each dining chair was not £85, but £84.
- The wood was bought in at a cost of £1.70 per kg instead of the expected cost of £1.80 per kg (Chapter 12, Example 12.15).
- The expected usage of wood for 1,100 chairs should have been 10 kg per chair (Chapter 12, Example 12.15 Step 2) × 1,100 chairs = 11,000 kg whereas actual usage was 11,600 kg.
- Anna expected each chair to take two hours to make and she expected to pay her employees £25 for each chair produced. In fact, she decided to pay her employees an hourly rate of £12.40 instead of a payment for each chair produced.
- The 1,100 chairs should have taken 2,200 hours to produce (1,100 × 2), but her wages records show that her two employees were paid for a total of 2,310 hours.
- Because of the autumn and winter weather being milder than anticipated, the heating costs came in at £200 lower than expected.

How can this information be used to explain the differences between the actual results and the expected results based on the increased levels of production and sales?

DIRECT MATERIAL PRICE AND USAGE VARIANCES

We saw in Illustration 13.3 that the wood for 1,100 chairs cost £19,720 against an expected cost of £19,800 (1,100 × £18 per chair in Anna's original estimates). This gave a total variance of £80. This is a favourable variance as Anna spent £80 less than expected on the wood used in production of her dining chairs. However, our additional investigations revealed two facts relating to the wood used in the chairs. The purchase price of wood was £1.70 per kg instead of the expected £1.80 and 11,600 kg of wood were used instead of the expected 11,000 kg. So the material was cheaper than expected but the usage was more than expected. Do these two differences explain the total variance of £80?

13

Figure 13.2 Direct material variances

Standard costing calls these two differences the direct material price variance and the direct material usage variance (Figure 13.2). The price variance shows how much of the difference is due to a higher or lower cost for direct material while the usage variance shows how much of the difference is due to the quantity of material used varying from what the standard says should have been used.

The direct material price variance is calculated in the following way:

	£
11,600 kg of wood should have cost (11,600 × £1.80)	20,880
11,600 kg of material actually cost	19,720
Direct material price variance	**1,160**

Does this make sense? The standard cost for wood is £1.80 per kg, whereas Anna paid £1.70 per kg, a difference of £0.10 per kg. Anna's employees used 11,600 kg of wood, so 11,600 × £0.10 = £1,160, the same answer as above.

Is this variance favourable or unfavourable? To answer this question you should ask whether the cost is higher or lower than the standard cost says it should be. In this case, the actual quantity of material used cost less than the standard cost says it should have done, so this is a favourable variance. Anna has spent less on wood for her chairs than the standard says she should have done.

However, while Anna has spent less on wood for her chairs than her standard says she should have spent, her craftsmen have used more material than anticipated in the standard. Each chair should use 10 kg of wood and so 1,100 chairs should have used 11,000 kg in total. As actual usage was 11,600 kg, Anna's employees have used 600 kg more than expected. The usage variance is calculated as follows:

	Kg
1,100 chairs should have used 10 kg of wood × 1,100 chairs	11,000
1,100 chairs actually used	11,600
Direct material usage variance in kg	(600)

	£
Direct material usage variance in kg × standard price per kg (600) × £1.80	(1,080)

Again, we can ask whether this variance is favourable or unfavourable. More material has been used than the standard says should have been used, so this variance is unfavourable. Anna's craftsmen have used more wood than they should have done and this has meant that her profit has been reduced as a result of this overusage.

DIRECT MATERIAL TOTAL VARIANCE

How do the price and usage variances relate to the total variance that we calculated earlier? This total variance was a favourable variance of £80 (£19,720 actual cost of the wood compared to £19,800 expected cost of wood for 1,100 chairs). Summarising our two variances above will give us this £80 total variance thus:

	£	Favourable/(Unfavourable)
Direct material price variance	1,160	Favourable
Direct material usage variance	(1,080)	(Unfavourable)
Direct material total variance	**80**	Favourable

WHY IS THIS RELEVANT TO ME?   Direct material price variance, direct material usage variance and direct material total variance

To enable you as a business professional to:

- Appreciate that variations in both the price and the usage of material should be used to explain the total direct material variance
- Calculate the direct material price variance and direct material usage variance
- Demonstrate that the total direct material variance is the sum of the direct material price variance and the direct material usage variance

13

SUMMARY OF KEY CONCEPTS   Are you confident you can state the formulae for the direct material total variance and the two sub-variances, direct material price variance and direct material usage variance? Go to the **online workbook** to revise these variances with Summary of key concepts 13.1.

MULTIPLE CHOICE QUESTIONS   Do you think that you could calculate the direct material variance and the sub-variances, direct material price variance and direct material usage variance? Go to the **online workbook** and have a go at Multiple choice questions 13.1 to test out your ability to calculate these figures.

DIRECT MATERIAL VARIANCES: INFORMATION AND CONTROL

We have calculated our variances, but what do they tell Anna and what use can she make of them? Our investigations and calculations show that cheaper material has been purchased and that this has saved Anna money on the material acquired. However, this money seems to have been saved at a cost. While the material is cheaper, more has been used than should have been and this suggests that the wood may not have been of the expected quality. Lower quality materials tend to lead to more wastage as they require more work to shape and fit them into the final product. This additional working has resulted in a higher usage as material was lost in the production process. Anna now needs to conduct further investigations to determine whether this lower cost material really is of lower quality. If so, she should in future demand only material of the requisite quality to minimise wastage and to guarantee the quality of the finished product.

Alternatively, Anna's employees might just have been careless in the way they handled the wood. More careful handling and more thoughtful workmanship might have resulted in less wastage and bigger savings from using this cheaper material. If this is the case, then her workers may need additional advice or training on how to make the best use of the material they are provided with so that wastage is reduced and profits increased. Price and usage variances thus point the way towards the areas that require further investigation to determine the reasons behind these variances and the means to resolve the problems arising.

WHY IS THIS RELEVANT TO ME?   Direct material variances: information and control

To enable you as a business professional to appreciate that:

- Unfavourable material variances are only indicators of problems that require management investigation, intervention and action to correct them

- Management must consider possible reasons for the variances that have arisen, along with potential solutions to ensure that unfavourable material variances do not persist

---

GO BACK OVER THIS AGAIN!   How confident are you that you can identify reasons for changes in the direct material price and usage variances? Go to the **online workbook** and complete Exercises 13.4 to test your skill in this area.

DIRECT LABOUR RATE AND EFFICIENCY VARIANCES

Our summary table of expected and actual costs in Illustration 13.3 shows that direct labour cost £28,644 against an expected cost to produce 1,100 chairs of £27,500. This is an unfavourable variance as Anna has incurred £1,144 more in direct labour costs than she expected to. Let's look first at the additional information uncovered by our investigations. Anna's employees were paid

Figure 13.3 Direct labour variances

not for the dining chairs that they produced but at a fixed rate per hour. This hourly rate was £12.40 instead of the expected £12.50 and the actual hours used in producing 1,100 chairs were 2,310 against an expected 2,200. Again, can these two differences explain the total variance of £1,144?

Just as for direct material, we can also calculate sub-variances for direct labour (Figure 13.3). The direct labour rate variance performs the same function as the direct material price variance by taking into account the unit cost of each hour paid for production. The direct labour efficiency variance looks at the time taken to make the actual goods and compares this with the hours that were expected to be used for that level of production. Where the hours taken are lower than they should have been, workers have been more efficient in producing goods. However, where more hours have been used to make the production than were expected, this will mean that labour has been less efficient than expected. In just the same way, the standard time to work through this chapter might be set at 10 hours, but different students will have very different experiences of how long studying this chapter will take them!

Direct labour rate variance is calculated in the following way:

	£
2,310 labour hours should have cost (2,310 × £12.50)	28,875
2,310 labour hours actually cost	28,644
Direct labour rate variance	**231**

Direct labour cost is lower than the standard cost says it should be for the hours actually worked, so this variance is favourable. This would be expected as the actual rate at which labour is paid is £12.40 per hour compared to the standard rate of £12.50 per hour. Thus you could have calculated this variance by taking the difference between the two hourly rates of £0.10 (£12.50 – £12.40) and multiplied this by 2,310 hours to give you the same answer of £231 less than 2,310 standard hours should have cost.

Again, while Anna has spent less on labour for her chairs than her standard says she should have done, her craftsmen have also used more hours than they should have spent in making the actual production. Each chair should use two hours of direct labour and so 1,100 chairs should have used 2,200 labour hours. As actual labour hours were 2,310, Anna's employees have taken 110 hours more than expected to make the actual production. The direct labour efficiency variance is calculated as follows:

	Hours
1,100 chairs should have used 1,100 × 2 hours	2,200
1,100 chairs actually used	2,310
Direct labour efficiency variance in hours	(110)
	£
Direct labour efficiency variance in hours × standard rate/hour (110) × £12.50	(1,375)

This variance is unfavourable as more labour hours have been used than the standard says should have been used in the production of 1,100 chairs. This means that Anna has incurred more cost and made a lower profit as a result of this increased usage and lower than expected efficiency of the workforce.

DIRECT LABOUR TOTAL VARIANCE

The sum of the direct labour rate and direct labour efficiency variances should equal the total variance that we calculated in Illustration 13.3. This total variance was £1,144 (£28,644 actual cost of direct labour compared to a £27,500 expected direct labour cost for 1,100 chairs). Summarising our two variances above will give us this £1,144 total variance thus:

	£	Favourable/Unfavourable
Direct labour rate variance	231	Favourable
Direct labour efficiency variance	(1,375)	(Unfavourable)
Direct labour total variance	**(1,144)**	(Unfavourable)

WHY IS THIS RELEVANT TO ME?   Direct labour rate variance, direct labour efficiency variance and direct labour total variance

To enable you as a business professional to:

- Appreciate that variations in both the rate at which labour is paid and the speed at which employees work should be used to explain the total direct labour variance

- Calculate the direct labour rate variance and the direct labour efficiency variance

- Realise that the total direct labour variance is the sum of the direct labour rate variance and the direct labour efficiency variance

---

SUMMARY OF KEY CONCEPTS   Are you sure you know how to calculate the direct labour total variance and its associated sub-variances, direct labour rate variance and direct labour efficiency variance? Go to the **online workbook** to check your understanding of how these variances are calculated with Summary of key concepts 13.2.

MULTIPLE CHOICE QUESTIONS   Are you convinced that you can calculate the direct labour total variance and its associated sub-variances, direct labour rate variance and direct labour efficiency variance? Go to the **online workbook** and attempt Multiple choice questions 13.2 to check your ability to calculate these figures.

DIRECT LABOUR VARIANCES: INFORMATION AND CONTROL

Again, merely calculating the variances is not enough: these variances have to be investigated and the causes, once identified, used to improve operations with a view to improving efficiency and making additional profit.

It seems that Anna can employ craftsmen at a slightly lower hourly rate than she had expected. This is helpful as a small amount shaved off the labour rate means additional profit for the business. Unfortunately, her craftsmen have taken rather longer than they should have done to make the 1,100 chairs over the course of the year. Why might this be? Under our analysis of the direct material variance (this chapter, Direct material variances: information and control), we suggested that the wood used in the chairs might be of lower quality and hence require more working and shaping before it could be incorporated into the finished chairs. If this were the case, then the additional hours taken in the production of the chairs could be accounted for by this additional working and shaping. Anna should therefore discuss this issue with her employees to find out why these additional hours were worked and whether there is a problem with the wood that is being used. A lower price for direct materials is always welcome, but if this lower price is causing additional costs to be incurred elsewhere in the production cycle, then higher quality materials at a higher price should be acquired. In this way, the higher quality materials will pay for themselves as lower labour costs will be incurred in making goods and more profit will be generated. Alternatively, Anna's craftsmen might just have worked more slowly to increase the number of hours they worked, thereby increasing their pay. To avoid this problem, Anna needs to think about incentivising her staff to work to the standard while still producing goods of the expected quality.

WHY IS THIS RELEVANT TO ME?   Direct labour variances: information and control

As a business professional you should understand:

- That direct labour rate and efficiency variances are only indicators of problems that require management investigation, intervention and action
- How to suggest possible reasons for the labour variances that have arisen, along with potential solutions to ensure that unfavourable variances do not persist

GO BACK OVER THIS AGAIN!   How easily do you think you can identify reasons for changes in the direct labour rate and efficiency variances? Go to the **online workbook** and complete Exercises 13.5 to test your skill in this area.

13

VARIABLE OVERHEAD VARIANCES

Anna does not incur any variable overheads in her business. If she did incur such overheads, the variances between standard and actual would be calculated in exactly the same way as for direct material and direct labour. First, there would be the variable overhead total variance, the total cost of variable overheads for actual production compared to the standard cost of variable overheads for actual production. This total variance would then be split down into the variable overhead expenditure variance and the variable overhead efficiency variance. To avoid disrupting the flow of our comparison and analysis of Anna's actual and expected profit, further discussion and an example of variable overhead variances is given at the end of this chapter (this chapter, Appendix: variable overhead variances).

FIXED OVERHEAD EXPENDITURE VARIANCE

Fixed overheads are, of course, fixed. Therefore, the only relevant consideration in analysing this variance is the expected expenditure compared to the actual expenditure (Figure 13.4). In Anna's case, she expected her fixed costs to be £7,800 (rent: £6,000, rates: £1,000, heating and lighting: £800) whereas the actual outcome was £7,600 (rent: £6,000, rates: £1,000, heating and lighting: £600). As we discovered from our investigations into Anna's accounting records, £200 less was spent on heating and lighting during the year as a result of milder than expected winter weather. This £200 fixed overhead expenditure variance is favourable as less was spent on fixed costs than was expected.

Figure 13.4 Fixed overhead expenditure variance

SUMMARY OF KEY CONCEPTS Do you think you can calculate the fixed overhead expenditure variance? Go to the **online workbook** to check your understanding of how this variance is calculated with Summary of key concepts 13.4.

FIXED OVERHEAD EXPENDITURE VARIANCE: INFORMATION AND CONTROL

As fixed overheads are fixed, businesses usually experience only small variations between expected and actual fixed costs. Organisations will not usually investigate fixed overhead expenditure variances in depth. There is little that can be done to reduce fixed costs that are mostly imposed from outside the business. On the other hand, since materials, labour and variable overheads are driven directly by internal business activity, time will be spent on investigating these variances as much more can be done to reduce unfavourable variances arising from operations under the direct control of management.

WHY IS THIS RELEVANT TO ME?   Fixed overhead expenditure variance

As a business professional you should appreciate that:

- Fixed overhead expenditure variance is the difference between total forecast expenditure on fixed overheads and actual fixed overhead expenditure
- Fixed overheads are largely outside the control of businesses
- Management time and effort will therefore focus upon investigating material, labour and variable overhead variances as businesses can take action to control and eliminate or exploit these variances

---

SALES VARIANCES

Our final variances relate to income, the sales variances.

Sales price variance

The first of these is the sales price variance (Figure 13.5). Anna's expectation was that she would sell her dining chairs for £85 each. However, further investigation revealed that her average selling price was only £84, a reduction of £1 per chair sold. Anna sold 1,100 chairs, so her sales price variance was 1,100 × £1 = £1,100. This is unfavourable as she received less income per chair than budgeted.

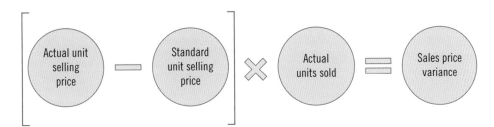

Figure 13.5 Sales price variance

Sales volume variance

We have now explained all the variances between Anna's expected and actual profit from the sale of 1,100 chairs as shown in Illustration 13.3, but there is one more variance we need to consider. Anna's original expectation was that she would sell 1,000 chairs and make a profit of £32,200. Her actual results show that she sold 1,100 chairs and made a profit of £34,236. The additional sales of 100 chairs give rise to another variance, the sales volume variance (Figure 13.6). This variance takes the additional standard contribution from each sale and multiplies this by the additional number of units sold to reflect the increased contribution arising from higher sales. This is logical as each additional sale will increase revenue by the selling price of one unit, but will also increase variable costs by the standard cost of direct material, direct labour and variable overhead for each additional unit of production and sales. Therefore, the contribution, the selling price less the variable costs, is used in this calculation. This variance is calculated as follows:

	Units
Actual units sold	1,100
Budgeted sales in units	1,000
Sales volume variance	100

	£
Sales volume variance at standard contribution 100 × £40	**4,000**

Is this variance favourable or unfavourable? As more sales have been made and more contribution earned, this is a favourable variance.

Anna will want to know why she is selling more chairs than budgeted and so she will investigate this increase with a view to selling even more. Similarly, she will also be keen to find out why her selling price is lower than budgeted and what factors in the market are pushing her selling price down.

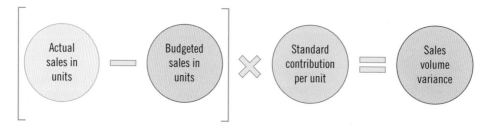

Figure 13.6 Sales volume variance

WHY IS THIS RELEVANT TO ME?   Sales price variance and sales volume variance

To enable you as a business professional to:

- Appreciate that variations in the selling price and in the volume of sales will have an impact upon the actual profit made compared to the expected profit
- Calculate the sales price variance and sales volume variance

SUMMARY OF KEY CONCEPTS Are you sure you know how to calculate the sales price variance and the sales volume variance? Go to the **online workbook** to check your understanding of how these variances are calculated with Summary of key concepts 13.5.

MULTIPLE CHOICE QUESTIONS Are you confident that you can calculate the sales price variance and the sales volume variance? Go to the **online workbook** and attempt Multiple choice questions 13.3 to check your ability to calculate these figures.

VARIANCES: SUMMARY

We can now summarise all our variances and reconcile Anna's forecast to her actual profit as follows. Anna's original expectation was that she would sell 1,000 dining chairs at £85 each and generate a profit of £32,200 so our starting point is this original expected profit.

	Unfavourable £	Favourable £	Profit £
Expected profit from selling 1,000 chairs at £85			32,200
Sales price variance	(1,100)		
Sales volume variance		4,000	
Direct material price variance		1,160	
Direct material usage variance	(1,080)		
Direct labour rate variance		231	
Direct labour efficiency variance	(1,375)		
Fixed overhead expenditure variance		200	
Total variances	(3,555)	5,591	
Add: favourable variances			5,591
Deduct: unfavourable variances			(3,555)
Actual profit for the year			**34,236**

WHY IS THIS RELEVANT TO ME? Summary of variances and reconciliation of expected to actual profit

To enable you as a business professional to:

* Present all your variances in summary form to explain the difference between expected and actual profit

NUMERICAL EXERCISES How confident do you feel handling extensive variance analysis questions? Go to the **online workbook** and have a go at Numerical exercises 13.2 to see how effectively you have absorbed the lessons of this chapter and how well you understand standard costing and variance analysis.

13

SHOW ME HOW TO DO IT   This chapter has involved a lot of tricky calculations and ideas. View Video presentation 13.1 in the **online workbook** to reinforce your knowledge of how standard costing and variance analysis is undertaken.

STANDARD COSTING: LIMITATIONS

Standard costing is a useful technique in comparing expected with actual financial performance. Where variances arise, these can be investigated to determine their causes and to identify ways in which unfavourable variances can be reduced and favourable variances maintained or enhanced. While setting standards encourages improvement and change for the better over time, standard costing also suffers from the following limitations:

- You will agree, I am sure, that this is a very complicated system and that this complexity can be discouraging when you first come across standard costing and variance analysis.

- It is also a time consuming system: a great deal of time will be needed to gather information from which to set the standards, to collect data from which to monitor standards against actual performance and to produce and evaluate variances.

- Time will also be needed to update standards for changes in costs owing to rising or falling material prices, wage costs, changes in overheads and selling prices.

- The information produced by variance analysis can be extensive and management may be overwhelmed by the volume of data presented to them.

- Standard costing systems tend to be rigid and inflexible: lack of flexibility should be avoided in the modern, ever changing business environment.

- However, modern computer systems should be able to assist management with the production of standard costs and variance analysis and in highlighting those variances that indicate that operations are out of control rather than within set tolerance limits. Profitability improvement depends upon careful cost control and such cost control is one of the key functions of business managers.

Given these limitations, it is probably not surprising to find that small and medium sized companies make no use of standard costing variance analysis. Give me an example 13.2 describes this failure to adopt this approach.

GIVE ME AN EXAMPLE 13.2   Adoption of standard costing variance analysis by small and medium sized companies in the UK

Management Accounting Practices of UK Small-Medium-Sized Enterprises published in July 2013 investigated the management accounting techniques and practices used by small and medium sized enterprises. While all the organisations surveyed undertook product costing, break-even analysis and working capital measures, none of the respondents engaged in standard cost variance analysis. However, the researchers considered that the failure to use this technique was appropriate for small and medium sized enterprises on cost-benefit grounds as the costs of obtaining the information were substantial while the benefits gained were very limited.

Source: www.cimaglobal.com

APPENDIX: VARIABLE OVERHEAD VARIANCES

Variable overheads are absorbed into products on the basis of the number of hours of activity incurred to produce one unit of production. The standard cost for variable overheads will estimate the number of hours products take to produce on either a labour or machine hour basis (see Chapter 11, Absorption costing: overhead allocation, to refresh your memory on how absorption cost bases work) and then allocate the variable overhead to each product on the basis of the standard number of hours required to produce one unit multiplied by the standard variable overhead cost per hour.

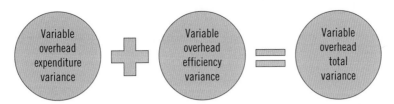

Figure 13.7 Variable overhead variances

Variable overhead variance calculations divide the total variance into variable overhead expenditure and variable overhead efficiency variances (Figure 13.7), in much the same way that the total direct labour variance is divided into labour rate and labour efficiency variances. The expenditure variance measures the difference between the variable overhead that should have been incurred for the level of production achieved and the actual expenditure. The variable overhead efficiency variance compares the difference between the actual hours taken to produce the actual production and the standard hours that actual production would have been expected to take. Think about how these variances are calculated in Example 13.2.

13

EXAMPLE 13.2

The Ultimate Chef Company manufactures food processors. Variable overhead incurred in the production of each food processor is set at 2½ hours at £6 per hour. During September, 1,000 food processors were produced. The employees of the Ultimate Chef Company were paid for 2,450 hours. The variable overhead cost for September was £14,540. Calculate:

- The variable overhead total variance

- The variable overhead expenditure variance

- The variable overhead efficiency variance

State whether each variance is favourable or unfavourable.

Variable overhead total variance

This is what the actual production should have cost and what it did cost.

	£
1,000 food processors should have cost 1,000 × 2½ hours × £6	15,000
1,000 food processors actually cost	14,540
Variable overhead total variance	**460**

Variable overhead expenditure variance

This is what the variable overhead should have cost compared with what it did cost for the actual hours worked.

	£
2,450 hours should have cost (2,450 × £6.00)	14,700
2,450 hours actually cost	14,540
Variable overhead expenditure variance	**160**

The variable overhead expenditure variance is favourable as less cost was incurred than expected for the actual number of hours used in production.

Variable overhead efficiency variance

This is how many hours should have been worked and how many were actually worked for the actual level of production.

	Hours
1,000 food processors should have used 1,000 × 2½ hours	2,500
1,000 food processors actually used	2,450
Variable overhead efficiency variance in hours	**50**

	£
Variable overhead efficiency variance in hours × standard rate/hour 50 × £6.00	**300**

The variable overhead efficiency variance is favourable as fewer hours were used than expected for the level of production achieved.

The variable overhead expenditure variance and the variable overhead efficiency variance can be summarised as follows to give the variable overhead total variance:

	£	Favourable/Unfavourable
Variable overhead expenditure variance	160	Favourable
Variable overhead efficiency variance	300	Favourable
Variable overhead total variance	**460**	Favourable

WHY IS THIS RELEVANT TO ME?   Variable overhead expenditure variance, variable overhead efficiency variance and variable overhead total variance

As a business professional you should now:

- Appreciate that variations in both the variable overhead expenditure and the speed of working should be used to explain the variable overhead total variance
- Be able to calculate the variable overhead total variance, variable overhead expenditure variance and variable overhead efficiency variance
- Understand that the variable overhead total variance is the sum of the variable overhead expenditure variance and the variable overhead efficiency variance

SUMMARY OF KEY CONCEPTS   Are you sure you know how to calculate the variable overhead total variance and the associated sub-variances, variable overhead expenditure variance and variable overhead efficiency variance? Go to the **online workbook** to check your understanding of how these variances are calculated with Summary of key concepts 13.3.

MULTIPLE CHOICE QUESTIONS   Are you confident that you can calculate the variable overhead total variance and its associated variances, variable overhead expenditure and variable overhead efficiency variances? Go to the **online workbook** and attempt Multiple choice questions 13.4 to check your ability to calculate these figures.

CHAPTER SUMMARY

You should now have learnt that:

- Selling price, material, labour, direct expenses, variable overhead and fixed overhead are the components that make up a standard cost
- Standard cost is an expected rather than an actual cost
- Standard costs are used in the planning and evaluation of operations
- Total variances between what should have been achieved and what was achieved explain the difference between actual and expected profits
- Variance analysis splits total variances into their constituent sub-variances arising from:

13

- Price (material), rate (labour) and expenditure (variable overhead) and
- Usage (material) and efficiency (labour and variable overhead)

● Sales variances are split into sales price and sales volume variances

● Variances help identify problems requiring further investigation and analysis to assist in the control of operations

 QUICK REVISION   Test your knowledge by attempting the activities in the **online workbook**, including flashcards on the key concepts, numerical exercises and Multiple choice questions. You can also try the further self-test questions which are available at www.oup.com/he/scott-i2a2e

END-OF-CHAPTER QUESTIONS

 Attempt the questions in the following sections and then look at the solutions which can be found in the **online workbook** to see whether there are areas that you need to revisit.

❯ RECALL AND REVIEW

❯ Question 13.1

Explain the difference between a standard cost and an actual cost and briefly describe the process of standard costing.

❯ Question 13.2

Hutcheon Limited is a manufacturing company which produces construction materials. The gross profit percentage of the company has been gradually reducing over the past two years. The board of directors asks you, the management accountant of the company, to determine the reasons for this downward trend. You believe that standard costing could help. What would you include in your report to the board of directors in terms of the benefits and limitations of standard costing?

❯❯ DEVELOP YOUR UNDERSTANDING

❯❯ Question 13.3

There are 30 apple trees in the orchard attached to Bill's farm. Bill reckons that each tree will be given five doses of fertiliser each year at a cost of £4 per tree and that 10 hours of labour per tree will be required to pick the apples from and prune each tree. Workers are paid £7.50 per hour.

13

At the end of the apple picking season, Bill calculates that the 30 trees only received four doses of fertiliser, although these cost £4.50 for each tree, and that the picking and pruning was undertaken at a cost of £8 per hour for 270 hours of labour.

Required

Calculate:

(a) The total expected costs of the orchard for the past year.

(b) The actual total costs of the orchard for the past year.

(c) Material total, price and usage variances.

(d) Labour total, rate and efficiency variances.

State whether the variances are favourable or unfavourable.

»Question 13.4

Fred bakes cakes. His budget indicates that he will produce and sell 1,000 cakes during March at a selling price of £15 each. At the end of March he calculates that his selling price was £15.50 for each cake produced and sold and that he has generated £14,725 in sales. His standard cost card for each cake shows that his variable cost of production is £6 per cake.

Required

Calculate for Fred for March:

(a) The sales price variance.

(b) The sales volume variance.

State whether the variances are favourable or unfavourable. Assuming that Fred's actual production costs are £6 per cake, prove that the sales price and sales volume variances explain fully his additional contribution for March.

»Question 13.5

Nadia and Co produces bathtubs. Standard variable overhead for the production of one bathtub is set at nine hours at £8.50 per hour. The budgeted fixed overhead is £55,000 per annum. In 2021, 7,300 labour hours were worked to produce 750 bathtubs. The actual fixed and variable overhead costs for 2021 were £58,000 and £61,900 respectively.

Required

Calculate the following variances stating whether each variance is favourable or unfavourable.

(a) The fixed overhead expenditure variance.

(b) The total variable overhead variance.

(c) The variable overhead expenditure variance.

(d) The variable overhead efficiency variance.

13

» Question 13.6

Alton plc produces sofas. The company's management accountant uses standard costing to control the costs. The standard cost card for each sofa is as follows:

	£
Direct material: 30 kg at £3 per kg	90
Direct labour: 4 hours at £10 per hour	40
Variable overhead: 4 hours at £2 per hour	8

The budgeted and actual results for 2021 are presented below.

	Budgeted		Actual	
	Details	£	Details	£
Sales	1,500 sofas at £200	300,000	1,320 sofas at £220	290,400
Direct material	1,500 sofas x 30 kg x £3	135,000	1,320 sofas x 32 kg x £3	126,720
Direct labour	1,500 sofas x 4 hours x £10	60,000	1,320 sofas x 3.5 hours x £12	55,440
Variable overhead	1,500 sofas x 4 hours x £2	12,000	1,320 sofas x 4 hours x £2.50	13,200
Total contribution		93,000		95,040
Total fixed costs		40,000		50,000
Profit for the year		**53,000**		**45,040**

Required

Calculate the following variances stating whether each variance is favourable or unfavourable:

- Sales volume variance
- Sales price variance
- Direct material price variance
- Direct material usage variance
- Direct material total variance
- Direct labour rate variance
- Direct labour efficiency variance
- Direct labour total variance
- Variable overhead expenditure variance
- Variable overhead efficiency variance
- Variable overhead total variance
- Fixed overhead variance

13

>> Question 13.7

Alton plc's board of directors would like to know what has caused the difference between the budgeted profit for the year and the actual profit that the company made. Based on your answers to Question 13.6:

(a) Prepare a statement reconciling budgeted profit to actual profit.

(b) Explain the difference between budgeted and actual sales, direct material, direct labour, variable overhead and fixed overhead and suggest possible reasons for the variances that have arisen.

>>> TAKE IT FURTHER

>>> Question 13.8

Sanguinary Services carries out blood tests for local hospitals, surgeries and doctors. The standard cost card for each blood test is given below.

	£
Chemicals used in blood tests: 10 millilitres at 50 pence/ml	5.00
Laboratory worker: 15 minutes at £16 per hour	4.00
Fixed overhead of the testing centre	2.00
Total cost	11.00
Charge for each blood test	15.00
Standard profit per blood test	**4.00**

The centre has fixed overheads of £72,000 per annum and plans to carry out 36,000 blood tests every year at the rate of 3,000 tests per month.

In April, the following results were recorded:

	Number
Blood tests carried out	**3,600**

	£
Chemicals used in blood tests: 33,750 millilitres at 48 pence/ml	16,200
Laboratory workers: 925 hours at £16.20 per hour	14,985
Fixed overhead of the testing centre	7,500
Total cost	38,685
Charge for each blood test 3,600 at £15.50	55,800
Profit for April	**17,115**

13

Required

(a) Calculate the profit that the centre expected to make in April, based on the original forecast of 3,000 blood tests in the month.

(b) Calculate the following:
- Sales volume variance
- Sales price variance
- Direct material total variance
- Direct material price variance
- Direct material usage variance
- Direct labour total variance
- Direct labour rate variance
- Direct labour efficiency variance
- Fixed overhead expenditure variance

Stating whether each variance is favourable or unfavourable.

(c) Prepare a statement reconciling the expected profit to the actual profit for April.

⋙ Question 13.9

Smashers Tennis Club runs coaching courses for its junior members. Each course lasts for ten weeks and is priced at £70 for each junior member. Smashers expects each course to attract 12 junior members. Each course is allocated 20 tennis balls for each participating junior at an expected cost of £10 for 20 balls. A professionally qualified tennis coach undertakes each hour-long coaching session over the ten weeks at a cost of £30 per hour.

The club administrator is reviewing the costs and income for the latest junior coaching course and she is trying to understand why the surplus from the course is £438 instead of £420. She tells you that the course actually attracted 16 juniors instead of the 12 expected and that a total of 400 balls had been allocated to and used by juniors on the course. Balls for the latest coaching course had cost 60 pence each. The coach had received an increase in her hourly rate to £33 per hour. The price for each course had been reduced by 10% on the original price in order to attract additional participants.

Required

(a) Calculate the original expected surplus from the coaching course.

(b) Calculate the expected surplus from the coaching course given that 16 juniors were enrolled.

(c) Calculate the actual income and costs for the course.

(d) Calculate variances for income and expenditure and present these in tabular form to reconcile the original expected surplus to the actual surplus.

13

>>> **Question 13.10**

Vijay Manufacturing produces garden gnomes. The standard cost card for garden gnomes is as follows:

	£
Plastic: 2 kg at £2.25 per kg	4.50
Labour: 0.5 hours at £8 per hour	4.00
Variable overhead: 4 machine hours at £0.75 per hour	3.00
Fixed overhead	1.00
Total cost	12.50
Selling price to Plastic Gnome Painters Limited	15.00
Standard profit per garden gnome	**2.50**

Fixed overheads total £24,000 and are allocated to production on the basis that 24,000 gnomes will be produced each year, 2,000 each month.

Vijay is reviewing the actual production and sales for the month of June. The weather has been wet and garden gnome sales have fallen from their normal levels. Consequently, the company has had to reduce the selling price in June to £14 per gnome in order to keep production and sales moving. Production and sales for the month were 1,800 gnomes. The input price per kg of plastic was £2.50 as a result of a sharp rise in the oil price but, because of reduced wastage and careful material handling, only 3,500 kg of plastic were used in June. Owing to the high level of unemployment in the area, Vijay has been able to pay his employees at the rate of £7.50 per hour. Total labour hours for the month were 950. Total machine hours for the month were 7,000 and the fixed and variable overheads totalled £1,600 and £5,500 respectively. Vijay has been trying to understand why his profit has fallen from its expected level for the month and has asked for your help. You are meeting him later on today to discuss his figures and to show him how his expected profit has fallen to the actual profit for the month.

Required

Draft figures for your meeting later on today with Vijay. Your figures should include:

(a) Calculations to show the profit Vijay expected to make from the production and sale of 2,000 garden gnomes in the month of June.

(b) Calculations to show the profit Vijay might have expected to make from the production and sale of 1,800 garden gnomes for the month of June.

(c) Calculations to show the profit Vijay actually did make for the month of June.

(d) A reconciliation statement showing all the necessary favourable and unfavourable variances to explain the difference between the expected profit for June calculated in (a) and the actual profit calculated in (c).

13

14 BUDGETING

LEARNING OUTCOMES

Once you have read this chapter and worked through the questions and examples in both this chapter and the online workbook, you should be able to:

- Discuss the ways in which budgets involve planning, communicating, coordinating, motivating and control functions

- Prepare budgeted monthly statements of profit or loss for an entity

- Determine the timing of cash inflows and outflows from budgeted income and expenditure

- Prepare a month-by-month cash budget for an entity

- Draw up a budgeted statement of financial position at the end of a projected accounting period

- Undertake comparisons between budgeted and actual income and expenditure to highlight variances in expected and actual financial performance

- Undertake sensitivity analysis to assess the effect that any changes in budget assumptions will have

INTRODUCTION

The word budget is all around us, every day. There are constant reminders of the national budget, individuals' budgets and business budgets. You yourself may have drawn up a budget for what you expected to spend during your first year at university. This budget might have been quite basic to start with, but, as you thought more about the costs you would be likely to incur, your budget would have been refined and become a more realistic means of planning your anticipated expenditure and its timing. However, budgeting can occur at a much simpler level. When you go out for the evening, the amount of money you take with you is your budget for that evening. In both cases, actual expenditure is likely to be very different from your original plan due to unforeseen costs—an expensive book or field trip for your course or a taxi home when you missed the last bus. This does not mean that the exercise was not worthwhile: planning ahead is important for both individuals and business organisations. Experience helps us to refine our future budgets so that the actual outcomes gradually become closer to our budgeted expectations.

WHAT IS BUDGETING?

For business people, a budget is the expression of a plan in money terms. That plan is a prediction of future income, expenditure, cash inflows and cash outflows. Once each stage of the plan is completed, then the actual results can be compared to expectations to determine whether actual outcomes are better, worse or the same as anticipated. As we saw in Chapter 13 on standard costing, such comparisons are a means of controlling an organisation's operations and taking action to reduce or eliminate unfavourable divergences from the plan while finding out the ways in which better than expected performance can be maintained and built upon.

WHY IS THIS RELEVANT TO ME?   What is budgeting?

As a business professional:

- You should appreciate that all businesses undertake budgeting
- You will be expected to play a significant role in the annual budgeting process
- Building an awareness of what budgeting is, what it involves and how to budget in practice will be essential knowledge

---

SUMMARY OF KEY CONCEPTS   Are you convinced you can define budgeting? Go to the **online workbook** to revise the definition with Summary of key concepts 14.1.

Give me an example 14.1 highlights the importance accorded to budgeting and forecasting by the business community.

GIVE ME AN EXAMPLE 14.1   Budgeting in business

The July 2009 CIMA report, *Management accounting tools for today and tomorrow*, surveyed the current and intended usage by business of more than 100 management accounting and related tools based on a questionnaire completed by 439 respondents from across the globe. The most commonly used technique in practice was financial year forecasting with 86% of respondents engaging in this activity.

The third most popular technique was cash forecasting which was used by 78% of those businesses surveyed. These two activities were the most popular budgeting tools across every size of company in the survey from small to very large. These findings indicate the very high priority that is accorded to budgeting and forecasting in the business community.

Source: www.cimaglobal.com

BUDGET OBJECTIVES AND THE BUDGETING PROCESS

Everyone has objectives, both individuals and organisations. It is not enough to have a vague hope that everything will work out and that objectives will be achieved without any planning or positive actions and a great deal of hard work being undertaken. Thus, individuals and organisations have to decide how they will achieve their objectives through careful planning on a step-by-step basis. A well-known phrase among university tutors is 'failing to plan is planning to fail'. This is just as true when you are writing an essay as it is when making projections for what a business will achieve in the next 12 months.

Budgets and the budgeting process thus assist organisations to focus upon achieving and the means to achieve their objectives in the ways shown in Table 14.1.

Table 14.1 The objectives of the budgeting process

Planning	Budgeting forces entities to look ahead and plan. Planning helps organisations think about the future and what they want to achieve, as well as helping them anticipate problems to determine how these will be overcome.
Communication	The directors will have plans to achieve certain objectives. However, if they do not tell everyone else involved in the organisation about those objectives, then they will not be achieved. Budgets communicate information to those persons and departments involved in achieving objectives to tell them what level of performance they have to attain to fulfil their part in reaching the desired goal.
Coordination and integration	Different departments have to work together to achieve objectives. The directors have to tell marketing what level of sales they need to achieve to reach the profit goal. Marketing then have to liaise with production to make sure that production can produce this number of goods and to the required timescale. Production has to make sure that purchasing is buying in the necessary raw materials to enable production to take place on schedule while personnel have to recruit the necessary workers to make the goods. Budgets thus coordinate and integrate business activities to give the organisation the best chance of achieving its goals.

Control	Budgeting enables an organisation to control its activities and check its progress towards achieving objectives by regularly comparing actual results with budgeted outcomes. Differences can then be investigated and action taken either to bring operations back on track or to exploit favourable trends further.
Responsibility	Responsibility for different parts of the budget is delegated to individual managers. One person alone cannot achieve everything on their own, so various managers work as part of a team, each with their own responsibility for hitting the targets assigned to them in the budget. These managers are then assessed and rewarded on the basis of their ability to meet their agreed objectives. Breaking down one big task into various smaller tasks and then making several managers responsible for achieving each of these smaller targets is a very good way to get things done.
Motivation	Budgets are used as motivating devices. Something too easy is not motivating and managers need to be challenged to achieve more. In the same way, your degree is challenging so that achieving your qualification motivates you and makes it worthwhile. As an incentive to achieve challenging budget targets, managers will be rewarded with bonuses. However, it is important to make sure that the targets are not completely unrealistic as impossible targets will result in managers giving up before they have even started.

WHY IS THIS RELEVANT TO ME?   Budgeting objectives and the budgeting process

As a business professional you should be aware of:

- What the objectives of the budgeting process are

- The roles budgeting plays in setting and achieving organisational goals

- What the budgeting process will expect of you

SUMMARY OF KEY CONCEPTS   Are you certain that you can summarise the objectives of budgeting and the budgeting process? Go to the **online workbook** to revise these objectives with Summary of key concepts 14.2.

GO BACK OVER THIS AGAIN!   Are you convinced that you understand the objectives of budgeting and the budgeting process? Go to the **online workbook** and attempt Exercises 14.1 to make sure you have fully grasped the principles.

GO BACK OVER THIS AGAIN!   Are you quite sure you understand how the budgeting objectives and the budgeting process work in practice? Go to the **online workbook** Exercises 14.2 and consider the scenario there to see how budgeting objectives and the budgeting process operate in everyday life.

14

BUDGETING: COMPREHENSIVE EXAMPLE

Now that we have defined a budget and considered what the organisational objectives in preparing budgets are, let's look in detail at the process of actually setting a budget through a practical example. This process involves several steps, which we will think about one by one.

Anna is considering the expansion of her business. She is planning to move her operations to a bigger workshop and has asked her bank for a loan with which to finance this expansion. In connection with her application for the loan, the bank has asked Anna to produce a budget covering sales, costs and cash flows for the next 12 months, together with a budgeted statement of financial position at the end of those 12 months. Anna has made a start on her budgets and has produced information for the first three months of the next financial year. However, she is finding budgeting difficult and has asked for your assistance in helping her to complete the remainder of the required information.

Step 1: setting the strategy and deciding on selling prices

Anna first has to decide what she wants to achieve and whether there are any obstacles she must overcome or which will stand in the way of her achieving her goals. She wants to expand, but she feels that the lack of finance is holding her back. However, her products are selling well and her customers are pleased with the quality of her output. Will she be able to finance her proposed expansion from current operations if the bank is not willing to help her? Budgeting will help her to answer this question. Figure 14.1 illustrates the first step in the budgeting process.

Figure 14.1 Budgeting step 1: setting the strategy and the selling prices

Her first decision will be to set her selling prices. Should she raise these, leave them at the same level or reduce the selling prices of each product? She has gone back to the costings for her three products that she presented in Chapter 12 (Limiting factor (key factor) analysis). These are reproduced in Illustration 14.1. Can she justify raising her selling prices? This will first depend on whether her costs are rising.

Illustration 14.1 Anna: selling prices and variable costs for dining chairs, coffee tables and kitchen cabinets

	Dining chairs £	Coffee tables £	Kitchen cabinets £
Selling price	85.00	50.00	80.00
Materials: wood	(18.00)	(12.60)	(10.80)
Materials: other	(2.00)	(5.40)	(9.20)
Direct labour	(25.00)	(18.00)	(30.00)
Contribution	**40.00**	**14.00**	**30.00**

14

Anna tells you that she has discussed the price of wood and other materials with her suppliers. They have reassured her that there are no price rises or material shortages anticipated in the next 12 months. This tells Anna that there will be no supply difficulties which will need to be planned for over the course of the coming year. At the same time she now knows that there are no expected increases in the cost of inputs to her products which would need to be built into her selling prices to pass on these cost increases to her customers.

Her workforce is loyal and they have stated that they have no intention of leaving in the next 12 months. Anna has looked into the current rates she is paying her workers and these are in line with market rates. The furniture makers' trade association informs her that labour costs are likely to remain steady over the course of the next year. Again, Anna now knows that she should not encounter any shortages of labour or pay rises which she would have to build into her budget for the coming year.

As her direct costs should remain unchanged for the next 12 months, it will be difficult for Anna to change her selling prices. She is happy with the levels of profit her sales are currently generating and, as she does not want to lose her customers through pitching her selling prices too high, she decides to leave the selling prices of each of her three products at the same level for the next 12 months.

WHY IS THIS RELEVANT TO ME?   Setting the strategy

To enable you as a business professional to appreciate that:

- Before the detailed budgeting process can begin, businesses have to decide what their object-ives and strategy are
- The strategy is directly responsible for the budgeted income and costs, cash inflows and cash outflows
- Setting targets for sales, profits or market share will determine the selling prices of products and services and these targets in turn will feed into the costs of providing those products and services

---

Step 2: the sales budget

Now that the pricing decision and the supply of materials and labour are clear, Anna's next thoughts will focus on her sales. Once decisions on strategy and prices have been made, this is exactly the right place to start the budgeting process as so many other costs and cash flows depend upon the volume of sales achieved. As we discovered in Chapters 11 and 12, Anna's direct costs for wood, other materials and labour will depend directly upon the number of products she sells: the more products she makes and sells, the more direct materials and direct labour cost she will incur. However, she will be unable to produce her material and labour budgets until she has set her sales budget in terms of units produced and sold. Figure 14.2 outlines this process.

14

Figure 14.2 Budgeting step 2: setting the sales budget

Illustration 14.2 Anna: budgeted sales in units of product for January, February and March

	January number	February number	March number	Total number
Dining chairs	150	200	350	700
Coffee tables	100	250	300	650
Kitchen cabinets	300	350	400	1,050

Anna has been talking to her customers to see how many of her products they propose buying in the near future. She has managed to determine that orders from customers for the first three months of the year are likely to be as shown in Illustration 14.2.

From these budgeted units of sales, Anna can now produce a sales budget in £s. This sales budget is presented in Illustration 14.3.

Illustration 14.3 Anna: budgeted sales in £s for January, February and March

	January £	February £	March £	Total £
Dining chairs	12,750	17,000	29,750	59,500
Coffee tables	5,000	12,500	15,000	32,500
Kitchen cabinets	24,000	28,000	32,000	84,000
Total sales for month	**41,750**	**57,500**	**76,750**	**176,000**

How did Anna arrive at the above figures? Monthly sales of each product are calculated by multiplying the monthly expected sales in units in Illustration 14.2 by the selling price for each product in Illustration 14.1. Thus, Anna expects to sell 150 dining chairs in January at a selling price of £85. This gives her a sales figure of 150 × £85 = £12,750 for this product line in January.

14

WHY IS THIS RELEVANT TO ME?   The sales budget

To enable you as a business professional to understand:

- How a sales budget is prepared
- The influence of projected sales volumes on the direct costs of making and selling products and providing services

NUMERICAL EXERCISES   Are you confident that you can produce a sales budget? Work your
way through the figures in Illustrations 14.1, 14.2 and 14.3 again to confirm your understanding of
how the monthly sales figures for each product were calculated and then go to the **online workbook**
and attempt Numerical exercises 14.1 to make sure you can produce a sales budget from monthly
budgeted sales units and budgeted selling prices.

Figure 14.3 Budgeting step 3: setting the direct costs budget

Step 3: calculate the direct costs of budgeted sales

Now that the sales budget has been set, the direct costs associated with those sales can be calculated. As already noted, direct costs are dependent upon the level of sales. In Anna's case, the
more units of each product her workshop makes, the more wood will be used, the more other
materials will be consumed and the more direct labour will be needed. Figure 14.3 outlines
this process.

Budgeted sales income for each month was calculated by multiplying the selling price by the
number of units produced and sold. In the same way, budgeted direct costs are found by multiplying the direct materials and direct labour by the number of units of sales. This gives the
budgeted material costs for wood shown in Illustration 14.4.

Illustration 14.4 Anna: budgeted costs for wood in January, February and March

	January £	February £	March £	Total £
Direct materials: wood				
Dining chairs	2,700	3,600	6,300	12,600
Coffee tables	1,260	3,150	3,780	8,190
Kitchen cabinets	3,240	3,780	4,320	11,340
Total direct materials (wood) for month	**7,200**	**10,530**	**14,400**	**32,130**

14

Illustration 14.2 tells us that Anna expects to sell 150 dining chairs in the month of January,
while Illustration 14.1 shows us that the wood for each chair costs £18.00; 150 chairs × £18.00
gives a total cost of wood for dining chairs in January of £2,700. Using the budgeted sales in
Illustration 14.2 for each product and the product costs for wood in Illustration 14.1, check the
calculation of the materials costs for wood in Illustration 14.4 to reinforce your understanding
of how we arrived at these costs.

In the same way and using the information in Illustrations 14.1 and 14.2, the budgeted costs
for other materials and direct labour for each product for each month have been calculated in

Illustrations 14.5 and 14.6. Other materials used in dining chairs amount to £2 per chair. Multiplying this cost of £2 per chair by the 150 chairs Anna expects to sell in January gives us a cost for other materials of £300 in that month. Similarly, labour costs of £25 per dining chair are multiplied by the 150 chairs budgeted for January to give a total labour cost for dining chairs in that month of £3,750.

Illustration 14.5 Anna: budgeted costs for other materials in January, February and March

Direct materials: other	January £	February £	March £	Total £
Dining chairs	300	400	700	1,400
Coffee tables	540	1,350	1,620	3,510
Kitchen cabinets	2,760	3,220	3,680	9,660
Total direct materials (other) for month	**3,600**	**4,970**	**6,000**	**14,570**

Illustration 14.6 Anna: budgeted costs for direct labour in January, February and March

Direct labour	January £	February £	March £	Total £
Dining chairs	3,750	5,000	8,750	17,500
Coffee tables	1,800	4,500	5,400	11,700
Kitchen cabinets	9,000	10,500	12,000	31,500
Total direct labour for month	**14,550**	**20,000**	**26,150**	**60,700**

WHY IS THIS RELEVANT TO ME?   The direct costs of budgeted sales

To provide you as a business professional with the knowledge and techniques to:

• Prepare budgets for direct costs based on budgeted sales

• Understand how direct cost budgets are compiled

NUMERICAL EXERCISES   Do you think you can produce a direct costs budget for materials and labour? Work your way through the figures in Illustrations 14.1, 14.2, 14.4, 14.5 and 14.6 again to confirm your understanding of how we arrived at the budgeted materials and labour cost figures for each product and then go to the **online workbook** and attempt Numerical exercises 14.2 to see if you can produce a direct materials and direct labour budget from monthly budgeted sales units and budgeted cost prices per unit.

Step 4: set the budget for fixed costs

The fixed costs budget will be different for every organisation and will depend upon what sort of resources are consumed by each entity as shown in Figure 14.4.

14

Anna expects her fixed costs and her capital expenditure for the next three months to be as follows:

- Rent on the new workshop of £3,000 will be paid in January to cover the months of January, February and March.

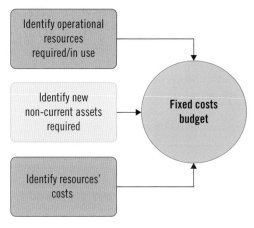

Figure 14.4 Budgeting step 4: setting the fixed costs budget

- New machinery and tools will cost £15,000 and will be delivered and paid for in January. These new non-current assets will have an expected useful life of five years and will be depreciated on the straight line basis.

- Anna anticipates that she will receive and pay an electricity bill in March covering the period 1 January to 15 March. She expects that this bill will be for around £1,500. Anna estimates that the new workshop will use a further £300 of electricity between 16 and 31 March. Each month of operation should be allocated an equal amount of electricity cost.

- An invoice for business rates of £1,200 on the new workshop will be received and paid on 15 February. These rates will cover the six-month period to 30 June.

- The insurance company requires a payment of £1,500 on 1 January to cover all insurance costs for the whole year to 31 December.

Step 5: draw up the budgeted monthly statement of profit or loss

Anna can now draw up her budgeted monthly statement of profit or loss from the information gathered together in steps 1–4 (Figure 14.5). This budgeted statement of profit or loss is presented in Illustration 14.7.

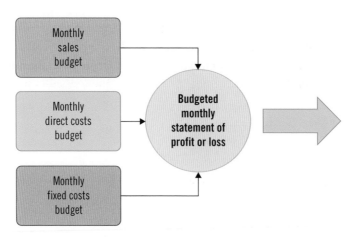

Figure 14.5 Budgeting step 5: draw up the budgeted monthly statement of profit or loss

Illustration 14.7 Anna: budgeted statement of profit or loss for January, February and March

	January £	February £	March £	Total £	Note
Sales	41,750	57,500	76,750	176,000	1
Cost of sales					
Direct material: wood	7,200	10,530	14,400	32,130	2
Direct material: other	3,600	4,970	6,000	14,570	3
Direct labour	14,550	20,000	26,150	60,700	4
Cost of sales	**25,350**	**35,500**	**46,550**	**107,400**	
Gross profit (sales – cost of sales)	16,400	22,000	30,200	68,600	
Expenses					
Rent	1,000	1,000	1,000	3,000	5
Rates	200	200	200	600	6
Machinery and tools depreciation	250	250	250	750	7
Electricity	600	600	600	1,800	8
Insurance	125	125	125	375	9
Net profit (gross profit – expenses)	**14,225**	**19,825**	**28,025**	**62,075**	

How did Anna calculate the budgeted results in Illustration 14.7? The following notes will help you understand how she determined the numbers in her budgeted statement of profit or loss:

1. The monthly sales are derived from Illustration 14.3.

2. Similarly, the direct materials for wood are given in Illustration 14.4.

3. Figures for other direct materials are given in Illustration 14.5.

4. Direct labour costs were calculated in Illustration 14.6. Check back to Illustrations 14.3–14.6 to make sure that the numbers in the statement of profit or loss have been correctly transferred from these workings.

5. While the rent of £3,000 was paid in January, this payment relates to three months, so the total expense is spread equally over the three months to which it relates. If you are at all unsure as to why this expense is presented in this way, you should revise this allocation of costs in the accruals basis of accounting in Chapter 3 (The accruals basis of accounting).

6. In the same way, the rates payment relates to the six months from January to June. The total cost of £1,200 is therefore divided by six months and £200 allocated as the rates cost to each month. The total cost for rates for the three months amounts to £600. How is the remaining £600 (£1,200 paid – £600 charged to the statement of profit or loss) classified in the accounts? Chapter 3, Prepayments and accruals, covers the subject of prepayments, expenses paid in advance that belong to a future accounting period.

7. Depreciation is another expense we tackled in Chapter 3 (Depreciation). The total cost of £15,000 is divided by five years, giving an annual depreciation charge on these new assets of £3,000. As there are 12 months in a year, a monthly depreciation charge of £3,000 ÷ 12 = £250 is allocated to each of the three months considered here.

8. The total electricity charge for the three months will be the £1,500 bill received and paid in the middle of March plus the £300 that has been used in the last two weeks of March. This £300 will be treated as an accrual (see Chapter 3, Prepayments and accruals), an expense incurred by the end of an accounting period giving rise to a liability and an expense that has not been paid by that period end date. The total electricity expense for the three months is thus £1,800. Dividing this figure by three gives us an expense of £600 for each month in the budgeted statement of profit or loss.

9. While the total insurance payment is £1,500, this cost covers the whole 12-month period. Therefore, the monthly charge for insurance in our budgeted statement of profit or loss will be £1,500 ÷ 12 = £125 per month, the remaining £1,125 (£1,500 – £375) being treated as a prepayment at the end of March.

WHY IS THIS RELEVANT TO ME?   The budgeted monthly statement of profit or loss

To enable you as a business professional to understand how:

- Budgeted statements of profit or loss you will be presented with have been drawn up
- To prepare your own budgeted monthly statements of profit or loss

---

NUMERICAL EXERCISES   Do you think you could put together a budgeted statement of profit or loss for a given time period using budgeted sales, materials, labour and fixed overheads? Work through Illustration 14.7 again to confirm your understanding of how we arrived at the figures in the budgeted statement of profit or loss and then go to the **online workbook** and attempt Numerical exercises 14.3 to make sure you can produce a budgeted statement of profit or loss from the sales, materials, labour and fixed overhead budgets.

SHOW ME HOW TO DO IT   Are you quite sure you understand how this budgeted statement of profit or loss in Illustration 14.7 was put together? View Video presentation 14.1 in the **online workbook** to see a practical demonstration.

14

Step 6: calculating cash receipts from sales

The budgeted statement of profit or loss for the first three months of the year in Illustration 14.7 shows that Anna expects to make a healthy profit of £62,075. However, as we have already seen in this book, profit does not equal cash (Chapter 6, Profit ≠ cash). The main concern of both entities and their banks will always be the cash flowing in and the cash flowing out, so it is important in any budgeting exercise to prepare the cash budget alongside the budgeted statement of profit or loss (Figure 14.6).

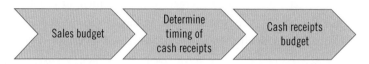

Figure 14.6 Budgeting step 6: cash receipts from sales budget

As we saw in Chapter 3 (Determining the amount of income or expense), sales are recognised as income in the months in which they occur, but cash from those sales will not necessarily be received in those same months. Where goods are purchased on credit, there is a time lag between the date of the sale and the day on which cash from that sale is received.

Based on her past experience and knowledge, Anna expects 30% of her customers to pay in the month of sale and the remaining 70% to pay in the following month. These expected monthly cash receipts from sales are shown in Illustration 14.8.

Illustration 14.8 Anna: budgeted cash receipts from sales in January, February and March

	January £	February £	March £	Total £
30% of sales received in month	12,525	17,250	23,025	52,800
70% of sales received next month	—	29,225	40,250	69,475
Total cash receipts per month	**12,525**	**46,475**	**63,275**	**122,275**

How were these cash receipts calculated? Anna expects to make total sales in January of £41,750 (Illustration 14.3); 30% of £41,750 is £12,525 received in January, the month of sale. Cash from the remaining 70% of January's sales will be received in the following month, February. This amounts to £29,225. You could calculate this number as 70% of £41,750 or just deduct the £12,525 already received from £41,750 to give you the same result. Work through the other budgeted sales and cash receipts in Illustrations 14.3 and 14.8 to ensure that you understand how the cash inflows from sales were calculated on the basis of Anna's expectations of when her customers will pay for the goods they have received.

Anna expects to make sales of £176,000 in the three months to the end of March (Illustrations 14.3 and 14.7). However, she has only collected £122,275 in cash (Illustration 14.8), a difference of £53,725. What does this difference represent and where should it be recorded in the budgeted accounts? Remember that this figure represents trade receivables due to the business, a current asset (Chapter 2, Current assets), which will be posted to Anna's budgeted statement of financial position at 31 March.

WHY IS THIS RELEVANT TO ME?   Calculating cash receipts from sales

To enable you as a business professional to understand:

- That, unless an entity sells for cash, sales do not equal cash receipts in the months in which the sales are recognised

- How to prepare budgets for receipts of cash from sales made to customers on credit terms

---

NUMERICAL EXERCISES   Are you convinced that you could produce a statement of budgeted cash inflows from sales? Work through Illustration 14.8 again to confirm your understanding of how we arrived at the budgeted cash receipts from sales and then go to the **online workbook** and attempt Numerical exercises 14.4 to make sure you can produce a statement of budgeted cash inflows from sales.

Step 7: calculating cash payments to direct materials suppliers and direct labour

Just as Anna's customers do not pay for their goods immediately, so Anna, as a customer of her materials suppliers, does not pay for all her direct materials in the month she receives them. Therefore, cash payments to suppliers have to be worked out in the same way as cash receipts from customers (Figure 14.7).

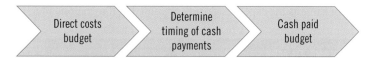

Figure 14.7 Budgeting step 7: cash payments from direct costs budget

Anna expects to pay for her purchases of wood as follows:

- 50% of the wood used in each month will be paid for in the actual month of use

- 30% of the wood used in each month will be paid for one month after the actual month of use

- 20% of the wood used in each month will be paid for two months after the actual month of use

Illustration 14.9 shows Anna's cash payments for wood.

Illustration 14.9 Anna: budgeted cash payments for wood for January, February and March

	January £	February £	March £	Total £
50% of wood used in month	3,600	5,265	7,200	16,065
30% of wood used one month ago	—	2,160	3,159	5,319
20% of wood used two months ago	—	—	1,440	1,440
Total cash payments per month	**3,600**	**7,425**	**11,799**	**22,824**

14

How were these cash payments for wood calculated? Anna's direct materials budget (Illustrations 14.4 and 14.7) shows that she expects to use wood costing £7,200 in January. This will be paid for as follows:

- 50% in month of use (January): £7,200 × 50% = £3,600

- 30% one month after the month of use: £7,200 × 30% = £2,160

- 20% two months after the month of use: £7,200 × 20% = £1,440

- Check: £3,600 + £2,160 + £1,440 = £7,200

On top of these payments for January's wood made in February and March are payments for wood used in those months, as well as March's payment for the wood used in February.

Illustration 14.9 shows that Anna will be paying £22,824 in cash for her wood purchases in the three months to 31 March, while her statement of profit or loss (Illustration 14.7) shows that she is incurring total direct materials costs for wood of £32,130. She therefore still has £9,306 to pay (£32,130 − £22,824), made up of £2,106 (20% of February's usage (£10,530 × 20%)) and £7,200 (50% of March's usage (£14,400 × 50%)). This figure of £9,306 represents a liability incurred and due to be paid to her suppliers. This amount will be recorded as a trade payable in Anna's budgeted statement of financial position at 31 March.

As well as her suppliers of wood, Anna also buys in other direct materials for use in producing her furniture. She intends to pay the suppliers of these other materials in the month in which these materials are used in production. Similarly, she will be paying her employees in the month in which production and sales are made. The cash outflows for other direct materials and direct labour in her monthly cash budget will be the same as the expenses already presented in Illustrations 14.5, 14.6 and 14.7.

WHY IS THIS RELEVANT TO ME?   Calculating cash payments for direct materials and direct labour

To enable you as a business professional to understand:

- That, unless an entity pays cash for all its direct materials and other purchases, direct materials do not equal cash payments in the months in which the costs are recorded

- How to prepare budgets for payments of cash to suppliers of direct materials and other purchases where these goods are purchased on credit terms

---

NUMERICAL EXERCISES   Are you confident that you could put together a budgeted statement of cash payments for direct materials and direct labour? Work through Illustration 14.9 again to confirm your understanding of how we calculated the budgeted cash payment figures for direct materials and direct labour and then go to the **online workbook** and attempt Numerical exercises 14.5 to see how accurately you can produce a budgeted statement of cash payments for direct materials and direct labour.

Step 8: draw up the monthly cash budget

Anna now has all the information from which to draw up her month-by-month cash budget. To do this she will look at the timing of her cash receipts from sales and the timing of her cash payments for direct materials and labour together with any other payments or inflows of cash, as shown in

Figure 14.8. Details of other payments of cash were given in step 4, the budget for fixed costs. In addition, Anna decides that she will be paying £10,000 of her own money into her business bank account on 1 January and that she will be drawing out £2,000 a month for her own personal expenses.

Her monthly cash budget for January, February and March is presented in Illustration 14.10.

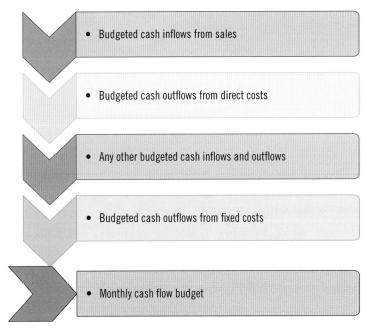

Figure 14.8 Budgeting step 8: draw up the monthly cash budget

Illustration 14.10 Anna: budgeted cash receipts and payments for January, February and March

	January £	February £	March £	Total £	Note
Cash received					
Sales	12,525	46,475	63,275	122,275	1
Capital introduced	10,000	—	—	10,000	2
Total cash receipts	**22,525**	**46,475**	**63,275**	**132,275**	
Cash paid					
Direct material: wood	3,600	7,425	11,799	22,824	3
Direct material: other	3,600	4,970	6,000	14,570	4
Direct labour	14,550	20,000	26,150	60,700	5
Rent	3,000	—	—	3,000	6
Machinery and tools	15,000	—	—	15,000	7
Electricity	—	—	1,500	1,500	8
Rates	—	1,200	—	1,200	9
Insurance	1,500	—	—	1,500	10
Drawings: personal expenditure	2,000	2,000	2,000	6,000	11
Total cash payments	**43,250**	**35,595**	**47,449**	**126,294**	
Cash receipts – cash payments	(20,725)	10,880	15,826	5,981	12
Cash at the start of the month	—	(20,725)	(9,845)		13
Cash at the end of the month	(20,725)	(9,845)	5,981		14

How did Anna produce her monthly cash budget for January, February and March? The following notes explain the numbers in each line of the cash budget.

1. The budgeted cash receipts from sales were calculated in Illustration 14.8.

2. Anna is paying in £10,000 of her own money on 1 January as noted.

3. The budgeted cash payments to suppliers of wood were presented in Illustration 14.9.

4. Anna is paying her suppliers of other direct materials in the month in which the other direct materials are used, so the cash payments to these suppliers are the same as the budgeted costs in Illustrations 14.5 and 14.7.

5. Likewise, direct labour is paid in the month in which production and sales take place so these cash payments are the same as the costs given in Illustrations 14.6 and 14.7.

6. Step 4 tells us that the rent is paid on 1 January. Although the cost of this rent is spread across the three months to which it relates in the statement of profit or loss (Illustration 14.7), the actual cash payment is budgeted to take place in January, so the whole £3,000 is recognised in the January cash payments.

7. In the same way, the cash outflow to buy the machinery and tools occurs in January so the whole of the £15,000 cash payment is recognised in January. Remember that depreciation is not a cash flow, just an accounting adjustment (Chapter 6, The indirect method and Table 6.1) that spreads the cost of non-current assets over the periods benefiting from their use, so depreciation does not appear in a cash budget. The actual outflow of cash to pay for the machinery and tools is £15,000 and this occurs in January so, just like the rent, this is the month in which this cash payment for these non-current assets is recognised.

8. Step 4 explains that the electricity bill received in March will be for £1,500 and that this electricity bill is paid in that month. Thus, £1,500 is the amount of cash that leaves the bank in March. The additional £300 accrual in the statement of profit or loss will be paid in a later period so no cash outflow is recognised in these three months for this amount which has not yet been paid.

9. Step 4 notes that the rates bill is paid in February and the full £1,200 payment is recognised in the cash budget as this is the actual amount paid in February regardless of the amounts that are allocated to each month in the budgeted statement of profit or loss.

10. Similarly, the insurance for the year is paid in January, so the whole cash payment of £1,500 is shown in January's column even though the cost in the statement of profit or loss is spread over the next 12 months.

11. Anna withdraws £2,000 a month from which to meet her personal expenditure so she recognises this as a cash payment each month.

12. After totalling up the cash receipts (inflows) and the cash payments (outflows), the receipts – payments line is presented. For January, total receipts in Illustration 14.10 are £22,525 while payments total £43,250. Thus, £22,525 – £43,250 = –£20,725, which means that there is a shortfall of cash in January and Anna's bank account will be overdrawn. January thus

14

shows greater payments than receipts of cash, while both February and March show a net inflow of cash, receipts in both months being greater than payments.

13. Cash at the start of the month is the cash balance at the end of the previous month. In the first month of a new business venture, as in Anna's case, this will be £Nil. In continuing businesses, this will be the budgeted or actual figure at the end of the last financial period.

14. The cash at the end of the month is the net cash inflow or outflow for the month plus or minus the cash or overdraft at the start of the month. In January, the net outflow for the month is £20,725 while the cash at the start of January is £Nil so (£20,725) +/− £Nil = (£20,725). At the end of February, there is a net cash inflow of £10,880 (total cash inflows of £46,475 − total cash outflows of £35,595). Adding this positive inflow of £10,880 to the negative balance at the start of the month (£20,725) gives us a lower overdraft at the end of February (£9,845), which then forms the opening balance at the start of March.

WHY IS THIS RELEVANT TO ME?   The monthly cash budget

To enable you as a business professional to understand:

• How cash budgets you will be presented with have been drawn up

• How to prepare your own monthly cash budgets

NUMERICAL EXERCISES   Are you sure that you could draw up a cash budget? Work through the figures in Illustration 14.10 again to confirm your understanding of how the cash budget was constructed and then go to the **online workbook** and attempt Numerical exercises 14.6 to make sure you can produce these budgeted statements.

SHOW ME HOW TO DO IT   How easily did you follow the preparation of Anna's monthly cash budget? View Video presentation 14.2 in the **online workbook** to see a practical demonstration of how the monthly cash budget in Illustration 14.10 was put together.

14

The importance of cash flow forecasts

The cash budget is the most important budgeted statement that you will ever produce. We have already seen in this book that cash generation is the critical task for businesses as, without adequate cash inflows, a business will be unable to meet its liabilities as they fall due and will collapse. Give me an example 14.2, from the Entrepreneur column in the *Financial Times*, emphasises how business professionals must continue to produce cash budgets no matter how high up an organisation they climb. If they do not, they are risking the very survival of their organisations.

> **GIVE ME AN EXAMPLE 14.2** Custodians of finance make the difference
>
> The weak link in many failed companies is the finance director. Better custody of borrowed or invested money by them would so often have prevented disaster. In most cases their words betray them as much as the numbers. I am indebted to John Dewhirst of Vincere, the turnaround specialists, for collecting some of the classic lines I discuss below.
>
> 'I don't do cash forecasts. I've never found them useful.'
>
> A lack of focus on cash is perhaps the greatest sin. A finance professional who does not prepare reasonably accurate projections of liquidity on a rolling basis is guilty of dereliction of duty. Often FDs drop such nitty gritty as they ascend the ranks, while some have historically enjoyed a cash cushion and never felt the pressure. They are the ones exposed when conditions deteriorate.
>
> Source: Luke Johnson, 2011, *Custodians of finance make the difference*, the Financial Times, 19 January. Used under licence from the Financial Times. All Rights Reserved.

> **WHY IS THIS RELEVANT TO ME?** The importance of cash budgets
>
> To emphasise to you as a business professional:
> - The critical importance of budgeting cash on a regular basis
> - The risks you run if you do not undertake regular cash budgeting

Step 9: draw up the budgeted statement of financial position

The final step in the budgeting process is to draw up the budgeted statement of financial position at the end of the budgeted period using the budgeted information already produced as shown in Figure 14.9. As we saw in Chapter 2, this statement summarises the assets and liabilities of an entity at the end of an accounting period, whether actual or budgeted. We have already looked at all the numbers that will go into Anna's statement of financial position when we prepared the budgeted statement of profit or loss and cash budget. Anna's budgeted statement of financial position is presented in Illustration 14.11, together with notes reminding you of the sources of the figures.

14

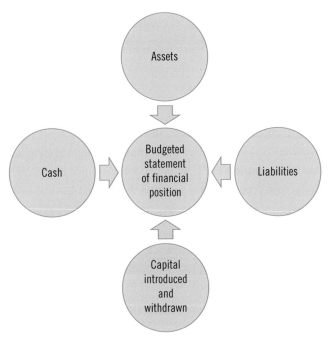

Figure 14.9 Budgeting step 9: draw up the budgeted statement of financial position at the period end

Illustration 14.11 Anna: budgeted statement of financial position at 31 March

	£	Note
Non-current assets		
Machinery and tools	14,250	1
Current assets		
Trade receivables	53,725	2
Insurance prepayment	1,125	3
Rates prepayment	600	4
Cash at bank	5,981	5
Total current assets	61,431	
Total assets	75,681	
Current liabilities		
Trade payables for wood	9,306	6
Electricity accrual	300	7
Total current liabilities	9,606	
Net assets: total assets − total liabilities (£75,681 − £9,606)	66,075	
Capital account		
Capital introduced	10,000	8
Net profit for the three months	62,075	9
Drawings	(6,000)	10
	66,075	

Notes to Anna's budgeted statement of financial position

1. Machinery and tools cost £15,000. Depreciation of £750 has been charged to the statement of profit or loss for the three months to the end of March (Illustration 14.7), so the carrying amount (cost – depreciation) of these assets is therefore £15,000 – £750 = £14,250.

2. The cash not collected from customers by the end of March. We calculated this figure in step 6.

3. The payment of £1,500 covers 12 months of insurance; £375 has been charged against profits as the insurance cost for the three months in the budgeted statement of profit or loss to the end of March (Illustration 14.7), so there is an insurance prepayment of nine months. Therefore, the insurance prepayment is £1,500 × 9/12 = £1,125.

4. Similarly, the payment of £1,200 covers six months of rates expenditure. At 31 March only three of the six months paid for have been used up and charged as an expense in the budgeted statement of profit or loss (Illustration 14.7), so there is a prepayment at 31 March of £1,200 × 3/6 = £600. This £600 represents the rates cost to be charged as an expense in the statement of profit or loss for April, May and June.

5. The cash at bank must equal the closing cash figure in the cash budget (Illustration 14.10).

6. This trade payables figure was calculated in step 7.

7. The electricity accrual is the expense incurred but not yet paid.

8. Anna introduced £10,000 into the business on 1 January in the cash budget.

9. Net profit for the three months is read off the budgeted statement of profit or loss in Illustration 14.7.

10. Drawings are the total amount that Anna has withdrawn from the business bank account for her own personal expenditure over the course of the three months. This figure appears in the cash budget in Illustration 14.10.

WHY IS THIS RELEVANT TO ME?   The budgeted statement of financial position

To enable you as a business professional to understand how:

- The budgeted statement of financial position is compiled from the budgeted statement of profit or loss and cash budget
- To prepare your own budgeted statements of financial position

---

NUMERICAL EXERCISES   Are you convinced that you could draw up a budgeted statement of financial position? Work through the above example again to confirm your understanding of how the statement of financial position was constructed and then go to the **online workbook** and attempt Numerical exercises 14.7 to make sure you can produce this statement.

SHOW ME HOW TO DO IT   How clearly did you understand how Anna's budgeted statement of financial position was put together? View Video presentation 14.3 in the **online workbook** to see a practical demonstration of how this statement was prepared.

Conclusions: financing expansion

What has Anna learnt from her budgeting exercise? At the start of the process, she had approached the bank for finance to start her new workshop. The bank asked her to undertake a budgeting exercise. By producing her budgets she now knows that, if everything goes exactly to plan, she will need to borrow a maximum of £20,725 (Illustration 14.10) from the bank as a result of her expansion. Happily, her cash budget also shows that this maximum borrowing of £20,725 will be paid off by the end of March, so any financing she needs will be very short term. A short-term overdraft with the bank would be the most appropriate form of financing for Anna.

Budgeting flowchart summary

We have now looked in detail at the budgeting process, the steps that are followed and the order in which those steps proceed. We can summarise the budgeting process in a flow chart. This flow chart is shown in Figure 14.10. Look back at the earlier sections of this chapter and relate each step to what you have learnt during our study of the budgeting process so far.

WHY IS THIS RELEVANT TO ME?   Budgeting flowchart summary

To provide you as a business professional with a:

• Map to help you draw up budgets and budgeted financial statements

• Logical step-by-step guide to the production of budgeted information

• Quick overview of the budgeting process to determine where each activity fits into the overall budgeting framework

14

GO BACK OVER THIS AGAIN!   A copy of this budgeting flowchart summary (Figure 14.10) is available in the **online workbook**: you might like to keep this on screen or print off a copy for easy reference while you revise the material in this chapter to provide you with a route map through the budgeting process.

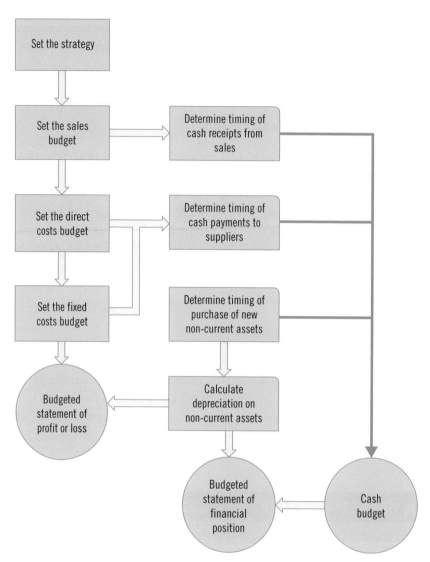

Figure 14.10 The budgeting process

BUDGETARY CONTROL: STATEMENT OF PROFIT OR LOSS

As we noted earlier in this chapter, budgets are used for control purposes. Once each month of actual activity is complete, comparisons are made between what was budgeted to occur and what actually happened. Figure 14.11 illustrates the budgetary control process. It is important to undertake this comparison activity every month so that variances from the budget can be determined and their causes investigated. It would be pointless waiting to complete a whole year of activity before any comparisons were made. By then it would be too late to undertake the

14

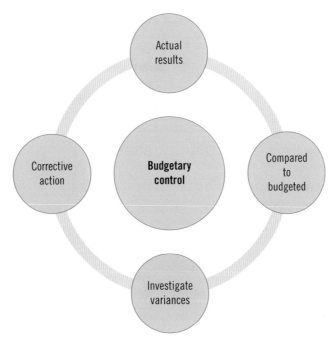

Figure 14.11 The budgetary control process

necessary action to correct budget deviations. In the same way, you do not wait until the end of the academic year to review feedback on your coursework, but instead look at the feedback on each assignment as it is returned so that you can make the necessary improvements in your next piece of assessment.

Monthly comparisons are an example of relevant accounting information (Chapter 1, What qualities should accounting information possess?). Monthly data is provided on a timely basis with a view to influencing managers' economic decisions in terms of, for example, what products to continue selling, whether to discount products that are not selling or to seek out cheaper sources of material if direct material prices from the current supplier are now too high. Comparisons are also confirmatory as well as predictive. The closer budgeted figures are to actual results in a month, the more likely budgeted figures for future months are to predict future outcomes accurately.

As an example, let's look at Anna's budgeted and actual results for January. These are shown in Illustration 14.12.

14

Illustration 14.12 Anna: budgeted v. actual statements of profit or loss for January

	January budget £	January actual £	January variances £
Sales	41,750	43,000	1,250
Cost of sales			
Direct material: wood	7,200	8,000	(800)
Direct material: other	3,600	3,550	50
Direct labour	14,550	14,500	50
Cost of sales	**25,350**	**26,050**	**(700)**
Gross profit (sales – cost of sales)	16,400	16,950	550
Expenses			
Rent	1,000	1,000	—
Rates	200	200	—
Machinery and tools depreciation	250	300	(50)
Electricity	600	600	—
Insurance	125	125	—
Net profit (gross profit – expenses)	**14,225**	**14,725**	**500**

In Illustration 14.12, numbers in brackets in the January variances column are classified as unfavourable, those variances that have reduced the budgeted profit, whereas figures without brackets are favourable, those variances that have increased the budgeted profit.

Now that we have produced our budget v. actual comparison, we can make the following observations.

Higher sales

- Sales are higher than budgeted. This suggests that the original estimates of product sales were a little lower than they should have been. If more products have been sold, Anna should find out why this has occurred and determine whether she can continue to exploit this favourable trend to make higher sales in the future.

- Alternatively, selling prices might have been higher than budgeted because of increased demand pushing prices up. Anna should do her best to maintain any higher selling prices as she will make more profit as a result.

- As there are two possible explanations for this sales variance, Anna will have to conduct further investigations to determine which of the two options is correct or whether it is a combination of both. The sales variance tells her to investigate further, but does not tell her the cause of this variance.

Direct costs

- The cost of wood used in production of goods sold rose in January. This, in itself, is not a surprise as higher production and sales will require more raw material input.

14

However, Anna will need to investigate whether the price of wood has increased or more wood than expected was used in production.

- Other direct material cost less than expected, suggesting lower prices than budgeted or more efficient usage by the workforce.

- Similarly, the cost of labour was lower despite the increased production and sales, suggesting that the workforce has been more productive than budgeted.

- Anna should try to encourage more efficient working as this will increase productivity and lower the costs per unit of production resulting in the generation of higher profits.

- To encourage this higher productivity, Anna might introduce a bonus scheme for her workers to give them a share in any increased profits. However, she will need to make sure that the bonus scheme does not encourage the workforce to work with less care and attention to detail so that the finished production, while taking less time to produce, is of lower quality.

Fixed costs

- Rent and insurance overheads should be as budgeted as these costs should be easily predictable in advance.

- The rates and electricity budget and actual figures are currently the same as we do not have any actual bills to work from. Remember that the rates bill is expected in February and the electricity bill will arrive in March. Once the actual bills are received Anna will be able to determine whether these costs are higher or lower than budgeted.

- The higher than budgeted depreciation figure suggests that the machinery and tools cost Anna more than anticipated, resulting in a higher monthly depreciation charge. Anna will need to check the actual payment for machinery and tools.

Net profit

- Overall, actual profits for January were higher than budgeted by £500.

- Based upon her investigations of the causes of the variances in January, Anna will aim to correct any unfavourable variances in the cost and usage of wood, while attempting to exploit the favourable variances in the sales to sell more goods or to sell goods at a higher price.

14

WHY IS THIS RELEVANT TO ME?   Budgetary control: actual v. budget comparisons: statement of profit or loss

As a business professional you will be expected to:

- Take on responsibility for any departmental budget you hold and to explain variations between budgeted and actual results

- Produce actual v. budget comparisons on a monthly basis

- Ask relevant questions when evaluating actual v. budget comparisons

GO BACK OVER THIS AGAIN!   Do you think you could suggest reasons for changes in budgeted v. actual sales and costs? Go to the **online workbook** and have a go at Exercises 14.3 to see if you can.

BUDGETARY CONTROL: CASH BUDGET

As well as comparing her budgeted and actual statements of profit or loss, Anna will also undertake a comparison of her budgeted and actual cash flows. As we noted at the start of this chapter, Anna needs additional finance from the bank to expand her business and move into the larger workshop. Her initial cash budget suggested that she would only need to borrow a maximum of £20,725. Because of the critical nature of cash inflows and outflows in her business operations, both Anna and her bank will be watching her cash position very closely to make sure that she does not exceed her borrowing capacity or her borrowing limits.

Anna produces her budgeted and actual cash flow comparisons for January in Illustration 14.13.

Illustration 14.13 Anna: budgeted v. actual cash inflows and outflows for January

	January budget £	January actual £	January variances £
Cash received			
Sales	12,525	13,760	1,235
Capital introduced	10,000	10,000	—
Total cash receipts	22,525	23,760	1,235
Cash paid			
Direct material: wood	3,600	4,000	(400)
Direct material: other	3,600	3,550	50
Direct labour	14,550	14,500	50
Rent	3,000	3,000	—
Machinery and tools	15,000	18,000	(3,000)
Electricity	—	—	—
Rates	—	—	—
Insurance	1,500	1,500	—
Drawings – personal expenditure	2,000	2,000	—
Total cash payments	43,250	46,550	(3,300)
Cash receipts – cash payments	(20,725)	(22,790)	(2,065)
Cash at the start of the month	—	—	—
Cash at the end of the month	(20,725)	(22,790)	(2,065)

What does this budgeted v. actual cash flow comparison tell Anna? She can draw the following conclusions:

- Her customers are paying more quickly than she expected. While she anticipated that 30% of her customers would pay in the month of sale, 32% of actual sales have paid in January

14

(£13,760 ÷ £43,000 (actual sales from the statement of profit or loss in Illustration 14.12) × 100%). Anna should try to persuade her customers to continue paying more quickly as this will improve her cash inflows and thereby reduce her borrowings more rapidly.

- While £400 more has been paid out for wood, this is consistent with Anna's intention that she would pay for 50% of the wood she used in the month of usage. As her actual usage was £8,000 (Illustration 14.12), she has paid half this amount in January.

- Payments for both other materials and labour are £50 less than expected, but these are the actual amounts used in January according to the budgeted v. actual statement of profit or loss (Illustration 14.12). Cash payments are thus in line with Anna's policy of paying in full for labour and other materials in the month in which they were used.

- Machinery and tools were budgeted to cost £15,000 but in fact cost £18,000. This is consistent with the increase in depreciation shown in the statement of profit or loss in Illustration 14.12. The machinery and tools are expected to have a five-year life, which gives an annual depreciation charge of £3,600 per annum (£18,000 ÷ 5) which equates to £300 per month (£3,600 ÷ 12). Anna tells you that the machinery and tools had been imported from Germany and that the increased cost was because of a fall in the value of the pound against the euro at the time the machinery and tools were bought and paid for.

- All other inflows and outflows of cash were as budgeted.

- As a result of the above differences in her planned cash inflows and outflows, Anna has borrowed an additional £2,065 from the bank in January. The sole cause of this problem was the payment for her machinery and tools. Her aim now will be to pay off this additional borrowing as quickly as possible by encouraging her customers to pay more promptly or trying to sell more products each month to increase her cash inflows while keeping outflows of cash as low as possible.

WHY IS THIS RELEVANT TO ME? Budgetary control: actual v. Budget comparisons: cash flow

As a business professional you must appreciate that:

- Cash is the lifeblood of business and without it businesses will run out of money and collapse

- Monitoring budgeted v. actual cash is thus just as (if not more) important as comparing budgeted v. actual profits

14

NUMERICAL EXERCISES   Are you sure that you could produce a comparison of budgeted v. actual cash flows? Go to the **online workbook** and have a go at Numerical exercises 14.8 to see if you can.

SENSITIVITY ANALYSIS

Anna has produced her budgets for the first three months of operations and predicted her maximum borrowings from the bank. However, what if her budgets don't turn out as she expects? How will this affect her profits and her cash flows? Given questions such as these, it is usual when budgeting to conduct sensitivity analysis to assess how profits and cash flows would turn out if certain expectations are changed. Thus, for example, a reduction in budgeted sales units might be applied, or an increase in direct costs of 10% or a fall in selling price of 10%. Spreadsheets make these 'what if?' calculations easy to undertake.

As an example, let's see what would happen to profits and cash flows if budgeted unit sales of Anna's products fell by 10% while keeping selling prices the same. We will adopt various short-cuts in producing our figures here, but all the calculations will be available in the online workbook.

First, let's look at the statement of profit or loss showing a 10% fall in numbers of products sold compared with Anna's original plans. This is shown in Illustration 14.14.

Illustration 14.14 Anna: budgeted statement of profit or loss for January, February and March assuming a 10% fall in the number of products sold while keeping selling prices the same

	January	February	March	Total	Note
	£	£	£	£	
Sales	37,575	51,750	69,075	158,400	1
Cost of sales	22,815	31,950	41,895	96,660	2
Gross profit (sales − cost of sales)	14,760	19,800	27,180	61,740	
Expenses					
Fixed costs	2,175	2,175	2,175	6,525	3
Net profit (gross profit − expenses)	**12,585**	**17,625**	**25,005**	**55,215**	

Notes on the above budgeted statement of profit or loss:

1. Sales volumes reduce by 10%, which results in sales 10% lower than those shown in Illustrations 14.3 and 14.7.

2. As sales volumes fall by 10%, cost of sales (direct costs) also falls by 10% as Anna's direct costs in producing 10% fewer goods will be 10% lower.

3. Budgeted fixed costs are made up of £1,000 (rent) + £200 (rates) + £250 (depreciation) + £600 (electricity) + £125 insurance to give total budgeted fixed costs per month of £2,175.

These are the same costs that we used in Illustration 14.7. Remember that fixed costs do not change with different levels of sales and production, so these costs are the same for the original budgeted sales and the revised budgeted sales volumes of 10% lower than originally planned.

14

Anna's original budgeted profit of £62,075 in Illustration 14.7 has now fallen to £55,215 given a 10% fall in sales volumes.

However, Anna's main concern was with finance and how much she would need to borrow from the bank. Surely the effect of this fall of 10% in sales volumes will increase the size of her projected overdraft? The effect of the 10% fall in sales volumes on the cash budget is shown in Illustration 14.15.

Illustration 14.15 Anna: budgeted cash inflows and outflows for January, February and March assuming a 10% fall in the number of products sold while keeping selling prices the same

	January £	February £	March £	Total £
Cash received				
Sales	11,273	41,827	56,947	110,047
Capital introduced	10,000	—	—	10,000
Total cash receipts	21,273	41,827	56,947	120,047
Cash paid				
Direct material: wood	3,240	6,683	10,619	20,542
Direct material: other	3,240	4,473	5,400	13,113
Direct labour	13,095	18,000	23,535	54,630
Rent	3,000	—	—	3,000
Machinery and tools	15,000	—	—	15,000
Electricity	—	—	1,500	1,500
Rates	—	1,200	—	1,200
Insurance	1,500	—	—	1,500
Drawings: personal expenditure	2,000	2,000	2,000	6,000
Total cash payments	41,075	32,356	43,054	116,485
Cash receipts – cash payments	(19,802)	9,471	13,893	3,562
Cash at the start of the month	—	(19,802)	(10,331)	
Cash at the end of the month	(19,802)	(10,331)	3,562	

Budgeted payments for rent, machinery and tools, electricity, rates, insurance and drawings across the three months under review do not change, so these stay the same in both Illustrations 14.10 and 14.15. Receipts from sales fall, but planned payments for wood, other materials and direct labour fall by more than the reduction in sales receipts. This has the effect of actually reducing the expected borrowings at the end of January from £20,725 to £19,802, so, even with lower sales volumes, Anna is borrowing less. Her cash balance at the end of three months is lower at £3,562 compared to the £5,981 shown in Illustration 14.10, but she still pays off the borrowings by the end of March as in her original budget.

The assumptions on which Anna's original budgets were based can be relaxed further to see what effect these changes will have on her budgeted statement of profit or loss, cash budget and projected statement of financial position and you can have a go at some of these in the online workbook.

The following extract, in Give me an example 14.3, from the directors' Viability Statement in the annual report and accounts of GlaxoSmithKline plc, shows how sensitivity analysis is used in practice to test the assumptions on which financial plans and forecasts are based and to determine whether these forecasts and plans are realistic and achievable.

GIVE ME AN EXAMPLE 14.3   Sensitivity analysis

The Plan has been stress tested in a series of robust operational and principal risk downside scenarios as part of the Board's review on risk. These include the potential effects of Brexit, which are not expected to be material, although there may be some short-term disruption. The downside scenarios consider GSK's cash flows, sustainability of dividends, funding strategy, insurance provision and recovery as well as other key financial ratios over the period. These metrics have been subject to sensitivity analysis, which involves flexing a number of the main assumptions underlying the forecasts both individually and in combination, along with mitigating actions that could realistically be taken to avoid or reduce the impact or occurrence of the underlying risk.

Source: GlaxoSmithKline plc annual report and accounts for the year ended 31 December 2018, p. 44

WHY IS THIS RELEVANT TO ME?   Sensitivity analysis

To enable you as a business professional to:

• Appreciate that original budgets will be subjected to sensitivity analysis to determine the effect of changes in budgeted numbers on budgeted profits and cash flows

• Undertake sensitivity analysis on budgeted information prepared by yourself and others

14

 GO BACK OVER THIS AGAIN!   How readily did you understand how the figures for Anna were calculated for the reduction in sales volumes of 10%? Take a look at Exercises 14.4 in the **online workbook** to view all the calculations involved in this exercise.

NUMERICAL EXERCISES Are you convinced that you could undertake sensitivity analysis on a set of budgeted figures? Go to the **online workbook** and have a go at Numerical exercises 14.9 to see what effect various changes would have on Anna's budgeted statement of profit or loss and cash budget for January, February and March.

CHAPTER SUMMARY

You should now have learnt that:

- Budgets perform planning, communicating, coordinating, motivating and control functions within organisations

- The sales budget is the starting point for all other budgeted figures and statements

- Entities prepare budgeted statements of profit or loss and cash budgets on a monthly basis

- Monthly comparisons are made between budgeted income and expenditure and budgeted cash inflows and outflows to ensure that operations are under control

- Businesses undertake comparisons between budgeted and actual income and expenditure to highlight variances in expected and actual financial performance

- Sensitivity analysis is applied to assumptions made in budgeted financial statements to determine how easily an entity could make a loss or require overdraft financing

QUICK REVISION Test your knowledge by attempting the activities in the **online workbook**, in- cluding flashcards on the key concepts, numerical exercises and Multiple choice questions. You can also try the further self-test questions which are available at www.oup.com/he/scott-i2a2e

END-OF-CHAPTER QUESTIONS

Attempt the questions in the following sections and then look at the solutions which can be found in the **online workbook** to see whether there are areas that you need to revisit.

❱ RECALL AND REVIEW

❱ **Question 14.1**

What is a budget? Why do firms spend time and money in the preparation of budgets? Explain how budgeting helps in the more effective management of a business.

14

> **Question 14.2**

Hermann plc prepares quarterly budgets. The following is the company's sales budget for 2022:

	Quarter 1	Quarter 2	Quarter 3	Quarter 4
Sales in units	5,500	8,400	7,300	4,100
Selling price per unit	£70	£70	£68	£68

Each unit of production and sales requires 2 kg of material costing £14 per kg, 1½ hours of direct labour costing £10 per hour and £5 of variable overhead. Total fixed costs for 2022 are budgeted at £200,000.

Required

Prepare budgeted statements of profit or loss for Hermann plc for each quarter of 2022 (your first task will be to calculate budgeted sales and budgeted costs).

>> DEVELOP YOUR UNDERSTANDING

>> **Question 14.3**

Dave is planning to start up in business selling ice cream from a van around his local neighbourhood from April to September. He wants to open a business bank account, but the bank manager has insisted that he provides a cash budget together with a budgeted statement of profit or loss for his first six months of trading and a budgeted statement of financial position at 30 September. Dave is unsure how to put this information together, but he has provided you with the following details of his planned income and expenditure:

- Dave will pay in £5,000 of his own money on 1 April to get the business started.
- He expects to make all his sales for cash and anticipates that he will make sales of £3,500 in April, £5,500 in May, £7,500 in each of the next three months and £2,500 in September.
- He will buy his ice cream from a local supplier and expects the cost of this to be 50% of selling price. Dave has agreed with his supplier that he will start paying for his ice cream in May rather than in the month of purchase.
- Dave intends to sell all his ice cream by the end of September and to have no inventory at the end of this trading period.
- Ice cream vans can be hired at a cost of £1,500 for three months. The £1,500 hire charge is payable at the start of each three-month period.
- Van running costs are estimated to be £250 per month payable in cash.
- Business insurance payable on 1 April will cost £500 for six months.
- Dave will draw £1,000 per month out of the business bank account to meet personal expenses.

Required
Provide Dave with:

- A cash budget for the first six months of trading.
- A budgeted statement of profit or loss for the first six months of trading.
- A budgeted statement of financial position at 30 September.

>> Question 14.4

Hena plc has a division that manufactures and sells solar panels. Demand for solar panels has picked up recently and the company is looking to increase its output. Hena plc's division currently manufactures 600,000 solar panels annually and is looking to double this capacity. A new factory has become available at an annual rent of £600,000 payable quarterly in advance. New plant and machinery would cost £1.8 million, payable immediately on delivery on 1 January. This new plant and machinery would have a useful life of 10 years and would be depreciated on a straight line basis with £Nil residual value. The directors of Hena plc are now wondering whether they should go ahead with the new solar panel factory. They have produced the following projections upon which to base their budgets.

Hena plc sells each solar panel for £150. Demand for the increased output is expected to be as follows:

- January: 20,000 panels
- February and March: 30,000 panels per month
- April: 40,000 panels
- May to August: 80,000 panels per month
- September: 60,000 panels
- October and November: 40,000 panels per month
- December: 20,000 panels
- All panels are sold to credit customers, 10% of whom pay in the month of sale, 60% in the month after and the remaining 30% two months after the month of sale.

Details of production costs are as follows:

- Materials cost is 30% of the selling price of the panels. Materials suppliers are paid in the month after production and sales have taken place.
- Production labour is 20% of the selling price; 70% of this amount is payable in the month of sale and the remainder, representing deductions from production wages for tax and national insurance, is paid to HM Revenue and Customs one month after production and sales have taken place.
- Other variable production costs of 10% of selling price are paid in the month of sale.

Fixed costs are estimated to be £50,000 per month and are to be treated as paid in the month in which they were incurred. Hena plc manufactures to order and sells all its production and has no inventories of solar panels at the end of the year.

Required
Using a spreadsheet of your choice, prepare the following statements for the next 12 months:

- A sales budget.
- A production costs budget.
- A monthly cash budget.
- A monthly budgeted statement of profit or loss.
- A budgeted statement of financial position at the end of the 12 months.

Advise the directors of Hena plc whether they should go ahead with the proposed expansion or not.

14

>> **Question 14.5**

The directors of Hena plc are impressed with your spreadsheet and your recommendation. However, they have new information that they would like you to build into your projections. The directors now expect that the selling price of panels will fall to £120 in the near future because of new competitors entering the market. Production materials, due to high levels of demand, will rise to 58% of the new selling price, while employees will have to be given a 5% pay rise based on production labour costs originally calculated in Question 14.4 to encourage them to stay. Other variable production costs will now fall to 10% of the new selling price. All other expectations in Question 14.4 will remain the same. The directors are now wondering if your recommendation would be the same once you have incorporated the above changes into your budget projections.

Required

Using the spreadsheet you have prepared for Question 14.4, prepare the following statements for the next 12 months on the basis of the directors' new expectations:

- A sales budget.
- A production costs budget.
- A monthly cash budget.
- A monthly budgeted statement of profit or loss.
- A budgeted statement of financial position at the end of the 12 months.

Advise the directors of Hena plc whether they should go ahead with the proposed expansion or not given the new information that has come to hand.

>> **Question 14.6**

John has recently completed a catering course. He decides to open a restaurant in Manchester. He recognises that before starting a new business he must ensure that sufficient cash is available in every single month of operation to meet all his expenses as they fall due. He has therefore prepared a list of expected receipts and payments of the restaurant for the first six months of operation (July to December):

- John will invest £6,000 of his own money into the business at the start of July.
- He estimates that sales for the first three months will be £4,000 per month and then sales will rise by 10% each month for the next three months. All sales will be for cash.
- A fitted out restaurant space will be rented for £1,000 per month. A deposit of the same amount is charged in the first month.
- £500 insurance for one year will be paid on 1 July.
- Advertising in the local newspaper will be taken out at a cost of £450 per month for the first three months. These adverts must be paid for before the local newspaper will run them.
- Purchases of food and beverages will amount to £1,600 per month for the first three months. Purchases of these items will then increase by 10% each month in line with sales. All purchases will be paid for in the month in which they are made.
- Wages of restaurant staff will amount to £2,000 each month.
- Utility bills (power, heating, water and telephone) will be £350 per month payable in September and December.

14

Required

(a) Prepare a monthly cash budget for John's restaurant for July to December.

(b) Advise whether John will require additional funding for his business and identify the months in which any additional funding will be required.

» Question 14.7

Given the results of the budgeting exercise in Question 14.6, John consults a financial advisor. The advisor believes that, considering the current economic situation, John should prepare his business plan on a worst case scenario before he starts trading. Her analysis suggests that food and drink purchase prices may increase by 12%, while sales revenue might fall by 8%. John therefore needs to think of other sources of financing such as a bank loan to prevent his business suffering a cash deficit.

Required

(a) Undertake sensitivity analysis on your results from Question 14.6 and prepare a cash budget for John's restaurant under the expected worst case scenario as suggested by the financial advisor.

(b) Advise whether John will require additional funding for his business and identify the months in which any additional funding will be required.

»»» TAKE IT FURTHER

»»» Question 14.8

Robert opens a business that produces and sells flowerpots. He pays £2,000 of his own money into the business bank account in September. Robert approaches you to help him produce a budget for the coming months. The following information is available:

(a) Flowerpots are produced in four sizes. The selling prices and variable costs of each flowerpot are presented below. Robert tells you that all sales are made for immediate payment in cash and that all costs and expenses are similarly paid in cash as they are incurred.

(b) Flowerpots: selling prices and variable costs

	Size A £	Size B £	Size C £	Size D £
Selling price	10	12	15	18
Materials: clay	2	3	5	6
Direct labour	2	4	4	6
Variable overhead	1	2	2	3

(c) Based on expected demand, Robert has drawn up the following budgeted sales in units for September to December:

14

	September Units	October Units	November Units	December Units
Size A	100	120	140	130
Size B	80	100	130	90
Size C	90	110	120	80
Size D	60	70	80	50

(d) Fixed costs

   i. Rent on the business premises is £800 per month and will be paid monthly.

   ii. £200 insurance will be paid on 1 September to cover all business activities from September to December.

   iii. Utility bills of £250 per month will be paid in October and December for power and heating used by the business.

   iv. General and administration expenses of £200 per month will be paid monthly.

   v. £240 will be paid on September 1 for radio advertising for the next four months.

Required

Prepare a monthly sales budget, variable costs budget, budgeted statements of profit or loss and cash budgets for September, October, November and December.

≫ Question 14.9

It is now August 2022. You have been asked by your head of department to prepare the monthly budgeted statement of profit or loss, the monthly cash budget and the budgeted statement of financial position for the 12 months ending 31 December 2023. You have been provided with the following details to help you in this task:

(a) Positive cash balances at the end of each month will earn interest at the rate of 0.5% of the month end balance and this interest will be receivable in the following month.

(b) Negative cash balances at the end of each month will be charged interest at the rate of 2% of the month end balance and this interest will be payable in the following month.

(c) Cash of £30,000 will be spent in March 2023 on new plant and equipment. The new plant and equipment will be brought into use in the business in the month of purchase.

(d) Your company produces three products: shirts, dresses and skirts. The cost cards for each product are as follows:

	Shirts £	Dresses £	Skirts £
Direct materials	10.00	12.00	6.00
Direct labour	12.00	15.00	7.50
Variable overhead	3.00	5.00	1.50
Total variable cost	**25.00**	**30.00**	**15.00**

14

(e) Selling prices are 140% of total variable cost. Payments for direct labour are made in accordance with note (i). 60% of the cost of materials is paid for one month after the month in which the materials were used in production, with the other 40% of materials being paid for two months after the month in which they were used in production. Where purchases of direct materials are greater than £20,000 in any one month, a 2½% discount is given on all purchases of direct materials in that month. When purchases of direct materials are greater than £25,000 in any one month, a 3½% discount is given on all purchases of direct materials in that month. Variable overhead is paid for in the following month.

(f) The marketing department has estimated that sales of each product for the year will be as follows:

2023	Shirts Number	Dresses Number	Skirts Number
January	500	300	800
February	600	350	900
March	750	400	700
April	900	700	650
May	1,000	800	500
June	1,000	1,200	400
July	800	1,000	350
August	700	600	200
September	950	400	500
October	650	300	600
November	850	450	750
December	1,100	600	850
Total	**9,800**	**7,100**	**7,200**

Your company sells its products directly to retailers. Retailers pay for the goods purchased as follows: 10% on delivery, 25% one month after delivery, 50% two months after delivery and the remaining 15% three months after delivery. All goods produced in the month are sold in the month and there are no inventories of finished goods or raw materials at the start or end of each month.

(g) The company rents its factory and offices and currently pays a total of £30,000 a year in rent. A rent review in March 2023 is expected to increase the annual factory rent to £36,000 from 1 August 2023. Quarterly rental payments in advance will be made on 1 February, 1 May, 1 August and 1 November 2023.

(h) Business rates for the six months to March 2023 will be paid on 1 October 2022 and the prepayment relating to January, February and March is shown in the budgeted statement of financial position at 1 January 2023 in note (k). Business rates of £7,500 per half year will be payable on 1 April 2023 and 1 October 2023. These business rates will cover the 12 months from 1 April 2023 to 31 March 2024.

14

(i)   Administrative and supervisory staff salaries are expected to total up to £9,000 a month. Sixty-eight per cent of staff salaries and direct labour costs are payable in the month in which they are incurred with the remaining 32% representing deductions for tax and national insurance being paid to HM Revenue and Customs in the following month.

(j)   An insurance premium of £6,000 is payable on 1 May 2023 covering all the insurance costs of the business for the 12 months to 30 April 2024.

(k)   The budgeted statement of financial position at 1 January 2023 is as follows:

	£
Non-current assets	
Plant, equipment and fittings: cost	120,000
Plant, equipment and fittings: accumulated depreciation	(36,000)
	84,000
Current assets	
Trade receivables (owed by customers)	122,000
Rent prepayment	2,500
Rates prepayment	3,600
Insurance prepayment	1,800
Bank interest receivable	17
Cash at bank	3,395
	133,312
TOTAL ASSETS	**217,312**
Current liabilities	
Trade payables (materials)	29,400
Trade payables (variable overhead)	7,200
Tax and national insurance (direct labour)	8,570
Tax and national insurance (admin and supervisory salaries)	2,752
Corporation tax payable	3,200
Dividend payable	5,000
Total liabilities	**56,122**
Net assets	**161,190**
Equity	
Share capital	50,000
Retained earnings	111,190
	161,190

Notes to the budgeted statement of financial position at 1 January 2023:

(i)   Plant, equipment and fittings have a useful economic life of five years. Depreciation on these assets is charged monthly on the straight line basis.

(ii) Sales for October, November and December 2022 are budgeted to be £60,000, £70,000 and £75,000 respectively.

(iii) Purchases of materials are budgeted to cost £20,000 in November 2022 and £21,400 (net of the 2½% discount) in December 2022.

(iv) The dividend payable is scheduled for payment in April 2023 and the corporation tax is due for payment on 1 October 2023.

Required

Prepare the monthly budgeted statement of profit or loss and cash budget for your company for the 12 months ended 31 December 2023 together with a budgeted statement of financial position at 31 December 2023.

⟫⟫ Question 14.10

Your friend is proposing to make a bid for a manufacturing business that has come onto the market. The business makes white plastic patio chairs. The purchase price for this business is £240,000. This purchase price is made up of plant, equipment and fittings (£180,000) with a useful life of five years, an inventory of raw materials (£20,000) and finished goods (£40,000). A delivery van will be purchased for £24,000 as soon as the business purchase is completed. The delivery van will be paid for in full in the second month of operations.

The following plans have been made for the business following purchase:

(a) Sales of plastic patio chairs, at a mark up of 60% (before discounts) on production cost (see (b) below), will be:

Month	January	February	March	April	May	June	July
Planned sales (units)	10,000	12,000	14,000	20,000	24,000	22,000	18,000

Thirty per cent of sales will be for cash. The remaining sales will be on credit with 60% of credit sales being paid in the following month and the remaining 40% paying what is owed two months after the month of sale. A discount of 10% will be given to selected credit customers, who represent 25% of gross sales.

(b) Production cost is estimated at £5.00 per unit. The estimated production cost is made up of:

- Raw materials: £4.00
- Direct labour: £1.00

Production will be arranged so that closing inventory of finished goods at the end of every month is sufficient to meet 60% of sales requirements in the following month. The valuation of finished goods purchased with the business is based upon the planned production cost per unit given in (a) above.

(c) The single raw material used in production will be purchased so that inventory at the end of each month is sufficient to meet half of the following month's production requirements. Raw material inventory acquired on purchase of the business is valued at the planned cost per unit as given in (b) above. Raw materials will be purchased on one month's credit.

14

(d) Costs of direct labour will be paid for as they are incurred in production.

(e) Fixed overheads are as follows: annual rent: £21,000, annual business rates: £8,100, annual heating and lighting: £7,500 and annual insurance: £1,500. Rent is payable quarterly in advance from 1 January. The business rates bill for January to March has been estimated at £1,800 and will be payable on 15 February, while the rates bill from April to September has been estimated at £4,200 and will be payable by monthly instalments from 1 April. Heating and lighting will be payable quarterly in arrears at the end of each three-month period. Annual insurance will be payable on 1 January.

(f) Selling and administration overheads are all fixed, and will be £114,000 in the first year. These overheads include depreciation of the delivery van at 25% per annum on a straight line basis.

(g) Selling and administration overheads will be the same each month and will be paid in the month in which they are incurred.

Required

Prepare a monthly cash budget and a monthly budgeted statement of profit or loss for the first six months of operations together with a budgeted statement of financial position at the end of June. As part of your budget, you should also produce a monthly production budget to calculate raw material purchases and a monthly sales budget to calculate both monthly sales and monthly cash receipts from sales.

PROCESS COSTING

15

INTRODUCTION

Our review of cost and management accounting thus far has focused on the costs and selling prices for solid units of production. The inputs to the production of wooden furniture in terms of materials and labour are easily distinguishable one from another. Likewise, the finished products are tangible and readily visible as individual units of production. However, what of products which are made in processes which involve the input and output not just of solid materials but of liquids or gases? These are processes in which the final output may not be immediately produced in readily divisible units. The production process for, for example, soft drinks or paints is continuous and it is very difficult to identify separate units of production until they are put into bottles, cans or tins. The outputs from one process can become the inputs to another process with the finished goods only being produced in the final process. Process costing is the costing method that is used to value the inputs and outputs from the oil, chemical, paper, food and drink industries. This chapter will therefore look at the ways in which process costing works in order to give a cost to units of production. In addition, we shall consider the way in which inventory is valued under process costing. Anna was able to value her wooden furniture on the basis of the material and labour inputs to each product together with an allocation of a proportion of production overhead (Chapter 11, Absorption costing and inventory valuation). By counting up her inventory of finished products and multiplying the total number of units by the cost price per unit she was able to derive a value for her inventory at the end of each accounting period very quickly and easily. But how should inventory for processes be valued at the end of each financial period? This valuation is made more difficult as a result of the continuous nature of the production process: at the end of the relevant period, some of the production may be only partially complete. How should this work in progress (WIP) be valued?

THE PROCESS ACCOUNT

As with all cost accounting techniques, the first step in process costing is to accumulate the costs in the cost account. In process costing, a process account is used to gather up these costs. The process account is a T account which gathers together the costs of inputs to a process. The inputs to the process, as in any other manufacturing operation, are materials, labour and overhead (Figure 15.1). Inputs to the process are posted to the debit (left hand) side of the process account while outputs appear on the credit (right hand) side. An example of a process account is shown in Illustration 15.1. Note that material inputs and outputs are expressed in money and unit terms, whereas labour and overhead are presented purely as costs expressed without any reference to quantities. In process costing, labour and overhead are known as conversion cost and this conversion cost is added to units of production. As always with T accounts, the totals on the two sides must be the same. In process costing, this means that both the quantities and the costs must be equal. From the example in Illustration 15.1, we can see that the cost per litre of output is the total cost of £60,000 divided by the total output of 5,000 litres = £12.

15

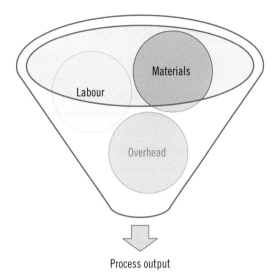

Figure 15.1 The process accounted for in the process account

Illustration 15.1 The process account

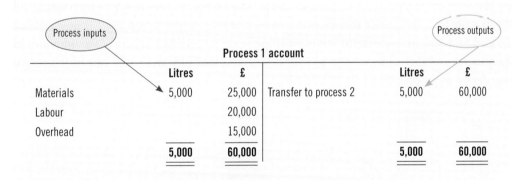

	Litres	£		Litres	£
Materials	5,000	25,000	Transfer to process 2	5,000	60,000
Labour		20,000			
Overhead		15,000			
	5,000	**60,000**		**5,000**	**60,000**

Process 1 account

Process inputs

Process outputs

WHY IS THIS RELEVANT TO ME?   The process account

To enable you as a business professional to understand:

- How the process account works
- The industrial situations in which process accounting is used to accumulate the cost of process inputs and to value process outputs

15

GO BACK OVER THIS AGAIN!   Are you sure that you understand how the process account works and what it is for? Go to the **online workbook** and have a go at Exercises 15.1 to check your understanding.

NORMAL LOSSES IN A PROCESS

In many if not all processes, the quantity of materials input to the process will not be the same as the quantity of materials of output from the process. This is as a result of evaporation, losses arising from chemical reactions or natural spoilage during the process (Figure 15.2). Lengthy experience and observation of these losses over time will enable entities to determine the normal level of losses that will be incurred each time the process is repeated. Normal losses are expected losses and are allowed for in the budget for each process. Normal losses in a process are usually expressed as a percentage of the quantity of materials input to the process. Normal losses are *never* given a value and are always valued at £Nil. The cost of normal losses is rolled up into the units of expected output from the process and valued as part of the units transferred to the next process or as units of finished product. Illustration 15.2 shows the way in which normal losses are accounted for in the process T account. In this case, the normal losses are expected to be 200 litres, leaving 4,800 litres of output transferred to process 2 (5,000 litres of input material – 200 litres of normal losses = 4,800 litres). While the normal loss is not valued in the process T account, the number of litres of normal loss is still added in to the credit side of the account as a deduction from the litres of input material to leave the number of litres transferred to process 2. Again, the two sides of the T account must balance: the 5,000 litres of input material is turned into 4,800 litres of output to process 2 + 200 litres of normal loss. From Illustration 15.2, we can see that the value of each litre of output to process 2 is now £60,000 divided by 4,800 litres = £12.50. The normal losses are thus valued as part of the output from the process and the value of these normal losses is carried forward in the cost of the output transferred to process 2.

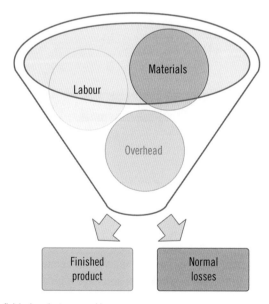

Figure 15.2 Process outcomes: finished product + normal losses

Illustration 15.2 The process account showing accounting for normal losses

	Litres	£		Litres	£
	Process 1 account				
Materials	5,000	25,000	Transfer to process 2	4,800	60,000
Labour		20,000	**Normal loss**	200	–
Overhead		15,000	Normal losses: quantified in units but not valued in £s		
	5,000	**60,000**		**5,000**	**60,000**

ABNORMAL LOSSES

Figure 15.3 presents the additional complication of abnormal losses. Abnormal losses arise when there are losses that exceed the expected normal loss. These abnormal losses are valued in the process account and are accounted for separately. Abnormal losses are not part of normal production so are not rolled up into the cost of expected finished production units from a process.

Illustration 15.3 presents the process account showing the normal losses of 200 litres and an abnormal loss of 100 litres. Normal losses are still not valued, being recorded as the expected number of litres of lost input material at £Nil value. Abnormal losses are valued at the unit cost of the expected finished output transferred from the process. As we saw in Illustration 15.2, the cost per litre of output transferred to process 2 is £12.50 (£60,000 ÷ 4,800 litres = £12.50 per litre). The cost of the 4,700 litres transferred to process 2 is thus 4,700 × £12.50 = £58,750 while the

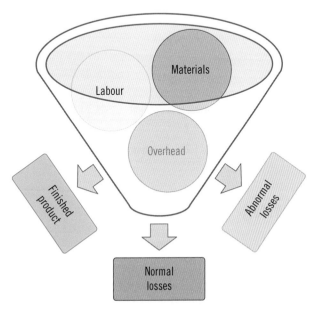

Figure 15.3 Process outcomes: finished product + normal losses + abnormal losses

abnormal loss of 100 litres is allocated a value of 100 litres × £12.50 (the unit cost of the expected finished output transferred from the process) = £1,250. Both sides of the process account must add up to 5,000 litres and £60,000 in total process inputs and total process costs.

Illustration 15.3 The process account showing the accounting for normal and abnormal losses

Process 1 account

	Litres	£		Litres	£
Materials	5,000	25,000	Transfer to process 2	4,700	58,750
Labour		20,000	Normal loss	200	–
Overhead		15,000	Abnormal loss	100	1,250
	5,000	**60,000**		**5,000**	**60,000**

Abnormal losses: quantified and valued at the cost of expected production

In the cost accounting system, the £1,250 of abnormal loss is transferred to an abnormal loss account as shown in Illustration 15.4. This abnormal loss represents a loss of expected finished production from a process and is charged as an expense to the costing statement of profit or loss at the end of the accounting period in which it arose. Highlighting this expense in this way reports the loss to the business and will encourage management to investigate the abnormal loss to determine whether it can be prevented in future or whether the loss was incurred as a result of a unique set of circumstances which will not be repeated.

Illustration 15.4 The abnormal loss account

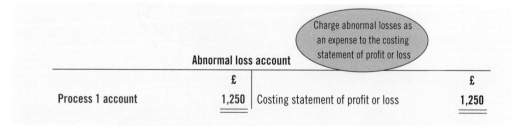

Charge abnormal losses as an expense to the costing statement of profit or loss

Abnormal loss account

	£		£
Process 1 account	1,250	Costing statement of profit or loss	1,250

ABNORMAL GAINS

As well as abnormal losses, processes can experience abnormal gains. Abnormal gains arise when the actual losses from the process are lower than the expected normal losses (Figure 15.4). As was the case with abnormal losses, abnormal gains are valued in the process account and accounted for separately. Illustration 15.5 presents the entries to the process account when abnormal gains arise. What has happened here? Instead of the expected 4,800 litres of output, 4,880 litres have been transferred to process 2. The output transferred to process 2 is valued at £12.50 per litre giving a total transfer value of £61,000. The normal loss is still included at 200 litres and

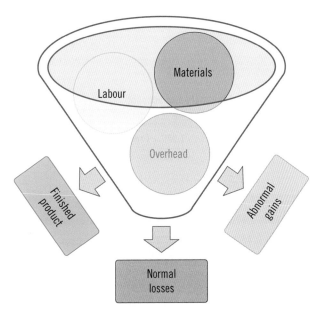

Figure 15.4 Process outcomes: finished product + normal losses + abnormal gains

£Nil value. But there are now 5,080 litres and £61,000 on the credit side of the process account so the abnormal gain is added to the debit side to balance the account. Eighty litres is the abnormal gain and this is valued at the finished production price per litre of £12.50 to give a total abnormal gain of £1,000.

Illustration 15.5 The process account showing normal losses and abnormal gains

Process 1 account

	Litres	£		Litres	£
Materials	5,000	25,000	Transfer to process 2	4,880	61,000
Labour		20,000	Normal loss	200	–
Overhead		15,000			
Abnormal gains	80	1,000			
	5,080	**61,000**		**5,080**	**61,000**

Abnormal gains: quantified and valued at the cost of expected production

In the cost accounting system, the £1,000 of abnormal gain is transferred to an abnormal gains account as shown in Illustration 15.6. This abnormal gain is then credited as income to the costing statement of profit or loss in the period in which it was incurred. Highlighting this additional income in this way will indicate to management that there may be ways in which to reduce the expected normal loss in the process. They will therefore be encouraged to investigate the gain to determine whether it can be maintained in the future or whether the gain arose as a result of an unrepeatable set of circumstances.

15

Illustration 15.6 The abnormal gains account

Credit abnormal gains
as income to the costing
statement of profit or loss

Abnormal gains account

	£		£
Costing statement of profit or loss	1,000	Process 1 account	1,000

WHY IS THIS RELEVANT TO ME?   Normal losses, abnormal losses and abnormal gains

To enable you as a business professional to understand:

- How losses and gains in processes are accounted for
- That normal losses are expected losses from a process
- That normal losses are quantified in units but are never given a value in £s
- That valuing and accounting for abnormal losses and gains separately encourages management to investigate the causes of these abnormal gains and losses

---

MULTIPLE CHOICE QUESTIONS   Are you convinced that you could account correctly for normal losses, abnormal losses and abnormal gains? Go to the **online workbook** and have a go at Multiple choice questions 15.1 to check your abilities in these areas.

SUMMARY OF KEY CONCEPTS   Can you remember what normal losses, abnormal losses and abnormal gains mean? Go to the **online workbook** to check your recollection with Summary of key concepts 15.1 to 15.3.

SHOW ME HOW TO DO IT   How certain are you that you have followed all the steps so far in completing the process account? View Video presentation 15.1 in the **online workbook** to see in detail the accounting entries involved in writing up the process account, recording normal losses, abnormal losses and abnormal gains.

DISPOSAL COSTS
Normal losses

Rather than just disappearing as a result of the evaporation of input materials, the losses from a process may take the form of actual waste products. These waste products will have to be disposed of and this disposal may incur a cost. Figure 15.5 shows that where the disposal of waste products does incur a cost, the disposal cost of normal losses has to be added to the process account thereby increasing the cost of finished production from the process. Illustration 15.7 presents the process account and the disposal cost account to reflect the cost of disposal of normal losses. In this illustration, each litre of waste product arising from the normal losses produced by the process incurs a disposal cost of £1.20. 200 litres of normal loss therefore incur

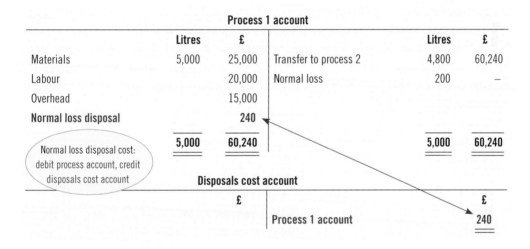

Figure 15.5 Accounting for the disposal costs of normal losses

a total disposal cost of 200 × £1.20 = £240. This cost is debited to the process account as an additional cost of the process, with the credit posting being made to the disposal costs account. The credit to the disposal costs account records the liability for disposal costs, a liability that will be discharged when the payment is made from the bank account (debit disposals cost account, credit bank account). Note that the normal loss is still not valued in the process account. The value of each litre of production transferred from process 1 to process 2 is now £60,240 total costs ÷ 4,800 litres of production from process 1 = £12.55.

Illustration 15.7 Accounting for the disposal cost of normal losses

Process 1 account

	Litres	£		Litres	£
Materials	5,000	25,000	Transfer to process 2	4,800	60,240
Labour		20,000	Normal loss	200	–
Overhead		15,000			
Normal loss disposal		**240**			
	5,000	**60,240**		**5,000**	**60,240**

Normal loss disposal cost: debit process account, credit disposals cost account

Disposals cost account

	£		£
		Process 1 account	240

MULTIPLE CHOICE QUESTIONS   Do you think you can account correctly for situations in which normal losses have a disposal cost? Go to the **online workbook** and have a go at Multiple choice questions 15.2 to check your understanding.

Abnormal losses

When there is a charge to dispose of waste products from a process, then both abnormal and normal losses will incur these disposal costs. How should we account for the disposal costs of abnormal losses? Whereas the cost of the disposal of normal losses is included in the calculation of total process costs, the cost of disposal of abnormal losses is not valued in the process account. Instead, the cost of disposal of abnormal losses is added to the abnormal loss account (Figure 15.6) and rolled up with the cost of any abnormal losses incurred in the process during each period. The cost of each unit of abnormal loss is valued on the basis of the cost of each unit of expected finished product from the process as before (this chapter, Abnormal losses).

15

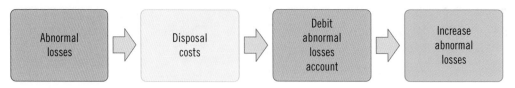

Figure 15.6 Accounting for the disposal costs of abnormal losses

Illustration 15.8 presents the process account, the disposal cost account and the abnormal loss account to illustrate these entries. The expected production from the process is 4,800 litres (5,000 litres of input material − 200 litres normal loss = 4,800 litres). The cost per litre of expected finished production is £60,240 ÷ 4,800 litres = £12.55 per litre. The value of the abnormal loss is thus 100 litres × £12.55 per litre = £1,255 while production transferred to process 2 is 4,700 litres × £12.55 per litre = £58,985. As before (this chapter, Abnormal losses), the total abnormal losses are reported separately as a cost in the costing statement of profit or loss for the period in which the abnormal losses arise. However, when disposal costs arise, the loss is not just the cost of lost production but the additional costs of disposing of these abnormal losses as well. This separate reporting encourages management to investigate these losses further to determine whether they can be prevented in future or whether the loss arose as a result of a unique set of circumstances which will not be repeated. The disposal cost account now shows a liability of £360 (£240 for the disposal of normal losses + £120 for the disposal of abnormal losses) which will be extinguished when the disposal cost is paid from the bank account (again, debit disposal cost account, credit bank account).

Illustration 15.8 Accounting for the disposal cost of normal and abnormal losses

Process 1 account

	Litres	£		Litres	£
Materials	5,000	25,000	Transfer to process 2	4,700	58,985
Labour		20,000	Normal loss	200	–
Overhead		15,000	**Abnormal loss**	100	1,255
Normal loss disposal		240			
Abnormal losses: debit abnormal loss account, credit process account	**5,000**	**60,240**		**5,000**	**60,240**

Abnormal loss account

	£		£
Process 1 account	1,255	Costing statement of profit or loss	1,375
Disposal cost account 100 × £1.20	120		
	1,375		**1,375**

Disposal cost account

	£		£
Abnormal loss disposal cost: debit abnormal loss account, credit disposal cost account		Process 1 account	240
		Abnormal loss account	120

15

WHY IS THIS RELEVANT TO ME?   Normal and abnormal losses: disposal costs

To enable you as a business professional to understand:

● How the disposal costs for both normal and abnormal losses in processes are accounted for

● That valuing and accounting for the disposal costs of abnormal losses separately encourages investigation by management with a view to eliminating these unexpected costs

MULTIPLE CHOICE QUESTIONS   Are you convinced that you can account correctly for the disposal costs of abnormal losses? Go to the **online workbook** and have a go at Multiple choice questions 15.3 to check your ability in this area.

SUMMARY OF KEY CONCEPTS   Can you remember how to account for the disposal costs of normal and abnormal losses? Go to the **online workbook** to revise the accounting entries with Summary of key concepts 15.4.

SHOW ME HOW TO DO IT   How certain are you that you have completely understood how to account for the disposal costs of normal and abnormal losses in the process account? View Video presentation 15.2 in the **online workbook** to see in detail how the disposal costs of normal and abnormal losses are accounted for.

SELLING LOSSES FROM A PROCESS
Normal losses

While organisations may incur a cost when disposing of the waste products from a process, it is just as likely that those waste products can be collected and sold to another entity for use in their own processes. Figure 15.7 summarises the way in which organisations should account for this income from the sale of losses from a process. As we shall see, the approach is very similar to the different accounting treatments for disposal costs for both normal and abnormal losses.

Illustration 15.9 presents the process account and the scrap account for the normal losses arising in our process. In this example, each litre of waste product can be sold for 96 pence (£0.96). As normal losses amount to 200 litres, this means that the normal losses from the process can be sold for £192 (200 × £0.96). The sale of the normal losses from the process creates an asset, a receivable. Money will be received from the sale of the normal losses (and any other losses) from

Figure 15.7 Accounting for the disposal proceeds from the sale of normal losses

15

Illustration 15.9 Accounting for the sale of normal losses from a process

Process 1 account

	Litres	£		Litres	£
Materials	5,000	25,000	Transfer to process 2	4,800	59,808
Labour		20,000	Normal loss scrap value	200	192
Overhead		15,000			
	5,000	**60,000**		**5,000**	**60,000**

Scrap account

	£		£
Process 1 account – normal loss	192		

Normal loss sale proceeds: debit scrap account, credit process account

the process. Therefore, the scrap account is debited with the sale proceeds from the normal losses to reflect the creation of this asset. The corresponding credit entry is to the process account. This may seem surprising as we have so far insisted that normal losses are not valued. However, normal losses are still not valued in the process account. The credit of £192 is not a valuation of the normal losses but of the scrap value of those normal losses. The money receivable from the sale of the normal losses reduces the total costs of the process by £192. The cost of each litre of finished product transferred to process 2 is now £12.46 ((£60,000 − £192) ÷ 4,800 litres of expected output from the process). Whereas the disposal costs of the normal losses increased the costs of the process in Illustration 15.7, the sale proceeds from the sale of the normal losses reduce the costs of the process in Illustration 15.9.

Abnormal losses

Illustration 15.10 presents the accounting entries to record the treatment of abnormal losses in a process and the sale proceeds arising from the sale of those abnormal losses when losses from the process can be sold. Abnormal losses continue to be valued at the expected cost of production from the process. As the cost of each litre of product has now been determined at £12.46 (this chapter, Illustration 15.9) after taking into account the sale proceeds from normal losses, the 100 litres of abnormal losses are valued at 100 × £12.46 = £1,246. The scrap value of the abnormal losses is not included in the process account. As in the case of the sale of normal losses (Illustration 15.9), the sale proceeds of the abnormal losses create an asset, a receivable, which is debited to the scrap account. The corresponding credit entry is made to the abnormal loss account and this has the effect of reducing the abnormal loss (Figure 15.8) that is charged to the costing statement of profit or loss for the period in which the abnormal losses arise. The abnormal loss continues to be reported separately to prompt management investigations to ensure that action is taken to avoid these abnormal losses in the future.

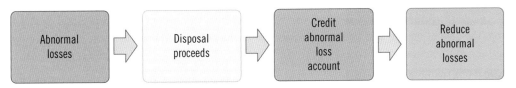

Figure 15.8 Accounting for the disposal proceeds from the sale of abnormal losses

Illustration 15.10 Accounting for the sale of abnormal losses from a process

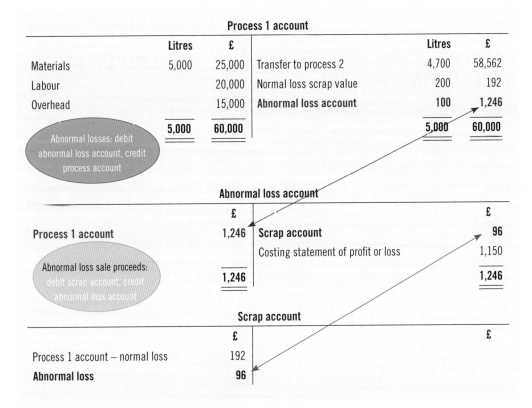

15

VALUING WORK IN PROGRESS AT THE END OF AN ACCOUNTING PERIOD

So far in this chapter we have assumed that processes all begin and end in an accounting period with no incomplete units of production at the start or at the end of the financial period. In real life situations, processes do not come to a complete stop at the end of each month or year with all processes completed and products transferred to finished goods or to the next process. Figure 15.9 shows that processes will usually generate finished product in a period but that the continuous nature of processes will give rise to partially completed production at the month or year end. This partially completed production is called work in progress, an asset that is included in inventory in the statement of financial position and as a deduction from production costs (cost of sales) in the statement of profit or loss. Work in progress represents products or processes that have been started but not completed by the period end date.

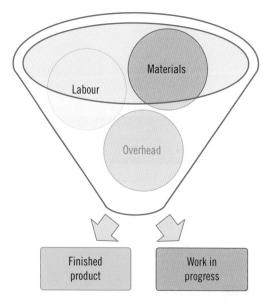

Figure 15.9 Process outcomes: finished product during the period + work in progress (production started but not yet finished) at the end of the period

As an example of work in progress, consider a builder who might have started the construction of a house three months ago. By the end of the accounting year, all the foundations have been completed, the walls have been built and the roof beams have been added, but there are no roof tiles, no windows or doors and no internal plastering or internal fittings have been started. This house would be classified as work in progress at the end of the financial year. To value this house, the builder will add up all the costs of materials, of labour and of overhead incurred up to the year-end date to determine a cost for the work done up to that point. The cost of this work in progress will be added to the closing inventory in both the statement of profit or loss and the statement of financial position. As we saw in Chapter 3 (Closing inventory), the cost or net realisable value (not selling price) of inventory at the end of an accounting period is a deduction from cost of sales with that inventory being carried forward to the next accounting period in the statement of financial position. In the next financial year, the house will be completed and sold to a buyer. All the costs incurred in building the house (the work in progress at the start of the year + all the materials, labour and overhead costs incurred in completing the house) will then be matched with the selling price to give the total profit on the sale.

In the same way, when a process is partially complete at the end of the month or year, the costs that have been incurred up to that point have to be calculated in order to determine the cost of this work in progress so that the current asset can be recognised and carried forward to the next accounting period. How is this valuation of work in progress in a process carried out? In process costing, this valuation is based on equivalent units. Equivalent units are an estimate of the whole number of units of complete output representing the incomplete process. This sounds confusing, so let's consider this in Example 15.1.

Scary Chemicals Limited operates a process in which 1,000 units of production are left in the process at the end of the month. However, these units are only 60% complete with respect to materials, labour and overhead. Therefore, the equivalent units are $1,000 \times 60\% = 600$ complete units. The completed units + the equivalent work in progress units are added together to find the number of units completed during the month. This total number of units is then used to determine the cost per unit for finished production and abnormal gains and losses (remember that normal losses are not valued). Figure 15.10 illustrates the equivalent units calculation.

Figure 15.10 The equivalent units calculation

15

EXAMPLE 15.2

Scary Chemicals Limited input 20,000 units of material to a new process at the beginning of September. At the end of the month, 16,000 units of finished production have been completed and there were 4,000 units of work in progress which is assessed as being 50% complete. The costs of the inputs to the process during the month were as follows:

- Materials: £43,200
- Labour: £51,300
- Overhead: £13,500

The following steps will be completed to determine the costs for finished production and work in progress.

Step 1: calculate the equivalent units of production

At this stage, the total costs of the process are irrelevant. The first stage in calculating the cost of each unit of output is to determine the number of equivalent units produced in the month. Illustration 15.11 presents the calculation of the equivalent units of production during September. 16,000 units are 100% complete, so this gives a total of 16,000 equivalent units (16,000 × 1.00). The remaining 4,000 units started in the month are 50% complete, so the equivalent units here are 4,000 × 0.50 = 2,000. The total equivalent units of production are thus 16,000 fully completed units + 2,000 units of work in progress = 18,000.

Illustration 15.11 Scary Chemicals Limited: equivalent units of production for September

	Total units	× % complete	= Equivalent units
Step 1: Output completed	16,000	100%	16,000
Step 1: Work in progress	4,000	50%	2,000
Total units	**20,000**		**18,000**

Step 2: calculate the cost per equivalent unit of output and work in progress

Total costs now become relevant. In Example 15.2, total costs for September are £43,200 (materials) + £51,300 (labour) + £13,500 (overhead) = £108,000. Producing 18,000 equivalent units (Step 1) has cost £108,000. Therefore, the cost per equivalent unit of production is £6 (£108,000 total costs divided by 18,000 equivalent units).

Step 3: calculate the total cost of output and work in progress

Each equivalent unit of production and work in progress has a cost of £6, so we can now value our finished production and work in progress as follows:

Cost of output of completed production: 16,000 units × £6 per unit (Step 2) = £96,000

Cost of work in progress 2,000 units × £6 per unit (Step 2) = £12,000

£96,000 + £12,000 = £108,000, the total cost of production for September

Step 4: complete the process account

Illustration 15.12 presents the completed process account for the month. The units of output started in September in terms of materials are 20,000 of which 16,000 were completed during the month with 4,000 units of work in progress at the end of the month, so both units columns total up to 20,000. The cost of materials, labour and overhead are debited to the process account and add up to £108,000. The credits to the account are £96,000, the completed production transferred to the production account, together with £12,000 work in progress, inventory carried forward to October. This work in progress will be completed in October to produce finished goods ready for transfer to the production account.

Illustration 15.12 Scary Chemicals Limited process account for September (Example 15.2)

Scary Chemicals Limited: process account

	Units	£		Units	£
Materials	20,000	43,200	Completed production	16,000	96,000
Labour		51,300	Work in progress c/f	4,000	12,000
Overhead		13,500			
	20,000	**108,000**		**20,000**	**108,000**

CLOSING WORK IN PROGRESS: VARYING COMPLETION PERCENTAGES OF COSTS

In Example 15.2, the valuation of work in progress was straightforward as all inputs of materials, labour and overhead into the units at the month end were estimated as being 50% complete. What procedure should be followed if there are differing levels of completion for the inputs to work in progress? In many processes, all the materials will be added at the start, but the labour and overhead will be added evenly throughout the entire process. How will these differing levels of completion affect the values calculated for finished goods and work in progress at the end of the accounting period? Again, an example (Example 15.3) will show us the method to follow in valuing finished output and work in progress.

EXAMPLE 15.3

Let's extend Example 15.2. All the costs are the same as in that example, but the completion of the work in progress units is as follows: material input to work in progress is 80% complete, whereas labour and overhead are 50% complete. We shall follow the same steps as in Example 15.2 in order to calculate the value of the completed units and the value of work in progress at the end of September.

Step 1: calculate the equivalent units of production

As in Example 15.2, the first step will be to work out the equivalent units produced in the month. However, there will be two sets of equivalent units to calculate. The first will be for materials and the second for labour and overhead. Illustration 15.13 presents the calculation of the equivalent units of production during September for both materials and for labour and overhead. Sixteen thousand units are 100% complete and have been transferred to completed production, so this gives a total of 16,000 equivalent units (16,000 × 1.00) for both materials and for labour and overhead. Four thousand units have been started in September, but are not complete by the end of the month. These units are 80% complete with regards to materials, so 4,000 × 80% means that materials in work in progress represent 3,200 equivalent units. Following the same approach for labour and overhead gives us 4,000 × 50% = 2,000 equivalent units of finished product. Adding the equivalent units of output of finished production and work in progress gives us 19,200 equivalent units of materials (16,000 + 3,200) and 18,000 equivalent units of labour and overhead (16,000 + 2,000).

Illustration 15.13 Scary Chemicals Limited: equivalent units of material and labour and overhead for September (Example 15.3)

	Materials			**Labour and overhead**		
	Total units	× % complete	= Equivalent units	Total units	× % complete	= Equivalent units
Step 1: Output	16,000	100%	16,000	16,000	100%	16,000
Step 1: WIP	4,000	80%	3,200	4,000	50%	2,000
Total units	**20,000**		**19,200**	**20,000**		**18,000**

Step 2: calculate the cost per equivalent unit of output and work in progress

Where there are varying completion percentages for materials and conversion cost, two calculations are required to work out the cost per equivalent unit of material and the cost per equivalent units of labour and overhead.

Materials

The total cost of materials input into the process during the period is £43,200. The cost per unit of completed output and work in progress for 19,200 equivalent units of material is therefore £43,200 ÷ 19,200 = £2.25. The materials in completed production and work in progress will therefore be valued at £2.25 per equivalent unit of material input.

Labour and overhead

The total cost of labour and overhead input into the process during the period is £51,300 (labour) + £13,500 (overhead) = £64,800. The cost per unit of completed output and work in progress for 18,000 equivalent units of labour and overhead is therefore £64,800 ÷ 18,000 = £3.60. The labour and overhead in completed production and work in progress will be valued at £3.60 per equivalent unit of labour and overhead input.

15

Step 3: calculate the total cost of output and work in progress

We now have our costs per equivalent unit for the various inputs into the process, so we can value our finished production and work in progress as follows:

Cost of output of completed production: 16,000 units of material × £2.25 per unit (Step 2) + 16,000 units of labour and overhead × £3.60 per unit (Step 2) = £93,600

Cost of work in progress 3,200 units of material × £2.25 (step 2) + 2,000 units of labour and overhead × £3.60 (step 2) = £14,400

£93,600 + £14,400 = £108,000 so the total cost of production for the period is completely allocated between finished production and work in progress.

Step 4: complete the process account

Illustration 15.14 presents the completed process account for September. The units of output started in the period in terms of materials are 20,000 of which 16,000 were completed during the month with 4,000 units of work in progress at the end of the month, so both units columns total up to 20,000. Costs of materials, labour and overhead are debited to the process account and add up to £108,000 for the period. The credits to the account are £93,600, the completed production transferred to the production account as calculated in Step 3, together with £14,400 work in progress, inventory carried forward to October. Again, this work in progress will be completed in the next month to produce finished goods ready for transfer to the production account.

Illustration 15.14 Scary Chemicals Limited: process account for September (Example 15.3)

Scary Chemicals Limited: process account

	Units	£		Units	£
Materials	20,000	43,200	Completed production	16,000	93,600
Labour		51,300	Work in progress c/f	4,000	14,400
Overhead		13,500			
	20,000	**108,000**		**20,000**	**108,000**

WHY IS THIS RELEVANT TO ME?   Valuing work in progress at the end of an accounting period

To enable you as a business professional to understand:
- How work in progress and completed production are valued on the basis of equivalent units
- How to account for differing levels of completion for different inputs to a process

15

UNIT COSTS WHEN THERE IS OPENING AND CLOSING WORK IN PROGRESS

Closing work in progress in a process at the end of one accounting period becomes the opening work in progress at the start of the next accounting period. Materials, labour and overheads are then added, finished goods are produced and the closing work in progress becomes the next period's opening work in progress. This continuous progression is shown in the process cycle in Figure 15.11. What effect will this opening work in progress have on the valuation of production

15

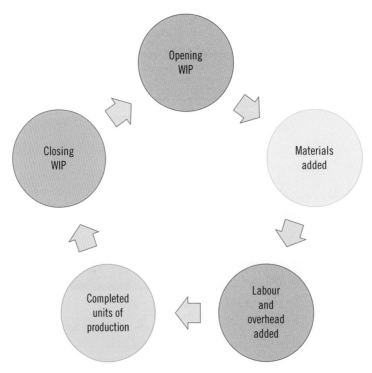

Figure 15.11 The process cycle

completed during the accounting period and on the valuation of work in progress at the end of that accounting period? When there is opening work in progress in a process, there are two options by which to value a process's finished production and closing work in progress: the first in first out method and the average cost method. Let's look at each of these methods in turn to see how they affect the values of finished production and closing work in progress.

VALUING FINISHED PRODUCTION AND CLOSING WORK IN PROGRESS: THE FIRST IN FIRST OUT METHOD

Figure 15.12 Valuing finished production and work in progress: the first in first out method

Figure 15.12 presents the order in which production is completed when valuing finished production and closing work in progress using the first in first out method. This method assumes that the opening work in progress units in a process are the first to be completed in the next accounting period. Therefore, the first additions of materials, labour and overhead to a process go towards finishing the partially completed units brought forward from the last financial period. Once these opening work in progress units are complete, then new units are started and completed during the accounting period. These units started and completed during the period are 100% complete with respect to materials, labour and overhead. At the end of the month, there will be closing work in progress, units of production that have been started but which are only partially complete at the end of that accounting period. The equivalent units approach is used once more in order to value the units completed during the period and the closing work in progress. Let's continue with the figures from Example 15.3 in Example 15.4.

EXAMPLE 15.4

In October, Scary Chemicals Limited produced a total of 26,200 units of finished production from its new process. The company incurred materials costs of £59,070 and labour and overheads added to the process totalled up to £91,350. At the end of October, the work in progress (5,000 units) was 40% complete with respect to materials and 16% complete with respect to labour and overhead. Work in progress at the start of October is the closing work in progress detailed in Example 15.3.

Step 1: calculate the equivalent units of production

Illustration 15.15 presents the equivalent units table for the process for October. Example 15.3 tells us that at the end of September, there were 4,000 units of partially completed production. These units of work in progress are the opening work in progress at the beginning of October.

15

Under the first in first out method of valuing finished production and closing work in progress, these are the first units to be completed in October. These opening work in progress units are 80% complete with respect to materials at the end of September: therefore, to complete these units, a further 20% (100% − 80%) of materials will need to be added to the process. The equivalent units of material used in completing this opening work in progress are thus 4,000 × 20% = 800. This makes sense as Illustration 15.13 shows us that the equivalent units of material carried forward in closing work in progress are 3,200. The 3,200 equivalent units of material in opening work in progress brought forward + the 800 equivalent units of material added to the process in October = 4,000 completed equivalent units of material.

Illustration 15.15 Scary Chemicals Limited: equivalent units table for October using the first in first out method to value finished production and closing work in progress

		Materials			Labour and overhead	
Finished output	**Total units**	**% to complete**	**Equivalent units**	**Total units**	**% to complete**	**Equivalent units**
Opening WIP completed	4,000	× 20%	800	4,000	× 50%	2,000
Other units started and finished in October	22,200	× 100%	22,200	22,200	× 100%	22,200
Total production in period	26,200		23,000	26,200		24,200
Closing WIP	5,000	× 40%	2,000	5,000	× 16%	800
	31,200		**25,000**	**31,200**		**25,000**

The same approach is used to determine the equivalent units of labour and overhead added to the process in October to complete the units of opening work in progress. Illustration 15.13 tells us that the closing work in progress at the end of September is 50% complete with respect to labour and overhead so a further 50% (100% − 50%) of labour and overhead will need to be added to the process to complete the conversion cost of these units brought forward at the start of October. Fifty per cent × 4,000 means that there are 2,000 equivalent units of labour and overhead used to complete the conversion of the opening work in progress into finished product. Again, we can see that this is correct as Illustration 15.13 shows 2,000 equivalent units of labour and overhead in closing work in progress + 2,000 equivalent units of labour and overhead added in October = 4,000 equivalent units. Once the 800 equivalent units of material and the 2,000 equivalent units of labour and overhead are added to the opening work in progress, then these units of production will be 100% complete.

During October 26,200 units of finished production were produced. These 26,200 units include the completion of the 4,000 units of work in progress brought forward from September. Therefore, the number of equivalent units started and completed during October was 26,200 − 4,000 = 22,200.

The equivalent units of closing work in progress can now be calculated. Five thousand units of production were started but not completed during the month. These units were 40% complete with respect to materials, so this gives equivalent units of material of 5,000 × 40% = 2,000. Likewise, labour and overhead in these 5,000 units is 16% complete so there are 5,000 × 16% = 800 equivalent units of labour and overhead in closing work in progress.

There were 31,200 units of production worked on during October, but these 31,200 units were only equivalent to 25,000 units of material and 25,000 units of labour and overhead.

Step 2: calculate the cost per equivalent unit of output and work in progress

Under the first in first out method of valuing finished production and closing work in progress, the costs of opening work in progress are ignored in the cost per equivalent unit calculations. Therefore, the costs incurred in the period are used to determine the cost per equivalent unit of materials and labour and overhead.

Materials

The cost of materials incurred in October was £59,070. The cost per equivalent unit of completed output and closing work in progress for 25,000 equivalent units of material is therefore £59,070 ÷ 25,000 = £2.3628. The materials in completed production and closing work in progress will therefore be valued at £2.3628 per equivalent unit of material input.

Labour and overhead

The total cost of labour and overhead incurred in October was £91,350. The per equivalent unit cost of completed output and closing work in progress for 25,000 equivalent units of labour and overhead is therefore £91,350 ÷ 25,000 = £3.654. The labour and overhead in completed production and closing work in progress will therefore be valued at £3.654 per unit of labour and overhead input.

Step 3: calculate the total cost of output and closing work in progress

We now have our cost per equivalent unit for the various inputs into the process, so we can calculate the values for our finished production and closing work in progress.

The cost of output of completed production is shown below (all figures are rounded to the nearest whole £):

	£
Opening work in progress cost brought forward from September (part of the total cost of production of completed output in October)	14,400
Completion of opening work in progress:	
• 800 equivalent units of material: 800 × £2.3628	1,890
• 2,000 equivalent units of labour and overhead: 2,000 × £3.654	7,308
Production started and finished in October	
• 22,200 equivalent units of material: 22,200 × £2.3628	52,454
• 22,200 equivalent units of labour and overhead: 22,200 × £3.654	81,119
Total cost of completed output during October	**157,171**

15

The closing work in progress is valued as follows, again rounding to the nearest whole £:

	£
• 2,000 equivalent units of material: 2,000 × £2.3628	4,726
• 800 equivalent units of labour and overhead: 800 × £3.654	2,923
Total cost of work in progress at the end of October	**7,649**

Step 4: complete the process account

We now have all the relevant numbers with which to complete the process account for October which is presented in Illustration 15.16. Four thousand units of work in progress were brought forward from September at a valuation of £14,400 so this is the first debit to the process account, the asset at the start of the month. Costs incurred during the month are debited to the process account as these are the costs added to the process thereby building up the inventory asset. Production completed in the month is a credit to the account as the finished production is transferred to the goods for sale account. The remaining credit entry is the closing work in progress, the balance left on the process account of production started but not finished in October which will form the opening balance on the process account for November.

Illustration 15.16 Scary Chemicals Limited: process account for October (Example 15.4) valuing finished production and closing work in progress using the first in first out method

Scary Chemicals Limited: process account for October					
	Units	£		Units	£
WIP b/f	4,000	14,400	Completed in month	26,200	157,171
Materials	27,200	59,070	WIP c/f	5,000	7,649
Conversion		91,350			
	31,200	**164,820**		**31,200**	**164,820**

WHY IS THIS RELEVANT TO ME? Valuing finished production and closing work in progress: the first in first out method

To enable you as a business professional to understand:

• That the first in first out method of valuing finished production and closing work in progress assumes that the opening work in progress brought forward is the first production to be completed

• How to calculate the equivalent units for material and conversion cost when finished production and closing work in progress are valued using the first in first out method

• How to determine the values for finished production and closing work in progress when using the first in first out method

15

MULTIPLE CHOICE QUESTIONS Are you certain that you understand and can apply the first in first out method of valuing finished production and closing work in progress in calculating equivalent units and in the valuation of finished production and closing work in progress? Go to the **online workbook** and have a go at Multiple choice questions 15.6 to check your understanding and abilities in this area.

SUMMARY OF KEY CONCEPTS Can you recall the steps involved in calculating equivalent units when valuing finished production and closing work in progress using the first in first out method? Go to the **online workbook** to check your recollection with Summary of key concepts 15.7.

SHOW ME HOW TO DO IT Did you completely understand how to calculate equivalent units, costs per equivalent unit, the value of finished goods and the value of closing inventory when using the first in first out basis? View Video presentation 15.5 in the **online workbook** to revise in detail how these calculations are made.

VALUING FINISHED PRODUCTION AND CLOSING WORK IN PROGRESS: THE WEIGHTED AVERAGE COST METHOD

The weighted average cost method involves calculating a weighted average cost for units produced from both opening work in progress and units started in the current period. Figure 15.13 shows that this method of valuing opening work in progress assumes that the opening work in progress units and the new units started in the accounting period are all mixed together. As a result of this mixing together, the resources put into the completion of the opening units and of the units started in the period cannot be identified separately. The new materials, the labour and the overhead added to the process during the month all go towards completing both the opening work in progress and the new units started in the period. Therefore this method does not assume that the opening work in progress units are finished first as the new inputs cannot be separately identified as first completing work in progress and then starting new units. At the end of each financial period, there will still be closing work in progress, units of production that have been started but which are only partially complete at the end of that accounting period. The equivalent units approach is still used to value the units completed during the period and the closing work in progress. To illustrate the weighted average cost method of valuing finished production and work in progress we shall use the same information as given in Example 15.4 and follow the same four steps.

Figure 15.13 Valuing finished production and closing work in progress: the weighted average cost method

Step 1: calculate the equivalent units of production

Illustration 15.17 presents the equivalent units table for the process for October. Whereas the first in first out method made a careful set of equivalent unit calculations to determine the material and conversion costs required to complete the units of opening work in progress, the weighted average cost method completely ignores the equivalent units of opening work in progress. The only concern when using the weighted average cost method is the number of units of production completed during the accounting period. In this case, a total of 26,200 units were completed in the month, the 4,000 units of work in progress at the start of the month + the 22,200 units started and completed in the month. These units are 100% complete during the period with respect to both materials and labour and overhead. At the end of the month, 5,000 units of production had been started but not yet finished, being 40% complete with respect to materials and 16% complete with respect to labour and overhead. These unfinished units of work in progress are accounted for in the usual way at the end of the month. As in the case of the first in first out method, there were 2,000 (5,000 units × 40% complete) equivalent units of material and 800 (5,000 units × 16% complete) equivalent units of labour and overhead at the end of October.

Illustration 15.17 Scary Chemicals Limited: equivalent units table for October using the weighted average cost method to value finished production and closing work in progress

	Materials			Labour and overhead		
	Total units	% complete	Equivalent units	Total units	% complete	Equivalent units
Output completed	26,200	x100%	26,200	26,200	x100%	26,200
Work in progress	5,000	x40%	2,000	5,000	x16%	800
Total units	31,200		28,200	31,200		27,000

Again, there were 31,200 units of production worked on during October, but these 31,200 units were equivalent to 28,200 units of material and 27,000 units of labour and overhead.

Step 2: calculate the cost per equivalent unit of output and work in progress

Under the weighted average cost method of valuing finished production and closing work in progress, the costs of opening work in progress are *not* ignored in the cost per equivalent unit calculations but are added to the material and conversion costs incurred in the period. Therefore, both the costs of opening work in progress and the costs incurred in the period are averaged to determine the cost per equivalent unit of materials and of labour and overhead. This adding together of the costs of opening work in progress and the costs incurred in the period means that completed units of opening WIP are each given a value of one full equivalent unit of production. The weighted average cost method assumes that all the units produced in a given period have the same unit cost and that a unit of part completed opening WIP has, when it has been completed, the same cost as a unit of output started and finished in the period.

15

Materials

The cost of materials in opening work in progress was £7,200 (Example 15.3). The cost of materials in October was £59,070. The combined material cost for the month was thus £7,200 work in progress + £59,070 cost of materials for October = £66,270. The cost per equivalent unit of completed output and closing work in progress for 28,200 equivalent units of material is therefore £66,270 ÷ 28,200 = £2.35. The materials in completed production and closing work in progress will therefore be valued at £2.35 per equivalent unit of material input.

Labour and overhead

The cost of labour and overhead in opening work in progress was £7,200 (Example 15.3). The cost of labour and overhead in October was £91,350. The combined labour and overhead cost for the month was therefore £7,200 + £91,350 = £98,550. The per equivalent unit cost of completed output and closing work in progress for 27,000 equivalent units of labour and overhead is thus £98,550 ÷ 27,000 = £3.65. The labour and overhead in completed production and closing work in progress will therefore be valued at £3.65 per unit of labour and overhead input.

Step 3: calculate the total cost of output and closing work in progress

We now have our cost per equivalent unit for the various inputs into the process, so we can calculate the values for our finished production and closing work in progress.

	£
Completed production in October	
• 26,200 equivalent units of material: 26,200 × £2.35	61,570
• 26,200 equivalent units of labour and overhead: 26,200 × £3.65	95,630
Total cost of completed output during October	**157,200**

The closing work in progress is valued as follows:

	£
• 2,000 equivalent units of material: 2,000 × £2.35	4,700
• 800 equivalent units of labour and overhead: 800 × £3.65	2,920
Total cost of work in progress at the end of October	**7,620**

Step 4: complete the process account

The process account for October can now be completed. This process account is presented in Illustration 15.18. Four thousand units of work in progress were brought forward from September at a valuation of £14,400 so this is still the first debit to the account, the asset at the start of the month. Costs incurred during the month are again debited to the process account as these

15

are the costs added to the process as the inventory asset is produced. Production completed in the month is a credit to the account as the finished production is transferred to the goods for sale account. The remaining credit entry is the closing work in progress, the balance left on the process account of production started but not finished in October which will form the opening balance on the process account for November.

Illustration 15.18 Scary Chemicals Limited: process account for October (Example 15.4) valuing finished production and closing work in progress using the weighted average cost method

Scary Chemicals Limited: process account for October

	Units	£		Units	£
WIP b/f	4,000	14,400	Completed in month	26,200	157,200
Materials	27,200	59,070	WIP c/f	5,000	7,620
Conversion		91,350			
	31,200	164,820		31,200	164,820

WHY IS THIS RELEVANT TO ME? Valuing finished production and closing work in progress: the weighted average cost method

To enable you as a business professional to understand:

• That the weighted average cost method of valuing finished production and closing work in progress pools the values of opening work in progress and costs incurred in a period in determining the weighted average value for units of finished production and closing work in progress

• That only the units completed in the period and the closing work in progress count as equivalent units when using the weighted average cost method of valuing finished production and closing work in progress

• How to determine the values for finished production and closing work in progress when using the weighted average cost method

MULTIPLE CHOICE QUESTIONS Are you confident that you understand and can apply the weighted average cost method of valuing finished production and closing work in progress in calculating equivalent units and in the valuation of finished production and closing work in progress? Go to the **online workbook** and have a go at Multiple choice questions 15.7 to check how well you have understood the techniques applied.

SUMMARY OF KEY CONCEPTS Are you able to recall how to calculate equivalent units when valuing finished production and closing work in progress using the weighted average cost method? Go to the **online workbook** to check your recollection with Summary of key concepts 15.8.

SHOW ME HOW TO DO IT Have you completely understood how to calculate equivalent units, costs per equivalent unit, the value of finished goods and the value of closing inventory when using the weighted average cost basis? View Video presentation 15.6 in the **online workbook** to go over in detail again how these calculations are made.

CHAPTER SUMMARY

You should now have learnt that:

- Process transactions are recorded in a process account

- A process account is a T account with columns for units of input and output and values of inputs and outputs

- Normal losses are never valued in process costing

- Normal losses are expected losses so any costs associated with normal losses are rolled up into the cost of completed production

- Abnormal gains and losses are valued on the basis of the unit cost of expected production from a process

- Abnormal gains and losses are reported separately in the costing statement of profit or loss to focus management's attention on these unexpected costs and revenues

- The disposal cost of normal losses increases the costs of production in the process account

- The disposal cost of abnormal losses increases the expense on the abnormal loss account

- Income received from the disposal of normal losses decreases the costs of production in the process account

- Income received from the disposal of abnormal losses decreases the expense on the abnormal loss account

- In order to value finished goods and closing work in progress in a process equivalent units are calculated for materials and for labour and overhead consumed in each accounting period

- Equivalent units = the number of units in a process × the percentage completion of those units

- Finished production and closing work in progress can be valued using either the first in first out method or the weighted average cost method

- The first in first out method of valuing finished production and closing work in progress assumes that the first units completed in a period are those units brought forward in closing work in progress from the previous accounting period

- The first in first out method of valuing finished production and closing work in progress calculates equivalent units in a period as completion of opening work in progress + units started and finished in a period + units in closing work in progress

- The weighted average cost method of valuing finished production and closing work in progress assumes that the resources used to complete opening work in progress and the units started and finished in the period are indistinguishable

- The weighted average cost method of valuing finished production and closing work in progress calculates equivalent units in a period as units completed in the period + units in closing work in progress

- The weighted average cost method of valuing finished production and closing work in progress averages the costs brought forward in opening work in progress and costs incurred in the period to calculate an average cost for each equivalent unit of material and of labour and overhead

QUICK REVISION   Test your knowledge by attempting the activities in the **online workbook**, including flashcards on the key concepts, numerical exercises and Multiple choice questions. You can also try the further self-test questions which are available at www.oup.com/he/scott-i2a2e

15

END-OF-CHAPTER QUESTIONS

Attempt the questions in the following sections and then look at the solutions which can be found in the **online workbook** to see whether there are areas that you need to revisit.

❯ RECALL AND REVIEW

❯ Question 15.1

Describe the accounting treatment for the following and briefly explain whether they are included in calculating the cost of production or not.

- Normal losses
- Abnormal losses
- Abnormal gains
- Disposal costs of normal losses
- Disposal costs of abnormal losses
- Proceeds from the sale of normal losses
- Proceeds from the sale of abnormal losses

❯ Question 15.2

Candy Limited produces chemicals. The following information is related to Production process 5:

Materials	15,000 kg at a cost of £4.00 per kg
Labour	2,000 hours at a cost of £10.00 per hour
Overhead	2,000 hours at a cost of £1.50 per hour
Normal loss	1,000 kg
Abnormal loss	500 kg
Normal loss disposal cost	£1 per kg
Abnormal loss disposal cost	£2 per kg

Required

Draw up the process account for Production process 5 and show the cost of finished production to be transferred to Production process 6.

❯❯ DEVELOP YOUR UNDERSTANDING

❯❯ Question 15.3

Iron Bar Limited produces soft drinks. A new product, Aloo Brew, has been developed and has just gone into production. During March, 30,000 litres of materials were input to the process at a cost of £7,425. Labour on the production process for the month cost £4,950 and overheads for the product for March totalled up to £2,625. Thirty thousand litres of Aloo Brew were produced in March and sent to the bottling section. There was no work in progress at the start or the end of the month and the expected normal loss from the Aloo Brew process is 0% of materials input.

Required

For Aloo Brew for March:

- Draw up the process account.
- Calculate the per litre cost of production.

>> Question 15.4

The Big Bang Chemical Company produces explosives for use in the mining industry. All explosives are produced in chemical processes involving the input of materials, labour and overheads. The following data apply to the product Whimper for October:

- 12,000 kilograms of materials were input to the process at a cost of £51,000.
- Process labour cost £27,000.
- Overheads for the month were £19,200.
- Normal losses are expected to be 10% of input materials.
- A total of 10,600 kilograms of Whimper were produced in October and transferred to finished goods for sale.
- There was no opening or closing work in progress of Whimper at the beginning or end of the month.

Required

For the production of Whimper in October:

- Calculate the expected normal loss in kilograms.
- Determine whether there is an abnormal loss or abnormal gain during production of the product in the month.
- Calculate the per kilogram cost of production of the product.
- Draw up the process account for the month.

>> Question 15.5

The refining process operated by Inedible Oils plc generated 24,000 litres of engine oil during June. Inputs to the process during the month were 25,000 litres of unrefined oil costing £52,875, labour costing £22,325 and overheads of £28,200. Normal losses are expected to be 6% of the quantity of materials input to the process. There was no opening or closing work in progress at the start or end of the month.

Required

For the production of engine oil in June:

- Calculate the expected normal loss in litres.
- Determine whether there is an abnormal loss or abnormal gain during production in the month.
- Calculate the per litre cost of production of the product.
- Draw up the process account for the month.

15

» Question 15.6

SCT Limited produces moisturising cream. Normal losses are expected to be 12% of the quantity of input materials. The waste products produced as normal and abnormal losses can be sold for 80 pence per litre. Input costs for August were:

- 7,500 litres of material at a cost of £26,500.
- Labour costing £11,880.
- Overheads of £8,540.

Actual production in August was 6,450 litres of moisturising cream. There was no opening or closing work in progress at the start or end of the month. SCT received the cash for all the scrap units sold from the process on 31 August.

Required

For the production of moisturising cream in August:

- Calculate the expected normal loss in litres.
- Determine whether there is an abnormal loss or abnormal gain during production in the month.
- Calculate the per litre cost of production of the product.
- Draw up the process account, the abnormal loss or abnormal gain account and the scrap account for the month.

» Question 15.7

Mr Threshy produces luxury ice cream. The process inputs for April were as follows:

- Materials: 30,000 litres at a cost of £0.66 per litre.
- Labour: 1,000 hours at a cost of £10 per hour.
- Overhead: 1,000 hours at a cost of £5 per hour.

During the process, the materials undergo regular skimming to produce the uniquely creamy Mr Threshy luxury ice cream. The materials skimmed off are disposed of at a cost of 20 pence per litre for both normal and abnormal losses. Normal losses are expected to be 20% of input materials. In April, 23,750 litres of ice cream were produced from the process. There was no opening or closing work in progress in the process at the beginning or end of the month. The disposals cost for the month was paid on 30 April.

Required

For the production of ice cream in April:

- Calculate the expected normal loss in litres.
- Determine whether there is an abnormal loss or abnormal gain during production in the month.
- Calculate the per litre cost of production of the product.
- Draw up the process account, the abnormal loss or abnormal gain account and the disposals cost account for the month.

15

⟫⟫ TAKE IT FURTHER

⟫⟫ Question 15.8

Mobo Chemicals Limited operate a refining process to produce cooking oils. At 1 December, the work in progress in the refining process was made up as follows:

- Materials: £26,187.
- Labour and overhead: £18,450.
- 10,000 work in progress units, 80% complete with respect to materials and 50% complete with respect to labour and overhead.

During December, materials costing £105,350 and labour and overhead costing £147,600 were added to the process. Completed output from the process for the month was 40,000 litres of cooking oils.

At 31 December, there were 5,000 units of work in progress, 60% complete with respect to materials and 20% complete with respect to labour and overhead.

Required

Present the two process accounts for Mobo Chemicals Limited on the basis that:

1. Finished production and closing work in progress are valued using the first in first out method.

2. Finished production and closing work in progress are valued using the weighted average cost method.

⟫⟫ Question 15.9

Giant Plant Fertilisers Limited produces liquid fertilisers for industrial agricultural use. At 1 May, the work in progress in the process was made up as follows:

- Materials: £51,660.
- Labour and overhead: £15,213.
- 12,000 work in progress units, 70% complete with respect to materials and 35% complete with respect to labour and overhead.

During May, materials costing £442,800 and labour and overhead costing £304,260 were added to the process. Completed output from the process for the month was 84,800 litres of liquid fertiliser.

At 31 May, there were 20,000 units of work in progress, 68% complete with respect to materials and 37% complete with respect to labour and overhead.

Required

Present the two process accounts for Giant Plant Fertilisers Limited on the basis that:

1. Finished production and closing work in progress is valued using the first in first out method.

2. Finished production and closing work in progress is valued using the weighted average cost method.

15

⟫⟫ Question 15.10

Acetic Industries Limited operates a two stage process in the production of vinegar. Details of the inputs and outputs to the two processes in July are presented below.

Process 1

Inputs for the month:

- 47,000 litres of material at a cost of £129,250.
- Labour costing £31,300.
- Overheads of £20,870.

Production in July and other details relating to Process 1 are as follows:

- Normal loss is expected to be 5% of the quantity of input materials.
- Actual output from Process 1 to Process 2 in the month was 44,000 litres.
- Normal and abnormal losses from Process 1 can be sold for £1.20 per litre. At 31 July, no cash had yet been received for the scrap value of the losses incurred in the month.
- There was no opening or closing work in progress in Process 1. All output during the month was transferred into Process 2 at cost.

Process 2

There were 6,000 units of work in progress at the start of July. Opening work in progress in Process 2 was made up of £22,800 of materials and £12,960 of labour and overhead. Opening work in progress was 100% complete with respect to materials and 50% complete with respect to labour and overhead.

All input materials in July came from Process 1. There was no other material input to the process. Labour and overhead costs incurred in July totalled up to £207,360. Forty-six thousand litres of vinegar were completed in Process 2 during the month and transferred to finished goods. No losses are expected from Process 2 and no losses were incurred during July.

Four thousand litres of vinegar were in progress at 31 July. These work in progress units were 100% complete with respect to materials and 50% complete with respect to labour and overhead.

Required

Write up the process accounts for Processes 1 and 2 for July together with any other accounts relevant to the two processes. Your answer should value the output and closing work in progress from Process 2 using both the first in first out and weighted average cost methods of valuing finished production and closing work in progress.

15

CAPITAL INVESTMENT APPRAISAL

LEARNING OUTCOMES

Once you have read this chapter and worked through the questions and examples in both this chapter and the online workbook, you should be able to:

- Understand what is meant by the term capital investment

- Understand why businesses undertake capital investment appraisal when making long-term investment decisions

- Explain how the four main capital investment appraisal techniques work

- Apply the four main capital investment appraisal techniques to capital investment decisions

- Explain the advantages and limitations of each of the four main capital investment appraisal techniques

- Understand the idea of the time value of money

INTRODUCTION

In the last few chapters we have looked at the costing of products and services and the role of cost accounting in various short-term decision-making and planning techniques as well as considering the management of short-term working capital in Chapter 9. These short-term decision-making techniques and working capital management aim to maximise contribution and profits over periods of a few weeks or months. What techniques should be applied if we want to maximise our value over the long term? This question arises when businesses want to make long-term investment decisions involving the outlay of significant amounts of money and resources (capital investment). What contribution and profits will any new investments make to the business? Will the new investments be valuable in the long run rather than just being profitable over short periods? Will the contribution and profits be higher than the returns we could generate from alternative investment options or from just putting the money into an interest paying bank account? These are important questions to ask when businesses are considering the investment of considerable sums of money in new projects and ventures. Businesses want to know if the contribution generated by these new investments will return their original cost and more. If a long-term investment fails to return the money originally invested, there would be little point undertaking the project in the first place.

WHAT IS CAPITAL INVESTMENT?

In Chapter 2 we considered the distinction between non-current assets and current assets. As we discovered, current assets are short-term assets (inventory, receivables and cash). In Chapter 9 we looked at how the cash arising from sales of inventory and the cash received from trade receivables is used to fund a business's short-term working capital requirements. Inflows of cash from inventory and trade receivables pay for the day-to-day expenditure that arises in running a business, such as payments for wages, rent, rates, electricity and heating as well as paying short-term liabilities as they become due.

However, non-current assets and new long-term investments require funding in order to maintain or expand a business's operations. Assets wear out or become outdated. Failure to replace and renew assets means that businesses are operating less efficiently and less profitably than they should. Without investment in new assets and new projects, businesses will not survive over the long term. When new investment is undertaken, this gives rise to new non-current assets that will be used to generate revenues, profits and cash over several years. Expenditure on these new non-current assets is termed capital expenditure, spending money now to benefit the future through the acquisition of these long-lasting, long-term assets. Consider Example 16.1.

16

EXAMPLE 16.1

If you were in charge of a haulage business, every few years you would need to invest in a new fleet of lorries. This fleet of lorries would then be used to generate revenue for several years before they themselves were replaced with a new fleet. Paying for these new vehicles would require long-term investment today. If the company did not currently have the cash on hand with which to pay for these new assets, these long-term funds would be provided by lenders in the form of loans (non-current liabilities as we saw in Chapter 2) or by shareholders in the form of new share capital subscribed by the shareholders (considered in Chapter 7).

Businesses undertake capital investment appraisal to determine whether new investments will be worthwhile and whether they will generate more cash than they originally cost.

WHY IS THIS RELEVANT TO ME?   Capital investment

To enable you as a business professional to:

- Appreciate the need for businesses to invest continually in new long-term assets from which to generate increased revenue, profits and cash

- Reinforce your ability to distinguish between short-term working capital management and long-term capital investment

---

GO BACK OVER THIS AGAIN!   Are you sure that you can distinguish between short- and long-term investment decisions? Go to the **online workbook** Exercises 16.1 to make sure you can make these distinctions.

WHY IS CAPITAL INVESTMENT APPRAISAL IMPORTANT?

Capital investment appraisal is essential when considering investments in new projects or in new assets. Without this appraisal, we will not be able to decide whether our investment is likely to be worthwhile in financial terms. Think about the points raised in Example 16.2.

EXAMPLE 16.2

When choosing the university at which you wanted to study, you might have weighed up the benefits and drawbacks from your current course compared with the benefits and drawbacks of choosing another programme at another university. Your thoughts will have centred not just on financial considerations: you might have reflected on the nightlife, the sporting facilities and the academic reputation of your chosen university among many other things. But at some point you will have taken into account the costs of studying at a particular college compared with the costs of studying elsewhere and the likely career and salary opportunities that would be open to you upon completion of your chosen course.

In the same way, businesses will want to know whether proposed investments are likely to represent a valuable addition to current operations and whether a positive return will be generated for shareholders. If not, there is no point in undertaking the project. Businesses will want to take on all projects that capital investment appraisal techniques suggest will make a positive return. However, cash for investment purposes, like many other resources, is often in short supply. Therefore, entities will undertake capital investment appraisal to determine which one of the several options competing for funds is the most valuable project in which to invest, given the levels of risk involved. Again, a simple example (Example 16.3) will illustrate these ideas.

16

EXAMPLE 16.3

If you have spare cash to invest, there are many banks, building societies and other investments competing for your money. You will weigh up each of the available options on the basis of which investment will give you the highest rate of interest, but also consider which investment is likely to be the safest home for your savings. It would be pointless putting your cash into an investment paying a high rate of interest if you were likely to lose all your money when the investment collapsed into liquidation.

Finally, the future is uncertain. What might seem like a good investment now might not look like such a good idea two years down the line. Therefore, managers have to exercise due care and attention when investing shareholders' money into projects in the expectation that they will produce the best outcomes for investors and other stakeholders. Capital investment appraisal is a further example of managers exercising control over an entity's operations as illustrated in Give me an example 16.1.

GIVE ME AN EXAMPLE 16.1   Capital investment appraisal

The following extract from the published report of Rio Tinto plc illustrates the rigorous approach adopted by company management to investing in current operations and in evaluating new investment opportunities.

We will continue to focus on maximising returns from our assets over the short, medium and long term. We will also maintain our disciplined and rigorous approach and invest capital only in projects that we believe will deliver returns that are well above our cost of capital.

Source: Rio Tinto plc annual report and accounts 2019
https://www.riotinto.com/en/invest/reports/annual-report

WHY IS THIS RELEVANT TO ME?   Capital investment appraisal

As a business professional you will be expected to:

- Understand the importance of evaluating long-term investment projects and what they will contribute to an organisation
- Be involved in capital investment decisions and appraise both the financial and non-financial aspects of these decisions
- Undertake the necessary capital investment appraisal of long-term projects you are proposing yourself

16

GO BACK OVER THIS AGAIN!   Are you confident that you can describe capital investment appraisal and explain why it's needed? Go to the **online workbook** Exercises 16.2 to make sure you appreciate what capital investment appraisal involves.

WHAT FINANCIAL INFORMATION WILL I NEED TO UNDERTAKE CAPITAL INVESTMENT APPRAISAL?

Capital investment appraisal relates to future events, so a substantial amount of estimation is required when undertaking this technique, as shown in Figure 16.1. All costs and revenues associated with a proposed project are expressed in terms of cash inflows and cash outflows.

The first piece of information required will be the cost of the new capital investment in £s. This is easily acquired as this cost will be readily available from the supplier of the new assets. In our haulage business example (Example 16.1), the capital investment will be the cost of the new lorries. This could be the list price or the list price less a discount for the purchase of several vehicles, but it is an easily ascertainable cost. If the capital investment involves the construction of a new building, then cost will be the cost of acquiring the land plus the construction costs. Again, the cost of the land will be a verifiable fact from the price the seller requires for the land, while the cost of the building will be the contract price determined by the engineers and designers at the construction company chosen to complete the project.

More difficult will be the estimates of revenue and costs arising from the new investment in each year of the proposed project's life. Demand for the new product or service will have to be determined along with the associated costs of providing the service or producing the product. Current demand and current revenue arising from that demand can be calculated quite easily, but future demand and future revenue will depend upon many uncertainties. Demand might fall to zero very quickly as a result of superior services and products from competitors or it might rise very rapidly as the business becomes the leading provider in the sector. Technology might reduce costs very quickly or costs might rise as a result of demand for particular raw materials that are in short supply. Whatever the revenues and costs, they will be subject to a high degree of estimation and in many ways will just represent a best guess.

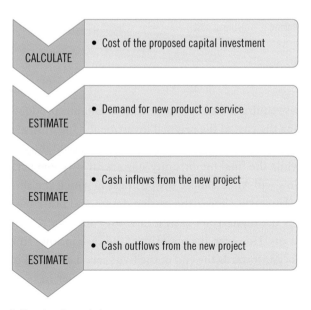

Figure 16.1 Steps in the capital investment appraisal process

16

CAPITAL INVESTMENT APPRAISAL TECHNIQUES:
COMPREHENSIVE EXAMPLE

To illustrate the capital investment appraisal techniques that are used in practice we will now turn to a comprehensive example.

Anna is looking to expand by diversifying into different areas of business. She currently has £500,000 to invest in acquiring the assets of an existing business from its owners. She has identified a stonemason, a furniture workshop and a garden design and build company as possible targets for her new investment. Market research and costings indicate that the net cash inflows (revenue – expenditure) into the three businesses over the next five years are expected to be those shown in Illustration 16.1.

Illustration 16.1 Anna: cash flows from the three possible capital investment projects

	Stonemason	Furniture workshop	Garden design and build
	£000	£000	£000
Investment cost (an outflow of cash)	(500)	(500)	(500)
Net cash inflows in year 1	160	190	50
Net cash inflows in year 2	160	180	100
Net cash inflows in year 3	160	170	150
Net cash inflows in year 4	160	160	250
Net cash inflows in year 5	160	150	350
Cash inflow from sale of the investment at the end of year 5	200	100	300
Total net cash inflows	1,000	950	1,200
Total net cash inflows – investment cost	500	450	700

All three businesses require the same initial investment, but produce differing total cash inflows after deducting the cost of the original investment. One business is expected to provide a steady income throughout the five years, one produces high initial cash inflows, but these then decline, while the final opportunity starts with very low net cash inflows, which then grow rapidly. How will Anna choose the business in which she should invest? Initially, it would appear that Anna will choose the garden design and build business for her investment as this produces the highest net cash inflow over the five years along with a higher resale value for the assets. However, the majority of the cash inflows from the garden design and build operation occur towards the end of the five years. Later cash inflows are much less certain (and hence riskier) than cash inflows that occur earlier in the other projects' lives. The following capital investment appraisal techniques can be used to help Anna make her decision.

16

CAPITAL INVESTMENT APPRAISAL TECHNIQUES

There are four commonly used techniques when undertaking capital investment appraisal. These are:

- Payback
- Accounting rate of return (ARR)
- Net present value (NPV)
- Internal rate of return (IRR)

We will look at each of the above techniques in detail to show how each of them works and what each of them tells us about the positive or negative financial returns from each project.

Payback

This method calculates the number of years it will take for the cash inflows from the project to pay back the original cost of the investment. An investment of £1,000 into a deposit account that pays 5% interest per annum would provide you with annual interest of £50 (£1,000 × 5%). To repay your initial investment of £1,000 would take 20 years (£1,000 ÷ £50). In the same way, businesses assess how long the cash inflows from a project would take to repay the initial investment into the project.

GO BACK OVER THIS AGAIN!   Are you certain that you can calculate a simple payback period? Go to the **online workbook** and have a go at Exercises 16.3 to make sure you can undertake these calculations successfully.

Looking at Anna's investment opportunities, let's consider the payback from the first option, the stonemason. To calculate the payback period, a payback table is drawn up to show how long the project will take to pay back the original investment. The first column of the table (see Table 16.1) lists the annual cash inflows and outflows, while the second column presents the initial investment outflow less the cash inflows received each year.

In Table 16.1 the investment of £500,000 is made at the present time and so is shown as the initial outflow of cash from the project. Investments made at the start of a project, the present time, are conventionally referred to as being made in year 0 or at time 0. As cash flows into the project, so the initial investment is paid back and the investment in the project not yet paid back falls.

At the end of year 1, after deducting the first year's cash inflows of £160,000, there is £500,000 − £160,000 = £340,000 still to be recovered from the project before the full £500,000 is paid back. In year 2, the project generates another £160,000, so at the end of year 2 there is still £340,000 − £160,000 = £180,000 required from the project before the initial investment is repaid in full. This process is repeated until the cumulative cash flows show £Nil or a positive number. At this point, the initial investment has been paid back by cash inflows into the project.

Table 16.1 shows that the stonemason project would repay the initial investment of £500,000 at some time between the end of years 3 and 4 as the cumulative cash flows (original investment − net cash inflows) turn positive by the end of year 4.

However, we can be more precise. Only £20,000 out of the £160,000 cash inflow in year 4 is required to repay the investment in the project that has not yet been repaid by the cash inflows

Table 16.1 Anna: payback table for the investment in the stonemason business

	Cash flows £000	Cumulative £000
Initial investment year 0	(500)	(500)
Net cash inflows year 1	160	(340)
Net cash inflows year 2	160	(180)
Net cash inflows year 3	160	(20)
Net cash inflows year 4	160	140
Net cash inflows year 5	160	300
Cash inflow from sale of the investment at the end of year 5	200	500

in years 1, 2 and 3. Therefore, the exact payback period for an investment in the stonemason business would be:

$$3 \text{ years} + \frac{£20,000}{£160,000} = 3.125 \text{ years}$$

As 0.125 years is roughly equivalent to 1½ months (12 × 0.125), the initial investment of £500,000 at time 0 is fully repaid after 3 years and 1½ months.

NUMERICAL EXERCISES   Do you think you can calculate a payback period for a project? Work your way through the above example again to confirm your understanding of how we arrived at the payback period for the stonemason project and then go to the **online workbook** and attempt Numerical exercises 16.1 and 16.2 to make sure you can apply this investment appraisal technique to the other two investments that Anna is considering.

Payback: the decision criteria

When using the payback method of capital investment appraisal, the project chosen is always the investment that pays back its initial cash outlay most quickly. In Anna's case, on the basis of payback, she would choose to invest in the furniture workshop as this repays the initial outlay of £500,000 in less than three years while the other two projects repay the same initial investment in more than three years, as shown in Figure 16.2.

Would this be a good decision? If Anna is concerned with just the speed of her cash recovery, then the furniture workshop would be the correct choice as her initial investment is returned to her in the shortest possible time. The payback calculation is easy to make and easy to understand, but it does not consider the time value of money (see this chapter, The time value of money). It also ignores the cash flows after the payback period is complete. In the case of the furniture workshop, a further £450,000 is generated from this project after the initial investment is paid back, whereas the garden design and build project yields a further £700,000 after payback, £250,000 more than the cash inflows from the preferred investment on the basis of the payback period.

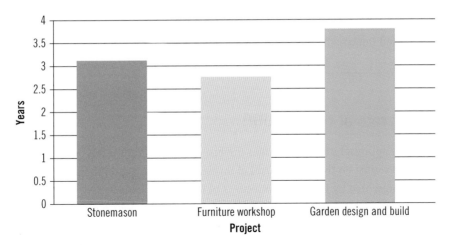

Figure 16.2 Payback periods in years of the three investment opportunities available to Anna

Should the payback period be the sole criterion upon which to base an investment decision? The answer to this question is 'no'. Payback will be just one of the criteria upon which any investment decision is based. Further decisions have to be made about the long-term revenue generation prospects of the investment. You probably noticed that the cash inflows from the furniture workshop are reducing year by year and that the resale value of the assets of this business is significantly lower than the resale value of the assets in the other two projects under consideration. Any further investment in this business after the five-year period will probably generate lower cash inflows than the other two options, so, from a longer-term point of view, an investment in the furniture workshop is probably not the best use of Anna's money if she wants to maximise the potential returns on her investment.

Looking at the other investment options, the garden design and build, while presenting the longest payback period, shows rising cash inflows each year that accelerate towards the end of the five-year period. Therefore, this might well be a better investment for the longer term as demand for this business's services seems to be rising sharply and might be expected to increase even further after the end of year 5. The stonemason business shows steady inflows of cash each year, but no increase or decrease in demand. This would seem to be the safest investment, but it is not one that will perform beyond expectations.

WHY IS THIS RELEVANT TO ME?   Payback method of capital investment appraisal

To enable you as a business professional to:

● Calculate a payback period for a proposed investment

● Understand the criteria on which to take an investment decision based on payback

● Understand the advantages and limitations of the payback method

● Appreciate that capital investment decisions have to be based on not just one but several criteria

16

Accounting rate of return (ARR)

This investment appraisal method averages the projections of accounting profit to calculate the expected rate of return on the average capital invested, as summarised in Figure 16.3. Accounting profit is represented by the net cash inflows of the project over its life, less the total depreciation (remember that depreciation is not a cash flow—refer back to Chapter 6, The indirect method, to revise this point—but is treated as an expense in arriving at accounting profit). The total accounting profit projections are divided by the number of years the project will last to give the average profit over the life of the investment. This is then divided by the average capital employed over the life of the project to determine the ARR.

Let's see how the ARR would be calculated for the stonemason business and then you can practise this technique on the other two potential investment opportunities.

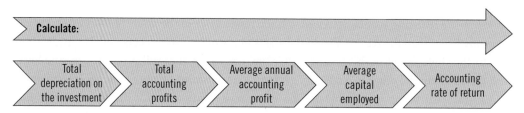

Figure 16.3 Steps in calculating the accounting rate of return (ARR) on an investment

ARR Step 1 calculate the total depreciation on the investment

First, we will need to calculate the total depreciation on the investment in the stonemason project. Remember that the total depreciation provided on non-current assets is given by the assets' cost – the residual value of those assets (Chapter 3, Residual value and the annual depreciation charge).

From Illustration 16.1:

- The cost of the assets is £500,000

- The residual value is the cash inflow from the sale of the investment at the end of year 5 of £200,000

Therefore, total depreciation over the five years of the project's life is:

£500,000 (cost) − £200,000 (residual value) = £300,000

16

ARR Step 2 calculate the total accounting profits

Total accounting profits are the total net cash inflows – the total depreciation. Total net cash inflows into the stonemason project are £160,000 for five years, a total of £800,000. The resale value of the assets is not included in the net cash inflows as this figure is used to calculate both the total depreciation on the project's assets and the average capital investment over the project's life.

Total accounting profits are thus £800,000 (net cash inflows) − £300,000 (depreciation) = £500,000.

ARR Step 3 calculate the average annual accounting profit

The average annual accounting profit is then £500,000 ÷ 5 years = £100,000 per annum.

ARR Step 4 calculate the average capital employed

The average capital employed in the stonemason project is found by adding together the original cost of the investment and the resale value of the assets at the end of the project and dividing this total figure by 2.

From Illustration 16.1:

- The cost of the assets is £500,000
- The residual value is the cash inflow from the sale of the investment at the end of year 5 of £200,000

Therefore, average capital employed in the stonemason business over the five years is:

(£500,000 (cost) + £200,000 (residual value)) ÷ 2 = £350,000

ARR Step 5 calculate the accounting rate of return

The ARR is then the average annual accounting profit divided by the average capital employed in the project:

$$\frac{£100,000 \text{ (average annual profit)}}{£350,000 \text{ (average capital employed over the five years)}} \times 100\% = 28.57\%$$

NUMERICAL EXERCISES   How confident are you that you can calculate an accounting rate of return for a project? Work your way through the above example again to confirm your understanding of how we arrived at the accounting rate of return for the stonemason project and then go to the **online workbook** and attempt Numerical exercises 16.3 and 16.4 to make sure you can apply this investment appraisal technique to the other two investments that Anna is considering.

16

Accounting rate of return: the decision criteria

The investment decision based on the ARR requires us to choose the proposed investment with the highest ARR, provided that this meets or exceeds the required ARR of the business. Assuming that the ARR meets Anna's target rate of return, the project that she will choose will be the garden design and build project as it produces an accounting rate of return of 35% compared with the furniture workshop, which has an accounting rate of return of 30%, as shown in Figure 16.4. This approach produces a quite different decision when compared to the payback method of investment appraisal.

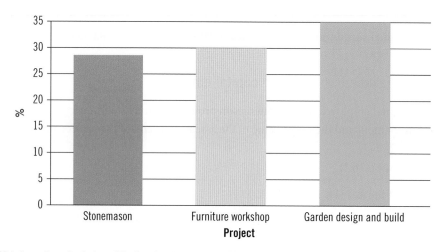

Figure 16.4 Accounting rate of return of the three investment opportunities available to Anna

While the ARR is easy to calculate and is based on accounting profits, it does suffer from some serious limitations:

- As with the payback method of investment appraisal, the ARR ignores the time value of money.

- The ARR is a percentage rather than the total profits generated by an investment, so projects with the same ARR could have hugely different cash flows, one with very low net cash inflows and one with very large net cash inflows. Managers will always prefer larger cash flows to smaller ones, but reliance on the relative measure of ARR might lead to the selection of a project with a higher rate of return but lower net cash inflows. In Anna's case the same project has both the highest accounting rate of return and the highest cash inflows, but this may not always be the case.

- ARR does not differentiate between projects (as payback does) that have the majority of the net cash inflows in the early stages of the project's life. As we have already noted, early cash inflows can be predicted with more accuracy and so are preferred by businesses as the money is in the bank rather than just being a potential future inflow of cash.

16

WHY IS THIS RELEVANT TO ME?   Accounting rate of return method of capital investment appraisal

To enable you as a business professional to:

- Calculate the ARR for a proposed investment
- Appreciate the criteria on which to make an investment decision based on the ARR
- Understand the advantages and limitations of the ARR method of capital investment appraisal

SUMMARY OF KEY CONCEPTS   Can you remember how the accounting rate of return is calculated and what its advantages and limitations are? Go to the **online workbook** to check your knowledge with Summary of key concepts 16.2.

Companies' use of the payback and accounting-based measures of investment appraisal is illustrated in Give me an example 16.2.

GIVE ME AN EXAMPLE 16.2   Companies' use of payback and accounting measures in evaluating investment opportunities

Do companies use payback and accounting based measures in practice to evaluate investment opportunities? The following extract from Next plc's Annual Report and Accounts for the 52 weeks to 26 January 2019 shows that they do.

New Space

Branch profitability of the portfolio opened or extended in the last 12 months was 21% of VAT inclusive sales. Payback on the net capital invested was 27.5 months, which is marginally beyond our internal payback hurdle of 24 months and reflective of the difficulty in predicting new store performance in the current environment.

Source: Next plc annual report and accounts 2019, p. 23

The time value of money

Before we consider the final two investment appraisal techniques, net present value (NPV) and the internal rate of return (IRR), we need to think about the time value of money. We noted earlier that both the payback and ARR methods of capital investment appraisal ignore this aspect of the investment decision. So why is the time value of money so important? And what do we mean when we talk about the time value of money? This approach to investment appraisal recognises that £1 received today is worth more than £1 received tomorrow. There are various reasons why today's money is more valuable than tomorrow's.

Firstly, inflation will reduce the value of our cash: £1 will buy more today than it will buy this time next year. For example, if a litre of petrol costs £1.40 today, we can buy 30 litres of petrol for £42 (30 × £1.40 = £42). However, if the inflation rate is 5% per annum, this means that in one year's time, one litre of petrol will cost £1.47 (£1.40 × 1.05). Our £42 will now only buy us 28.57

16

litres of petrol (£42 ÷ £1.47), as the purchasing power of our £42 has fallen as a result of inflation. Therefore, given that inflation reduces the value of our money and what we can buy with it, it makes sense to receive cash today rather than receiving cash tomorrow.

We can combat the effects of inflation by investing our money to generate interest to maintain our purchasing power. £1 invested today at an annual interest rate of 5% will give us £1.05 in a year's time, our original £1 plus 5% interest. If the inflation rate over the same period has been 5%, we will be no worse off and our purchasing power will have remained the same. In our example above, £42 today invested at a rate of 5% would give us £44.10 (£42 × 1.05) in one year's time. With this £44.10 we could buy £44.10 ÷ £1.47 = 30 litres of petrol so the purchasing power of our money has been maintained.

However, if we can invest our £1 for a year at an interest rate of 5% while inflation is only 3%, at the end of the year we would need our original £1 plus a further 3p to buy the same goods in a year's time that £1 will buy today. We will thus be 2p better off as our £1.05 is more than the £1.03 we need for consumption in one year's time. If we cannot have our money today, we will demand something in return to compensate us for waiting for cash that is receivable in the future. By investing our money in the bank or in a project, we are missing out on using the cash today so there is an opportunity cost element to this investment. A higher return on the cash is the compensation we expect for forgoing consumption today.

Finally, money that we will receive in the future is more risky than money we receive today because of the uncertainty that surrounds future income. Investing money carries the risk that we will not receive any interest as well as the risk that our original investment will not be repaid in full. Therefore, investors require a particular level of return to compensate them for the risk they are taking by investing their money. In the same way, businesses require a rate of return to compensate them for risking their capital in a particular venture. The riskier the venture is, the higher the rate of return that will be required to invest in that venture, as shown in Give me an example 16.3.

GIVE ME AN EXAMPLE 16.3   Higher risk = higher return

Two bailout packages totalling €240 billion were advanced to the Greek government in May 2010 and October 2011. In April 2015 growing fears that Greece would fail to repay what it owed to its international creditors, thereby forcing the country out of the European single currency, caused the value of Greek bonds to fall dramatically. As a result, anyone investing their money in Greek two-year bonds on 15 April 2015 would have seen the returns on these bonds rise to 27%. This very high return is due to the risk that the Greek government will be unable either to pay the interest or to repay the capital value of those bonds. Clearly, the higher the risk, the higher the return that investors will demand for taking on that risk. By contrast, the price that investors were paying for German 10-year government bonds (which are considered an ultra-safe investment) on the same day meant that their returns from their investment in these bonds were close to zero.

Source: https://www.wsj.com/articles/greek-government-bonds-plunge-on-ratings-downgrade-1429180492

WHY IS THIS RELEVANT TO ME?   The time value of money

To enable you as a business professional to:

- Understand that inflation erodes the value of today's money and reduces its future purchasing power
- Appreciate that money received today has more purchasing power than money received tomorrow
- Appreciate that cash expected in the future is less certain and so riskier
- Understand that investors will require a certain rate of return on money invested in order to compensate them for the risks they are taking in investing their money
- Appreciate that investing money in a project involves an opportunity cost as that money cannot be used for something else while it is invested in the project

GO BACK OVER THIS AGAIN!   Are you certain that you have grasped the concept of the time value of money? Go to the **online workbook** and have a look at Exercises 16.4 to make sure you understand this concept and then have a go at Exercises 16.5 to check your grasp of this subject.

MULTIPLE CHOICE QUESTIONS   Are you sure that you understand the time value of money? Go to the **online workbook** and have a go at Multiple choice questions 16.1 to test your understanding.

Business investment and the time value of money

In the same way, businesses invest money with the expectation that their investments will earn them a return in the future. Businesses will determine the acceptable level of return to compensate them for the risks involved in investing and use this level of return to discount expected future cash inflows and outflows to a present value. Present value expresses expected future inflows and outflows of cash in terms of today's monetary values. Discounting to present value thus expresses all a project's cash inflows and outflows in the common currency of today, thereby facilitating a fair comparison of projected cash inflows and outflows for different investment proposals.

The acceptable level of return is referred to as the business's cost of capital and is sometimes known as the hurdle rate of return. If an investment clears the hurdle—that is, the NPV is greater than or equal to £Nil—then it means that the project will deliver a positive return and generate more profit for the business over time than has to be invested at the beginning of the project.

Net present value

Anna estimates that her expected rate of return is 15%. This is the rate of return that she feels will compensate her for the risk she is taking in investing in a new business of which she has no experience. Applying this rate of return to the stonemason project produces the NPV results shown in Illustration 16.2.

16

Illustration 16.2 Anna: net present value of the investment in the stonemason business discounted at a rate of 15%

	Cash flows £000	× Discount factor 15%	= Net present value £000
Cash outflow year 0	(500)	1.0000	(500.00)
Net cash inflows year 1	160	0.8696	139.14
Net cash inflows year 2	160	0.7561	120.98
Net cash inflows year 3	160	0.6575	105.20
Net cash inflows year 4	160	0.5718	91.49
Net cash inflows year 5	160	0.4972	79.55
Cash inflow from sale of the investment at the end of year 5	200	0.4972	99.44
Stonemason investment: net present value of the project discounted at a rate of 15%			**135.80**

How did we arrive at these figures?

The initial investment is always made at the start of the project, time 0, and so is already expressed in terms of today's money. Therefore, there is no need to discount this figure to present value as today's money is already stated at its present value. This figure is thus multiplied by a discount rate of 1.0000.

All cash inflows are assumed to be received at the end of each year of the project and so are discounted to present value as though they are received at the end of year 1, at the end of year 2, at the end of year 3 and so on, right up to the last expected cash inflow or outflow associated with the project. This is an important convention of the NPV and IRR capital investment appraisal techniques, but is obviously unrealistic as, in reality, cash will flow into and out of projects throughout the year. However, it is an assumption you need to be aware of and this assumption is made to keep the models as simple as possible.

Discount factors are presented in Table 1 in the Appendix. Check that the figures given in Illustration 16.2 are the discount rates for time intervals 1, 2, 3, 4 and 5 for a 15% discount rate. If you ever need to derive your own discount rates, you would divide 1 by $(1 + $ the interest rate being used$)^n$ where n is the number of years into the project. In Anna's case, this is 1 divided by $(1 + 0.15)$ for year 1, 1 divided by $(1 + 0.15)^2$ for year 2, 1 divided by $(1 + 0.15)^3$ for year 3 and so on. Check that these calculations do give you the discount factors shown in Illustration 16.2 by working out these figures on your calculator now. Keep Table 1 in the Appendix handy for the remaining examples in this chapter and when you attempt the various activities in the online workbook.

Just as we saw with statements of cash flows in Chapter 6, cash outflows are shown in brackets while cash inflows are shown without brackets. This convention is also applied when calculating NPVs. Thus the initial investment, which is an outflow of cash, is shown in brackets while the inflows of cash are shown without brackets. Totalling up the NPV of the outflow and the NPVs of all the inflows gives us a positive NPV of £135,800 for the stonemason project.

16

NUMERICAL EXERCISES Are you confident that you can calculate a net present value for a project? Work your way through the above example again to confirm your understanding of how we arrived at the net present value for the stonemason project and then go to the **online workbook** and attempt Numerical exercises 16.5 and 16.6 to make sure you can apply this investment appraisal technique to the other two investments that Anna is considering.

SHOW ME HOW TO DO IT How clearly did you understand the calculation of a proposed project's net present value? View Video presentation 16.1 in the **online workbook** to see a practical demonstration of how the net present value calculation is carried out.

Net present value: the decision criteria

Projects discounted at the business's cost of capital resulting in either an NPV of £Nil or a positive NPV are accepted. If a company has several projects under consideration, then all projects with a positive or £Nil NPV are taken on. Where more than one project is competing for investment capital, then the project with the highest NPV is accepted first. If investment capital is available to undertake a further project, then the project with the second highest NPV is accepted and so on until all the available capital for investment has been allocated to projects. Proposed projects with a negative NPV are rejected and are not developed beyond the evaluation stage.

In Anna's case, she can only invest in one of the three projects as her capital for investment is limited to £500,000. Figure 16.5 shows that the garden design and build project gives the highest NPV of £183,850, well above the project with the second highest NPV, the stonemason business. The furniture workshop, which was ranked first on the basis of payback and second on the basis of ARR, is now the worst performing project on the basis of NPV. Therefore, Anna will accept the garden design and build project on the basis of the evaluation provided by the NPV method of investment appraisal.

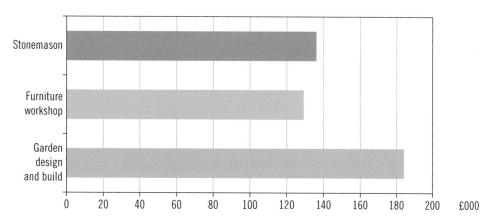

Figure 16.5 Net present value of the three investment opportunities available to Anna

Net present value: advantages

The NPV technique has the following advantages:

- Unlike the payback and ARR investment appraisal techniques, NPV does take into account the time value of money. This makes it a superior method of evaluating and differentiating between several projects.

16

- NPV discounts all cash inflows and outflows from a project into today's money to enable a fair comparison between projects to be made.

- NPV accounts for all the cash inflows and outflows from a project.

- Cash inflows that arise later in the project's life are riskier than cash inflows that arise earlier. The use of discount factors enables users of this technique to reflect this increased risk arising from later cash inflows as these cash inflows are worth less in current money terms.

- The NPV technique can be used in conjunction with the payback approach to determine when NPVs become positive (see this chapter, Discounted payback and Table 16.2). The further into the future this happens, the riskier the project is.

Net present value: limitations

However, as with all investment appraisal techniques, the NPV approach also suffers from the following disadvantages:

- This method is more difficult to understand than the simpler payback method.

- The technique makes the very large assumption that cash inflows and outflows and discount rates can be predicted with the required level of accuracy.

WHY IS THIS RELEVANT TO ME?   Net present value method of capital investment appraisal

To enable you as a business professional to:

- Calculate a net present value for a proposed investment project

- Appreciate the criteria on which to make an investment decision based on the net present value method

- Understand the advantages and limitations of the net present value method

---

 SUMMARY OF KEY CONCEPTS   Can you remember how net present value is calculated and what its advantages and limitations are? Go to the **online workbook** to revise these with Summary of key concepts 16.3.

Discounted payback

Before we move on to consider the internal rate of return investment appraisal method, it is worth noting that the net present value and payback methods of investment appraisal can be combined to calculate the discounted payback period. This method takes the discounted cash flows under the net present value approach and then determines when those discounted cash flows will turn positive after taking into account the original investment in a project. Table 16.2 presents the discounted payback for the stonemason project.

Table 16.2 Anna: discounted payback table for the investment in the stonemason business

	Cash flows	Cumulative
	£000	£000
Initial investment year 0	(500.00)	(500.00)
Discounted cash inflows year 1	139.14	(360.86)
Discounted cash inflows year 2	120.98	(239.88)
Discounted cash inflows year 3	105.20	(134.68)
Discounted cash inflows year 4	91.49	(43.19)
Discounted cash inflows year 5	79.55	36.36
Discounted cash inflow from sale of the investment at the end of year 5	99.44	135.80

Table 16.2 tells us that the discounted payback period is between four and five years. Only £43,190 out of the £79,550 discounted cash inflow in year 5 is required to repay the investment in the project that has not yet been repaid by the discounted cash inflows in years 1 to 4. Therefore, the exact discounted payback period for the investment in the stonemason business would be:

$$4 \text{ years} + \frac{43.19}{79.55} \times 12 = 4.543 \text{ years}$$

0.543 years is equivalent to 6½ months (12 × 0.543), so the initial investment of £500,000 at time 0 is fully repaid after 4 years and 6½ months under the discounted payback approach to investment appraisal.

NUMERICAL EXERCISES   Are you sure that you can calculate a discounted payback period for a project? Work your way through the above example again to confirm your understanding of how we arrived at the discounted payback period for the stonemason project and then go to the **online workbook** and attempt Numerical exercises 16.7 and 16.8 to make sure you can apply this investment appraisal technique to the other two investments that Anna is considering.

WHY IS THIS RELEVANT TO ME?   Discounted payback method of capital investment appraisal

To enable you as a business professional to:

- Calculate the discounted payback period for a proposed investment project
- Understand how the net present value and payback methods of investment appraisal are combined to determine the discounted payback period for a proposed investment project

16

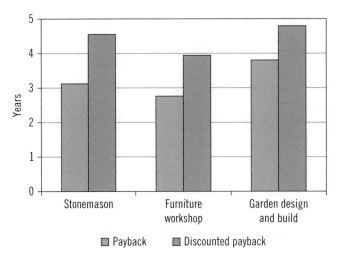

Figure 16.6 Payback and discounted payback of the three investment projects available to Anna

The discounted payback results are shown in Figure 16.6 together with the original payback results (Figure 16.2). The discounted payback decision would be the same as the payback decision with the furniture workshop paying back the initial investment more quickly than the other two investment opportunities. However, the decision to choose the furniture workshop investment on the basis of the discounted payback period would still suffer from the same limitations as outlined earlier (this chapter, Payback: the decision criteria) so Anna has not gained much additional information as a result of these additional calculations.

Internal rate of return (IRR)

The IRR is linked to the NPV technique and is the discount rate at which the NPV of the project is £Nil. The IRR is thus the discount rate at which a project breaks even, the discount rate at which the present value of the cash outflows is equal to the present value of the cash inflows.

To calculate the IRR, a process of trial and error is used. Project cash flows are discounted at successively higher rates until a negative NPV is given for that project. The IRR is then estimated using a mathematical technique called interpolation. This technique is illustrated later.

Figure 16.7 illustrates the IRR, the discount rate which gives an NPV of £Nil. The NPV of a project at various discount rates is determined and plotted on the graph. As the discount rate increases, the NPV of the project falls. The point at which the NPV line crosses the *x* axis on the graph is the point at which the NPV is £Nil and this is the IRR.

All this may sound very complicated, so let's see how the IRR is calculated using the proposed investment in the stonemason business. We saw in Illustration 16.2 that a discount rate of 15% gave a positive NPV of £135,800 for this project. Using a discount rate of 26% to discount the stonemason project will give us the NPV shown in Illustration 16.3.

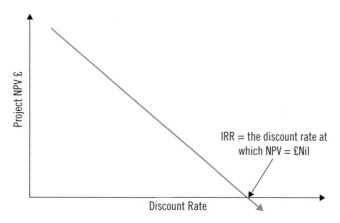

Figure 16.7 Graphical presentation showing the internal rate of return, the point at which the NPV of a project is £Nil

Illustration 16.3 Anna: net present value of the investment in the stonemason business discounted at a rate of 26%

	Cash flows £000	× Discount factor 26%	= Net present value £000
Cash outflow year 0	(500)	1.0000	(500.00)
Net cash inflows year 1	160	0.7937	126.99
Net cash inflows year 2	160	0.6299	100.78
Net cash inflows year 3	160	0.4999	79.98
Net cash inflows year 4	160	0.3968	63.49
Net cash inflows year 5	160	0.3149	50.38
Cash inflow from sale of the investment at the end of year 5	200	0.3149	62.98
Stonemason investment: net present value of the project discounted at a rate of 26%			**(15.40)**

We now know the following facts:

- A discount rate of 15% gives us a positive NPV of £135,800 (Illustration 16.2).

- A discount rate of 26% gives us a negative NPV of £15,400 (Illustration 16.3).

- Therefore, the discount rate that will give us a £Nil NPV lies somewhere between 15% and 26%.

Calculating the internal rate of return

This discount rate is given by the following calculation:

$$15\% + \frac{135.80}{(135.80 + 15.40)} \times (26\% - 15\%) = 24.88\%$$

16

How did we arrive at this IRR of 24.88%?

- We know that a discount rate of 15% gives a positive return, so this will be our starting point.
- What we don't know is where the NPV line crosses the *x* axis on the graph, the point at which the NPV of the project is equal to £Nil (Figure 16.7).
- Therefore, we have to estimate the discount rate at which the NPV is £Nil.
- Our NPV has to fall by £135,800 before we reach the discount rate that gives an NPV of £Nil.
- The total difference between the two results is £135,800 + £15,400 = £151,200 whereas we only need our NPV to fall by £135,800 before a net present value of £Nil is reached.
- Therefore, if we divide £135,800 by £151,200 and then multiply this fraction by the difference between the positive (15%) and negative (26%) discount rates, this will tell us how far along the line between 15% and 26% the IRR is.
- Adding the 15% to this result gives us an IRR of 24.88%.

NUMERICAL EXERCISES   Are you confident that you can calculate an internal rate of return for a project? Work your way through the above example again to confirm your understanding of how the internal rate of return was calculated for the stonemason project and then go to the **online workbook** and attempt Numerical exercises 16.9 and 16.10 to make sure you can apply this investment appraisal technique to the other two investments that Anna is considering.

SHOW ME HOW TO DO IT   How easily did you follow the calculation of a proposed project's internal rate of return? View Video presentation 16.2 in the **online workbook** to see a practical demonstration of how the internal rate of return calculation is carried out.

Internal rate of return: the decision criteria

Where a project has an IRR higher than an entity's required rate of return on investment projects, then the project should be accepted. Where projects are competing for resources, then the project with the highest IRR would be selected for implementation. In Anna's case, Figure 16.8 shows that the furniture workshop now comes out on top again with an internal rate of return of 25.31% compared with the garden design and build's IRR of 25.00% and 24.88% on the investment in the stonemason. However, the IRR evaluation requires the project originally selected under the net present value technique to be preferred where the decision under the IRR investment appraisal technique differs from the original NPV outcome. This makes sense as the NPV of the garden design and build investment discounted at a rate of 15% was £183,850 compared with a NPV of £128,890 for the furniture workshop investment discounted at the same rate. As we noted earlier, managers will always prefer a higher cash inflow to a lower one.

16

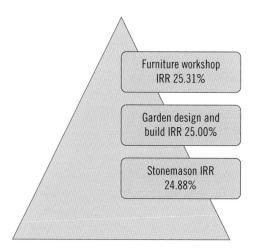

Figure 16.8 Internal rate of return of the three investment opportunities available to Anna

Internal rate of return: advantages

The IRR has the following advantages:

- As with the NPV technique, the time value of money is taken into account. This gives the IRR the same advantages as the NPV technique when compared with the ARR and payback investment appraisal methods.

- In the same way as NPV, the IRR method accounts for all the cash inflows and outflows from a project and discounts all these figures into today's money.

- Similarly, cash inflows that arise later in the project are riskier than cash inflows that arise earlier in the project. The use of discount factors enables users of this technique to reflect this increased risk arising from later cash inflows as these cash inflows are worth less in current money terms.

- The IRR technique tells us the percentage discount rate that will give an NPV of £Nil, the break-even NPV for a project. Thus, the technique does not require entities to specify in advance what their cost of capital is, but allows users to determine whether the rate of return is acceptable or not.

- The IRR provides more information than the NPV technique in that it tells users which project gives the highest rate of return where all projects have a positive NPV when discounted at the entity's cost of capital.

Internal rate of return: limitations

- Just as you found with the NPV technique, the IRR is difficult to understand! However, with practice and thought you will become familiar with this technique and be able to apply it in practice.

16

- The IRR, like the ARR, is a percentage rather than an absolute figure, so there is a risk that projects with a higher internal rate of return will be accepted even when the net present value of the cash flows from other projects discounted at the entity's cost of capital is higher. Hence the requirement that the IRR does not overrule the original decision under the NPV technique. As we saw in Chapter 8 (Ratios, figures or both?), the absolute magnitude of the figures must be considered alongside any ratios or percentages calculated when making decisions.

- The IRR cannot be used if cash flows are irregular. Where cash flows turn from being inflows to outflows and back again, a project will have two or more internal rates of return as the NPV line will cross the x axis in two or more places (illustration of this is beyond the scope of the present book).

WHY IS THIS RELEVANT TO ME?　Internal rate of return method of capital investment appraisal

To enable you as a business professional to:

- Calculate an IRR for an investment project
- Appreciate the criteria on which to make an investment decision based on the IRR
- Understand the advantages and limitations of the IRR method

---

SUMMARY OF KEY CONCEPTS　Can you remember the formula to calculate the internal rate of return and what its advantages and limitations are? Go to the **online workbook** to revise these with Summary of key concepts 16.4.

What use do companies make of discounted cash flow measures in practice? Have a look at Give me an example 16.4 to see the ways in which GlaxoSmithKline plc uses discounted cash flow techniques to evaluate investment projects.

MAKING A FINAL DECISION

Which project should Anna choose to invest in? Based on our earlier results and the results from the Numerical exercises, we can draw up a table to show us the rankings of the projects based on the results of each of the four capital investment appraisal techniques we have applied to the three proposals. These results are shown in Table 16.3.

The investment in the stonemason fails to come out on top on any of the investment appraisal criteria. Therefore, on purely financial grounds, investment in this project would be rejected. The other two projects are ranked first on the basis of two techniques, second once and third once.

> ### GIVE ME AN EXAMPLE 16.4 Companies' use of discounted cash flow measures in evaluating investment opportunities
>
> The following extracts from the annual report of GlaxoSmithKline plc illustrate the use of both the NPV and the IRR methods of investment appraisal used in evaluating investment opportunities (R&D = Research and Development):
>
> In 2010, we calculated that our estimated R&D internal rate of return (IRR) was 11% and stated a long-term aim of increasing this to 14%. We continue to improve the financial efficiency of our R&D and in February 2014 announced an estimated IRR of 13%. We continue to target 14% on a longer-term basis. Our estimated IRR is an important measure of our financial discipline and our strategic progress to improve the economics of R&D. It also underpins our strategy to
>
> create more flexibility around the pricing of our new medicines.
>
> Source: GlaxoSmithKline plc, annual report 2014, p. 27
>
> We have a formal process for assessing potential investment proposals in order to ensure decisions are aligned with our overall strategy. This process includes an assessment of the cash flow return on investment (CFROI), as well as its net present value (NPV) and internal rate of return (IRR) where the timeline for the project is very long term. We also consider the impact on earnings and credit profile where relevant.
>
> Source: GlaxoSmithKline plc, annual report 2014, p. 68

However, as already noted under internal rate of return, where the IRR technique gives a different result from the NPV technique, then the original choice under the NPV technique should be the project selected. In this case, the garden design and build will be accepted by Anna on the basis of the capital investment appraisal techniques applied to the three proposals. The garden design and build has the highest NPV and the highest ARR, as well as seeming to offer the highest net cash inflows and the highest growth potential among the projects on offer.

Table 16.3 Anna: summary of rankings based on the results of each of the four capital investment appraisal techniques applied to the three proposed investments

Capital investment appraisal technique	Stonemason	Furniture workshop	Garden design and build
	Ranking	Ranking	Ranking
Payback and discounted payback	2	1	3
Accounting rate of return	3	2	1
Net present value	2	3	1
Internal rate of return	3	1	2

16

POST INVESTMENT AUDIT

In previous chapters we have placed emphasis on the need to compare actual outcomes to expectations. Capital investment decisions are no exception to this approach. Once the investment in new non-current assets has been made and cash is flowing in from each new project, then managers will gather relevant information to evaluate how precise or how inaccurate their expectations and forecasts were. A post investment audit will be conducted to compare actual and forecast cash inflows and outflows. The aim of this comparison is to improve the accuracy of future capital investment appraisal proposals in order to minimise unfavourable outcomes. At the end of each project's life, the post investment audit will consider all aspects of the project and compare these with the expectations in the original proposal. Recommendations for improving the capital investment appraisal process will then be made and submitted to management for consideration and implementation.

SENSITIVITY ANALYSIS

In Chapter 14 sensitivity analysis was applied to budgets to determine the extent to which the outcome would change if the assumptions on which the budget was based were relaxed. In the same way, capital investment appraisal can be subjected to sensitivity analysis to see what the result would be if the cash inflows were reduced or increased by 10% or 20%, if the cost of the investment were increased by 10% or 20% and if the cost of capital were increased or decreased. By undertaking these additional calculations, a more informed investment decision can be made.

CHAPTER SUMMARY

You should now have learnt that:

- Capital investment involves the acquisition of new non-current assets or the investment in projects with the aim of increasing sales, profits and cash flows to the long-term benefit of a business.

- Capital investment appraisal is undertaken to evaluate the long-term cash generating potential of investment projects.

- Capital investment appraisal of new projects is important in assisting decision makers in allocating scarce investment capital resources to projects that will maximise the profits of the entity in the long run.

- Payback, accounting rate of return, net present value and internal rate of return calculations assist in the appraisal of capital investment projects.

- All four capital investment appraisal techniques offer both advantages and limitations when used in capital investment decisions.

- Money received tomorrow is less valuable than money received today.

16

END-OF-CHAPTER QUESTIONS

Attempt the questions in the following sections and then look at the solutions which can be found in the **online workbook** to see whether there are areas that you need to revisit.

❯ RECALL AND REVIEW

❯ Question 16.1

Describe the four commonly used capital investment appraisal techniques which are used to evaluate investment projects. Your answer should also explain how the outcome of each technique will determine whether a project should be undertaken or not.

❯ Question 16.2

The following table summarises the results of a capital investment appraisal exercise. There are four projects under evaluation and you have been asked to determine which project should receive investment funding. Which one of the four projects should be selected?

	Project A	Project B	Project C	Project D
Discounted payback	60 months	54 months	50 months	55 months
ARR	16%	19%	14%	18%
NPV	£181,000	£185,000	£159,000	£175,000
IRR	15%	14%	12%	10.5%

❯❯ DEVELOP YOUR UNDERSTANDING

Note to Questions 16.3–16.10: don't forget to use Table 1 in the Appendix when calculating the NPV and IRR of an investment project.

❯❯ Question 16.3

Podcaster University Press is evaluating two book proposals, one in accounting and one in economics. The directors are keen on both books but have funding for only one and they cannot decide which book to publish. Details of the two books are as follows:

Accounting book

The accounting book requires an investment of £450,000 to be made immediately. The book will produce net cash inflows of £160,000 in years 1 to 3 and £100,000 in years 4 and 5. The non-current assets involved in the book's production are expected to have a resale value of

16

£50,000 after five years. It is the directors' intention to sell the non-current assets from this project at the end of year 5 to realise the £50,000 cash inflow.

Economics book

The economics book requires an immediate investment of £600,000. The book will produce net cash inflows of £240,000 in year 1, £200,000 in year 2, £160,000 in year 3 and £105,000 in years 4 and 5. The non-current assets bought to print this book are expected to have a resale value of £100,000 at the end of the project. It is the directors' intention to sell the non-current assets from this project at the end of year 5 to realise the £100,000 cash inflow. Podcaster University Press has a cost of capital of 10%.

You should use a discount rate of 20% when calculating the IRR of the two book projects.

Required

Evaluate the two book projects using the payback, ARR, NPV and IRR methods of investment appraisal. Which project will you recommend and why will you recommend this project?

≫ Question 16.4

Zippo Drinks Limited is considering an investment into its computerised supply chain with a view to generating cash savings from using the benefits of currently available technology. Two options are under consideration. Option 1 will cost £200,000 and operate for five years, while Option 2 will cost £245,000 and remain operational for seven years. Given the longer implementation period, Option 2 will not realise any cash savings until the end of year 2. Neither investment will have any resale value at the end of its life. Because of the scarcity of investment capital, Zippo Drinks Limited can only undertake one of the supply chain projects. The directors of the company are asking for your help in evaluating the two proposals. The cash savings from any new investment in the years of operation are expected to be as follows:

	Option 1 £000	Option 2 £000
Year 1	50	–
Year 2	70	80
Year 3	80	85
Year 4	70	86
Year 5	60	101
Year 6	–	81
Year 7	–	71

Zippo Drinks Limited has a cost of capital of 15%.

For your IRR calculations, you should discount the two projects using a 19% discount rate.

Required

Calculate the payback periods, ARRs, NPVs and IRRs of the two supply chain investment proposals. On the basis of your calculations, advise the directors which of the two investments they should undertake. You should also advise them of any additional considerations they should take into account when deciding which project to adopt.

16

» Question 16.5

You are considering a five-year lease on a small restaurant serving light meals, snacks and drinks. The five-year lease will cost £80,000 and the lease will have no value at the end of the five years. The costs of fitting out the restaurant will be £30,000. After five years, you expect the restaurant fittings to have a scrap value of £2,000. You anticipate that net cash inflows from the restaurant will be £35,000 in the first year, £45,000 in the second year, £60,000 in the third year, £65,000 in the fourth year and £55,000 in the final year of operation. You have been approached by a fellow entrepreneur who is also very interested in the restaurant. She has proposed that you pay the £80,000 to take on the lease while she will fit out the restaurant at her own expense and pay you £40,000 per annum as rent and profit share. You expect a return of 12% per annum on any capital that you invest.

You are now uncertain whether you should fit out and run the restaurant yourself or sub-let the restaurant to your fellow entrepreneur. Running the restaurant yourself results in an IRR of 33.84% while allowing your fellow entrepreneur to run the restaurant and pay you rent and a share of the profits generates an IRR of 41.10%.

Required

Evaluate the above alternatives using the payback, ARR and NPV capital investment appraisal techniques. Which of the two options will you choose? In making your decision, you should also consider any other factors that you would take into account in addition to the purely financial considerations.

» Question 16.6

A manufacturing company intends to purchase a new piece of equipment to increase its production capacity. The equipment will cost £150,000 and it is expected that this equipment will have a resale value of £25,000 at the end of the project. The asset is budgeted to contribute the following cash inflows during each of the five years of the project's life:

	£
Year 1	60,000
Year 2	50,000
Year 3	40,000
Year 4	30,000
Year 5	20,000

The managers of the company are particularly keen to know how long it will take to recover the initial investment in the equipment.

Required

(a) Calculate the time required for the project to pay back its original investment.

(b) How would your answer change if the time value of money is taken into consideration? The company's expected rate of return is 10%.

(c) Explain the reasons why the time value of money should be considered in capital investment decisions.

16

>> Question 16.7

Ocean Solutions is a company operating in the oil and gas industry. The company is considering three potential projects for investment. The proposed projects will start in 2023 and will all have a six-year life. At the end of the projects' lives, all the facilities installed must be dismantled and the area surrounding the gas field must be returned to its pre-project condition. As a result, decommissioning expenditure will be incurred at the end of each project. Limited capital for investment and limited human resources mean that the company can only undertake one of these projects. Ocean Solutions' required rate of return is 12%. The following table summarises the expected cash inflows and outflows for each investment project:

		Gas field A £m	Gas field B £m	Gas field C £m
Initial investment		28.0	24.0	31.0
Cash inflows	2023	4.0	5.9	7.0
	2024	6.5	8.0	12.0
	2025	9.0	12.0	14.3
	2026	13.0	15.2	17.0
	2027	15.0	13.0	12.5
	2028	8.6	9.0	7.0
Decommissioning expenditure		10.0	8.3	15.0

Required

Evaluate the three projects using the NPV and IRR capital investment appraisal techniques. Using the results of your calculations, advise Ocean Solutions' directors on which project should be selected. To find the IRR of each project, you should discount the cash flows of Project A at 16%, of Project B at 30% and of Project C at 24%.

>>> TAKE IT FURTHER

>>> Question 16.8

Brando Limited is considering four possible investment projects. Each proposed project will last for eight years and will have a resale value at the end its life. Due to capital constraints only one of the four projects can be undertaken. The company's expected rate of return is 10%. The board of directors of the company has called upon your expertise in order to evaluate the four investment projects and to recommend which project the company should select.

The projects' initial investment, cash inflows and resale values are as follows:

		Project 1 £	Project 2 £	Project 3 £	Project 4 £
Initial investment		100,000	120,000	90,000	115,000
Cash inflows	Year 1	15,000	12,000	10,000	14,000
	Year 2	17,500	14,000	12,000	15,500
	Year 3	19,000	17,000	13,500	18,000
	Year 4	21,000	18,000	15,500	22,000
	Year 5	20,000	19,500	17,000	25,000
	Year 6	18,500	20,500	20,000	21,000
	Year 7	16,000	23,000	19,500	10,000
	Year 8	13,000	22,000	18,000	8,000
Resale value at the end of year 8		40,000	50,000	30,000	15,000

Required

Calculate the payback periods, ARRs, NPVs and IRRs of the four projects. Based on your calculations, advise the directors which of the four investment projects Brando Limited should undertake.

⟫ Question 16.9

Ambulators Limited makes prams and pushchairs. The company is currently evaluating two projects that are competing for investment funds.

The first project is the introduction to the market of a new pram. The new pram will require an initial investment of £3,300,000 in marketing and enhanced production facilities and each new pram will sell for £450 over the life of the product. Market research has shown that demand for the new pram is expected to be 5,000 units in the first year of production, with demand rising by 20% per annum on the previous year's sales in years 2 to 5. At the end of year 5, a new improved pram will have entered production and the investment in the new pram will have a residual value of £Nil.

The second project is a new pushchair. This will require an initial outlay on marketing and enhanced production facilities of £2,200,000. Each new pushchair will sell initially in the first year of production and sales for £220, but the directors expect the price to rise by £10 each year in each of years 2 to 5. Market research has projected that initial demand will be for 6,000 pushchairs in year 1 and that demand will rise by 10% per annum on the previous year's sales in years 2 to 5. At the end of year 5, the production facilities will be used to produce a new pushchair and will be transferred to the new project at a valuation of £500,000.

Both projects are competing for the same capital resources and only one of the projects can be undertaken by the company.

16

The cost cards for the new pram and the new pushchair are as follows:

	Pram £	Pushchair £
Direct materials	150.00	80.00
Direct labour	75.00	40.00
Variable overhead	25.00	10.00
Fixed overhead	50.00	20.00
Total cost	**300.00**	**150.00**

Fixed production overhead allocated to the cost of each product is based on 5,000 units of production for prams and 6,000 units of production for pushchairs. Fixed costs do not include depreciation of the new investment in each project.

Ambulators Limited has a cost of capital of 11%.

Required

For the proposed investment in the new pram or pushchair, calculate for each project:

- The payback period.
- The ARR.
- The NPV.
- The IRR.

You should round your sales projections to the nearest whole unit of sales.

The directors would like to hear your views on which project they should accept. Your advice should take into account both the financial aspects of the decision and any other factors that the directors of Ambulators Limited should consider when deciding which project to invest in.

≫≫ Question 16.10

Chillers plc manufactures fridges and freezers. The company is considering the production of a new deluxe fridge-freezer. The fridge-freezer will sell for £600 and the company's marketing department has produced a forecast for sales for the next seven years as follows:

Year	Units sold
2023	3,500
2024	4,000
2025	4,500
2026	5,250
2027	5,750
2028	5,500
2029	5,250

16

Variable costs are budgeted to be 40% of selling price. Fixed costs arising from the sale and production of the new deluxe fridge-freezer are expected to be £1,200,000 per annum. Fixed costs exclude depreciation of the new investment.

As a result of the introduction of the new deluxe fridge-freezer, the company expects to lose sales of 2,000 standard fridge-freezers each year over the next seven years. These standard fridge-freezers sell for £350 each with variable costs of 35% of selling price. The reduction in sales of standard fridge-freezers will save cash expenditure on fixed costs of £395,000 per annum.

The initial expenditure on the production line for the new deluxe fridge-freezer has been estimated at £2,000,000. At the end of seven years, this production line will have a scrap value of £100,000.

Chillers plc has a required rate of return on new investment of 13%.

Required

For the proposed investment in the new deluxe fridge-freezer, calculate:

- The payback period.
- The ARR.
- The NPV.
- The IRR.

Advise the directors of Chillers plc whether the project should go ahead or not.

16

17 CORPORATE GOVERNANCE AND SUSTAINABILITY

LEARNING OUTCOMES

Once you have read this chapter and worked through the questions and examples in both this chapter and the online workbook, you should be able to:

- Understand the control problems that arise within limited liability companies as a result of shareholders appointing directors to run the companies in which they invest

- Describe how the agency problem arises whenever a task is delegated to another party

- Define what is meant by the term corporate governance

- Describe the roles and responsibilities of the various participants in the corporate governance process

- Outline how corporate governance is used to monitor and control directors' actions and decisions to focus on the long term sustainable success of a business

- Describe how the Corporate Governance Code and other regulations work together to assure the integrity of the financial reporting process

- Appreciate that the modern corporation has responsibilities beyond just generating a profit for shareholders

- Describe corporate social responsibility reporting and what it involves

- Define the term sustainability

- Appreciate that the modern business entity is expected to present more than just financial information about its operations and activities

- Discuss how information about a range of performance measures beyond mere financial measures is beneficial to an organisation and its long-term survival
- Define the five fundamental principles of ethics for professional accountants

INTRODUCTION

Directors are appointed by shareholders to run companies on their behalf (Chapter 1, Control, accounting and accountability) (Figure 17.1). Shareholders firstly want to know that the resources entrusted to the directors are being used effectively and efficiently to generate profits and dividends. As shareholders are not involved in the day-to-day running of the company, their only source of financial information about their company is the annual report and accounts. The annual report and accounts are prepared by the directors. Shareholders thus have an information asymmetry problem: the directors know all about the company but shareholders know only what they are told (Figure 17.1). As a result of this information asymmetry, various other questions arise for shareholders. How can they be sure that what the directors are telling them in the annual financial statements is a fair representation of what has actually happened during the past 12 months? Are the directors hiding anything? Do the annual financial statements tell them everything they need to know for decision-making purposes? Apart from the financial results, how can shareholders be sure that the directors are running the business honestly, ethically and in accordance with the law? Is their company a good corporate citizen or are the directors engaging in illegal or morally suspect behaviour? What controls are there on the directors to make sure that they always take the right decisions and always act in the long-term best interests of the shareholders?

These questions also arise as a result of the agency problem. In these situations, someone (the agent) is entrusted to undertake a task by someone else (the principal). In the case of limited companies, the shareholders are the principals who appoint the directors as their agents (Figure 17.1).

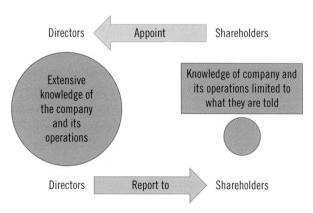

Figure 17.1 Information asymmetry between directors and shareholders

17

In an ideal world, the aims and objectives of the shareholders and of the directors would be exactly the same. However, the agency problem means that agents will always act in their own best interests and not in those of their principals. Directors will therefore seek to maximise the short-term profits of the company and thereby their own remuneration rather than taking decisions now that will generate long-term benefits for the shareholders. This is not a problem in small companies in which shareholders and directors are the same persons. But in listed companies (public limited companies, plcs), directors do not remain in their posts for lengthy periods of time, so, by the time today's investments pay off in say five or 10 years' time, the directors may no longer be employed by the company and so they will gain no benefit from considering the long-term interests of shareholders at the expense of their own short-term advantage.

Happily, help is at hand. The Companies Act 2006 together with corporate governance as enshrined in the Corporate Governance Code provides rules and guidance on many aspects of organisational management with a view to ensuring that entities are fully under control, that directors are not exceeding their powers and that business entities are run for the long-term benefit of stakeholders and not just to satisfy the short-term interests of directors. This chapter will consider in outline how these legal and governance rules work in order to limit shareholders' concerns over the running of their companies.

WHY IS THIS RELEVANT TO ME?   The information asymmetry and agency problems

To enable you as a business professional to understand:

- What is meant by the terms agency problem and information asymmetry
- The control problems that arise when shareholders delegate the running of companies to directors
- The causes of the problems that may arise from information asymmetry and the agency problem

---

GO BACK OVER THIS AGAIN!   Do you fully appreciate the control problems that arise in limited liability companies as a result of the agency problem and information asymmetry? Go to the **online workbook** and have a go at Exercises 17.1 to check your understanding.

CORPORATE GOVERNANCE: A BRIEF HISTORY

Following a series of financial scandals and corporate collapses in the late 1980s and early 1990s which had undermined the credibility of reported financial information and eroded trust in business, the Financial Reporting Council, the London Stock Exchange and the accountancy profession established the Committee on the Financial Aspects of Corporate Governance with Sir Adrian Cadbury as its chair. The aim of the committee was to consider the ways in which investor confidence in the honesty and accountability of listed companies should be restored. The Committee's report in 1992 was named after its chair and is always known as the Cadbury Report. All the proposals in the Cadbury Report were built on existing good practice, but the report gave them much more formal recognition and established the basis on which all publicly listed and public interest companies would henceforth be governed.

CORPORATE GOVERNANCE: A DEFINITION

What is meant by the term corporate governance? Section 2.5 of the Cadbury Report provides the following definition:

> Corporate governance is the system by which companies are directed and controlled. Boards of directors are responsible for the governance of their companies. The shareholders' role in governance is to appoint the directors and the auditors and to satisfy themselves that an appropriate governance structure is in place. The responsibilities of the board include setting the company's strategic aims, providing the leadership to put them into effect, supervising the management of the business and reporting to shareholders on their stewardship. The board's actions are subject to laws, regulations and the shareholders in general meeting.

The original report produced by the Cadbury Committee has been updated over the intervening years to embrace additional aspects in corporate governance. However, the main features are clear from the above quotation. The current Corporate Governance Code is built up of the principles, more detailed provisions and associated guidance. The aim of the Corporate Governance Code is to ensure that shareholders and boards of directors interact and work together to ensure that their company is effectively directed and controlled. Before we consider how the Code shows how effective direction and control can be achieved, let's look at the different parties who play a role in the corporate governance process.

SUMMARY OF KEY CONCEPTS   Can you remember the definition of corporate governance? Go to the **online workbook** to revise this definition with Summary of key concepts 17.1.

CORPORATE GOVERNANCE: THE PARTIES INVOLVED

Figure 17.2 sets out the key participants in the corporate governance process. These participants and their corporate governance roles and responsibilities will each be considered in turn. Once these roles and responsibilities are clear, we can then determine how the interaction of the various parties aims to ensure that publicly listed and public interest companies are effectively directed and controlled in order to address the concerns that shareholders have.

The board of directors: executive and non-executive directors

All companies have a board of directors who are responsible for running the company. The board of directors is made up of two categories of director: executive and non-executive. Both executive and non-executive directors are elected by the shareholders. The executive directors are responsible for the day-to-day running and management of the company, implementing policies and dealing with all the operational issues that arise on a daily basis. Executive directors are employees of the company and are remunerated on the basis of their employment contracts with the company.

17

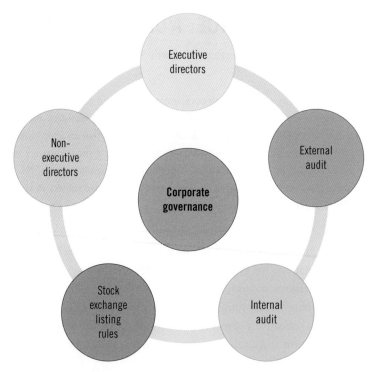

Figure 17.2 The key parties involved in the Corporate Governance process

Non-executive directors, on the other hand, do not perform any executive management functions. They are thus not involved in any day-to-day running of the business. Despite being members of the board of directors, non-executive directors are not employees of the company but charge fees for their services rather than receiving a salary.

Non-executive directors attend monthly board meetings and also set up and run various board committees. These board committees are composed of non-executive directors only and they fulfil critical functions in relation to financial reporting (the audit committee), directors' remuneration (the remuneration committee) and the nomination of new board members (the nomination committee). Figure 17.3 summarises the roles and responsibilities of both the executive and the non-executive directors.

WHY IS THIS RELEVANT TO ME?   Board of directors: executive and non-executive directors

To enable you as a business professional to understand:

- The different roles of the executive and non-executive directors in the running of listed and public interest companies
- That executive directors are excluded from membership of the audit, remuneration and nomination committees

17

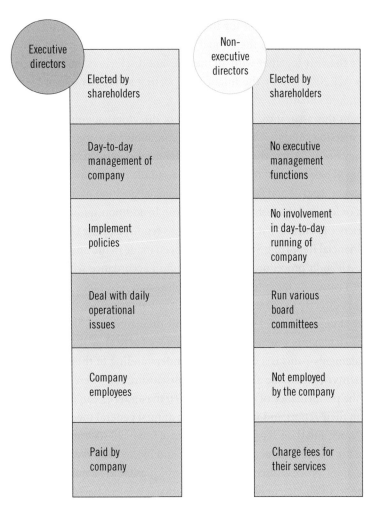

Figure 17.3 The roles and responsibilities of the executive and the non-executive directors

---

SUMMARY OF KEY CONCEPTS Are you certain you can describe the different duties and roles of executive and non-executive directors? Go to the **online workbook** to check your recollection with Summary of key concepts 17.2.

GO BACK OVER THIS AGAIN! Are you confident that you can distinguish between the roles of the executive and non-executive directors? Go to the **online workbook** and have a go at Exercises 17.2 to check your ability in this area.

External audit

The directors prepare the financial statements for their company on an annual basis. As we noted earlier (this chapter, Introduction: the information asymmetry and agency problems) accounting results for the year might not reflect all the relevant facts and figures. Alternatively, because directors control the financial reporting process and content, the annual report and accounts might be presented in a more favourable way than is warranted in order to secure greater financial

17

rewards and continued employment for the directors. Therefore, shareholders require reasonable assurance that the figures in the annual report and accounts present a true and fair view of the results for the year together with all the relevant disclosures and details required by both the Companies Act 2006 and by the financial reporting standards issued by the International Accounting Standards Board.

In order to gain this assurance, shareholders (not directors) appoint auditors annually at the annual general meeting. Auditors are qualified accountants who are completely independent of the company they are auditing. They review the financial statements presented by the directors, undertake testing of balances and transactions on a sample basis in order to verify that the financial statements present a true and fair view of the financial position of the company at the year end and of the profit or loss and the cash flows for the year. In addition, auditors use their expert knowledge and experience to ensure that all the disclosures required by the Companies Act 2006 and by International Financial Reporting Standards have been made in full and that no material information is omitted. All audit procedures are carried out in accordance with International Standards on Auditing (ISAs) issued by the International Auditing and Assurance Standards Board (IAASB).

Auditors report directly to shareholders without any interference from the directors in order to safeguard the independence of their report and their findings. The audit report comments on the financial statements prepared by the directors (note that the auditors do not prepare the financial statements—this is a common misunderstanding of the auditors' role). Where the financial statements do not make all the relevant disclosures or where directors have obstructed the auditors in the performance of their duties, then the auditors can inform the shareholders of their concerns in their report and in person at the annual general meeting.

The auditors' work and their reports enable users of financial statements to place a high degree of confidence in the audited financial information and in the audit reports attached to them. The auditor and the audit process also facilitate the workings of the capital markets which require assurance on the truth and fairness of financial information as a basis for the buying and selling of shares. Audited information is also used as a reliable basis for both investment in and lending to limited liability companies.

WHY IS THIS RELEVANT TO ME?   External audit

To provide you as a business professional with:

- A brief overview of the role of external auditors in the financial reporting regime

- A foundation for your later studies in auditing

SUMMARY OF KEY CONCEPTS   Do you think you can describe the role and responsibilities of external audit? Go to the **online workbook** to check your abilities in this area with Summary of key concepts 17.3.

GO BACK OVER THIS AGAIN!   Are you certain you understand the role and activities of external auditors? Go to the **online workbook** and have a go at Exercises 17.3 to check your understanding.

17

Internal audit

The internal audit function on the other hand is set up by the board of directors. As the name indicates, internal audit activities are undertaken by individuals working within the organisation. Whereas external audit is narrowly focused on the truth and fairness of the annual financial report and accounts and their compliance with the relevant legislation and International Financial Reporting Standards, internal audit is given a very much wider ranging remit. While external audit aims to verify past results, internal audit is focused on not just past but also current operations, as well as being forward looking and proactive. Internal audit concentrates attention upon the entire range of organisational operations involving an assessment of the effectiveness of the risk management, control and governance procedures alongside an evaluation of the integrity and accuracy of the reporting and internal control systems. Internal audit reports provide evaluations of every aspect of a business's activity with a view to improving and enhancing those activities to further the business's objectives and to help it achieve its aims. The aim of internal audit is always to add value to an organisation and its activities.

In the same way as external audit, internal audit, despite being staffed by employees of the business, aims to provide independent reports of its findings. This independence is enhanced by reporting not to the executive directors (who might be criticised by internal audit or seek to limit the internal auditors' range of activities) but to the independent non-executive directors on the audit committee. Internal auditors are not involved in the day-to-day operations of a business (you cannot be independent when you are evaluating your own work) but stand back from daily operational activities to present an objective overview of operations and activities, their effectiveness and their compliance with the legal and ethical obligations of the entity. This organisational independence from management enables unrestricted evaluation of management activities and personnel. Figure 17.4 presents a comparison of internal and external audit.

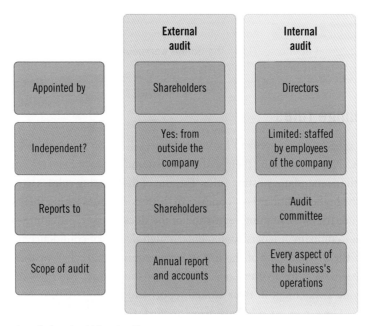

Figure 17.4 A comparison of external and internal audit

17

Directors have a responsibility to ensure that organisational operations and activities are fully under control and that assets are adequately safeguarded (for example, how easily could cash be stolen from a business?). To fulfil these responsibilities, the board of directors will set up an internal control system which puts in place checks and balances whose aim is both to prevent fraud and errors occurring and to result in their discovery if they do. Internal audit will assess and evaluate these internal control systems to determine their effectiveness and their ability to prevent the theft of assets and the occurrence of errors. In addition, a rigorous review of the internal controls will enable internal auditors to assess the reliability of information used in the financial and management reporting systems as well as evaluating an organisation's full compliance with laws and regulations.

WHY IS THIS RELEVANT TO ME?   Internal audit

To enable you as a business professional to appreciate:

- The extensive and wide ranging role of internal auditors within organisations

- The differences in the roles and responsibilities of both internal and external auditors

- How internal auditors continually monitor management and operations in shareholders' best interests

---

SUMMARY OF KEY CONCEPTS   Are you sure that you can describe the roles and responsibilities of internal audit? Go to the **online workbook** to check your abilities in this area with Summary of key concepts 17.4.

GO BACK OVER THIS AGAIN!   Are you confident that you understand what internal auditors do? Go to the **online workbook** and have a go at Exercises 17.4 to check your understanding.

GO BACK OVER THIS AGAIN!   Are you able to distinguish between the roles and responsibilities of internal and external auditors? Go to the **online workbook** and have a go at Exercises 17.5 to check your abilities in this area.

Stock exchange rules

Public limited companies can apply to have their shares listed on a recognised stock exchange. All companies accepted and listing their shares on the London Stock Exchange must ensure that they comply with the mandatory listing rules. The aim of these listing rules is to protect investors and to uphold the highest standards of conduct in those companies listing their shares. The listing rules guarantee the efficiency and regulation of the stock market, providing, in the same way as auditors do for company financial statements, a high degree of confidence in the operations and integrity of the market. One of the listing rules requires that all companies listing on the Stock Exchange should abide by the Corporate Governance Code. The rules dictate that listed companies provide a statement in their annual report and accounts stating how the principles in the Corporate Governance Code have been applied. Confirmation of compliance with the Code's provisions is also required. In situations where listed companies have not complied with the Code's principles, they must provide an explanation of their non-compliance. This regime is referred to as 'comply or explain'. This oversight by the Stock Exchange provides an additional safeguard for investors. Compliance with the listing rules ensures that boards of directors study the Code to make sure that they do comply. Studying the Code in this way will help the directors to determine whether their company is complying or not. Where they are not complying, they can take steps to make sure that their procedures and operations are in full compliance.

WHY IS THIS RELEVANT TO ME? Stock exchange rules

To enable you as a business professional to appreciate:

● The role of the Stock Exchange rules and oversight in corporate governance

● The disclosures companies have to make in their annual reports and accounts to certify compliance with the Stock Exchange rules

---

SUMMARY OF KEY CONCEPTS Are you quite sure you understand the role of the Stock Exchange rules in corporate governance? Go to the **online workbook** to check your understanding with Summary of key concepts 17.5.

ADDRESSING SHAREHOLDER CONCERNS

Now that the participants in the corporate governance process are clear, we can consider the ways in which these participants, the Companies Act 2006 and the Corporate Governance Code work together to meet shareholders' concerns. These concerns fall under various headings, so we shall consider each issue in turn under a separate heading.

Long-term success v. short-term profits

Firstly, let's consider how the Corporate Governance Code addresses the issue of whether the directors' focus should be on long-term success or short-term profits. Shareholders invest for the long term, whereas the expectation is that directors will aim to achieve the highest short-term profits possible in order to maximise their remuneration. These opposing aims pull in opposite directions, as shown in Figure 17.5.

Figure 17.5 The opposing aims of directors and shareholders

17

Given this tension between the two sets of opposing interests, shareholders will want reassurance that it is their long-term interests that are at the centre of directors' attention and decision making. Both the Companies Act 2006 and the Corporate Governance Code recognise this conflict and give shareholders' interests priority. The Companies Act 2006 and the Corporate Governance Code together emphasise that it is the long-term success of the company that counts. Section 172(1) of the Companies Act 2006 imposes a duty on directors to promote the success of the company and requires directors to consider the likely consequences of any decision in the long term. This long-term focus is given further emphasis in the Corporate Governance Code which states that '[a] successful company is led by an effective and entrepreneurial board, whose role is to promote the *long-term sustainable success* of the company, generating value for shareholders and contributing to wider society' (Corporate Governance Code, Section 1 Board Leadership and Company Purpose, Principle A, emphasis added). This aim of long-term sustainable success recurs twice in the Introduction and is reiterated in Section 5 of the Code which deals with directors' remuneration: 'Remuneration policies and practices should be designed to support strategy and promote *long-term sustainable success*. Executive remuneration should be aligned to company purpose and values, and be clearly linked to the successful delivery of the company's *long-term strategy*' (Corporate Governance Code, Section 5 Remuneration, Principle P, emphasis added). In these ways, the Corporate Governance Code and the Companies Act 2006 seek to ensure that shareholders' long-term interests are fully prioritised and are not subordinated to the short-term interests of the directors. Should the directors fail to consider the long-term sustainable success of the company in their actions, then shareholders can remove those directors from office at the next annual general meeting.

Company decision making

Directors should thus work together as a board, to make decisions as a body not as individuals acting alone. However, shareholders will worry that the board of directors might not be acting in the best interests of the business, might be taking unnecessary risks or might include directors who are acting on their own initiative without consulting the other directors about the decisions they are taking. As we have seen, Principle A of the Corporate Governance Code emphasises that 'a successful company is led by an effective and entrepreneurial board, whose role is to promote the long-term sustainable success of the company'. The board is thus required to work as a unit and to take decisions together rather than individual directors making decisions without consulting the board as a whole. How does this work in practice? Give me an example 17.1 presents Taylor Wimpey's statement relating to management processes and division of responsibility in the company's Corporate Governance report. This example illustrates the directors' collective responsibility for decision making over a very wide range of matters exercised by the board working together as a complete unit in order to prevent risky individual actions in key strategic and operational decisions.

GIVE ME AN EXAMPLE 17.1   Collective decision making by the board

Taylor Wimpey plc's annual report and accounts for the year ended 31 December 2019 (page 74) notes that the schedule of matters specifically reserved for the decision of the board can be found on the company's website at https://www.taylor wimpey.co.uk/corporate/our-company/governance/ our-policies.

Consultation of the documents on the website shows that this schedule of matters covers 'strategy and management, capital and structure, financial reporting and controls, internal controls, contracts, communication, board membership and other appointments, remuneration, delegation of authority, corporate governance matters, policies and other'.

Source: https://www.taylorwimpey.co.uk/corporate/our-company/governance/our-policies

As well as collective responsibility for decisions, the Code emphasises that a clear division of responsibilities should exist within the board of directors. The executive directors are responsible for running the business on a day-to-day basis while the non-executive directors' role is to run the board and its associated committees. Principle G of the Code establishes that 'the board should include an appropriate combination of executive and non-executive (and, in particular, independent non-executive) directors, such that no one individual or small group of individuals dominates the board's decision making. There should be a clear division of responsibilities between the leadership of the board and the executive leadership of the company's business.' (Corporate Governance Code, Section 2 Division of Responsibilities) so that every board member participates in the decision-making process. In order to ensure that there is a clear division of responsibilities, the Code requires that 'the roles of chair and chief executive should not be exercised by the same individual' (Corporate Governance Code, Section 2 Division of Responsibilities, Provision 9). This clear division of responsibilities ensures that no one person has unrestricted decision-making responsibility. In situations in which one individual makes all the decisions, then risks are increased as opposing views and counsels are ignored, and there is no restraining hand to rein in dominant personalities. Splitting the leadership of the company and requiring key decisions to be taken by the board of directors as a whole will reassure shareholders that the direction of the business is fully under control and extreme or excessively risky actions are being avoided.

This all sounds like a very good control mechanism on the executive directors but what is to prevent the executive directors simply overwhelming the non-executive directors through sheer force of numbers and forcing their policies through? This problem is addressed in Section 2 of the Code. Provision 11 states that 'at least half the board, excluding the chair, should be non-executive directors whom the board considers to be independent'. This provision thus aims to ensure that the non-executive directors cannot be dominated by the executive directors to enable effective enforcement of corporate governance in each and every company. Give me an example 17.2 presents an example of how this works in practice. Principle G in the Corporate Governance Code thus enables non-executive directors to fulfil their roles successfully so that they 'provide constructive challenge, strategic guidance, offer specialist advice and hold management to account' (Corporate Governance Code, Section 2 Division of Responsibilities, Principle H).

17

GIVE ME AN EXAMPLE 17.2   Non-executive and executive director numbers

The board of Taylor Wimpey plc is made up of three executive directors, one non-executive chair and five non-executive directors. The five non-executive directors and the chair have a wide range of experience in industries including construction, business services, economics, politics, financial services, property and retail. Through this structure, the board has a balance of skills, experience and independence in combination with the executive directors' knowledge and experience in both the construction industry and finance. The number of non-executive directors comfortably exceeds the number of the executive directors so that the non-executive directors can fulfil their oversight and advisory roles effectively.

Source: https://www.taylorwimpey.co.uk/corporate/investors/2019-annual-report

---

WHY IS THIS RELEVANT TO ME?   Company decision making

To enable you as a business professional to appreciate that:

- The executive directors run the business on a day-to-day basis
- The non-executive directors run the board and its associated committees
- The Corporate Governance Code requires that no one individual or group of individuals should have unfettered powers of decision making and control
- All board members both executive and non-executive participate in the decision-making process
- The chair and chief executive roles are exercised by different individuals

---

GO BACK OVER THIS AGAIN!   Are you sure you understand the roles of the various parties in the decision-making process in companies? Go to the **online workbook** and have a go at Exercises 17.6 to check your appreciation of the Corporate Governance Code requirements in this area.

Board effectiveness

As we have seen, the Corporate Governance Code requires companies to be headed by an effective board (this chapter, Long-term success v. short-term profits). But how is this effectiveness achieved and what steps should directors be taking to ensure that they are effective? Directors should avoid complacency and just following the same approaches as in the past. They should question and test the strategy and direction of the company to make sure that the strategy adopted by the company is the most effective means of achieving the company's long-term goals. There should be procedures in place to ensure that directors are fulfilling their roles and responsibilities effectively and they should actively question their own effectiveness and review what they have achieved to determine what they might have done better. What does the Corporate Governance Code have to say about these aspects of board effectiveness?

Various principles and provisions of the Code deal with the factors, summarised in Figure 17.6, essential in promoting the effectiveness of the board and of the individual board members. Section 3 of the Code (Composition, Succession and Evaluation) states the principle that '[t]he board and its committees should have a combination of skills, experience and knowledge' (Corporate Governance Code, Principle K). While skills, experience and knowledge are essential to effective performance, directors must also have sufficient time in which to fulfil their duties (Corporate Governance Code, Principle H and Provision 15). Accurate, timely and clear information (Corporate Governance Code, Principle F) together with appropriate policies, processes and resources (Corporate Governance Code, Principle I) will be essential in helping all the directors to fulfil their roles. Feedback on performance provided by both their fellow directors and by outside parties will tell each director whether they are meeting the requirements of the role. Shareholders are also involved in the assessment process as they are given a regular say on their directors' performance through the opportunity to re-elect the directors or to reject their reappointment. The current directors will not be in their posts indefinitely so a continuous flow of new blood onto boards to replace those retiring and to reinforce and strengthen the directors as a body is also required. This flow of new blood will be met through careful succession planning.

Non-executive directors have considerable knowledge, skills and experience gained in running other businesses as they are recruited from other publicly listed companies or other senior positions. This prior experience brings valuable insights and knowledge to boards of directors to ensure that these boards are effective in directing and controlling their companies. The non-executive directors provide an advisory and oversight function on the board. In this role, Principle H in Section 2 of the Code states that they should 'provide constructive challenge, strategic guidance, offer specialist advice and hold management to account'. The non-executive directors' role is to take an independent, broad overview of the business

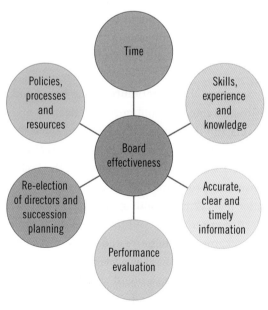

Figure 17.6 The requirements for board effectiveness in the Corporate Governance Code

and its progress to ensure that it is moving in the right direction and adopting the correct strategies through which to achieve its aims. As they are not employees of the company, non-executive directors are able to adopt a much more objective overview of the business which executive directors, due to their close involvement in the day-to-day affairs of the company, cannot take.

'Annual evaluation of the board should consider its composition, diversity and how effectively members work together to achieve objectives. Individual evaluation should demonstrate whether each director continues to contribute effectively' (Corporate Governance Code, Section 3 Composition, Succession and Evaluation, Principle L). In addition, Provision 21 of the Code requires 'formal and rigorous annual evaluation of the performance of the board, the chair and individual directors'. The same provision recommends a three-yearly externally facilitated board evaluation to avoid the problems of internal bias and a complacent approach when conducting such evaluations. Once the three-yearly report has been received 'the chair should act on the results of the evaluation by recognising the strengths and addressing any weaknesses of the board. Each director should engage with the process and take appropriate action when development needs have been identified' (Corporate Governance Code, Section 3 Composition, Succession and Evaluation, Provision 22). The non-executive directors are required to meet annually without the chair being present in order to evaluate the chair's performance (Corporate Governance Code, Section 2 Division of Responsibilities, Provision 12). As well as appraisal by their peers both inside and outside the company, the directors and their performance are subjected to appraisal by the shareholders through the annual re-election process at the annual general meeting. The re-election process is not just a rubber stamping exercise allowing the existing directors to continue in their roles for another year since 'the board should set out in the papers accompanying the resolutions to elect each director the specific reasons why their contribution is, and continues to be, important to the company's long-term sustainable success' (Corporate Governance Code, Section 3 Composition, Succession and Evaluation, Provision 18). Real thought thus has to go into justifying the re-election of each director each and every year. Appraisals of this kind ensure that all the directors are fulfilling their responsibilities effectively and act as a timely corrective to any shortcomings in this respect.

Shareholders will be concerned about continuity on the board and the ability of the board to renew itself effectively to guarantee the continued effectiveness of the board into the future. How will today's star players and the enhanced performance that they have generated be replaced? Will these replacements perform to the same high levels of expectation? The Corporate Governance Code, Principle J states that 'appointments to the board should be subject to a formal, rigorous and transparent procedure, and an effective succession plan should be maintained for board and senior management. Both appointments and succession plans should be based on merit and objective criteria and, within this context, should promote diversity of gender, social and ethnic backgrounds, cognitive and personal strengths'. Such an approach to succession will ensure the continuity of board effectiveness. Diversity on the board will encourage a wide range of opinions and ideas and a board with a suitable balance of skills will enable the shareholders to be confident that all the different aspects of controlling and directing the company are covered.

17

WHY IS THIS RELEVANT TO ME?   Board effectiveness

To enable you as a business professional to understand:

- The steps boards of directors will take to ensure they fulfil their roles effectively
- That non-executive directors provide an oversight function on boards
- How board effectiveness is assessed, maintained and enhanced

GO BACK OVER THIS AGAIN!   Are you confident you can say how boards ensure they are effective? Go to the **online workbook** and have a go at Exercises 17.7 to check your understanding.

Ensuring the integrity of financial statements

One of the most important duties of the board of directors is to prepare and present the annual financial statements. As we have seen earlier in this chapter, the shareholders' main concern relates to the completeness of the annual report and financial statements and whether they present a true and fair view of the profits or losses, cash flows and financial position of the company in compliance with the reporting requirements of both the Companies Act 2006 and of International Financial Reporting Standards.

What provisions are there in the Corporate Governance Code to ensure that the information presented in the annual report and financial statements shows a true and fair view of profits, cash flows and the statement of financial position and that all the information presented is complete and unbiased?

As the financial statements are audited by independent auditors from outside the company, the auditor's report already adds credibility to the financial information presented (this chapter, External audit). However, there is a risk that the directors may bully the auditor into accepting a reduction in the disclosures made or to agree to accounting treatments that are biased, reflecting the concerns of the directors rather than the true and fair view required by the Companies Act 2006. What guiding principles does the Corporate Governance Code provide with a view to preventing such misleading financial statements?

Principle M of the Code states that 'the board should establish formal and transparent policies and procedures to ensure the independence and effectiveness of internal and external audit functions and satisfy itself on the integrity of financial and narrative statements'. The Code (Section 4) then goes on to require that 'the board should present a fair, balanced and understandable assessment of the company's position and prospects' (Corporate Governance Code, Section 4 Audit, Risk and Internal Control, Principle N and Provisions 25 and 27). These duties are imposed on the board as a whole, so all the members of the board of directors, both executive and non-executive, have to read, review and consider the financial statements to ensure that they adhere to these requirements. Further safeguards are added in the Code's provisions. As noted earlier (this chapter, The board of directors: executive and non-executive directors), the audit committee is made up of non-executive directors. There should be at least three independent non-executive directors on the audit committee, at least one of whom should have recent, relevant financial experience

17

(Corporate Governance Code, Provision 24). This recent relevant financial experience will enable the audit committee to assess whether the report and financial statements present a fair, balanced and understandable assessment of the company's position and prospects as mandated by the Corporate Governance Code. This provision also requires the audit committee members to have competence relevant to the sector in which the company operates. This competence gives the audit committee a benchmark against which to evaluate the report and financial statements of an organisation and will enable the audit committee members to see potential gaps or potentially misleading information due to their in-depth sector knowledge and experience.

Provision 25 also emphasises the audit committee's role in meeting the requirements of the Code with respect to the financial statements. The audit committee's main role and responsibilities should include (among others):

- 'monitoring the integrity of the financial statements of the company and any formal announcements relating to the company's financial performance, and reviewing significant financial reporting judgements contained in them.

- providing advice (where requested by the board) on whether the annual report and accounts, taken as a whole, is fair, balanced and understandable, and provides the information necessary for shareholders to assess the company's position and performance, business model and strategy' (Corporate Governance Code, Section 4 Audit, Risk and Internal Control, Provision 25).

As well as reviewing the final report and financial statements to ensure that they meet the requirements of the Code, the audit committee is also charged with various duties that relate to ensuring the integrity of the financial records upon which the report and accounts are based. Thus, Provision 25 also requires the audit committee to review the company's internal financial controls and internal control and risk management systems. Alongside this duty, the audit committee is tasked with monitoring and reviewing the effectiveness of the company's internal audit function and assessing the effectiveness and independence of the external audit process. The audit committee makes recommendations on the appointment, reappointment and removal of the external auditor for the shareholders' consideration. Where the external auditor's independence appears to have been compromised, the audit committee can recommend the removal of the external auditor to the shareholders.

In addition to overseeing the external audit process, the audit committee and the external auditors meet on a regular basis to discuss the financial statements and any issues arising. These meetings between the members of the audit committee and the external auditors help to maintain auditor independence and the integrity of the external audit process: there are no executive directors on the audit committee who might pressure the external auditors in the ways suggested earlier, so the external auditors are free to express their opinions on the financial statements and any shortcomings they have identified. As the audit committee members are non-executive directors with a purely oversight role and whose fees are not affected by the financial results, there is no incentive for the audit committee members to pressure the external auditors into accepting less than complete or misleading disclosures. Give me an example 17.3 provides extracts from the audit committee report of Taylor Wimpey plc to illustrate the issues we have been considering in this section to show you how these principles and provisions of the Code work in practice.

17

GIVE ME AN EXAMPLE 17.3   The audit committee's role and responsibilities

'AUDIT COMMITTEE REPORT

Dear Shareholder,

On behalf of the Board, I am pleased to present the report of the Audit Committee . . .

The Committee supports the Board in fulfilling its corporate governance responsibilities, including the Group's risk management and internal control framework; internal audit process; financial reporting practices; the preparation and compliance of the Company's Annual Report and Accounts; and the external audit process . . .

The Committee continues to hold meetings with the external auditor and the Head of Internal Audit, independent of the Executive, and these assist in ensuring that reporting, forecasting and risk management processes are subject to rigorous review throughout the year . . .

The Committee is confident that its composition; balance; and expertise can give shareholders confidence that the financial; reporting; risk; and control processes of the Company are subjected to the appropriate level of independent, robust and challenging oversight.'

Source:https://www.taylorwimpey.co.uk/corporate/investors/2019-annual-report

WHY IS THIS RELEVANT TO ME?   Ensuring the integrity of the financial statements

To enable you as a business professional to understand:

- How the Corporate Governance Code requires the board of directors as a whole to present a fair, balanced and understandable assessment of the company's position and prospects

- The ways in which the audit committee monitors the integrity of the financial statements

- That the audit committee is responsible for monitoring and reviewing the internal control and risk management systems of a company

- That the audit committee monitors the performance of the internal and external auditors

- The way in which the audit committee helps to maintain the independence and integrity of the external audit process

GO BACK OVER THIS AGAIN!   Do you think you understand how the integrity of the financial statements is assured? Go to the **online workbook** and have a go at Exercises 17.8 to check your understanding.

Directors' remuneration

As the directors run the company, what is to stop them deciding their own remuneration and paying themselves excessive amounts at the shareholders' expense? What restraints are there on the directors to prevent them abusing their position in this way?

The main principles stated in Section 5 of the Corporate Governance Code require that '[r]remuneration policies and practices should be designed to support strategy and promote long-term sustainable success. Executive remuneration should be aligned to company purpose and values, and be clearly linked to the successful delivery of the company's long-term strategy. A formal and transparent procedure for developing policy on executive remuneration and determining director and senior management remuneration should be established. No director should be

17

involved in deciding their own remuneration outcome' (Corporate Governance Code, Section 5 Remuneration, Principles P and Q). As a result of these clear principles, directors are unable to set their own remuneration. The remuneration of the executive directors is decided by the remuneration committee which is staffed entirely by non-executive directors (Corporate Governance Code, Provision 32). As the non-executive directors are responsible for evaluating the executive directors' performance (this chapter, Board effectiveness), they are in a very good position to determine the executive directors' remuneration. In this way, the Corporate Governance Code seeks to ensure that directors' remuneration is not excessive for the levels of profits and performance achieved.

Other provisions in the Corporate Governance Code go further in seeking to ensure that directors work for the benefit of shareholders. Firstly, Provision 36 aims to align directors' interests closely with those of shareholders, stating: 'remuneration schemes should promote long-term shareholdings by executive directors that support alignment with long-term shareholder interests.' Directors who own shares in the company will focus much more on the long-term sustainable success and value maximisation of that company than on increasing short-term profit and remuneration. Secondly, where directors' performance is not up to the required level, Provision 37 of the Corporate Governance Code allows remuneration schemes to set out the terms under which amounts can be recovered or withheld. Likewise, Provision 39 seeks to ensure that failure is not rewarded: 'The remuneration committee should ensure compensation commitments in directors' terms of appointment do not reward poor performance. They should be robust in reducing compensation to reflect departing directors' obligations to mitigate loss.' Again, the objective of these provisions is to promote shareholders' interests over those of the directors in pursuit of the long-term sustainable success of the company.

Shareholder communications

The final shareholder concern relates to communications from their directors and how effective these are. Yet shareholders are not the only stakeholders in companies and it is expected that communications are made to all stakeholders. Section 1 of the Corporate Governance Code presents the main principle in this area: 'In order for the company to meet its responsibilities to shareholders and stakeholders, the board should ensure effective engagement with, and encourage participation from, these parties' (Corporate Governance Code, Section 1 Board Leadership and Company Purpose, Principle D). Formal communications with shareholders take place through the annual report and accounts and through the annual general meeting. But the Code recommends further, non-formal communications with shareholders: 'In addition to formal general meetings, the chair should seek regular engagement with major shareholders in order to understand their views on governance and performance against the strategy. Committee [audit, nomination and remuneration] chairs should seek engagement with shareholders on significant matters related to their areas of responsibility. The chair should ensure that the board as a whole has a clear understanding of the views of shareholders' (Corporate Governance Code, Section 1 Board Leadership and Company Purpose, Provision 3). Give me an example 17.4 presents an example of the very extensive shareholder engagement activities that are undertaken in practice. As a result of such extensive engagement activities, shareholders can be confident that they are fully informed of developments and other matters that affect them as shareholders and that their views and concerns are taken into account by the directors.

17

GIVE ME AN EXAMPLE 17.4   Shareholder engagement

'Engagement with shareholders and consideration of their interests

The Board actively seeks and encourages engagement with shareholders, including its major institutional shareholders and shareholder representative bodies. The Board fully supports the principles of the 2018 UK Corporate Governance Code and also welcomes and acknowledges the Stewardship Code, both of which aim to foster a more proactive governance role by major shareholders. The Board has put in place arrangements designed to facilitate contact with shareholders concerning business, governance, remuneration and other relevant topics. This provides the opportunity for meetings between shareholders and the Chair, the Independent Non Executive Directors (including the Senior Independent Director), as well as the Chief Executive, Group Finance Director and Group Operations Director and other executives including the Company Secretary as appropriate, in order to establish a mutual understanding of objectives.

The Company also operates a structured programme of investor relations, based on formal announcements and publications covering the Full Year and Half Year results. This includes engagement with shareholders and shareholder representative bodies at meetings with individual Directors to establish a mutual understanding of objectives. In addition, the Chair meets with the Company's institutional shareholders from time to time, both proactively and upon request, in order to discuss the Company and its performance, governance and remuneration policies.

An annual consultation exercise is undertaken by the Remuneration Committee, in conjunction with which the Chair of the Committee engages directly with shareholders and their representative bodies. In developing the proposed new Remuneration Policy, the Remuneration Committee took into account wider workforce remuneration and related policies, to ensure that incentives and rewards were aligned with wider Group remuneration principles and with Group culture and sought feedback from major shareholders and their representative bodies as part of the annual consultation.

At the Company's AGM – both before, during and after the meeting; Directors actively engage with shareholders who have attended. In addition, there are a series of 'roadshows' following the announcement of the Group's Full Year and Half Year results.

All Directors receive formal reports and briefings during the year about the Company's investor relations programme and consider detailed feedback through surveys; direct contact; and also other means, which are taken into account when considering major strategic and operational alternatives open to the Company.

The Company is, of course, also always very pleased to hear from and engage with our private shareholders and has, for example, hosted the United Kingdom Shareholders Association at our Chobham Manor development in November 2019. Individual shareholders were able to meet with Regional management for a presentation and Q&A, which was followed by a tour of the development.'

Source:https://www.taylorwimpey.co.uk/corporate/investors/2019-annual-report

---

CORPORATE SOCIAL RESPONSIBILITY REPORTING

So far in this chapter, the main focus of corporate governance has been upon the directors of the company and their relationship with the shareholders. However, there are other stakeholders to consider together with a wider reporting and operational role for entities. Our discussions in Chapter 1 (The users of accounting information) reviewed the interests and information needs of other parties such as employees, customers, suppliers, the government and the general public. Should companies and businesses also be taking these other parties into account both in their operations and in their annual reports? Do companies have any reporting responsibilities beyond informing shareholders of profits generated and dividends paid?

The US economist, Milton Friedman, famously took a very strong line against businesses adopting any other approach than that of generating profit. Writing in *The New York Times Magazine* (13 September 1970), Friedman quoted the following lines from his 1962 book *Capitalism and Freedom*:

> There is one and only one social responsibility of business—to use its resources and engage in activities designed to increase its profits so long as it stays within the rules of the game, which is to say, engages in open and free competition without deception or fraud.

On this view of a business, companies only exist to make a profit for shareholders, and directors' sole responsibility is towards those shareholders. This view ignores entirely the effect that businesses and the products they produce have on the natural environment, on consumers, on communities and on other interested parties. As long as a profit is being made and made legally, nothing else is seen to matter. By extension, this argument proposes that directors should only report financial data and ignore any other performance measures and indicators.

By the 1960s, however, commentators and business people had begun to challenge the view that business had no other responsibilities beyond the mere generation of profit. Stakeholder theory presents the idea that directors and managers should balance the interests of all stakeholders (those with a stake or interest in a business) and not favour one group of interests over another. Employee welfare and development and a concern for the local environment and the people living within it were suggested as other measures that entities should consider when planning operations, designing new products and reporting on performance. This corporate social responsibility reporting approach is illustrated in Figure 17.7.

In the UK, this corporate social responsibility approach has also received attention in the Companies Act 2006. Section 172 of the Act sets out directors' duties in detail (emphasis added):

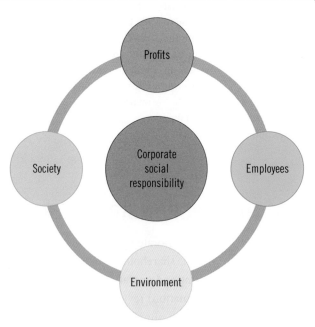

Figure 17.7 The corporate social responsibility reporting model for companies

Duty to promote the success of the company

Section 172 (1) A director of a company must act in the way he considers, in good faith, would be most likely to promote the success of the company for the benefit of its members as a whole, and in doing so have regard (amongst other matters) to—

(a) The likely consequences of any decision in the long term,

(b) The interests of the company's employees,

(c) The need to foster the company's business relationships with suppliers, customers and others,

(d) The impact of the company's operations on the community and the environment,

(e) The desirability of the company maintaining a reputation for high standards of business conduct, and

(f) The need to act fairly as between members of the company.

Notably, as indicated by the highlighted sections, directors are not just required to promote the success of the company for the benefit of shareholders (members) but for the benefit of other stakeholders and society as a whole as well. We saw in Chapter 1 (The users of accounting information) that there are various other user groups of financial accounting information besides shareholders, lenders and other creditors and it is the additional interests of these groups that the Companies Act 2006 requires directors to take into account.

This requirement to consider other interested parties as well as shareholders now extends to presenting information in the strategic report presented to shareholders. Section 414C of the Companies Act 2006 states that the following information should be presented by companies quoted on a stock exchange:

i. 'environmental matters (including the impact of the company's business on the environment),

ii. the company's employees, and

iii. social, community and human rights issues,

including information about any policies of the company in relation to those matters and the effectiveness of those policies.'

The Corporate Governance Code revised in 2018 also recognises the wider responsibility of business in its introduction: 'Companies do not exist in isolation. Successful and sustainable businesses underpin our economy and society by providing employment and creating prosperity. To succeed in the long-term, directors and the companies they lead need to build and maintain successful relationships with a wide range of stakeholders.' Provision 5 of the Corporate Governance Code takes up this theme stating: 'the board should understand the views of the company's other key stakeholders and describe in the annual report how their interests and the matters set out in section 172 of the Companies Act 2006 have been considered in board discussions and decision-making. The board should keep engagement mechanisms under review so that they remain effective.' The other main stakeholder identified in the Corporate Governance Code is the company's workforce, but this does not preclude consideration of others with a stake in the enterprise as shown in Give me an example 17.5.

17

GIVE ME AN EXAMPLE 17.5 Engaging with other stakeholders

The Directors are required by law to act in a way that promotes the success of the Company for the benefit of shareholders as a whole. In so doing the Company must, in accordance with Section 172 of the Companies Act 2006, also have regard to wider expectations of responsible business behaviour, such as having due regard to the interests of, and actively engaging with, its employees; the need to engage and foster business relationships with suppliers, customers and others; the need to act fairly as between members of the Company; the likely consequences of any decision in the long term; the desirability of maintaining a reputation for high standards of business conduct; and the impact of the Company's operations on the community and the wider environment . . .

During the year, the Board specifically discussed this requirement on several occasions and concluded that its existing processes and decision-making properly take into account both the duty to shareholders and the wider considerations with regard to other stakeholders as referred to above.

The Board concluded that its key stakeholders continue to be as listed in last year's Annual Report, namely:

Our customers, who buy the Company's product.

Our employees.

Our partners in the supply chain, who are suppliers and subcontractors to the Company's business operations.

Our shareholders, who invest in the Company.

The communities in which the Company operates.

In addition, the Board also specifically took into account the potential impact of the Company's operations on:

The health and safety of its employees, customers and visitors to its sites and offices.

The environment.

Engagement with wider stakeholders

Engagement with each of these stakeholders and consideration of their respective interests in the Company's decision-making process, took place during the year as described on this page and on pages 77 to 81.

The Board continues to engage with its key stakeholders and the feedback from this engagement will continue to inform the Board's thinking and decision-making in relation to strategy and the oversight of the day to day operations of the Group.

Engagement with employees

During the year, we have engaged with employees on a number of issues related to them, namely the impact of Brexit; feedback from the results of the 'TalkBack' employee survey; the development of the new Taylor Wimpey Values; and further proposals to facilitate agile working. In addition, feedback was sought following briefings given on Group plans, progress and initiatives. As we consider our employees to be one of the key resources that enable us to drive success, we also encourage their involvement in driving the Company's performance through encouraging participation in the all-employee share schemes . . . We consider our employees' feedback to be an essential component of our efforts to move forward as a Company, and more information on how we have considered their views in Board decision-making can be found in the following pages.

Source:https://www.taylorwimpey.co.uk/corporate/investors/2019-annual-report

---

WHY IS THIS RELEVANT TO ME? Corporate social responsibility reporting

To enable you as a business professional to appreciate:

- That the current view is that annual reports should report information relevant to a wider range of stakeholders than just shareholders

- The directors' duties as set out in company legislation and the Corporate Governance Code
- The wide-ranging duties that directors must fulfil in promoting the success of the company
- That directors should consider a wider range of interests than just those of shareholders

SUMMARY OF KEY CONCEPTS   Can you recall all the requirements of the directors' duty to promote the success of the company? Go to the **online workbook** to revise these requirements with Summary of key concepts 17.6.

The rationale for corporate social responsibility reporting

Why have business organisations bought into the corporate social responsibility debate? Why have they chosen, voluntarily, to consider and report to a wider set of stakeholders on aspects of their operations which do not immediately generate additional profit for their shareholders?

Business organisations exist only to serve society, so society is the ultimate shareholder in every business. Therefore, society's concerns and interests should be awarded the same level of attention and importance as those of investors. As the Corporate Governance Code recognises, business does not operate independently of society and its expectations, therefore companies should be accountable not just to shareholders but also to society as a whole. This accountability would extend to the products produced and sold by a business and the resources entrusted to it. Employees should be treated with due consideration and enabled to fulfil their potential within the organisations they work for. Customers should not be harmed by the products they buy, while suppliers should be treated fairly and not pressured to reduce their selling prices to enable buying organisations to profit at their expense. The public at large should expect organisations to avoid polluting the air, land and water sources and that all waste products from processes and operations are handled safely to protect individuals and the wider environment from harm.

Today's consumers want reassurance that the products they buy are sourced and produced ethically without causing harm either to the environment or to those individuals producing those products. Shareholders also want to be confident that the profits made by their companies are not generated from exploiting workers or the environment. Companies are eager to protect their reputations as reputational damage is difficult and time consuming to repair and can adversely affect sales and profits. Looking after the workforce, ensuring that suppliers are paid on time, looking into supply chains to check for unethical or environmentally unfriendly practices are all part of the risk management that organisations undertake to protect their reputation and shareholders' investment. Disclosing information on these aspects of company performance helps the public and other interested parties to assess the social responsibility of businesses and assists in enhancing each organisation's reputation for fair dealing and adherence to ethical principles. Customers like to buy goods and services from organisations which share their values, so considering other aspects of performance and reporting on these helps both to present entities in a positive light and to boost revenue and profits. Such actions also help to build the reputation of the business and show that it is caring for the long-term interests of all its stakeholders, not just the short-term interests of the directors and shareholders.

17

WHY IS THIS RELEVANT TO ME?   The rationale for corporate social responsibility

To enable you as a business professional to appreciate:

- That companies are accountable to society as a whole not just to investors
- That there are rational business advantages to adopting socially responsible policies
- That the reputation of a company is a valuable asset which requires protection from damage

---

GO BACK OVER THIS AGAIN!   Are you sure that you appreciate the reasons why companies adopt and report socially responsible attitudes and activities? Go to the **online workbook** and have a go at Exercises 17.9 to check your understanding.

SUSTAINABILITY AND ENVIRONMENTAL REPORTING

The ultimate long-term strategy for every business is to make its activities sustainable. What does this mean? *Our Common Future* (the Brundtland report) presented by the World Council on Environment and Development in 1987 defines sustainable development as that which 'meets the needs of the present without compromising the ability of future generations to meet their own needs'. This vision requires that all demands placed upon the natural environment by people and business organisations be met without reducing the capacity of the environment to provide for future generations. Businesses are therefore expected to concern themselves with issues such as climate change and energy use and to pay proper attention to the effects of their operations on the natural environment.

Unilever is one company that has been developing and reporting its sustainability strategy over many years. Give me an example 17.6 presents Unilever's strategy for sustainable business which forms part of the group's sustainable living plan.

GIVE ME AN EXAMPLE 17.6   Unilever's strategy for sustainable growth

'Unilever has been a purpose-driven company from its origins. Today, our purpose is simple but clear – to make sustainable living commonplace.

We are living in an increasingly uncertain and volatile world. Temperatures are rising, droughts are more frequent, food supplies are increasingly scarce, the gap between rich and poor is growing and billions still do not have access to basic hygiene and sanitation. These challenges are compounded as the global population continues to expand.

Every day, 2.5 billion people use our products. We see first-hand how people the world over are already affected by these changes which pose new challenges for us: fluctuating commodity prices, unstable markets and a shortage of sustainable raw materials. Business as usual is no longer an option.

With change though, comes opportunity. The Business & Sustainable Development Commission, co-founded by Unilever, concluded that successful delivery of the Sustainable Development Goals (SDGs) – which seek to tackle 17 of world's most urgent challenges – will create market opportunities of at least $12 trillion a year.

Businesses that thrive in the future will be those that serve society today. That's why, in 2010, we launched the Unilever Sustainable Living

Plan – our blueprint for sustainable growth. The Plan is helping us to drive more profitable growth for our brands, save costs, mitigate risk and build trust among our stakeholders.

We know that the biggest challenges facing the world cannot be addressed by one company alone. So we're also working to help transform the system in which business is done. By being part of the solution to challenges, businesses have the opportunity to win the trust of consumers while helping create societies and economies in which they can grow and succeed.'

Source: https://www.unilever.com/sustainable-living/our-strategy/

Unilever is just one example of many businesses that have adopted sustainability and corporate social responsibility as part of their long-term strategy. Any annual report that you look at will provide details on these sustainability and CSR strategies together with statistics relating to what has been achieved over the past year and how improvements have been made. Have a look at Taylor Wimpey plc's Sustainability report for 2019, especially pages 36–8, available at https://www.taylorwimpey.co.uk/corporate/sustainability/2019-sustainability-review.

The rationale for adopting and reporting a sustainability strategy

As we have seen in this chapter, businesses must consider long-term sustainable success, not just a boost in short-term profits. A sustainability strategy represents the ultimate focus on the long term with the aim of ensuring the business's survival into the indefinite future. This approach accords well with shareholders' long-term investment horizon (this chapter, Long-term success v. short-term profits). However, there are many other benefits that a sustainability strategy brings. Give me an example 17.7 presents just four of the benefits generated by or expected from Unilever's adoption of its sustainable living plan.

GIVE ME AN EXAMPLE 17.7   Benefits of Unilever's sustainable living plan

Since the adoption of its sustainable living plan, Unilever has generated the following benefits:

- An average annual total shareholder return of around 13% on its shares over the 10 years from December 2009 to December 2019 compared to an average annual total shareholder return of around 5% on the FTSE 100 (Unilever is a constituent company of the FTSE 100), a total shareholder return over 10 years of 240% v. a return of 60% for the FTSE 100 as a whole.

- A reduction in water abstraction of 47% per tonne of production since 2008.

- A reduction of 65% per tonne of production in CO_2 emissions from energy used in the group's factories, with the aim that by 2020 CO_2 emissions from energy from the group's factories will be at or below 2008 levels despite significantly higher production volumes.

- A reduction of 96% in total waste per tonne of production since 2008.

Sources: https://www.unilever.com/Images/uslp-performance-summary-2019_tcm244-549815_en.pdf

17

Give me an example 17.7 shows that Unilever's strategic focus on sustainability has generated considerable benefits for shareholders in line with Friedman's insistence on profit generation as the only social responsibility of business. These benefits have been realised in the form of total shareholder returns significantly above the average and reduced costs arising from both reduced resource usage and reduced waste. Positive news generates headlines for businesses together with favourable market reactions to both products and share prices. In these ways, adopting a sustainability strategy produces benefits for both shareholders and the environment and demonstrates that what is good for the environment also turns out to be good for shareholders and investors.

Companies are also recognising their wider duty of care to the public and the planet and their obligation to look after the natural resources entrusted to them. All stakeholders have an interest in the wellbeing of the planet. As a result of this interest, a stewardship report that focuses on the environment and on how natural resources have been managed and preserved is required by all these stakeholders alongside the financial results. Where damage has been caused to land, air or water, stakeholders will expect directors to report on the steps that have been taken to repair this damage and to prevent further damage in the future.

Environmental and sustainability reporting will assist companies in managing the risks that arise from any business activity. Actively seeking to avoid polluting natural resources will reduce the impact of economic penalties against organisations. The Deepwater Horizon oil spill in 2010 is estimated to have cost BP $61.6 billion (https://www.ft.com/content/ff2d8bcc-49e9-11e6-8d68-72e9211e86ab) and resulted in a fall in the share price which has not yet been recovered over the intervening ten years. Sound risk management policies are also applied by the capital markets: any potential investment which appears too risky will not attract funding or will be required to pay a higher rate of interest to compensate for the increased risk attached to the project (Chapter 16, The time value of money). Based on this principle, capital markets take into account not just ordinary business risks but also environmental risks and the environmental policies of companies seeking inward investment. Companies with more effective environmental risk management policies will attract funding at lower interest rates as the risks are lower. Ethical investment funds will withhold investment from companies which do not adopt a suitably responsible approach to the environment while socially responsible investors will avoid companies that fail to do the right thing. Again, this twin-pronged approach benefits shareholders in reducing costs and increasing profits.

Sustainability information presented is relevant in that it assists consumers and investors in making rational economic decisions. The disclosure of such details indicates a fully transparent approach to reporting and shows the organisation as having nothing to hide. Such disclosure is also part of good corporate governance which dictates that all entities should report on all of their activities and their total impact. Competitive advantage may be another benefit of sustainability reporting as consumers favour organisations adopting a responsible approach to the use of natural resources and the environment over those with a less responsible approach.

WHY IS THIS RELEVANT TO ME?   Sustainability and environmental reporting

To enable you as a business professional to understand:

- How a sustainability approach enables businesses to promote their long-term success
- The commercial, finance, financial and reputational advantages gained by organisations promoting and reporting a sustainable and environmentally conscious approach in their businesses

17

GO BACK OVER THIS AGAIN! Are you confident that you appreciate the reasons why companies adopt sustainability and environmentally responsible approaches in their businesses? Go to the **online workbook** and have a go at Exercises 17.10 to check your understanding.

PROFESSIONAL ACCOUNTANTS' ETHICAL PRINCIPLES

The International Ethics Standards Board for Accountants® (IESBA) sets out five fundamental principles of ethics for professional accountants. These ethical principles are adopted by the accounting bodies in each individual country. The five fundamental principles of ethics set out by IESBA in section 110.1 A1 of its *Handbook of the International Code of Ethics for Professional Accountants* are:

- Integrity: professional accountants must be straightforward and honest in all their professional and business dealings and relationships.

- Objectivity: professional accountants must be objective in all their professional and business judgements and dealings. They must not allow their objectivity and independent judgement to be compromised by any bias, conflicts of interest or the undue influence of others.

- Professional competence and due care: professional accountants must pass the examinations of their chosen professional body and fulfil certain specified minimum levels of experience during their period of training in order to become a member of their chosen accounting body. However, professional accountants' education and learning does not stop once they have gained their qualification. The IESBA states that professional accountants must keep their professional knowledge and skills up to date to enable them to provide the requisite competence and professional levels of service to their clients or their employers. Continuing professional education will enable professional accountants to update their knowledge of current technical and professional standards and current legislation to ensure that they are able to display the required professional competence and due care in all the tasks they undertake.

- Confidentiality: all information acquired by professional accountants in the course of their professional work must be kept confidential and not disclosed to other parties without the express permission of their clients or employers or in situations where there is a legal or professional duty to disclose such information.

- Professional behaviour: professional accountants must comply with all relevant legislation and regulations and must avoid any actions that might bring discredit upon both themselves and the accounting profession as a whole.

Source: https://www.ifac.org/system/files/publications/files/IESBA-Handbook-Code-of-Ethics-2018.pdf

These five fundamental ethical principles set out the standard of behaviour required from each and every professional accountant. Failure to comply with or breaching these principles will result in the professional accountant's member body taking disciplinary action against the individual member. In practice, ethical dilemmas will arise and it is up to professional accountants to apply these fundamental ethical principles in resolving these dilemmas and in managing any conflicts that do occur. You will meet examples of these dilemmas in your later studies. For now, however, you just need to be aware of these fundamental ethical principles.

WHY IS THIS RELEVANT TO ME? Professional accountants' ethical principles

To enable you as a business professional to:

● Understand the five fundamental ethical principles for professional accountants

● Appreciate that professional accountants are bound by these ethical principles in all their professional activities

SUMMARY OF KEY CONCEPTS Can you recall all five ethical principles for professional accountants? Go to the **online workbook** to revise these principles with Summary of key concepts 17.7.

CHAPTER SUMMARY

You should now have learnt that:

● Agency and information asymmetry problems arise when shareholders appoint directors to run companies on their behalf

● Shareholders need to be assured that directors are acting in the shareholders' best long-term interests and not in their own short-term interests

● Corporate governance is the system by which companies are directed and controlled

● Effective corporate governance involves executive directors, non-executive directors, external auditors, internal audit, the Stock Exchange listing rules and shareholders

● Executive directors run the company, non-executive directors run the board

● Non-executive directors make up the membership of the audit committee, the nominations committee and the remuneration committee

● External auditors report on the truth and fairness of the annual financial statements and their compliance with legislation and International Financial Reporting Standards

● Internal audit undertakes investigations and reports on every aspect of a company's operations, internal control, strategy and corporate governance

● The Corporate Governance Code and the Companies Act 2006 require directors to promote the long-term success of their company

● Effective corporate governance requires that the board should include an appropriate combination of executive and non-executive directors, such that no one individual or small group of individuals dominates the board's decision making

● All directors should run the business together as a body

● At least half of the directors on each board of directors should be independent non-executive directors

17

- Boards of directors and shareholders evaluate each director's performance

- The audit committee monitors the integrity of the annual report and accounts, receives reports from internal audit, monitors and evaluates internal control and oversees the external audit process and the external auditor

- Companies have a wider duty than just making profit for the shareholders

- Business organisations serve society and so are accountable to society as a whole

- Adopting socially responsible, environmentally friendly and sustainable business practices helps to generate long-term success for businesses through commercial, financing, reputational and risk minimisation advantages

- Integrity, objectivity, professional competence and due care, confidentiality and professional behaviour are the IESBA's five fundamental principles of ethics for professional accountants

QUICK REVISION Test your knowledge by attempting the activities in the **online workbook**, including flashcards on the key concepts, numerical exercises and Multiple choice questions. You can also try the further self-test questions which are available at www.oup.com/he/scott-i2a2e

END-OF-CHAPTER QUESTIONS

Attempt the questions in the following sections and then look at the solutions which can be found in the **online workbook** to see whether there are areas that you need to revisit.

❯ RECALL AND REVIEW

❯ Question 17.1

Explain what is meant by information asymmetry and the agency problem and the reasons why these problems arise.

❯ Question 17.2

Briefly describe the key parties involved in the corporate governance process and explain their roles and responsibilities.

❯❯ DEVELOP YOUR UNDERSTANDING

❯❯ Question 17.3

Explain the rationale behind the requirements of the Corporate Governance Code.

❯❯ Question 17.4

Explain the rationale behind corporate social responsibility reporting.

❯❯ Question 17.5

Why is sustainability such an important issue for businesses today?

17

>> Question 17.6

Describe the role of the audit committee in the corporate governance process.

>> Question 17.7

The Corporate Governance Code requires that no one individual or small group of individuals should dominate the board's decision making. Explain the mechanisms designed to ensure that the board of directors' decisions are made on a collective basis.

>>>TAKE IT FURTHER

>>> Question 17.8

'The aim of the Corporate Governance Code is control.' Discuss.

>>> Question 17.9

'The only responsibility of business is to generate a profit.' Discuss.

>>> Question 17.10

'The proper function of accounting is the measurement of profits and cash flows and the presentation of assets and liabilities.' Discuss.

APPENDIX

Table 1 Present value of £1 at compound interest $(1 \div r) - n$

Periods of n	Discount rate as a percentage									
	1%	2%	3%	4%	5%	6%	7%	8%	9%	10%
1	0.9901	0.9804	0.9709	0.9615	0.9524	0.9434	0.9346	0.9259	0.9174	0.9091
2	0.9803	0.9612	0.9426	0.9246	0.9070	0.8900	0.8734	0.8573	0.8417	0.8264
3	0.9706	0.9423	0.9151	0.8890	0.8638	0.8396	0.8163	0.7938	0.7722	0.7513
4	0.9610	0.9238	0.8885	0.8548	0.8227	0.7921	0.7629	0.7350	0.7084	0.6830
5	0.9515	0.9057	0.8626	0.8219	0.7835	0.7473	0.7130	0.6806	0.6499	0.6209
6	0.9420	0.8880	0.8375	0.7903	0.7462	0.7050	0.6663	0.6302	0.5963	0.5645
7	0.9327	0.8706	0.8131	0.7599	0.7107	0.6651	0.6227	0.5835	0.5470	0.5132
8	0.9235	0.8535	0.7894	0.7307	0.6768	0.6274	0.5820	0.5403	0.5019	0.4665
9	0.9143	0.8368	0.7664	0.7026	0.6446	0.5919	0.5439	0.5002	0.4604	0.4241
10	0.9053	0.8203	0.7441	0.6756	0.6139	0.5584	0.5083	0.4632	0.4224	0.3855
11	0.8963	0.8043	0.7224	0.6496	0.5847	0.5268	0.4751	0.4289	0.3875	0.3505
12	0.8874	0.7885	0.7014	0.6246	0.5568	0.4970	0.4440	0.3971	0.3555	0.3186
13	0.8787	0.7730	0.6810	0.6006	0.5303	0.4688	0.4150	0.3677	0.3262	0.2897
14	0.8700	0.7579	0.6611	0.5775	0.5051	0.4423	0.3878	0.3405	0.2992	0.2633
15	0.8613	0.7430	0.6419	0.5553	0.4810	0.4173	0.3624	0.3152	0.2745	0.2394
16	0.8528	0.7284	0.6232	0.5339	0.4581	0.3936	0.3387	0.2919	0.2519	0.2176
17	0.8444	0.7142	0.6050	0.5134	0.4363	0.3714	0.3166	0.2703	0.2311	0.1978
18	0.8360	0.7002	0.5874	0.4936	0.4155	0.3503	0.2959	0.2502	0.2120	0.1799
19	0.8277	0.6864	0.5703	0.4746	0.3957	0.3305	0.2765	0.2317	0.1945	0.1635
20	0.8195	0.6730	0.5537	0.4564	0.3769	0.3118	0.2584	0.2145	0.1784	0.1486
21	0.8114	0.6598	0.5375	0.4388	0.3589	0.2942	0.2415	0.1987	0.1637	0.1351
22	0.8034	0.6468	0.5219	0.4220	0.3418	0.2775	0.2257	0.1839	0.1502	0.1228
23	0.7954	0.6342	0.5067	0.4057	0.3256	0.2618	0.2109	0.1703	0.1378	0.1117
24	0.7876	0.6217	0.4919	0.3901	0.3101	0.2470	0.1971	0.1577	0.1264	0.1015
25	0.7798	0.6095	0.4776	0.3751	0.2953	0.2330	0.1842	0.1460	0.1160	0.0923

				Discount rate as a percentage							
11%	12%	13%	14%	15%	16%	17%	18%	19%	20%	25%	30%
0.9009	0.8929	0.8850	0.8772	0.8696	0.8621	0.8547	0.8475	0.8403	0.8333	0.8000	0.7692
0.8116	0.7972	0.7831	0.7695	0.7561	0.7432	0.7305	0.7182	0.7062	0.6944	0.6400	0.5917
0.7312	0.7118	0.6931	0.6750	0.6575	0.6407	0.6244	0.6086	0.5934	0.5787	0.5120	0.4552
0.6587	0.6355	0.6133	0.5921	0.5718	0.5523	0.5337	0.5158	0.4987	0.4823	0.4096	0.3501
0.5935	0.5674	0.5428	0.5194	0.4972	0.4761	0.4561	0.4371	0.4190	0.4019	0.3277	0.2693
0.5346	0.5066	0.4803	0.4556	0.4323	0.4104	0.3898	0.3704	0.3521	0.3349	0.2621	0.2072
0.4817	0.4523	0.4251	0.3996	0.3759	0.3538	0.3332	0.3139	0.2959	0.2791	0.2097	0.1594
0.4339	0.4039	0.3762	0.3506	0.3269	0.3050	0.2848	0.2660	0.2487	0.2326	0.1678	0.1226
0.3909	0.3606	0.3329	0.3075	0.2843	0.2630	0.2434	0.2255	0.2090	0.1938	0.1342	0.0943
0.3522	0.3220	0.2946	0.2697	0.2472	0.2267	0.2080	0.1911	0.1756	0.1615	0.1074	0.0725
0.3173	0.2875	0.2607	0.2366	0.2149	0.1954	0.1778	0.1619	0.1476	0.1346	0.0859	0.0558
0.2858	0.2567	0.2307	0.2076	0.1869	0.1685	0.1520	0.1372	0.1240	0.1122	0.0687	0.0429
0.2575	0.2292	0.2042	0.1821	0.1625	0.1452	0.1299	0.1163	0.1042	0.0935	0.0550	0.0330
0.2320	0.2046	0.1807	0.1597	0.1413	0.1252	0.1110	0.0985	0.0876	0.0779	0.0440	0.0254
0.2090	0.1827	0.1599	0.1401	0.1229	0.1079	0.0949	0.0835	0.0736	0.0649	0.0352	0.0195
0.1883	0.1631	0.1415	0.1229	0.1069	0.0930	0.0811	0.0708	0.0618	0.0541	0.0281	0.0150
0.1696	0.1456	0.1252	0.1078	0.0929	0.0802	0.0693	0.0600	0.0520	0.0451	0.0225	0.0116
0.1528	0.1300	0.1108	0.0946	0.0808	0.0691	0.0592	0.0508	0.0437	0.0376	0.0180	0.0089
0.1377	0.1161	0.0981	0.0829	0.0703	0.0596	0.0506	0.0431	0.0367	0.0313	0.0144	0.0068
0.1240	0.1037	0.0868	0.0728	0.0611	0.0514	0.0433	0.0365	0.0308	0.0261	0.0115	0.0053
0.1117	0.0926	0.0768	0.0638	0.0531	0.0443	0.0370	0.0309	0.0259	0.0217	0.0092	0.0040
0.1007	0.0826	0.0680	0.0560	0.0462	0.0382	0.0316	0.0262	0.0218	0.0181	0.0074	0.0031
0.0907	0.0738	0.0601	0.0491	0.0402	0.0329	0.0270	0.0222	0.0183	0.0151	0.0059	0.0024
0.0817	0.0659	0.0532	0.0431	0.0349	0.0284	0.0231	0.0188	0.0154	0.0126	0.0047	0.0018
0.0736	0.0588	0.0471	0.0378	0.0304	0.0245	0.0197	0.0160	0.0129	0.0105	0.0038	0.0014

Table 2 Annuity table: the present value of £1 received or paid per year at a compound rate of interest $1/r - \{1/[r(1 + r)n]\}$

Periods of n	Discount rate as a percentage									
	1%	2%	3%	4%	5%	6%	7%	8%	9%	10%
1	0.990	0.980	0.971	0.962	0.952	0.943	0.935	0.926	0.917	0.909
2	1.970	1.942	1.913	1.886	1.859	1.833	1.808	1.783	1.759	1.736
3	2.941	2.884	2.829	2.775	2.723	2.673	2.624	2.577	2.531	2.487
4	3.902	3.808	3.717	3.630	3.546	3.465	3.387	3.312	3.240	3.170
5	4.853	4.713	4.580	4.452	4.329	4.212	4.100	3.993	3.890	3.791
6	5.795	5.601	5.417	5.242	5.076	4.917	4.767	4.623	4.486	4.355
7	6.728	6.472	6.230	6.002	5.786	5.582	5.389	5.206	5.033	4.868
8	7.652	7.325	7.020	6.733	6.463	6.210	5.971	5.747	5.535	5.335
9	8.566	8.162	7.786	7.435	7.108	6.802	6.515	6.247	5.995	5.759
10	9.471	8.983	8.530	8.111	7.722	7.360	7.024	6.710	6.418	6.145
11	10.368	9.787	9.253	8.760	8.306	7.887	7.499	7.139	6.805	6.495
12	11.255	10.575	9.954	9.385	8.863	8.384	7.943	7.536	7.161	6.814
13	12.134	11.348	10.635	9.986	9.394	8.853	8.358	7.904	7.487	7.103
14	13.004	12.106	11.296	10.563	9.899	9.295	8.745	8.244	7.786	7.367
15	13.865	12.849	11.938	11.118	10.380	9.712	9.108	8.559	8.061	7.606
16	14.718	13.578	12.561	11.652	10.838	10.106	9.447	8.851	8.313	7.824
17	15.562	14.292	13.166	12.166	11.274	10.477	9.763	9.122	8.544	8.022
18	16.398	14.992	13.754	12.659	11.690	10.828	10.059	9.372	8.756	8.201
19	17.226	15.678	14.324	13.134	12.085	11.158	10.336	9.604	8.950	8.365
20	18.046	16.351	14.877	13.590	12.462	11.470	10.594	9.818	9.129	8.514
21	18.857	17.011	15.415	14.029	12.821	11.764	10.836	10.017	9.292	8.649
22	19.660	17.658	15.937	14.451	13.163	12.042	11.061	10.201	9.442	8.772
23	20.456	18.292	16.444	14.857	13.489	12.303	11.272	10.371	9.580	8.883
24	21.243	18.914	16.936	15.247	13.799	12.550	11.469	10.529	9.707	8.985
25	22.023	19.523	17.413	15.622	14.094	12.783	11.654	10.675	9.823	9.077

	Discount rate as a percentage										
11%	**12%**	**13%**	**14%**	**15%**	**16%**	**17%**	**18%**	**19%**	**20%**	**25%**	**30%**
0.901	0.893	0.885	0.877	0.870	0.862	0.855	0.847	0.840	0.833	0.800	0.769
1.713	1.690	1.668	1.647	1.626	1.605	1.585	1.566	1.547	1.528	1.440	1.361
2.444	2.402	2.361	2.322	2.283	2.246	2.210	2.174	2.140	2.106	1.952	1.816
3.102	3.037	2.974	2.914	2.855	2.798	2.743	2.690	2.639	2.589	2.362	2.166
3.696	3.605	3.517	3.433	3.352	3.274	3.199	3.127	3.058	2.991	2.689	2.436
4.231	4.111	3.998	3.889	3.784	3.685	3.589	3.498	3.410	3.326	2.951	2.643
4.712	4.564	4.423	4.288	4.160	4.039	3.922	3.812	3.706	3.605	3.161	2.802
5.146	4.968	4.799	4.639	4.487	4.344	4.207	4.078	3.954	3.837	3.329	2.925
5.537	5.328	5.132	4.946	4.772	4.607	4.451	4.303	4.163	4.031	3.463	3.019
5.889	5.650	5.426	5.216	5.019	4.833	4.659	4.494	4.339	4.192	3.571	3.092
6.207	5.938	5.687	5.453	5.234	5.029	4.836	4.656	4.486	4.327	3.656	3.147
6.492	6.194	5.918	5.660	5.421	5.197	4.988	4.793	4.611	4.439	3.725	3.190
6.750	6.424	6.122	5.842	5.583	5.342	5.118	4.910	4.715	4.533	3.780	3.223
6.982	6.628	6.302	6.002	5.724	5.468	5.229	5.008	4.802	4.611	3.824	3.249
7.191	6.811	6.462	6.142	5.847	5.575	5.324	5.092	4.876	4.675	3.859	3.268
7.379	6.974	6.604	6.265	5.954	5.668	5.405	5.162	4.938	4.730	3.887	3.283
7.549	7.120	6.729	6.373	6.047	5.749	5.475	5.222	4.990	4.775	3.910	3.295
7.702	7.250	6.840	6.467	6.128	5.818	5.534	5.273	5.033	4.812	3.928	3.304
7.839	7.366	6.938	6.550	6.198	5.877	5.584	5.316	5.070	4.843	3.942	3.311
7.963	7.469	7.025	6.623	6.259	5.929	5.628	5.353	5.101	4.870	3.954	3.316
8.075	7.562	7.102	6.687	6.312	5.973	5.665	5.384	5.127	4.891	3.963	3.320
8.176	7.645	7.170	6.743	6.359	6.011	5.696	5.410	5.149	4.909	3.970	3.323
8.266	7.718	7.230	6.792	6.399	6.044	5.723	5.432	5.167	4.925	3.976	3.325
8.348	7.784	7.283	6.835	6.434	6.073	5.746	5.451	5.182	4.937	3.981	3.327
8.422	7.843	7.330	6.873	6.464	6.097	5.766	5.467	5.195	4.948	3.985	3.329

Table 3 Future value of £1 at compound interest $(1 + r)n$

Periods of n	Discount rate as a percentage									
	1%	2%	3%	4%	5%	6%	7%	8%	9%	10%
1	1.010	1.020	1.030	1.040	1.050	1.060	1.070	1.080	1.090	1.100
2	1.020	1.040	1.061	1.082	1.103	1.124	1.145	1.166	1.188	1.210
3	1.030	1.061	1.093	1.125	1.158	1.191	1.225	1.260	1.295	1.331
4	1.041	1.082	1.126	1.170	1.216	1.262	1.311	1.360	1.412	1.464
5	1.051	1.104	1.159	1.217	1.276	1.338	1.403	1.469	1.539	1.611
6	1.062	1.126	1.194	1.265	1.340	1.419	1.501	1.587	1.677	1.772
7	1.072	1.149	1.230	1.316	1.407	1.504	1.606	1.714	1.828	1.949
8	1.083	1.172	1.267	1.369	1.477	1.594	1.718	1.851	1.993	2.144
9	1.094	1.195	1.305	1.423	1.551	1.689	1.838	1.999	2.172	2.358
10	1.105	1.219	1.344	1.480	1.629	1.791	1.967	2.159	2.367	2.594
11	1.116	1.243	1.384	1.539	1.710	1.898	2.105	2.332	2.580	2.853
12	1.127	1.268	1.426	1.601	1.796	2.012	2.252	2.518	2.813	3.138
13	1.138	1.294	1.469	1.665	1.886	2.133	2.410	2.720	3.066	3.452
14	1.149	1.319	1.513	1.732	1.980	2.261	2.579	2.937	3.342	3.797
15	1.161	1.346	1.558	1.801	2.079	2.397	2.759	3.172	3.642	4.177
16	1.173	1.373	1.605	1.873	2.183	2.540	2.952	3.426	3.970	4.595
17	1.184	1.400	1.653	1.948	2.292	2.693	3.159	3.700	4.328	5.054
18	1.196	1.428	1.702	2.026	2.407	2.854	3.380	3.996	4.717	5.560
19	1.208	1.457	1.754	2.107	2.527	3.026	3.617	4.316	5.142	6.116
20	1.220	1.486	1.806	2.191	2.653	3.207	3.870	4.661	5.604	6.727
21	1.232	1.516	1.860	2.279	2.786	3.400	4.141	5.034	6.109	7.400
22	1.245	1.546	1.916	2.370	2.925	3.604	4.430	5.437	6.659	8.140
23	1.257	1.577	1.974	2.465	3.072	3.820	4.741	5.871	7.258	8.954
24	1.270	1.608	2.033	2.563	3.225	4.049	5.072	6.341	7.911	9.850
25	1.282	1.641	2.094	2.666	3.386	4.292	5.427	6.848	8.623	10.835

					Discount rate as a percentage						
11%	12%	13%	14%	15%	16%	17%	18%	19%	20%	25%	30%
1.110	1.120	1.130	1.140	1.150	1.160	1.170	1.180	1.190	1.200	1.250	1.300
1.232	1.254	1.277	1.300	1.323	1.346	1.369	1.392	1.416	1.440	1.563	1.690
1.368	1.405	1.443	1.482	1.521	1.561	1.602	1.643	1.685	1.728	1.953	2.197
1.518	1.574	1.630	1.689	1.749	1.811	1.874	1.939	2.005	2.074	2.441	2.856
1.685	1.762	1.842	1.925	2.011	2.100	2.192	2.288	2.386	2.488	3.052	3.713
1.870	1.974	2.082	2.195	2.313	2.436	2.565	2.700	2.840	2.986	3.815	4.827
2.076	2.211	2.353	2.502	2.660	2.826	3.001	3.185	3.379	3.583	4.768	6.275
2.305	2.476	2.658	2.853	3.059	3.278	3.511	3.759	4.021	4.300	5.960	8.157
2.558	2.773	3.004	3.252	3.518	3.803	4.108	4.435	4.785	5.160	7.451	10.604
2.839	3.106	3.395	3.707	4.046	4.411	4.807	5.234	5.695	6.192	9.313	13.786
3.152	3.479	3.836	4.226	4.652	5.117	5.624	6.176	6.777	7.430	11.642	17.922
3.498	3.896	4.335	4.818	5.350	5.936	6.580	7.288	8.064	8.916	14.552	23.298
3.883	4.363	4.898	5.492	6.153	6.886	7.699	8.599	9.596	10.699	18.190	30.288
4.310	4.887	5.535	6.261	7.076	7.988	9.007	10.147	11.420	12.839	22.737	39.374
4.785	5.474	6.254	7.138	8.137	9.266	10.539	11.974	13.590	15.407	28.422	51.186
5.311	6.130	7.067	8.137	9.358	10.748	12.330	14.129	16.172	18.488	35.527	66.542
5.895	6.866	7.986	9.276	10.761	12.468	14.426	16.672	19.244	22.186	44.409	86.504
6.544	7.690	9.024	10.575	12.375	14.463	16.879	19.673	22.901	26.623	55.511	112.455
7.263	8.613	10.197	12.056	14.232	16.777	19.748	23.214	27.252	31.948	69.389	146.192
8.062	9.646	11.523	13.743	16.367	19.461	23.106	27.393	32.429	38.338	86.736	190.050
8.949	10.804	13.021	15.668	18.822	22.574	27.034	32.324	38.591	46.005	108.420	247.065
9.934	12.100	14.714	17.861	21.645	26.186	31.629	38.142	45.923	55.206	135.525	321.184
11.026	13.552	16.627	20.362	24.891	30.376	37.006	45.008	54.649	66.247	169.407	417.539
12.239	15.179	18.788	23.212	28.625	35.236	43.297	53.109	65.032	79.497	211.758	542.801
13.585	17.000	21.231	26.462	32.919	40.874	50.658	62.669	77.388	95.396	264.698	705.641

ANNOTATED STATEMENTS

Illustration 2.1: Bunns the Bakers plc: annotated statement of financial position at 31 March 2021

Economic resources controlled by the entity as a result of past events. An economic resource is a right that has the potential to produce economic benefits. The monetary value of assets must be measurable in such a way that a faithful representation is achieved.

Intangible assets have no material substance and include intellectual property rights, patents, licences and trademarks.

Assets with material substance including land and buildings, vehicles, machinery, fittings and equipment.

Inventories comprise of raw materials for use in the production process and of finished goods for sale and goods bought in for resale.

Money due from customers for goods supplied on credit terms and other money due from other parties external to the business.

Present obligations of the entity to transfer economic resources as a result of past events. The monetary value of liabilities must be measurable in such a way that a faithful representation is achieved.

Amounts owed to suppliers for goods provided on credit and other money due to other parties external to the business.

Liabilities the entity must meet that are due for payment more than 12 months after the statement of financial position date.

The number of shares in issue multiplied by the par (face) value of each share.

Profits earned by the business in earlier accounting periods not yet distributed as dividends to the shareholders.

Amounts received on the issue of share capital over and above the par (face) value of each share.

Assets not purchased for resale in the normal course of business. Non-current assets are held for long-term use within the business to produce goods or services.

Holdings of shares and loans in other companies

Short-term assets whose economic benefits will be used up by the entity within the next 12 months. Current assets change constantly during the trading cycle as inventory is turned into goods for sale and then into cash and new inventories are bought in and turned into more goods for sale and into more cash in an ever repeating cycle.

Cash held within the business and in bank current and short-term deposit accounts.

Short-term liabilities that will be paid within the next 12 months. As with current assets, current liabilities are constantly changing as liabilities paid are replaced by new liabilities incurred.

Bank overdrafts and loan instalments due within the next 12 months.

Tax payable to local taxation authorities on the profits made by the business during the last trading year.

Long-term liabilities due to be paid by the business more than 12 months after the statement of financial position date.

Loan instalments that are due more than 12 months after the statement of financial position date.

The residual interest in the assets of the entity after deducting all of its liabilities. Remember that assets − liabilities = equity.

	2021 £000	2020 £000
ASSETS		
Non-current assets		
Intangible assets	50	55
Property, plant and equipment	11,750	11,241
Investments	65	59
	11,865	11,355
Current assets		
Inventories	60	55
Trade and other receivables	62	75
Cash and cash equivalents	212	189
	334	319
Total assets	12,199	11,674
LIABILITIES		
Current liabilities		
Current portion of long-term borrowings	300	300
Trade and other payables	390	281
Current tax liabilities	150	126
	840	707
Non-current liabilities		
Long-term borrowings	2,700	3,000
Long-term provisions	200	200
	2,900	3,200
Total liabilities	3,740	3,907
Net assets	8,459	7,767
EQUITY		
Called up share capital	2,500	2,400
Share premium	1,315	1,180
Retained earnings	4,644	4,187
Total equity	8,459	7,767

Revenue, cost of sales, gross profit, distribution and selling costs, administration expenses and operating profit all form the trading part of the statement of profit or loss.

Sales income earned in an accounting period. Revenue represents sales made in the ordinary course of business, in this case from selling bakery and related goods.

Gross profit = Revenue − Cost of sales

The costs of selling and distributing goods such as advertising, transporting bakery goods from the main bakery to the shops, costs of running the shops and shop wages.

Operating profit = Gross profit − Distribution and selling costs − Administration expenses

Interest received and receivable on surplus cash deposited with the company's bank.

Illustration 3.1: Bunns the Bakers plc: annotated statement of profit or loss for the years ended 31 March 2021 and 31 March 2020

	2021 £000	2020 £000
Revenue	10,078	9,575
Cost of sales	(4,535)	(4,596)
Gross profit	5,543	4,979
Distribution and selling costs	(3,398)	(3,057)
Administration expenses	(1,250)	(1,155)
Operating profit	895	767
Finance income	15	12
Finance expense	(150)	(165)
Profit before tax	760	614
Income tax	(213)	(172)
Profit for the year	**547**	**442**

Note: income and profit figures are shown without brackets while items of expenditure are shown in brackets. This is to help you understand which items are subtracted and which items are added to determine the result (profit or loss) for the year.

The direct costs of making the sales included in Revenue. These could be the costs of making bakery goods (including ingredients and bakers' wages) or the direct costs of buying in related products for resale.

All the costs of running the trading operation that do not fall under any other heading including legal expenses, audit, accountancy and directors' salaries. All these costs are essential in running the business but they cannot be allocated to the costs of making and producing or distributing and selling the goods sold.

Finance income and finance expense form the financing part of the statement of profit or loss.

The tax charged on the profit for the year. For UK companies, this tax is called Corporation Tax.

Profit for the year (also called profit after tax) = profit before tax − income tax

Interest paid and payable on borrowings used in financing the business's operations.

Profit before tax = operating profit + finance income − finance expense

Illustration 6.1: Bunns the Bakers plc annotated statement of cash flows for the years ended 31 March 2021 and 31 March 2020

Cash flows from operating activities reconciles the profit for the year to the cash generated from operations in the year by adjusting for certain non-cash transactions in the statement of profit or loss and changes in working capital.

Depreciation and amortisation of non-current assets are not cash flows but an accounting adjustment to reflect the benefits of non-current assets used up in each accounting period. The cash outflow associated with non-current assets is the actual cash paid to acquire them.

Cash generated from day to day trading activities from which to finance day-to-day operations. Surplus cash can be used for expansion and investment.

Taxation arises on profits from operations so taxation paid is deducted from cash flows from operating activities.

Cash invested in new long-term capacity from which to generate new income by expanding and improving the business.

Cash received from the sale or scrapping of non-current assets.

Cash raised from or paid to long-term providers of finance.

Cash raised from the issue of new share capital.

Capital element of long-term borrowings repaid in the year to the providers of long-term debt finance from operating cash inflows.

Cash and cash equivalents on the statement of financial position at the end of last year.

Profit (or loss) for the year is found in the statement of profit or loss.

Figures for income tax expense, finance expense and finance income are found in the statement of profit or loss.

(Increase)/decrease in inventories, (increase)/decrease in trade and other receivables and increase/(decrease) in trade payables represent the cash effects of movements in working capital over the course of the accounting year.

Profits and losses on the disposal of property, plant and equipment are the difference between sale proceeds and carrying amount and are thus not a cash flow. The cash flow associated with disposals of property, plant and equipment are the actual cash receipts from the sale of the assets.

Cash inflows and outflows from long-term investing.

Investment of surplus cash from which to generate interest or dividend income to boost profits.

Interest received from investing surplus cash in current or non-current asset investments.

Interest paid on long- and short-term borrowings as a return to lenders for providing debt finance to the company.

Net increase in cash and cash equivalents = net cash inflow from operating activities (£1,219) – net cash outflow from investing activities (£891) – net cash outflow from financing activities (£305) = £23.

Dividends paid to shareholders as a return on their investment in the company.

Cash and cash equivalents at the end of the current year on the statement of financial position.

	2021	2020
Cash flows from operating activities	**£000**	**£000**
Profit for the year	547	442
Income tax expense	213	172
Finance expense	150	165
Finance income	(15)	(12)
(Increase)/decrease in inventories	(5)	8
Decrease in trade and other receivables	13	9
Increase/(decrease) in trade and other payables	109	(15)
Amortisation of intangible non-current assets	5	7
Depreciation of property, plant and equipment	394	362
(Profit)/loss on disposal of property, plant and equipment	(3)	4
Cash generated from operations	**1,408**	**1,142**
Taxation paid	(189)	(154)
Net cash inflow from operating activities	1,219	988
Cash flows from investing activities		
Acquisition of property, plant and equipment	(910)	(600)
Acquisition of investments	(6)	(11)
Proceeds from sale of property, plant and equipment	10	47
Interest received	15	12
Net cash outflow from investing activities	(891)	(552)
Cash flows from financing activities		
Proceeds from the issue of ordinary share capital	235	148
Dividends paid	(90)	(72)
Repayment of current portion of long term borrowings	(300)	(300)
Interest paid	(150)	(165)
Net cash outflow from financing activities	(305)	(389)
Net increase in cash and cash equivalents	**23**	47
Cash and cash equivalents at the start of the year	189	142
Cash and cash equivalents at the end of the year	**212**	189

Note: cash inflows (money coming in) are shown without brackets while cash outflows (money going out) are shown in brackets. Work through the above statement of cash flows, adding the figures without brackets and deducting the figures in brackets to help you understand how the cash inflows and outflows add up to the subtotals given.

TERMINOLOGY CONVERTER

Terms used in this book	Equivalent term or terms
Absorption costing	Full costing
Allowance for receivables	Provision for doubtful debts
Capital	Equity
Capital and reserves	Equity
Carrying amount	Net book value
Cash conversion cycle	Operating cycle, working capital cycle
Cost of capital	Hurdle rate of return
Equity	Capital, capital and reserves
Finance expense	Interest payable
Finance income	Interest receivable
Inventory	Stock
Inventory days	Stock days
Irrecoverable debts	Bad debts
Nominal ledger	General ledger
Payables	Creditors
Payables days	Creditor days
Purchase day book	Purchases listing
Purchase returns day book	Purchase returns listing
Receivables	Debtors
Receivables days	Debtor days
Revenue	Turnover, sales
Sales day book	Sales listing
Sales returns day book	Sales returns listing
Statement of financial position	Balance sheet
Statement of profit or loss	Income statement, statement of financial performance, profit and loss account

GLOSSARY

Abnormal gains This is a term used in process costing to describe and value the outputs from a process that are over and above the expected output from that process.

Abnormal losses This is a term used in process costing to describe and value outputs from a process that are below the expected output from that process.

Absorption costing The cost of products including all the direct costs of production and a proportion of the indirect costs of production based on normal levels of output.

Accountability Managers provide an account of how they have managed resources placed in their care. In this way, those appointing managers can assess how well their managers have looked after the resources entrusted to them.

Accounting The summarising of numerical data relating to past events and presenting this data as information to managers and other interested parties as a basis for both decision-making and control purposes.

Accounting equation Assets – liabilities = equity or assets = liabilities + equity. As equity includes the difference between income and expenditure, the equation can be expanded to assets + expenses = liabilities + equity + income.

Accounting rate of return An investment appraisal technique that averages the projections of accounting profit to calculate the expected rate of return on the average capital invested.

Accruals Expenses incurred during an accounting period but not paid for until after the accounting period end are still recognised as a liability in the statement of financial position and as an expense in the statement of profit or loss.

Accruals basis of accounting All income and expenditure are recognised in the accounting period in which they occurred rather than in the accounting period in which cash is received or paid.

Acid test ratio See Quick ratio.

Activity-based costing Overhead costs are allocated to products on the basis of activities consumed: the more activities that are associated with a particular product, the more overhead is allocated to that product and so the higher its cost and selling price will be.

Actual v. budget comparisons A comparison of planned outcomes with actual outcomes on a monthly basis as a means of exercising control over operations.

Adverse variances Unfavourable variances.

Agency problem This problem arises in situations in which one person (the agent) is appointed to undertake a task by the principal. Agency theory says that the agent will always act in their own best interests, not in the best interests of the principal.

AGM Annual general meeting.

Allowance for receivables The allowance for receivables is calculated as a percentage of trade receivables after deducting known irrecoverable debts. This allowance is an application of the prudence concept, assuming that not all trade receivables will pay what is owed. Also referred to as the provision for doubtful debts.

Annual general meeting A meeting held every year by limited liability companies at which shareholders consider and vote on various significant resolutions affecting the company.

ARR See Accounting rate of return.

Articles of Association A document that covers the internal regulations of a company and governs the shareholders' relationships with each other.

Assets Defined by the IASB Conceptual Framework as 'a present economic resource controlled by the entity as a result of past events'.

Attainable standard A standard that can be achieved with effort. This standard is neither too easy nor so difficult as to be unattainable.

Balance sheet Another term for the statement of financial position.

Bond A long-term loan to an organisation with a fixed rate of interest and a fixed repayment date.

Bonus issues An issue of shares to shareholders from retained earnings. A bonus issue does not raise any cash. Bonus issues are recorded in the statement of financial position at the par value of the shares issued.

Books of prime entry The first point at which a transaction is recorded in the accounting system. Books of prime entry are the sales day book, the sales returns day book, the purchase day book, the purchase returns day book, the cash book, the petty cash book and the payroll.

Break-even point The point at which sales revenue = fixed + variable costs. At the break-even point, an entity makes neither a profit nor a loss. Break-even point can be expressed in £s or units of sales. Break-even point cannot be used when more than one product or service is produced and sold. The break-even point is calculated by dividing total fixed costs by the contribution per unit of sales.

Budget The expression of a plan in money terms. That plan is a prediction or a forecast of future income, expenditure, cash inflows and cash outflows.

Budgetary control Comparisons between budgeted and actual outcomes to determine the causes of variances between planned and actual results. The causes of differences are then identified to enable remedial action to be taken.

Budgeting The process of drawing up the budget.

Business entity Any organisation involved in business. Businesses may be sole traders, companies with limited liability or partnerships.

Business entity convention The business is completely separate from its owners. Only business transactions are included in the business's financial statements.

Cadbury Report The name by which the report of the Committee on the Financial Aspects of Corporate Governance published in 1991 is most commonly known.

Capital account The equity part of the statement of financial position for sole traders. The capital account is the sum of the opening capital balance plus the profit for the year (minus a loss for the year) minus any drawings made by the sole trader during the year.

Capital investment The acquisition of new non-current assets with the aim of increasing sales, profits and cash flows to the long-term benefit of a business.

Capital investment appraisal An evaluation of the long-term cash generating capacity of capital investment projects to assist decision makers in allocating scarce investment capital resources to projects to maximise long-run profits.

Carrying amount Cost or fair value of a non-current asset— the accumulated depreciation on that non-current asset. Net book value is an equivalent term that you might also come across to describe the result of deducting accumulated depreciation from the cost or fair value of a non-current asset.

Cash book A book of prime entry that records cash receipts and cash payments.

Cash budget A detailed summary on a month-by-month basis of budgeted cash receipts and cash payments.

Cash conversion cycle Inventory days + receivables days – payables days. Also known as the working capital cycle or the operating cycle.

Cash flow cycle The time it takes a business to convert inventory into a sale and to collect cash either at the point of sale or from trade receivables with which to pay trade payables.

Cash flows from financing activities One of the three sections in the statement of cash flows. This section represents the cash raised from the issue of share capital and loans and the cash spent in repaying borrowings and paying interest and dividends.

Cash flows from investing activities One of the three sections in the statement of cash flows. This section represents the cash spent on buying new non-current assets, the cash received from selling surplus non-current assets and the cash received from interest and dividends on investments made.

Cash flows from operating activities One of the three sections in the statement of cash flows. This section represents the cash generated from sales less the cash spent in both generating those sales and in running the organisation.

Comparability An enhancing qualitative characteristic of financial information. Information should be comparable over time. The usefulness of information is enhanced if it can be compared with similar information about other entities for the same reporting period and with similar information about the same entity for other reporting periods. Comparability does not mean consistency, although consistency of presentation and measurement of the same items in the same way from year to year will help to achieve comparability. Similarly, comparability does not mean uniformity of presentation.

Compensating error These arise when two or more errors cancel each other out.

Complete reversal of entries Transactions are posted to the correct accounts, but the debit and credit entries are reversed. Amounts debited and credited to the accounts to correct complete reversal of entry errors must be twice the original amount of the transaction, firstly to reverse the incorrect entry and then to add what should have been debited or credited originally.

Confidentiality One of the IESBA's five fundamental principles of ethics for professional accountants. This principle states that all information acquired by professional accountants in the course of their professional work must be kept confidential and not disclosed to other parties without the express permission of their clients or employers or in situations where there is a legal or professional duty to disclose such information.

Consistency The presentation or measurement of the same piece of accounting information on the same basis each year.

Contribution Selling price less the variable costs of making that sale.

Conversion cost This term is used in process costing to indicate the labour and overhead incurred in a process to turn raw materials into the output from the process. Conversion cost is added to the cost of raw materials added to the process to calculate the cost of completed units.

Corporate governance The system by which companies are directed and controlled.

Corporate social responsibility Social and environmental considerations are integrated into the management of the operations of an organisation. May be abbreviated to CSR.

Cost accounting '[The] gathering of cost information and its attachment to cost objects (for example a product, service, centre, activity, customer or distribution channel in relation to which costs are ascertained), the establishment of budgets, standard costs and actual costs of operations, processes, activities or products; and the analysis of variances, profitability or the social use of funds' (*CIMA Official Terminology*).

Cost allocation The process of allocating costs, both direct and indirect, to products or services.

Cost centre A division of an entity to which attributable costs are allocated.

Cost drivers The level of activity associated with each cost pool used to allocate costs to products under activity-based costing.

Cost object 'A product, service centre, activity, customer or distribution channel in relation to which costs are ascertained' (*CIMA Official Terminology*).

Cost of capital The level of return on an investment that is acceptable to a business given the level of risk involved. Also known as the hurdle rate of return.

Cost of sales The direct costs attributable to the sale of particular goods or services.

Cost pools The allocation of indirect costs of production associated with particular activities in an activity-based costing system.

Cost-volume-profit analysis A management accounting technique used to determine the relationship between sales revenue, costs and profit. Abbreviated to CVP.

Costing The process of determining the cost of products or services.

Creditor days See Payables days.

Creditors Persons to whom entities owe money. See also Payables.

Credits A term used in double-entry bookkeeping. Credit accounts represent liability, capital and income accounts. Credit entries to a credit account increase the balance on liability, capital and income accounts as well as reducing the balance on asset and expense accounts.

Current assets Short-term assets that will be used up in the business within one year. Examples include inventory, trade receivables, prepayments and cash.

Current liabilities Short-term liabilities due for payment within one year of the year-end date. Examples include trade payables, taxation and accruals.

Current ratio Current assets divided by current liabilities. Used in the assessment of an entity's short-term liquidity. This ratio should be used with caution in the evaluation of an entity's liquidity.

CVP See Cost-volume-profit analysis.

Debenture A long-term loan to an organisation with a fixed rate of interest and a fixed repayment date.

Debits A term used in double-entry bookkeeping. Debit accounts represent asset and expense accounts. A debit entry to a debit account will increase the balance on asset and expense accounts as well as reducing the balance on liability, capital and income accounts.

Debt ratio Total liabilities divided by total assets. An indicator of how reliant an entity is upon external parties to fund its assets.

Debtor days See Receivables days.

Debtors Persons who owe money to an entity. See also Trade receivables.

Depreciation The allocation of the cost of a non-current asset to the accounting periods benefiting from that non-current asset's use within a business. Depreciation is *not* a way of reflecting the market value of assets in financial statements and it does not represent a loss in an asset's value.

Direct cost The costs of a product or service that are directly attributable to the production of a product or the delivery of a service. Direct costs may be variable or fixed.

Direct labour efficiency variance The time taken to make the goods actually produced compared with the standard time that should have been taken to make those goods multiplied by the standard rate per hour.

Direct labour rate variance What labour hours actually cost compared with what the standard says the labour hours should have cost for the actual level of production achieved.

Direct material price variance What the materials for actual production cost compared with what the standard says they should have cost for that level of production.

Direct material usage variance The actual quantity of materials used to make the goods actually produced compared with the standard quantity that should have been used to make those goods multiplied by the standard cost per unit of material.

Direct method An approach to preparing the statement of cash flows that involves disclosing the gross cash receipts from sales and the gross cash payments to suppliers.

Directors Persons appointed by the shareholders at the annual general meeting to run a limited company on their behalf.

Discounting Future cash inflows and outflows are discounted to their present value using an entity's cost of capital.

Discounts allowed An allowance given to trade receivables against amounts owed to encourage early payment of amounts owed. A sales invoice presents two prices: the price after taking the discount into account and the price if the discount is not taken up. Sales are initially recorded at the discounted price. Discounts allowed not taken up by customers are added to the value of sales.

Discounts received Suppliers reward their customers with discounts for early payment or quantity purchases. Discounts received are a source of income in the statement of profit or loss, a deduction from cost of sales and a deduction from trade payables.

Distributable reserves Retained earnings available for distribution to shareholders as a dividend.

Distribution The distribution of retained profits to shareholders as a dividend. A distribution is not an expense of a company but a deduction from retained earnings.

Dividend A distribution of profits to shareholders.

Dividend cover A comparison of the total dividend for an accounting period to the profit after taxation and after preference dividends. This ratio is used to assess the expected continuity of dividend payments. The higher the ratio, the more likely the dividend payment will continue into the future.

Dividend per share The total dividend for a period divided by the number of ordinary shares in issue multiplied by 100 to give a figure of dividend per share in pence.

Dividend yield The dividend per share as a percentage of the current share price.

Double entry An accounting methodology which recognises that every transaction has two effects on the figures in the financial statements.

DPS See Dividend per share.

Drawings Amounts taken out of a business by a sole trader for personal rather than business use. Drawings are in effect a repayment of the amounts owed by the business to the owner. Drawings are not an expense but a deduction from capital. Drawings are not permitted in limited liability companies.

Dual aspect The recognition that each accounting transaction has a double effect on the amounts stated in the financial statements.

Duality principle Each transaction has an equal and opposite effect on two or more accounts.

Earnings per share The profit after taxation and after preference dividends divided by the number of ordinary shares in issue multiplied by 100 to give a figure of earnings per share in pence.

Economic resource A right that has the potential to produce economic benefits.

Efficiency ratios Measures of non-current asset turnover and revenue and profit per employee to determine how well an organisation has used its resources to generate profits.

EGM Extraordinary general meeting.

EPS See Earnings per share.

Equity The capital of an entity on its statement of financial position. Equity is, in theory, the amount the owners of the business would receive if all the business assets and liabilities were sold and settled at the amounts stated in the statement of financial position. Defined by the IASB Conceptual Framework as 'the residual interest in the assets of the entity after deducting all its liabilities'.

Equity share capital This is an equivalent term for ordinary share capital.

Equivalent units Expressing partially completed units in a process at the end of an accounting period as the equivalent number of fully completed units.

Error of commission A transaction is posted to the correct type of account (income, expense, asset, liability or capital) but the wrong account is debited or credited.

Error of omission A transaction is completely missed out of the double-entry record.

Error of original entry The correct accounts are debited and credited to the double-entry record, but the wrong amount is recorded.

Error of principle A transaction is posted to the wrong type of account.

Exceptional income Income and expenditure that arise from transactions that are not in the ordinary course of business.

Expenses Defined by the IASB Conceptual Framework as 'decreases in assets, or increases in liabilities, that result in decreases in equity, other than those relating to distributions to holders of equity claims'.

Extraordinary general meeting A meeting called by the directors of a limited company to request the approval of shareholders for certain business transactions. An extraordinary general meeting is any meeting of the shareholders as a body other than the annual general meeting.

Fair value The amount at which an asset could be sold or a liability settled in the open market.

Faithful representation A fundamental qualitative characteristic of financial information. Financial information must not only represent relevant economic phenomena (transactions and events), but it must also faithfully represent the phenomena that it purports to represent. Perfectly faithful representation of economic phenomena in words and numbers requires that the information presented must have three characteristics: it must be complete, neutral and free from error.

Favourable variances Differences between actual and budgeted results arising from higher income or lower expenditure.

Financial accounting The reporting of past information to parties external to the organisation.

First in first out A method of stock valuation. The units of product that were acquired at the earliest date are those that are sold first. In process costing, an assumption is made that the work in progress units at the start of the accounting period are the units that were completed first before any production of new units commenced.

Fixed cost A cost that does not vary in line with production or sales over a given period of time.

Fixed overhead expenditure variance The difference between the actual fixed overhead expenditure incurred and the budgeted level of fixed overhead expenditure.

Gearing ratio Long- and short-term borrowings divided by the total statement of financial position equity figure × 100%. A measure designed to help financial statement users assess whether an entity has borrowed too much money. The gearing ratio should be used in conjunction with the interest cover ratio in making this assessment.

General ledger See Nominal ledger.

Going concern A business that has sufficient demand for its products and sufficient sources of finance to enable it to continue operating for the foreseeable future.

Gross pay The contractually agreed rate of pay × the hours worked before any deductions for income tax (PAYE) or national insurance (NIC).

Gross profit Sales less the direct costs of making those sales.

Gross profit percentage The gross profit of an organisation divided by the sales figure × 100 %.

Historic cost The original cost of an asset or liability at the time it was purchased or incurred.

IAASB International Auditing and Assurance Standards Board.

IAS International Accounting Standard.

IASB International Accounting Standards Board.

Ideal standard The best that can be achieved. Ideal standards tend to be unrealistic and unachievable as they would only ever be attained in a perfect world.

IESBA The International Ethics Standards Board for Accountants.

IFRS International Financial Reporting Standard.

Income Defined by the IASB Conceptual Framework as 'increases in assets, or decreases in liabilities, that result in increases in equity, other than those relating to contributions from holders of equity claims'.

Income statement An equivalent term for the statement of profit or loss.

Indirect cost Costs that cannot be attributed directly to units of production. Also known as overheads.

Indirect method An approach to preparing the statement of cash flows that ignores total inflows and outflows of cash from operations. Instead, the operating profit for a period is adjusted for increases or decreases in inventory, trade receivables, prepayments, payables and accruals and for the effect of non-cash items such as depreciation and profits and losses on disposal of non-current assets in order to determine the cash flows from operations.

Information asymmetry This arises in situations in which one party knows much more about a subject than another as a result of a principal delegating a task to an agent.

Insolvency The inability of an entity to repay all that it owes to its creditors.

Integrity One of the IESBA's five fundamental principles of ethics for professional accountants. This principle requires professional accountants to be straightforward and honest in all professional and business relationships.

Interest cover Trading profit divided by finance cost (interest payable). This ratio shows how many times interest payable on borrowings is covered by operating profit. The higher the ratio, the more likely entities will be able to continue paying the interest on their borrowings.

Internal rate of return The discount rate applied to the cash flows of a capital investment project to produce a net present value for the project of £Nil.

Inventory A stock of goods held by a business.

Inventory days Inventory divided by cost of sales × 365 days. This ratio measures the average stockholding period, the length of time an entity holds goods as stock before they are sold.

IRR See Internal rate of return.

Irrecoverable debts Trade receivables from which cash will not be collected. Irrecoverable debts are an expense in the statement of profit or loss, not a deduction from sales. Also known as bad debts.

ISA International Standard on Auditing.

Key factor = Limiting factor.

Last in, first out (LIFO) A method of stock valuation. The units of product that were acquired at the most recent date are those that are sold first.

Liabilities Defined by the IASB Conceptual Framework as 'a present obligation of the entity to transfer an economic resource as a result of past events'.

Limiting factor A scarcity of input resources, such as materials or labour, is referred to as a limiting factor in the production of goods or services. When input resources are scarce, entities calculate the contribution per unit of limiting factor to maximise their profits in the short term.

Liquidity The ability of entities to meet payments to their creditors as they become due.

Loan notes A long-term loan to an organisation with a fixed rate of interest and a fixed repayment date.

Management accounting Cost and management accounting is concerned with reporting accounting and cost information to users within an organisation to assist those internal users in making decisions and managing the business.

Margin of safety The difference between the current level of sales in units and the break-even point in units of sales.

Marginal cost The additional cost incurred in producing one more unit of product or delivering one more unit of service. Also known as the variable cost of production.

Materiality The IASB Conceptual Framework defines materiality thus: 'Information is material if omitting it or misstating it could influence decisions that . . . users . . . make on the basis of financial information about a specific reporting entity. In other words, materiality is an entity-specific aspect of relevance based on the nature or magnitude, or both, of the items to which the information relates in the context of an individual entity's financial report.'

Memorandum of Association This document covers a limited company's objectives and its powers and governs the relationship of the company with the outside world.

Money measurement The measurement of financial results in money terms.

National insurance Both employees and employers make national insurance contributions. For employees, this is a deduction from their salary and determines employees' entitlement to certain state benefits. For employers, national insurance contributions are levied on the value of each employee's gross pay. Often abbreviated to NIC.

Net present value The total of the discounted future cash inflows and outflows from a project. Projects with a positive net present value are accepted, while projects with a negative net present value are rejected.

Net profit The surplus that remains once all the expenses have been deducted from total income.

NIC See National insurance.

Nominal ledger Also known as the general ledger. The nominal ledger is an alphabetical listing of all the double-entry accounts of an entity.

Non-current asset turnover Revenue is divided by non-current assets to determine how many £s of sales are generated from each £ of non-current assets.

Non-current assets Assets held within the business long term for use in the production of goods and services. Non-current assets are retained within the business for periods of more than one year and are not acquired with the intention of reselling them immediately or in the near future.

Non-current liabilities Liabilities due for payment more than 12 months from the statement of financial position date.

Normal level of production The expected level of production achievable within an accounting period. This level is used as the basis for allocating fixed overhead costs to products and in the valuation of inventory at the year end.

Normal losses The expected losses from a process. Normal losses are never given a monetary value.

Normal standard What a business usually achieves.

NPV See Net present value.

Objectivity One of the IESBA's five fundamental principles of ethics for professional accountants. This principle states that professional accountants should not compromise professional or business judgements as a result of bias, conflict of interest or the undue influence of others.

Operating cycle Another term for the cash conversion cycle or working capital cycle. See Cash conversion cycle.

Operating profit The profit that remains after all the costs of trading, direct (cost of sales) and indirect (distribution and selling costs and administration expenses), have been deducted from sales revenue.

Operating profit percentage Determines profitability on the basis of revenue less all operating costs before taking into account the effects of finance income, finance expense and taxation.

Opportunity cost Opportunity cost is the loss that is incurred by choosing one alternative course of action over another, the benefits given up to use a resource in one application rather than taking the next best alternative course of action. Opportunity cost is only a relevant consideration when resources are limited: when resources are unlimited there is no opportunity cost.

Ordinary share capital The most common form of share capital issued by companies conferring on holders the right to receive all of a company's profits as dividends and to vote at company meetings. Also known as equity share capital.

Par value The face value or nominal value of a share.

Payables = liabilities. A payable is an obligation to make a transfer of cash or other assets to another organisation or person in the future.

Payables days Trade payables divided by cost of sales × 365 days. This ratio measures the average period taken to pay outstanding liabilities to trade suppliers.

Payback The number of years it will take for the cash inflows from a capital investment project to pay back the original cost of the investment.

PAYE Pay as you earn. This is a deduction from gross pay to reflect the income tax due on each payment of wages or salary to an employee.

Performance ratios Ratios of particular interest to an entity's shareholders as they measure the returns to the owners of the business.

Period costs Fixed costs incurred in the administration, marketing and financing of an entity relating to the period in which they are incurred.

Periodicity The preparation of financial statements for a set period of time, usually one year.

Petty cash book A record of cash received from the bank and cash expenditure on small items such as stamps, office refreshments and cleaning. Petty cash is used to pay expenses to suppliers who do not offer credit terms to businesses.

Pre-emption rights The rights of existing shareholders to subscribe to new issues of share capital before those shares can be offered to non-shareholders.

Preference share capital Preference shares receive a fixed rate of dividend that is paid before the ordinary shareholders receive any dividend. Money subscribed for preference share capital is returned to preference shareholders before any amounts are returned to ordinary shareholders on the winding up of a company. However, preference shareholders have no right to vote in company general meetings.

Prepayments Amounts paid in advance for goods and services to be provided in the future. These amounts are recognised as prepayments at the statement of financial position date and as a deduction from current period expenses.

Present value The discounting of future cash inflows and outflows to express all cash flows in the common currency of today, thereby facilitating a fair comparison of projected cash inflows and outflows for evaluating different capital investment proposals.

Price/earnings ratio The current market price of a share divided by the latest earnings per share figure. The ratio provides an indication of how long it would take for that share to pay back its owner in earnings if the share were purchased today and earnings remained the same for the foreseeable future.

Prime cost The total direct cost of producing one product or one unit of service.

Process costing The collection and assignment of costs to products or outputs produced in a process. Process costing is used to value products or outputs that are indistinguishable from one another.

Production cost The total direct costs of producing one product or one unit of service plus the proportion of fixed production overheads allocated to products and services on the basis of the normal level of production.

Professional behaviour One of the IESBA's five fundamental principles of ethics for professional accountants. This principle states that professional accountants must comply with all relevant legislation and regulations and must avoid any actions that might bring discredit upon both themselves and the accounting profession as a whole.

Professional competence and due care One of the IESBA's five fundamental principles of ethics for professional accountants. This principle states that professional accountants should gain their qualification and then keep their professional knowledge and skills up to date to enable them to provide the requisite competence and professional levels of service to their clients or their employers.

Profit The surplus remaining after all expenses are deducted from total income.

Profit after tax The profit that remains once all the expenses and charges have been deducted from sales revenue and any other income for the accounting period added on. Also known as profit for the year or profit for the period.

Profit after tax percentage Profit for the year or period (= profit after tax) divided by revenue × 100%.

Profit and loss account Another term for the statement of profit or loss.

Profit before tax Sales – cost of sales – distribution and selling costs – administration expenses + finance income – finance expense.

Profit before tax percentage Profit before tax divided by revenue × 100%.

Profit for the year = Profit after tax.

Profit per employee Calculated by dividing the number of employees during an accounting period into the operating profit for the period.

Profitability An assessment of the profits made during an accounting period by comparing current period profits and profitability percentages to those of previous periods.

Prudence The process of exercising caution in the production of financial statements in the expectation of less favourable outcomes. Prudence is only exercised under conditions of uncertainty.

Purchase day book A listing of all purchase invoices by date, supplier, internal invoice number, gross amount, VAT and net amount. The net amount of each purchase invoice is categorised into different types of expenditure ready for posting to the nominal ledger accounts.

Purchase ledger A record of invoices and credit notes received from and cash paid to each trade payable. The purchase ledger is a record outside the double-entry system but the total of all individual purchase ledger balances should be equal to the closing balance on the trade payables control account.

Purchase listing This is an equivalent term for the purchase day book.

Purchase returns The cancellation of a purchase by returning goods to suppliers. The accounting effect of purchase returns is to reduce expenses in the statement of profit or loss and trade payables in the statement of financial position.

Purchase returns day book A listing of all credit notes (negative purchases) received from suppliers by date, supplier, internal credit note number, gross amount, VAT and net amount. The net amount of each credit note is categorised into different types of expenditure ready for posting to the nominal ledger accounts.

Purchase returns listing This is an equivalent term for the purchase returns day book.

Quick ratio Also known as the acid test ratio. The quick ratio compares current assets that are readily convertible into cash with current liabilities as a measure of an entity's short-term ability to pay what it owes over the next 12 months. This ratio

should be used with caution in the evaluation of an entity's liquidity.

Ratio(s) The expression of the relationship(s) between two different figures.

Realisation Profits should not be anticipated until they have been earned through a sale.

Receivables Amounts of money owed to an entity by parties outside the organisation.

Receivables days Trade receivables divided by sales × 365 days. This ratio measures the average period taken to collect outstanding debts from credit customers.

Reducing balance A method of allocating depreciation on non-current assets to accounting periods benefiting from their use. This method uses a fixed percentage of cost in the first year of an asset's life and then applies the same percentage to the carrying amount of assets in accounting periods subsequent to year 1. The reducing balance method allocates a smaller charge for depreciation to each successive accounting period benefiting from a non-current asset's use. Residual value is ignored when calculating reducing balance depreciation.

Relevance A fundamental qualitative characteristic of financial information. To be relevant, information must be capable of making a difference in the decisions made by users. Relevant information may be predictive and assist users in making predictions about the future or it may be confirmatory by assisting users to assess the accuracy of past predictions. Relevant information can be both predictive and confirmatory.

Relevant costs The costs that will be incurred if a certain course of action is followed. Relevant costs are the costs that influence decision making.

Residual value The amount which the original purchaser of a non-current asset thinks that the asset could be sold for when the time comes to dispose of it.

Return on capital employed Operating profit (profit before interest and tax) divided by the equity of an entity plus any long-term borrowings × 100%.

Revenue Sales of goods and services made by an entity in the ordinary (everyday) course of business.

Revenue per employee Calculated by dividing the revenue for an accounting period by the number of employees employed during that accounting period.

Rights issues An issue of shares to existing shareholders at a discount to the current market price. This is not the issue of shares at a discount, which would be illegal under the Companies Act 2006.

ROCE See Return on capital employed.

Sales = revenue.

Sales day book A listing of all sales invoices by date, customer, invoice number, gross amount, VAT and net amount. The net amount of each sales invoice may be categorised into different types of sales ready for posting to the nominal ledger accounts.

Sales ledger A record of invoices and credit notes sent to and cash received from each trade receivable. The sales ledger is a record outside the double-entry system but the total of all individual sales ledger balances should be equal to the closing balance on the trade receivables control account.

Sales listing = sales day book.

Sales price variance The difference between the standard selling price and the actual selling price multiplied by the actual quantity sold.

Sales returns The cancellation of a sale by a customer returning goods. The accounting effect of sales returns is to reduce sales in the statement of profit or loss and trade receivables in the statement of financial position.

Sales returns day book A listing of all credit notes (negative sales) by date, customer, credit note number, gross amount, VAT and net amount. The net amount of each credit note may be categorised into different types of sales ready for posting to the nominal ledger accounts.

Sales volume variance The actual sales – budgeted sales in units multiplied by the standard contribution per sale.

Sensitivity analysis Changing the assumptions on which forecasts are based to determine the effect of those changes on expected outcomes.

Share capital A source of very long-term financing for limited companies. All limited companies must issue share capital that will remain in issue for as long as the company exists.

Share premium The amount subscribed for shares in a limited company over and above the par value of each share.

Shareholders Owners of share capital in limited companies. Shareholders may be either ordinary shareholders or preference shareholders.

Stakeholder theory The theory that a business's moral and ethical values should be applied in the management of organisations for the benefit of all stakeholders rather than just for the benefit of shareholders.

Standard costing The costs and selling prices of products are estimated with a reasonable degree of accuracy. Comparisons of actual and standard outcomes are then undertaken to determine the variances between expected and actual outcomes with a view to revising standards where necessary.

Statement of cash flows A summary of the cash inflows and outflows of an entity for a given period of time.

Statement of financial position A summary of the assets, liabilities and equity of an entity at a particular point in time.

Statement of profit or loss A statement of income and expenditure for a particular period of time. Also referred to as the income statement or the profit and loss account. The statement of profit or loss also forms part of the statement of financial performance presented by entities.

Stewardship The process of looking after resources entrusted to a person.

Stock A different term for inventory.

Stock days See Inventory days.

Straight line A method of allocating the cost of non-current assets to the accounting periods benefiting from their use. The

straight line method allocates the same charge for depreciation to each accounting period benefiting from a non-current asset's use within a business.

Sunk costs Sunk costs are past costs which have no influence over future decision making. Sunk costs represent expenditure that has already been incurred which no future action will change or alter.

Sustainability The long-term objective of business entities, aiming to remain in operational existence for the indefinite future.

T account Used in double entry to record and accumulate transactions. Each T account has a debit (left hand) and credit (right hand) side. The balance on each T account at the end of each accounting period is carried forward as an asset, liability or equity or written off to the statement of profit or loss as an expense or income.

Time value of money Money received today is worth more than money received tomorrow due to the impact of inflation and the uncertainty surrounding the receipt of money in future time periods.

Timeliness An enhancing qualitative characteristic of financial information. The decision usefulness of information is enhanced if it is available to users in time for it to be capable of influencing their decisions. While the decision usefulness of information generally declines with time, information that can still be used in identifying trends continues to be timely in the future.

Trade payables control account A summary account adding the opening credit balance of trade payables to the purchase day book totals for the accounting period and deducting the purchase returns day book totals, cash paid and discounts received in order to arrive at the closing trade payables balance at the end of the accounting period. The balance on the trade payables control account should be the same as the total of all the individual supplier balances on the purchase ledger.

Trade receivables Amounts owed to an entity by customers for goods and services supplied on credit.

Trade receivables control account A summary account adding the opening debit balance of trade receivables to the sales day book totals for the accounting period and deducting the sales returns day book totals, cash received and irrecoverable debts in order to arrive at the closing trade receivables balance at the end of the accounting period. The balance on the trade receivables control account should be the same as the total of all the individual customer balances on the sales ledger.

Trial balance A listing of all the debit and credit balances on the nominal ledger. The total debit balances should be equal to the total credit balances. If they are not then an error in the double-entry process has occurred.

Turnover The term used in financial statements in the UK to represent sales or revenue.

Understandability An enhancing qualitative characteristic of financial information. Understandability should not be confused with simplicity. Financial statements that excluded complex information just because it was difficult to understand would not result in relevant information that was faithfully presented. Reports that excluded such information would be incomplete and would thus mislead users. Readers of financial reports are assumed to have a reasonable knowledge of business and economic activities in order to make sense of what they are presented with but when they are unable to understand the information presented, then the IASB recommends using an adviser. To help users understand information presented, that information should be classified, characterised and presented clearly.

Unfavourable variances Differences between actual and budgeted results arising from lower income or higher expenditure.

Unsecured Loans for which no assets of an entity have been pledged in the event that the entity fails to repay the amounts borrowed.

Variable cost The costs of a product or service that vary directly in line with the production of a product or delivery of a service. Also known as the marginal cost of a product or service.

Variable overhead efficiency variance The time taken to make the goods actually produced compared with the standard time that should have been taken to make those goods multiplied by the standard variable overhead rate per hour.

Variable overhead expenditure variance The variable overhead actually incurred in the production of goods compared with the standard expenditure that should have been incurred for the level of actual production.

Variances Differences between expected, forecast or budgeted and actual financial results.

Verifiability A qualitative characteristic of financial information that enhances the usefulness of information that is relevant and faithfully represented. Verifiability provides users with assurance that information is faithfully presented and reports the economic phenomena it purports to represent. To ensure verifiability, it should be possible to prove the information presented is accurate in all major respects. The accuracy of information should be capable of verification by observation or recalculation.

Weighted average cost A method of valuing closing inventory. The weighted average cost valuation divides the total costs incurred in an accounting period by the number of units produced or purchased during the same period to calculate the average cost of each unit of production or goods for resale. This average cost is then used to calculate the costs of goods for resale or finished goods and work in progress produced during the period.

Work in progress Units of production which are partially complete at the end of an accounting period. Units of work in progress are completed in the next accounting period.

Working capital Current assets less current liabilities.

Working capital cycle See Cash conversion cycle. This is another term for the cash conversion cycle which is also known as the operating cycle.

INDEX

Note: Tables and figures are indicated by an italic *t* and *f* following the page number.

A

Ablynx 65
abnormal gains 554–6, 555*f*
abnormal losses 553–4, 553*f*
  disposal costs 557–9, 558*f*
  selling losses 560–2, 561*f*
absorption costing 417–26, 419*f*, 422*f*, 424*t*, 425*t*
  v. activity-based costing 432–5
  administration, marketing and finance overheads 429
  inventory valuation 420–1
  v. marginal costing 449–50
  problems with 429–30
  selling price, setting a 420
  service department overheads 427–8, 427*t*, 428*t*
accountability 12–14, 13*f*
accounting
  branches of 22–6
  control and accountability 12–14, 13*f*
  defined 10–12, 10*f*
accounting equation 56, 130*f*
  double entry 130–1, 131*f*
accounting information
  business decision making, role in 14–16, 15*f*
  cost v. benefit 21
  limitations 29–30
  materiality 20–1
  qualitative characteristics 16–22, 17*f*, 17*t*, 19*t*
  users of 22–6, 24*t*
    cost and management accounting 25–6
    financial accounting 22–5, 24*t*
accounting principles and conventions 283–5
accounting profession 26–7
  ethical principles 643–4
accounting rate of return (ARR) 592–3, 592*f*
  decision criteria 594–5, 594*f*, 607, 607*t*
accounting standards 27
  development process 28, 28*f*
  see also International Accounting Standard; International Accounting Standards Board;

International Financial Reporting Standards
accruals 283
  preparation of financial statements 108, 113
  statement of cash flows 280, 281
  statement of profit or loss and statement of financial position 94–5, 95*f*
accruals basis of accounting 91–3, 92*f*, 93*f*
  absorption costing 421
  closing inventory 106
  depreciation 102
  interest received 290
  preparation of financial statements 108, 110, 113
  and statement of cash flows 267
  statement of profit or loss 91–3, 92*f*, 93*f*, 280
acid test ratio *see* quick ratio
activity-based costing 430–5
  v. absorption costing 432–5
  how it works 431–2
actual v. budget comparisons
  cash flow 534–5
  statement of profit or loss 530–4
administration expenses
  absorption costing 429
  statement of profit or loss 83–4, 84*f*, 85*f*
adverse variances 484
agency problem 617–18
allowance for receivables 200
  preparation of financial statements 108
  statement of profit or loss 104–5
annotated statements 653–5
annual accounts
  limited companies 7–8
  public limited and private limited companies 9–10
annual general meeting (AGM)
  external auditors 622
  limited companies 6–7
  shareholder communications 634
annuity table 649*t*
Articles of Association
  limited companies 8
  share issues at par value 310

asset utilisation ratios 336–8, 336*f*, 350*t*
assets 42–5
  accounting equation 56
  composition of total assets 46*f*
  defined 42–3
  faithful representation 43–4
  statement of financial position 40, 40*f*, 42–50, 64
    drawing up 60, 61, 62
    recognition 44, 45*f*
  tangible 46, 47
  valuation 63–4
  see also current assets; intangible assets; non-current assets
Association of Chartered Certified Accountants (ACCA) 26
attainable standard 482–3, 483*f*
audit
  external *see* external audit
  internal *see* internal audit
  post investment 608
audit committee 631–3
auditors 7–8
  computer systems, tests of 183

B

bad debts *see* irrecoverable debts
balance sheet *see* statement of financial position
Balfour Beatty plc 310
bank account
  bank reconciliation 216–20
  cash payments 211, 212
  cash received 196
  non-current assets, disposal of 229
  petty cash book 220
  sales day book 191
bank finance 302–6, 302*f*
  see also bank loans; overdrafts
bank loans 302, 304–5, 304*f*, 305*t*
  budgeting 512, 529, 534, 535, 537
  contract 373
  timing of payments 373–4
bank overdrafts *see* overdrafts
bank reconciliation 216–20
bank statements 19*t*
bankruptcy 361

board of directors 619–21, 621*f*
  company decision making 626–7
  corporate social responsibility 637
  effectiveness of board 628–31, 629*f*
  financial statements, ensuring the
    integrity of 631
  shareholder communications 634
bonds 306–7
bonus issues 312, 314
Boohoo.com 340
books of prime entry 184, 184*f*, 228
borrowings
  long-term 54
  risky 378–81
  see also bank loans
BP 642
break-even point 453–5, 453*f*
  assumptions 472
  cost-volume-profit analysis 458
  graphical illustration 455, 455*f*
  high and low fixed costs 459
  margin of safety 455–6, 456*f*
  sensitivity analysis 456–7
  target profit 457–8
Brundtland Report 640
budget 509
  cash *see* cash budget
budgetary control 531*f*
  cash budget 534–5
  statement of profit or loss 530–4
budgeted monthly statement of profit or
  loss 517–19, 518*f*
  budgetary control 530–4
  sensitivity analysis 536
budgeted statement of financial
  position 526–9, 527*f*
budgeting 508–9, 539–48
  example 512–30
  nature of 509–10
  objectives 510–11, 510*t*
  process 510–11, 530*f*
  sensitivity analysis 536–9
business decision making *see* decision
  making
business entity 115, 283
business entity convention 58
business organisations 300–1, 316–19
  types 3–10
    limited companies 4–10, 5*f*
    partnerships 4, 5*f*
    public limited and private limited
     companies 9*f*, 9–10
    sole traders 3–4, 3*f*

C

Cadbury Report 618, 619
capital
  cost of 597
  introduced 301–2
  see also working capital
capital account 58–9, 59*f*
  see also equity
capital investment 584–5

capital investment appraisal 583–4,
  608–15
  decision making 606–7, 607*t*
  financial information for 587
  importance 585–6
  post investment audit 608
  sensitivity analysis 608
  steps 587*f*
  techniques 588–90
    accounting rate of return 592–5,
     592*f*, 594*f*
    discounted payback 600–2, 601*t*,
     602*f*
    internal rate of return 602–6,
     603*f*, 605*f*
    net present value 597–600, 599*f*,
     604
    payback 589–92, 590*t*, 591*f*, 595,
     602*f*, 602
    time value of money 595–7
capital structure ratios 375–8, 376*f*,
  376*t*, 381*t*
capitalising reserves 312
Carillion 361
carrying amount 96–7, 97*t*, 103
  efficiency ratios 333
  non-current assets, disposal of 229,
    230, 231
  reducing balance depreciation 100
  statement of cash flows 285–7
cash *see* cash and cash equivalents
cash account, finding missing figures
  from T accounts 232–3
cash and cash equivalents
  not equal to profits 263–5
  preparation of financial
    statements 107, 112–13
  statement of cash flows 255, 262–3,
    270
  statement of financial position 48–9,
    60–1
  see also cash flow cycle; cash flows
    from financing activities; cash
    flows from investing activities;
    cash flows from operating
    activities; cash paid; cash
    received; cash refunds
cash book 196
  bank reconciliation 216–20
  cash payments 211
  cash receipts 196
cash budget 520, 520*f*, 522–5, 523*f*
  budgetary control 534–5
  importance 525–6
  sensitivity analysis 537
cash conversion cycle 367*f*, 370–2,
  371*f*, 381*t*
cash equivalents *see* cash and cash
  equivalents
cash flow cycle
  liquidity 361–3
  manufacturers 361–2, 362*f*
  retailers 361–2, 361*f*

cash flows from financing
  activities 256–7, 260–2, 261*f*
cash flows from investing
  activities 256–7, 259–60, 259*f*
cash flows from operating
  activities 256–9
  statement of cash flows
    direct method of preparation
     279–80
    indirect method of
     preparation 279–83
cash paid 211–14
  calculation
    from expenses T account 276–8
    from trade payables control
     account 214–15
  cash book 196
  petty cash book 220
  purchase ledger 213–14
  purchases and cash paid system 185,
    201*f*, 202
  to suppliers 274–6
  trade payables control account 215
cash received 196–8
  calculation from trade receivables
    control account 273–4
  cash book 196
  petty cash book 220
  sales and cash received system 186*f*,
    187
  sales ledger 198–9
cash refunds
  purchases and cash paid system 201*f*,
    202
  sales and cash received system 186*f*,
    188
chairperson 627, 628
Chartered Institute of Management
  Accountants (CIMA) 26
  break-even point and cost-volume-
    profit analysis 458
  budgeting 510
  cost accounting and cost objects
    defined 396
  cost allocation 426
  management accounting
    defined 398–9
  profitability 409
  relevant costs 473
  standard costing variance analysis 498
  variance analysis 482
Chartered Institute of Public Finance
  and Accounting (CIPFA) 27
Citigroup 380
closing inventory
  cost calculation methods 115–18
  at end of accounting period 172–3
  preparation of financial
    statements 110, 113
  statement of profit or loss 106–7
Committee on the Financial Aspects
  of Corporate Governance
  (Cadbury Committee) 618, 619

communication
  as budgeting objective 510*t*
  with shareholders 634–5
Companies Act 2006
  corporate governance 618, 625
    external audit 622
    financial statements, ensuring the
      integrity of 631
    long-term success v. short-term
      profits 626
  corporate social responsibility 636–7
  dividends 315
  limited companies 7, 8
  pre-emption rights 313
  public limited and private limited
    companies 9
  rights issues 312–13
  share issues at par value 310
Companies House 7, 8
comparability
  accruals basis of accounting 91
  cost and management
    accounting 403
  as qualitative characteristic of
    accounting information 16, 17*f*,
    17*t*, 18*t*
  ratio analysis 347–9
compensating error 234*t*
competence, professional 643
complete reversal of entries 234*t*
conduct, standards of 27
confidentiality 643
consistency 283
  ratio analysis 347
contribution 447–8, 448*f*
  break-even point 453–4, 456–7
  cost-volume-profit analysis 458
  high and low fixed costs 459
  limiting factor analysis 468–72
  margin of safety 455–6, 456*f*
  marginal v. absorption costing
    449–50
  marketing and selling price 459–61
  outsourcing decisions 464–8
  sensitivity analysis 456–7
  special orders 461–4
  target profit 457–8
control
  accounting and accountability
    12–14, 13*f*
  as budgeting objective 510*t*
conversion cost 550
coordination, as budgeting
  objective 510*t*
corporate bonds 306–7
corporate governance 616–18, 644–6
  codes 27
  corporate social responsibility
    reporting 635–9, 636*f*
    rationale 639–40
  defined 619
  history 618
  parties involved 619, 620*f*

board of directors 619–21, 621*f*
  external audit 621–2, 623*f*
  internal audit 623–4, 623*f*
  stock exchange rules 624–5
public limited companies 10
shareholder concerns,
  addressing 625
  board effectiveness 628–31, 629*f*
  company decision making 626–8
  directors' remuneration 633–4
  financial statements, ensuring the
    integrity of 631–3
  long-term success v. short-term
    profits 625–6, 625*f*
  shareholder communications 634–5
sustainability reporting 642
Corporate Governance Code 618, 619
  board effectiveness 628–30, 629*f*
  company decision making 626–7
  corporate social responsibility 637,
    639
  directors' remuneration 633–4
  financial statements, ensuring the
    integrity of 631–2
  long-term success v. short-term
    profits 625–6
  shareholder communications 634
  shareholder concerns 625
  stock exchange rules 624–5
corporate social responsibility 635–6,
  636*f*
  reporting 636–40, 636*f*
cost
  indirect 415, 416
  inventory 106
  opportunity 452–3, 596
  period 429
  production 419*f*, 419
  sunk costs 451–2
  see also direct cost; fixed cost;
    marginal cost; prime cost;
    relevant costs; total cost;
    variable cost
cost accounting 395–6, 405–7
  defined 396–8
  v. financial accounting 400–2, 401*f*
    information 402–5, 404*f*
  roles 396*f*, 399
  users of accounting information 25–6
cost allocation 398*f*, 398
  absorption costing 417–26, 424*t*,
    425*t*
    v. activity-based costing 432–5
    administration, marketing and
      finance overheads 429
    inventory valuation 420–1
    problems with 429–30
    selling price, setting a 420
    service department
      overheads 427–8, 427*t*, 428*t*
  activity-based costing 430–5
    v. absorption costing 432–5
cost-benefit rule 404

cost cards 418
  standard 480, 483–4
cost centre 431
cost drivers 431, 433
cost object 396–8, 397*f*
cost of capital 597
cost of sales
  preparation of financial
    statements 113
  statement of profit or loss 83, 84*f*,
    85*f*, 88
cost pools 431, 433
cost-volume-profit (CVP) analysis 458
costing 408–9, 411, 438–45
  importance 409–10
  limitations and assumptions 435–8,
    436*f*
  selling price, setting a 411, 420
  short-term decision making 446–7,
    473–8
    absorption costing 449–50
    contribution analysis 448*f*, 448,
      453–72
    marginal costing 449–50, 472–3
    opportunity costs 452–3
    relevant costs 451–2, 459–73
    scope 447
    sunk costs 451–2
  see also absorption costing; activity-
    based costing; process costing;
    standard costing
credit notes
  purchase ledger 209, 210
  purchases and cash paid system 201*f*,
    202
  sales and cash received system 186*f*,
    187
  sales ledger 194, 195
creditor days *see* payables days
credits
  accounting equation 129–30, 129*f*, 130*f*
  dual aspect concept 66
  T accounts 129–30, 129*f*, 130*f*
current assets 45, 47–9
  and non-current assets, distinction
    between 49–50
  preparation of financial
    statements 107, 108
  statement of financial position 40,
    45, 47–9
    drawing up 60, 61, 62
  valuation 63
current liabilities 54
  preparation of financial
    statements 107, 108
  statement of financial position 53–5
    drawing up 60, 61, 62
  timing of payments 373–5
  valuation 63
current ratio 363–4, 381*t*
  limitations 374
  traditional view 366–7
current value (fair value) 63–4

D

debentures 306–7
debits
    accounting equation 129–30, 129f, 130f
    dual aspect concept 66
    T accounts 129–30, 129f, 130f
debt ratio 376f, 376t, 377–8, 381t
debtor days *see* receivables days
debts, irrecoverable *see* irrecoverable debts
decision making
    accounting information, role of 14–16, 15f
    corporate governance 626–8
    long-term *see* capital investment appraisal
    short-term *see* short-term decision making
deferred tax 48, 54
Deloitte 459
depreciation 96–7, 97t
    accounting rate of return 592
    methods 99–102, 100t, 101f
        choice of 101–2
    non-current assets, disposal of 229, 230
    preparation of financial statements 108, 114
    reducing balance *see* reducing balance
    residual value and annual depreciation charge 97–8, 98t
    statement of cash flows 276, 277, 278, 279, 285–7
    straight line *see* straight line depreciation
    what it is and is not 102–3
direct cost 412–13, 413t
    activity-based costing 431
    cost cards 418
    prime cost 419f, 419
direct labour efficiency variance 490–2, 491f
direct labour rate variance 490–2, 491f
direct labour total variance 491f, 492–3
direct labour variances 490–2, 491f
    information and control 493
direct material price variance 487–9, 488f
direct material total variance 489
direct material usage variance 487–9, 488f
direct material variances 487–9, 488f
    information and control 490
direct method 269–78, 279
directors 12–13
    agency problem 617–18
    appointment of 7
    corporate governance 618, 619–21, 620f, 621f
        board effectiveness 628–30, 629f
        company decision making 626–8

effectiveness of board 628–30, 629f
        external audit 621–2
        financial statements, ensuring the integrity of 631
        internal audit 623–4
        long-term success v. short-term profits 625–6, 625f
        remuneration 633–4
        shareholder communications 634
    corporate social responsibility 636–7
    roles and responsibilities 619–20, 621f
    and shareholders, information asymmetry between 617, 617f
    stock exchange rules 625
    see also executive directors; non-executive directors
discounted payback 600–2, 601t, 602f
    decision criteria 607t
discounting
    net present value 599
    time value of money 597
discounts allowed, statement of profit or loss 105
discounts received
    preparation of financial statements 108
    statement of profit or loss 105–6
    trade payables control account 215
disposal costs, process costing 556–9, 557f, 558f
distributable reserves 315–16
distribution 315
distribution and selling costs 83, 84f, 85f
dividend cover 338f, 344, 345, 350t
dividend payout ratio 342, 343, 345, 350t
dividend per share (DPS) 338f, 342–3, 345, 350t
dividend yield 338f, 343–4, 345, 350t
dividends 13, 307–8, 315
    distributable and non-distributable reserves 315–16
    final 315
    interim 315
    ordinary share capital 308, 309f
    performance ratios 338
        see also dividend cover; dividend payout ratio; dividend per share; dividend yield
    preference share capital 308, 309f
    statement of cash flows 260, 261f, 289
double entry 66, 127–8, 173–84, 238–52
    accounting equation 56, 130–1, 131f
    bank reconciliation 216–20
    cash payments 211–14
    cash received 196–8
    cost and management accounting 402, 403
    dividends 315
    errors

potential 233–5, 234t
    when the trial balance does not balance 235–7
    journals 238
    nominal ledger 228
    non-current assets, disposals of 229–31
    payroll system 222–7
    petty cash 220–2
    purchase day book 203–6
    purchase ledger 208–10
    purchase returns day book 206–8
    purchases and cash paid system 201–3, 201f
    sales and cash received system 185–8, 186f
    sales day book 188–9, 190–2
    sales ledger 194–6, 198–9
    sales returns day book 192–4
    share issues at par value 310
    T accounts 129–30, 129f, 130f
        closing off 160–71
        example 124–71
        missing figures, finding 232–3
        posting accounting transactions to 132–6
        separate accounts for inventory and purchases 171–3
        trial balance 137–9, 154–60
    trade payables control account 214–16
    trade receivables control account 199–201
    transactions and transaction systems 184–5
    trial balance, when it does not balance 235–7
    VAT 190
drawings 58, 301
    business entity assumption 115
dual aspect 66, 283
    statement of financial position 66–9
duality principle 69
    accounting equation 56, 131
due care 643

E

earnings per share (EPS) 338f, 339–40, 345, 350t
efficiency ratios 332–8, 333f, 336f, 350t
EMI plc 380
employer's NIC (expense) account 226–7
environmental reporting 640–3
equity
    accounting equation 56
    components 57–60, 57f, 59f
    defined 56
    statement of financial position 40f, 40, 57–60
    drawing up 60, 61, 62
    see also capital account

equity share capital *see* ordinary share
    capital
equivalent units 563, 563*f*
    closing work in progress 564
    opening work in progress
        first in first out valuation
            method 569–71
        weighted average cost valuation
            method 574–5
    varying completion percentages of
        costs 566
error of commission 234*t*
error of omission 234*t*
error of original entry 234*t*
error of principle 234*t*
errors
    double entry
        potential errors 233–5, 234*t*
        when the trial balance does not
            balance 235–7
    freedom from 17*t*
    internal control systems 624
ethical rules of conduct 27, 643–4
exceptional income 81, 82, 82*f*
executive directors 619–21, 620*f*, 621*f*
    board effectiveness 630
    company decision making 627–8
    financial statements, ensuring the
        integrity of 631
    internal audit 623
    remuneration 634
    roles and responsibilities 619, 621*f*
expenses
    accounting equation 131, 131*f*
    defined 80–1
    direct costs 412–13, 413*t*
    preparation of financial
        statements 107, 108–10, 113,
        114
    statement of profit or loss 77–8,
        83–5, 88
    determining expenses 89–90, 90*t*
Experian 54–5
external audit 620*f*, 621–2
    financial statements, ensuring the
        integrity of 631, 632
    and internal audit, comparison
        between 623*f*
extraordinary general meeting (EGM) 7

F

fair value 63–4
faithful representation 16, 17*f*, 17*t*, 18*t*
    assets 43–4
    financial accounting v. cost and
        management accounting 403
    liabilities 51
favourable variances 484
final dividend 315
finance expense
    statement of cash flows 291–2
    statement of profit or loss 84, 85*f*, 88
finance income

statement of cash flows 290
    statement of profit or loss 81, 82*f*, 88
finance overheads, absorption
    costing 429
financial accounting
    v. cost and management
        accounting 400–2, 401*f*
    information 402–5, 404*f*
    objectives 22–3
    users of accounting information 22–
        5, 24*t*
        questions asked by user
            groups 23–5, 24*t*
financial information *see* accounting
    information
Financial Reporting Council (FRC) 27,
    618
financial stability
    ratios 375–8, 376*f*, 376*t*, 381*t*
    risky borrowings 378–81
financial statements, ensuring the
    integrity of 631–3
financing activities, cash flows
    from 256–7, 260–2, 261*f*
financing business 300–1, 316–19
    bank finance 302–6, 302*f*, 304*f*, 305*t*
    capital introduced 301–2
    distributable and non-distributable
        reserves 315–16
    dividends 315
    public limited companies 306–14
    sole traders and partnerships 301–2
Finsbury Food Group plc 102
First Group plc 57–8
first in, first out (FIFO) 116, 117, 118,
    569–73, 569*f*
fixed cost 414–17, 415*f*, 416*f*, 417*t*
    absorption costing v. marginal
        costing 449
    assumptions 435–6
    break-even point 453–5, 455*f*
    budget 516–17, 517*f*
    contribution 448
    high and low 459
    marginal costing 449, 472
    stepped 436*f*, 436
fixed overhead expenditure
    variance 494–5, 494*f*
formation documents 8
freedom from error 17*t*
Friedman, Milton 636, 642
full costing *see* absorption costing
future value 651*t*

G

gearing ratio 376*f*, 376*t*, 377, 381*t*
general ledger 228
general meetings
    annual *see* annual general meeting
    extraordinary 6
    limited companies 6–7
    ordinary shareholders 308, 309*f*
    preference shareholders 308, 309*f*

German bonds 596
GlaxoSmithKline plc 538, 607
going concern 254, 283–4
Greek bonds 596
Greggs plc
    cash flows
        from financing activities 261–2
        from investing activities 260
        from operating activities 258
    comparisons with other
        companies 349
    profits 77
gross pay 223, 225
gross profit 79
    preparation of financial
        statements 113
    statement of profit or loss 85, 86*f*
gross profit percentage 327*f*, 328–9,
    350*t*
    interpretation 320–30, 331

H

historic cost 284
    v. fair value 63–4
HM Revenue and Customs
    income tax 223, 224
    national insurance
        employee's 223, 224
        employer's 224, 226–7
    VAT 190, 191, 196, 204
hurdle rate of return 597

I

ideal standard 482, 483*f*
income
    accounting equation 131, 131*f*
    defined 79–80
    exceptional 81, 82, 82*f*
    finance *see* finance income
    statement of profit or loss 77–8, 81–3
        determining income 89–90, 89*t*
    see also revenue
income statement *see* statement of profit
    or loss
income tax
    payroll system 222, 223, 224, 225
    statement of profit or loss 84–5, 85*f*
    transactions and transaction
        systems 185
incomplete records 232–3
incorporation 6, 7
indirect cost 415, 416
    see also absorption costing; activity-
        based costing
indirect method 257, 278–83, 282*t*
inflation 595–6
information asymmetry 617, 617*f*, 618
insolvency 361
Institute of Chartered Accountants
    in England and Wales
    (ICAEW) 27
Institute of Chartered Accountants in
    Ireland (ICAI) 27

Institute of Chartered Accountants in
    Scotland (ICAS) 27
intangible assets 45, 46
    cash flows from investing
        activities 259, 259f
    statement of financial position 45, 46
        drawing up 62
integration, as budgeting objective 510t
integrity 643
interest 596
interest cover 376f, 376t, 378, 381t
    risky borrowings 380
interest paid
    cash flows from financing
        activities 261, 261f
    see also finance expense
interest received
    cash flows from investing
        activities 259, 259f
    see also finance income
interim dividend 315
internal audit 620f, 623–4
    and external audit, comparison
        between 623f
    financial statements, ensuring the
        integrity of 632
internal control systems 624
internal rate of return (IRR) 598,
        602–3, 603f
    advantages 605
    calculation 603–4
    decision criteria 604, 605f, 607, 607t
    GlaxoSmithKline plc 607
    limitations 605–6
International Accounting Standard
        (IAS) 28
    IAS 1 Presentation of financial
        statements 85
    IAS 2 Inventory 106, 118, 421
    IAS 7 Statement of cash flows 255–6
    list of 31
International Accounting Standards
        Board (IASB) 27, 28–9
    accruals accounting 91
    assets defined 42
    cash equivalents 262
    cost v. benefit of accounting
        information 21
    drawings and the business entity
        convention 115
    equity defined 56
    expenses defined 80
    Exposure Drafts 28
    external audit 622
    fair value 284
    financial statements 267
    freedom from error 17t
    income defined 79–80
    liabilities defined 50
    liquidity and solvency 360
    materiality defined 20
    objective of financial reporting 22–3
    prudence 284

qualitative characteristics of
        accounting information 16–17
    statement of financial position 64, 65
    see also International Financial
        Reporting Standards
International Accounting Standards
        Committee 28
International Auditing and Assurance
        Standards Board (IAASB) 622
International Ethics Standards Board
        for Accountants (IESBA) 643
International Financial Reporting
        Standard (IFRS) 28
    financial statements, ensuring the
        integrity of 631
    list of 30–1
International Standards on Auditing
        (ISA) 622
inventory
    closing see closing inventory
    opening 171–2
    statement of cash flows 280, 281
    statement of financial position 47
    valuation 420–1
inventory days 368t, 369–70, 381t
    cash conversion cycle 367f, 370–2, 371f
investments
    cash flows from investing
        activities 256–7, 259–60, 259f
    statement of financial position 47
irrecoverable debts
    preparation of financial
        statements 108, 113, 114
    statement of profit or loss 103–4
    trade receivables control account 200

J
joint ventures 48
journals 238

K
key (limiting) factor 468–72

L
labour
    direct costs 412–13, 413t
    see also direct labour variances
last in, first out (LIFO) 116, 117, 118
legal identity, separate 6
liabilities 50–5
    accounting equation 56
    composition of total liabilities 53f
    defined 50–1
    faithful representation 51
    statement of financial position 40,
        40f, 53–5, 65
        drawing up 60, 61, 62
        recognition 51–2, 52f
    valuation 63–4
    see also current liabilities;
        non-current liabilities
limited companies 4–10, 5f

corporate governance see corporate
        governance
    long-term finance 306–14
    private 9–10
    public see public limited companies
    statement of financial position 57–8,
        57f
    tax liabilities 374
limited liability 6
limited liability partnerships (LLPs) 4
Limited Liability Partnerships Act
        2000 4
limiting factor 468–72
liquidity
    cash flow cycle 361–3, 361f, 362f
    IASB 360
    ratios 363–7, 381t
Lloyds Bank 303–4, 305t
loan notes 306–7
loans 80
    bank see bank loans
    debentures 306–7
    long-term borrowings 54
    received 260, 261f
    repaid 261, 261f
London Stock Exchange 618, 624
long-term borrowings 54
long-term decision making see capital
        investment appraisal
long-term provisions 54
long-term solvency
    ratios 375–8, 376f, 376t, 381t
    risky borrowings 378–81
long-term success v. short-term
        profits 625–6, 625f
loss on asset disposal 98–9
    statement of cash flows 282

M
machinery account 230
machinery accumulated depreciation
        account 230
make or buy (outsourcing)
        decisions 464–8, 466f
management accounting 395–6, 405–7
    defined 398–400
    v. financial accounting 400–2, 401f
        information 402–5, 404f
    roles 396f, 399
    users of accounting information
        25–6
margin of safety 455–6, 456f
marginal cost 412
    v. absorption costing 449–50
        assumptions 472–3
        outsourcing decisions 465
market value of an entity 65
marketing
    overheads 429
    and selling price 459–61
Marks and Spencer plc 314, 341
matching see accruals
materiality 20–1, 284

materials
    direct costs 412–13, 413*t*
    see also direct material variances
Memorandum of Association
    limited companies 8
    share issues at par value 310
missing figures, finding from
        T accounts 232–3
money measurement 284
motivation, as budgeting objective 510*t*

N

national insurance (NIC)
    employee's 222, 223, 224, 225
    employer's 224, 226–7
    transactions and transaction
        systems 185
Nestlé 89, 90
net book value *see* carrying amount
net pay 224
net present value (NPV) 597–9
    advantages 599–600
    decision criteria 599, 599*f*, 607, 607*t*
    GlaxoSmithKline plc 607
    and internal rate of return 604, 605,
        606
    limitations 600
net profit *see* profit for the year
net realisable value 106
Next plc
    bonds 306–7
    borrowings 379, 380
    capital investment appraisal
        techniques 595
    out-of-date goods, effect on profit
        margins 366
    price/earnings ratio 341
Nichols plc 49
nominal ledger 228
non-current asset disposals
        account 229, 230, 231
non-current asset turnover 333*f*, 333–4,
        350*t*
non-current assets 45–6
    capital investment 584–5
    cash flows from investing
        activities 259, 259*f*
    and current assets, distinction
        between 49–50
    depreciation *see* depreciation
    disposal of 229–31, 282, 285–7
    preparation of financial
        statements 107, 108, 110
    profits and losses on disposal of 98–9
    statement of cash flows 282, 285–7
    statement of financial position 40, 45–8
        drawing up 60, 61, 62
    valuation 63
non-current liabilities 54–5
    statement of financial position 40,
        54–5
        drawing up 60, 61, 62
    valuation 63

non-distributable reserves 315–16
non-executive directors 619–21, 620*f*,
        621*f*
    audit committee 631–2
    board effectiveness 629–30
    company decision making 627–8
    financial statements, ensuring the
        integrity of 631–2
    internal audit 623
    remuneration 634
    roles and responsibilities 620, 621*f*
normal level of production 418
normal losses 552–3, 552*f*
    disposal costs 556–7, 557*f*, 558–9
    selling losses 559–60, 559*f*, 561–2
normal standard 483*f*, 483

O

objectivity 643
Ocado 314
opening inventory 171–2
operating activities, cash flows from
        see cash flows from operating
        activities
operating cycle *see* cash conversion
        cycle
operating profit 79
    statement of profit or loss 85–6, 86*f*
operating profit percentage 327*f*,
        330–3, 331*t*, 332*f*, 350*t*
opportunity cost 452–3, 596
ordinary share capital 307, 308, 309*f*
Our Common Future (Brundtland
        Report) 640
outsourcing decisions 464–8, 466*f*
overdrafts 302–4, 302*f*
    preparation of financial
        statements 107
    timing of payments 374
    working capital 372
overhead allocation *see* cost allocation
overhead variances
    fixed 494–5, 494*f*
    variable 494, 499–501, 499*f*

P

par value 57, 310, 311
partnerships 4, 5*f*
    capital introduced 301–2
    limited liability 4
pay as you earn *see* PAYE
payables days 368*t*, 369–70, 381*t*
    cash conversion cycle 367*f*, 370–2,
        371*f*
payback 590–1, 590*f*, 595, 602*f*, 602
    decision criteria 590–2, 591*f*, 607*t*
    discounted *see* discounted payback
PAYE (pay as you earn) 223, 225
    see also income tax
PAYE and NIC control account 226,
        227
payout ratio 342, 343, 345, 350*t*
payroll system 185, 222–7

pensions
    contributions 222, 223–4, 225–6
    control account 226
    statement of financial position 54
performance ratios 338–45, 338*f*, 350*t*
period costs 429
periodicity 284
petty cash book 220–2
planning, as budgeting objective 510*t*
pre-emption rights 313
preference share capital 307, 308, 309*f*
    dividends 315
Premier Foods plc 46
Premier League football clubs 459
prepayments
    preparation of financial
        statements 108, 113, 114
    statement of cash flows 280, 281
    statement of financial position 48, 94
    statement of profit or loss 94, 94*f*
present value
    net *see* net present value
    table 647*t*
    time value of money 597
price/earnings (P/E) ratio 338*f*, 340–2,
        345, 350*t*
prime cost 419
    activity-based costing 431
    components 419*f*
private limited companies 9–10
process costing 549–50, 577–82
    abnormal gains 554–6, 555*f*
    abnormal losses 553–4, 553*f*
    disposal costs 556–9, 557*f*, 558*f*
    normal losses 552–3, 552*f*
    process account 550–1, 551*f*
    selling losses 559–62, 559*f*, 561*f*
    work in progress, valuing at end of
        an accounting period 562–5,
        562*f*, 563*f*
        first in, first out method 569–73,
            569*f*
        unit costs when there is
            opening and closing work in
            progress 568–9, 568*f*
        varying completion percentages of
            costs 565–8
        weighted average cost
            method 573–6, 573*f*
process cycle 568*f*
product differentiation 463
production cost 419*f*, 419
professional accounting bodies 26–7
professional behaviour 643
professional competence 643
profit
    on asset disposal 98–9, 231, 282
    categories of 85–6, 86*f*
    costs, importance of 409–10
    distributable reserves 315
    Friedman on 636, 642
    importance 77
    not equal to cash 263–5

selling price, setting a 411
short-term, v. long-term
success 625–6, 625f
statement of profit or loss 77–8,
85–6, 86f
target 457–8
see also gross profit; operating profit;
profit before tax; profit for the
year
profit after tax see profit for the year
profit after tax percentage 327f, 330–3,
331t, 332f, 350t
profit and loss account see statement of
profit or loss
profit before tax 79
statement of profit or loss 86, 86f
profit before tax percentage 327f,
330–3, 331t, 332f, 350t
profit for the year 79
preparation of financial
statements 114
statement of profit or loss 86, 86f
profit per employee 333f, 334–6, 350t
profit per unit of input resource 336–8,
336f, 350t
profitability 323–4, 323t, 327–32, 327f,
331t, 332f, 350t
financial statements, need for 325–6
property, plant and equipment
cash flows from investing
activities 259, 259f
statement of cash flows 285–7
statement of financial position 47, 62
provision for doubtful debts see
allowance for receivables
prudence 104, 284
public limited companies (plcs) 9f, 9–10
corporate governance 624
long-term finance 306–14
purchase day book 203–6
purchase ledger 209, 210
trade payables control account 215
purchase invoices
purchase ledger 209, 210
purchases and cash paid system 201f,
202
purchase ledger 208–10, 228
cash payments 213–14
purchase listing see purchase day book
purchase returns
preparation of financial
statements 108, 113
statement of profit or loss 106
purchase returns day book 206–8
purchase ledger 209, 210
trade payables control account 215
purchase returns listing see purchase
returns day book
purchases and cash paid system 185,
201–3, 201f
purchases listing see purchase day
book
purchasing power 596

Q

quick ratio (acid test ratio) 364–6, 381t
limitations 374
traditional view 366–7

R

ratio analysis 320–2, 352–60, 383–91
advantages 326–7
capital structure ratios 375–8, 376f,
376t, 381t
comparisons with other
companies 347–9
consistency, importance of 347
current liabilities 373–5
efficiency ratios 332–8, 333f, 336f,
350t
financial statements
evaluation 322–3
need for 325–6
liquidity and the cash flow cycle 361–
3, 361f, 362f
liquidity ratios 363–7, 381t
need for 323–5
performance ratios 338–45, 338f, 350t
profitability ratios 327–32, 327f, 331t,
332f, 350t
return on capital employed 346–7
risky borrowings 378–81
tables of ratios 350t, 381t
working capital 367–72, 367f, 368t,
381t
importance 372–3
realisation 106, 284
receivables days 368t, 369–70, 381t
cash conversion cycle 367f, 370–2,
371f
reducing balance 99–100, 100t, 101f
choice of 101
refunds see cash refunds
Registrar of Companies 8
regulation of the accounting
profession 26–7
relevance 16, 17f, 17t, 18t
cost and management
accounting 403
relevant costs 451–2
assumptions 472–3
limiting factor analysis 468–72
marketing and selling price 459–61
opportunity costs 452–3
outsourcing decisions 464–8
special orders 461–4
residual value 97–8, 98t, 99–100
responsibility, as budgeting
objective 510t
retained earnings/profits
bonus issues of shares 312
dividends 315
statement of financial position 57,
58, 62
return on capital employed
(ROCE) 346–7, 350t

returns see purchase returns; sales
returns
revenue
break-even point 453–5, 453f
preparation of financial
statements 107, 108–10, 112–13
statement of profit or loss 77–8, 81,
82f, 88
determining revenue 89–90, 89t
see also income
revenue per employee 333f, 334–6, 350t
rights issues 312–14
Rio Tinto plc 399, 586
risk
borrowings 378–81
time value of money 596
Rolls Royce Holdings plc 82, 189, 421
Ryanair 346, 348

S

salaries see payroll system
sales
cost of see cost of sales
see also income; revenue
sales and cash received system 184,
185–8, 186f
sales budget 513–15, 514f
sales day book 188–9, 190–2, 195
sales invoices
sales and cash received system 185,
186f
sales day book 188–9
sales ledger 194, 195
sales ledger 194–6, 228
cash receipts 198–9
trade receivables control account 200
sales listing see sales day book
sales per unit of input resource 336–8,
336f, 350t
sales price variance 495, 495f, 496
sales returns
preparation of financial
statements 108, 113
statement of profit or loss 106
sales returns day book 192–4, 195
sales returns listing see sales returns
day book
sales variances 495–7, 495f, 496f
sales volume variance 495–6, 496f
Salesforce.com 254
Sanofi 65
selling losses, process costing 559–62,
559f, 561f
selling price
and marketing 459–61
setting a 411, 420
sensitivity analysis 456–7
budgeting 536–9
capital investment appraisal 608
separate legal identity, limited
companies 6
service department overheads 427–8,
427t, 428t

share-based payments
   cash flows from financing
      activities 261–2
   cash flows from operating
      activities 258
share capital 306–7
   bonus issues 312, 314
   cash flows from financing
      activities 260, 261*f*
   limited companies 6
   ordinary 307, 308, 309*f*
   performance ratios
      dividend per share 338*f*, 342–3,
         345, 350*t*
      earnings per share 338*f*, 339–40,
         345, 350*t*
   preference *see* preference share
      capital
   rights issues 312–14
   share issues at par value 57, 310, 311
   shares issued at a premium 310–11
   statement of financial position 57, 62
share premium 57, 62
shareholders 6, 12–13
   agency problem 617–18
   audit 7–8
   bonus issues of shares 312
   corporate governance 618, 619, 625
      board effectiveness 628–31, 629*f*
      communications with
         shareholders 634–5
      company decision making 626–8
      directors' remuneration 633–4
      external audit 622
      financial statements, ensuring the
         integrity of 631–3
      long-term success v. short-term
         profits 625–6, 625*f*
   and directors
      appointment of 7
      information asymmetry
         between 617, 617*f*
   general meetings 6–7
   limited liability 6
   ordinary share capital 308
   pre-emption rights 313
   preference share capital 308, 309*f*
   rights issues 313
   voting rights 7
short-term decision making 446–7, 473–8
   absorption costing 449–50
   contribution analysis 448*f*, 448,
      453–72
   marginal costing 449–50, 472–3
   opportunity costs 452–3
   relevant costs 451–2, 459–73
   scope 447
   sunk costs 451–2
sole traders 3–4, 3*f*
   capital introduced 301–2
   statement of financial position
      58–9, 59*f*
solvency
   IASB 360
   long-term *see* long-term solvency

special orders 461–4
stakeholder theory 636
standard cost cards 480, 483–4
standard costing 437, 479–80, 501–7
   different standards 482–3, 483*f*
   direct labour variances 491*f*
      information and control 493
      rate and efficiency 490–2, 491*f*
      total 492–3
   direct materials variances 488*f*
      information and control 490
      price and usage 487–9
      total 489
   limitations 498
   nature of 480–1
   overhead variances
      fixed 494–5
      variable 494, 499–501, 499*f*
   sales variances 495
      price 495, 495*f*, 496
      volume 495–6, 496*f*
   setting the standard 483–7
   summary 497–8
standards *see* accounting standards;
      conduct, standards of
start-up capital 301
statement of cash flows 253–5, 292–9
   annotated 655
   cash and cash equivalents 262–3
   cash flows
      from financing activities 260–2, 261*f*
      from investing activities 259–60,
         259*f*
      from operating activities 257–9
   constructing the 256–63
   IAS 7 presentation format 255–6
   interaction with other financial
      statements 254, 265–8, 268*f*
   in isolation 265–8
   preparation
      direct method 269–78, 279
      indirect method 257, 278–83, 282*t*
      using T accounts 271–2, 276–8,
         285–92
   profit not equal to cash 263–5
   ratio analysis 325
   risky borrowings 380
   value of 265–6
statement of financial performance *see*
      statement of profit or loss
statement of financial position 39–75,
      40*f*
   accounting equation 56
   accruals 94–5
   allowance for receivables 104–5
   annotated 653
   assets 42–50
      composition of total assets 46*f*
      definitions 42–3
      recognition 44, 45*f*
   closing inventory 106–7
   drawing up the 60–3
   equity 56–60
      components 57–60, 57*f*, 59*f*
      definitions 56

   interaction with other financial
      statements 254, 266–8, 268*f*
   liabilities 50–5
      composition of total liabilities 53*f*
      definitions 50–1
      recognition 51–2, 52*f*
      preparation 107–15
   prepayments 94
   ratio analysis 325, 360
   terminology 42
   valuation of assets and liabilities 63–4
   value of 266–7
   what it shows/does not show 64–6
statement of profit or loss 76–126
   accruals 94–5, 95*f*
   accruals basis of accounting 91–3,
      92*f*, 93*f*, 280
   adjustments 103–7
   annotated 654
   budget 517–19, 518*f*
      budgetary control 530–4
      sensitivity analysis 536
   cash flows, calculation of 271–2
   cash paid for expenses, calculation
      of 276
   depreciation 96–7, 97*t*
      methods 99–102, 100*t*, 101*f*
      what it is and is not 102–3
   expenses 83–5
      defined 80–1
      determining the amount of 89–90,
         90*t*
   income 81–3
      defined 79–80
      determining the amount of 89–90,
         89*t*
   interaction with other financial
      statements 254, 265–8, 268*f*
   by nature 87–8
   non-current assets, profits and losses
      on disposal of 98–9
   preparation 107–15
   prepayments 94, 94*f*
   profit, categories of 85–6
   ratio analysis 325
      profitability ratios 327, 328
   residual value and annual
      depreciation charge 97–8, 98*t*
   terminology 78–9
   value of 266–7
stewardship 13
stock *see* inventory
stock days *see* inventory days
stock exchanges
   corporate governance 620*f*, 624–5
   debentures, bonds and loan
      notes 306
   shares 9
straight line depreciation 97*t*, 99, 100,
      101*f*
   choice of depreciation method 101, 102
   preparation of financial
      statements 114
   residual value and effect on straight
      line depreciation charge 98*t*

sunk costs 451–2
suspense account 235–6
sustainability 616–18, 640–3, 644–6
    defined 640
    rationale for adopting and reporting a
        sustainability strategy 641–3

T

T account 129–30, 129f
    cash flows, calculation of 271–2, 285
        cash paid for expenses 276–8
        cash paid to trade payables 274–6
        cash received from trade
            receivables 273–4
        dividends paid 289
        interest paid 291–2
        interest received 290
        property, plant and
            equipment 285–7
        tax paid during the year 287–8
    debits and credits 129–30, 129f, 130f
    missing figures, finding 232–3
    nominal ledger 228
    posting accounting transactions
        to 132–6
    process costing 550
    trial balance 137–9
        example 154–60
tangible assets 46, 47
target profit 457–8
tax
    current liabilities 54
    deferred 48, 54
    limited liability companies 374
    PAYE 223, 225
    statement of cash flows 257, 287–8
    statement of financial position 54
    VAT see VAT
    see also income tax
Taylor Wimpey plc
    audit committee 633
    company decision making 626–7
    corporate social responsibility 638
    non-current assets 47–8
    non-executive and executive director
        numbers 628
    operating profit margin 410
    shareholder communications 635
Ted Baker
    out-of-date goods, effect on profit
        margins 366
    price/earnings ratio 341
    profits 77
    sales and profit per unit of input
        resource 337–8
Terra Firma 380
Thrive Renewables 311
time value of money 595–7
timeliness 17, 17f, 17t, 18t
    cost and management
        accounting 403
timing of payments 373–5
total cost 416–17, 416f, 417t

break-even point 453–5, 455f
Toyota 468
trade payables
    preparation of financial
        statements 113
    statement of cash flows 280, 281
    statement of financial position 53–4,
        62, 90, 90t
trade payables control account 214–16
    cash payments 211, 212
        purchase day book 204
    purchase ledger 208–9, 210, 213–14
    purchase returns day book 207, 208
trade receivables
    allowance for receivables see
        allowance for receivables
    irrecoverable debts 103–4
    preparation of financial
        statements 108, 113, 114
    sales ledger 194
    statement of financial position 48,
        89, 89t
        indirect method of
            preparation 280, 281
trade receivables control account 199–
    201
    cash received 197
        calculation of 273–4
    sales day book 191
    sales ledger 194, 195
    sales returns day book 193, 194
transactions and transaction
        systems 184–5
transposition errors 234t
trial balance 137–9
    example 154–60
    nominal ledger 228
    potential errors 233, 234t
    when it does not balance 235–7
turnover see revenue

U

understandability 17, 17f, 17t, 18t
    financial accounting v. cost and
        management accounting 403
unfavourable variances 484
Unilever 640–2
unincorporated businesses 58–9, 59f
    see also sole traders
unsecured loans 305t

V

value added tax see VAT
variable cost 412, 414f, 414, 416–17,
        416f, 417t
    absorption costing 449
    assumptions 435, 436–7
    break-even point 453–5, 455f
    contribution 448f, 448
    marginal costing 449, 472
variable overhead efficiency
        variance 494, 499f, 499,
        500–1

variable overhead expenditure
        variance 494, 499f, 499, 500,
        501
variable overhead total variance 499f,
        499, 500, 501
variable overhead variances 494,
        499–501, 499f
variance analysis 437, 479–80, 481–2,
        501–7
    different standards 482–3, 483f
    direct labour variances 491f
        information and control 493
        rate and efficiency 490–2, 491f
        total 492–3
    direct materials variances 488f
        information and control 490
        price and usage 487–9
        total 489
    limitations 498
    overhead variances
        fixed 494–5, 494f
        variable 494, 499–501, 499f
    sales variances 495
        price 495, 495f, 496
        volume 495–6, 496f
    setting the standard 483–7
    summary 497–8
variances 481
    favourable 484
    unfavourable 484
VAT 190
verifiability 16, 17f, 17t, 18t
    financial accounting v. cost and
        management accounting
        403

W

wages see payroll system
wages and salaries control account 225,
        226
    cash payments 211, 212
weighted average cost (AVCO) 116,
        117, 118, 573–6, 573f
Whitbread plc 340
work in progress (WIP)
    closing 562–5, 562f, 563f
    opening
        first in first out valuation
            method 569–73, 569f
        weighted average cost valuation
            method 573–6, 573f
    unit costs when there is opening and
        closing WIP 568–9, 568f
    varying completion percentages of
        costs 565–8
working capital
    cycle see cash conversion cycle
    defined 367
    importance 372–3
    ratios 367–72, 367f, 368t, 381t

X

Xu Ji Electric Co. Ltd 435